WITHDRAWN

Emarketing Excellence

Now in its fourth edition, the hugely successful *Emarketing Excellence* is fully updated, keeping you in line with the changes in this dynamic and exciting field and helping you create effective and up-to-date customer-centric e-marketing plans.

A practical guide to creating and executing e-marketing plans, it combines established approaches to marketing planning with the creative use of new e-models and e-tools. This new edition seamlessly integrates social media technology like Facebook check-in, social networking, tablets and mobile applications into the mix, demonstrating how these new ways to reach customers can be integrated into your marketing plans. It also includes brand new sections on online marketing legislation and QR codes, plus an expanded section on email marketing, the most commonly used e-marketing tool.

Offering a highly structured and accessible guide to a critical and far-reaching subject, *Emarketing Excellence* (fourth edition) provides a vital reference point for all students of business or marketing, and marketers and e-marketers involved in marketing strategy and implementation, who want a thorough yet practical grounding in e-marketing.

Dave Chaffey is CEO of Smart Insights (www.smartinsights.com), an online publisher and analytics company providing advice and alerts on best practice and industry developments for digital marketers and e-commerce managers. He also works as an independent Internet marketing trainer and consultant for Marketing Insights Limited, and has consulted on digital marketing and e-commerce strategy for a range of companies. Dave is a visiting lecturer on e-commerce courses at various universities including Birmingham, Cranfield, Derby, Manchester Metropolitan and Warwick. He is also a tutor on the IDM Diploma in Digital Marketing course, for which he is Senior Examiner.

PR Smith (www.prsmith.org) is a best-selling marketing author, international speaker and adviser. His five other books are renowned for their 'edutainment' style. His SOSTAC® Planning System is used by organizations around the world (and in the top three business models of all time – as voted by members of the Chartered Institute of Marketing). Paul advises and trains organizations that embrace change and creativity in Asia, Africa and Europe. He is also the author and founder of the Great Sportsmanship Programme (www.greatsportsmanship.org), which uses social media to mobilize communities into sportsmanship.

Emarketing Excellence

Planning and optimizing your digital marketing

Fourth edition

Dave Chaffey and PR Smith

 Routledge
Taylor & Francis Group

LONDON AND NEW YORK

1st edition published 2001
2nd 2005
3rd 2008
by Butterworth Heinemann/ Elsevier

This edition published 2013
by Routledge
2 Park Square, Milton Park, Abingdon, Oxon OX14 4RN

Simultaneously published in the USA and Canada
by Routledge
711 Third Avenue, New York, NY 10017

Routledge is an imprint of the Taylor & Francis Group, an informa business

© 2013 Dave Chaffey and PR Smith

British Library Cataloguing in Publication Data
A catalogue record for this book is available from the British Library

Library of Congress Cataloging in Publication Data
Chaffey, Dave, 1963–
    Emarketing excellence: planning and optimizing your digital marketing /
    Dave Chaffey and PR Smith. – 4th ed.
        p. cm.
    Includes bibliographical references and index.
    1. Internet marketing. I. Smith, P. R. (Paul Russell), 1957– II. Title.
    HF5415.1265.S615 2012
    658.8'72–dc23   2012018941

ISBN: 978-0-415-53335-5 (hbk)
ISBN: 978-0-415-53337-9 (pbk)
ISBN: 978-0-203-08281-2 (ebk)

Typeset in Iowan Old Style
by Keystroke, Station Road, Codsall, Wolverhampton

Printed and bound in Great Britain by Bell & Bain Ltd., Glasgow

Contents

Figures

Tables

Preface to the fourth edition

The constant innovation in digital technologies and the ways in which we interact with them have continued relentlessly since the third edition of *Emarketing Excellence*.

WHAT'S NEW IN THIS EDITION?

The two big changes are social and mobile. Social media has already revolutionized marketing and mobile marketing has (finally) become mainstream. We believe social media marketing is so important that we've created a new chapter on this (Chapter 5; many readers asked us for this too). There are many other new concepts we have introduced, which 'veterans' will realize are simply new ways of describing best practice in digital marketing. For example, we have added content marketing, digital body language, inbound marketing, marketing automation, remarketing, 'earned, owned and paid media', the Ladder of Engagement and many more. With additional digital marketing channels and platforms, the complexity of managing e-marketing has become more challenging, and for this reason, Chapter 9 now focuses on this.

Despite this, we believe that in some ways, we've gone backwards in the world of marketing. Despite the wonderful new tools available to marketers (many of which are free or cost-effective), we think, overall, that customers are still confronted with an awful lot of sloppy marketing. Web sites that underperform; Facebook questions or comments that aren't answered; telephone or email leads that aren't followed up; poor integration with offline communications that complicate or even contradict basic marketing principles. Time-compressed, information-fatigued customers are angry and satisfaction levels are wavering.

That's the bad news. The good news is that it is relatively easy to be outstanding and we show examples where companies have achieved this. It is relatively easy to give customers the attention they deserve (we've moved from 'getting attention to giving attention'). It is easier to learn about customer needs. It's also easier to tailor and target relevant content and relevant products and services to the right customer. It's a question of systems – organizing processes and systems and resources in a more cost-effective manner. So if you follow all the advice in this book, you will be an outstanding world-class marketer delivering exceptional satisfaction to a growing number of loyal and engaged customers. The fundamentals of marketing excellence have not changed.

Many of the predictions that we made in previous editions have proved true. We forecast that customers would start to consolidate their choices to fewer, better, added-value sites and services. We also said that being customer-centric online was essential to create real value-added customer experiences that nurture customer satisfaction and ultimately, highly profitable repeat business. Nothing too surprising there, you might say. What is surprising is that many organizations are only at an early stage of developing their online marketing capabilities. Many have not implemented or refined many of the core digital marketing techniques that we describe in this book, such as search engine optimization, partner marketing, personalized web recommendation, A/B and multivariate testing and automated email contact strategies. Indeed, many companies are far from an 'always-on' approach to digital marketing, with campaigns running without in-flight adjustment and web sites only being refreshed every few years, where improvements to customer journeys and brand messaging are urgently needed.

Many of the permission-based approaches to e-marketing we recommended in earlier editions are now legal requirements due to European and US privacy laws such as the Privacy and Electronic Communications Directive (2002/58/EC) and the US 'CAN-SPAM' laws. E-marketers also now have to make sure that their web sites are accessible, to be compliant with the Disability and Discrimination Act (replaced in 2010 by the Equality Act). This is also good practice since it assists with search engine optimization.

Despite all of this, the fundamental principle remains the same – stick close to customers. Talk to them. Listen to them (in communities and social networks). Develop processes for systematically analysing customer comments, ratings and engagement levels. Compare this with competition. Understand customers better than they understand themselves. Become customer experts. Be crystal clear about the target markets, what they are, how you access them, how you can help them, how you position your services.

Use marketplace analysis and modelling to understand your offering and how you compare to competition both in reality and in customers' perceptions. Then develop credibility before raising visibility. After that, strong and clear value propositions help to win customers' and prospects' permission (permission marketing). Use e-marketing analysis techniques such as surveys, audience data and web analytics to improve your online offering. You can then refine your proposition and develop relations (relationship marketing) through effective, usable web sites and timely reminders (whether by opt-in email, text messages, direct mail or even telephone (permission allowing).

But remember, both today and into the future, that customers don't only go online to save time and money, while selecting and purchasing products; they go online via web or mobile to spend time, to socialize and simply for entertainment. The now familiar social networks – such as Facebook and, in the business arena, LinkedIn – are now where many of us spend time, sometimes discussing brands, but for most of the time just socializing. And of course when we're socializing, we mostly don't want to be constantly interrupted by marketing messages – so customer engagement has become a key challenge. Systems to tell others what we think about products and brands are also important as is user-generated content.

Many readers will be moving on from their initial e-strategies to the next generation of e-strategies or developing a long-term e-marketing roadmap to introduce new approaches. We hope this book helps to move you along the evolutionary path towards e-plans that really help to boost performance in an integrated way. Although the benefits of digital marketing span right across an organization's functions (customer feedback, customer service, product enhancement, sales, finance/payment, delivery, administration and marketing), we tend to link it strongly to marketing communications plans. The reality is that any e-marketing plan needs to be part of a marketing communications plan and it also should be part of a broader marketing plan. Needless to say, the e-marketing plan should fit in with the overall business plan and goals.

Enjoy the read, enjoy the digital ride towards being a world-class e-marketer and let us know what you think via our sites/pages: Dave (www.smartinsights.com) and Paul (www.facebook.com/PRSmithMarketing).

HOW IS *EMARKETING EXCELLENCE* STRUCTURED?

Emarketing Excellence has been developed to help you learn efficiently. It has supported students on many university and college business and marketing courses and a range of specialist qualifications in digital marketing offered by the Chartered Institute of Marketing (CIM)/the Communications Advertising and Marketing (CAM) Education Foundation; Econsultancy/Manchester Metropolitan University; and the Institute of Direct and Digital Marketing (IDM). It is structured around ten self-contained chapters, each of which supports learning through a clear framework based on sections with clear learning outcomes, summaries and self-test questions. The E-marketing Insight boxes give varied perspectives from practitioners and academics, while the E-marketing Excellence boxes give examples of best practice. We have also included numerous tips and best practice checklists for you to compare your e-marketing against and to help you develop a plan.

Chapter 1 Introduction to e-marketing

This chapter introduces e-marketing and its benefits and risks. It describes the difference between e-commerce, e-business and digital marketing; the alternative digital communications channels and technology platforms; the dangers of sloppy e-marketing; how to present a business case for increasing your online activities and the benefits – Sell, Speak, Serve, Save and Sizzle. We also explain core concepts such as social, inbound and content marketing that are at the heart of e-marketing.

Chapter 2 Remix

The digital world affects every aspect of business, every aspect of marketing and every aspect of the marketing mix. Some argue that physical distribution, selling and pricing absorb the biggest impact. In fact, all the elements of the marketing mix are affected by this new world. This chapter shows you exactly how to evaluate the options for varying your organization's marketing mix.

Chapter 3 E-models

The business world is changing faster than ever before. Old approaches and models are being turned on their heads. In this chapter, we show you how to assess your online marketplace, review new business, revenue and communications models, and develop budget models.

Chapter 4 E-customers

This chapter looks inside the online customer's mind. We explore customers' issues, worries, fears and phobias, as well as other motivators for going online . . . and show how marketers can respond to these behaviours. We also look at on-site behaviour, the online buying process, web analytics and the many influencing variables. We finish with a look to the future, your future and how to keep an eye on the e-customer.

Chapter 5 Social media marketing

This is where the online world gets really interesting. We're excited about the potential of social media marketing! It's one of the biggest opportunities in marketing we've seen for years. But, if it's ad hoc or unmanaged, it won't be fully effective and can even be damaging. It definitely cannot be ignored and warrants its own strategy. That's why we've devoted a separate chapter to it, showing you how to create a structured plan for social media marketing.

Chapter 6 Site design

This chapter will make you think about web sites a little differently. We go beyond best practice in usability and accessibility, to show you how to design commercially led sites which deliver results. Commercially led site designs are based on creating compelling, persuasive mobile and desktop experiences which really engage visitors through relevant messages and content, encouraging them to stay on the site and return to it.

Chapter 7 Traffic building

Sadly, it's not always the best products that succeed, but rather reasonably good ones that (a) everyone knows about; and (b) everyone can easily find when they need them. The same is true of web sites. This chapter shows you how to build traffic – how to acquire the right visitors to your site in order to achieve the right marketing outcomes for you. You will receive a briefing on the different digital communications channels, including search engine marketing, online PR, online partnerships, interactive advertising, opt-in email and viral marketing. We will also show you that success with your online communications also means gaining different forms of visibility on partner sites which are themselves successful in traffic building.

Chapter 8 e-CRM

Online customer relationship management (CRM) is packed with fundamental common-sense principles. Serving and nurturing customers into lifetime customers makes sense as existing customers are, on average, five to ten times more profitable. At the heart of this is a good database – the marketer's memory bank, which, if used correctly, creates arguably the most valuable asset in any company. In this chapter, we show you how to develop integrated email contact strategies to deliver relevant messages throughout the customer lifecycle, automating and optimizing wherever possible.

Chapter 9 Managing digital marketing

Managing digital marketing requires a constant review of new digital marketing opportunities. A major transformation to e-business and social business in organizations is needed to implement these new capabilities fully. This chapter explores the challenges and changes needed in a company to manage always-on digital marketing effectively. Topics covered include the transformation to social business, automation, measurement, optimization and making the business case for these changes.

Chapter 10 E-planning

E-marketing planning involves marketing planning within the context of the e-business e-environment. So, not surprisingly, the successful e-marketing plan is based on traditional marketing disciplines and planning techniques, adapted for the digital media environment and then mixed with new digital marketing communications techniques. This chapter shows you how to create a comprehensive e-marketing plan, based on the well-established principles of the SOSTAC® Planning System (Smith, 2011).

WHO IS THIS BOOK FOR?

Marketing and business professionals

- *Marketing managers* responsible for defining an e-marketing strategy, implementing strategy or maintaining the company web site alongside traditional marketing activities.

- *Digital marketing specialists* such as new media managers, e-marketing managers and e-commerce managers responsible for directing, integrating and implementing their organizations' e-marketing.

- *Senior managers and directors* seeking to identify the right e-business and e-marketing approaches to support their organizations' strategy.

- *Information systems managers and chief information officers* also involved in developing and implementing e-marketing and e-commerce strategies.

- *Technical project managers or web masters* who may understand the technical details of building a site, but want to enhance their knowledge of e-marketing.

Students

This book has been created as the core text for the CIM e-Marketing Professional Development Award and the IDM Digital Marketing qualifications. As such, *Emarketing Excellence* will support the following students in their studies:

- *Professionals studying for recognized qualifications* The book provides comprehensive coverage of the syllabus for these awards.

- *Postgraduate students on specialist master's degrees in electronic commerce, electronic business or e-marketing and generic programmes in marketing management, MBA, Certificate in Management or Diploma in Management Studies* which involve modules or electives for e-business and e-marketing.

- *Undergraduates on business programmes* which include marketing modules on the use of digital marketing. This may include specialist degrees such as electronic business, electronic commerce, Internet marketing; and marketing or general business degrees such as business studies, business administration and business management.

- *Postgraduate and undergraduate project students* who select this topic for final-year projects or dissertations – this book is an excellent source of resources for these students.

- *Undergraduates completing work placement* who are involved with different aspects of e-marketing such as managing an intranet or company web site.

- *MBA* – we find that this book actually gives non-marketing people a good grounding in marketing principles, business operations and, of course, e-marketing.

WHAT DOES THE BOOK OFFER TO LECTURERS TEACHING THESE COURSES?

This book is intended to be a comprehensive guide to all aspects of deploying e-marketing within an organization. It builds on existing marketing theories and concepts, questions the validity of these models in the light of the differences between the Internet and other media, and references the emerging body of literature specific to e-business, e-commerce and e-marketing. Lecturers will find that this book has a good range of case study examples to support their teaching. Web links given in the text and at the end of each chapter highlight key information sources for particular topics.

LEARNING FEATURES

A range of features has been incorporated into *Emarketing Excellence* to help the reader get the most out of it. They have been designed to assist understanding, reinforce learning and help readers find information easily. The features are described in the order that you will find them.

At the start of each chapter

- *Overview*: a short introduction to the relevance of the chapter and what you will learn.
- *Overall learning outcome*: a list describing what readers can learn through reading the chapter and completing the self-test.
- *Chapter topics*: chapter contents and the learning objectives for each section.

In each chapter

- *E-marketing Excellence boxes*: real-world examples of best practice approaches referred to in the text.
- *E-marketing Insight boxes*: quotes, opinions and frameworks from industry practitioners and academics.

- *E-marketing Best Practice Checklists*: to enable you to evaluate and improve your current approaches or plan a new initiative.
- *Practical E-marketing Tips*: Do's and Don'ts to improve your web site, email or database marketing.
- *Definitions*: key e-marketing terms are emphasized in italic and the glossary contains succinct definitions.
- *Web links*: where appropriate, web addresses are given for further information, particularly those serving to update information.
- *Section summaries*: these are intended as revision aids and to summarize the main learning points from the section.

At the end of each chapter

- *Summary*: these are also intended as revision aids and to summarize the main learning points from the chapter.
- *References*: these are references to books, articles or papers referred to within the chapter.
- *Further reading*: supplementary texts or papers on the main themes of the chapter. Where appropriate, a brief commentary is provided on recommended supplementary reading on the main themes of the chapter.
- *Web links*: these are significant sites that provide further information on the concepts and topics of the chapter. All web site references within the chapter – for example, company sites – are not repeated here. The web site address prefix 'http://' is omitted for clarity except where the address does not start with 'www'.
- *Self-test questions*: short questions which will test understanding of terms and concepts described in the chapter and help relate them to your organization.

At the end of the book

- *Glossary*: a list of definitions of all key terms and phrases used within the main text.
- *Index*: all key words and abbreviations referred to in the main text.

References

Smith, P.R. (2011) *The SOSTAC® Guide to Writing the Perfect Plan*. Self-published e-book available on Amazon and Kindle.

Acknowledgements

We are fortunate to have shared our journey of understanding how best to use digital marketing with thousands of students and many marketing professionals and we thank you for sharing your experiences with us. We'd particularly like to thank all the practitioners who have shared their experiences on applying digital marketing which feature on www.smartinsights.com and in this edition of *Emarketing Excellence*.

We really do appreciate the effort made by the digital marketing specialists who have shared their knowledge as expert commentators on www.smartinsights.com, or made creative comments and posts on the PR Smith Marketing Facebook page, some of which appear in this book. These specialists include: Mike Berry, Steve Dempsey, John Horsley, Richard Sedley and Ze Zook (marketing strategy); Dan Barker, Ben Jesson, Pritesh Patel and Jon Clifford (analytics); Dan Bosomworth, Paul Fennemore, Katy Howell, Jay Cooper and Marie Page (social media marketing); Rene Power and Jean Paul de Clerck (B2B marketing); Rob Thurner (mobile marketing); Chris Soames, James Gurd and John Newton (search marketing); Mel Henson (copywriting); Paul Rouke, Gerry McGovern and Paul Schwartfeger (usability); Mark Brownlow, Kath Pay and Tim Watson (email marketing); Neil McLennan (behavioural ads and remarketing); Adam Sharp and Ben Smart (automated marketing and CRM); Kat Mayfield (review marketing); and Steve Harris.

Also thanks to the many occasional contributors who contact us and share their expertise and experiences.

We also want to thank the team at Taylor & Francis for their help in the creation of this book, especially Amy Laurens, our editor, and Rosie Baron, the editorial assistant.

Finally, thanks to the Chaffey clan – Sal, Zoe and Sarah; and the Smith clan – Beverley, Aran, Cian and Lily. Their collective patience is very much appreciated.

Get updates on
this chapter

Chapter **1**

Introduction to e-marketing

We have a vision – to be the first fashion company that is fully digital end-to-end. The experience is that the customer will have total access to Burberry across any device, anywhere, but they will get exactly the same feeling of the brand, feeling of the culture, regardless of where, when and how they [are] accessing [it].

To any CEO who is sceptical today about social enterprise, you have to be totally connected with everyone who touches your brand. If you don't do that, I don't know what your business model is in five years.

Angela Ahrendts, Burberry CEO

OVERVIEW

This chapter introduces e-marketing and its benefits and risks. It describes the difference between e-commerce, e-business and e-marketing; the alternative digital communications channels; the dangers of sloppy e-marketing; how to present a business case for increasing your online activities, and the benefits of doing so – Sell, Serve, Speak, Save and Sizzle.

OVERALL LEARNING OUTCOME

By the end of this chapter, you will be able to:
- Describe the development of the electronic marketspace
- Outline an approach to developing an e-marketing plan
- Describe the key benefits of e-marketing.

CHAPTER TOPIC	LEARNING OBJECTIVE
1.1 Introduction	Outline the benefits and risks of e-marketing
1.2 The connected world	Outline the characteristics of the new marketspace
1.3 B2C, B2B, C2B and C2C	Identify different forms of collaboration between marketplace members
1.4 E-definitions	Describe the difference between e-commerce, e-business and e-marketing
1.5 Sloppy e-marketing	Avoid basic e-marketing mistakes
1.6 Objectives	Outline the five basic e-marketing objectives
1.7 Objective – Sell	Define objectives for selling to the customer online
1.8 Objective – Serve	Define objectives for serving the customer online
1.9 Objective – Speak	Define objectives for speaking to the customer online
1.10 Objective – Save	Define objectives for saving online
1.11 Objective – Sizzle	Define objectives for enhancing the brand online
1.12 Introduction to e-strategy	Outline approaches to achieving e-marketing objectives
1.13 Tactics, action and control	Outline e-marketing tactics, actions and control

1.1 Introduction

This chapter introduces you to the world of *e-marketing*; its background and its benefits. It introduces the key concepts you need to succeed in e-marketing, plus examples of good and bad e-marketing. Chances are your organization is already actively engaged in e-marketing, so in this chapter, and throughout the book, we give you a planning framework and checklists to evaluate and improve your current e-marketing practices or plan new initiatives.

The chapter is structured using a simple *aide-mémoire*, called SOSTAC®. SOSTAC® is used by thousands of professionals to produce all kinds of plans (marketing plans, corporate plans, advertising plans and e-marketing plans). In later chapters and, in particular, Chapter 10, we provide a step-by-step guide to creating an e-marketing plan. In this chapter, we'll use SOSTAC® to provide a structure for an initial review.

INTRODUCING SOSTAC® PLANNING FOR E-MARKETING

SOSTAC® stands for Situation analysis, Objectives, Strategy, Tactics, Actions and Control (Figure 1.1). It is described in more detail in Smith (2011) and Smith and Taylor (2004) who note that each stage is not discrete, but there is some overlap during each stage of planning – previous stages may be revisited and refined, as indicated by the reverse arrows in Figure 1.1 below. For creating an e-marketing plan, the planning stages are:

- *Situation analysis* means 'where are we now?' (In the context of this chapter, this includes definition of 'e' terms, growth in users and change in the marketplace, as well as examples of good and bad e-marketing.)
- *Objectives* means 'Where do we want to be?' What do we want to achieve through online channels, what are the benefits? We describe the five 'Ss' as the main objectives of, reasons for, or benefits of being online, which you should exploit.
- *Strategy* means 'How do we get there?' Strategy summarizes how to fulfil the objectives. What *online value propositions (OVPs)* should we create, and what positioning should drive the overall marketing mix and the promotional mix, right down to the different *contact strategies* for different segments, and which digital media channels should be selected? Getting your digital strategy right is crucial. As Kenichi Ohmae says (1999), 'There's no point rowing harder if you're rowing in the wrong direction'.
- *Tactics* reviews the tactical tools and the details of the marketing mix which is covered in Chapter 2 and the communications mix which is covered in Chapter 7.
- *Actions* refers to action plans and project management skills – essential skills which we won't go into in this chapter.
- *Control* looks at how you know if your e-efforts are working, and what improvements can be made – again, we won't delve in too deeply in this chapter.

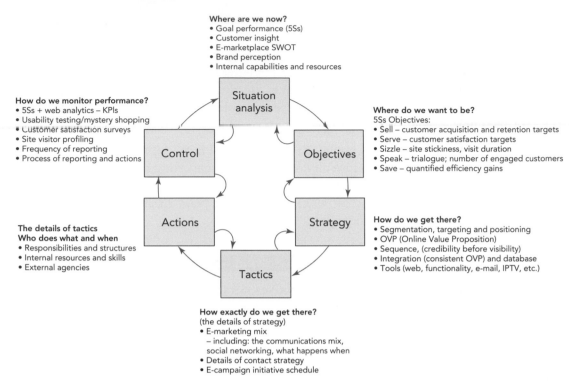

Where are we now?
• Goal performance (5Ss)
• Customer insight
• E-marketplace SWOT
• Brand perception
• Internal capabilities and resources

How do we monitor performance?
• 5Ss + web analytics – KPIs
• Usability testing/mystery shopping
• Customer satisfaction surveys
• Site visitor profiling
• Frequency of reporting
• Process of reporting and actions

Where do we want to be?
5Ss Objectives:
• Sell – customer acquisition and retention targets
• Serve – customer satisfaction targets
• Sizzle – site stickiness, visit duration
• Speak – trialogue; number of engaged customers
• Save – quantified efficiency gains

The details of tactics
Who does what and when
• Responsibilities and structures
• Internal resources and skills
• External agencies

How do we get there?
• Segmentation, targeting and positioning
• OVP (Online Value Proposition)
• Sequence, (credibility before visibility)
• Integration (consistent OVP) and database
• Tools (web, functionality, e-mail, IPTV, etc.)

How exactly do we get there?
(the details of strategy)
• E-marketing mix
  – including: the communications mix,
    social networking, what happens when
• Details of contact strategy
• E-campaign initiative schedule

Figure 1.1   SOSTAC® planning framework. SOSTAC® is a registered trade mark of PR Smith (www.prsmith.org)

SECTION SUMMARY 1.1

Introduction

The SOSTAC® planning framework is used to structure this chapter. SOSTAC® is:

- Situation analysis – where are we now?
- Objectives – where do we want to be?
- Strategy – how do we get there?
- Tactics – which tactical tools do we use to implement strategy?
- Actions – which action plans are required to implement strategy?
- Control – how do we manage the strategy process?

1.2 Situation – the connected world

Let's consider the current situation of e-marketing – where the marketplace migrates into the *electronic marketspace*. How significant is this change? Fixed and mobile access to the Internet is continuing to grow rapidly and seamlessly across borders and into an online world already inhabited by over a billion customers. Given its scale and the benefits it offers to these customers and businesses, it is a big part of the future of all businesses. The Internet is far more than 'just another channel to market' – a misguided phrase that is still heard surprisingly frequently. We will explain how the Internet can and should be used to transform how a business communicates with its audience and delivers enhanced brand experiences.

Despite the vast number of people (and businesses) buying online, don't you think it's a little weird when you consider that millions, billions and even trillions of dollars, pounds and euros pass seamlessly through wires interconnecting lots of devices all around the world? Google has built a billion-dollar business simply by charging for mouse clicks, some costing up to US$50! Perhaps it's even weirder when you consider that in future a lot of it will be wireless. In China, there are already more mobile phone subscribers than the population of the United States.

THE CONNECTED WORLD

The most common way of accessing the Internet remains the desktop computer or laptop. What are the up-and-coming ways of accessing the Internet? *Interactive digital TV, mobile phones and mobile apps*, planes, trains and automobiles all access the Internet. Cars can also be 'connected' so that they can alert roadside repair companies to your location before you actually break down. Just about anything can be wired up, courtesy of the powerful combination of computer chips and cordless or wireless technology, including higher speed data transfer protocols such as *3G, 4G* and *Bluetooth* for data transfer between mobile phones and other hand-held devices. Digital marketers need constantly to evaluate the tremendous range of platforms as they evolve.

E-MARKETING INSIGHT

Digital marketing platforms

Although the desktop access platform has been dominant for years and remains significant, mobile marketing platforms are becoming more important. These are the main platforms that the digital marketer needs to evaluate and manage:

Desktop, laptop and notebook platforms

1 *Desktop browser-based platform*. This is traditional web access through the consumer's browser of choice whether Internet Explorer, Google Chrome or Safari. The app store on Chrome gives a new way to reach audiences.

2 *Desktop apps*. Apple users are accessing paid and free apps from their desktop via the Apple App Store while Microsoft Windows users have their equivalent gadgets. This gives opportunities for brands to engage via these platforms.

3 *Email platforms*. While email isn't traditionally considered as a platform, it does offer a separate alternative to browser and app-based options to communicate with

prospects or clients, whether through editorial or advertising, and email is still widely used for marketing.

4 *Feed-based and API data exchange platforms.* Many users still consume data through RSS feeds, and Twitter and Facebook status updates can be considered a form of feed or stream where ads can be inserted.

5 *Video marketing platforms.* Streamed video is often delivered through the other platforms mentioned above, particularly through browsers and plug-ins, but it represents a separate platform. Television channels delivered through streaming over the Internet known as IPTV are related to this platform.

Major social networks like Facebook, Google+, LinkedIn and Twitter can also be called platforms; some call them ecosystems because of their supporting interfaces and tools. These are accessed across platforms.

Mobile phone and tablet platforms

The options on mobile hardware platforms are similar in many ways to the desktop. Since they can be used in different locations, there are many new opportunities to engage consumers through *mobile marketing* and *location or proximity-based marketing*. The main platforms are:

1 *Mobile operating system and browser.* There are mobile browsers which are closely integrated with the operating system.

2 *Mobile-based apps.* Apps have to be developed specifically for the mobile operating system, whether it is Apple iOS, Google Android, RIM or Windows.

Other hardware platforms

There are a host of other and growing platforms through which to communicate with customers; for example:

1 *Gaming platforms.* Whether it's a PlayStation, Nintendo or Xbox variety of gaming machine, there are increasing options to reach gamers through ads or placements within games; for example, in-game ads.

2 *Indoor and outdoor kiosk-type apps.* For example, interactive kiosks and augmented reality options to communicate with consumers.

3 *Interactive signage.* The modern version of signage is closely related to kiosk apps and may incorporate different methods such as touch-screen, Bluetooth or QR codes to encourage interactivity. The E-marketing Insight box below gives a futuristic example.

Tesco Homeplus opens subway virtual store in South Korea

In South Korea, Tesco Homeplus has significantly fewer stores than the market leader E-mart. Based on research which showed that many Koreans tend to shop in stores near their homes for convenience, Tesco trialled a virtual store to reach these shoppers.

Virtual displays were implemented in a similar way to actual stores from the display to merchandise, but smartphone QR code readers are used to shop with and after checkout, the goods are delivered to the customer's home (Figure 1.2).

Figure 1.2   Tesco home shopping service in South Korea

Source: Cheil Worldwide (http://www.canneslions.com/inspiration/_archive_advert.cfm?id=548309&_playlist_d=5528)

RESEARCH, TRENDS AND FORECASTS

To effectively plan your e-marketing to predict your results, you need to tap into the wealth of research about current Internet usage and future trends. In Table 1.1, we summarize a selection of free and paid-for services to help you analyse your e-marketplace. In Chapter 3 on e-models and Chapter 4 on e-customers, we explain how you should analyse your online marketplace to help understand and exploit the online potential.

Table 1.1 Tools for assessing your e-marketplace

Service	Description
1 **Alexa** (www.alexa.com). Free tool, see also www.compete.com. Also use the Google syntax related:domain.com to find related sites.	Free service owned by Amazon which provides traffic ranking of individual sites compared to all sites. Works best for sites in Top 100 000. Sample dependent on users of the Alexa toolbar.
2 **Hitwise** (www.hitwise.com). Paid tool, but free research available at http://weblogs. hitwise.com.	Paid service available in some countries to compare audience and search/site usage. Works through monitoring IP traffic to different sites through ISPs.
3 **Netratings** (www.netratings.com). Paid tool.	Panel service based on at-home and at-work users who have agreed to have their web usage tracked by software. Top rankings on site gives examples of most popular sites in several countries.
4 **Comscore** (www.comscore.com). Paid tool.	A similar panel service to Netratings, but focusing on the US and UK. A favoured tool for media planners.
5 **ABCE Database** (www.abce.org.uk). Free tool. (Choose ABCE Database.)	The Audit Bureau of Circulation (Electronic) gives free access to its database of portals (not destination sites) who have agreed to have their sites audited to prove traffic volumes to advertisers.
6 **Search keyphrase analysis tools. Compilation available from** www.davechaffey.com/ seo-keyword-tools.	Tools such as the Google Keyword tool and Google Traffic Estimator can be used to assess the popularity of brands and their products reflected by the volume of search terms typed into Google and other search engines.
7 **Forrester** (www.forrester.com).	Paid research service offering reports on Internet usage and best practice in different vertical sectors such as financial services, retail and travel. Free research summaries available in press release section and on its marketing blog (http://blogs. forrester.com).
8 **Gartner** (www.gartner.com).	Another research service, in this case focusing on technology adoption within companies. Also see Jupiter research (www.jupiterresearch.com) who often have good reports on e-mail marketing best practice.
9 **IAB** (US: www.iab.net, UK: www.iab.uk.net, Europe: www.iabeurope.eu).	The Internet or Interactive Advertising Bureau has research focusing on investment in different digital media channels, in particular display ads and search marketing. In 2007, the UK was leading in online ad expenditure, accounting for over 15% of ad investment.

Table 1.1 *(Continued)*

Service	Description
10 **IMRG** (www.imrg.org).	The Internet Media in Retail Group has compilations on online e-commerce expenditure in the UK which, as of the time of writing, was averaging around £5 billion per month or over 10% of all retail spend.

SECTION SUMMARY 1.2

Situation – the connected world

More customers are spending an increasing part of their lives in the virtual world. Marketers need to analyse demand by consumers for online services and respond to customers' needs in this new connected world.

1.3 Situation – B2C, B2B, C2B and C2C

The options for digital communications between a business and its customers are summarized in Figure 1.3. Traditionally, the bulk of Internet transactions are between business and business or industrial and commercial markets, known as **B2B** (business-to-business); and between business and consumer markets (like cars and cola), known as business-to-consumer (**B2C**).

B2B AND B2C

This is where the bulk of online business occurs. Once upon a time, marketing used to learn from the *fast-moving consumer goods (FMCG)* manufacturers like Guinness, Coca-Cola and Heinz, while industrial marketing, or B2B marketing, was considered by some to be less exciting. This is no longer the case, with relatively new B2B brands like Eloqua, Hubspot, Smart Insights and Salesforce using *content marketing* to fuel dramatic growth.

In 2001, Ford and General Motors combined forces through the *B2B marketplace* Covisint (www.covisint.com) and moved their then US$300 billion and US$500 billion supply chains online. Today, Covisint is no longer an open marketplace, instead it is used by a handful of motor manufacturers. The benefits of online B2B commerce are now more about identifying products in electronic catalogues from a range of suppliers, selecting the best option and then managing the paperwork and workflow electronically through e-procurement. The eBay auction model has not really taken hold in B2B, although eBay does have its own B2B auction facility (http://business.ebay.com) and Alibaba.com has created a billion-dollar business focused on Asia.

	From: Supplier of content/service	
	Consumer	Business (organization)
To: Consumer of content/service Business (organization)|Consumer	**Consumer-to-Consumer (C2C)** • eBay • Peer-to-peer (Skype) • Social networks and blogs • Product recommendations	**Business-to-Consumer (B2C)** • Transactional: Amazon • Relationship-building: BP • Brand-building: Unilever • Media owner: News Corp • Comparison intermediary: Kelkoo, Pricerunner
	Consumer-to-Business (C2B) • Group and Priceline • Consumer-feedback, communities or campaigns	**Business-to-Business (B2B)** • Transactional: Euroffice • Relationship-building: BP • Media-owned: Emap business publications • B2B marketplaces: EC21

Figure 1.3   Options for online communications between an organization and its customers

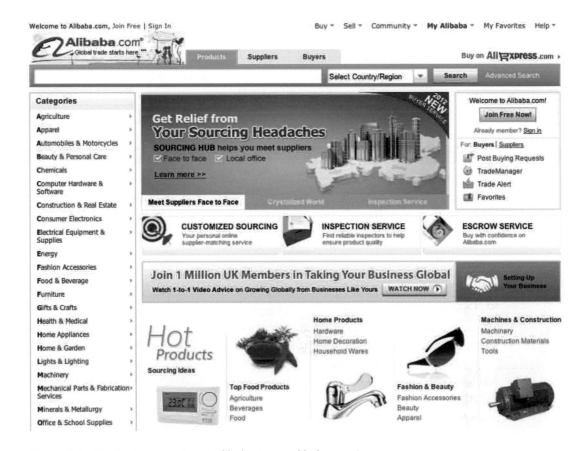

Figure 1.4   Product categories at Alibaba (www.alibaba.com)

PRACTICAL E-MARKETING TIP

Sourcing skills online

If you need to source web or email templates or scripts, it may be worth considering using an online web skills marketplace such as oDesk (www.odesk.com), Guru.com (www.guru.com) or Elance (www.elance.com), although care is needed in selecting the right agency or person, based on recommendations or testimonials.

C2C AND C2B

Whether you are B2C or B2B, don't forget C2C and C2B. C2C models and the *social media* to support them have proved one of the most disruptive examples of online business technology. An early indication of the popularity of C2C was the growth of online consumer auctions at eBay and in niche communities focusing on interests such as sport, films or pastimes. More recently, a dramatic growth in C2C interactions has been fuelled by the growth of social networks: the 'Big 4' – that's Facebook, Google+, LinkedIn and Twitter – are now key to reaching many customers through 'social outposts' and key influencers on these platforms. Social interactions are now so important that they are reducing consumption of other forms of digital media and traditional media, so all companies need to develop a strategy to engage these consumers. That's why we devote Chapter 5 to developing a social media strategy.

Customer-to-business models may play a significant role in some B2B or B2C sectors. In this model, a potential buyer approaches a marketplace of sellers who then compete for the sale. In the consumer market, Priceline (www.priceline.com) and price comparison sites such as Kelkoo follow this model. Groupon has established a group-buying model where previous models like LetsBuyIt.com failed. C2B also involves customers developing their own content online, which is known as user-generated content (UGC), with businesses facilitating it. For example, many smaller travel companies, such as Superbreak (www.superbreak.com) and Travel Republic (www.travelrepublic.co.uk) have exploited the approach originally adopted by TripAdvisor (www.tripadvisor.com). Do you have a plan for UGC?

E-MARKETING EXCELLENCE

Argos and RS Components exploit new markets

When catalogue retailer Argos (www.argos.co.uk) launched its web site, it found that sales were not limited to its core B2C market. Around 10 per cent of the site's customers were B2B – the web provided a more convenient purchase point than the previous retail chain. It has since changed its product offering to accommodate this new segment. Conversely, B2B company RS Components found that a significant proportion of sales were B2C, so reaching new customers via its online presence.

TYPES OF ONLINE PRESENCE

When assessing the relevance and potential of e-marketing for a business, remember that different business types offer different opportunities and challenges. Chaffey and Ellis-Chadwick (2012) identify five main types of online presence or components possible as part of a site:

1 *Transactional e-commerce site.* Manufacturers, e-retailers, travel or financial services providers make their products available for online purchase. The main business contribution is through sale of these products. The sites also support the business by providing information for consumers who prefer to purchase products offline.

2 *Services-oriented relationship building or lead-generation web site.* Provides information to stimulate purchase and build relationships. Products are not typically available for purchase online. Information is provided through the web site, along with email marketing, to inform purchasing decisions. The main business contribution is through encouraging offline sales and generating enquiries or leads from potential customers. Such sites also help by adding value for existing customers by providing them with information of interest to them.

   Visit these sites: B2B examples are management consultants such as Pricewaterhouse Coopers (www.pwc.com) and Accenture (www.accenture.com). Most car manufacturers' sites may be services-oriented rather than transactional.

3 *Brand-building site.* Provides an experience to support the brand. Products are not typically available for online purchase, although merchandise may be. The main focus is to support the brand by developing an online experience of the brand through content marketing integrated with social media outposts. They are typical for low-value, high-volume, fast-moving consumer goods (FMCG brands).

   Visit these sites: Lynx (www.lynxeffect.com/uk) and Guinness (www.guinness.com).

4 *Portal or media site.* The main purpose of these types of *intermediaries* or publishers is to provide information and content. The term portal refers to a gateway to information or a range of services such as a search engine, directories, news, blog content, shopping comparison, etc. This is information both on the site and via links through to other sites. Online publishers have a diversity of options for generating revenue, including advertising, commission-based sales (affiliate marketing) and selling access to content through subscription or pay-per-view.

   Visit these examples: Yahoo! (www.yahoo.com), the *Financial Times Online* (www.ft.com) or TripAdvisor (www.tripadvisor.com).

5 *Social network or community site.* A site enabling community interactions between different consumers (C2C model). Typical interactions include posting comments and replies to comments, sending messages, rating content and tagging content in particular categories. Well-known examples include Facebook and LinkedIn, but there are many less well-known niche communities that may be important within a market. In addition to distinct social network sites, social interactions can be integrated into other site types through plug-ins or *application programming interfaces (APIs)*. The Facebook APIs are very important in integrating Facebook 'Like' buttons and content into sites through services such as the Facebook social plug-in.

Remember that these are not clear-cut categories of web sites, since many businesses will have sites which blend these elements, but with different emphasis depending on the markets in which they operate.

To engage their audience and so increase advertising revenue, social networking sites are also looking to provide many of these services through *social network company brand pages*, sometimes called 'social outposts' for short. Vets Now is a great example of an engaging brand page.

E-MARKETING INSIGHT

E-marketing in action. Vets Now creates a community through a Facebook Park Bench and Scratching Post

Vets Now is the UK's leading provider of Out of Hours emergency veterinary care, but it's not a 'megabrand', so it really shows what you can achieve if you get the communications strategy right. Park Bench (for dog owners) and Scratching Post (for cat owners) not only give a great route to interact with the audience, but have also driven tens of thousands of registrations to a 'My Pet Profile' Facebook app, where owners can create a profile for their pet. Some 17 per cent of fans convert to the app where they can share stories, follow other pets and meet other pet owners like them.

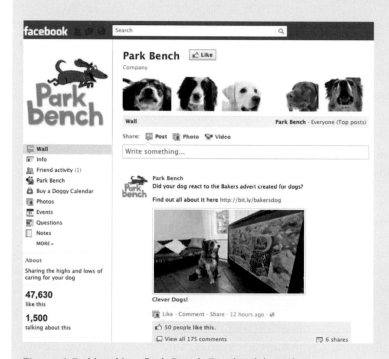

Figure 1.5   Vets Now Park Bench Facebook brand page

Source: Blog post by Marie Page on SmartInsights.com published 31 January 2012 (www.smartinsights.com/social-media-marketing/facebook-marketing/case-study-what-makes-these-some-of-the-most-engaged-facebook-pages-in-the-uk/).

The Vets Now team have worked hard to build a community through posting on the Facebook wall for each brand, where they have found the following types of update to be the most shareable and engaging.

1 Short status updates
2 Status updates that invite fans to 'fill in the blanks'
3 Photo galleries
4 Longer updates uploaded in the form of notes
5 Weekly 'Ask a Vet' sessions
6 Facebook polls have been great for engagement and viral spread but also superb as a customer research tool
7 The wall is open to fans to post their own updates and photos
8 A competition requiring 'Likes' of the Park Bench.

SECTION SUMMARY 1.3

Situation – B2C, B2B, C2B and C2C

E-marketing involves collaboration between different parties that can be characterized by four main interactions:

1 B2C – business-to-consumer (B2C e-tail is arguably the most talked about)
2 B2B – business-to-business (less talked about, but with the most transactions)
3 C2C – customer-to-customer interactions (best known as consumer auctions, but can also be achieved as B2C and B2B social networks or communities)
4 C2B – customer-to-business (novel buying models where customers approach the business on their own terms or generate content to support the business).

1.4 Situation – e-definitions

There are many terms with the e-prefix and many different interpretations. Within any organization, developing a common understanding for terms such as e-commerce, e-business and e-marketing, and how they interrelate and who will manage them, is important to enable development of a consistent, coherent strategy.

E-commerce is primarily about selling online or the ability to transact online. This includes e-tailing, online banking and shopping – which involve transactions where buyers actually buy and shoppers actually shop. Some suggest that e-commerce includes all online transactions such as responding to an enquiry or an online catalogue search.

E-commerce itself does not include the marketing or the back office administration processes that are required to run a business. *E-business* has a broader perspective involving the automation of all the business processes in the value chain – from procurement or purchasing of raw materials, to production, stock holding, distribution and logistics, sales and marketing, after sales, invoicing, debt collection and more.

E-marketing, Internet marketing or digital marketing is at the heart of e-business – getting closer to customers and understanding them better, adding value to products, widening distribution channels and boosting sales through running e-marketing campaigns using *digital media channels* such as search marketing, online advertising and affiliate marketing which we will explain later in this chapter. It also includes using the web site to facilitate customer leads, sales and managing after-sales service. As with mainstream marketing, e-marketing is a way of thinking, a way of putting the customer at the heart of all online activities; e.g. getting different user groups to test your web site on different browsers in different settings on different connections.

E-MARKETING – THE DYNAMIC DIALOGUE

Simply put, e-marketing is marketing online whether via web sites, online ads, opt-in email, interactive kiosks, interactive TV or mobiles. It involves getting close to customers, understanding them better and maintaining a dialogue with them. It is broader than e-commerce since it is not limited to transactions between an organization and its stakeholders, but includes all processes related to marketing.

This dynamic dialogue is at the heart of good marketing. E-marketing builds on the database (of customers and prospects) and creates a constant flow of communications between customers and suppliers and between customers themselves. Dynamic means what it says. Dynamic does not mean static *brochureware* web pages – you do still see them! It's a two-way flow of communications – an ongoing discussion between customer and supplier. The power of this dialogue is that it not only engages audiences, but gives associated boosts to *search engine optimization (SEO)* and *social media optimization (SMO)* through the backlinks and social sharing that it creates which give positive ranking signals to the search engine.

Brian Solis, a social media specialist says in his book *Engage* (Solis, 2011) that: 'SEO + SMO – Amplified Findability'.

E-marketing can help create a business which is customer led . . . where the customer participates – through a constant dialogue, a dynamic dialogue, expressing interests, requesting products and services, suggesting improvements, giving feedback . . . where ultimately, the customer drives the business.

PRACTICAL E-MARKETING TIP

Do you right touch?

Savvy digital marketers understand the importance of building an integrated multi-channel touch or contact strategy which delivers customized communications to consumers through search or *behavioural targeted* display ads, emails and web recommendations and promotions. Every customer interaction or response to a communication should be followed up by a series of relevant communications delivered via the right combination of channels (web, email, phone, direct mail) to elicit a response or further dialogue. This is contextual or 'Sense and Respond' marketing, where the aim is to deliver relevant messages which fit the current context of what the customer is interested in according to the searches they have performed, the type of content they have viewed or the products they have recently purchased.

We call this 'right touching':

Right Touching is:

A *Multi-channel Communications Strategy*

Customized for *Individual Prospects* and *Customers* forming *segments*

Across a *defined customer lifecycle*

Which . . .

Delivers the *Right Message*

Featuring the *Right Value Proposition* (product, service or experience)

With the *Right Tone*

At the *Right Time*

With the *Right Frequency and Interval*

Using the *Right Media/Communications channels*

To achieve . . .

Right balance of value between both parties

(Dave Chaffey, www.smartinsights.com)

You can see that right touching is not easy; all the permutations mean that businesses often get it wrong. That's why we think it's one of the biggest challenges for companies across customer acquisition, retention and growth. We return to this topic in Chapter 8 on E-CRM where we explain how to develop the right contact strategy.

E-MARKETING CHECKLIST – RIGHT TOUCHING

To what extent are you incorporating right touching into your e-marketing? Use this checklist from customer acquisition to retention:

☑ 1 *Search marketing:* when a prospect uses a search engine to search for a company or brand name or a specific category or product, a paid search ad from the company or content in the *natural search results* as explained in Chapter 7.

☑ 2 *Behavioural targeting or online advertising:* when a prospect interacts with content on a media site or searches on a specific term, a sequence of follow-up ads known as *behavioural retargeting* should be displayed as they visit other sites within a network and the destination site of the merchant paying for the advertising.

☑ 3 *Multi-touches across different digital media channels for acquisition.* Use tracking and develop *attribution models* through *web analytics* to understand the sequence and combination of different digital media channels (search, *affiliates*, display ads or *aggregators*) which generate the most cost-effective response. How do you allocate the channel to the outcome? Do you simply do '*last click wins*' or do you weight across the different touch points as we discuss in Chapter 3?

☑ 4 *Customer lifecycle model and welcome strategy*: when a prospect subscribes to an email newsletter, enquires about a service or makes a first purchase, a welcome communications strategy should be in place which uses a sequence of email and possibly personalized web recommendations, direct mail and phone communications to educate

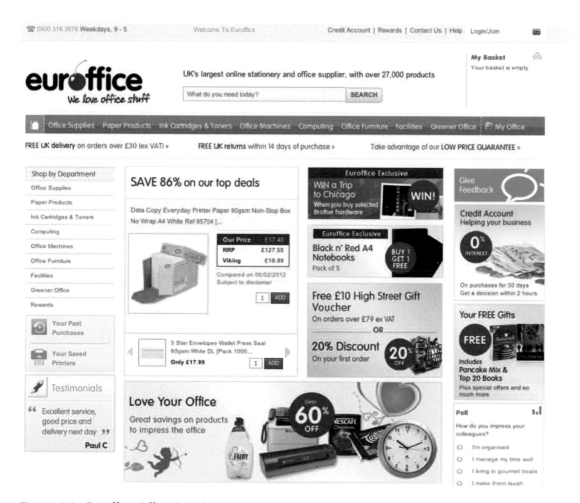

Figure 1.6   Euroffice Office Supplies serving B2C and B2B markets (www.euroffice.co.uk)

the customer about the brand or product and generate the initial sale. This should aim at building a relationship and then developing commitment from first-time visitor, to repeat visitor to qualified prospect, to first-time customer and then repeat customer, so increasing customer lifetime value.

☑   5 *Reducing online attrition*: when a shopper abandons their shopping basket, a combination of communications should seek to win them back. Alternatively, after a quotation, for example, for a car policy, follow-up emails should remind customers about the benefits of taking out the policy.

☑   6 *Delivering relevant recommendations for retention and growth*. When an existing customer returns to a site, a personalized container should be available on every page to deliver relevant personalized promotions. Amazon recommendations are the best-known examples; another is office supplier Euroffice (www.euroffice.co.uk, Figure 1.6) which delivers relevant recommendations to prospects and customers according to their position in the lifecycle, segment and previous purchases. Similarly, dynamic content panels within emails do the same.

☑   7 *Following up on customer product or promotion interest*. When a customer clicks on a link in an email or interacts repeatedly with content on a site, is there an automated workflow triggering an email, direct mail or phone reminder about the offer?

☑   8 *Getting the frequency right*. Effective right touching requires that messages stay engaging, relevant and do not become too intrusive or too repetitive. So you should put limits on the maximum number of emails that are sent in a period (e.g. one a month or one a week) and the interval between them (e.g. an interval of at least 3 days).

☑   9 *Getting the channel right*. Right channelling means using the best channel(s) for the customer, which fit their preferences, and the right channel for the company, which gives them the best combination of cost and response. It means that you may be able to upweight email communications for some customers because they interact and respond to them, so reducing costs of direct mail. But other customers on an email list may not respond to or dislike email, and so direct mail is upweighted to them.

☑ 10 *Getting the offer right*. Offers will vary in effectiveness according to the audience targeted and this will be shown by their profiles and customer journeys indicated by the media and content they have consumed. Can you identify the Next Best Product for previous purchasers? So right touching requires that testing is built-in to deliver the right messages and right sequences of communications for different audiences.

THE CUSTOMER-LED BUSINESS

Let's get back to the fundamentals. Although different business models and marketing models have emerged, the same basic marketing principles apply whether online or offline:

● Get close to customers, listen to them
● Involve them
● Serve them
● Add value

- Find the best ones
- Nurture them into lifelong customers and advocates
- And, of course, test, test, test, measure and improve.

To help define e-marketing in more detail, let's look at what marketing is. The UK Chartered Institute of Marketing defines marketing as: *'The management process responsible for identifying, anticipating and satisfying customer needs profitably'.*

What does e-marketing involve?

Now let's consider how e-marketing can fulfil the definition of marketing, if properly implemented. Let's break up the definition into manageable chunks: *E-marketing can identify, anticipate and satisfy customer needs efficiently.*

Taking a web site as a major part of e-marketing, consider how a web site can fulfil the definition of marketing (identify, anticipate and satisfy customer needs profitably). It can:

- *Identify* needs from customer comments, enquiries, requests and complaints solicited via the web site's email facility, bulletin boards, chat rooms and, of course, sales patterns (seeing what's selling and what's not), and by observing new customer groupings identified by data mining through customer data, sales and interests (recorded using *web analytics* which reveal insights into interests determined by pages visited). Don't forget *online surveys* assessing satisfaction and requesting suggestions for service or product improvements. Finally, there is a proliferation of online secondary sources of research such as those given in Table 1.1 (above), many of which provide free in-depth insights into customer needs.

- *Anticipate* customer needs by asking customers questions and engaging them in a dynamic dialogue built on trust. And, of course, a little bit of what Amazon calls *collaborative filtering* helps the company to identify and anticipate what customers might like, given that buyers of similar books have similar interests. Customers often welcome suggested books from Amazon. And today's sophisticated profiling techniques allow many companies to do their own *data mining* to discover and anticipate buyers' needs. This is old technology. More recent sophisticated *profiling* technology allows some companies to analyse your interests without even knowing your name – courtesy of the *cookie* – a bit of code sent to your access device when you visit certain sites. So without knowing your name, it knows your interests. It recognizes your device and records which types of sites you visit (interests you have). So when you visit a web site and an unusually relevant banner ad drops down, this is no coincidence – cookies have anticipated your desires and needs.

- *Satisfy* needs with prompt responses, punctual deliveries, order status updates, helpful reminders, after-sales services and added value services combined with the dynamic dialogue. The dialogue maintains permission to continue communicating and then adds value by delivering useful content in the right context (right time and right amount).

- *Efficiently* means in an automated way (or partially automated) . . . an efficient, yet hopefully not impersonal, way (i.e. it allows tailor-made technology to increase the marketer's memory as the relationship effectively blossoms during the customer's life – increasing *lifetime value*).

And if the web site is integrated with customer relationship management (*CRM*) systems and *mass customization*, then the relationship deepens and needs are completely satisfied in a very efficient automated two-way process. This also, of course, provides some protection from the inevitable onslaught of competition.

SECTION SUMMARY 1.4

Situation – e-definitions

E-commerce generally refers to paid-for transactions, whether B2C or B2B, but some commentators include all communications between customers and business. E-business is broader, including e-commerce, and is a means to optimize all business processes that are part of the internal and external value chain. E-marketing is best considered as how e-tools such as web sites, CRM systems and databases can be used to get closer to customers – to be able to identify, anticipate and satisfy their needs efficiently and effectively.

1.5 Situation – sloppy e-marketing

Identifying, anticipating and satisfying customer needs is all simple common sense. Yet common sense is not common. Sloppy e-marketing has become commonplace . . . broken sites, delayed deliveries, impersonal responses, non-responses.

Whether it's unclear objectives, lack of strategy or simply lousy execution, good e-marketing is still relatively rare.

E-MARKETING INSIGHT

Online customers demand service

It's a well-known saying that if you have a good experience with a brand, you may tell one person; but if you have a bad experience, you tell ten others. Today, through online sharing of experiences, the experiences can be shared much more widely. Smart Insights (2012a) reported that 'over 44 per cent of adults now use the web to share grievances about products, with new customers expecting to interact with companies online and get a speed response'. At the same time, many companies are ignoring comments by customers made on the social networks, with one survey showing that '95% of customer Facebook posts were ignored by brands' (Smart Insights, 2012b). Some are even facilitating it; for example, McDonald's asked its Facebook followers and Twitter fans to share their experiences under a hash tag #McDStories, which was hijacked by customers complaining about negative experiences. The report recommends that to minimize the impact of customer complaints:

● The customer service operation is equipped to monitor and engage with a targeted spectrum of media.

- Companies fully understand where, why and how their customers are using social media before making any social media marketing changes.
- A balance is struck across different types of media – telephone, email, web, social network and mobile.
- The power of online communities is recognized, and customers are encouraged to help each other.
- Relationships are nurtured with advocates who wield particular influence on the Internet.
- Specialist tools are used to measure the impact of customers' online activity.

Chapter 3 on changing e-models shows why many of the old-world models, business models, marketing models, distribution models, pricing models and advertising models do not fit the new world of e-marketing. New models are required and the e-models chapter invites you to create some new models and examine other new emerging models. Whether marketing offline or online, do not forget the basics of good business – carefully thought-through ideas, attention to detail and excellent execution can be the difference between success and failure.

Sloppy e-marketing is also often evident through inefficient design of customer experiences on site. Take the example of a transactional site, where there are many opportunities to lose the customer's order. It's no wonder that average conversion rates remain well below 5 per cent (based on a Smart Insights [2011] compilation; see Figure 1.7).

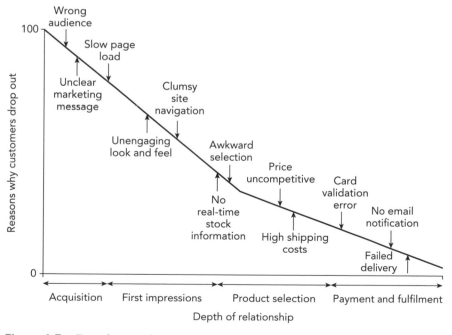

Figure 1.7   E-marketing sloppiness causes high attrition rates

Situation – sloppy e-marketing

There are many examples of poor e-marketing. This may result from unclear objectives, lack of strategy or simply lousy execution. Marketers should assess and minimize the risks before embarking on e-marketing.

1.6 Objectives

One reason why many new businesses, and in particular new e-businesses, go horribly wrong is often because objectives are not clearly agreed, and companies keen to get on with it jump straight to tactical e-tools (such as web sites and banner ads) without first agreeing clearly defined objectives and razor-sharp strategies.

The following sections on objectives cover the purpose or reasons why businesses go online. They examine the kind of clear objectives and goals that will drive good e-marketing.

So before making the change to e-marketing, first be clear: Why do you want to go online? What are the objectives? What advantages and benefits are expected?

You must be clear why you're getting into e-marketing and the areas on which you want to focus as you improve your e-marketing. What are the objectives? Apart from competitive paranoia? What are the benefits? There are five broad benefits of, reasons for or objectives of e-marketing:

1 Grow sales (through wider distribution, promotion and sales).
2 Add value (give customers extra benefits online).
3 Get closer to customers (by tracking them, asking them questions, creating a dialogue, learning about them).
4 Save costs (of service, promotions, sales transactions and administration, print and post), and so increase profits on transactions.
5 Extend the brand online. Reinforce brand values in a totally new medium.

There is a section on each of these 'objectives'.

All these e-marketing objectives can be summarized as the 5Ss – Sell, Serve, Speak, Save and Sizzle. These are covered in the next five sections. Once you have defined (and quantified) 'where you are going' (your objectives), you can then decide 'how to get there' – strategy. First, consider objectives.

You should set specific goals for objectives in each of the five areas, as shown in Table 1.2.

Table 1.2 Objectives for the 5Ss of e-marketing

Benefit of e-marketing	How benefit is delivered	Typical objectives
Sell – Grow sales	Achieved through wider distribution to customers you can't readily service offline or perhaps through a wider product range than in-store or lower prices compared to other channels.	• Achieve 10% of sales online in market • Increase online sales for product by 20% in year • Increase conversion rate by 5%
Serve – Add value	Achieved through giving customers extra benefits online or inform product development through online dialogue and feedback.	• Increase conversion rate by 5% increase interaction with different content on site • Increase dwell time duration or pages per view on site by 10% (sometimes known as stickiness) • Increase number of customers actively using online services (at least once per month) to 30%
Speak – Get closer to customers	This is creating a two-way dialogue through web and email forms and polls; conducting online market research through formal surveys; and informally monitoring chat rooms to learn about them. Also speak through reaching them via key influencers through e-PR.	• Grow email coverage to 50% of current customer database • Survey 1,000 customers online each month • Increase visitors to community site section or increase ratings/reviews and discussions by 5%
Save – Save costs	Achieved through online email communications, sales and service transactions to reduce staff, print and postage costs.	• Generate 10% more sales for same communications budget • Reduce cost of direct marketing by 15% through email • Increase web self-service to 40% of all service enquiries and reduce overall cost-to-serve by 10%
Sizzle – Extend the brand online	Achieved through providing a new proposition and new experience online while at the same time appearing familiar.	• Add two new significant enhancements to the customer online experience • Rework online value proposition messaging • Improve branding metrics such as: brand awareness, reach, brand favourability and purchase intent

E-MARKETING INSIGHT

Ultralase grow visits and sales through clearly defined objectives

Ultralase (www.ultralase.com, Figure 1.8), is a company offering laser eye treatment – a high-value consumer service. Their market is characterized by intense competition with other suppliers such as Optimax, Optical Express and Accuvision. Before developing a digital strategy, Ultralase had relatively low brand awareness and was struggling with a long sales cycle and relatively uninformed customers. The main communications disciplines used were:

- Press
- Direct mail
- PR
- Brochures

Their web site integrates with these offline channels and shows how the 5Ss can be applied as objectives which inform site features and communications:

- *Sell* – a prominent call to action 'above-the-fold' of the site encourages permission marketing with an offer of a DVD which is still relevant for a high-involvement decision and is aimed to ultimately lead to a consultation.
- *Serve* – service quality is shown by records of customer treatment on a separate domain (http://thegiftofsight.com). Service is delivered by specially formulated frequently asked questions (FAQs).
- *Speak* – the site highlights three key user tasks responding to consumer concerns; i.e. quality, cost and booking a consultation.
- *Save* – Ultralase have invested in online media such as search marketing and PR which can be more cost-effective than offline media to drive awareness when prospects are looking for this service. The content on the site also reduces the need for more expensive brochures in mailings.
- *Sizzle* – the site features patients' stories and makes surgeons more accessible. Key messages are delivered through a high-impact carousel at the top of the page.

As we review the 5Ss, we will relate them to Ultralase.

SECTION SUMMARY 1.6

Objectives

Organizations need to be clear about the objectives of e-marketing, so that the appropriate resources can be directed at achieving these objectives. A useful framework for developing objectives is the 5Ss of Sell, Serve, Speak, Save and Sizzle.

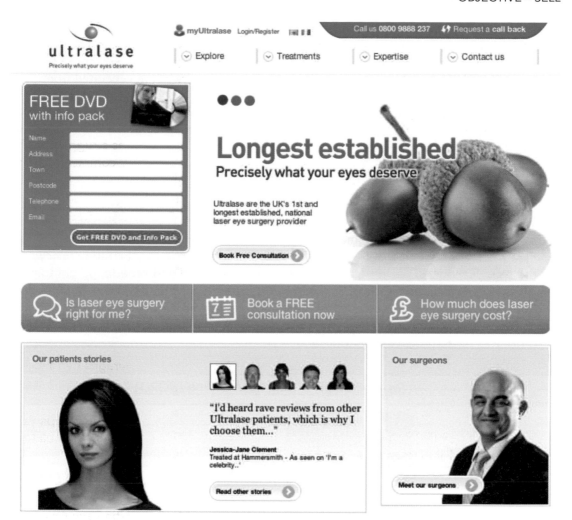

Figure 1.8   Ultralase (www.ultralase.com)

1.7 Objective – sell – using the Internet as a sales tool

Just about anything can be sold online, from books to bikes, jobs to jets, turbines to toys and chemicals to kidneys. Although just about anything can be sold online, the Internet has a greater impact on some industries than others, particularly education, entertainment and advisory services – many of which can be digitized and delivered down the line.

Companies must be able to sell or transact online to meet these customers' new online needs. A key objective to set is the *direct online revenue contribution* for different products and different markets. This defines the proportion of sales transactions completed online. For example, a bank might try to achieve 15 per cent of its insurance sales online in the UK.

But remember that many other products and services are partly bought online. Shoppers browse online, collecting information, prices and special offers before visiting stores and showrooms or picking up the phone to negotiate better deals. So *mixed-mode selling* is a must! Organizations have to support customers who want to be able to buy both online and offline. Therefore it is essential to accommodate those who want to buy online and those who just want to browse. For example, BMW find that approximately half of their test drives are generated from their web site.

E-MARKETING INSIGHT

Understanding cross-channel customer behaviour using ROPO

Some commentators have coined the term ROPO, standing for 'Research Online Purchase Offline', although Research Offline Purchase Online is another behaviour which can also be important as customers use their smartphones to scan online prices in-store. Figure 1.9 gives a useful matrix for summarizing these behaviours. This study reviewed the role of the Internet in the decision process for mobile and broadband contracts involving the Vodafone web site and stores in Germany, based on a panel of 16,000 web users and questionnaires about their intent and purchase. For both of these services, the contract was signed online by around a third of the audience. However, a significant proportion signed the contract offline.

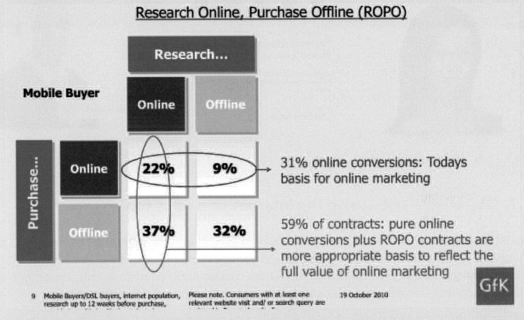

Figure 1.9   ROPO matrix showing main cross-channel customer behaviours

Source: Google (2010)

'Clicks-and-mortar' organizations offer customers the reassurance of a real presence (building/mortar) along with the easy accessibility of the Internet. So another objective to set is the *indirect online revenue contribution* – the proportion of sales that are influenced by digital communications. Ultralase will have objectives for the number of leads generated from the web site, either directly or by phone. A similar objective is the *reach* of the web site within its target audience. Ultralase will be able to work back to assess the number and the cost of leads generated by different channels, such as paid search and display advertising.

E-MARKETING INSIGHT

Tagging value events to assess the influence of a web site and digital channels on sales

The key types of outcomes or 'value events' that will be useful for a business, such as enquiries or sales on a site, should be defined. These value events are particularly important for a business-to-business vendor, or a consumer brand with non-transactional sites which don't sell products online. Pages on which these value events occur can be tagged through web analytics systems. For example, the free tool Google Analytics (www.google.com/analytics) allows you to set up 'conversion goals' by indicating which page(s) are valuable, and you can then attribute a dollar value to each; e.g. US$1 for a newsletter sign-up. You can then see which referring channels and content on the site influence sales and contribute to achieving other goals in its Multi-Channel Funnels feature. Alternatively, other web analytics systems allow scripting (coding) within the HTML of a page, sometimes known as 'spotlight tags', to indicate whether it is a valuable page.

Typical value events include:

- Sale (by tagging a sales confirmation page)
- Lead (by tagging an enquiry or document download form)
- Newsletter registration (tagged confirmation page)
- Searches (tagging a search results page)
- Product page views (tagging product pages)
- Product document downloads (tagging document download pages).

Don't forget offline value events such as sales generated by phone numbers. You should aim to track these through using unique phone numbers, perhaps for different parts of the site.

Going back to the BMW example, why not take it to the next level and offer the web visitor who wants a real test drive delivery of the vehicle for the weekend? Assuming that the visitor is screened and fits the ideal profile and suitable insurance is taken out, wouldn't this close the sales cycle and accelerate mixed-mode selling?

The real crunch may come when businesses realize the power of the Internet's potential for distribution – extending the availability of many products and services without physically having to display a product. Take EDF Energy's London Eye, for example. The service could be extended and distributed to a much wider audience than London's immediate tourist market. Anyone around the world could log on to a live web cam (camera) and take the 30-minute virtual ride to enjoy stunning views at night or by day. This service could be revenue generating while promoting tourism simultaneously. Equally, the Louvre, the Pyramids and many more attractions can now extend their distribution of both the point of purchase (i.e. buying a ticket) and the point of consumption (enjoy the view from your home). Sales and distribution opportunities abound.

So online sales will continue to grow. But there are other additional benefits of or objectives for e-marketing including serving, speaking, saving and sizzling. You can explore each of these at your leisure.

SELLING WHAT TO WHOM

There is a tendency, when setting online sales objectives, to use a low-risk approach of selling existing products into existing markets. This is the market penetration approach shown in Figure 1.10, which you may recognize as the Ansoff matrix – used by marketers for over 40

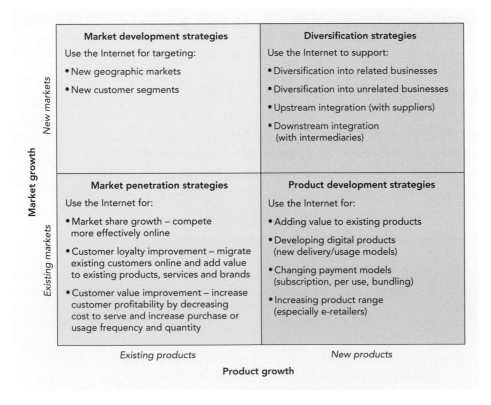

Figure 1.10   Online opportunities for product and market innovation

years to determine strategic priorities. We will see in later chapters that objectives should also be set for selling new digital products into new markets as appropriate.

E-MARKETING EXCELLENCE

EasyJet sells

EasyJet was founded by Stelios Haji-Ioannou, the son of a Greek shipping tycoon, who reputedly used to 'hate the Internet'. In the mid-1990s, Haji-Ioannou reportedly denounced the Internet as something 'for nerds', and swore that it wouldn't do anything for his business. However, he decided to experiment with a prototype site, and sat up and took notice when sales started to flow from the site. Based on early successes, easyJet decided to invest in the new channel and proactively convert customers to using it. To help achieve this, they set an initial target of 30 per cent of seats by the year 2000. By August 2000, the site accounted for 38 per cent of ticket sales and by 2001, for over 90 per cent of seats. By 2007, phone sales were down to just single digit percentages, but significant enough for the phone channel to be retained. Of course, this success is based on the relative ease of converting direct phone sale customers to online customers.

SECTION SUMMARY 1.7

Objective – sell

The clearest benefit of e-marketing is the capability to sell from an online presence. Although this may not be practical for all products, an online presence is still important in supporting the buying decision leading to sales through traditional channels. You should use your web analytics system to tag different types of value event web pages which indicate that your goals are being achieved. An online presence also offers opportunities to sell into new markets and reach particular segments.

1.8 Objective – serve – using the Internet as a customer-service tool

Another e-marketing objective is serving or adding value. How can a web site help customers improve their experience or add value to their experience? Take newspapers. Newspapers can allow readers to create their own newspapers through personalization. They are no longer constrained by publication times, but can be accessed at any time. Their readers can set up alerts to be notified by email as soon as an event breaks.

Ultralase provides a range of information to serve its audience and answer their questions as shown in Figure 1.8. This includes a suitability checker, an online forum, a Q&A service, an information pack on a DVD and, of course, an appointment booker.

Another example: for customers who like their wines, the Marks & Spencer web site tests its visitors' knowledge of labels and grapes. And if, having chosen a wine, you're unsure of what to eat, Ragu's web site offers free recipes (and encourages visitors to send the recipe to a friend).

If, after dinner, you're not sure which toothpaste to use, visit the Mentadent web site where visitors can get samples of toothpaste and free oral care advice. Visitors can even email questions to a resident dentist.

Social media give new and important customer service channels. Yet research has shown that many companies ignore comments by customers made on their Facebook pages or through the @ symbol in Twitter. Savvy companies like Dell review all negative and positive brand mentions using social listening tool Radian6 and then respond accordingly. Others use specialist tools such as Get Satisfaction, Kampyle or UserVoice to get responses (see http:://bit.ly/smartlistening for examples).

E-MARKETING EXCELLENCE

Assessing online customer engagement

How effectively you serve and speak to your online audience is indicated by measures of online customer engagement, an important concept we will refer to throughout *Emarketing Excellence*. You should assess customer engagement both for web site visitors and email subscribers and break it down by different online segments such as different audience types and visitors referred from different sources such as search engines or online ads.

You should assess online customer engagement using the checklist shown in Table 1.3.

Table 1.3 Measures of online customer engagement

Engagement metric	Engagement tactic
1 **% of non-home page entry visits:** Your home page isn't necessarily the most important page on your site. People might arrive on other pages so make sure your messages are distributed throughout the site.	**Use run-of-site OVP messages:** Use promotional messages across the site that explain the essence of your offer (not just on the home page).
2 **Bounce rate:** The percentage of visitors who enter a site or page and leave immediately.	**Use a run-of-site sign-up:** Place value-based messages and calls-to-action prominently throughout your site. For example, see the email sign-up on www.thomson.co.uk.
3 **Duration:** Duration on site, or better, pages per visit.	**Use heatmaps or overlays to assess engagement:** Tools like ClickDensity show what people click on and how soon. Helps you refine the clarity of your messages and calls-to-action.

Table 1.3 (Continued)

Engagement metric	Engagement tactic
4 **Marketing outcomes:** Assign values to outcomes/events and use them to assess the success rate; e.g. newsletter sign-up, 2 points; register CV, 5 points, etc.	**Get your scent right:** Experiment with design or language variations in hyperlinks and images to see what is attractive to visitors. For example, Dell have menu options to appeal to different sizes of business.
5 **Micro or step conversion rates:** Assess the effectiveness of your site and drop-off at every stage of the customer acquisition-to-conversion lifecycle.	**Interactive sales advisers:** Replicate the steps you would use in a physical sales situation, considering types of questions asked, etc., and tailor responses to visitors accordingly. If a visitor dwells on a page offer for a long time encourage them to enter a chat session.
6 **Brand search-term strength:** Assess the number of people searching on your brand name or URL through time to assess how powerful your brand is in attracting new and repeat visitors.	**Generate awareness:** This could be through above-the-line advertising online or offline or sponsorships, for example, to generate awareness. But previous visitors and customers will also search on your brand if they have had a favourable experience.
7 **Email activity level:** Use email communication for on-going engagement with customers. Check levels of activity and response.	**Refined touch strategy:** Develop a strategy that looks at message type, triggers, outcomes required, the right medium for messages and the right sequence, etc.
8 **Define activity levels or hurdle rates (for different activities):** Set metrics to review different types of user activity; e.g. number of new users in last 60 days, number of active or dormant users, etc.	**Personalize by activity or lifecycle of content in web or email pods:** Offer users different messages depending on their status; i.e. message for new visitors will differ from message to regular, registered users.
9 **Emotional response:** Conduct benchmarking research with users to assess their emotional responses to aspects such as look and feel, design, messaging, etc.	**Multivariate testing:** Test different permutations of buttons, messaging, etc., to see what the highest uplift is.
10 **Outcomes:** Beyond the use of analytics tools, play programmes to find out what people think, including aspects such as relevance, believability and likeability, etc.	**Use secondary navigation to highlight next steps:** Use a combination of images and text for menus to invite users to do something else on your site.

SERVING THE B2B AUDIENCE

Examples of excellent added value, online, can also be found in B2B markets. Companies like FedEx, GE and Dell add value through their web sites all the time. They also build switching costs as customers become more and more locked into their excellent services.

Take GE Power Systems – they have created a web-based tool called a 'turbine optimizer' which enables operators of any GE turbine to measure and improve their machine's efficiency by comparing its performance against any similar turbines anywhere in the world.

Dell adds value by integrating its web help system into a customer's own Enterprise Resource Planning (ERP) system as Dell Premier, a corporate B2B sub-brand. This means that when a customer orders online from Dell, this triggers both Dell's system and the customer's own system simultaneously, which in turn updates both systems as to orders, approvals, budgets, stock, etc. This also makes switching suppliers more difficult.

Intel adds value by sharing relevant information with its customers. The company track its stocks (inventories) second by second and makes this information available to its customers. Customers return the favour with information about their own stocks.

A web site's main purpose is to help customers (and other stakeholders such as suppliers and distributors). The big question to ask is: 'How can my web site help my customers? How can I add extra value?' The search for new ways to add value is continuous.

Added value, extra service, call it what you want, becomes part of the product or service. Web sites can become part of a product or service. Do you agree?

E-MARKETING INSIGHT

Patricia Seybold on adding value to B2B services

Seybold (1999) defines eight success factors to achieve e-marketing. Two of these refer to adding value and they still ring true today. She says:

- *'Let customers help themselves.'* This 'customer self-service' can be enquiring about delivery of a product or obtaining after-sales support.
- *'Help customers do their jobs.'* Give information about best practice to help professionals complete their day-to-day work.

E-MARKETING EXCELLENCE

EasyJet serves

When easyJet customers have a query, the easyJet contact strategy is to minimize voice calls through providing carefully structured frequently asked questions (FAQs) and email forms.

Objective – serve

A web presence can be used to add value for customers at different stages of the buying process, whether pre-sales, during the sale or post-sales support.

1.9 Objective – speak – using the Internet as a communications tool

A web site and 'outposts' on social media and other partner sites are powerful new communications channels to increase awareness, build brand, shape customer opinion and communicate special offers. While marketing investment to increase awareness used to focus on paid media with additional PR activity, new categories of owned and earned media have become more important.

Today's main types of media are:

1 *Paid media*. Paid or bought media are media where there is investment to pay for visitors, reach or conversions through search, display ad networks or affiliate marketing. Offline traditional media like print and TV advertising and direct mail remain important, accounting for the majority of paid media spend.

2 *Earned media*. Traditionally, earned media has been the name given to publicity generated through PR invested in targeting influencers to increase awareness about a brand. Earned media also includes word of mouth that can be stimulated through viral and social media marketing and includes conversations in social networks, blogs and other communities. It's useful to think of earned media as developed through different types of partners such as publishers, bloggers and other influencers including customer advocates. Think of earned media as different forms of conversations occurring both online and offline; these still all require investment.

3 *Owned media*. This is media owned by the brand. Online, this includes a company's own web sites, blogs, mobile apps or their social presence on Facebook, LinkedIn, Google+, Twitter or YouTube. Offline-owned media may include brochures or retail stores.

Many brands haven't adjusted their way of thinking about speaking to their audience. Use the framework shown in Figure 1.11 for reviewing the balance in companies in which you're involved.

The E-Marketing Excellence box 'EasyJet speaks – using the web as a PR tool' (below) illustrates some approaches. As well as speaking to customers, the Internet provides a tool to listen to customers – to get closer to them. In the last 100 years, marketers have got worse at knowing customers. We've become separated and distanced by middlemen, distributors, agents, retailers, advertising agencies and market research agencies. The world of e-marketing opens up the opportunity to get close to customers again . . . to speak to them and to listen to them in ways that were not previously possible. Your web presence gives great opportunities to get feedback from customers on your brand and communications using the tools we have listed at http://bit.ly/smartlistening.

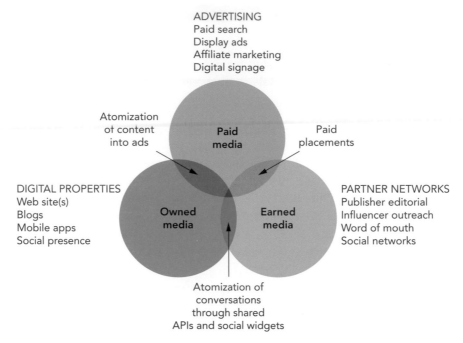

ADVERTISING
Paid search
Display ads
Affiliate marketing
Digital signage

Atomization
ot content
into ads

**Paid
media**

Paid
placements

DIGITAL PROPERTIES
Web site(s)
Blogs
Mobile apps
Social presence

**Owned
media**

**Earned
media**

PARTNER NETWORKS
Publisher editorial
Influencer outreach
Word of mouth
Social networks

Atomization of
conversations
through shared
APIs and social widgets

Figure 1.11   Categories of media: paid, owned and earned

FROM OUTBOUND TO INBOUND MARKETING

Traditional media are predominantly *push media* where the marketing message is broadcast from company *to* customer and other stakeholders. During this process, there is limited interaction with the customer, although interaction is encouraged in some cases, such as the direct-response advert or mail-order campaign.

In digital media it is often the customer who initiates contact with a brand and who is *seeking* information or an experience through visiting a web site or company outpost. In other words, it is a *pull* mechanism where it is particularly important to have good visibility in search engines when customers are entering search terms relevant to a company's products or services. Amongst marketing professionals this powerful new approach to marketing is now commonly known as *inbound marketing* (Shah and Halligan, 2009). Inbound marketing is powerful since advertising wastage is reduced. Content and search marketing can be used to target prospects with a defined need – they are proactive and self-selecting. But this is a weakness since marketers may have less control than in traditional communications where the message is pushed out to a defined audience and can help generate awareness and demand. Advocates of inbound marketing such as Dharmesh Shah and Brian Halligan (2009) argue that content, social media and search marketing have a huge role to play in generating demand.

HOW CONTENT MARKETING DRIVES CONVERSATIONS

Success in today's permission marketing requires exceptional, compelling content. To emphasize the importance of content marketing to gaining permission, encouraging sharing and ongoing engagement through web sites and social media, the concepts of *content marketing* and content strategy have developed to describe best practice approaches. By content we refer to the combination of static content forming web pages, but also dynamic rich media content which encourages interaction. Videos, podcasts, user-generated content and interactive product selectors should also be considered as content which should be refined to engage site visitors.

You can see the challenge that content strategy presents since there are so many different types of content delivered in different forms to different places on different access platforms, yet it is increasingly important to engage customers in social media. These elements of content marketing need to be planned and managed:

1 *Content engagement value.* Which types of content will engage the audience – is it simple product or services information, a guide to buying product(s), or a game to engage your audience?

2 *Content media.* These include plain text, rich media such as Flash or Rich Internet applications or mobile apps, audio (podcasts) and hosted and streamed video. Even plain text offers different format options, from HTML text to e-book formats and PDFs.

3 *Content syndication.* Content can be syndicated to different types of partner sites through feeds, *APIs,* microformats or direct submission by email. Content can be embedded in sites through widgets displaying information delivered by a feed.

4 *Content participation.* Effective content today is not simply delivered for static consumption; it should enable commenting, ratings and reviews. These also need to be monitored and managed both in the original location and where they are discussed elsewhere.

5 *Content access platforms.* These include different digital access platforms such as desktops and laptops of different screen resolution and mobile devices. Paper is also a content access platform for print media.

The infographic in Figure 1.12 shows an overall process for inbound marketing integrating inbound and content marketing.

Using digital media channels to speak with your audiences on other sites

Online marketers have a fantastic range of communications tools that they can use to speak to their audience when they are not on their site, and to encourage them to visit the site. In Chapter 7, we review the six main options for traffic building (shown in Figure 7.2) and discuss how to make the right media investment decisions. For now, we will just introduce these key digital media channels.

1 *Search engine marketing* (SEM) – placing messages on a search engine, encouraging click-through to a web site when the user types a specific keyword phrase. The two main disciplines are search engine optimization (SEO) to boost a company's position in the natural search listings and paid search marketing which uses sponsored ads, typically on a Pay Per Click (PPC) basis.

   Search marketing is great for targeting audiences at the moment of intent. It can help create a level playing field where small companies can be listed alongside well-known brands to

Figure 1.12   Inbound marketing infographic

Source: First10 (2012)

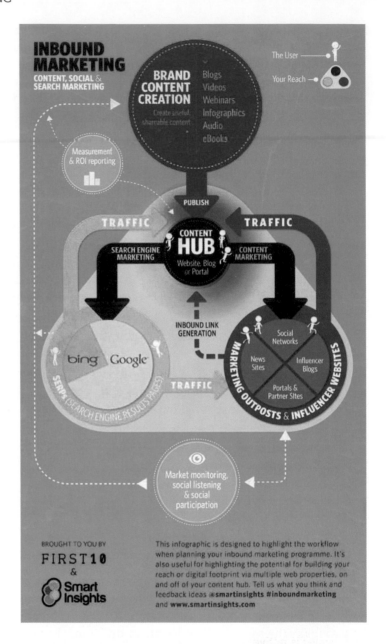

increase awareness of them and drive response. That's if the small companies can get SEO right or afford to compete in paid search marketing.

2 *Online PR* – Maximizing favourable mentions of your company, brands, products or web sites on a range of third-party web sites such as media sites, social networks and blogs, which are likely to be visited by your target audience.

Online PR can offer a low-cost route to increase awareness of your brand, it can also help attract visitors and increase *backlinks* to a site, which as we will see in Chapter 7, is useful for SEO.

3 *Online partnerships* – Creating and managing long-term arrangements to promote your online services on third-party web site or email communications. Different forms of partnership include link building, affiliate marketing, online sponsorship and co-branding.

Smart online marketers realize the value of partnerships in extending their reach into their audiences via other sites.

4 *Interactive advertising* – Use of online display ads, such as banners, skyscrapers and rich media ads, to achieve brand awareness and encourage clickthrough to a target site.

5 *Opt-in email* – Renting opt-in email lists, placing ads in third-party e-newsletters, making deals with third parties for co-registration or co-branding of emails, or building your own in-house email list and sending e-newsletters or email campaigns.

The main aim of email marketing for acquisition is to generate awareness of brands or offerings or direct response to achieve registration or leads.

6 *Social media marketing* – Social media marketing can and should integrate with all of these other communications approaches. Social media helps amplify a message through comments and sharing of social networks, viral marketing or word-of-mouth marketing.

As we have said, your site also needs to speak with, not speak at, your audience. The database behind the web site is a warehouse full of valuable information about customers and their patterns of purchasing, responses to promotions and much more. *Data mining* the *data warehouse* can reveal intriguing insights into buyer behaviour.

Combine the database with *collaborative filtering* (or rules such as 'if buy product "A", then likely to want product "C"') and the e-marketer has a very powerful weapon . . . the dynamic dialogue about relevant products.

Speak to customers, monitor their purchases, suggest other relevant products and all in a helpful, non-intrusive manner. If your local delicatessen remembers your name and asks if you'd like to try some particular pâté because they remember you bought a particular type of cheese last time, then you welcome this dialogue. The same applies here, except that this can be automated. This helps to create a dynamic dialogue with the customer.

E-MARKETING INSIGHT

EasyJet speaks – using the web as a PR tool

EasyJet is active in using the web as a PR tool. Here are some examples:

- EasyJet jets were emblazoned with oversize 'www.easyJet.com' logos.
- EasyJet ran a competition to guess the losses of rival airline Go and received 65,000 entries and also enhanced press coverage.
- Owner Stelios Haji-Ioannou has a personal views page, 'message from Stelios'.
- Standard press-release pages are regularly updated.

Objective – speak

One of the many benefits of e-marketing is getting close to customers again. Speaking to them. You can explore the other benefits (selling, serving, saving and sizzling) now or later.

1.10 Objective – save – using the Internet for cost reduction

Another e-marketing objective is 'saving'. This is what will catch the financial director's ear together with 'sell', since the two together increase profitability – saving money, time and effort. Savings emerge in digital media channels, customer service, transactional costs and, of course, print and distribution.

Good systems help customers to service themselves. This obviously saves money, and, if done in a simple, speedy and efficient manner, increases customer satisfaction.

FedEx estimated that it saves between US$2 and US$5 when they service customers via the web site rather than over the phone. This saves many millions of dollars per annum. Similarly, Dell showed that it saved between US$5 and US$10 per customer which adds up to many millions. Cisco saves hundreds of millions of dollars every year now through its web-based customer services.

Other estimates suggest that there are huge savings in transactional costs when they are completed online. For example, the cost of an over-the-counter transaction in a bank is over US$1 compared to 1 cent when completed online.

Ultralase saves money in a range of ways – first by using the most cost-effective digital media channels such as affiliates and paid search which are Pay Per Performance media. Then it uses its site to qualify visitors; since visitors can self-serve, that means fewer inbound phone calls to manage and phone conversations can focus on the customers who need or prefer this type of service. It also saves money through sending emails rather than post (remember right touching).

In addition to the efficiency gains of e-systems, many businesses negotiate better deals online (from suppliers anywhere in the world). These businesses can also enjoy new economies of scale from the higher purchasing power emerging from the new online purchasing alliances like GM and Ford, mentioned in Section 1.3.

Other savings are found in print and distribution. Annual reports, sales literature, user manuals and much more can be stored and distributed electronically – saving storage space, paper, trees, fuel (transport) and, of course, money and time.

Some companies find other savings by using the Internet for cheaper phone calls. Other companies find savings by soliciting cost-saving ideas from their employees, customers and even general visitors to their web sites.

Other companies find that their web operations not only save money, but also generate extra revenues through banner advertising. Busy sites attract traffic. Advertisers need audiences, so some sites allow advertisers to advertise on their web sites, for a price.

Introducing allowable Cost Per Acquisition (CPA)

Cost Per Acquisition (CPA) is crucial in controlling media and is often used to control the level of bids. For example, to control online advertising or paid search marketing, it is vital that you calculate and define a target or *allowable cost per acquisition* for different types of product.

Your actual CPA will be dependent on a combination of conversion rate and cost per click.

Cost Per Acquisition (CPA) = (100/site conversion rate) × Cost Per Click

This can be simplified to:

Cost Per Acquisition (CPA) = Cost Per Click/conversion rate

For example, CPA is £40, with a CPC of £2 and a conversion rate of 5 per cent. To set target goals for allowable CPA depends on the value delivered by the customer acquisition across their lifetime; i.e. we also need to factor in the revenue generated from an individual product sale, total basket size or predicted lifetime value, typically over a five-year period.

A final note on CPA is that you need to take into account telephone sales influenced by the web site and the contribution that the media channel makes to developing brand awareness, familiarity and favourability. For example, display advertising may not be justified in terms of CPA alone, but it may support sales through other digital channels such as paid search.

E-MARKETING EXCELLENCE

EasyJet saves on call-centre expansion

The Internet is important to easyJet since it helps to reduce running costs, important for a company where each passenger generates a small profit. Part of the decision to increase the use of the Internet for sales was to save on the building of a £10 million contact centre which would have been necessary to sustain sales growth if the Internet was not used as a sales channel.

As an example, a 1999 sales promotion offered 50,000 seats to readers of *The Times*. The scalability of the Internet helped to deal with demand since everyone was directed to the web site rather than the company needing to employ an extra 250 telephone operators.

SECTION SUMMARY 1.10

Objective – save

So e-marketing saves money in many different ways. Of all the benefits of e-marketing (selling, serving, speaking, saving and sizzling), saving is the one that will help to present any business case, as the financial fraternity relate to savings very quickly. The other benefits of e-marketing (selling, serving, speaking and sizzling) will strengthen your business case.

1.11 Objective – sizzle – using the Internet as a brand-building tool

The Internet offers new opportunities to build and strengthen the brand – to add some 'sizzle' to the brand. To add extra value (or 'added value'), extend the experience and enhance the image. Ask yourself, 'What experience could a web site deliver that would be truly unique and representative of the brand?' A newspaper that allows you to build your own newspaper and have it delivered electronically as an app; or a car manufacturer that allows you to build your own car; or a camera company that allows you to learn how to use its cameras by simulating taking photographs with different settings and allowing you to compare and contrast the results (and also gives you tips on how to maintain your camera and protect your films and photos, and invites you to send your best photos in to a competition). A travel company that gives you a 'virtual friend' – after you tell them what your interests are (via an online questionnaire), the 'friend' suggests ideas for things you would like to do in the cities you choose to explore. Cosmetics companies offer online games, screensavers, viral emails, video clips and soundtracks to enhance the online brand experience. This extra sizzle can enhance the brand in a way that can only be done online.

Drinks brand Bacardi (www.bacardi.com) sizzles online by maintaining the club scene atmosphere with their OVP including a pulsating beat, BAT radio, video clips and cocktail recipes, although delivered through a Flash rich media application – search engine optimization doesn't matter too much to them since the brand is so strong!

Brands are important as they build trust, recognition and, believe it or not, relationships between the buyer and the supplier. Sometimes brand imagery is the only real differentiator between products.

The brand is affected by both reality and perception: the *reality* of the actual experience enjoyed (or suffered) when using the brand; the *perception*, or image, associated with the particular product. In addition to the real experience, these perceptions are built through advertising, sales promotions, direct mail, editorial exposure (PR), exhibitions, telesales, packaging, point of sale, web sites and the most potent communications tool, word of mouth.

All of these communications tools work both online and offline; for example, banner ads, incentives, offers and promotions. *Opt-in email* remains a powerful tool for customer communications.

And packaging and point of sale are still required in the online world as some sites recreate the shopping mall experience. As the visitor selects stores and aisles, packaging and point-of-sale skills are still required.

These all contribute to the brand, as does the experience – the quality of the experience, both online and offline. Remember that sloppy web sites damage the brand. Slow email responses damage the brand. Non-responses can kill it.

There is no doubt that e-marketing can help to build the brand. Many analysts see e-marketing as a way to build both the brand image and the overall company value – yet another benefit of e-marketing. You can see the other benefits or objectives of e-marketing – adding value, getting closer to customers, selling and saving, whenever you need to build your business case.

Ultralase (see Figure 1.8 above) has worked hard at developing its content and online services so that it now offers much more than a brochure site, with detailed technical information, a forum and a Q&A service.

SECTION SUMMARY 1.11

Objective – sizzle

Objectives should also consider how to enhance a brand by adding value online. This can include adding to the experience of the brand through interactive facilities. Protecting the brand through achieving trust about security and confidentiality is also important.

1.12 Introduction to e-strategy objectives

Strategy summarizes how you achieve your objectives. Strategy is influenced by both the prioritization of objectives (sell, serve, speak, save and sizzle) and, of course, the amount of resources available.

You should think of e-marketing strategy as a channel strategy where electronic channels and digital media support other communications and distribution channels. It requires clear prioritization as to how the channel should be used. Your e-marketing strategy should identify target markets, positioning, online value proposition (OVP), the choice of mix of digital media channels to acquire new customers, and contact strategies to welcome and develop existing customers.

E-channel strategies are most effective when they are creating differential value for all parties to a transaction compared to other channels. But e-channels do not exist in isolation, so we still need to manage channel integration and acknowledge that the adoption of e-channels will not be appropriate for all products or services or generate sufficient value for all partners.

Key elements of an e-channel strategy, which we explore in more detail in Chapter 10, are:

1 It delivers against the goals that we have set through the 5 Ss.
2 It defines and communicates the specific benefits as to why customers should use the e-channel, which we refer to throughout this book as the *online value proposition (OVP)*. For B2B office supplier Euroffice (see Figure 1.6 above), the OVP centres on the next-day delivery, price guarantee and the rewards programme which are promoted prominently on their site. For Ultralase (see Figure 1.8 above), the OVP is the services and content available to help visitors decide on the best treatment and supplier.
3 It prioritizes audiences for whom e-channel adoption is most appropriate. Online services will not be equally effective for all customer segments, so decide which you will target. Ultralase needs to serve both fast customer leads where customers decide to enquire relatively quickly, and more considered leads where the customer does a lot of research before deciding to ask for further information.
4 It prioritizes products sold or purchased through the e-channel. Some will be more appropriate than others.

5 It specifies the mix of digital media channels used to acquire new customers and balances this against targets of sales revenues and profitability. This will be constrained by the objective of cost of customer acquisition. So, e-channel strategy guides the choice of target markets, positioning and propositions, which in turn guide the optimum marketing mix, sequence of e-tools (such as web sites, opt-in email, e-sponsorship, viral marketing), service level and evolutionary stage.

E-strategy also affects the traditional marketing mix as the *product* can be extended online, the *place* of purchase can be expanded, not to mention web *price* transparency, online *promotions* and the *people* who service the web site enquiries, the automated *processes* and the importance of having a professional presence or *physical evidence*. The remix required for e-marketing is examined in Chapter 2.

LINKING STRATEGY TO OBJECTIVES

One essential part of e-strategy is the development of the dynamic dialogue and the eventual full use of the integrated database potential. Regardless of how the customer comes into contact, he or she must be dealt with as a recognizable individual with unique preferences. The fully integrated database is essential so that the customer's name, address and previous orders are recalled and used appropriately in email sequences and with web personalization. This requires careful planning, as described in Chapter 8.

So, to summarize, the components of e-strategy include:

- Crystal-clear objectives (what you want to achieve online)
- Target markets, positioning and propositions
- Optimum mix of tactical e-tools (web site, banner ads, etc.)
- Evolutionary stage (what stage you want to be at)
- Online marketing mix (particularly service levels)
- Dynamic dialogue (ongoing with the customer)
- Integrated database (recognize and remember each customer whether via web or telephone).

Strategy is crucial. As Kenichi Ohmae observed (1999): 'There's no point rowing harder if you are rowing in the wrong direction'.

This is just a brief glimpse at e-strategy. It is examined in more depth in Chapter 10.

SECTION SUMMARY 1.12

Introduction to e-strategy

E-strategy defines a company's approach to achieving its e-marketing objectives. It should include the range of tactical e-tools and a revised marketing mix.

1.13 Tactics, action and control

Tactics are the details of strategy. Tactical e-tools include the web site, opt-in email, digital media channels such as paid search and display advertising, virtual exhibitions and sponsorship. Tactics require an understanding of what each e-tool can and cannot do. Tactics may also involve where and how each tool is physically used, whether with a kiosk, interactive TV, mobile or alternatives (such as microwave).

Each one is a mini project requiring careful planning and good project management skills combined with tactical 'nous' and creativity. Action, or implementation, also requires an appreciation of what can go wrong from cyber libel to viruses, mail bombs, hackers and hijackers, cyber squatting and much more . . . contingency planning is required. What happens when the server goes down or a virus comes to town? What happens if one of the e-tools is not working, or is not generating enough enquiries? Something has to be changed.

To help keep your tactics focused on customer-centric content marketing, we recommend the PRACE framework (Figure 1.13) as a way to reach and engage customers to meet business objectives. PRACE stands for:

- *Step 1 Plan.* It's all too easy to build a basic web site or a presence on a social network without a strategy, without thinking about how it will support your goals to build your brand. Planning involves working through the tried and trusted marketing fundamentals of customer research, segmentation, positioning and development of value propositions.
- *Step 2 Reach.* Reach means building awareness of a brand, its products and services on other web sites and in offline media in order to build traffic by driving visits to different web presences like your main site, microsites or social media sites.
- *Step 3 Act.* Act is about persuading site visitors or prospects to take the next step on their journey when they initially reach your site or social network presence. It may mean finding out more about a company or its products, searching to find a product or reading a blog post. It's about engaging the audience through relevant, compelling content and clear navigation pathways so that they don't hit the back button. The *bounce rates* on many sites are greater than 50 per cent, so getting the audience to act or participate is a major challenge, which is why we have identified it separately.
- *Step 4 Convert.* Conversion is where the visitor commits to forming a relationship which will generate commercial value for the business. It's about delivering on marketing goals such as leads or sales on web presences online and offline.
- *Step 5 Engage.* Here we're building deeper customer relationships through time in order to achieve retention goals. Encouraging advocacy or recommendations through word of mouth is a key part of engagement.

But how do you know if it's going well? Performance is measured against the detailed targets. Time has to be made for a regular review of what's working and what's not. Good marketers have control over their destinies. They do not leave it to chance and hope for the best. They reduce risk by finding what works and what doesn't – so that e-tactics, or even the e-strategy can be changed if necessary.

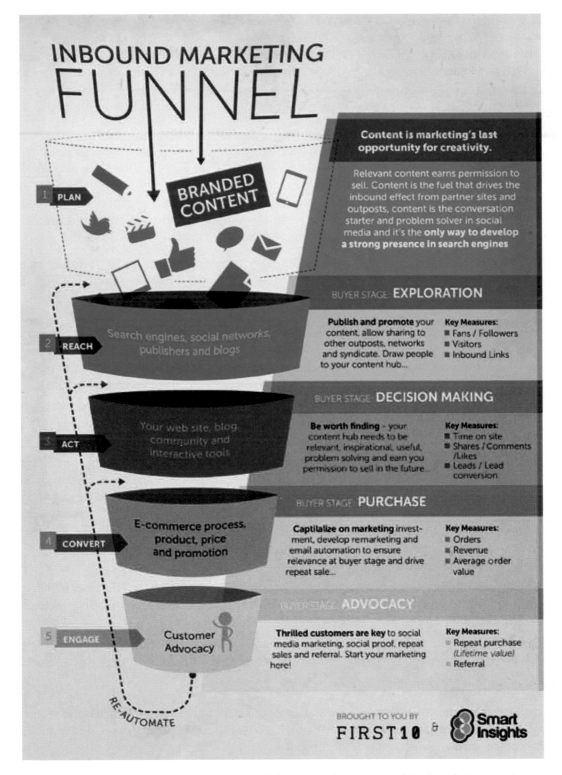

Figure 1.13   Using the PRACE framework to link business objectives to digital marketing tactics

Real marketers also want constantly to improve. Which tools are giving the best return on investment? Why? Other control mechanisms include measuring the number of hits, number of unique visitors, number of conversions (visitors that purchase or subscribe), churn rate (number of people who ask to be taken off the subscription list or database).

Some companies ask managers to present 'Learnings' alongside their actual performance. 'Learnings' mean anything they have learned from the marketplace during the last period. This forces a culture of constant improvement.

Finally, control also includes *competitive intelligence*, monitoring your competitors – what they're doing; what they're repeating; what works for them; what they're stopping.

Good marketers also have contingency plans or practise risk management. What happens if plan 'A' doesn't work? What happens if the competition cuts prices? Or worse still, what happens if the server goes down and your network crashes? Do you have a second server? Good marketers think things through.

Whither web analytics?

Developing a good system of *web analytics* is vital for controlling your digital communications. Using web analytics means applying tools like Google Analytics to help you check whether your objectives are being achieved; it should also be used for ongoing improvements.

Web analytics also provide tactical insights such as the opportunity of seeing what are the most popular pages (i.e. what's of interest to customers) and how long they spend on specific pages. Comparing enquiries (visitors) to sales (customers) reveals conversion ratios. How good are you at converting an enquiry into a sale or a sample? This ratio is important and should be watched carefully. High traffic (visitors) and low sales give a low *conversion ratio* and suggest that the web site needs to be improved, whereas low traffic and high sales give a high conversion ratio which suggests that the web site design is fine, but perhaps more resources need to be spent on generating traffic.

Web analytics, online feedback tools and questionnaires can work together. For example, the analytics system can reveal items or pages that are not popular. The feedback tools show why and what users are interested in. We'll discuss this more in Chapter 7.

So to conclude: e-marketing will continue to grow despite the vast array of sloppy sites and services. Winners will address these issues. Winners will plan strategically for both the evolutionary stages and the specific e-marketing objectives: sell, serve, speak, save and sizzle.

SECTION SUMMARY 1.13

Tactics, action and control

Tactics are the details of strategy. Tactical e-tools include the web site, opt-in email, banner ads, virtual exhibitions and sponsorship. Actions include project planning and implementation, while control involves assessing the results against objectives.

CHAPTER SUMMARY

1 SOSTAC® is a planning framework suitable for e-marketing and can be used for developing all types of plans, including e-marketing plans. It stands for Situation analysis, Objectives, Strategy, Tactics, Actions and Control.

2 The connected world connects businesses to consumers using an ever-increasing range of platforms from mobiles to tablets to cars.

3 E-marketers need to assess the particular relevance of B2C, B2B, C2B and C2C marketing to their organization.

4 E-marketing and e-commerce are a subset of e-business that involve the automation of all business processes. E-marketing can assist in all elements of marketing – providing new techniques to identify, anticipate and satisfy customer needs efficiently.

5 Sloppy e-marketing can arise from poorly defined objectives, lack of strategy or poor execution. Risk assessment can minimize the risks of this occurring.

6 Clear objectives are required for e-marketing in order that resources can be directed at achieving these objectives, and we can measure whether our targets are being achieved.

7 The first of the 5S objectives is 'Sell'; using the Internet as an additional sales channel to reach new and existing customers.

8 The second of the 5S objectives is 'Serve'; using the Internet for customer service and adding value. Value can be added using a range of techniques including 24/7 access to support information and online tools.

9 The third of the 5S objectives is 'Speak'; using the Internet as a communications tool for inbound, outbound and social communications integrated with other media. Developing a content marketing strategy is essential to fuel your inbound marketing.

10 The fourth of the 5S objectives is 'Save'; using the Internet to increase efficiency and so reduce costs.

11 The fifth of the 5S objectives is 'Sizzle'; using the Internet as a brand-building tool, by increasing brand awareness and enabling interaction with the brand. Your Sizzle is communicated through your online value propositions (OVPs).

12 E-strategy entails defining approaches to achieve e-marketing objectives using a range of tactical e-tools and a revised marketing mix.

13 Tactics are the details of strategy. Tactical e-tools include the web site, opt-in email, banner ads, virtual exhibitions and sponsorship. The PRACE framework ensures that tactics are focused on business goals from Planning your strategy, Reaching your audience, encouraging them to Act and Convert and ongoing Engagement and advocacy.

References

Chaffey, D. and Ellis-Chadwick, F. (2012) *Digital Marketing: Strategy, Implementation and Practice*, 5th edition. Financial Times/Prentice Hall, Harlow.

First10 (2012) Content marketing infographic, published 14 February 2012 at: <u>www.</u>

smartinsights.com/content-management/content-marketing-strategy/a-content-marketing-and-inbound-marketing-blueprint/

Google (2010) New GfK ROPO study with Vodafone. Blog post, 20 October at: http://google barometer.blogspot.com/2010/10/new-gfk-ropo-study-with-vodafone.html

Ohmae, K. (1999) *The Borderless World: Power and Strategy in the Interlinked Economy*. Harper Business, New York.

Seybold, P. (1999) *Customers.com*. Century Business Books, Random House, London.

Shah, D. and Halligan, B. (2009) *Inbound Marketing: Get Found Using Google, Social Media, and Blogs*. John Wiley & Sons, Inc., Hoboken, NJ.

Smart Insights (2011) Ecommerce conversion rate compilation. Blog post by Dave Chaffey, 4 April at: www.smartinsights.com/ecommerce/ecommerce-analytics/ecommerce-conversion-rates/

Smart Insights (2012a) New report shows how and why customer service must change due to social media use. Blog post by Dave Chaffey, 2 February at: www.smartinsights.com/customer-relationship-management/customer-service-and-support/social-media-customer-service/

Smart Insights (2012b) 95% of Facebook posts ignored by brands. Blog post by Danyl Bosomworth, 20 June at: www.smartinsights.com/social-media-marketing/facebook-marketing/95-of-facebook-posts-ignored-by-brands/

Smith, P.R. (2011) *The SOSTAC® Guide to Writing the Perfect Plan*. Self-published E-book available on Amazon and Kindle.

Smith, P.R. and Taylor, S. (2004) *Marketing Communications: An Integrated Approach*, 4th edition. Kogan Page, London.

Solis, S. (2011) *Engage: The Complete Guide for Brands and Businesses to Build, Cultivate, and Measure Success in the New Web*. Wiley, New York.

Further reading

Chaffey, D. (2011) *E-Business and E-Commerce Management: Strategy, Implementation and Practice*, 5th edition. Financial Times/Prentice Hall, Harlow. Chapter 8 introduces the concept of e-marketing and its relationship with e-commerce and e-business.

DTI (2003) *Business in the Information Age – International Benchmarking Study 2003*. Department of Trade and Industry, London.

Web links

ClickZ (www.clickz.com) has articles and statistics on a wide range of e-marketing tactics.

Econsultancy (www.econsultancy.com). Detailed insights and events about e-marketing best practice.

Emarketer (www.emarketer.com). A compilation of research reports showing trends in Internet adoption and usage.

Emarketing Excellence book home page (www.davechaffey.com/E-marketing). An index of all e-marketing links for each chapter in this book.

Interactive Media in Retail Group (www.imrg.org). Trade body for e-retailers reporting on growth and practice within UK and European e-commerce.

International Telecommunications Union (ITU) (www.itu.int/ti/industryoverview/index. htm). Choose Internet indicators. This presents data on Internet and PC penetration in over 200 countries.

Marketing Sherpa (www.marketingsherpa.com). Case studies and news about e-marketing.

New Media Age (www.nma.co.uk). A UK digital marketing trade weekly.

New Media Knowledge (www.nmk.co.uk). Articles and events relating to new media developments.

Net Imperative (www.netimperative.com). Updates and reports on the UK new media landscape.

PR Smith blog (www.prsmith.org). Insights on the development of SOSTAC® plus videos from the marketing experts.

Revolution Magazine (www.revolutionmagazine.com). Keep up to date on e-marketing best practice for the range of new media with the UK trade monthly for digital marketing.

Smart Insights (www.smartinsights.com). Covers all the latest developments and best practices in digital marketing to support this book. Edited by Dave Chaffey. See www.smartinsights. com/book-support for content relevant to the chapters of this book.

Self-test

1 Summarize each element of the SOSTAC® framework.

2 Describe how customers and companies are becoming interconnected.

3 Assess the potential for B2C, B2B, C2B and C2C interactions via your online presence.

4 Devise a diagram outlining the difference between e-business, e-marketing and e-commerce.

5 List your experiences of sloppy e-marketing.

6 Describe the need for objectives and the characteristics of suitable objectives.

7 Outline 'Sell' e-marketing objectives for your organization.

8 Outline 'Serve' e-marketing objectives for your organization.

9 Outline 'Speak' e-marketing objectives for your organization.

10 Outline 'Save' e-marketing objectives for your organization.

11 Outline 'Sizzle' e-marketing objectives for your organization.

12 Summarize e-strategies to achieve the objectives you have described in Questions 7 to 11.

13 Summarize the main tactical e-tools used by your organization in the context of the PRACE framework and the concepts of content and inbound marketing.

Get updates on
this chapter

Chapter **2**

Remix

A marketer is like a chef in a kitchen . . . a mixer of ingredients.

Bartels (1963)

The digital world affects every aspect of business, every aspect of marketing and every aspect of the marketing mix. Some argue that physical distribution, selling and pricing absorb the biggest impact. In fact, all the elements of the marketing mix are affected by this new world. This chapter shows you exactly how to evaluate the options for varying your organization's marketing mix.

OVERALL LEARNING OUTCOME

By the end of this chapter, you will be able to:

- Understand the online implications of each element of the marketing mix
- Extend each element of the mix into the online world
- Begin to plan each element of the mix in the online world.

CHAPTER TOPIC	LEARNING OUTCOME
2.1 Introduction	Identify the different elements of the marketing mix and where they fit into the e-marketing plan
2.2 What is the marketing mix?	Appreciate the many different approaches to the marketing mix
2.3 Beyond the mix	Identify the marketing skills required to take you beyond the mix
2.4 The mix is morphing	Assess the full potential of extending any product online
2.5 Product	The mix is morphing, particularly when social media merges product, place and promotions
2.6 Price	Review your pricing and consider some dynamic pricing models
2.7 Place	Identify the online distribution issues and challenges
2.8 Promotion	Discuss the problems and opportunities of the online communications mix
2.9 People	Analyse why online service requires a delicate balance of people and automation
2.10 Physical evidence	Identify the digital components that give 'evidence' to customers and check that your web site has them
2.11 Process	List the components of process and understand the need to integrate them into a system
2.12 An extra 'P' – partnerships	So much of marketing today is based on strategic partnerships, marketing marriages and alliances that we have added this 'P' in as a vital ingredient in the marketing mix

2.1 Introduction to remix

The *marketing mix* is a well-established conceptual framework that helps marketers to plan their approach to each market. At worst, it provides a checklist of decisions which marketers must make. At best, marketers integrate, or mix, these decisions together and allocate their resources accordingly. In this chapter we examine how the mix applies today. Online developments affect every aspect of business, every aspect of marketing and every aspect of the marketing mix. So do we have to throw out the old marketing mix concept or can it still be applied? Is a radical remix needed?

There is a debate amongst marketers about which mix is the most appropriate, regardless of whether it is online or offline. Some feel that the traditional version of the mix simply misses the mark. There are others who feel it is a useful starting point. Some argue that physical distribution, selling and pricing absorb the biggest impact from the Internet. In fact, all the elements of the mix are affected by the online world.

The e-marketing mix is changing as products become services, services become customer-driven, and customers create communities that extend the brand into new online experiences. It's a new type of mix. While 'people', or staff, used to do all the customer service, now there are 'new people' (customers), who help each other in creating new customer experiences. These new people are users who generate new products, new promotional materials including advertisements, reviews and ratings (positive and negative, as for automotive companies Chrysler and Honda, although they are approved or deleted by the marketing team); new customer services such as 'ask and answer services' where customers share answers to other customers' questions (as offered by www.homedepot.com).

Although an extra element of the mix is suggested at the end of the chapter, this chapter does not seek to create a new mix, but examines how the old mix is radically changed by the fast-changing digital environment. Figure 2.1 (below) summarizes the main elements of the marketing mix and key issues of how the mix is changed in the digital environments that are explored in this chapter.

The overall balance of the marketing mix is strategic and the details of the mix are tactical. For example, deciding whether to heavily discount prices and raise a high profile in a broad array of down-market web sites and communities is strategic. The tactical details would list the sites and communities and relevant prices.

Of course, a balanced mix itself is not enough to ensure success. Too many clever start-up companies and many existing companies do not have all of the facets required to run a business. To ensure that a business (or even just the new online aspects of a business) actually works (for the customer), you need to ensure first that there is a market, and second that you can supply it; i.e. that the basic business is fit for purpose and that the appropriate technology, product/service design, production process and marketing process, sales process, delivery process, cash-flow process and after-sales support process are all in place along with the 3Ms resources – men (and women – the human resource), money (budgets) and minutes (time) – required to service it. All of this must be 100 per cent in place at the same time, because if any single element fails, then so does the whole.

Figure 2.1   The 7Ps of the classic marketing mix

However, customers don't care about an organization's facets or internal processes; they just want the right product/service to be available to them at the right time, in the right place and at the right price. The old 4Ps all carefully balanced. And since increasingly all products are becoming services (as they also offer online product experiences), we need to add the remaining 3Ps for services – people, processes and physical evidence – to the required mix online.

SECTION SUMMARY 2.1

Introduction to Remix

The marketing mix is a well-established conceptual framework that helps marketers to structure their approach to each market. It should be re-examined and reapplied for the online world.

2.2 What is the marketing mix?

The *marketing mix* rose to prominence in the early 1960s, although it was first referred to in 1949 at an American Marketing Association conference. Around the start of the 1960s,

Canadian Jerome McCarthy (1960) coined the term the '*4Ps*': *product, price, place, promotion*. The four Ps are controllable variables which, when planned and carefully mixed together in the right way, satisfy customers. In 1963, Bartels said: 'A marketer is like a chef in a kitchen . . . a mixer of ingredients'.

So what are the ingredients that marketers need to mix together to satisfy customer needs? Some of the controllable factors include: product quality, product availability, product image, product price and service.

Since that time many have argued that the *4Ps* worked for products rather than services. American academics Booms and Bitner then developed the *7Ps*, sometimes known as the service mix (Booms and Bitner, 1981). They considered that the extra Ps – people, processes and physical evidence – were crucial in the delivery of services. People create and deliver a service – if they aren't happy, the service falls apart. Processes are even more important as the process of production is not behind closed doors (as in the case of products), but open for all to see. In addition, crystal-clear processes have proven themselves critical in the successful use of social media. Finally, when buying intangible services, many customers rely on cues given from tangible, or physical, evidence (such as uniforms, badges and buildings).

EXTENDING THE MIX

Some feel that for interactive marketing, Peppers and Rogers's *5Is* (1997) should replace the *7Ps* in the information age. Do your online efforts support:

- *Identification* – customer specifics
- *Individualization* – tailored for lifetime purchases
- *Interaction* – dialogue to learn about customers' needs
- *Integration* – of knowledge of customers into all parts of the company
- *Integrity* – developing trust through non-intrusive marketing such as *permission marketing*?

The 5Is do not supplant the 7Ps, but rather are complementary to them since the 5Is define the process needed, whereas the 7Ps are the variables that the marketer controls.

Because of its origins in the 1960s, the marketing mix suggests a push marketing which does not explicitly acknowledge the needs of customers. Consequently, some marketing analysts feel that the marketing mix can lead to a product orientation rather than a customer orientation. To mitigate this effect, Lautenborn (1990) suggested the 4Cs framework, which considers the 4Ps from a customer perspective. In brief, the 4Cs are:

- Customer needs and wants (from the product)
- Cost to the customer (price)
- Convenience (relative to place)
- Communication (promotion).

Subsequently, Rothery (2008) developed the 4Es framework.

- Experience – means a product is an experience (including online experience)
- Every place – means place or distribution should be everywhere the customer wants it
- Exchange – means price (as money or credit is exchanged for product or services)
- Evangelism – promotion becomes evangelism.

Frenchman Albert Frey (1961) tried to simplify the mix and cluster it all into two simple groups:

- The offering (product, packaging, service and brand)
- The methods/tools (distribution channels, personal selling, advertising and sales promotion).

MIXING THE MIX

Regardless of the approach to the mix, the same principle applies – stick close to customers; listen to them using social media or formalized marketing research to learn what they need; and supply it better than the competition by mixing the right mix.

Marketers mix the mix in different ways, sometimes with astonishing degrees of success. The mix can be mixed in different ways to satisfy different segments.

Should more be spent on distribution systems (systems, stock, delivery vehicles) and less on advertising? Or perhaps prices should be reduced to generate more demand (which requires more stock)? Or would a price reduction damage the brand perception? Should 'people' or service staff be increased, whether in the stores, in deliveries, over the phone or on social media? There is an endless array of possible ways to mix the mix. One key point to remember, however, is that the mix is tactical. Marketing-mix decisions should only be made after marketing strategy has been agreed. Strategy includes the 'positioning' (how a brand should be seen or perceived or positioned in the mind of a customer). Strategy also includes defining which segments are going to be targeted. Segmentation, targeting and positioning are the three major components of strategy (see Chapter 10 on e-planning).

With the increased price transparency made possible through price comparison sites, it can be difficult to compete online as a trusted brand differentiating on premium service quality alone. Some online shoppers do not remain loyal to a favourite brand if a competitor is running a special offer.

This type of purchasing seems to start with the product and then selection of a supplier on price, but with a preference for known brands where there is a higher level of trust. Many sites now start with reviews of products, with alternative listings of suppliers listed by price. For example, Reevoo (www.reevoo.com, Figure 2.2) rates products according to individuals' opinions. Of course, customers buy in a variety of different ways or journeys (see Chapter 3 on e-models for more detail).

Online shopping comparison site Bizrate (see Figure 2.3) has a different approach, with more in-depth ratings by consumers of online stores, based on a broad range of variables from: 'ease

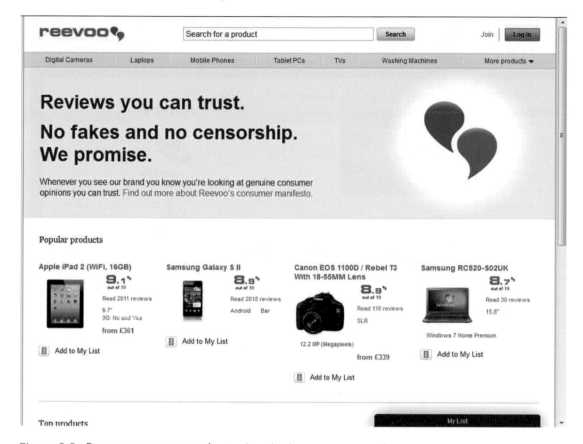

Figure 2.2   Reevoo consumer product rating site (www.reevoo.com)

of ordering; product selection; product info; price; web site quality; on-time delivery; product representation; customer support; privacy policies and shipping and handling'. The trick is knowing which variables are most important for the ideal customer. You need to know what your targeted 'ideal' customers base their decisions on: is it best price, best quality, best delivery, service, best image, best environment?

Today's dynamic customer communities give guidance which other consumers find trustworthy.

Sometimes tough decisions mean chopping and changing the mix. For example, faster and wider distribution might mean more money spent on stock and delivery vehicles and less money spent on advertising.

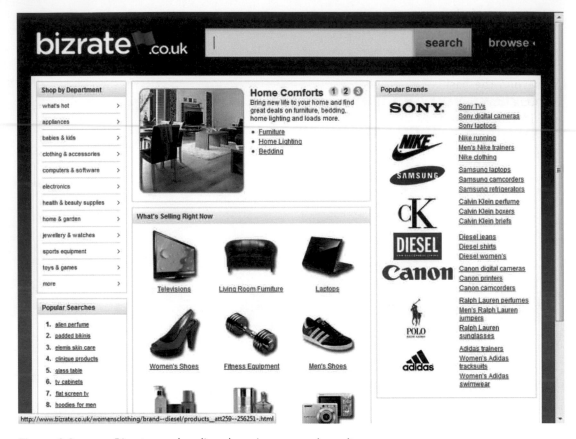

Figure 2.3   www.Bizrate.co.uk online shopping comparison site

What is the marketing mix?

Marketing touches every part of the corporation. One way of structuring, or categorizing, the set of decision variables is through the marketing mix. There are several different approaches, including the 7Ps. These have to be re-evaluated for the new media. The 7Ps which are explored in this chapter are:

- Product
- Price
- Place
- Promotion
- People
- Physical evidence
- Processes
- Plus a new 'P' – partnerships.

2.3 Beyond the mix

The previous section showed that there are many different approaches to the marketing mix such as the 4Ps, 4Cs, 4Es, 5Is and 7Ps. On top of all of this, today's marketers need skills that go beyond the basic mix. By the end of this section, you will know what skills you need. Although the mix provides a useful framework for marketers, other factors also need to be considered. Decisions on the mix are not made until marketing strategy first determines *target markets* and required *brand positionings*.

In our discussion of the online value proposition, we add specific issues that are important online, such as the quality of content, delivery of personalized messages and participation in social networks. In Chapter 4, we explain how, from a customer-centric point of view, you should review your digital activities against the Cs of Content, Customization, Community (and participation), Convenience, Choice and Cost reduction.

Marketers also need to know how to manage alliances (partnerships and marketing marriages), databases and how to build customer relationships that nurture *lifetime customers* who might give you more *'share of wallet'* (this means customers spend more with you on additional products or services from your product range or from your list of approved supplier partners).

Everything today is about relationships. The choice of mix should help to grow relationships:

- Relationship marketing means keeping customers happy for life.
- Strategic alliances and partnerships are all about relationships.
- Supply chain management is increasingly built on relationships – sharing data and systems and budgets.
- If the trends towards *consolidation* (customers choosing fewer suppliers) and *commoditization* (competition producing similar products) continue, then much business will be won and lost depending on the relationship between buyer and supplier.

Marketers have to understand relationships and how to make them work – whether online or offline – with customers and suppliers.

As we will see in Chapter 8 on e-customer relations management, relationships blossom when important things are, first, remembered (like your name and preferences) and, second, acted upon (such as your birthday or wedding anniversary). As organizations become accessible 24/7/365 through a wide range of devices and people, an integrated database can help you remember names, needs, events and a lot more (in both B2C and B2B markets).

E-MARKETING INSIGHT

Segmentation and positioning according to Professor Peter Doyle

Doyle on segmentation – segmentation is the key to marketing. If there is one golden rule for upcoming marketers, then it is segmentation. Why? For two reasons. First, people are heterogeneous. Different customers want different things. So to satisfy customers, you have to provide different solutions for different customers. The second reason is that people are prepared to pay different prices.

Doyle on positioning – positioning is central to marketing strategy. Positioning refers to how a brand is perceived in the minds of a target group of customers. Positioning is the encapsulation of two key concepts. The first is the target market – what is your choice of segment? Second – what will make the customer prefer your product to competitors'? How can we achieve a differential advantage?

(Smith, 2002)

SECTION SUMMARY 2.3

Beyond the mix

Before choosing the marketing mix, marketing strategy first determines target markets and required brand positionings. Then excellent marketers think beyond the short-term mix and think 'long term'. This means choosing a mix that nurtures 'lifetime customers' and grows 'share of wallet'. Ask how each marketing-mix decision affects customer relations. Relationship marketing permeates all the decisions that marketing managers have to make about the mix. Excellent marketers have database skills, partnership skills and relationship skills built into all their decisions regarding the marketing mix.

2.4 The mix is morphing

By the end of this section, you will understand how the digital world brings several Ps (i.e. product, promotion and place) together, particularly when considering apps and widgets.

Social media has changed everything. Generating conversations on social media platforms enhances the product experience (product), promotes the brand (promotions), and spreads the accessibility of a brand (place) and is totally dependent on well-trained teams (people) who are given crystal-clear systems and processes (processes).

Social media has deepened the impact of digital media. This has not gone unnoticed by the world's best marketers such as Unilever, which moved its digital marketing budget out of the media mix (promotion) and into the marketing mix (product and promotions) when they realized that social media content and dialogue also impacted on the product experience.

The search for added value (improved product experiences) is now relentless, whether through new product features, or more likely through enhanced online experiences via new features available from iPhone apps and widgets (more on this later). Are apps product, promotion, place or all three morphed together?

APPS AND WIDGETS MERGE PLACE, PRODUCT AND PROMOTION

Apps and widgets improve the customer experience (product), delivering the experience wherever you are (place), and all of this simultaneously promotes the product (promotion). Widgets can be built (commissioned by a brand), bought (from another widget creator) or borrowed (often for free) from places like Google gadgets, which enables individuals to personalize their home page with content from brands they like. Widgets are embedded into a web site so that visitors enjoy added-value functions. Widget creators often encourage web sites to embed their widget in as many web sites as possible (as it contains a link back to the widget owner's web site). There are widgets for everything from news feeds, to sports feeds to fun and games to weather forecasts and great quotations. Creative brands can develop or sponsor these across a range of platforms from desktop (PC and Mac apps), browser (e.g. Google Chrome apps and web services) to mobile apps.

As more and more online customers access online experiences (shopping, information, entertainment) via mobile (as opposed to PC), marketers enjoy additional options to help customers. They can optimize the web site for mobile phone access (more later, see Chapter 6) and/or develop mobile apps (see Figure 2.4) which bring new experiences to people and spread the brand far and wide.

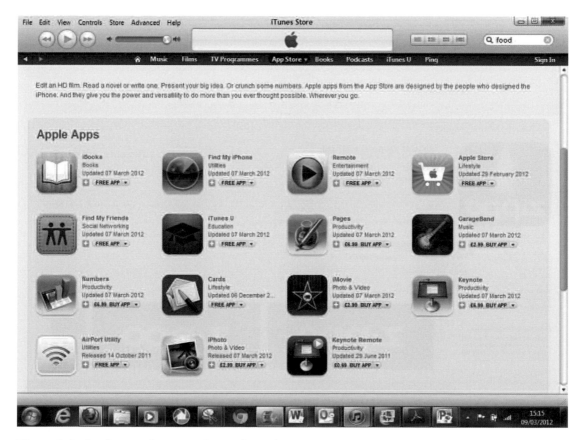

Figure 2.4   Apple apps (www.apple.com/itunes)

E-MARKETING INSIGHT

Adding value through apps

Creative apps must also add value, be user friendly, available across different platforms – especially Android, iOS and Windows mobile – and be maintained as platforms are upgraded. Here are a few examples: the Burger King app shows the nearest branch, and lets the user choose, order and select a pick-up time. The Ikea app drops furniture photos from a catalogue into a photograph of your living room so you can see what it looks like in your room before you buy. Orange's GlastoNav app showed users who was on which stage at Glastonbury and provided directions to the various stages and tents amidst the massive sprawling mass of the festival site. Nike's joint venture with Apple's iPod enabled joggers to access a jogging community web site, log their runs and connect with and compare to other joggers by using their iPods (or their iPhones) and a Nike+ branded transmitter (that fits into some specially designed Nike shoes or can be attached to shoes).

The Virtual Zippo® Lighter app (Figure 2.5) allows customers to hold up a flickering burning lighter flame before a concert starts without burning their hands. It has 10 million fans despite its ratings only getting 3 stars (out of 5) for current and previous versions.

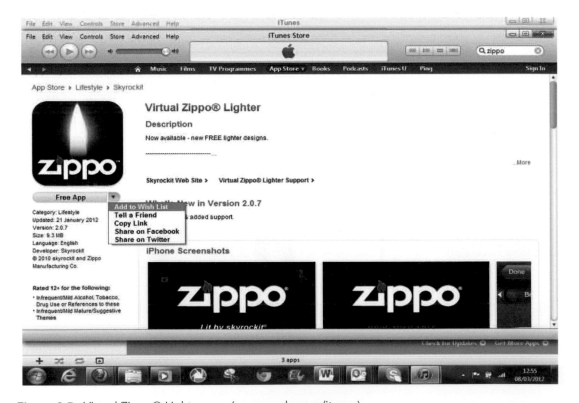

Figure 2.5   Virtual Zippo® Lighter app (www.apple.com/itunes)

Gibson's guitar app includes a guitar tuner, a metronome and a chord chart, all of which are extremely useful for any guitarist (see Figure 2.6, 2.7 and 2.8).

Figure 2.6   Gibson's free app helps guitarists; they can choose a tuning on the 'Mode' page so the tuner will only track notes for that particular tuning (www.gibson.com/en-us/lifestyle/features/gibson-guitar-app-0302/)

Figure 2.7   The Gibson app also features a standard metronome that allows users to choose a specific BPM or tap the screen three times to automatically set the tempo. Other key features of the app include over 30 chord charts with finger markings to help the user with mastering the chord (www.gibson.com/en-us/lifestyle/features/gibson-guitar-app-0302/)

Figure 2.8   The Gibson app also announces new products, artist activity, news stories, interesting and factual features, exclusive contests and special events (www.gibson.com/en-us/lifestyle/features/gibson-guitar-app-0302/)

Kraft's iFood Assistant delivers recipes and has a feature that creates a shopping list that automatically includes the ingredients for the chosen recipes. It even identifies the locations of nearby grocery stores and which aisles stock the items.

Probably one of the most unusual apps is Unilever's; Domestos was behind a fun Flushtracker app that allowed users to track the course of their toilet flush through the sewer system (see Figure 2.9).

Figure 2.9   Unilever's Domestos Flushtracker app (www.flushtracker.com/index.php?page=start)

SECTION SUMMARY 2.4

Widgets and apps, in particular, add an exciting dimension to the traditional marketing mix since they add value, promote the brand and put it into everyone's pocket via their phone – effectively bringing several Ps together (i.e. product, promotion and place).

2.5 Product

By the end of this section, you will understand online value propositions, be able to assess the potential of extending your product online and spot opportunities for other products online. You will also be able to begin to assess your overall business as a result of the online opportunity.

The online world offers a host of new opportunities and prompts these product-related questions:

- What benefits do you deliver to your customers?
- Can they be delivered online?
- What other benefits might your customers like?
- Can these benefits be delivered online?
- What is your business? Can it be delivered online?

DIGITAL PRODUCTS

Amidst the 'e' explosion, Ghosh (1998) suggested that companies should consider how to modify product and add *digital value*. These are two huge questions that, even today, can reshape your whole business.

E-MARKETING INSIGHT

Digital value

Ghosh talks about developing new products or adding digital value to customers. He urges companies to ask:

1 Can I afford additional information or transaction services for my existing customer base?
2 Can I address the needs of new customer segments by repackaging my current information assets or by creating new business propositions using the Internet?
3 Can I use my ability to attract customers to generate new sources of revenue such as advertising or sales of complementary products?
4 Will my current business be significantly harmed by other companies providing some of the value I currently offer?

He suggests you need to analyse each feature of your product or service and ask how can each of these features be improved or adapted online.

These changes can be substantial – one such example is Hughes Christensen, an oil drilling tool company, which discovered that it had a much more lucrative online oil drilling advisory service.

There is no doubt that every product or service can find some added value online. Even for soft drinks such as Pepsi and Tango, there is a shift from physical interactions to non-physical brand experiences.

So it's not just digitizable products and digitizable services that extend themselves into the online world, but any products from any business. Layer apps and widgets on top of this and products or services can create a much better customer experience.

Obviously the entertainment, education and advice services are ideal, but, surprisingly, so are complex industrial products (witness the GE turbine optimizer referred to in Chapter 1). In fact the more complex the product, the more online opportunity there is, since there is a need to educate, train, test, install and service – most of which can be integrated online. Figure 2.10 shows how the online presence can help customers to make complex product selections. Visitors select their requirements and suitable models are indicated using a *Rich Internet Application (RIA)*. While these applications can provide a compelling customer experience, care has to be taken with respect to search engine optimization (SEO), since the search engines may not readily index and link to specific product pages.

Figure 2.10   Helping customers to make decisions (www.tv.philips.com/)

Even less complex but high-involvement consumer purchases such as cars can be aided online through 'mixed mode' or ROPO purchasing (Research Online Purchase Offline).

Remember to keep asking, 'How can I help my customer?' 'What information do my ideal target customers seek?' 'How can I save customers' time?' 'How can I add value to their online experience when they visit my site?' Ultimately, ask, 'How can I help my customers?'

'How can I excel at giving them this online?' Communities of customers can be tapped into to help answer this question. This is the idea of the *prosumer* – the proactive consumer who participates in the design of products or services.

The product or customer experience is increasingly important online, as there is a school of thought that suggests that all products eventually become services. Cohen *et al.* (2006) from the Harvard Business School believe that 'all products become services' as the after-sales market opens up new opportunities. But many organizations still treat the after-market services as an afterthought – perhaps because the 'after market' is deemed to be complicated or outside the safety zone and therefore difficult to manage. But they point out that many US organizations will generate their growth primarily from the 'after market' by adding services, updates and upgrades, consultancy, installations and training.

E-MARKETING INSIGHT

QR codes (Quick Read codes) add another layer to existing products and services

Quick Read (QR) codes can also enhance two of the 'Ps': promotion and place. These codes let users easily use a smartphone camera to scan a type of barcode to get digital information (web site, video clip, article, photo deal or a shop). They add these layers of information and can be used in many creative ways to enhance a product experience, add extra information or even bring a supermarket to you (see Figure 1.2 in Chapter 1).

Figure 2.11   New York's Central Park QR codes allow visitors to enhance their experience

Source: Agency Magma, New York. Director: PhillyK

In New York's Central Park, QR codes allow visitors to enhance their experience while walking through Central Park. Visitors can relive movie scenes by watching famous movie clips when standing in the same location (and scanning a particular QR code). Visitors can watch and listen to a full orchestra perform in a particular spot in the park where they previously performed, or learn about the stones or plants in the park just by scanning a QR code (posted on a sign or a poster) with a mobile phone (which has a QR code reader app). Do remember if directing visitors to a web site to ensure that the web site is optimized for mobile display screens (Chapter 6).

Products are consumed (and created) differently – many customers want to interact with the brand and with other customers in new-found communities of kindred spirits who want to share information, ideas, problems, challenges and solutions, and maybe even friendship. Perhaps the online need for communities is a reflection of the offline breakdown of communities. Some customers like membership privileges, exclusive areas. Chapter 4, on e-customers, suggests that the couch potato may only be a slothful slob because of the absence of interactive technology, which now allows hundreds of thousands to interact with online programmes, as demonstrated by the BBC's guidelines for new programmes: 'find, play, share'. 'Find' embraces distribution or place – ensuring that viewers can find the content easily. 'Play' means the product itself, and 'Share' combines product with promotion and distribution, as programmes and their communities of interest are nurtured to extend the product experience online, to talk to each other, to tell each other and ensure that relevant people can access it wherever they congregate. Although this is for digital products, this approach for a product brief may extend into many other non-digital products and services.

Some companies set their production processes according to UGC (user-generated content). Consider the t-shirt company whose customers post their designs online, the community votes for the most popular designs and the company manufactures accordingly (see Chapter 3).

Of course, customers have been determining products' functionality for many years now as mobiles are used for texting and taking photos (in fact, mobile photos are now outstripping photos taken by cameras). Customers also consume vast quantities of entertainment via their phones (in fact, more than the whole of Hollywood movies in cinemas; see Chapter 4).

Finally, digital product and service portfolios can expand to meet the growing diversity of tastes being generated online by the many customer niches online, otherwise known as *The Long Tail* (Anderson, 2006).

The success of the Pebble wristwatch (www.getpebble.com) is a great example of using prosumers to help with new product development through crowdsourcing, technically known as 'open innovation'.

Pebble used Kickstarter (www.kickstarter.com/projects/597507018/pebble-e-paper-watch-for-iphone-and-android) to get customers to pledge to buy the product in return for early delivery or other exclusive offers. Kickstarter supports new product development and start-ups through crowdsourcing, concept testing and amplification of the buzz around a new product.

E-MARKETING INSIGHT

Alvin Toffler and the prosumer

The prosumer concept was introduced in 1980 by futurist Alvin Toffler in his book *The Third Wave*. According to Toffler, the future would once again combine production with consumption. In *The Third Wave*, Toffler saw a world where interconnected users would collaboratively 'create' products. Note that he foresaw this over ten years before the web was invented!

Alternative notions of the prosumer, all of which are applicable to e-marketing, are catalogued at Word Spy (www.wordspy.com/):

1 A consumer who is an amateur in a particular field, but who is knowledgeable enough to require equipment that has some professional features ('professional' +'consumer')

2 A person who helps to design or customize the products they purchase ('producer' +'consumer')

3 A person who creates goods for their own use and also possibly to sell ('producing' + 'consumer')

4 A person who takes steps to correct difficulties with consumer companies or markets and to anticipate future problems ('proactive' + 'consumer').

An example of the prosumer idea is illustrated by BMW, who, prior to the launch of a new model, set up an interactive web site where users could design their own dream roadster. The information was stored automatically in a database and as BMW had previously collected data on its most loyal customers, the database could give a very accurate indication of which combinations were the most sought after and should therefore be put into production.

The Ladder of Engagement in the next chapter explores the prosumer in more detail.

THE EXTENDED PRODUCT

Online opportunities for enhancing product value can also be identified. Ask: 'How can I move beyond the core product?' The different elements of the *extended product* can be highlighted or delivered online. What other products and services would a customer really value? Which of these services can be produced cost-effectively and better than competitors?

The extended product also includes incorporating tools to help users during their use of the product or service.

The extended product contributes to perceptions of quality. Quality and credibility are inextricably linked. 'Develop credibility before raising visibility' makes sense, otherwise you end up making a lousy low-profile company into a lousy high-profile company. Credibility requires quality products and services – these can be demonstrated by:

- Endorsements
- Awards
- Testimonies
- Customer lists and numbers
- Customer comments
- Warranties
- Guarantees
- Money-back offers
- White papers
- Staff photographs
- Social proof such as the number of subscribers, circlers, fans or followers on social networks.

Remember also – you need to analyse the competition continuously. What is their core and extended product offering? That's the easy bit. Increasingly, the hard bit is knowing who your competition is, as boundaries and categories collapse. Witness Yahoo! offering electricity and Virgin offering telephone services; it seems there are no boundaries, just shares of wallet based on relationship marketing. This means that once a supplier wins a customer's trust, it is possible that the customer will consolidate their number of suppliers and start to buy a wider range of products and services from the same supplier. If the relationship is right, the share of wallet can grow. This brings us back to the online value proposition – what exactly is being offered to the customer? Can you summarize your company's OVP?

ONLINE VALUE PROPOSITION

The *online value proposition* (previously called Internet value proposition) can be different to the offline proposition. Ideally, the proposition should exploit some of the unique advantages of being online which include: immediacy, interactivity and depth of content, faster, more convenient, easier as well as cheaper to buy online, better experience online, new experiences online, more resources or information online . . .

The OVP must somehow reinforce core brand values and clearly summarize what a customer can get from you online that they cannot get elsewhere (including competitors and offline offers). This is quite a task and requires very careful consideration of customer needs, competitive offering, company strengths and resources available. Many sites – in fact, most sites – do not achieve this. Observe competitors' sites and their offerings, can you distinguish between them? A cleverly created advertising strap line appearing on a web site can summarize the offering. More detailed pages in offline communications or on the web site (e.g. under the 'About Us' option) can describe the proposition more fully. Here are a few OVPs that appear to match the strap lines:

- AutoTrader – The biggest and best car site on the planet – www.autotrader.com
- Boosey & Hawkes – A world of music – www.boosey.com

- Flickr – Share your photos. Watch the world – www.flickr.com
- Great Sportsmanship Programme – Mobilising communities into sportsmanship – www.greatsportsmanship.org
- Kelkoo – Compare. Buy. Save – www.kelkoo.com
- Wordtracker.com – Find the keywords you need to succeed online – www.wordtracker.com/
- YouTube – Broadcast yourself – www.youtube.com

Web guru, Jakob Nielsen, has an interesting exercise which assesses whether a web site communicates effectively during the first 10 seconds:

Guideline 1

1 Collect the taglines from your own site and your three strongest competitors.
2 Print them in a bulleted list without identifying the company names.
3 Ask yourself whether you can tell which company does what.
4 More important, ask a handful of people outside your company the same question.

Guideline 2

1 Look at how you present the company in the main copy on the home page.
2 Rewrite the text to say exactly the opposite.
3 Would any company ever say that?
4 If not, you're not saying much with your copy, either.

The OVP is more than the sum of features, benefits and prices; it should encompass the complete experience of selecting, buying and using the product or service. The traditional categories of the different elements of the marketing mix are beginning to blur as proposition merges with product experience. About time too, as all of the mix must be seamlessly integrated.

Since the OVP is a core digital marketing concept, we refer to it throughout this book. In Chapter 4, we explain how, from a customer-centric point of view, you should review your site against the 6Cs of Content, Customization, Community (and participation), Convenience, Choice and Cost reduction.

> ### E-MARKETING INSIGHT
>
> #### Testing propositions (and prices) – analytics is the first role I fill
>
> First, you can assign (different) propositions randomly to visitors on first arrival to test interest/sales. I would typically run this against a large control group (being offered the current main proposition) to both protect commercial results and detect the effect of

any external influences that may otherwise wrongly influence the experiment. Free tools like Google Website Optimiser provide information as tests run that help assign a confidence to a temporary result. In my experience, the only way to ensure valid tests and improved business results is to bring in the best analytical brain you can find. Analytics is the first role I fill when I build a digital team, it's that important . . .

(Smart Insights, 2011a)

SECTION SUMMARY 2.5

Product

Find the ideal product that you can deliver, can afford, are good at, can protect and go for it. The online world allows you to create a whole range of new versions, variations and even new products and services. Finally, play to your strengths and exploit your distinctive competitive advantage by having a strong and clear OVP.

2.6 Price

Pricing and *price models* are being turned upside down by the Internet. In 2007, UK rock band, Radiohead, launched their CD online with a 'pay whatever you want' price tag. Reports suggested that many downloaded the album for free. Have you noticed how price models are changing online? Imagine being paid one day and the next day having to pay for delivering the same service? AOL used to pay ABC News for content. Now ABC pays AOL to place its content on AOL pages. It's also happened in advertising. Audiences used to pay for the media; now the media pays audiences to watch their ads.

In this section you will see why you need to review your prices and your pricing models regularly as transparent and dynamic pricing has an impact on all markets.

NEW PRICING APPROACHES

New *buying models* require new pricing approaches.

Name-your-price services such as Priceline (www.priceline.com), transparent pricing, group pricing (e.g. Groupon and Living Deals) and global sourcing (particularly by giant procurement mergers like Ford and Chrysler) are forcing marketers to radically rethink their pricing strategies.

Companies which can offer digital products such as written content, music or videos now have more flexibility to offer a range of purchase options at different price points, including:

- *Subscription.* This is a traditional publisher revenue model, but subscription can potentially be offered for different periods at different price points; e.g. 3 months, 12 months or 2 years.
- *Pay Per View.* A fee for a single download or viewing session at a higher relative price than

the subscription service. Music service Napster offers vouchers for download in a similar way to a mobile phone company 'Pay As You Go' model.

- *Bundling.* Different channels or content can be grouped at a reduced price compared to Pay Per View.

- *Ad-supported content.* There is no direct price set here; instead, the publisher's main revenue source is through adverts on the site (either *CPM* display advertising on-site using banner ads and skyscrapers; or *CPC* which stands for 'Cost Per Click', more typical of search ad networks). Other options include *affiliate* revenue from sales on third-party sites or offering access to subscriber lists. The UK's most popular newspaper site, the *Guardian* (www. guardian.co.uk), trialled an ad-free subscription service, but like many online publishers, has reverted to ad-supported content.

For all of these, it is necessary to have a sound *digital rights management (DRM)* solution in place to minimize copying.

A growth in competition is caused partly by global suppliers and partly by globalized customers searching via the web, which puts further pressure on prices. Many online companies enjoy lower margins with more efficient web-enabled databases and processes. They also cut out the middleman and his margin. So they revel in the ultra-competitive nature of online global markets.

And there's more . . . barter, countertrade, strategic alliances, technology transfer, licences, leasing as well as auctions, and reverse auctions where sellers compete to supply a buyer, counter auctions . . . are all putting downward pressure on prices. On the other hand, web sites can track customer segments and their sensitivity to prices against their activity on the site, or past purchase habits recorded in host databases or stored in cookies held on the user's computer (with their permission); for example, if a customer's history shows two visits to a particular product page, then an automatic online coupon might nudge the unsure customer to buy. In theory, marketers with well-managed databases can tailor prices to discrete segments at optimum prices.

PRICING UNDER PRESSURE

Pricing is under pressure through the continual trend towards *commoditization*. Something new is commoditized almost every day. Once buyers can (a) specify exactly what they want, and (b) identify suppliers, they can run *reverse auctions*. Qualified bidders undercut each other – for both business and consumer products. Colvin (2000) reported that through medicineonline. com elective procedures such as laser eye corrections or plastic surgery required by a particular customer are fought over by rival practices.

Price transparency is another factor. As prices are published on the web, buyer comparison of prices is more rapid than ever before. Storing prices digitally in databases potentially enables shopping bots and robot shoppers to find the best price. Price comparison sites have been around since the 1990s, in different sectors; e.g. MoneySupermarket (www.moneysupermarket. com, Figure 2.12).

Figure 2.12   MoneySupermarket.com (www.moneysupermarket.com)

So, such comparison sites create customer empowerment which leads to further downward pressure on prices. This is what happens when customers want to take control of the relationship rather than the other way around.

And it's not going to get any easier to sustain old prices. A prototype next-generation e-commerce server from the University of Washington uses gaming strategies to decide when to bargain even harder during the negotiation of complex contracts.

Prices are complex; options for the price package include:

- Basic price
- Discounts
- Add-ons and extra products and services
- Guarantees and warranties
- Refund policies
- Order cancellation terms
- Revoke action buttons.

Ironically, the money-rich and time-poor customers in B2C markets may be much slower than buyers in B2B markets where transaction values are often higher, so savings are more significant. Business-to-business marketplaces such as EC21 (Figure 2.13), known as exchanges or hubs, and auctions will grow in significance.

Much routine and repetitive buying will be carried out in these B2B exchanges. Major corporations are already buying through online exchanges and auctions.

Marketers (and buyers) will need new skills – defining the strengths and weaknesses of various exchanges and auctions.

Experienced business people know the impact of buying efficiencies. Martin Butler estimates that a 5 per cent saving in procurement equals the same contribution as a 30 per cent increase in sales for many manufacturing companies (Butler, 2001).

Marginal costing may be required – for many digitized products, the marginal cost is almost zero. Some companies (such as software vendors) are redefining their business, becoming service providers and giving the product away at cost. They make their money on selling the add-ons and extras. A very different pricing model or just a traditional loss-leader approach?

Figure 2.13   EC21 global B2B marketplace (www.ec21.com)

Some call it *second layer selling*. For example, companies sell end-of-term cars from corporate fleets, contract hire and leasing companies and car rental companies to affinity groups such as large employers. The cars themselves are sold at cost, while the add-ons and extras make a profit – insurance, finance, recovery services.

Interestingly, many of the most successful brands are not the cheapest in their category. Customers are prepared to pay premium prices for perceived quality. In addition, research by Apollo (2007) reveals that exposure to television commercials reduces shoppers' sensitivity to price changes.

One final pricing consideration is moving from fixed prices to rental and leasing prices. Cars, computers, flight simulators and now even music can be hired or leased.

E-MARKETING EXCELLENCE

GlaxoSmithKline reduces prices through reverse auctions

Healthcare company GlaxoSmithKline started using online reverse auctions way back in 2000 to drive down the price of its supplies. For example, it bought supplies of a basic solvent for a price 15 per cent lower than the day's spot price in the commodity market, and Queree (2000) reported that, on other purchases of highly specified solvents and chemicals, the company (then SmithKline Beecham) was regularly beating its own historic pricing by between 7 per cent and 25 per cent. She said: 'FreeMarkets, the company that manages the SmithKline Beecham auctions, quotes examples of savings achieved by other clients in these virtual marketplaces: 42% on orders for printed circuit boards, 41% on labels, 24% on commercial machinings and so on.'

The reverse auction process starts with a particularly detailed Request for Proposals (RFP) from which suppliers ask to take part, and then selected suppliers are invited to take part in the auction. Once the bidding starts, the participants see every bid, but not the names of the bidders. In the final stages of the auction, each last bid extends the bidding time by one more minute. One auction scheduled for two hours ran for four hours and 20 minutes and attracted more than 700 bids!

PRICE MONITORING

Pricing is such an important variable, but it can be complex when there are hundreds or even thousands of products competing in a busy marketplace packed with competitors that constantly change their prices. In price-sensitive marketplaces, not knowing that your competitors have increased their prices could cost you tens of thousands of pounds in lost revenue in a short space of time. Equally, not knowing that your competitors have cut their prices can push a brand outside of a price-sensitive market. There are services like Competitor Pricewatch (www.cpw.uk.com see Figure 2.14a and 2.14b) which deliver price reports hourly, daily or weekly so that a busy marketing team can address any potential price problems within the first 10 minutes of their day, releasing them from time-consuming, and often incomplete, manual price reports – thereby freeing up their time to get on with more pressing matters, in the knowledge that they are on top of the constantly changing price points.

SECTION SUMMARY 2.6

Price

The Internet is changing pricing for ever. Prices are under pressure. Pricing structures and options are becoming more complex. It is crucial to get the pricing right in the short, medium and long term. Review new price structures in your markets, driven by customers looking for lower prices available through a range of online tools including reverse auctions, customer unions, commoditization, cybermediaries, intermediaries, infomediaries and shopping bots.

2.7 Place

To understand the significance of place, consider which is the most successful *brand* in the soft drinks markets? The answer is Coca-Cola, not Pepsi. It is readily available almost whenever and wherever customers could need it. Their excellent *distribution* gives them the edge.

This logic also transfers to the electronic marketspace. Esther Dyson (1999) says: 'You put coke machines in places where you think people might want to drink a coke. On the Internet you put Amazon buttons in places where there might be people inclined to buy books'.

Place and promotion overlap when organizations extend their presence online with links from other sites or with microsites in relevant places as the brand gets wider promotion, and simultaneously increases its distribution (place) as the brand is, effectively, available for purchase more widely online. Place means the place of purchase, distribution and, in some cases, consumption. Some products exploit all three aspects of place online; for example, digitizable products such as software, media and entertainment. Widgets can extend distribution across many other web sites. Apps (once downloaded) can extend distribution into the hands of millions of customers via their mobiles. And QR codes can bring distant (and even past) experiences closer. *Proximity marketing* and *location-based marketing* bring promotions to the customer as they physically move closer to a distribution point. Foursquare and Facebook Places enable customers to reveal their locations to friends and discover nearby Deals. Customers get rewarded with special offers for checking into a venue. In the USA, Gap gave away 10,000 pairs of jeans through Deals to drive people into its stores. Interestingly, check-in behaviour patterns differ between the USA and EU countries (see Chapter 4). 'More and more large brands are turning to location based services to find out more about and communicate with their customers, and to offer them deals and promotions for their loyalty' (Gray, 2011).

So it's not just digitizable products and services – all products and services can extend themselves online by considering their online representation for place of purchase and distribution. Even perishable goods such as food and flowers are sold online as customers like the increased convenience and reduced cost of ordering online, often using delivery partners for offline fulfilment. Distribution channels can radically change. Amazon (1994) and eBay (1995) are relative newcomers on the retail scene.

Price Report

This report will allow you to compare any of your products directly against your competitors.

Please make a selection from the drop down below and click 'Show Price Details'.

Product Type	Books ▼
Product	--- Select Product --- ▼ (Optional)
Freetext Search	

☐ Show hidden items   500 ▼ records per page

SHOW PRICE DETAILS >>

Export results to excel

Item Name	Supplier	Price	Admin Price	Shipping	Total	< % >	Correct	Visibility	Ignore
Alan Sugar: What You See Is What You Get	Your Price	19.99		free	19.99			👁	⊘
Alan Sugar: What You See Is What You Get		9.62		free	9.62	-51.89%	✓	👁	⊘
Alan Sugar: What You See Is What You Get		12.00		free	12.00	-39.97%	✓	👁	⊘
Alan Sugar: What You See Is What You Get		16.10		free	16.10	-19.46%	✓	👁	⊘
Alan Sugar: What You See Is What You Get		20.00		2.00	22.00	10.06%	✓	👁	⊘
Alan Sugar: What You See Is What You Get	Average Price	15.54		0.40	15.94				
Derren Brown: Confessions of a Conjuror	Your Price	9.50		free	9.50			👁	⊘
Derren Brown: Confessions of a Conjuror		8.31		free	8.31	-12.53%	✓	👁	⊘
Derren Brown: Confessions of a Conjuror		8.94		not submitted	8.94	-5.89%	✓	👁	⊘
Derren Brown: Confessions of a Conjuror		9.09		free	9.09	-4.32%	✓	👁	⊘
Derren Brown: Confessions of a Conjuror		9.74		free	9.74	2.53%	✓	👁	⊘
Derren Brown: Confessions of a Conjuror		12.99		free	12.99	36.74%	✓	👁	⊘
Derren Brown: Confessions of a Conjuror		12.99		2.00	14.99	57.79%	✓	👁	⊘
Derren Brown: Confessions of a Conjuror	Average Price	10.22		0.29	10.51				
E-Business and E-Commerce Management: Strategy, Implementation and Practice	Your Price	40.01		free	40.01			👁	⊘
E-Business and E-Commerce Management: Strategy, Implementation and Practice		36.89		free	36.89	-7.80%	✓	👁	⊘
E-Business and E-Commerce Management: Strategy, Implementation and Practice		37.31		free	37.31	-6.75%	✓	👁	⊘
E-Business and E-Commerce Management: Strategy, Implementation and Practice		38.04		free	38.04	-4.92%	✓	👁	⊘
E-Business and E-Commerce Management: Strategy, Implementation and Practice		46.52		free	46.52	16.27%	✓	👁	⊘
E-Business and E-Commerce Management: Strategy, Implementation and Practice		46.99		2.00	48.99	22.44%	✓	👁	⊘
E-Business and E-Commerce Management: Strategy, Implementation and Practice	Average Price	40.96		0.33	41.29				
Great Expectations	Your Price	3.50		free	3.50			👁	⊘
Great Expectations		2.76		free	2.76	-21.14%	✓	👁	⊘
Great Expectations		2.99		free	2.99	-14.57%	✓	👁	⊘
Great Expectations		2.99		free	2.99	-14.57%	✓	👁	⊘
Great Expectations		2.99		free	2.99	-14.57%	✓	👁	⊘
Great Expectations		2.99		2.00	4.99	42.57%	✓	👁	⊘
Great Expectations	Average Price	3.04		0.33	3.37				
Rainbow Good News Bible	Average Price	12.67		0.40	13.07				
The Da Vinci Code	Your Price	10.49		free	10.49			👁	⊘
The Da Vinci Code		5.09		free	5.09	-51.48%	✓	👁	⊘
The Da Vinci Code		5.59		free	5.59	-46.71%	✓	👁	⊘
The Da Vinci Code		6.33		free	6.33	-39.66%	✓	👁	⊘
The Da Vinci Code		6.39		free	6.39	-39.08%	✓	👁	⊘
The Da Vinci Code		7.99		2.00	9.99	-4.77%	✓	👁	⊘
The Da Vinci Code	Average Price	6.96		0.33	7.31				
The Girl with the Dragon Tattoo (Millennium Trilogy Book 1)	Your Price	8.50		free	8.50			👁	⊘
The Girl with the Dragon Tattoo (Millennium Trilogy Book 1)		2.50		free	2.50	-70.59%	✓	👁	⊘
The Girl with the Dragon Tattoo (Millennium Trilogy Book 1)		3.88		free	3.88	-54.35%	✓	👁	⊘
The Girl with the Dragon Tattoo (Millennium Trilogy Book 1)		3.89		free	3.89	-54.24%	✓	👁	⊘
The Girl with the Dragon Tattoo (Millennium Trilogy Book 1)		4.79		free	4.79	-43.65%	✓	👁	⊘
The Girl with the Dragon Tattoo (Millennium Trilogy Book 1)		7.99		2.00	9.99	17.53%	✓	👁	⊘
The Girl with the Dragon Tattoo (Millennium Trilogy Book 1)	Average Price	5.26		0.33	5.59				

1

Figure 2.14a   www.pricewatch.com

With permission of Jon Clifford, Pricewatch

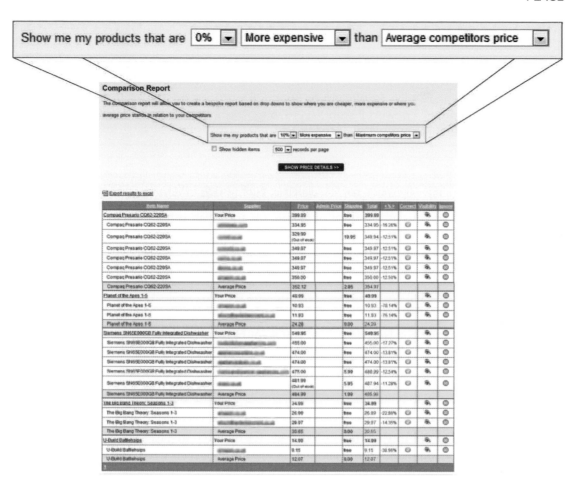

Figure 2.14b www.pricewatch.com allows search and compare using different criteria

With permission of Jon Clifford, Pricewatch

Price follows place?

Using channel data as a pricing factor has proven more successful. As historical data is accumulated, it is possible to really offer competitive prices to those customers identified as high value at the point of application. An accurate value/propensity model can use the wealth of information available from digital visitors (geography, visit trigger/ campaign, past visits, customer history, etc.) to drive truly personalized pricing. In this example, price follows place and both price and promotion reflect the individual customer (Smart Insights, 2011a).

> **Promotion follows place?**
>
> Ads can follow people – so that depending where they are, a more specific relevant ad appears on their phone or in their browser or as a text message. 'This kind of location based marketing is akin to placing an intimate outdoor poster ad in the palm of a potential customer – powerful stuff', says Doug Chisholm, managing director of Rippll (location-based marketing) (Gray, 2011).

ADS (PROMOTION) FOLLOW CUSTOMERS ONLINE (PLACE) – 'REMARKETING'

This involves placing your ads in front of people (as they visit other sites within the Google ad network) who have already expressed an interest in your business; e.g. who have previously:

- Visited your web site
- Signed up for a newsletter
- Abandoned a shopping cart
- Or even bought your goods/service (and you want to reach them after a specific number of days).

WHICH PLACE? REPRESENTATION

Berryman *et al.* (1998) highlighted the importance of place in e-commerce transactions when they identified the three different locations for online purchases shown in Figure 2.15 below. When many companies think about making their products available online, they tend to think only of selling direct from their web site (a). However, other alternatives for selling products are from a neutral marketplace (b) such as EC21 (www.ec21.com, Figure 2.13) and also through going direct to the customer (c). An example of this is a business-to-business auction such as that described for GlaxoSmithKline in Section 2.6 where the supplier goes to the customer's site to bid. Companies need to consider the alternatives for online *representation*.

NEW DISTRIBUTION MODELS

So place is vital and an explosion of radically new ideas has occurred in the online world of distribution in the last five years. Here are a few:

- *Disintermediation* – this is removing the middleman to deal direct with customers instead of through agents, distributors and wholesalers. Note that this can create channel conflict as middlemen feel the squeeze. For example, Hewlett-Packard sells a lot of equipment to hospitals. But when hospitals started going directly to the HP site, first for information and second to place orders, it posed a big question: do we pay commission to the sales representative for this?
- *Reintermediation* – this is the emergence of new types of middlemen who are brokers, such as Bizrate, which unites buyers with sellers.

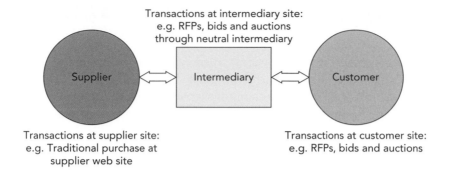

Figure 2.15   Alternative representation locations for online purchases

- *Infomediation* – a related concept where middlemen hold data or information to benefit customers and suppliers.
- *Channel confluence* – this has occurred where distribution channels start to offer the same deal to the end customer.
- *Peer-to-peer services* – music swapping services such as Napster and Gnutella opened up an entirely new approach to music distribution with both supplier and middleman removed completely, providing a great threat, but also an opportunity to the music industry.
- *Affiliation* – affiliate programmes can turn customers into sales people. Many consider sales people as part of distribution. Others see them as part of the communications mix. Amazon.com sees its 400,000 affiliate partners as a huge asset which creates part of their distinctive competitive advantage.
- *Group purchasing* – facilitated by Groupon and Living Deals. Millions of people are alerted to special, limited, heavily discounted offers negotiated by group purchasing groups, and clusters of them reply.

One last way of extending an organization's reach or distribution (and promotion channels) is to create a *widget* (covered in Section 2.4) and make it available for other organizations to embed on their own site to add value to their customers. Google gadgets offers many free widgets ranging from Einstein Quotes, to calendars, to changing photos. YouTube has a classic widget that allows (and encourages) other web sites to seamlessly link YouTube content into the other organization's web site.

This approach is sometimes called *atomization* to suggest how the content on a site is broken down into smaller fundamental units such as features, blog postings or comments, which can then be distributed via the web through links to other sites. Widgets are another aspect of atomization where data can be exchanged between the widget and the server on which it is hosted. The syndication and distribution of content from one site to other sites or readers which access it via *RSS feeds* is another example of atomization.

Excellent distribution requires a deep understanding of when and where customers want products and services. Partnership skills are also required as much distribution is externally sourced, whether order fulfilment, warehousing, logistics or transport.

SECTION SUMMARY 2.7

Place

Distribution, or place, is crucial to the success of any enterprise. Assuming your organization has a reasonable product or service, online or offline the principle is the same: increase your representation and make it widely and readily available to target customers. Marketers today need to think of multi-channels for distribution to ensure they make their products and services easily available to as many ideal customers as possible.

2.8 Promotion

The Internet extends and integrates all ten online communications tools. This section summarizes the opportunities and the challenges of online communications that are explored in more detail in Chapter 7 on traffic building. First, we consider the range of online promotion tools that are available. We then give guidelines as to how these tools can best be exploited.

ONLINE COMMUNICATIONS TOOLS

Online promotion is continuing to grow in importance and gaining an increasing share of marketers' budgets and efforts – whether it is a text message that changes behaviour immediately, or key words that attract more enquiries, or contextual banner ads that change attitudes, or viral marketing that makes people talk about a brand. Online channels can do things that offline communications simply cannot; e.g. some web sites can promote, communicate and create a brand experience which is unique to the online users. Take the soft drink, Tango; it is renowned for its irreverence and fun approach. Tango.com brings the irreverence alive in a way that only the Internet can with games such as 'The Shocking Adventures of Nylon Neddie'.

The complete promotional mix or communications mix – the ten communications tools (advertising, selling, sales promotion, PR, sponsorship, direct mail, exhibitions, merchandizing, packaging and word of mouth) – can be used to communicate or promote in the online or offline world. They can all be extended online in new and dynamic ways. Think about their online equivalents. Table 2.1 summarizes the online equivalents of these established communications tools.

Although web sites can be considered a separate communications tool, they are best thought of as an integrator of all ten tools shown in Table 2.1.

Table 2.1 Online executions of different communications tools

Promotional mix	Online executions
1 Advertising	Interactive display ads, Pay Per Click search advertising
2 Selling	Virtual sales staff and chat and affiliate marketing
3 Sales promotion	Incentives, rewards, online loyalty schemes
4 PR	E-news releases, e-newsletters, social networks, links and virals
5 Sponsorship	Sponsoring an online event, site or service
6 Direct mail	Opt-in email, e-alerts, e-newsletters and *web response*
7 Exhibitions	Virtual exhibitions and white paper distribution
8 Merchandizing	Web site design, promotional ad serving on retail sites, personalized recommendations
9 Packaging	Photographs of real packaging displayed online
10 Word of mouth	Social media plus viral, affiliate marketing, e-mail a friend, reviews

E-MARKETING INSIGHT

Chevrolet's Tahoe advertisements break new ground

Back in 2006, Chevy needed to escape the tightly controlled, painstakingly monitored, woefully predictable confines of the 30-second TV spot and roam the online jungle. But everybody's doing that now. So, Chevy marketers thought, let's take this thing a notch further – let's have an online contest to see who can create the best TV ad for the new Tahoe – the wikification of the 30-second spot.

The contest ran for 4 weeks and drew more than 30,000 entries, the vast majority of which faithfully touted the vehicle's many selling points – its fully retractable seats, its power-lift gates, its relative fuel economy. But then there were the rogue entries, the ones that subverted the Tahoe message with references to global warming, social irresponsibility, war in Iraq and the psychosexual connotations of extremely large cars. On its own web site, the Tahoe now stood accused of everything but running down the Pillsbury Doughboy . . . Attack ads were piling up on its site, spilling over onto YouTube.

'Right now, consumers are engaged with new forms of media in a way they haven't been before and probably won't be forever. That is an opportunity', says ad agency senior executive, Ed Dilworth.

The Tahoe campaign has to be judged a success. The microsite attracted 629, 000 visitors by the time the contest winner was announced. On average, those visitors spent more than 9 minutes on the site, and nearly two-thirds of them went on to visit www.chevy.com; for 3 weeks running, www.chevyapprentice.com funneled more people to the Chevy site than either Google or Yahoo did. Once there, many requested information or left a cookie trail to dealers' sites. Sales took off too, achieving 25 per cent market share, outpacing its nearest competitor, the Ford Expedition, 2 to 1. In March, the month the campaign began, its market share hit nearly 30 per cent. By April, according to auto-information service Edmunds, the average Tahoe was selling in only 46 days (as opposed to 4 months).

'When you do a consumer-generated campaign, you're going to have some negative reaction', Dilworth says. 'But what's the option – to stay closed? That's not the future. And besides, do you think the consumer wasn't talking about the Tahoe before?' They were, of course; the difference is that in the YouTube era, the illusion of control is no longer sustainable.

More and more, however, consumers are doing this stuff on their own. YouTube is full of unsolicited Chevy 'ads' that are far more sophisticated than anything the Tahoe Apprentice campaign yielded, pro or con.

Consumer-generated advertising has led to some seriously upside-down behaviour. Brands that once yelled at us now ask what we have to say. No longer content to define our identity (Gap kids, the Marlboro man), they ask us to help define theirs.

(Rose, 2006)

GUIDELINES FOR EFFECTIVE PROMOTION

The online promotional challenges that marketers need to respond to can be summarized by the six key issues of the promotional mix, integration, creativity, interaction, globalization and resourcing.

1. Promotional mix

E-marketers need to mix the *promotional mix*. This involves deciding on the optimum mix for different online promotional tools. Think about whether you use the full range of promotional tools in Table 2.1 (above) and whether you are using the most cost-effective techniques for acquiring and retaining your target customers.

E-MARKETING INSIGHT

Blogs – a powerful tool in the promotional mix

When Renault wanted to promote its new range of cars, it invited 13 bloggers from France, Germany, Great Britain, Italy and Spain writing about high-tech, trends, innovation and scientific themes to a conference session by CEO Carlos Ghosn and tests of vehicles in the ZE range. This generated 22 articles delivering 900,000 exposures to the message whilst boosting Renault's visibility on social networks and simultaneously bumping up its search engine rankings.

(Smart Insights, 2011b)

2. Integration

Both online and offline communications must be integrated. All communications should support the overall positioning and *online value proposition* which the e-marketing strategy defines.

You need a single consistent message and a single integrated database – which recognizes and remembers customers' names and needs regardless of which access devices are being used (TV, telephone, PC, iPad or mobile device).

Online integration is difficult enough. Online and offline integration requires even more management skills.

3. Creativity

Today's marketer can exploit the vast untapped creative opportunities presented by the Internet. The only limitation is your imagination. Imagine sponsoring a virtual experience. Or sending opt-in e-mails that make customers sit up and take notice. Or developing the ultimate virtual exhibition. Or creating a 'must have' viral that becomes a 'must share' viral.

E-MARKETING INSIGHT

Ten golden rules of IMC

1 Get management support for IMC (integrated marketing communications) by ensuring they understand its benefits to the organization.

2 Integrate at different levels by putting IMC on the agenda of different meetings; integrate horizontally between managers in different functions such as distribution and production; and ensure that PR, advertising and sales are integrating their efforts.

3 Maintain common visual standards for logos, typefaces and colours.

4 Focus on a clear marketing communications strategy. Have clear communications objectives. Have clear positioning statements. Link core values into every communication.

5 Start with a zero budget – build a new communications plan by specifying the resources needed and prioritizing communications activity accordingly.

6 Think customers first. Identify the stages before, during and after each purchase and develop a sequence of communications activities that help the customers through each stage.

7 Build relationships and brand values. All communications should strengthen customer relationships. Ask how each communication tool enables you to do this. Customer retention is as important as customer acquisition.

8 Develop a good marketing information system which defines who needs what information when. IMC defines, collects and shares vital information.

9 Share artwork and other media. Consider how advertising imagery can be used across mail shots, new releases and the web site.

10 Be prepared to change it all. Constantly search for the best communications mix.

(Smith and Zook, 2011)

Of course, creativity must fit the overall communications strategy relevant to a specific target market and positioning consistent with the overall brand positioning.

4. Interaction

Next comes the extra layer of creativity – interaction (or engagement). This is where the online opportunity can really create some 'sizzle'. This enhances the experience and deepens the impact (and also creates an opportunity to collect customer data). As mentioned in Chapter 1, 95 per cent of Facebook posts are ignored by brands despite the fact that the more people that are interacting, commenting and clicking – the more news feeds you will appear on.

So 'Enable your wall, or get off of Facebook' (Rezab, 2011).

Systematic harvesting and presenting of customer reviews is a process which can be managed by third-party companies like Reevoo. The reviews then appear wherever a product appears for sale online. Collecting reviews, posting them wherever the product is displayed, encouraging customers to write and share their reviews have a powerful impact on sales. One test suggested that increasing reviews up to 50 boosts conversion rates from 2 per cent to 4 per cent, due to the effect of 'social proof'. See Chapter 3 on e-models.

5. Globalization

Then, of course, there are the added complications of a global audience. Web sites and social media platforms give access to a global market. Caution needs to be exercised when entering international markets. See the Priceline E-marketing Excellence box below for some examples of the cultural and business practices that need to be considered for the Japanese market. Also see Chapter 4 on e-customers for examples of localized brand names that restrict sales in international markets.

E-MARKETING EXCELLENCE

Adjusting the offering for the Japanese market

When Priceline (www.priceline.com) tried to enter the Japanese market, they hit a number of barriers. These still serve as a lesson and reminder of the need for 'cultural customization'.

1 Web site design – Japanese read from right to left.
2 Profit margins – Japanese negotiate fiercely. They do thorough research. Priceline may not get such good margins in this market.
3 No cancellations policy – contracts in Japan 'are not perceived as final agreements. Traditionally, if either party has remorse there are renegotiations'.
4 One-hour acceptance or rejection of bids – Japanese don't like to make snap decisions.
5 Bargain hunting – bargaining and price hunting is not talked about. Talking about haggling is tacky.
6 Customer service – it is useful to know whether your Japanese friend has understood you or not.
7 Giveaways – avoid giving gifts, in Japan with an even number of components, such as an even number of flowers in a bouquet. Never give four of anything.

6. Resourcing

The online communications opportunity is infinite. However, resources to design and maintain the content, interactions and the database are not infinite. Resources are also needed to service customer enquiries whether online or offline.

Some companies switch resources out of telephone customer service into social media customer service via, for example, Facebook. Resourcing needs to be planned carefully and you must expect to grow social media resources over time. Why bother? With the right resources, online promotions – and, in particular, social media resources – can boost awareness, affection, preferences, relationships which ultimately build stronger brands, which in turn builds sales, gives early warning signs and generates free market research (customer feedback).

The rush to develop, for example, a Facebook presence without a plan, systems and processes and even resources is dangerous. Develop a plan that includes a content plan, response plan, data plan (what to do with the data), processes (checking Facebook routinely) and people who are trained and briefed.

Even ensuring consistent use of the brand requires time, energy and money.

Finally, remember that all communications are wasted if the rest of the mix is wrong; for example, a poorly targeted product.

SECTION SUMMARY 2.8

Promotion

All ten communications tools should be reviewed for how they can be extended and enriched online. Online communications challenges include: mix, integration, creativity, globalization and resourcing. Take advantage of the characteristics of the new media through promotion that is dynamic, carefully targeted, highly relevant and helps to build an ongoing relationship

Table 2.2 E-marketing checklist – integrated communications

1　Does senior management support integrated marketing communications and the importance of the brand?
2　Do you integrate at different levels by putting IMC and the brand on the agenda of different meetings; horizontally between managers in different functions such as distribution and production, the web master and the sales team, etc.?
3　Do you have design guidelines or a brand book which maintains common visual standards for logos, typefaces and colours?
4　Is there a clear marketing communications strategy with clearly defined brand values, brand positioning and brand personality which is linked into the core of every communication?
5　Do you start from scratch with a zero budget and define exactly what is required – build a new communications plan by specifying the resources needed and prioritizing communications activity accordingly?
6　Do you think customers first and identify a contact strategy (a sequence of communications) for different customer segments who are at different stages in the customer lifecycle?
7　Do you build relationships and brand values with all communications? Do you ask: 'How does this help the customer? Does this strengthen my brand?'
8　Do you have a good marketing information system which defines, first, who needs what information when and, second, which communications tools are working better than others?
9　Do you always consider how campaigns and traffic-generating ideas can be integrated with other tools and techniques? Do you share artwork across all the communications mix – both online and offline?
10　Are you prepared constantly to improve by closely monitoring what works and optimizing the best communications tools?

based on the permission and trust of the customer. Use the checklist in Table 2.2 to assess how integrated your communications are.

2.9 People

In services marketing, people, or staff, are considered a crucial element of the marketing mix. As more products add online services to enhance their offerings, 'people' become more and more important. By the end of this section, you will understand how service needs a balance of people and automation and what the key management challenges are.

WHY ARE PEOPLE IMPORTANT?

As well as experience of the marketplace, people (and process) are key – real people, real buildings and established integrated systems that deliver goods and services. People are important since everyone in your organization is an ambassador and a sales person for your company. People do business with people. Hence IBM coined the phrase 'Social Business', which includes almost all staff engaging in conversations, solving problems, giving service and making sales courtesy of social media platforms.

Given that everyone represents the company, you can see the importance of having happy staff.

Happy Staff = Happy Customers = Happy Shareholders

The challenge, of course, is to recruit the right people, train them (including brand values and social media best practice) and reward or motivate them appropriately. The real issue is that we have got worse at customer service (as highlighted in Chapters 1, 4 and 8). We are sitting on a customer service time bomb. This is in a turbulent environment where customer expectations are rising, and often, satisfying these rising expectations is not enough to keep customers loyal. However, we ignore customer service at our peril.

DELIVERING ONLINE SERVICE

Remember the 90:10 ratio? Some suggest that web sites should adopt the 90:10 ratio as the value or service to sales pitch ratio. This implies that the bulk, 90 per cent, of your web site should be designed to service customers.

How well does your site make use of the following?

- *Auto-responders.* These automatically generate a response when a customer emails an organization or submits an online form.
- *Email notification.* Automatically generated by a company's systems to update customers on the status of their order: for example, order received, item now in stock, order dispatched.
- *Call-back facility.* Customers fill in their phone number on a form and specify a convenient time to be contacted. Dialling from a representative in the call centre occurs automatically at the appointed time and the company pays, which is popular.
- *Real-time live chat.* A customer support operator in a call centre can type responses to a site visitor's questions; for example, a widely deployed technology such as LivePerson (www.liveperson.com).
- *Frequently asked questions (FAQs).* For these, the art is in compiling and categorizing the questions so that customers can easily find (a) the question and (b) a helpful answer.
- *Ask and answer services* provide a moderated service where customers help each other by answering each other's questions.
- *On-site search engines.* These help customers to find what they're looking for quickly and are popular when available. Some companies have improved conversion-to-sale rates greatly by improving the clarity of the results that the search engines return. Site maps are a related feature.
- *Co-browsing.* Here, the customer's screen can be viewed by the call-centre operator in combination with callback or chat.
- *Virtual assistants.* These come in varying degrees of sophistication and usually help to guide the customer through a maze of choices.
- *Customer reviewers and assistants.* Online social media enable organizations to recruit customers to help shape their service for other customers through reviews and comments.

- *Tailored customer landing pages* (e.g. to create a specific landing page for, say, a variety of different propositions, or even keyphrases used in a PPC campaign; i.e. each phrase links to a slightly different landing page which highlights a particular keyphrase or proposition).

IS AUTOMATION ALWAYS BEST? INBOUND CONTACT STRATEGIES

The concept of *'customer self-service'* or *'web self-service'* is prevalent in e-marketing. Customer self-service enables customers to obtain the information they need faster and saves the business money. However, we need to pause and ask whether all customers want to conduct all their interactions online.

Think of buying an air ticket via the web. This is fine if you have a particular flight in mind, and it is available. If it is not, our experience is that it is quicker to talk to a customer representative who is knowledgeable about the alternatives available.

Some online customer segments just want to browse, others want to find specific information and others again want to buy or get customer support. Of the segment that wants to buy, a sub-segment wants to buy offline and needs personal contact either via phone, letter, or personal visit. Alternatively, they cannot find the information they need online in the *FAQs* or via the online search engine. At this point, the customer will want to contact the company by email or phone. Inbound contact strategies aim to control the volume and medium of enquiries and responses. Responses may be by *auto-responder*, email, phone or real-time chat with sales staff. As in this example, clear indications have to be given of when the service is available; and to manage demand, services are often only promoted when visitors are more engaged with the site. Some companies offering complex products have found a benefit in displaying a chat window automatically after a customer has been on a page for a certain length of time.

Many companies, such as the Nationwide Building Society (www.nationwide.co.uk), use an *inbound contact strategy* of customer choice or *'customer preferred channel'*. The easyJet E-marketing Excellence box in Section 1.7 shows that you can give customers a choice, but steer them towards using the web as a contact tool.

A key figure for measuring the effectiveness of your inbound contact strategy is the average number of contacts needed to resolve an issue. Remember that many questions will not be answered by the first email. Companies need to decide whether the best strategy is to switch the customer to phone or online chat to resolve the issue, rather than bouncing multiple emails between customer and contact centre. Two-way interactions such as voice, online chat and co-browsing (where the customer's screen can be viewed by the call-centre operator) will be more effective in resolving an issue immediately. Automated marketing and digital body language can be very effective too (see Section 2.11 on Process).

KEEPING CONTENT FRESH

Many organizations now have many thousands of web pages (sometimes in several languages as well as different versions for mobiles as well as PC/laptop). To keep the content fresh, up to date and relevant to the customer has significant management and resource implications. We will see later how *content management systems (CMSs)* are essential to the consistency and management of any large site, since they enable *content owners* in different parts of the organization to update the content they are responsible for. They also provide workflow facilities which can automatically prompt a content owner to update content and use email to remind other staff to review and authorize publication. But having the right technology is only part of the story. Managers of content owners must have strategies to keep content fresh. These may include:

1 *Regular update dates* such as start of month for some content types like news or promotions.
2 *Triggers for publication.* Every new press release or product or price change must go on-site.
3 *Ownership of content in job description.* The quality of content, including freshness, is part of staff performance appraisal (this is a 'stick' approach).
4 *Explaining benefits of content update to content owners.* Showing that updates will save the content owner time; e.g. in explaining things on the phone or by helping them sell more (this is a 'carrot' approach).
5 *Using the CMS to set content expiry dates.* For certain content types, expiry dates can be set and an email alert sent to the content owner.
6 *Publish dates of when pages on-site were last updated.* Some organizations use a chart to show which pages are updated least frequently to shame staff into taking ownership!
7 *Real-time content delivery* takes articles or items from a database, so partially automating the update process (the database still needs to be updated).

TRAINING AND RESOURCING

Of course, staff need to be trained and motivated whether they man the web site, the telephones, the field sales or the reception. What happens if a web transaction fails and the customer calls the centre? Can call-centre staff access the web database to complete the transaction, or do they have to collect all the details again? Can call-centre staff be retrained to service customers via Livechat, Facebook or other social media platforms (see Chapter 8 for an example of how switching resources from phones to Facebook can be very effective in speedily solving problems and boosting customer relationships – if staff are suitably trained in content and systems/processes)? A seamless, integrated contact database is also required.

A key resourcing issue is whether to identify specific staff to handle contacts from different channels or whether to empower staff to answer questions from a variety of channels. Current thinking suggests that the latter approach is best since this increases the variety of work and results in more knowledgeable staff who can answer customers' queries more effectively.

It is worth investing in continual staff training as well as in online tools. Benchmark research from Harvard (Kotter and Heskett, 1992) revealed that companies which invest in all three key stakeholders (employees, customers and shareholders) out-perform those that invest in only two or fewer.

A final point is that although some consider that the Internet 'marginalizes the role of direct customer contact', it is also used to recruit quality staff. Most potential recruits these days check out web sites as a matter of course. If they don't, they're probably not management material!

People

People/staff are important. People are the differentiating factor that has helped many 'clicks-and-mortar' companies out-perform the virtual companies. In fact, service – before, during and after a sale – is required if repeat business is to be enjoyed. Contact strategies should be developed that give customers choice of contact, but minimize costly interactions with staff. Automated services help, but people are also required. Beware of the customer service time bomb. It is a delicate balancing act, but bear them both in mind when integrating online and offline marketing activities. Recruitment, training and motivation are required. And remember, happy staff = happy customers = happy shareholders.

2.10 Physical evidence

The aim of this section is to highlight the different aspects of physical evidence a web site can display and check that your web site has them.

As services are intangible, customers look for reassurance that the service is going to be alright. They look for cues such as a well-designed site (as well as endorsements) to give them clues about the quality of the intangible service.

In the offline world, physical evidence includes buildings, uniforms, logos and more. In the online world, the evidence is digital. Imagine the impression that a broken window would give to a customer. Similarly, a web site with a typo sends the same worrying messages. So the web site becomes a significant part of the physical evidence.

In the online world, customers look for other cues and clues to reassure themselves about the organization. So first, a reassuring sense of order is required. This means that web sites should be designed in an uncluttered style with a consistent look and feel that customers feel comfortable with, as explained in Chapter 6 on site design. Remember that you need to win a visitor's trust, as you are about to ask them for three new currencies: their time, their privacy (data) and their credit card (security). So, here are some factors that reassure nervous visitors:

- Guarantees
- Refund policies
- Privacy policies

- Security icons
- Trade and professional body memberships
- Awards
- Customer lists
- Customer endorsements
- Third-party/institutional endorsements
- International Standards (ISO . . .)
- Independent reviews
- News clippings
- Ethical policies
- Community links
- Full address and contact details (you are legally obliged to do this if you are selling anything from the site)
- Text only version
- Error free (proof read everything)
- Reliable response systems.

Plus the big four reasons why people come back to a site:

- High-quality content
- Ease of use (navigation)
- Quick download (NB mobile)
- Frequently updated.

Physical evidence should help to integrate the online and offline world. Many retailers such as the Carphone Warehouse (www.carphonewarehouse.com) use coupons printed out online which can be redeemed for a discount at a store. This helps conversion-to-sale rates and also tracks how the online presence is impacting the offline sales.

Remember that physical evidence emerges in the offline world – if goods and services are delivered offline, then the normal physical evidence is required; i.e. professional packaging, paperwork, delivery vehicles and uniforms can all reinforce the right message.

Equally they can damage the brand if they are not managed. Imagine a scruffy delivery person in a filthy, broken-down van belching fumes stopping outside your home or office. The offline evidence would damage the online evidence. So, both need to be managed carefully.

Physical evidence

Customers look for online cues and clues for reassurance. Web sites can provide these in the form of high-quality site design and reassurance – through guarantees, refund policies, privacy policies, security icons, trade body memberships, awards, customer lists, customer endorsements, independent reviews, news clippings and more. Encourage web site visitors to print coupons or white papers as physical evidence to keep your company at the front of their minds.

Offline activities can provide reassurance in the form of professional-looking buildings, delivery vans and uniforms. Evidence, whether physical or digital, needs to be managed constantly.

2.11 Process

Process refers to the internal and sometimes external processes, transactions and internal communications that are required to run a business. Excellent execution of these is vital. By the end of this section, you will be able to identify the components of process and understand how they need to be integrated into a database. Given that we are sitting on a customer service time bomb (Chapter 8), there is a golden opportunity to develop lifetime customers through deep and engaging customer service processes online.

THE IMPORTANCE OF PROCESS

How many people do you talk to who have had bad experiences online with major brands? How many have you had yourself in the last week? Excellent processes are where e-commerce ends and e-business begins. Unintegrated e-commerce sites create problems, as exemplified by US online toy stores whose web sites and associated processes did not link into an information system explaining to customers when stocks were unavailable. Add in social media, and the importance of having crystal-clear processes that work for both the customer and the staff becomes even greater.

Developing a systematic listening team as well as a system to use the information means details like: Who monitors what? Who compiles the analysis and the reports? Who responds to comments on blogs and in group discussions on LinkedIn? Who analyses the comments, complaints, suggestions, worries, issues and opportunities? What happens to this information? What kind of decisions does it affect? How often? Processes become the key to success in the new approach to making strategic sense of social media chaos in the Ladder of Engagement (Smith and Zook, 2011), as demonstrated in the next chapter.

Traditional offline services have processes continually on view, with the manufacturing process for goods behind closed doors. Online services and their process of production are not as visible since many of the processes operate in systems unseen by the customer. Some of the process, or system, is on view, like menus, form filling, shopping baskets, follow-up emails and, of course, the interactions on web sites. It is on this part of the process and its outputs that customers will judge service.

It seems that many companies have not yet learned how to optimize these processes – 80 per cent of potential buyers exit before they make their purchase. This suggests that ordering is too complicated or confusing, or the system simply doesn't work smoothly.

OPTIMIZING INTERNAL PROCESSES

To understand the importance of process, consider a simple online enquiry and subsequent online sale of a book. How should the system work? Think about which events or actions need to take place for the order to be fulfilled and for the customer to be satisfied.

These are some of the events that need to happen, and they must be backed up by an efficient, seamless process:

- Customer wants to check availability – Does the site show the number in stock and when next available if out of stock? See Dabs.com (www.dabs.com) for good practice.
- Product specification or price is changed – Is the change seamlessly reflected in the web site and price lists or catalogues?
- Customer places order – Is the site updated to indicate the changed number in stock? Is the customer notified by email that their order has been processed? Is the finance system updated to include the new order within the month's revenue?
- Customer makes email enquiry – Can the system cope when a wave of telephone calls and emails hit and respond promptly and accurately?
- Product dispatched – Is the customer notified of this event by email? Can they track their order if required?

Optimization involves minimizing the people involved with responding to each event and providing them with the right information to serve the customer. Minimizing human resources can occur through redesigning the processes and/or automating them through technology. The problem is that many sites simply do not have efficient systems in place. They lack the logistical and fulfilment infrastructure required to trade online.

Processes continue beyond the sale with after-sales service, generating customer feedback, upselling, cross-selling, product development and improvement built in as part of the processes.

The front-end customer interface – whether this is a web site, interactive TV screen, mobile phone screen or even a telephone sales person – must integrate with the back-end systems which are out of sight in the back offices and warehouse. This is easier said than done.

A well-managed process integrates into the business processes and systems which, in turn, shave costs and slash inventories. Some companies take orders and payment immediately and ask third-party suppliers to supply directly. So stock (and working capital required to fund stock) is reduced to zero. In fact, because the company receives payment from the customer and doesn't pay the supplier for 30 or 60 days, the company generates surplus cash. This creates negative working capital because instead of having to fund stock with working capital, the supply process is so tight it generates its own funds.

E-MARKETING INSIGHT

Automated marketing and digital body language

Automated 'Sense and Respond' marketing looks at the behaviour of a visitor (or a group of visitors) and sets rules to generate automated responses; e.g. if Visitor A visits several pages including the shopping basket, but does not purchase, they will get an automatic email with an offer of help (whether a sales call or more information or asking if they needed any particular information); whereas visitor B who downloads a white paper and spends several minutes on the product details page will get a different email offering additional information or personal advice from an engineer. The rules become a set of processes that allow highly relevant information or questions to be sent to the prospect to help them and move them towards the next step of the buying process. Visitor C may already have bought a product, but will be pleasantly surprised when an email arrives asking if everything is ok and if they'd like any more information regarding the page they visited. It's all about helping prospects and customers.

OPTIMIZING EXTERNAL PROCESSES

Reviewing processes and systems can help organizations to radically redesign supply and distribution chains, and in the process, compete much more effectively.

For many organizations, Jack Welsh's well-known internal slogan 'Destroy Your Business.com' (before the dotcoms do) makes a lot of sense just from the process side alone. Reinvent the business process so that it's faster, lighter on resources and, most importantly, makes the customer happy.

Classic marketing empathizes with the customer – what kind of problems, priorities and procedures do they need? What will delight them? Then build the process that caters for the many diverse types of customers out there.

How value chains need to be revised is another aspect of process that is considered in Chapter 9 on e-business.

SECTION SUMMARY 2.11

Process

Good processes and systems can create competitive advantage. There are lots of poor processes that kill sales and damage the brand. Processes can have a huge impact on your organization.

2.12 An extra 'P' – partnerships

Perhaps there is a new P in the mix, 'partnerships' or marketing marriages or alliances. Kenichi Ohmae (Smith, 1996) said that no company can succeed globally without partners. Most organizations today would agree with this and have staff dedicated to partnership marketing. It is not surprising, a few years after Ohmae's comment, to find award-winning e-marketing campaigns revealing a common pattern – partnerships. Although increasingly important in the offline world of marketing, clever partnerships are also emerging as keys that open the doors to vast new markets. Hence the emergence of alliance managers. Here are a few examples:

Ford Galaxy teamed up with Tesco and AOL to gain access to a million new online customers within its target audience of 30–44-year-old women with children. Ford also wanted to be associated with brands that have already improved its target audience's lives.

MUtv (the TV channel devoted to Manchester United) partnered with Sky and Century Radio in an attempt to develop its product so it could create an exciting proposition which quickly attracted 379,000 unique users in 98 countries. Combine this with MORI's estimated MUFC global fan base of 70 million and you can see the potential.

In the online world, many e-retailers now have staff dedicated to managing online partnerships, particularly for *affiliate marketing*, which is covered in Chapter 7.

Some companies have people specializing in partnerships; other companies employ agencies to be their partners or even agencies to find their partners, whether through a blogger outreach programme (to connect with more bloggers) or an affiliate marketing campaign (to recruit more affiliate marketers). There is no doubt that partnerships need to be identified, recruited and nurtured for success.

E-MARKETING INSIGHT

Live 8 and O$_2$ team up

The highly innovative and highly effective partnership between the Live 8 charity and O$_2$, the mobile service provider, proved that partnerships can achieve what previously seemed impossible. This account is based on O$_2$'s *New Media Age* Awards (2006) submission.

Situation

The twentieth anniversary of Live Aid saw the hastily prepared Live 8 event snatching global headlines. Live 8 needed to raise over £1 million, promote its concert, create a way of selecting over 100,000 concert ticket holders and then distribute the tickets – all within two weeks. O$_2$ approached Live 8 to run the ticketing process via text. The operator realized that the Live 8 concert was going to be the biggest music event for 20 years and that demand for tickets would outweigh supply.

Objective

1 To develop a fair mechanism to select 130,000 guests for the Live 8 Charity Concert and ultimately distribute 130,000 Live 8 concert tickets safely and securely in just two weeks.

2 To raise at least £1.6 m in revenue for Live 8 (to offset some of the costs of putting on the event and distributing 130,000 tickets quickly and securely at low cost).

Strategy

O_2 worked with Mobile Interactive Group (MIG), using its Vote Winner platform to run the competition, having publicized the competition questions and the O_2 short-code in all national newspapers and on radio and TV stations.

Tactics

The ticket competition entry mechanism went live on 6 June 2005. In order to meet the requirement for a speedy and fair entry process, a multiple-choice question was agreed with Live 8. After seven days, the competition closed and 66,500 winners were notified via text message that they had won a pair of tickets.

Action

Each winner was sent a unique PIN which they then had to enter at the O_2 web site. Each text message entered into the competition cost £1.50, all of which went to Live 8. A standard network charge of between 10p and 12p was applied to all messages to cover network costs. O_2 didn't make any money from the project. At its peak the system received 611 messages a second, compared to 500 a second for *Big Brother* (the popular TV show). Within tight deadlines they provided a simple yet effective call-to-action and an excellent customer experience.

Control

The Live 8 ticketing operation was recorded by the *Guinness Book of Records* as the largest-ever text competition. Nearly 2.1 million people entered and the campaign raised over £3 m for the Live 8 Charity Concert for Africa, which went on to raise the profile of Africa's plight and win concessions for Africa, including debt cancellation for many countries.

SECTION SUMMARY 2.12

An extra 'P' – partnerships

We cannot do everything ourselves. Partnerships can help enormously, but they require skilled management.

CHAPTER SUMMARY

1 The marketing mix must be re-examined for the online world since there are many new opportunities to vary the mix to take advantage of the characteristics of digital media.

2 The main elements of the traditional marketing mix are product, price, place, promotion, people, processes and physical evidence. Alternative models such as the 5Is of identification, individualization, interaction, integration and integrity have been developed in recognition of the potential of one-to-one/relationship marketing online.

3 Relationship building and service quality are vital with the trends towards consolidation and commoditization. Building relationships and increasing loyalty are required to increase profitability.

4 The mix is much more dynamic today as prices follow place, and apps, widgets and QR codes add layers to products and expand reach into new places. Promotions-follow-place propositions are constantly optimized and elements are morphing. Overall, the marketing mix is morphing as all the 'Ps' are challenged, improved and merged by new digital technologies.

5 *Product.* Products can be extended online by offering new information-based services and interaction with the brand to create new brand experiences.

6 *Price.* Reduction in market prices and changes in purchase, distribution and usage of products are considered when specifying the place element of the mix. Disintermediation, countermediation and reintermediation are major marketplace changes which must be responded to. The atomization of content and services through widgets and feed syndication is another trend.

7 *Promotion.* Online options for all elements of the promotional mix – from advertising, selling, sales promotion, PR, sponsorship, direct mail, exhibitions, merchandizing, packaging to word of mouth – should all be reviewed for the promotion part of the mix. Key issues in devising the promotional mix are integration, interaction, creativity, globalization and resourcing.

8 *People.* People are a significant contributor to the mix since service quality is a key differentiator online or offline. Organizations need to decide on the best balance of automated online customer service and traditional human service to provide customers with service quality and choice while at the same time minimizing service costs. Online social media enable organizations to recruit customers to help shape their service for other customers through reviews and comments.

9 *Physical evidence.* The quality of the site is the physical evidence online, so it is important to reassure customers buying intangible services through a site that meets acceptable standards of speed and ease of use. This can be supplemented by certification by independent organizations.

10 *Process.* All processes impact on customers in terms of product and service quality. In the online context, it is particularly important to revise processes by integrating front- and back-office systems to provide an efficient response to customer support requests and fulfilment.

11 *Partnerships.* Marketing marriages and alliances can be potent, but need experienced management.

References

Anderson, C. (2006) *The Long Tail: Why the Future of Business is Selling Less of More*. Hyperion, New York.

Apollo (2007) US consumer research project. Arbitron and the Nielsen Company. World Advertising Research Centre (WARC), London.

Bartels, F. (1963) *The History of Marketing Thought*. Richard D. Irwin, Homewood, IL.

Berryman, K., Harrington, L., Layton-Rodin, D. and Rerolle, V. (1998) Electronic commerce: three emerging strategies. *McKinsey Quarterly*, 1, pp. 152–9.

Booms, B.H. and Bitner, M.J. (1981) Marketing strategies and organizational structures for service firms. In *Marketing of Services*, eds J. Donnelly and W. George. American Marketing Association, Chicago, IL, pp. 451–77.

Butler, M. (2001) Techno business. *Winning Business*, January, p.75.

Cohen, M., Agrawal, N. and Agrawal, V. (2006) Winning in the aftermarket. *Harvard Business Review*, 84(5), pp. 129–38.

Colvin, G. (2000) Value driven, you might get your next face lift online. *Fortune*, 29 May.

Dyson, E. (1999) [Article title unobtainable.] www.medialifemagazine.com/newspapers/archives/jan00/news20104.html, 31 December.

Frey, A. (1961) *Advertising*, 3rd edition. Ronald Press Company, New York.

Ghosh, S. (1998) Making business sense of the Internet. *Harvard Business Review*, March–April, pp. 126–35.

Gray, R. (2011) Location is where it's at. *The Marketer*, February. Available at: www.themarketer.co.uk/articles/features/location-is-where-its-at/

Kotter, J. and Heskett, J. (1992) *Corporate Culture and Performance*. Free Press, New York.

Lautenborn, R. (1990) New marketing litany: 4Ps passé, 4Cs take over. *Advertising Age*, 1 October, p. 26.

McCarthy, J. (1960) *Basic Marketing: A Managerial Approach*. Richard D. Irwin, Homewood, IL. *New Media Age* Awards (2006) Centaur, London.

Peppers, D. and Rogers, M. (1997) *One to One Future*, 2nd edition. Doubleday, New York.

Queree, A. (2000) *Financial Times* technology supplement, 1 March.

Rezab, J (2011) Companies respond to just 5% of questions on Facebook. Econsultancy, 17 October at: http://econsultancy.com/uk/blog/8149-companies-respond-to-just-5-of-questions-on-facebook

Rose, F. (2006) And now, a word from our customers, *Wired*, 14 December.

Rothery, G. (2008) The matchmaker. *Marketing Age*, November/December.

Smart Insights (2011a) Remixing your marketing mix online. Roberto Hortal, 18 October at: www.smartinsights.com/digital-marketing-strategy/online-marketing-mix/remixing-your-marketing-mix-online/

Smart Insights (2011b) Using blogger networks to amplify a marketing campaign. Dave Chaffey, 16 September at: www.smartinsights.com/online-pr/online-pr-outreach/blogger-networks/.

Smith, P.R (1996) The Marketing CDS. www.prsmith.org, London.

Smith, P.R. (2002) The Marketing CDs. www.prsmith.org, London.

Smith, P.R. (2011) *Marketing Communications – An Integrated Approach*, 5th edition. Kogan Page, London.

Toffler, A. (1980) *The Third Wave*. Bantam Books, New York.

Further reading

Bickerton, P., Bickerton, M. and Pardesi, U. (2000) Exploiting your global niche – the best marketing mix. Chapter 6 in *CyberMarketing*. Chartered Institute of Marketing series. Butterworth-Heinemann, Oxford.

Chaffey, D., Mayer, R., Johnston, K. and Ellis-Chadwick, F. (2003) The Internet and the marketing mix. Chapter 5 in *Internet Marketing: Strategy, Implementation and Practice*. Financial Times/Prentice Hall, Harlow.

Cumming, T. (2001) Set marketing strategies and targets. Chapter 6 in *Little E, Big Commerce*. Virgin Business Guides, London.

Smith, P.R. and Taylor, J. (2004) Marketing and the integrated communications mix. Chapter 1 in *Marketing Communications: An Integrated Approach*. Kogan Page, London.

Web links

Bizrate (www.bizrate.com). An example of an online shopping comparison site.

Chris Anderson's Long Tail blog (www.thelongtail.com). In-depth blog by the author of *The Long Tail* which relates to the product element of the marketing mix.

CIM 10-minute guide to the marketing mix. (www.cim.co.uk/filestore/resources/10min guides/marketingmix.pdf). A fairly detailed introduction to the marketing mix with further links.

E-marketing Excellence book update page (www.smartinsights.com/digital-marketing-strategy/online-marketing-mix/). A page showing updates related to this chapter.

Introduction to the marketing mix (http://businesscasestudies.co.uk/business-theory/marketing/marketing-mix-price-place-promotion-product.html). The Times 100 – a student and teacher business studies resource centre – has a basic introduction to the marketing mix and case studies of it in practice.

New Media Age awards (www.nmaawards.co.uk). Has awards in innovation across different business sectors.

PaidContent (www.paidcontent.org). Discusses the economics and revenue models for online publishing.

Smart Insights marketing mix advice (www.smartinsights.com/digital-marketing-strategy/online-marketing-mix/remixing-your-marketing-mix-online/). A collection of articles applying the marketing mix to e-commerce, content and social media marketing.

Self-test

1 For each element of the marketing mix (7Ps), list two differences introduced by the digital world.

2 How appropriate are the 5Is of identification, individualization, interaction, integration and integrity as a replacement for the marketing mix?

3 What is the principal way in which product can be varied through an online presence?

4 Summarize in one sentence how an online presence can be used to enhance brands.

5 Explain the reasons for price transparency and marketing responses to this phenomenon.

6 Describe the relevance of disintermediation and reintermediation to your organization and actions that have been/should be taken.

7 Summarize online applications of advertising, PR, direct selling and word-of-mouth promotional mix tools.

8 Recommend a channel contact strategy for inbound communications to your organization.

9 How does the concept of physical evidence relate to your organization's web site?

10 Assess how your online presence contributes to the main business processes and to what extent they have been streamlined by the move online.

11 What impact do apps, widgets and QR codes have on the marketing mix?

Chapter **3**

E-models

We've moved from 'The Attention Economy (push)' to 'The Attraction Economy (pull)' to 'The Participation Economy (share)'.

Roberts (2010)

The business world is changing faster than ever before. Old approaches and models are being turned on their head. In this chapter, we show how to assess your online marketplace, review new business, revenue and communications models and develop budget models.

By the end of this chapter, you will:

- Appreciate the changing nature of business models because of social media
- Appreciate digital revenue models
- Review and select models which are appropriate for your business.

CHAPTER TOPIC	LEARNING OBJECTIVE
3.1 Introduction	Outline the changes to existing models and new models
3.2 Online revenue models	Review alternatives for generating revenue, particularly from advertising
3.3 Intermediary models	Understand the role of different intermediaries in influencing online sales
3.4 Attribution models	Assess approaches for reconciling media spend to different digital channels
3.5 Communications models	Describe differences in communications models and how they can be exploited
3.6 Customer information processing models	Assess differences in customer information processing that occur online
3.7 Customer buying models	Summarize changes to buying models and assess their implications
3.8 Loyalty models	Assess the relevance of new loyalty models
3.9 Social media models	Explain the drivers for the increase in social media
3.10 Social business models and the Ladder of Engagement	Review shifts in the fundamental business model driven by social media

3.1 Introduction to e-models

Whether business models, revenue models, communications models or buying models, old models are being replaced by new and revised models. This chapter explores some of the changes to existing models and shows how they can be incorporated into e-marketing planning to make sure you are maximizing your online sales and return on investment. Some of the budgeting models we review are also vital for controlling spend in the different online media channels we will cover in Chapter 7 on traffic building.

It is the fluid, flexible and agile businesses that embrace the new models enabled by technology and exploit the opportunities presented by the new economy. 'The best leaders, it turns out, are the most insatiable learners' (Taylor, 2012).

Before exploring the different models, let's clarify what is a model. A model is anything that represents reality. It could be a model aeroplane, a map, a diagram, algebra or a formula. Here, we are particularly interested in descriptive models that describe a process – the current way in which a business operates in its dealings with customers and intermediaries such as media sites or price comparison engines. In Chapter 9, we review changes with other e-business partners like suppliers and distributors.

There are many different implications of change across a variety of models:

- Customers develop new patterns of media consumption and product selection, and brands need to be visible at the right time in the right place as consumers use search engines, review sites and affiliates to choose their preferred supplier. So online marketers need to review their *online marketplace models* to understand their digital marketspace.
- Businesses cross categories as supermarkets become banks, as radical changes to *business models* and *revenue models* are enacted.
- 'Markets become conversations' (Levine *et al.* 2000), where dialogue between customers and between employee and customer drive the relationships.
- *Value chains* and *distribution channels* are restructured as existing channel partners are bypassed and new channel partners and *value networks* are formed and reformed.
- Your suppliers or distributors may seek new revenue from online ads and affiliate links and this offers new opportunities for you to reach your audience online.
- Marketing becomes transparent as customers manage the relationship with companies rather than the other way around. Systems and control mechanisms are opened up to customers.
- Brand equity changes from being visually driven to interactively driven.
- Businesses can become what Charles Handy (1995) calls a 'box of contracts', as many functions are outsourced to form a *virtual business*.

EMBRACING NEW MODELS EQUIPS YOU FOR SURVIVAL

Positive psychologists have shown that some people tend to frame the world optimistically, others pessimistically. Optimists often have an edge: in our (McKinsey) survey, three-quarters of the respondents who were particularly good at positive framing thought they had the right skills to lead change, while only 15 percent of those who weren't thought so.

For leaders who don't naturally see opportunity in change and uncertainty, those conditions create stress. When faced with too much stress (each of us has a different limit), the brain reacts with a modern version of the 'fight, flight, or freeze' instinct that saber toothed tigers inspired in early humans. This response equips us only for survival, not for coming up with creative solutions. Worse yet, in organizations such behaviour feeds on itself, breeding fear and negativity that can spread and become the cultural norm.

(Barsh et al., 2010)

SECTION SUMMARY 3.1

Introduction to e-models

Models describe the process by which business is conducted between an organization, its customers, suppliers, distributors and other stakeholders. Managers constantly need to review how going 'digital' can change existing models and offer new models that can deliver competitive advantage.

3.2 Online revenue models

A knowledge of the range of options for generating revenue online is useful, both for intermediary sites such as media owners, portals and affiliates and for transactional sites where the main transactional revenue may be supplemented by ad revenue, for example. It is also useful from a media-buying perspective when promoting your site, since when viewed from the reverse direction, these are all options, which we explore further in Chapter 7, that you have for paying for visitors, either when approaching site owners direct or via a media agency. So you need to review the options and select a media mix which delivers the best return on investment (ROI). We present budgets based on these online media selling/buying models in Chapter 10.

In addition to direct selling online and brokering online sales through an auction arrangement, there are nine main ad revenue models that a budding web entrepreneur or established site owner can use to generate revenue.

1 *Revenue from subscription access to content.* A range of documents can be accessed for a period of a month or typically a year. For example, *The Financial Times* online (www.ft.com) has a three-tier subscription model according to the types of content you can access, varying from £100 to £400 per year.

2 *Revenue from Pay Per View access to documents.* Here payment occurs for single access to a document, video or music clip which can be downloaded. It may or may not be protected with a password or DRM.

For example, we pay to access detailed best practice guides on Internet marketing from Marketing Sherpa.

3 *Revenue from CPM display advertising on site* (e.g. banner ads, skyscrapers or rich media). CPM stands for 'Cost Per Thousand' where M denotes 'mille'. The site owner such as FT.com charges advertisers a rate-card price (for example, £50 CPM) according to the number of its ads shown to site visitors. Ads may be served by the site owner's own ad server or more commonly through a third-party ad network service. With display ad networks, space can be bought at a lower rate because it is known as a blind ad buy – CPM rates are lower because it is not known where the ads will be placed.

4 *Revenue from CPC advertising on site (Pay Per Click text ads)*. CPC stands for 'Cost Per Click'. Advertisers are charged not simply for the number of times their ads are displayed, but according to the number of times they are clicked. These are typically text ads, similar to sponsored links within a search engine, but delivered over a network of third-party sites such as Google Adsense (www.google.com/adsense), Yahoo! Content Match (http://searchmarketing.yahoo.com/srch/contentmatch.php), Microsoft Content Ads (http://advertising.microsoft.com/advertise/search/content-advertising) or MIVA (www.miva.com). For example, Dave Chaffey's site (www.davechaffey.com) uses Google Adsense by inserting JavaScript at different points in the page to automatically serve contextual ads related to the content, so a page about email marketing has ads about email services which can be bought on a CPM (site-targeted) or CPC basis.

For us, the search content networks are one of the biggest secrets in online marketing. Search engines such as Google generate over a third of their revenue from the display network (the network of sites that get paid by Google for allowing Google to place ads on their sites), but some advertisers do not realize that their ads can be displayed beyond search engines and so do not get their ads served in this highly targetable network. Google is the innovator and offers options for different formats of ad units including text ads, display ads, streamed videos and now even Cost Per Action as part of its Pay Per Action scheme.

5 *Revenue from sponsorship of site sections or content types (typically fixed fee for a period) – fixed price deal, CPA or CPC deal.* A company can pay to advertise a site channel or section. For example, HSBC bank sponsors the Money section on the Orange portal. This type of deal is often struck for a fixed amount per year. It may also be part of a reciprocal arrangement, sometimes known as a 'contra-deal' where neither party pays. However, it is a negotiated deal, so it may also have CPA or CPC elements.

6 *Affiliate revenue (typically CPA, but could be CPC)*. Affiliate revenue is commission-based; for example, Dave Chaffey displays Amazon books on his site http://blog.davechaffey.com and receives around 5 per cent of the cover price as a fee from Amazon. Such an arrangement is sometimes known as Cost Per Acquisition (CPA). Amazon, and others, offer a tiered scheme where the affiliate is incentivised to gain more revenue the more they sell. Hence this is often called a pay-per-performance ad deal.

Increasingly, this approach is replacing CPM or CPC approaches where the advertiser has more negotiating power. For example, way back in 2005, manufacturing company Unilever started negotiating CPA deals with online publishers where it paid for every email address captured by a campaign rather than a traditional CPM deal.

However, it depends on the power of the publisher who will often receive more revenue overall for CPM deals. After all, the publisher cannot influence the quality of the ad (the creative message) or the incentivization to click which will affect the clickthrough rate on the ad and therefore the CPM.

7   *Subscriber data access for email marketing.* The data a site owner has about its customers is also potentially valuable since it can send different forms of email to its customers if they have given their permission that they are happy to receive email either from the publisher or third parties. The site owner can charge for adverts placed in its newsletter or can deliver a separate message on behalf of the advertiser (sometimes known as list rental). A related approach is to conduct market research with the site customers.

8   *Access to customers for online research.* An example of a company that uses this approach to attract revenue from surveys is the teen site Dubit.

9   *Freemium models.* In the *freemium model,* free feature-limited or 'taster' access is given to content or an online service. Time-limited trials may also be considered 'freemium', but strictly it refers to a continuously available free service where the majority of customers use your service for free and the minority pay.

The model is most commonly applied to online software services or online publishing. The benefits of the freemium model for the brands operating it are:

- Increased conversion to sale due to ease of conversion from interest to trial of service to paid service (a much smaller proportion will convert to a paid service because of the risk that it may not offer value) – this is dependent on the quality of the service
- Increased awareness of the service through sharing of experiences by freemium users compared to paid users (amplification through network effects)
- Other revenue models are possible through freemium use such as advertising or affiliate. Google is the ultimate example of a freemium service where Adwords is the revenue model.

Disadvantages of this model include the incremental user cost of offering the service although this is likely to be relatively low for digital services. Getting the balance right between free and paid features is difficult. If the service quality or experience is poor, this can potentially damage take-up of paid services.

The Evernote app for capturing ideas and thoughts or the Dropbox filesharing service are other examples of a freemium service. Many millions of people use these services for free and will probably never pay.

ASSESSING THE BEST FORM OF REVENUE MODEL

Considering all of these approaches to revenue generation together, the site owner will seek to use the best combination of these techniques to maximize the revenue. To assess how effective different pages or sites in their portfolio are at generating revenue, they will use two approaches.

The first is eCPM, or effective Cost Per Thousand. This is a measure of the total revenue the site owner can generate when 1,000 pages are served. Through increasing the number of ad units on each page, this value will increase. This is why you will see some sites which are cluttered with ads. The other way to assess page or site revenue-generating effectiveness is Revenue Per Click (RPC) and the similar Earnings Per Click (EPC), actually based on 100 clicks to make it more meaningful for affiliates who will only generate revenue for a small percentage of clicks out from their sites. Basic revenue model evaluation spreadsheets based on these variables are available from http://bit.ly/smartdownloads.

SECTION SUMMARY 3.2

Online revenue models

There is a wide array of online revenue models for media owners to consider, from traditional CPM and fixed sponsorships through to the upstarts CPC and CPA. With contextual advertising options available from the main search networks and with the growth of display ad networks, there are now options for all site owners to review their ad revenue potential.

3.3 Intermediary models

It is vital that marketers understand their position in the online marketplace. This is your 'click ecosystem' which describes the flow of online visitors between search engines, media sites, other intermediaries, your competitors and you. Prospects and customers in your online marketplace will naturally turn to search engines to find products, services, brands and entertainment. Search engines act as a distribution system which connects searchers for different phrases to sites. Companies need to analyse consumer use of keyphrases entered from generic searches for products or services, more specific phrases and brand phrases incorporating their brand and competitor names. They also need to assess using services listed later in this section, to discover which online intermediaries or competitors have the best share of these phrases or are popular in their own right as well-known brands that attract visitors directly.

Online marketplace analysis is fundamental to developing an e-marketing strategy for an organization. It is also useful at an early stage in planning an online marketing campaign to indicate which type of sites you plan to partner with for promotion and the type of search terms which may need to be purchased for Pay Per Click advertising.

To help summarize the linkages and traffic flows in your e-marketplace, we urge you to create an e-marketplace map (Figure 3.1). This shows the relative importance of different online intermediaries in the marketplace and the flow of clicks between your different customer segments, your company site(s) and different competitors via the intermediaries. You need to know which sites are effective in harnessing search traffic and either partner with them or try to grab a slice of the search traffic yourself, as explained in Chapter 7.

Intermediary models introduce some concepts we will refer to more fully in later sections; the main members of the e-marketplace model are:

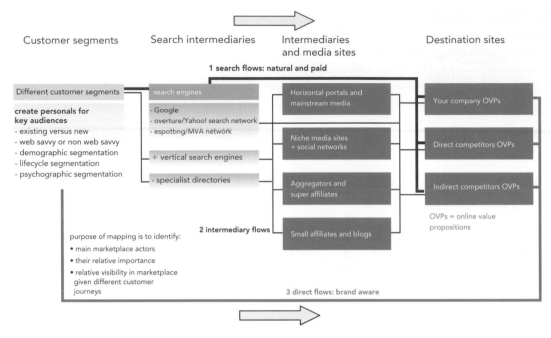

Figure 3.1 Map showing flow of different audiences via search engines to intermediaries and destination sites

1 *Customer segments*. To explore the right intermediaries, we need first to identify different segments to understand their online media consumption, buyer behaviour and the type of content and experiences they will be looking for from intermediaries and your web site. Personas are used to understand the preferences, characteristics and online behaviours of different groups as described in Chapters 4 and 6.

2 *Search intermediaries*. These are the main search engines in each country – typically, Google, Yahoo! and Microsoft Live Search, but others are important in some markets such as China (Baidu) and Russia (Yandex). Use audience data from comScore (www.comscore.com), Experian Hitwise (www.hitwise.com) and Nielsen Netratings (www.nielsen-online.com) to find out their relative importance in your country. You will need to know the most important phrases and which sites the visitors are directed to as shown in Figure 3.2, for example. Tools such as the Google Keyword Tool and Google Traffic Estimator (accessed from www.google.com/ads/agency/toolkit.html) are helpful to determine the popularity of phrases.

Since search is so important, we recommend creating a 'gap analysis' showing the potential audience against the actual audience for your target keyphrases. You do have a comprehensive keyphrase list of consumer search behaviours? Many don't. Summarize it on a marketplace map.

For example, in the financial sector, MoneySupermarket.com is an important potential partner if you are offering fixed-rate mortgages. The aggregator receives more search clicks than any of the major high street banks or building societies for all searches for fixed-rate mortgages.

Websites receiving traffic from terms in Fixed Rate Mortgages

Week ending 9 June 2012

	Websites (44 returned)	Search Clicks ▼	Paid:Organic Rate	
1	MoneySupermarket.com	16.57%	33.79%	66.21%
2	Money.co.uk	14.51%	5.70%	94.30%
3	Britannia Building Society	6.22%	16.52%	83.48%
4	This is Money	5.75%	0.00%	100.00%
5	Santander	4.11%	100.00%	0.00%
6	Nationwide Building Society	4.05%	0.00%	100.00%
7	Which 4 U	3.82%	100.00%	0.00%
8	Knowyourmoney.co.uk	3.47%	100.00%	0.00%
9	moneyfacts.co.uk	3.07%	0.00%	100.00%
10	BestMortgage.co.uk	2.91%	100.00%	0.00%

Figure 3.2 Example showing the sites receiving traffic from UK Internet searches for fixed-rate mortgages

Source: Experian Hitwise (www.hitwise.com)

3 *Intermediaries and media sites*. Media sites and other intermediaries such as affiliates are often successful in attracting visitors via search or direct since they are mainstream brands. You should assess potential partners in the categories shown in Figure 3.1 such as:

  1 *Mainstream news media sites or portals* include traditional sites, e.g. FT.com or *The Times*; or pure play ones, e.g. Google News, an aggregator

  2 *Niche/vertical media sites*, e.g. E-consultancy, ClickZ.com in B2B

  3 *Price comparison sites* (also known as aggregators), e.g. MoneySupermarket.com, Kelkoo, Shopping.com, uSwitch

  4 *Superaffiliates*. Affiliates gain revenue from a merchant to whom they refer traffic, using a commission-based arrangement based on the proportion of sale or a fixed amount. They are important in e-retail markets, accounting for tens of percent of sales

  5 *Niche affiliates or bloggers*. These are often individuals, but they may be important influencers; for example, in the UK, Martin Lewis of moneysavingexpert.com receives millions of visits every month. Smaller affiliates and bloggers can be important collectively.

4 *Destination sites*. These are the sites that the marketer is trying to generate visitors for, whether these are transactional sites, like retailers, financial services or travel companies or manufacturers or brands. Figure 3.1 mentions OVP or online value proposition which is a summary of the unique features of the site which are described in more detail in Chapter 2. The OVP is a key aspect to consider within planning – marketers should evaluate their OVPs against those of competitors and think about how they can refine them to develop a unique online experience.

Well-known, trusted brands which have developed customer loyalty are in a good position to succeed online since a common consumer behaviour is to go straight to the site through entering a URL or from a bookmark or email. Alternatively, they may search for the brand or URL.

PRACTICAL E-MARKETING TIP

Brand strength

Use web analytics to track the popularity of your brand and how this varies through time with seasonality, offline and online campaigns. You can also see the number of direct visitors arriving straight on the site. You can also access reports showing visitors searching on your brand name, your URL, misspellings and in combination with different products. You need to protect your brand from 'brand hijacking' in the search engines, as described in Chapter 7.

THE LONG TAIL MARKETPLACE MODEL (ZIPF'S LAW)

The significance of the long tail model was brought to prominence by Chris Anderson's book *The Long Tail* and his blog (www.thelongtail.com). We introduced it in Chapter 2. Formerly known as Zipf's law, it refers to any large collection of items ordered by size or popularity. It describes how the frequency or popularity of items declines in a regular way. It is known as the long tail phenomenon since although a handful of items are very popular, there are many, many others which, although not popular individually, collectively can be important if marketers want their services to appeal to a range of potential customers. Niche goods and services can be as economically attractive as mainstream goods and services since the potential aggregate size of the many small markets can be large. Furthermore, profitability may be greater on the tail. See Chapter 4, Section 4.1 for more on the long tail.

E-MARKETING INSIGHT

About Zipf's law

Zipf's law states that in a large collection ordered or ranked by popularity, the second item will be around half the popularity of the first one, and the third item will be about a third of the popularity of the first one. In general:

The kth item is 1/k the popularity of the first.

Zipf's law can be applied to describe the exponential decrease in preferences for using, selecting or purchasing from a choice of items. Since the tail is long, it is a mistake to concentrate marketing efforts only on the most popular items since many customers or prospects will have a different behaviour and will have different content or product preferences. The flip side of this logic is that if you have limited resources, you should concentrate your efforts on the head.

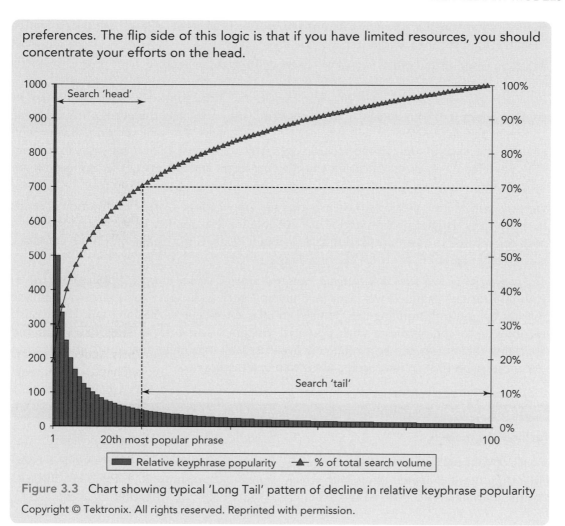

Figure 3.3 Chart showing typical 'Long Tail' pattern of decline in relative keyphrase popularity

Online marketers will encounter the long tail a lot. Here are some of the situations, and the implications:

1 *Popularity of search terms within a category or for an individual site.* A typical pattern is shown in Figure 3.3. Implication: keyphrase analysis used to determine search engine optimization and Pay Per Click marketing is most effective when hundreds of potential phrases are analysed for each customer need, rather than only the five or ten top keyphrases.

We have found these tips for targeting the long tail through search include:

- Target keyphrases with four or more keywords through SEO and Pay Per Click; within SEO, refer to these longer phrases within the <title> of your web page or blog posting
- Use the Google Keyword Tool (https://adwords.google.com/select/keywordtoolexternal) to identify different qualifiers such as 'geography' used to search for a more common phrase; e.g. 'marketing recruitment Manchester' is a geographic qualifier

- Use synonyms; e.g. include reference to online marketing, digital marketing and e-marketing within an article
- Target singular and plural versions – users will search for each.

2 *Popularity of content within a web site*. Implication: the more pages you have with different content relevant to your audience, the more likely you are to meet the needs of your diverse audience and the more they will engage with the content. But you should use your web analytics package to identify the top 20 pages which are most visited and then make sure they are effective in communicating your key messages and achieving the actions you are looking for.

3 *The popularity of items purchased from an e-retail site*. Implication: a larger inventory will result in more sales. Higher profit margins are possible for less popular items since consumers may be prepared to pay more for difficult-to-obtain items. Chris Anderson (2006) discusses this effect at length in his book *The Long Tail*.

4 *The popularity of web sites in a category measured through unique visitors*. Implication: the e-communications channels we cover in Chapter 7 such as interactive advertising, affiliate marketing and link building can be used to take advantage of the long tail. Using such techniques to communicate with potential visitors visiting niche sites like blogs and specialist directories can be a relatively low-cost way to achieve reach in comparison to expenditure on the top ten portals of the web or a category.

SECTION SUMMARY 3.3

Intermediary models

Analysis of your online marketplace can help you to understand customer behaviour in order to identify potential search terms with which you should promote your company and also potential partner sites or media buys.

3.4 Attribution models

We know that different customers buy in different ways. Some visit your web site just once and immediately buy (this makes analysing what works easy). Others visit several times before buying (or 'converting'). Some visitors actually remember and insert a specific web address (URL) into a browser and arrive at a site 'directly'. Or, as is often the case, they perform multiple searches and will be referred by different types of site. Different customers take different journeys (using different channels) to buy the same product. Channels include display ads; paid search (PPC); email; partners/affiliates/blog links; online PR; social media platforms, etc. Conversion means achieving a goal which could be making a sale, or a customer making an enquiry, taking a trial, registering for a newsletter, registering for blog post updates, etc.

Purchase intent jumps after first visit

Achieving and measuring repeat visits is worthwhile, since according to Flores and Eltvedt (2005), on average, purchase intent sees a double digit increase after someone has been to a site more than once.

Setting up clear 'Goals' in Google Analytics is the first step to understanding which sources of traffic, and which campaigns, are most effective. The second step *is tagging different media channels as explained in Chapter 7* (see E-marketing Insight box – reviewing different types of traffic sources with web analytics).

You cannot build the best picture of which channels are influencing sales if your agencies are using different tracking tools and reporting separately on different media channels; for example, the ad agency reports on display advertising, the search agency on Pay Per Click, the affiliate manager on affiliate sales. Instead, it is important to use a unified tracking system which typically uses common tags across all media channels. Common unified tracking solutions are available from the likes of Microsoft (Atlas), and Google (DoubleClick DART) and Google Analytics Multi-Channel Funnels feature.

To simplify the understanding of media effectiveness, for companies with a unified tracking method, a common approach is to attribute or credit the sale or other outcome to the last click, in this case, affiliate 2. This is a good approach in that it avoids double counting – a marketer wouldn't want to credit both affiliate 1 and affiliate 2 with 5 per cent commission on basket value. However, it doesn't reflect the role of the mix of media such as display advertising and natural search in influencing the sale. A common phenomenon in online advertising is the display advertising *halo effect* where display ads indirectly influence sales. These are sometimes known as 'view-throughs' or post-impression effects. A more sophisticated approach is to weight the responsibility for sale across several of the different referrers according to a model, so just considering the affiliates – affiliate 1 might be credited with 30 per cent of the sales value and affiliate 2 with 70 per cent, for example.

Measuring the 'last click wins' (last-click attribution model) only reveals which channel the customer came from on their final visit when converting. This ignores the impact of previous ads, clicks or visits from different channels. See Figure 3.7 below.

Analysing goal assists in football and in marketing

Just as football managers analyse the number of 'assists' a player makes (by giving a good pass to another player who scores), marketing managers need to know what channels (or tools) actually 'assist' the web site goal conversions. Players who make assists are often as important as the ones scoring the goals.

	Basic Channel Grouping	Assisted Conversions ↓
1.	Organic Search	138
2.	Direct	96
3.	Referral	43
4.	Social Network	23
5.	(Other)	11
6.	Paid Advertising	8
7.	Feed	6
8.	Email	2

Figure 3.4   Assisted Conversion Path report

Source: Patel (2012)

Patel (2012) analysed a B2B client who had 18–24-month buying cycles and included multiple campaigns in between. He used the new Multi-Channel Funnel reports in Google Analytics as they 'provide marketers with much more detailed insights into the first and last interactions visitors have with a website before conversion' (in this case into an enquiry/lead).

Patel tested the new Assisted Conversion and Conversion Path reports in Google Analytics V5 over a four-week period. Assisted Conversions identify which sources of traffic played a part (assisted) in converting a visitor (in this case into a lead/enquiry).

The Assisted Conversion Path report revealed *the relative importance of different media channels in influencing conversion.*

The different channel types are also explained in Chapter 7.

Having identified the top assists, marketing managers need to analyse the journeys that delivered these conversions. Google Analytics now shows the *Top Conversion Paths* which reveal the history of a series of visits. The *Top Conversion Paths* report (where visitors make two visits or more) shown in Figure 3.5 revealed the following:

This report shows the grouped combination of channels which resulted in conversion. For example, the above report shows that two Direct visits (initial interaction and final interaction) lead to the most conversions (32). Hence the importance of a short, easy-to-remember URL address, used prominently across all online and offline media. It also suggests that brand awareness campaigns are working. Patel suggests that 'If Direct visits [are] not top of the list for you then maybe you should think about a brand awareness campaign'.

The second most popular conversion path (with 22 conversions) is two visits from non-branded search terms. Hence the importance of optimizing your web site for keyphrases (non-brand

Figure 3.5 Conversion paths taken when visitors require at least two visits

Source: Patel (2012)

name keyphrases to facilitate a search which does not contain your company name or product names). Note: Patel actually created his own groupings so he could see 'brand' and 'non-brand' search terms. The default report does not show this.

Path 5 of Figure 3.5 shows 13 conversions after two interactions (or visits) – the first interaction came from a generic (non-branded) search term (which suggests the SEO is working), while the second visit came from directly inserting the correct URL (which suggests (a) the content was good enough to make a visitor want to remember the exact URL address; and (b) the URL was easy to remember).

In Path 25 of the same report (Patel, 2012; see Figure 3.6 overleaf), brand awareness is generated or enhanced by the content on a social platform. Some time later, the same visitor searches (using a generic or non-branded term/phrase), sees the brand on the search results and clicks to land on the site and convert. Who said social and search don't go hand in hand?

Social sites do help to keep the brand front of mind (i.e. in the 'considered set' of possible brand choices). The transparency of social sites should be reassuring, while the content (and transparent comments/discussions around the brand) can win trust.

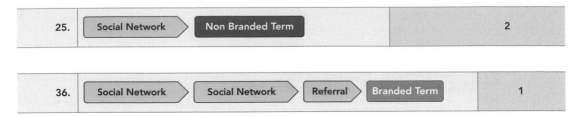

Figure 3.6   Social and search go together

Source: Patel (2012)

It is worth remembering two things when using Multi-Channel Funnels analysis (Top Paths Analysis): (1) always set up your analytics to separate visitors who search using generic terms from those who search using your brand name; (2) remember that although these reports give an insight, they do not give a completely accurate analysis as all of this is cookie-dependent, and many visitors use several different devices (each device being counted as a new visitor) and some visitors' systems delete cookies, so each visit will trigger a new cookie, suggesting a new visitor rather than a returning visitor.

Figure 3.7 provides another way of looking at the different journeys customers take when hiring an Avis car (adapted from Paget, 2011).

Note: if customer journeys are relatively simple and most visitors are converting on the first visit, then attribution modelling is not necessary. As a rule of thumb, if more than three-

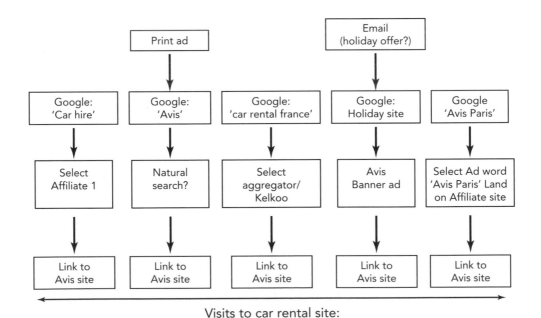

Figure 3.7   Avis Car customer journeys

Source: Adapted from Paget (2011)

quarters of your visitors convert on a single visit, then attribution modelling (or Multi-Channel Funnelling) is less important.

Note: 'view-throughs' (where someone sees a display ad but doesn't click on it) can be included through ad serving systems (but not Google Analytics).

Consider now an even more complex purchase path for a higher-value, more considered purchase with a longer purchase path (Figure 3.8). Center Parcs Holidays incidentally see their customers migrating online (70 per cent of bookings are made online compared to 20 per cent back in 2008). Their customers tend to research the holiday carefully. Center Parcs need to decide whether to use more expensive generic keywords to help the final conversion. Sixty days' worth of data were analysed to see how different channels performed. Each channel contribution was reviewed and credit given where it was due. The system attempts to give some credit (for an assist) to various channels; e.g. 50 per cent credit is given to a display ad view, while more credit – say, 60 per cent – is given to a display ad (or PPC) if it has been clicked on.

- 42 per cent clicked on a PPC ad and booked with no other channel involved in the booking
- 52.1 per cent clicked on an organic search, then on a PPC ad and made a booking
- 4.8 per cent viewed a display ad and then clicked on a PPC ad and made a booking.

In this case, a more detailed review of attribution is warranted.

The analysis can go onto the next level to consider the optimum sequence of media.

See this excellent visualization (Figure 3.9) presented by Media Vest (MVi) agency at the ad:tech conference way back in 2006 for a travel client, showing that brands with large budgets have been using this approach for some time (Chaffey, 2010).

D = display banner ad
S = paid search (PPC)
X = aggregator (or comparison site like Kelkoo)

Figure 3.8 Number of exposures required before conversion

Source: Center Parcs case study by Ignition One Research (2010)

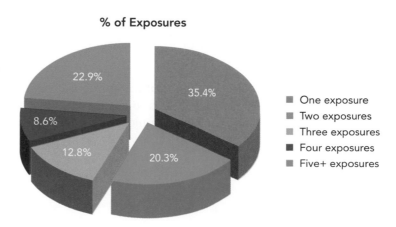

% of Exposures

- One exposure
- Two exposures
- Three exposures
- Four exposures
- Five+ exposures

Channels	Sequence	% Conversions	Channel Allocation
2	DS	34.01%	74.75%
	SD	20.98%	
	XS	8.35%	
	SX	7.33%	
	DX	2.24%	
	XD	1.83%	
3	DSD	7.74%	18.53%
	SDS	5.30%	
	SXS	3.05%	
	DXD	1.02%	
	DXS	0.81%	
	XSX	0.41%	
	SDX	0.20%	
4	SDSD	1.63%	4.48%
	DSDS	1.43%	
	DXDX	0.41%	
	DSDX	0.20%	
	DSXD	0.20%	
	DXDS	0.20%	
	DXSD	0.20%	
	SDSX	0.20%	
5	DSDSD	1.02%	1.43%
	SDSDS	0.41%	
6	DSDSDS	0.20%	0.61%
	SDSDSD	0.20%	
	SDSDXS	0.20%	
7	DSDSDSD	0.20%	0.20%

Figure 3.9 Sequence of media

This revealed that the highest conversions occurred when customers either:

- [DS] saw a display ad and went to the site (or was it a 'view-through'?); subsequently saw a paid search ad and went to the site (for a second time?) and converted
- [SD] saw a paid search ad which took them to the site; subsequently saw a banner ad and went to the site and converted.

This analysis identifies how display ads might prompt a later search. The old 'last click wins' omits these insights.

A further analysis will also look at the *latency* or interval between visits. Ultimately, e-marketing can drill down to very granular details to isolate and identify which channels (or tools) are performing. Now consider how communications models actually work on the end user.

E-MARKETING CHECKLIST – YOUR ONLINE TRACKING CAPABILITIES

Here is a checklist to assess your tracking capabilities:

Q1 Do you have unified tracking across all media?

- ☑ What high-level reporting do you have that enables you to compare cost (CPA), value (*ROI*, ROAS or *LTV*) and conversion across all media?
- ☑ What granularity do you have; i.e. how far can you break down by?

  - ○ Media, by referrer type
  - ○ Category or product(s) initially purchased
  - ○ Customer type (e.g. size of business/consumer, value or purchase activity over different time periods/lifecycle stages)
- ○ Paid and natural search keyphrases – can these be tracked down to campaign, ad group and triggering keyword level in each search network, and can these be compared to actual search terms entered by visitors?

Q2 How do you attribute sales to referring media? Do you use:

- ☑ Last referrer
- ☑ First referrer
- ☑ Weighted mix between the two – especially paid search
- ☑ Have you successfully removed duplication through using common tagging codes?
- ☑ Do you analyse the halo effect of combined media/channel impressions?

Q3 How well do you understand your sales cycle?

That is, what analysis have you done on sequence and consideration period for searches or affiliate referrals based on 'cookied' visitors; i.e. do you understand this pattern?

Which cut-off point do you use to assess contributions from different media such as display ads? Usually, a period of 30 days is a standard for a product like a holiday, but it could be shorter for books or CDs, for example.

Q4 Do you assess traffic quality on types of value events (other than sales)?

This is a detailed insight to identify opportunities for further improvement to media and sites – it can be argued that it is irrelevant if the Cost Per Acquisition is too high. A simpler approach is bounce rates by media type; i.e. percentage of visitors progressing beyond the first page.

Q5 Have you checked the accuracy of your campaign management systems?

Campaigns will be tracked by different sources such as page-tags on a web analytics system, tags on a campaign management system, ad-serving systems or log files. Differences between these should be assessed and minimized although different data collection will likely always generate discrepancies. The important aspect is to make tracking consistent through time. Tag position on the page can be important and if a page is slow to load, then this may not be registered as a click in the analytics system, although the ad-serving system has recorded it. Tags may just be plain wrong through human error, so this also needs to be checked.

E-MARKETING INSIGHT

The display ad halo effect – what do online site visitors do when they see an ad?

Clickthrough rates on ads tend to be very low, with most compilations showing response rates well below 1 per cent. This phenomenon is known as banner blindness. This phenomenon is well known and we consider how to counter it in Chapters 6 and 7, but it is worth considering that not everyone who sees an ad clicks – this is the halo effect.

SECTION SUMMARY 3.4

Attribution models

New tracking models using tracking and analytics ensure that online media spend is allocated to media which are influencing sales. You need to plan to gain a single de-duplicated unified view of all digital referrers. Once this has been achieved, the next challenge is working out how the combination of digital media to which consumers have been exposed impacts on sales.

3.5 Communications models

This section primarily explores how multi-stage communications models are moving into web-based community communications models. Brief reference is also made to other communications models including viral marketing, affiliate marketing and permission-based marketing.

In the last millennium, mass communications models were popular – with a simple model showing the sender (marketer) sending a message directly to the customer:

Then opinion leaders and opinion formers were identified as important elements in communications models. So they were targeted to help encourage word-of-mouth spread. Here the sender sends a message and some of it goes directly to the customer and some is picked up by opinion formers who subsequently pass the message on to customers.

Add in some feedback and interaction and you've got conversations, with the arrows also indicating flowbacks to the sender and other customers – a trialogue:

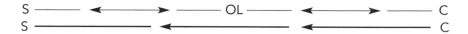

> ### E-MARKETING INSIGHT
>
> **Harnessing the trialogue**
>
> Walmsley (2007) believes that the main impact of media was not to find new ways to connect brands to consumers as originally anticipated, but in connecting those consumers, or 'people' as they like to be called, to each other. So, the age of trialogue has arrived and brands need to reinterpret themselves as facilitators.
>
> Walmsley believes that this trialogue will influence every aspect of marketing from product design through to product recommendation. An example where product design is influenced is Threadless (www.threadless.com), the online t-shirt store, which only carries designs its users have uploaded, and manufactures only those that get a critical mass of votes.
>
> The potency of trialogue derives from the opportunity that brands now have to talk to people, but also to be a small part of billions of their conversations. This is the point where user-generated content meets brands – an area fraught with difficulty for the unwary yet rich with opportunity for the creative (see Section 3.10 on the Ladder of Engagement).

Think about who are the opinion formers and opinion leaders in your marketplace. Separate online from offline influencers. They may include business leaders, celebrity users, journalists, public speakers, consultants, professional bodies and awards, influential networks, accrediting bodies, chat-room moderators, news groups, etc. Word of mouth works much more quickly online than offline.

Now comes the interesting bit. With the Internet came the easier facilitation of customer communities – where customers talk to each other (C2C) and back to the company (C2B) and also back to opinion formers and influencers. And now brands can encourage customers to write reviews which, ultimately, help other customers (see Section 3.7 on buying models for more on accelerating reviews).

The flow of communications eventually becomes like a web of communications between customers and opinion leaders – all built around the brand. The company facilitates these conversations. In doing so, it keeps close to customers as it can look and listen to what's being said. It can also communicate easily with the customers and ultimately develop strong relationships. News groups, blogs, Facebook pages, discussion rooms (hosted by the brand) discuss the brand, its applications, problems, issues, ideas, improvements and a broader array of topics linked with some of the brand values. In a sense, a web of conversations is being spun around the brand (see Figure 3.10).

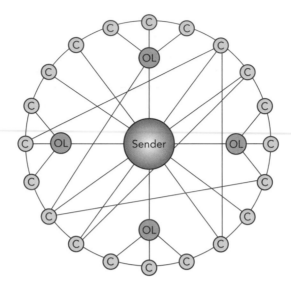

Figure 3.10   A web of conversations – accelerating word of mouth [C = customer; OL = opinion leader]

Referrals are part of C2C and eventually C2B as the referred customer contacts the business. Viral marketing is an extension of this C2C (consumer-to-consumer) or P2P (peer-to-peer) model where customers pass the message on. This is accelerated word of mouth. Clever, creative messages with interesting ideas, amazing images, special offers, announcements and invitations are good for viral marketing.

Affiliate marketing also spreads awareness of a brand amongst a community of relevant customers, who in turn talk to each other and can spread ordinary or clever viral messages within their own communities.

Implicit in all of these communications models is *permission-based marketing*. In this time-compressed, information-cluttered world, customers resent unsolicited SPAM. E-marketers must get permission to send messages. If the customer agrees, a message is eventually sent. There is more on permission-based marketing in Chapter 8.

ADVERTISING

All the models are changing. None more so than advertising. Advertising agencies are confronted by another big shift in their communications models. They have to move from 'getting attention' to 'giving attention'. This presents new challenges to agencies used to winning attention and creating brand awareness. Now, when visitors land on the brand's site, it is the brand that must pay attention. And they are starting to, courtesy of Facebook's Open Graph, which effectively lets brands present visitors with information tailored to their specific interests. New sites and apps are now sharing information from Facebook about users so that they can tailor offers, features and services to each individual's interests and tastes (as determined by whatever information that individual has made public on Facebook) – even if that individual has never visited that particular site before. For example, participating web sites like www.CNN.com will display tailored information, goods and services relevant to a particular visitor's specific interests – without the visitor even having to sign in at that web site or provide it with any information (as long as the visitor is signed into Facebook). 'Companies from Eventbrite to TripAdvisor to Amazon's Diapers.com to *The New York Times* have used the Open Graph to recommend everything from concerts to news articles and vacation destinations based on what users' Facebook friends are liking and sharing' (Halligan, 2011).

Test thousands of messages to optimize

To make the most of the advertising opportunities on social media, marketers must take this targeting to the extreme . . . Create custom messaging for as many different target groups as feasible, get really granular and test enough variations, ideally thousands, to properly optimise your campaign.

(Manning, 2012)

After that, marketers can tailor their messages and offers in a more optimized way, having discovered what works best for different types of customer group. Note that many brochure-ware sites do not take full advantage of the online opportunities and merely use the web to replicate other media channels by delivering a uniform message to all web site visitors.

E-MARKETING INSIGHT

Ads tracking you down! Targeting individuals in companies

If we are in a sales cycle with a large company there will be multiple decision makers, but our sales rep may only be talking to one of them – the others might be hard to find. We might run a Facebook or Linkedin campaign targeting employees of that company to ensure our brand message reach[es] everyone involved in the sales cycle.

(Joe Chernov, vice-president, content marketing, Eloqua, cited in Manning, 2012)

Ads tracking you down! Targeting individuals going for lunch

It is possible to mine real-time conversations. If McDonald's sees that you tagged it in a post ('going to McDonald's for lunch'), it can offer you coupons before you arrive. This is where Facebook's potential dominance becomes obvious – the ability to mine the real-time conversations of more than 750 million users is not really available on any other platform. (For a while, Facebook has been testing ads based on real-time posts.) (Slutsky, 2011)

Note: once audiences paid for the media which carried the ads; today many marketers pay the audience for consuming the media with incentives such as free phones if they accept ads.

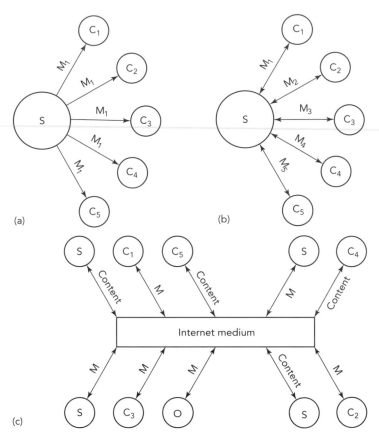

Figure 3.11   The differences between one-to-many and one-to-one communications online. S, the sender (the marketer) sends a message (M) to customers (C). (a) Old communications model (one-to-many); (b) one-to-one communications online; (c) many-to-many communications online

Adapted from Chaffey *et al.* (2003)

SECTION SUMMARY 3.5

Communications models

This section explored how multi-stage communications models are moving into web-based community communications models offering tailored messages targeted to specific groups and even individuals. Brief reference was also made to other communications models including viral marketing, affiliate marketing and permission-based marketing. New models bring new opportunities.

3.6 Customer information processing models

This section is a short one and leads you into the next chapter on e-customers by raising more questions than answers about online information processing.

There are many models for information processing, some so complex that they render themselves relatively useless in terms of practical application. We are going to look briefly at two of the more practical information processing models – one for display ads and one for web sites.

Consider first, Rossiter and Bellman (1999) developed the ALEA model that describes the online advertising experience as a process whereby attention is gained, followed by learning. If the consumer's emotional responses to the ad content are positively or negatively reinforced, further attention may be paid to the ad and further learning may take place until the brand's attributes are accepted.

This ALEA model is a 'heterarchy' of possible responses and does not specify a definitive sequence except that (1) attention must precede learning and emotional responses; and (2) learning and emotional responses must precede acceptance.

Rossiter and Bellman (1999) hypothesize that sustained attention is directly related to the evaluative intensity of the consumer's emotional response to a content node encountered during a visit to a web ad.

They also theorize that brand attitude will be directly affected by the appropriateness of the sequence of emotions encountered during a visit to an online advertisement and by the appropriateness of the final emotion experienced. Furthermore, they propose that consumers with a high-category need tend to process the online ad linearly in a 'hierarchy of effects' sequence (a logical pattern of pages), while those with a low-category need should process fewer pages of the site in a random order.

By contrast, Hofacker's model (2001; see Chapter 4, Section 4.5 for more detail) has five stages of information processing which can be used to review the effectiveness of an ad or a promotional container, or the overall page template layout on a site:

1 Exposure – is the message there long enough for a customer?
2 Attention – what grabs the attention – movement, colour . . . ?
3 Comprehension and perception – how does the customer interpret the stimulus?
4 Yielding and acceptance – is the information accepted by the customer?
5 Retention – how well can the customer recall their experience?

Each stage acts as a hurdle, since if the site design or content is too difficult to process, the customer cannot progress to the next stage. The e-marketer fails.

A final thought on the difficulty of grabbing a customer's attention. An interesting social experiment about perception, taste and the priorities of people was carried out by the *Washington Post* (Weingarten, 2007; see Figure 3.12).

The following extract by Nonnenmocher (2012) is a blog post that paraphrases the original article.

> *A man sat at a metro station in Washington, DC and started to play the violin; it was a cold January morning. He played six Bach pieces for about 45 minutes. 1,100 people went through the station during this time . . .*

Three minutes went by, and a middle aged man noticed there was [a] musician playing. He slowed his pace, and stopped for a few seconds, and then hurried up to meet his schedule. A minute later, the violinist received his first dollar tip: a woman threw the money in the till and without stopping, and continued to walk. A few minutes later, someone leaned against the wall to listen to him, but the man looked at his watch and started to walk again. Clearly he was late for work.

The one who paid the most attention was a 3 year old boy. His mother tagged him along, hurried, but the kid stopped to look at the violinist. Finally, the mother pushed hard, and the child continued to walk, turning his head all the time. This action was repeated by several other children. All the parents, without exception, forced them to move on.

In the 45 minutes the musician played, only 6 people stopped and stayed for a while. About 20 gave him money, but continued to walk [at] their normal pace. He collected $32. When he finished playing and silence took over, no one noticed it. No one applauded, nor was there any recognition.

The violinist was Joshua Bell, one of the most talented musicians in the world. He had just played one of the most intricate pieces ever written, on a violin worth $3.5 million dollars.

Figure 3.12   People rush past one of the world's greatest violinists as they screen out information in their busy lives

The Washington Post/Getty Images

Two days before his playing in the subway, Joshua Bell sold out at a theatre in Boston where the seats averaged $100.

This is a real story. Joshua Bell playing incognito in the metro station was organized by the Washington Post. The outlines were: in a commonplace environment at an inappropriate hour: Do we perceive beauty? Do we stop to appreciate it? Do we recognize the talent in an unexpected context?

One of the possible conclusions from this experience could be: If we do not have a moment to stop and listen to one of the best musicians in the world playing the best music ever written, how many other things are we missing?

(Nonnenmocher, 2012)

SECTION SUMMARY 3.6

Customer information processing models

Understanding how customers process information helps marketers to communicate more clearly. We have looked at models by Rossiter and Bellman for banner ads and also Hofacker for web sites.

3.7 Customer buying models

What goes through a customer's mind moments before they purchase? What stages do they go through when making a purchase? To sell, you have to know how and why people buy. By the end of this section, you will be able to select and draw a suitable buying model for online customers.

The choice of model obviously depends on the type of purchase and the type of buyer. We are going to consider an online consumer making a purchase. We will consider two different purchasing scenarios – one for a *high-involvement purchase* (e.g. a car or a smartphone) and one for a low-involvement routine purchase (e.g. a can of cola). Chapter 4 on e-customers considers these in much more detail. In this short section, we'll outline the models in action.

HIGH-INVOLVEMENT PURCHASES

For a high-involvement purchase like a car, customers go through a rigorous buying process from: problem identification to information search to evaluation to decision to buy through to post-purchase.

As we will see (Chapter 4, Section 4.6 goes into this in much more detail), a good web site (and/or good ads and recommendations) help buyers move through all, or most, of these stages in the buying process. Some buyers prefer to browse online and buy offline (or just test drive), while others prefer to test, browse and buy online.

The introductory chapter emphasized the importance of being able to offer this *mixed mode* of online and offline sales. The integrated database and integrated communications should be able to identify prospects online and close sales offline, even if it means delivering a test-drive car to the door. Surprisingly, many businesses are still struggling to integrate their databases.

LOW-INVOLVEMENT PURCHASES

Obviously, not all purchases require this much effort. There are many, many low-involvement purchases that we make every day, which do not warrant this kind of effort. Despite being almost 100 years old, and criticized by some, the *AIDA* model of attention (awareness), interest, desire and action is still used by many professionals.

There are many buying models such as *ATR* or awareness, trial and reinforcement – generate awareness, facilitate an easy trial and then reinforce it with advertising from then on. There are many adaptations which web sites can use. The Tektronix Learn-Buy-Use model shows how this approach can be used to deliver relevant content that supports sales and branding objectives.

E-MARKETING EXCELLENCE

Tektronix extends the ATR model

A business-to-business example of a high-involvement purchase is illustrated by test-and-measurement provider company Tektronix (www.tektronix.com), using a web microsite to support its e-business suite. It uses the approach shown in Figure 3.13. The site's *online value proposition* used to deliver this experience centres on a resource centre known as myTek which enables relevant content to be delivered by email throughout the customer lifecycle.

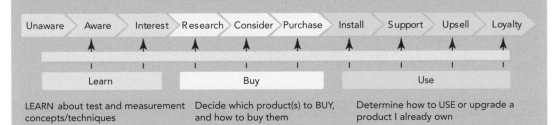

Figure 3.13 Model used to design content and services for the Tektronix web site (www.tektronix.com)

Increasingly today, reviews lie at the heart of any high-involvement buying model. Based on more than 1 million product page visits, *research by Reevoo suggests that increases in the number of reviews have a direct correlation with increases in sales.* High volumes of reviews seem to make the scores you show more trustworthy. Reviews equal 'trust and social proof' which are important during the 'Research, Consider and Purchase' stages.

How reviews bump up conversions

Figure 3.14 shows that increasing reviews from zero reviews to 50 reviews can increase sales conversions from 2 per cent to 4 per cent (or even going from zero to 10 reviews can increase conversions from 2 per cent to 3 per cent).

Brands should consider the buying process as ongoing. Therefore 'Purchase' is just one stage in the ongoing buying process. Securing reviews should be added as another component in the buying model. Improving your post-purchase follow-up emails is one place to start. Actively soliciting reviews generates vital customer feedback, nurtures brand loyalty and encourages other prospective buyers to buy your product or service.

Figure 3.15 shows that without actively encouraging reviews, occasional negative reviews can give a skewed view of a product or service which often destroys trust and confidence. Poorly managed reviews can misrepresent a brand, as it often only takes just one or two negative reviews created by competitors or a negative customer to reduce sales conversions significantly.

Figure 3.16 shows that accumulating more reviews can reduce doubt and increase sales conversions. See more on FUDS (Fears, Uncertainties and Doubts) in Chapter 4 on e-customers. So the actual purchase of a product or service is not the end of the marketing process, but rather it is literally in the middle of the buying model.

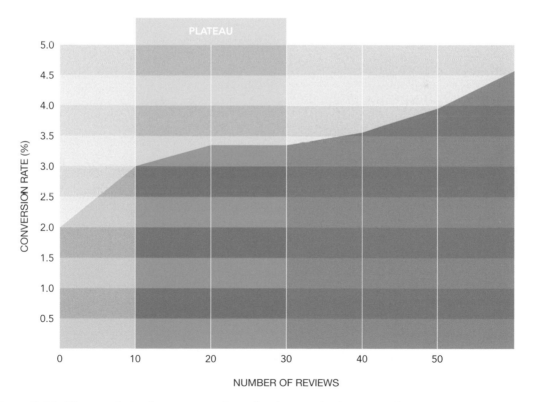

Figure 3.14   The correlation between number of reviews and sales conversion

Source: Reevoo

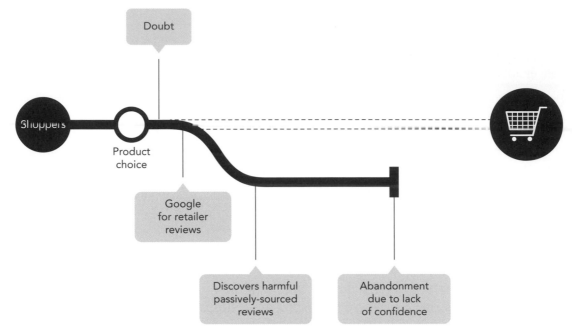

Figure 3.15   Occasional negative reviews can misrepresent a brand

Source: http://b2b.reevoo.com/products/reputation

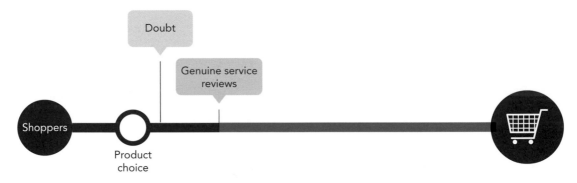

Figure 3.16   More reviews can reduce doubt and increase sales

Source: http://b2b.reevoo.com/products/reputation

SECTION SUMMARY 3.7

Customer buying models

Online marketers must check to see that their online activities (web sites, kiosks or other e-tools) accommodate all the stages of the buyer's buying process – whether linear problem solving, AIDA, ATR or others.

3.8 Loyalty models

Are you loyal to a brand online? Why – what makes you loyal? By the end of this section, you will know the components of loyalty.

We know that repeat business is, on average, five times more profitable than new business. On the other hand, low loyalty has a high cost as constantly recruiting new customers is expensive.

You need to identify and target your ideal customers and then move them up the Ladder of Loyalty (Considine and Murray, 1981) and a proportion of them up the Ladder of Engagement (Smith and Zook, 2011 – see Section 3.10 for more) so that they become loyal lifetime customers who also spend more of their 'share of wallet' with you on an extended product portfolio if the brand loyalty is sufficiently strong, as in the case of Tesco. In fact, move customers on to becoming advocates spreading your message. So how do you develop loyalty and strong relations with customers? Quality product, quality service and quality sites are basic prerequisites. In fact, satisfying customers should be replaced by delighting customers, since many satisfied customers still defect. On top of this, we are getting worse at customer service (Cerasale and Stone, 2004; Rezab, 2011 – see also Chapter 8). After this comes privacy and security. Respect and protect your customers' privacy. Ensure and reassure them of security. Add value to the relationship and reinforce brand values at every opportunity. Integrate your products and services into your customers' systems. Extend the partnership and share systems – this provides a certain amount of 'lock-in' where customers avoid the disruption caused by changing suppliers.

Going back to 'added value', rewarding customers is one way of adding value to the relationship. There are a number of innovative approaches emerging to reward and encourage online customer loyalty. All involve the visitor being offered some form of reward for buying. Rewards may take a number of different forms; e.g. credits, click miles. Remember there's always room for creativity. Take the Coca-Cola auction. Coca-Cola has amalgamated the loyalty notion with the auction model. In the physical world, the potential bidder collects Coke can ring pulls; once registered, these can be used to bid for a range of products. Vouchers are another method – visitors to www.richersounds.co.uk can print a 'buy one, get one free' voucher and then visit the store to redeem it. This approach can be used to increase sales and enhance the value of a site by increasing and retaining the user base.

It is important to explore ways to develop a loyal online customer base. Evidence suggests that site users return to their favourite group of sites, similar to their favourite store, as over time, customers tend to consolidate the number of sites they visit. Many emerging pure play companies are relying on the growth of their user base rather than the growth of loyalty among their existing user base. This has yet to be proven as a sound strategic approach – many companies following this approach have closed as funding has ceased to be available. Eventually, repeat business, lifetime loyalty and relationship marketing will separate the winners from the losers. Loyalty is so important that it pops up in every chapter of this book. Chapter 8 addresses e-CRM in much more detail.

The IDIC loyalty model

Peppers and Rogers (1997) have applied their classic work on building one-to-one relationships with the customer to the web. They suggest the IDIC approach as a framework
for using the web effectively to form and build relationships. IDIC stands for:

1 *Customer identification.* This stresses the need to identify each customer on their first
   visit and subsequent visits. Common methods for identification are the use of cookies
   or asking a customer to log on to a site.
2 *Customer differentiation.* This refers to building a profile to help segment customers.
   Characteristics for differentiating customers are described in Section 4.9.
3 *Customer interaction.* These are interactions provided on-site such as customer-service
   questions or creating a tailored product.
4 *Customer communications.* This refers to personalization or mass-customization of
   content or emails according to the segmentation achieved at the acquisition stage.
   Approaches for personalization are explained in Section 8.6.

ACHIEVING CUSTOMER ADVOCACY AND NET PROMOTER SCORE

Advocacy is another key aspect of loyalty; some argue it is the ultimate measure, with the
answer to the ultimate question 'Would you recommend us?' needing to be 'Yes' for as many
of your customers as possible. The importance of assessing advocacy, and putting in place
structures to support it have been highlighted in the concept of the *Net Promoter Score* which
has been advocated by Reicheld (2006). This is based on economic analysis of the customer
base of a company. For Dell, reports estimate that the average consumer is worth US$210 (five-
year Net Present Value), whereas a detractor costs the company US$57 and a promoter
generates US$328. See Chapter 10, Section 10.7 on control for examples of the value of a 'like'
or a 'share'. The value of promoters is generated by positive word of mouth and they also
naturally have higher retention and spend rates. At the same time, the influence of detractors
needs to be assessed since they can create negative word of mouth.

Think about how the Net Promoter Score concept applies online. In this chapter, we have
seen the increasing importance of social networks and these provide a platform for both
promoters and detractors. Brands need to think about how they facilitate promotion within
the web environment and manage the comments of detractors. An example of the type of
problem that can occur is indicated by the Land Rover car brand – a search for this marque
shows the message *'DO NOT PURCHASE a Land Rover Discovery 3 – you will live to regret it if you
have a similar experience to me as countless other owners have too'* in the natural listings, thanks to
a critical posting on a forum. This appeared despite the site owner having approached Land
Rover. Maybe time for some *negative SEO* to help to reduce the position of this company in the
natural listings.

On a positive note, there is a lot a site owner can do to facilitate advocacy within their site: check out our checklist of ideas to consider how to influence and manage online advocacy.

E-MARKETING CHECKLIST – INFLUENCING AND MANAGING ADVOCACY ONLINE

Facilitating online advocacy:

☑ Page template contains 'forward/recommend to a friend', 'share', 'like' and 'comment' options.

☑ Email has 'forward to a friend' option.

☑ Enable customer feedback and showcase positive experiences; e-retail sites contain options for rating and commenting on products (see Reevoo.com).

☑ Business sites have prominent testimonial and case study sections with pull-outs featuring customer success stories.

☑ Sites indicate 'wisdom of crowd' through showcasing top-selling products or most-read and commented-on features.

☑ Involve customers more in shaping your web services and core product offerings.

Managing online detractors:

☑ Use online reputation management tools (www.davechaffey.com/online-reputation-management-tools) for notification of negative (and positive) comments.

☑ Develop a process and identify resources for rapidly responding to negative comments using a natural and open approach.

☑ Assess and manage the influence of negative comments within the natural listings of search engines.

☑ Practise fundamental marketing principles of listening to customer comments about products and services and aim to rectify them to win back the situation!

SECTION SUMMARY 3.8

Loyalty models

Quality product, quality service and quality sites are basic prerequisites to achieve online customer loyalty. Reward schemes can also be used to enhance loyalty. A plan is needed to facilitate and leverage the comments of advocates and manage negative comments by detractors.

3.9 Social media models

In Chapter 6, we will explore frameworks to help manage different aspects of digital marketing. In this chapter, we will look at models showing the power of the network effect or social graph.

Take a target audience of 20 people. Here's how Lilley (2007) calculates how many messages can spread around, depending on what media is being used.

- A *broadcast network* is based on a 'one to many' model (e.g. TV advertising). It is called a Sarnoff network (after David Sarnoff, the broadcasting legend). A hypothetical Sarnoff network with 20 viewers has a score of 20. The network score is simply the number of nodes (audience members) = 20.

- A *telephone and email network* is based on a 'many to each other' model. It is called a Metcalfe network (after Bob Metcalfe, one of the inventors of the Ethernet). This communications model allows everyone to contact each other. Because everyone can call each other, the total possible number of calls or emails is 20 squared, or 400. This is potentially much more powerful for communicating messages among people than a Sarnoff network. The network score is node to the power of 2 or $20^2 = 400$.

- A *social network* is an 'immensely more powerful category of network' based on a 'many belong to numerous networks' model. It is called a Reed network (after David Reed, who observed that people in social situations belong to more than just one network). The possible value of a Reed network is 2 to the power of the number of nodes on the network. Take the same group of 20 people in a social situation, whether virtual or real. This generates a network score of $2^{20} = 1,000,000+$ (1,048,576!).

Moving from a broadcast network to a telephone/email network, even if only 10 per cent of the people pass the message on (maybe a special offer, or perhaps a criticism), it still means that 40 messages will be sent around. This is twice as powerful as the TV network, which only had a possible total of 20 messages being received. Moving on to the Reed network (social media network), if 10 per cent spread the message, that generates 100,000+ possible messages that can be received. Or, even if only one-tenth of 1 per cent pass the message on, it would still generate 1,000+ messages, which is 50 times more powerful than the old TV model with just 20 messages.

Now consider just one social network, LinkedIn, which is sometimes referred to as Facebook for businesspeople. It is a powerful tool. Once registered (which is free), businesspeople start connecting with other businesspeople, effectively building their own networks. If an individual has, say, even just 170 connections (contacts), LinkedIn calculates that the individual becomes part of a network of approximately 3 million people (Smith and Zook, 2011).

Remember, social media has grown so rapidly because we are social animals. We like to communicate, be part of a community, interact with each other. So when someone was clever enough to come up with a way to let all your friends know when you discover a new band, or see a great movie – with just one click, then it simply had to be a huge success. It facilitates a fundamental need for communicating.

WHAT WILL WEB 3.0 BRING?

While Web 2.0 was about social media, community participation, user-generated content, ratings, interaction, liking, sharing and data exchange, no one is 100 per cent clear what Web

3.0 will bring. It is probably going to be more immersive, virtual, 3D and with far more intelligent recommendations and tailored relevant content, syndicated content, data feeds, data exchange between networks and automated decisions.

There will be increased use of semantic markup leading to the semantic web envisioned by Tim Berners-Lee in 2001. It seems semantic markup will be needed to develop artificial intelligence applications which recommend content and services to web users without them actively having to seek them and apply their own judgement as to the best products and brands (i.e. an automated shopping comparison service) (as suggested by the use of standardized data feeds between shopping comparison sites and Google Base).

This represents the Holy Grail where we have a 'web that thinks like you' as it has been described. More immersive customer experiences may increase. Web 3.0, the semantic web, may combine virtual worlds (including augmented reality) with intelligent systems, creating whole new opportunities for those who embrace the technology. The University of Tokyo already has perfect virtual rain that looks like and probably feels like water dropping on to a surface (as you insert your hand into projected data images).

E-MARKETING INSIGHT

Nielsen's 90–9–1 rule of participation inequality: encouraging more users to contribute

To encourage online community participation is a challenge, since the majority of visitors to a community lurk or don't participate. Usability expert Jakob Nielsen (2007) gives examples of participation on Wikipedia (just 0.2 per cent of visitors are active) and Amazon (fewer than 1 per cent post reviews). He says that *'in most online communities, 90% of users are lurkers who never contribute, 9% of users contribute a little, and 1% of users account for almost all the action'*.

He explains:

- *90% of users are lurkers (i.e., read or observe, but don't contribute).*
- *9% of users contribute from time to time, but other priorities dominate their time.*
- *1% of users participate a lot and account for most contributions: it can seem as if they don't have lives because they often post just minutes after whatever event they're commenting on occurs.*

While it isn't possible for a site to turn around this distortion, completely, he does describe some strategies. First, there should be easy methods for a visitor to contribute, clicking a rating or commenting without registering. Second, automate contributions, but show related recommendations or most-read articles. Third, provide templates. Fourth, reward users by giving them accolades for contribution, and, finally, promote participation through design or featuring top reviewers.

E-MARKETING INSIGHT

Microsoft digital advertising solutions

Guidelines for advertisers in social networks

With the tremendous increase in social networks over the past few years, there are now many opportunities for advertising within social networks either through buying ad space, or – more interestingly – creating brand space, brand channels or widgets that enable consumers to interact with or promote a brand. The digital advertising part of Microsoft recommends these approaches for interacting with consumers in this space (Microsoft, 2007).

1 *Understand consumers' motivations for using social networks.* Ads will be most effective if they are consistent with the typical life stage of networkers or the topics that are being discussed.

2 *Express yourself as a brand.* Use the web to show the unique essence of your brand, but think about how to express a side of the brand that is not normally seen.

3 *Create and maintain good conversations.* Advertisers who engage in discussions are more likely to resonate with the audience, but once conversations are started, they must be followed through.

4 *Empower participants.* Social network users use their space and blogs to express themselves. Providing content or widgets so they can associate themselves with a brand may be appealing. For example, in the first six months from the launch of charity donation widgets, 20,000 have been used online and they became one of the biggest referrers to the JustGiving web site, driving more people to fundraising pages to make donations (JustGiving, 2009).

5 *Identify online brand advocates.* Use reputation management tools to identify influential social network members who are already brand advocates. Approach the most significant ones directly. Consider using contextual advertising such as Microsoft content ads or Google Adsense to display brand messages within their spaces when brands are discussed.

The golden rule: behave like a social networker

Microsoft recommends this simple fundamental principle which will help content created by advertisers to resonate with social networkers: behave like the best social networkers through:

- Being creative
- Being honest and courteous (ask permission)
- Being individual
- Being conscious of the audience
- Updating regularly.

METCALFE'S LAW PROVES THE POWER OF COMMUNITY

Metcalfe's law refers to the power of an interconnected network to enable collaboration and extend the reach of an organization. It originates from Bob Metcalfe, a co-founder and former chief executive of networking company 3Com, who said: *'The power of the network increases exponentially by the number of computers connected to it. Therefore, every computer added to the network both uses it as a resource while adding resources in a spiral of increasing value and choice.'*

More succinctly, the value of a network grows by the square of the size of the network. The bigger the network, the more valuable it is and the more valuable a new member.

The biggest implication of Metcalfe's law for digital marketing is potentially in the value created from setting up online communities among your organization's staff, partners and customers. For networks set up within companies (intranets) or between partners (extranets), Metcalfe's law suggests that value will be increased the more employees or partners are active users.

Where communities are created as part of a business proposition, the law shows the importance of supporting the growth of the network through the difficult initial phase until a 'critical mass' of participants is achieved. Many communities never make it through this phase.

Mark Zuckerberg, the founder of Facebook, has used the concept of the social graph to explain the power of links between people to show the scale of Facebook's 'reach'. Facebook has the largest social graph between individuals and these are now connected across web sites through the Facebook API (Open Graph). This enables companies like Nike and Spotify to increase awareness of their services as Facebook Friends see these services being used.

SECTION SUMMARY 3.9

Social media models

This section explored the power of social media, why it has grown so rapidly and how it affects customers (namely participation) and what Web 3.0 might bring. To tap into communities, brands need to plan for more open conversations with consumers, listening carefully and then responding.

3.10 Social business models and the Ladder of Engagement

The Ladder of Engagement is intended to show how customers can drive the business (using the new social media culture) through mobilizing customer engagement in a carefully structured way. This section is mostly reproduced from PR Smith and Ze Zook's *Marketing Communications – Integrating Offline and Online with Social Media* (2011).

CUSTOMER ENGAGEMENT CREATES STRONGER BRANDS AND MORE ADVOCATES

Marketers who understand and influence customer engagement better than their competitors are more likely to develop stronger brands and more loyal customers. Engaged customers are more likely to become brand zealots. Therefore it is important to identify engaged customers and start a brand ambassador programme to further strengthen the relationship and energize their word of mouth.

The ideal customer, or most valuable customer, does not have to be someone who buys a lot. The ideal customer could be an influencer who is a small irregular buyer but who posts ratings and reviews, as the reviews could influence another 100 people.

Another reason for brands to engage with customers as much as customers engage with brands is offered by American social media guru, Brian Solis, who says:

> *Social media has democratized influence, forever changing the way businesses communicate with customers and the way customers affect the decisions of their peers. With platforms like Twitter, YouTube, and Facebook, anyone can now find and connect with others who share similar interests, challenges, and beliefs – creating communities that shape and steer the perception of brands. Without engagement in these communities, we miss major opportunities to shape our stories.*
>
> *(Solis, 2010)*

The Ladder of Engagement, however, goes far beyond shaping stories and messages as it ultimately goes through to shaping products, services, processes and even the very way a business is run.

IDENTIFYING ENGAGED CUSTOMERS IS IMPORTANT

Monitoring the quantity and frequency of blog posts, comments, forum discussions, reviews and profile updates helps to identify opportunities and also acts as an early alert system to any future problems or opportunities. Chapter 6 explains how it's important to target influencers or brand evangelists rather than just purchasers. Some companies ask customers to give a product rating or even post a product review as a standard part of their after-sales contact strategy. Today, independent review companies like Reevoo.com specialize in helping brands get more reviews from customers. The more engaged customers actually identify themselves by their own self-selection (or their decision to write a review).

A customer who doesn't care about the product is likely to be less committed or less emotionally attached to the brand. On the other hand, a customer who is engaged is likely to be more emotionally connected to the brand. Marketers need to know about the sentiment, opinion and affinity a person has towards a brand. This is often expressed through repeat visits, purchases, product ratings, reviews, blogs, discussion forums and, ultimately, their likelihood to recommend a friend.

E-MARKETING INSIGHT

Product reviewers want to engage more

'70% of customers who left reviews for products wanted to help improve those products and they purchased more products, more often than non-reviewers did' (Aarons *et al.*, 2009).

Is customer engagement (a) measured and (b) used to improve products, services and processes? If not, why not, as it is free customer research (albeit skewed by coming from existing customers only and ignoring potential new prospects)? It is possible to increase some customers' level of engagement by moving them up from giving a product rating, to writing a product review, to joining a discussion, to suggesting ideas, to screening ideas, to testing ideas and eventually to buying the ideas when they become products or services. Many of these will become brand champions, evangelists or brand ambassadors. This is why moving some customers up the 'Ladder of Engagement' is valuable.

E-MARKETING INSIGHT

If you were paying attention you get the answers to questions you didn't think to ask

When the customer feels that the provider of a brand or a service that is important to them is engaging with them with some reciprocity, and the company is really demonstrating that it is listening, that is inherently very motivating. People welcome the chance to have a meaningful input into these products and services. Members have the sense of feeling like insiders – because they get an advance preview of what's to come and better still they're getting a voice in further defining and redefining what is to come . . . if you were paying attention you get the answers to questions you didn't even think to ask.

(O'Dea, 2008)

The Ladder of Engagement

Moving customers up the Ladder of Engagement creates brand loyalty, unleashes brand zealots, and can help improve an organization's processes, products and services. This can also create sustainable competitive advantage as customers become more engaged and more loyal to the brand in which they are involved.

The lower half of the ladder encourages customers to engage via product ratings, reviews and discussions. The upper half of the ladder is higher-level user-generated content (UGC), which encourages customers to become co-creators of content, products, services and even systems for the organization. This is sometimes referred to as crowdsourcing. The highest level of co-creation occurs when customers co-create the products that they subsequently buy (see examples in sub-section on 'collaborative co-creation' below).

Not everyone will rise to the top of the ladder. In fact, Nielsen suggests that only 1 per cent of web site visitors will; 90 per cent lurk, 9 per cent occasionally contribute and 1 per cent regularly contribute. He calls it the 90–9–1 rule (see Section 3.9). But those 1 per cent are important: hence the importance of identifying engaged customers.

A TNS *Digital Life* global study (2010) suggests that 61 per cent of Britons do not want to engage with brands through social media, although 33 per cent of Britons have commented

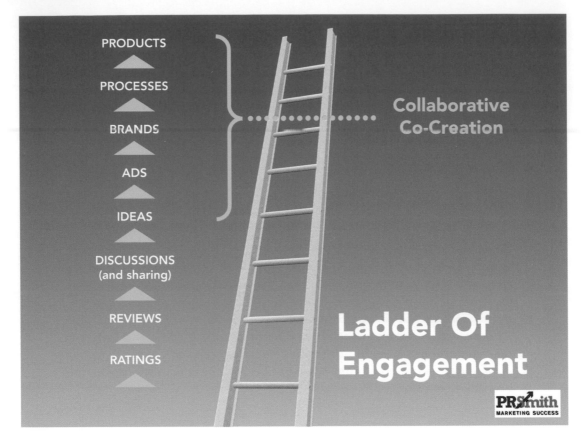

Figure 3.17   The Ladder of Engagement

Smith and Zook (2011)

about brands online somewhere (not necessarily on the brand's own social platforms). Either way, it is more than just 9 per cent occasionally contributing. Having said that, not everyone wants to engage with a packet of frozen peas, but some products and services play a more important part in people's lives and hence are more likely to be worthwhile engaging with.

While moving customers and other stakeholders up the Ladder of Engagement strengthens brand loyalty and boosts sales, it does require careful planning, systems and resources. Using the Ladder of Engagement is a long-term strategic decision.

E-MARKETING INSIGHT

The beginning of a beautiful relationship

Remember that the second visit to a web site is the beginning of a relationship. Therefore it is always worth asking the question: what is a brand doing to bring relevant visitors back to the site?

At the highest end of the ladder, the virtual circle completes itself as customers shape new products. It is a self-fulfilling system. As the customers create the product, they create their own demand. However cutting-edge this is, it does require the basic business skills of systems of communications, registration, processing, feedback, rewarding and putting into action. So back to basics – developing systems that work requires careful planning and rigorous testing. Here are some examples of how companies use the different steps on the Ladder of Engagement.

Ratings and reviews: Amazon

Amazon will try to engage customers by asking for a product rating, which takes just a few seconds. They then invite you to write a product review, which takes a few minutes. As mentioned, some companies make ratings and reviewing a standard part of their after-sales contact strategy. Customers value reviews from their peers. This shows that consumers are able to apply their own filters and, effectively, rate the ratings. There is a hierarchy of trust online, which starts with personal friends.

It is perhaps stating the obvious by declaring that reviews and recommendations (earned media) are far more effective than paid media (ads) in influencing customer purchase decisions. And a recommendation from a friend is a very potent influence on most B2C buying decisions (some would include B2B buying decisions also). A recommendation from a trusted friend conveying a relevant message is up to 50 times more likely to trigger a purchase compared to another recommendation (Bughin et al., 2010). Ninety-two per cent trust earned media (recommendations) as they have more credibility than paid media/ads (24 per cent) (Nielsen Wire, 2009). Conversion rates from earned media are five times higher than paid media (5 per cent+ conversion rate from earned media as opposed to 1 per cent conversion rate from paid media; Fugetta, 2011). Finally, recommendations can generate more traffic. Mork-Ulnes (2010) suggests that 25–40 per cent of all traffic comes from recommendations. See Section 3.6 on customer buying models for more on how to generate additional reviews.

E-marketing practice ask and answer: the Home Depot

One level of discussion is 'ask and answer', where customers ask questions and other customers answer them. The Home Depot (www.homedepot.com), a US DIY chain, invites customers to ask DIY questions and eventually they get other customers to answer the questions. Issues of liability for any careless advice obviously need to be addressed, and real experts may be preferred to casual customer experts.

Another type of discussion is where customers discuss the product or, in the case of the Great Moments of Sportsmanship, they passionately discuss sportsmanship stories. Those who do engage in discussions are usually passionate about the brand or, in this case, the principle of sportsmanship. They also reveal themselves as potential brand ambassadors. These discussions also generate answers to questions (see Figure 3.18) and sometimes new stories for publication on Twitter, Facebook, the blog and the next edition of the book (www.greatsportsmanship.org).

Figure 3.18 Discussions can be triggered on a blog, Facebook page, Twitter or forums

Source: www.greatsportsmanship.org

Collaborative co-creation

Now we move to the higher levels of engagement where customers and prospects collaborate on creating ideas, ads, systems and products and services.

IDEAS

Dell's IdeaStorm (www.ideastorm.com) generates ideas on how to improve the business and uses systemized suggestion boxes (Figure 3.19). Customers, and even non-customers, can suggest new products and features, as well as better ways of running the business; e.g. improvements in their processes. Dell has earned US$10 m from the early stages of IdeaStorm. This may seem tiny to a company of Dell's size, but remember, this is brand engagement, a form of brand promotion to the brand zealots, and it also contributes something to the bottom line.

Dell's Richard Binhammer says: 'Forget ROI and focus more broadly on business value'; i.e. across the six business areas which have fully embraced social media for different business reasons – marketing, product development, sales, online presence, customer service and communications. While other brands focus on one of these at a time, Dell has reached a point where they can 'inhale and exhale at the same time' (Bhargava, 2011).

People can generate a lot of ideas if they are given the platform and the encouragement. When BMW launched its virtual innovation agency to canvass suggestions from people all over the world, it received a staggering 4,000 ideas in the first week alone. The collaborative culture can work inside also, as demonstrated by Toyota's in-house suggestion scheme which generated 651,000 ideas in 2011. Even more remarkably, over 90 per cent of the suggestions were implemented. That's over half a million new ideas implemented in one year (Slone, 2010).

ADVERTISEMENTS

Co-creating ads is more common in the United States, where customers are asked to generate ads. In 2008, Chevrolet's Tahoe campaign team supplied graphics, music, photos and video clips and asked its audience to make an ad. The best one would be shown during the Super Bowl, the most sought-after TV spot in the world. It generated a huge response. The company also discovered some user-generated discontent (UGD), with several negative ads posted on YouTube. It took the brave decision to allow both positive and negative ads to be created – a classic double-sided argument, which generated more discussions and a lot of press coverage. By the time of the Super Bowl, the PR surrounding the user-generated ad campaign had boosted anticipation of the ads, and an enthralled audience watched with great intrigue.

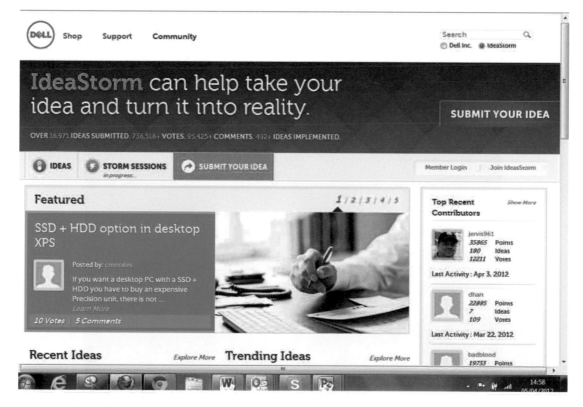

Figure 3.19 Dell's IdeaStorm

Source: www.ideastorm.com/

More recently, Unilever has declared crowdsourcing a success, following the August 2010 release of their first crowdsourced television advert. The Peperami ad was generated by ideas sent in as scripts or storyboards (Figure 3.20). The final ad was selected from 1,200 entries and cost just 30–40 per cent of the fee Unilever could have expected to pay a traditional agency.

Kraft Foods in Greece scored a hit with a user-generated 27-minute long-form ad for its Lacta chocolate bar. The crowd sourced the story and the casting, and some of the crowd even appeared as extras. The Love in Action campaign started using traditional TV advertisements to invite people to send in their love stories. Thirteen hundred love stories and one month later (it took a month to sift through the stories), the winning story was selected. Online polls voted for and selected the cast (full screen tests were put up online), the characters' names and even their costumes. Updates were posted on Facebook and Kraft's blog, which was followed by over 11,000 registered voters and 20,000 fans and eventually watched over 150,000 times. It created such a buzz that Greece's leading TV station, MEGA Channel, offered to screen it free of charge on 14 February as part of its Valentine's Day programming, which attracted a 12 per cent share of viewers and was seen by more than 335,000 people. Lacta sales are also up in a declining market (Hall, 2010).

BRAND NAMES

Co-creation can go way beyond ads and promotions; it can even generate brand names, if the basic systems are in place. Boeing created a buzz around the launch of the new 787, the Dreamliner, by inviting input from potential customers and passengers online. Indeed it was

Figure 3.20 Peperami's crowdsource ad boosted engagement and entertained customers, while reducing advertising costs

Source: www.campaignlive.co.uk/news/1022198/

Figure 3.21   Boeing Dreamliner: 500,000 voters decided the brand name
Source: www.boeing.com/commercial/787family/

the community that named the aircraft the Dreamliner, with some 500,000 votes cast online from 160 countries (O'Dea, 2008; Figure 3.21).

PRODUCTS AND SERVICES

Some say that user-generated content (UGC) has been used offline for many years now. The *X Factor* music talent TV show is a good example as it attracts users to generate their own content to potentially create new product concepts; the audiences then pay for the privilege of carrying out new product screening (which product gets most votes) and new product testing (votes again). You can see why this UGC and the system behind it is marketing utopia. LEGO has been collaborating with customers for years, asking children to suggest, create and screen new product ideas. They then financially reward 'those whose ideas go to market'.

Back to the online world. Peugeot invited its online audience to submit new product concepts; i.e. submit car designs. This attracted 4 million page views. Peugeot built a demonstration model of the winning design to exhibit at marketing events. It also partnered with software developers to put it into a video game.

Take product variations and product components. The *Great Moments of Sportsmanship* book is part of the Great Sportsmanship Programme which mobilizes whole communities into sportsmanship. Customers send in their sportsmanship stories for further discussion on the blog

Figure 3.22   www.Pods4jobs.com: UGC videos created by young people to help young people choose careers and courses

and possible inclusion in the next edition. The aim is to have totally user-generated future editions.

In the careers sector, there is a highly engaging UGC company whose product is 100 per cent user generated. Called Pods4jobs (www.pods4jobs.com), it is an online careers advice site with a difference – videos only and all created by the target market; i.e. mostly teenagers interviewing people at work, revealing a 'warts and all' insight into different careers. Here, kids interview their parents, aunts, uncles, grandparents, neighbours or anyone who has a career. Students shoot their own video, upload it and, if it is accepted, get a certificate of achievement.

Occasionally B2B is mixed with B2C, as in the case of the InnoCentive site, which allows 180,000 freelance scientists, engineers, entrepreneurs, students and academics to work on problems posed by industry, creating and selling solutions in return for cash rewards. Major players are involved, including NASA and *The Economist* as well as Accenture and Booz Allen Hamilton.

One outstanding UGC web site is www.threadless.com, whose loyal community of graphic designers, artists and generally creative people send in designs for new t-shirts (Figure 3.23). The community votes for the best one; they then produce it and sell it back to the community. The retail trade has spotted these high-quality and unusual t-shirts and now orders significant quantities of their limited-edition, high-quality products. Threadless has 1.5 million followers and a turnover of £20m.

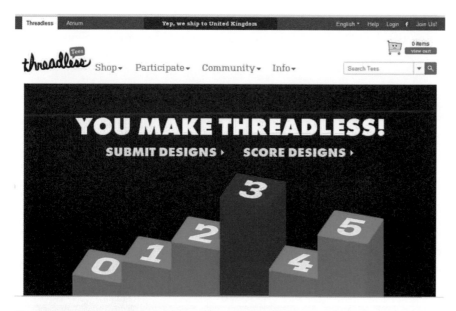

Figure 3.23   Threadless t-shirts (www.threadlesscom/)

IBM also uses open innovation for its Big Green Innovations unit. Likewise, Proctor & Gamble (P&G) revamped its innovation model by adopting open innovation back in 2008. Fifty per cent of P&G's Innovation & Research comes from external collaboration. Proctor & Gamble has gone from being an inward-looking organization ('Fortress P&G') to a corporation that relies on external collaboration for most of its innovation and research (Business and Innovation, 2008).

From Intel to Xerox, NASA to Novell and Vodafone to Virgin, more and more organizations are unleashing the collective brainpower of people outside their organization.

Successful UGC and even the lower levels of engagement are dependent on a vibrant, responsive audience and one of marketing's often forgotten fundamentals – systems and processes that work, and basic marketing principles of testing interfaces and back-office systems. Usability testing is a prerequisite. Remember, web sites are fun, but back office means business.

E-MARKETING INSIGHT

UGC enhances search results

'25% of search results for the world's top 20 largest brands are links to user-generated content' (Qualman, 2009).

All of these UGC systems draw from the basics of perfect marketing processes and the passionate attention to detail required if user-generated systems are to work successfully.

Ask: 'How well are we measuring the engagement of our different online audiences and then closing the loop by using the data to identify the advocates and deliver more relevant communications?'

E-MARKETING INSIGHT

BBC Radio Northern Ireland takes UGC to a new level

Co-creation and user-generated content have been around for a long time, as is the case with radio show phone-ins, whereby the audience's input and opinions are a key part of the programme. However, BBC Radio Northern Ireland took it to a new level back in 2007 when they felt that the audience input was so funny that they should make an animated TV show from it. They even kept, with permission, the callers' actual voices and dubbed them into the animation. Called *On the Air* by Flickerpix, some of the series is still on YouTube (Figure 3.24).

Figure 3.24   *On the Air* used real audience voices from the radio show in the animated TV programmes (www.flickerpix.com/projects/tv-series/on-the-air/)

E-MARKETING INSIGHT

Collaborative co-creation is a natural instinct – it's an unselfish gene

For generations, we have operated on the assumption that human beings are fundamentally selfish, and so we have built systems and organizations around monetary incentives, rewards, and punishments. That hasn't always worked very well.

Now the tide is starting to turn. In fields such as evolutionary biology, psychology, sociology, political science, and experimental economics, researchers are seeing evidence that human beings are more cooperative and behave far less selfishly than we have long assumed.

The success achieved by such collaborative offerings as Wikipedia, Craigslist, Facebook, and open source software has, in fact, a scientific basis. Dozens of field studies have identified highly successful cooperative systems, which are often more stable than those based on incentives. Moreover, researchers have found neural and possibly genetic evidence of a human predisposition to cooperate. Evolution may actually favour people who collaborate and societies that include such individuals.

Organizations would be better off helping us to engage and embracing our generous sentiments rather than assuming that we are driven purely by self-interest. We can build collaborative systems by encouraging communication, ensuring that claims about community are authentic, fostering a feeling of solidarity, being fair, and appealing to people's intrinsic motivations (Benkler, 2011).

MANAGING COLLABORATIVE CO-CREATION

This requires expert management skills covering legal rights, financial agreements, regular communications, project management; in fact, this also requires crystal-clear rules, clear leadership and transparent processes for setting goals and resolving conflict. As with any form of crowdsourcing, the key is to develop a cost-effective, consistent and fair filtering process from the very start.

Once mastered, however, the results can be fantastic as essentially the business becomes a pure customer-driven business – marketing utopia.

SOCIAL BUSINESS

Move over social media, here comes social business.

In the last millennium (around 1997), IBM introduced e-business. They were right. Now they are introducing 'Social Business'. We've seen how the Ladder of Engagement encourages businesses to become more customer-centric, particularly as they move up to the higher levels of engagement such as collaborative co-creation. Social media has helped many companies to become more customer-centric. Social media also facilitates the idea that 'people do business with people' (not companies). IBM discovered (Neisser, 2011) that adding IBM 'experts' to various web pages and testing this in A/B testing revealed dramatically improved page performance. The brand experience for an IBM customer is an experience with an IBM-er. Therefore, as Neisser suggests, employees need to become digital citizens by being comfortable with social media and being given time and resources to exploit it so that more people in decision-making units can enjoy the IBM experience with an IBM-er.

However, many large organizations are afraid of what their employees might do with social media even though they let those same employees talk to customers and prospects and stakeholders outside of the company via phone, fax, email and face-to-face. As Bhargava (2011) says, 'if you can't trust your employees to do the right things and make the right choices, then maybe you need to hire better people'.

Interestingly, Gartner (2009) reported that 'Social networks can ultimately destroy business models that are company-centric.' Hence the need for customer-centric social businesses. Gartner went on to say that by 2015, consumers will have an almost effortless ability to monitor quality, pricing, availability and business sentiment, and find alternatives. Witness e-customers' 'post literacy era where everyone and everything is rated' (see Section 4.11 in Chapter 4 on e-customers).

CHAPTER SUMMARY

1 Models describe the process by which business is conducted between an organization, its customers, suppliers, distributors and other stakeholders. Managers need constantly to review how electronic communications change existing models and offer new opportunities.

2 Online revenue models for media owners to consider include traditional CPM and fixed sponsorships, Cost Per Click models and Cost Per Acquisition affiliate models. Ads can also be displayed as part of a network.

3 Analysis of your online marketplace can help you understand customer behaviour in order to identify potential search terms with which you should promote your company and also potential partner sites or media buys.

4 New attribution models ensure that online media spend is allocated to media which are influencing sales. A single de-duplicated unified view of all digital referrers should be achieved to help understanding of how the combination of digital media to which consumers have been exposed to impacts on sales.

5 Communications models have enabled a change from many-to-one, to many-to-some and to one-to-one communication. Other new communications techniques are viral marketing, affiliate marketing and permission-based marketing.

6 Buying models can accommodate the linear process for high-involvement purchases, mixed-mode buying and traditional models such as AIDA and low-involvement ATR.

7 Hofacker's customer information processing model of exposure–attention–comprehension and perception–yielding and acceptance–retention is a valuable method of enhancing the communications efficiency of a web site.

8 A quality product, service and web site are basic prerequisites to build customer loyalty. The role of the web in advocacy and negative mentions should be assessed and monitored.

9 Business is undergoing massive changes in its business models, particularly since the introduction of social media.

10 The Ladder of Engagement model demonstrates how selected customers can become more engaged with a brand and ultimately how this can create a whole new business model. Social business models are next as employees are empowered to utilize social media.

References

Aarons, C., Edwards, A. and Lanier, X. (2009) Turning blogs and user-generated content into search engine results. *Marketing Vox and Nielsen BuzzMetrics SES Magazine*, 8 June.

Anderson, C. (2006) *The Long Tail: Why the Future of Business is Selling Less of More*. Hyperion, New York.

Barsh, J., Mogelof, J. and Webb, C. (2010) How centered leaders achieve extraordinary results. *McKinsey Quarterly Online*, October.

Benkler, Y. (2011) The unselfish gene. *HBR Magazine*, 27 July.

Bhargava, R. (2011) 10 big brand lessons from the Corporate Social Media Summit. *Social Media Today*, 22 June.

Bughin, J., Doogan, J. and Vetvik, O. (2010) A new way to measure word-of-mouth marketing. *McKinsey Quarterly*, April.

Business and Innovation (2008) Open for innovation. 1 October [complete source information unobtainable].

Cerasale, M. and Stone, M. (2004) *Business Solutions on Demand*. Kogan Page, London.

Chaffey, D. (2010) Digital media campaign attribution model. Blog post, 11 November at: www.smartinsights.com/traffic-building-strategy/media-attribution/media-conversion-attribution/

Chaffey, D., Mayer, R., Johnston, K. and Ellis-Chadwick, F. (2003) *Internet Marketing: Strategy, Implementation and Practice*, 2nd edition. Financial Times/Prentice Hall, Harlow.

Considine, R. and Murray, R. (1981) *The Great Brain Robbery*, Pasadena, CA.

Flores, L. and Eltvedt, H. (2005) Beyond online advertising – lessons about the power of brand websites to build and expand brands. Published in *Proceedings of ESOMAR Online Conference, Montreal*.

Fugetta, R. (2011) Five reasons you need to focus on earned media. *Ad Age Digital*, 18 May.

Gartner (2009) *Trip Report: Gartner Customer Relationship Management Summit 2009*. Gartner, Stamford, CT.

Hall, E. (2010) In Greece Kraft scores a hit for Lacta chocolate with crowdsourced film. *Advertising Age*, 24 March.

Halligan, K. (2011) Facebook marketing: the four biggest blunders hurting your brand. *Ad Age Digital*, 13 September.

Handy, C. (1995) *The Age of Unreason*, 3rd edition. Arrow Books , London.

Hofacker, C. (2001) *Internet Marketing*, 3rd edition. Wiley, New York.

Ignition One Research (2010) 5 steps to media attribution for increased ROI. At: http://bit.ly/betterattribution.

JustGiving (2009) JustGiving Widget version 2.0. Blog posting, 28 May at: http://blog.justgiving.com/community/encourage-the-use-of-justgiving-widgets/

Levine, R., Locke, C., Searls, D. and Weinberger, D. (2000) *The Cluetrain Manifesto*. Perseus Books, Cambridge, MA.

Lilley, A. (2007) Why Web 2.0 adds up to a revolution for our industry. *Media Guardian*, 1 October.

Manning, J. (2012) Digital: 5 social advertising endorsements. *The Marketer*, January/February.

Microsoft (2007) Word of the web guidelines for advertisers. Understanding trends and monetising social networks. Research report. Microsoft Digital Advertising Solutions.

Mork-Ulnes, N. (2010) Earned media optimization belongs in your digital marketing toolbox along with SEO and ad optimization. *Beyond Rethinking Digital*, 2 April.

Neisser, D. (2011) Move over Social Media; here comes Social Business. *Fast Company*, 11 September. At: www.fastcompany.com/1779375/move-over-social-media-here-comes-social-business

Nielsen, J. (2007) Participation inequality: encouraging more users to contribute. *AlertBox*, 9 October, 2006 at: www.useit.com/alertbox/participation_inequality.html

Nielsen Wire (2009) Global advertising: consumers trust real friends and virtual strangers the most, 7 July.

Nonnenmocher, J. (2012) Stop and smell the flowers. Post on the Joshua Bell story, 12 February at: www.GlorianaJoesCoffeeGarage.com

O'Dea, A. (2008) Innovation. *Marketing Age*, September/October.

Paget, J. (2011) Attribution modelling for social media. Smart Insights, 13 December.

Patel, P. (2012) Using Multi-Channel Funnels to analyse the impact of marketing channels on conversions. Smart Insights, 24 January at: www.smartinsights.com/google-analytics/google-analytics-campaign-tracking/influence-social-media

Peppers, D. and Rogers, M. (1997) *One to One Future*, 2nd edition. Doubleday, New York.

Reicheld, F. (2006) *The Ultimate Question: Driving Good Profits and True Growth*. Harvard Business School Publishing, Cambridge, MA.

Rezab, J. (2011) Companies respond to just 5% of questions on Facebook. E-consultancy, 17 October.

Roberts, K. (2010) Video interview with Saatchi & Saatchi Worldwide CEO Kevin Roberts by PR Smith.

Rossiter, J.R. and Bellman, S. (1999) A proposed model for explaining and measuring web advertising effectiveness. *Journal of Current Issues and Research in Advertising*, 21(11), pp. 13–31.

Slone, P. (2010) Want marketing innovation? Go for quantity. *The Marketer*, December/January.

Slutsky, I. (2011) Facebook's new location features look less like Foursquare, more like, well, Facebook. *Ad Age Digital*, 25 August at: http://adage.com/article/digital/facebook-s-location-features-foursquare/229461

Smith, P.R. and Zook, Z (2011) *Marketing Communications – Integrating Offline and Online with Social Media*. Kogan Page, London.

Solis, B. (2010) It's time to engage: please help share the news. Blog post, 26 February, at: www.briansolis.com/2010/02/its-time-to-engage-please-spread-the-word/ .

Taylor, B. (2012) Are you learning as fast as the world is changing? Harvard Business Review Blog Network, 26 January at: http://blogs.hbr.org/taylor/2012/01/are_you_learning_as_fast_as_th.html

TNS (2010) *Digital Life* (survey). At: http://2010.tnsdigitallife.com/

Walmsley, A. (2007) New media: the age of the trialogue. *The Marketer,* September.

Weingarten, G. (2007) Pearls before breakfast. *Washington Post Magazine,* 8 April.

Further reading

Schaeffer, M.W. (2012) *Return on Influence.* McGraw Hill, New York.

Smith, P.R. and Zook, Z. (2011) *Marketing Communications – Integrating Offline and Online with Social Media.* Kogan Page, London.

Web links

Connected Marketing (www.connectedmarketing.com). Blog and community that supports the book edited by Justin Kirby about approaches to viral marketing and achieving advocacy online.

Harvard Business Review (www.hbr.org). Strategy advice.

Hitwise blog (http://weblogs.hitwise.com). Sample reports from Hitwise on consumer search behaviour and the importance of different online intermediaries.

McKinsey Quarterly (www.mckinseyquarterly.com). Business strategy.

Net Promoter Score blog (http://netpromoter.typepad.com/fred_reichheld). Blog on achieving advocacy by Fred Reichheld and other specialists such as Paul Marsden (see also links in Chapter 9 on e-business).

Rough Type (www.roughtype.com). Nicholas Carr's blog on how technology is disrupting business models. Carr is a former editor of the *Harvard Business Review.*

Smart Insights online revenue model spreadsheets (www.smartinsights.com). Excel spreadsheets for modelling visitor volumes and campaign responses.

Wikinomics.com (www.wikinomics.com). Blog for the *Wikinomics* book by Don Tapscott and Anthony Williams.

Self-test

1 Summarize the main online revenue models.

2 Explain the concept of commoditization.

3 Do you think value networks or the external value chain is a more useful model for defining e-marketing strategy?

4 Explain the relevance of the prosumer concept to the modern marketer.

5 Describe how the B2B marketer can use the concept of e-procurement to enhance sales to existing and new customers.

6 Describe marketing tactics to accommodate changes to the distribution channel for your organization.

7 Outline the changes from traditional mass communication to new communications models.

8 Which e-marketing tactics should be developed to accommodate different buying models?

9 Apply Hofacker's model of customer information processing to your organization's web site.

10 Outline models to help build customer loyalty.

Chapter **4**

E-customers

We have only two sources of competitive advantage: the ability to learn more about our customers faster than the competition; the ability to turn that learning into action faster than the competition.

Jack Welch, former GE CEO

This chapter looks inside the online customer's mind. We explore customers' issues, worries, fears and phobias as well as other motivators for going online . . . and how marketers can respond to these behaviours. We also look at on-site behaviour, the online buying process and the many influencing variables. We finish with a look to the future, your future, and how to keep an eye on the e-customer.

OVERALL LEARNING OUTCOME

By the end of this chapter, you will:

- Understand online customers and their buying behaviour and how they differ from offline customers.
- Overcome the issues and concerns that online customers have.
- Begin to move e-customers through their online mental stages.

CHAPTER TOPIC	LEARNING OBJECTIVE
4.1 Introduction	Identify the changing customer expectations and how to satisfy them
4.2 Motivations	Evaluate and respond to the factors that encourage users to adopt and stay using the Internet
4.3 Expectations	Determine the facilities that customers require online
4.4 Fears and phobias	Evaluate and manage the fears and phobias that hinder online transactions
4.5 Online information processing	Recognize how visitors process information and how marketers can respond to this. Identify the online buying process
4.6 The online buying process	Support the buying process through traditional and digital channels
4.7 Relationships and loyalty	Understand online relationship marketing techniques that maintain relationship, and nurture loyalty
4.8 Communities and social networks	Assess the suitability of techniques used to foster online communities and how to build active/lively online communities
4.9 Customer profiles	Describe the profile characteristics of online customers, both B2C and B2B
4.10 Researching the online customer	Assess the process, techniques and measures used customer to research and assess online marketing effectiveness
4.11 The post-literate customer	Paint a picture of the future and the new online customer's changing behaviour patterns

4.1 Introduction to e-customers

Understanding customers is fundamental to successful marketing. Good marketers know their target customers inside out and upside down. They are able to put a microscope on their buyers. Understanding online customers is even more important, as the geographic and cultural spread is often much wider. Online customers also have different attitudes to both acquiring information and buying online. On top of this, the same person may both think and behave differently online than offline. So overall, e-marketers have to watch their online customers even more closely.

Online customers are changing. Not only do they talk back, they now shout back and even bite back if brands break their promise. For some time, customers have unlocked 'brand control' from marketers and set up their own brand discussions. Although they are still time-compressed and information-fatigued, they have found a new energy fuelled by social media which allows them to fulfil their age-old desire to communicate about what interests or concerns them. Customers now have a platform to raise their voices and some of them can't stop shouting! Some estimates suggest that even an excellent product or service can have up to 5 per cent of negative reviews (giving less than a 5/10 score).

Customers have been abused by businesses which dump sloppy service on them, again and again. Survey after survey reveals that we have, in fact, got worse at marketing over the last ten years. And customers are angry. They are also increasingly impatient and less forgiving. The clock is ticking. We are still sitting on a customer-service time bomb.

Surprisingly, we've gone backwards in marketing. We are in an era of declining marketing skills, as detailed in Chapter 8 on e-CRM. Meanwhile, automated customer-service telephone queuing systems and unworkable web sites have not helped. Robotic answer machines with self-service menus dump all the work on the information-fatigued, time-poor customer. Add web sites that don't work, with dead ends, error messages, complicated navigation, and – if you have the patience to struggle through all of that, electronic shopping carts that crash. The customer-service time bomb is ticking. The angry customer can be seen lurking amongst the many blogs and hate sites attacking brands. These can fuel an exponential spreading of negative word of mouth or ('word of mouse').

Customers will not tolerate bad service, and will gladly accept offers from competitors when they inevitably come knocking on their door. Add in customers who talk back and also who talk to each other using their new social media platforms of power. Social network sites facilitate customer discussions (Coca-Cola never asked for rockets, it just happened that customers discovered that mixing Coke and Mentos mints caused an explosive reaction and customers started posting videos of this phenomenon). Customers talk because they want to share opinions, others are hungry for fame and others want to meet new friends or simply transcend to another place.

Customers have unlocked 'control' from communications as user-generated content (UGC) is not totally controllable. Social media will continue to grow in line with the very human need for social contact. Customers have been mobilized by social media.

'His own company's online service was like a foreign country he had rarely visited'

Recently, I had problems with online banking. After lots of frustration with technical support, I rang my bank manager. In the past, whenever I had a problem he had been extremely helpful and made sure it was resolved immediately. This time around, things were different. 'I'm not technical,' he told me. He began to talk about his bank's online banking service as if it were a foreign country he had rarely visited. He was behaving like a typical senior manager when it came to IT. He wanted to wash his hands of responsibility. It was not his domain. IT, it seems, is not the responsibility of senior managers or CEOs. They have much more important things to do, obviously.

(McGovern, 2010)

We are possibly on the cusp of a customer revolution, bringing an end to accepting sloppy service and also an end to the mass-market dumb-downed customer. As *Wired* editor and author of *The Long Tail*, Chris Anderson, says:

For too long we've been suffering the tyranny of lowest-common-denominator fare, subjected to brain-dead summer blockbusters and manufactured pop. Many of our assumptions about popular taste are actually artifacts of poor supply-and-demand matching – a market response to inefficient distribution.

(Anderson, 2006)

Online digital markets facilitate obscure niche markets as easily as they do mass markets. In the online world it can be as profitable to serve 100 customers, spread across the world, with 100 different digital products as it is to serve 100 local customers one standardized product. This opens a gate to consumer taste which takes it away from the 'tyranny of the lowest dumb down denominator' (Anderson, 2006). Instead of a handful of powerful marketers recommending, and often determining, what is in and what is out – there is now a mobilized customer, generating their own particular recommendations and creating many smaller nice demands.

Although spread across the world, customers with similar interests can communicate and share thoughts through images, audio, video and text anywhere in the world. This means that clusters of customers with similar tastes and interests are connecting with each other to form new global niches and segments. Global markets are here; for example, Manchester United Football Club has an estimated 70 million fans around the world and Al Jazeera International's English-language TV news service has a 100 million audience worldwide. As media follows markets, media consumption may go global; therefore marketers must remember that brands with international ambitions must have a consistent global image – production should be international in catering for international audiences and content rights should be global. Creating content that users can pass on via their networks is an increasingly important channel of communication. When using these channels, brands must think global. Multiple local and conflicting brand identities will not work. In addition, localized brand names can often restrict brands from international sales. Smith and Zook (2011) list several restrictive brand names including: Sic (French soft drink); Pschitt (French soft drink); Lillet (French soft drink); Creap (Japanese coffee creamer); Irish Mist (in Germany, 'mist' means manure); Bum (Spanish potato crisp); Bonka (Spanish coffee); Trim Pecker Trouser (Japanese germ bread); Gorilla Balls (American protein supplement); My Dung (restaurant); Cul toothpaste (pronounced 'cue' in France, which means 'anus'); Scratch (German non-abrasive bath cleaner); Super-Piss (Finnish car lock anti-freeze); Spunk (jelly-baby sweet from Iceland). For more, see www.prsmith.org.

Think global, but act local – remember, not all consumers use Facebook and Twitter. They're banned in China. Weibo, China's Twitter, which blends Twitter and Facebook, is massively popular as users can post video, comment and debate with 140 Chinese characters (which means they can express three to four times more in that 140-character constraint).

The Internet – and broadband, in particular – has opened up the global village even more and changed business dynamics radically (see Chapter 3 on e-models and Section 3.10 in particular). It has created a level playing field for the smaller niche brands to compete with the established global players. Small brands have access to bigger, global, markets and can communicate directly with customers across the world in new and more meaningful ways – ways never dreamt of ten years ago. Power will be prised away from those major brands that are not prepared to change. *Social networks can ultimately destroy business models that are company-centric* (Gartner, 2009). See Section 3.10 on social business in the previous chapter for more.

Maybe it will be the database holders who take control. Imagine opening your fridge and as you take the last can of Guinness, the fridge asks you if you'd like to replace the beer online automatically with a competitor's new stout? It's the database holder who knows who drinks what beer, when and where, or at least simply records the last beer's bar code as it's taken out of the fridge. The key to accessing the customers' databases embedded in fridges and microwaves, cars, phones and PDAs is not the hardware, but the intelligence to know exactly when you might like to replace something with a special offer. The invasion of the infomediary starts here. Look at the data sharing as brands connect with Facebook's Open Graph (see Section 3.5 in Chapter 3 on e-models).

Along with changing customer needs comes changing media consumption patterns. TV used to be pushed at impassive couch potatoes. The web, on the other hand, was, and still is, a 'pull' medium. Content is pulled down to a computer with a conscious click. This viewer is in control. It turns out that the old heaving mass of supposedly slovenly couch potatoes actually like to be active, interactive, even participatory, to influence the programme, its result and even choose the time to view it (as well as enjoy the instant gratification of immediate online purchase and delivery wherever and whenever required). The era of 'appointment-to-view' TV is over. Perhaps the slothful couch potato was simply a function of the absence of interaction (technology) rather than intrinsic defects in human nature? As media technology and audiences move from push to pull, marketers are witnessing a radical increase in consumer sovereignty where informed customers can easily compare prices, alert each other to quality issues and brand messages and challenge marketers directly.

Customers continue to change their media habits; for example, in the EU, customers are consuming less TV, newspapers and magazines and more Internet, while radio remains steady (EIAA, 2007). E-customers also have a big appetite for small screens. Consumers around the world use their mobiles, PDAs and iPods to consume vast amounts of Internet content. More entertainment is consumed on mobile than on the big screens. Total global content on mobile networks (includes games, video and gambling) has been worth more than Hollywood movies annually since 2007.

Elsewhere, others customers use virtual worlds to meet new people, to break out of their old offline groups and even to escape from their bodies as men become women and women become men or other types of avatar, including animals and hybrids, in a new virtual world. Interestingly, some people with disabilities enjoy virtual worlds since there are no physical barriers and no discrimination – visitors can become whatever they want to be and can move, talk, dance, play games, do business and have fun just like anyone else.

Tim Guest (2007), in his book *Second Lives*, suggests that patients suffering from cerebral palsy find virtual worlds like a second life, fulfilling their desire to be free from the shackles of a wheelchair or free from the stigma of having a disability. In this sense, the online experiences have created a level playing field for all customers.

CONSUMERS VALUE PRIVACY AND TRUST

On this new level playing field, privacy, trust and time are emerging as new currencies that have a very high value in customers' minds. Customers are cautious about giving up private information. They are also busy and don't like wasting time (if you can save your customer time, they will like you even more). They expect you to protect their privacy (hence privacy statements are de rigueur for every web site). Equally, customers resent being asked for too much information or being asked for information when they haven't yet established any relationship. Many customers lie when filling in online forms – over half of those surveyed, as revealed by Adestra (2006), when they are asked for personal information.

Customers value their privacy. Many customers resent intrusive marketing invading their private time and space. So companies like Coca-Cola invite youth customers into Coca-Cola's world of sponsored music instead of invading the customer's space with ads. Customers want to choose when and where they receive information or ads. Having said this, customers welcome relevant help from companies which know how to genuinely save customer time or deliver them new experiences that enhance their lives or their jobs. Customers do like personal, tailored (relevant) communications, whether opt-in email or personalized web sites. It has been said that 'enlightened companies . . . remember information for helping customers not just information about them' (Wright, 2006: 51). This builds trust in the relationship.

Do people trust people more than web sites? Well, people trust well-known and well-respected brands. Why else would you give an unknown American your credit-card details and home address (when buying books off Amazon)? In the UK, several major brands score higher in trust than the church and the police. Well-managed brands are trusted as long as their promise is never broken. How do you feel when a web site remembers your name? And when it remembers your preferences? Are we content to have unconscious relationships with brands, robots and machines as well as people? Some sites display team members behind an organization as they know that 'people still do business with people'.

Trust is increasingly important as online customers live in a dangerous environment of privacy invasion and identity theft. If mobile subscription fraud is actually easier and more profitable than drug smuggling, then it will attract more criminal behaviour online. Criminal gangs are actively targeting mobile operators as telecoms fraud becomes a massive sector, and fears grow that social networking web sites can leave both an individual and a business dangerously exposed to fraud. Personal data can be compiled from public profiles that customers post about themselves in social network sites.

Money-rich, time-poor customers need to find information quickly and make transactions easily. Well-designed sites can satisfy impatient customers, build relationships and nurture loyalty through added relevant value. Today, visitors are reducing the number of sites they regularly visit, but they are spending more time on those selected sites. These 'sticky sites' keep visitors longer with relevant material and services that constantly, genuinely, help their customers. In return, customers are prepared to spend more of their 'share of wallet' on a broader range of products from a single site. Growing 'share of wallet' makes sense since it is 'five times cheaper to sell to an existing customer than a new one'; in fact, online, it can be ten times more profitable (Laurent and Eltvedt, 2005). Brand extensions, web rings, alliances and marketing marriages can extend a product range (and grow share of wallet from a customer) and satisfy a needy customer simultaneously.

Despite having a wider choice, customers are starting to consolidate their choice of preferred web sites. So this creates an opportunity for marketers to develop 'sticky' web sites that keep visitors on the site with easy-to-find, relevant information and services. Ask yourself what is on your site that might attract a visitor to come back a second time and, ultimately, regularly revisit the site and develop a strong relationship with the site or brand. Remember, the second visit is the start of the relationship. By getting it right now, there is a possibility of creating competitive advantage by developing a strong relationship with online customers which protects you from the inevitable onslaught of competition.

Finally, watch how B2B companies deliver e-marketing to their customers because B2B companies are often much more sophisticated than B2C companies at helping their customers. They perfect *scenario planning* to identify how online services can really help customers in their daily lives. The web site of a company like Kingspan Insulated Roof & Wall Systems actually helps architects to design and specify materials they need online quickly and efficiently. Other companies, like National Semiconductor, have, since 2002, been giving engineers (who design component parts for mobile phones and DVD players) access to their 'web-bench' – a sophisticated online design, test and redesign programme that allows them to do in 2 hours what previously took months. They have over 30,000 design engineers on-site generating 3,000 orders or referrals every day (one such order for an integrated socket for Nokia was for 40 million units). Learn from best practice wherever you can find it.

IDEAL CUSTOMERS

Now comes the important and interesting bit – knowing your customers. Who are your ideal customers? You have good and bad customers. Bad ones continually haggle about prices, pay late, constantly complain, grab all your promotions and leave you as soon as another company comes along. The ideal customers, on the other hand, are the ones that pay on time, give you as much notice as possible, share information, become partners giving you useful feedback. You know the ones – they are a pleasure to work with. But who are they? What makes them different? What do they really want? How can you help them even more? Are they online? Targeting, satisfying and keeping the ideal customer are crucial.

Ideal customers are worth more than you think. Pareto's 80:20 law suggests that 80 per cent of your sales comes from only 20 per cent of your customers. Some estimates suggest that your best 20 per cent of customers generate 140 per cent of your profits. This means that many of your other customers generate losses. A company's best customer could be worth 30 times the worst customer. Chris Anderson's (2006) long tail theory challenges Pareto and suggests otherwise.

Regardless, you need to know – who are your best customers? Are all of them online? So we need to know our ideal customer's profile – who they are, where they are, what they want, what they spend, any distinguishing characteristics. How do we recognize them on a database? What questions should we ask them about themselves? We need to know them better than they know themselves!

We need to understand their mindset, their attitudes and aspirations. We also need to know the barriers to buying online – their fears and phobias. We need to know where our proposition sits with their needs, their lives, their jobs – 'their worlds' – both online and offline.

We also need to know their purchasing process – the stages they move through and the information needs they have at each stage. We need to know their information processing stages: how they acquire information (what channels), how they learn about products and offers, what words they search with, what words (and images) arouse them to take action. How their perception screens out some offers and filters in others.

In general, the online customer is different to the offline customer. Despite living in an information-cluttered and time-compressed world, the online customer is empowered like never before: more information, transparent prices, more rights. They also realize the value of their time and attention. Witness the rise of permission-based marketing and the demise of the effectiveness of intrusion-based marketing. Remember, assumptions you might have about existing offline customers may not apply online. Even the same customer may display different characteristics online and offline.

ENGAGED CUSTOMERS = CUSTOMER ENGAGEMENT

If you can understand and influence engagement better than your competitors, then this will help you develop brand loyalty and, if used correctly, a real customer-driven business (see Section 3.10 on the Ladder of Engagement in Chapter 3).

The ideal customer, or most valuable customer, does not have to be someone who buys a lot. The ideal customer could be an influencer who is a small irregular buyer, but who posts ratings and reviews as his or her reviews can influence another 100 people. 'Engaged customers' are probably going to become brand zealots if we keep them engaged. Therefore it is important to identify 'engaged customers' and start a brand ambassador programme to further strengthen the relationship and energize their word of mouth.

We can monitor the quantity and frequency of blog posts, forum discussions, reviews, profile updates, etc. This identifies opportunities and also acts as an early warning system for any future problems. Consider targeting brand evangelists rather than just purchasers. Some companies actually ask customers to give a product rating or even post a product review as a standard part of their after-sales contact strategy. This way the more engaged customers identify themselves by their own self-selection.

You should use our engagement checklist (Table 4.1 below) to determine how involved a customer is with your products or services. A customer who doesn't care about the product is likely to be less committed or less emotionally attached to the firm providing the product. On the other hand, a customer who is engaged is likely to be more emotionally connected to the brand. We need to know about the sentiment, opinion and affinity a person has towards a brand. This is often expressed through repeat visits, purchases, product ratings, reviews, blogs and discussion forums and, ultimately, their likelihood to recommend a friend.

Ask yourself: 'How well are we measuring the engagement of our different online audiences and then closing the loop by using this data to identify the advocates and deliver more relevant communications?'

Table 4.1 Customer engagement checklist

Involvement

1 Does the customer segment buy your product or service more or less frequently compared to your competitors?
2 Does the customer frequently purchase (defined as more than 'x' purchases per month)?
3 Is the customer a frequent visitor to the web site (defined as more than 'x' visits per month)?
4 Does the customer spend above the average site visit duration ('x' minutes) each time they visit your site?
5 Does the customer engage in key service interactions? For example, choosing and comparing different products.
6 Does the customer engage in minor service interactions? For example, checking the status of the account.

Interaction

7 Does the customer visit the discussion areas or blogs?
8 Does the customer participate in discussions by posting comments regularly ('x' per month)?
9 Has the customer written a product review?
10 Has the customer created any other user-generated content (including uploading photos or videos)?
11 Has the customer made any connections relevant to the brand in social networks?

Intimacy

12 Does the customer express an opinion in customer service calls?

Influence

13 Does the customer refer other customers to the site?
14 Are you monitoring and acting on engagements in the above areas?

E-MARKETING INSIGHT

Pareto versus *The Long Tail*

Meet Robbie Vann-Adibé, the CEO of Ecast, a digital jukebox company whose bar-room players offer more than 150,000 tracks – and some surprising usage statistics. He hints at them with a question that visitors invariably get wrong: 'What percentage of the top 10,000 titles in any online media store (Netflix, iTunes, Amazon, or any other) will rent or sell at least once a month?'

Most people guess 20 percent, and for good reason: we've been trained to think that way. The 80:20 rule, also known as Pareto's principle (after Vilfredo Pareto, an Italian economist who devised the concept in 1906), is all around us. Only 20 percent of major studio films will be hits. Same for TV shows, games, and mass-market books – 20 percent all. The odds are even worse for major-label CDs, where fewer than 10 percent are profitable, according to the Recording Industry Association of America.

But the right answer, says Vann-Adibé, is 99 percent. There is demand for nearly every one of those top 10,000 tracks. He sees it in his own jukebox statistics; each month, thousands of people put in their dollars for songs that no traditional jukebox anywhere has ever carried. Suddenly, popularity no longer has a monopoly on profitability. The second reason for the wrong answer is that the industry has a poor sense of what people want. We equate mass market with quality and demand, when in fact it often just represents familiarity, savvy advertising, and broad if somewhat shallow appeal. Rhapsody streams more songs each month beyond its top 10,000 than it does its top 10,000. Google, for instance, makes most of its money off small advertisers (the long tail of advertising), and eBay is mostly tail as well – niche and one-off products.

(Anderson, 2006)

SECTION SUMMARY 4.1

Introduction to e-customers

This chapter explores online customers – who they are, why they go online, their expectations, their fears and their phobias. We examine their online buying process as well as their internal mental processes right through to forming relationships and building communities. The chapter finishes with a look at the future – the 'post-literate customer' – and shows you how to research the online customer.

4.2 Motivations

By the end of this section, you will be able to discuss why customers go online. We will try to lift the lid on online customers' heads, look inside their minds and explore what drives them online. Finally, we'll see how we can use this knowledge to get, and keep, more online customers.

Understanding customer motivations is not an option or a luxury. It is an absolute necessity for survival. If you don't know what customers want, then how can you satisfy them? If you can't satisfy them, how can you keep them or even attract them in the first place? Without this deep understanding of your customers, you're just shooting in the dark and hoping for the best – not the way to run a business.

So we need to know why customers go online? What are their motives? What needs are being satisfied?

FACEBOOK, CAVEMEN, CLEVER NETWORKERS, HERDS OR INDIVIDUALS?

Group behaviour is well documented in social studies. Marketers understand the natural impulse to follow the crowd. Some sociologists believe humans are just copying machines, basically. Because humans are social animals, a large percentage of an individual's brainpower is devoted to interacting with others, watching their behaviour and wondering what they think of us. We carry this legacy with us every time we buy a particular brand of washing powder or choose what movie to watch in the cinema. We have learned or evolved to be animals that are good at copying.

In the 1960s, the sales of domestic air conditioning were followed and mapped for years. Findings showed that the best way to predict who would buy air conditioning came down to whether a person's neighbour had it. People had to see it to be likely to copy it.

Think caveman. If everyone is running away, you don't ask why; you just run. Copying means you don't have to learn everything from scratch, and you can defend or protect yourself more easily because you react to things more quickly, so it makes sense from a survival viewpoint.

The Mexican wave – why? Because everyone in the crowd can see everyone else, and is aware of the group behaviour. The Mexican wave cannot be recreated in a shopping centre, because people can't see each other, nor can they see the group behaviour.

Facebook, on the other hand, is like a digital version of the Mexican wave, because people can see what all their friends are doing. They can not only see if their friends are online, but also what their friends are currently doing and what they have been up to in the past. If someone gets an invite to Facebook and joins, that person in turn sends invites to his or her friends. Wherever the herd moves next, people follow. The Internet just manifests or provides the mechanics for what we are naturally programmed to do.

If someone stands staring at the sky and pointing, that person is bound to get strange looks from passers-by, but get six or seven people standing together staring and pointing at the invisible spaceship and the crowd will swell.

Harnessing the knowledge of the herd has greater potential when it comes to building brand loyalty (Kearon, 2008).

WHY DO CUSTOMERS VENTURE ONLINE?

Socializing, catching up on news, shopping/browsing, being entertained and being educated are typical reasons people give for going online. So, socializing through email, chat rooms, blogs and social network sites is the killer application in the B2C markets. Billions of emails are sent every day and SMS (text) messages are catching up. Leveraging the strong desire to socialize should not be underestimated. It is one of Maslow's basic defined needs.

The second most popular activity is finding out about products, regardless of whether they are to be purchased online or offline, so we need to facilitate the process of mixed-mode buying – browsing online and buying offline.

Internet users are active, not passive; they enjoy their power and love to exercise it. Comparison shopping puts them in control. The empowered online customer has more knowledge than ever before from sharing information with others and from comparison sites or shopping bots. How well do you know the comparison sites for your products and services? Seek them out and monitor them continuously.

Surprisingly, not all online customers hate real physical shopping. They just like getting good deals and being in control. The convenience of online shopping may grow in importance as time-compressed customers realize the time-saving nature of online shopping. Time saving can satisfy several needs simultaneously as the time saved can be spent fulfilling a range of unfilled needs.

Incidentally, many products fail to sell in large volumes online since the products don't pass de Kare-Silver's 'electronic shopping test' (see E-Marketing Insight box below) which measures the likelihood of online retail purchases.

It's simple: if customers can't find the right information about your products and service propositions, then you don't even make it into the 'considered set' of brands being considered by a potential customer.

The third most popular online activity is entertainment. After adult entertainment come games, music and checking up on the latest news about the favourite band, sports team or celebrity.

It is no surprise that popular sites offer these key activities of socializing, product information, purchasing and entertainment through email and chat, search engines and product guides, shopping, community and games.

PRACTICAL E-MARKETING TIP

Support satisficing behaviour

When we create online services, we often base our designs for our customer experiences on rational models of how online users behave. However, research such as that by Penn (2005) reminds us that, in reality, consumers are often far from rational – they exhibit *satisficing behaviour* where they often act on impulse or make do with imperfect information, so we need to build this into our online designs and our design process by including calls-to-action and content which support slower, rational 'maximizer' behaviour and faster, less rational 'satisficer' behaviour. Some users will just act on impulse, so it should be easy to do that. Ultralase (www.ultralase.com) has a sign-up form on its home page, not hidden deep in the site; similarly LOVEFiLM (www.lovefilm.com) has used multivariate testing to highlight the 'Free Trial' message rather than the more rational 'Learn More' button which may introduce doubt.

E-MARKETING INSIGHT

Online customers – irrational animals?

We are still not terribly rational customers. As Oscar Wilde once remarked: '[M]an is a rational animal until he is asked to act within the dictates of reason.' So it continues – the illogical, irrational consumer is still on the rampage. Penn (2005) suggests that if the 'handed down' wisdom is that consumers make rational choices and, moreover, can explain those choices, then brain science suggests, more or less, the opposite. In this alternative view, unconscious processes mediate cognitive rational decision making, leading to a choice which can only be half understood (at best) by introspection. In other words, we can't always say with any reliability why we made a particular choice. Sometimes, we just 'do it', because 'we always do it'.

RESPONDING TO CUSTOMER MOTIVATIONS

Once you know why people go online, you can apply a very simple marketing formula:

1 Find out why people buy and what are their aspirations and expectations. Then . . .
2 Reflect the reasons, aspirations and expectations in your communications. This way you give customers what they want instead of what you want.

Of course, you have to be able to deliver the promised benefits. Otherwise repeat sales die, negative word of mouth spreads and the online activities damage the brand. Don't promise what you cannot deliver.

Existing offline customers can be encouraged to go online before they are besieged by other, competitive, online offerings. Remember someone, somewhere, is analysing and targeting your market right now.

Tempt customers by offering channel choice and, something customers can't get elsewhere, the *online value proposition (OVP)* detailed in Chapter 6. Tell them how it works and how they can use it. Other motivators such as the social aspect can be used: for home users, and sometimes for business users also, online activities are an important social tool, enabling conversations with participants known and unknown, from near and far. Also, useful member-get-member promotions amongst existing customers help members to help others with useful information about interesting offers. Word of mouth and referrals are powerful tools. Remember, reassurance is vital since security is a major fear and phobia. Section 4.4 below explores fears and phobias.

We suggest that you consider the 6Cs of customer motivation to help define the OVP (Chaffey, 2004):

1 *Content* – we know that relevant content is still king. Online content should provide something that supports other channels. Often this means more detailed, in-depth information to support the buying process or product usage. As well as text-based content which is king for business-to-business, there is also interactive content which is king for consumer sites and particularly brands. Remember that context is also king. Context provides the right information, personalized for the right segment, using the right media to achieve relevance.
2 *Customization* – *mass customization* of content delivers personalized content viewed as web site pages or email alerts. This is commonly known as personalization or tailoring of content according to individuals or groups – see www.siebel.com for a great example.

3 *Community* (and participation) – community, these days known as 'social networks'. Online channels such as the Internet are known as 'many-to-many' media, meaning that your audiences can contribute to the content. For consumer retail, review sites such as Epinions (www.epinions.com) are important for informing customer perceptions of brands. Similarly, in business markets, some specialist communities have been set up. For example, E-consultancy (www.e-consultancy.com) has forums and reviews which discuss issues in the supply of e-business services.

4 *Convenience* – convenience is the ability to easily find, select, purchase, and in some cases, use products, from your desktop at any time; the classic 24/7 availability of a service.

5 *Choice* – the web gives a wider choice of products and suppliers than traditional media. The success of online intermediaries such as Kelkoo (www.kelkoo.com) and Screentrade (www.screentrade.com) is evidence of this.

6 *Cost reduction* – the Internet is widely perceived as a relatively low-cost place of purchase. In the UK, Vauxhall has keyed into this perception by offering Vauxhall Internet Price (VIP); in other words, lower prices than through dealer-based distribution. Similarly, a key component of the easyJet OVP when it launched was single tickets that were £2.50 cheaper than tickets bought through phone bookings. This simple price differential together with the limited change in behaviour required from phone booking to online booking has been a key factor in the easyJet online ticketing channel effectively replacing all other booking modes.

E-MARKETING INSIGHT

de Kare-Silver's electronic shopping test

This assesses the consumer's propensity to purchase a retail product using the Internet; de Kare-Silver suggests factors that should be considered in the electronic shopping test:

1 *Product characteristics.* Does the product need to be physically tried or touched before it is bought?

2 *Familiarity and confidence.* Considers the degree to which the consumer recognizes and trusts the product or brand.

3 *Consumer attributes.* These shape the buyer's behaviour – are they amenable to online purchases in terms of access to the technology, skills available and do they no longer wish to shop for a product in a traditional retail environment?

Typical results from the evaluation, where products are scored out of 50 for suitability for electronic commerce, are:

- Groceries (27/50)
- Mortgages (15/50)

- Travel (31/50)
- Books (38/50).

According to de Kare-Silver (2000), any product scoring over 20 has good potential, since the score for consumer attributes is likely to increase through time. Given this, he suggests companies will regularly need to review the score for their products.

Understanding what motivates people online is critical for marketers to be able to use the magic marketing formula (identify needs, reflect them and deliver a reasonable product or service). However, B.J. Fogg at Stanford University suggests that targeting a customer's relevant motivations is just one of three key variables that need to be in place in order to change the behaviour of a customer. Fogg says:

> *Three things have to happen to change behaviour:*
>
> 1 *Trigger (call to action) e.g. email alert from facebook (note the 'trigger' comes to me in the course of my normal behaviour – this is very important)*
> 2 *Be motivated (being told you've been tagged in a photograph generally makes people want to see the photograph*
> 3 *Have to have the ability to do the behaviour (one click link to see the photo). If these 3 things come together at the very same moment – they change behaviour.*
>
> *(Fogg, 2009)*

Actually understanding these variables as well as customer expectations, fears, phobias, relationships and their information processes and buying processes is required. Let's now look at customer expectations.

SECTION SUMMARY 4.2

Motivations

B2C customers are motivated to go online for a range of reasons – social, shopping, entertainment. B2B customers are driven by cost savings, speed and selling. Enlightened companies realize there are other motivators such as enhanced customer relationships. In addition to delivering an excellent product or service, find what motivates your customers and then reflect it through your online and offline communications – a simple formula for success.

4.3 Expectations

By the end of this section, you will begin to know how to manage customer expectations. This section reviews what customers expect when they visit a web site and how to deliver these expectations.

WHAT ARE THE ONLINE EXPECTATIONS?

Online customers have raised expectations. They expect higher standards in terms of service, convenience, speed of delivery, competitive prices and choice. They also want, if not expect, to be in control, secure and safe. The problem with raised expectations is that first, they are crushed more easily; and second, they can damage the brand if not fulfilled.

Online customers expect fast service and fast delivery. The Internet and everything associated with it suggests speed. If online businesses do not deliver speedily, then online customers are disappointed, annoyed, angry and sometimes vociferous. Even if delivery takes the same time as the retail store, the online customers often expect a little more (whether it is a price discount, wider choice or whatever). This is the problem with raised expectations.

Separate research from Microsoft and Google shows that it only takes a quarter of a second's delay in page loading time for customer frustration to build. Microsoft found that a delay of 2 seconds resulted in a 4 per cent loss in revenue (Dixon *et al.*, 2010). Customers are impatient. They expect immediate information. Any delays will be penalized by abandoning web sites and conversion rates falling through the floor. So deliver fast page downloads – customers don't like to wait; e.g. page download speeds falling from 2 seconds to 4 seconds can cut conversion rates from 3.75 per cent to 2.2 per cent. Put it another way: reducing page loading time from 4 seconds to 2 seconds increases conversion rates by approximately 70 per cent. This can be huge. For some companies, this increase in conversion rates is the difference between survival and failure. There is a correlation between download speeds and conversion rates (Soames, 2012). Other research (Tagman, 2012) suggests that just 1 second's delay in page-load can cause 7 per cent loss in customer conversions.

Now consider a customer's expectations when buying a book online. Top of the list of online customer expectations is minimizing the time on-site and delivering what is promised, but there are many other requirements (see the E-Marketing Excellence box on 'Customer expectations for an online purchase', below).

Online customers, quite reasonably, expect things to work – they expect to find what they want easily and buy what they want easily. The Internet is a quagmire for the destruction of both raised expectations and even ordinary expectations.

Also, customer expectations change over time. *An increasing number of customers prefer to access online information via mobile only. Some customers abandon email and only use Facebook (in fact, by 2010, Boston University had stopped giving out email addresses as students prefer, and now expect, to only use Facebook for their information feeds).*

Sadly, it seems there are many exceptions to perfect service as discussed in the introduction. Customer service is critical; poor customer service rather than price or features is the number one reason why customers don't remain loyal to a company.

So if online access via mobile is increasing, it is logical for customers to expect reasonable web sites (via mobile). But do all companies cater for this growing need and growing expectation? Mobile-friendly sites essentially improve customer service.

Customers do not expect to see tiny overpacked web sites when they search via mobile, but that's what many will find. With their expectations crushed, they'll leave these web sites behind and migrate to other sites that have bothered to present them with mobile-optimized sites where they will enjoy a better user experience which makes them want to do business with the site. With less space, ensure that the key tasks that customers expect to be able to carry out are optimized; e.g. key messages; links to site pages; click to call phone number; and link to view full web site.

Buy? Get free consultation? Customers don't expect to see all the pages a regular site has, but they do expect to be able to easily find the main key tasks quickly.

Note: web sites built on blog engines such as WordPress can install a widget and very quickly become mobile-friendly – so that traffic coming onto the web site from mobiles is detected and a basic mobile-friendly version of the site is automatically presented.

So, the most significant expectation is customer service and we need to work hard to deliver this across the many interactions between company and customer before, during and after the buying process. Section 4.5 discusses the online buying process. Chapter 8 explores customer service and relationship management in much more detail. Now let's explore customer fears and phobias.

E-MARKETING INSIGHT

Customer expectations for an online retail purchase

Our expectations are informed by our peers and by past experience. So when we shop online, we expect, or indeed demand, that the experience will be superior to traditional shopping. The list of requirements is long.

1 Easy to find what you're looking for by searching or browsing.
2 Site is easy to use, pages are fast to download with no bugs.
3 Price, product specification and availability information on site to be competitive and correct, but we probably prefer great customer services to great prices – this is what will keep us loyal.
4 Specification of date, time and delivery to be possible.
5 Email notification when order is placed and then dispatched.
6 Personal data remain personal and private and security is not compromised.
7 Verification for high-value orders.
8 Delivery on time.
9 Returns policy enabling straightforward return or replacement.

. . . and finally, quick online or offline answers to questions when the expectations above aren't met. This means traceability through databases, someone who knows your order status and can solve your problems.

MANAGING CUSTOMER EXPECTATIONS

Customers' expectations can be managed, met and exceeded. How do we do this? Here are three stages:

1 *Understanding expectations.* Managing the expectations of the demanding customer starts with understanding these expectations. Use customer research and site benchmarking to help with this. Use standard frameworks to establish the gap between expectation and delivery and prioritize to solve the worst shortcomings. Use scenarios to identify the customer expectations of using the services on your site.

2 *Setting and communicating the service promise.* Expectations can best be managed by entering into an informal or formal agreement as to what service the customer can expect through customer-service guarantees or promises (see the E-marketing Excellence box below). It is better to under-promise than over-promise. A book retailer that delivers the book in two days when three days were promised will earn the customer's loyalty better than the retailer who promises 1 day, but delivers in two!

3 *Delivering the service promise.* Commitments must be delivered through on-site service, support from employees and physical fulfilment. If not, online credibility is destroyed and a customer may never return. Detailed techniques on delivering the service promise are given in the E-marketing Excellence box on 'Service guarantees and promises' below.

E-MARKETING EXCELLENCE

Service guarantees and promises

These can be made for a range of aspects:

- Information accuracy (product specifications, price, availability and delivery times) must all be accurate. How many customers did the retailer (who mistakenly offered television sets for sale at £2.99) lose when it informed customers who had placed orders that it would not honour the order?

- Email response. How long will the company take to respond for different sorts of enquiries?

- Security guarantees. What happens if security is compromised?

- Delivery guarantees. What happens if delivery is late?

- Return guarantees. What happens if the product is unsuitable?

Price promises. If you are offering the best prices, this should not be an empty promise. If a company uses an *attack e-tailing* approach, then frequent comparison with competitors' prices and real-time adjustment to match or better them are required. This approach is important on the Internet because of the transparency of pricing and availability of information made possible through shopping comparison sites such as Kelkoo. As customers increasingly use these facilities, then it is important that price positioning is favourable.

Service promises can also be formalized in a service-level agreement (SLA). If a business purchases a hosting service from an Internet service provider, its obligations and what it will do if they are not met will be clearly laid out in an SLA.

Expectations

Managing customers' expectations is even more challenging in the online world because of raised expectations. We need to:

1 Understand the customer's expectations for service delivery and the gap with current delivery.
2 Make clear service promises through privacy statements, promises and guarantees on security, delivery, price and customer-service response times.
3 Deliver the service promise through a fast, easy-to-use site (including a mobile-optimized site), with competitive pricing backed up by excellent customer service and perfect fulfilment.

Not rocket science – just common sense.

4.4 Fears and phobias

By the end of this section, you will understand the fears and phobias that occupy some customers' minds when going online. You will also know how to address these issues.

The average consumer is not fearful of turning on the TV or radio or picking up a telephone. Perhaps the biggest difference about the Internet is the often unconscious fear associated with it, and as marketers, we have to deal with this. You probably don't have these fears (since you're reading this book). But many of your potential customers do. Now we're going to ask you to do what good marketers are good at: empathize – empathize with customers, imagine how they feel when going online, particularly when going online for the first time, or going to make their first online purchase.

Consider the fears you think your customers might have: security risks such as identity theft and stolen credit-card details, hackers, hoaxes, viruses, SPAM and lack of privacy – Big Brother syndrome – probably top your list. Then we have e-nasties such as cyber stalkers, hate mail, fake mail, mail bombs, cults and paedophiles lurking in children's chat rooms. Many of these fears are based on reality. Others fear having their computer taken over remotely by a malicious or criminal hacker. You may also have noted less significant anxieties such as not knowing what to do, fear of getting lost, fear of too much information or fear of inaccurate information. These fears centre on lack of customer control.

There are also fears about how the Internet will destroy the lives of individuals, families, and so the whole of society. Safety needs such as security, protection, order and stability are of great importance in our hierarchy of needs. So too, the need to be loved is strong online. People still want to be loved or accepted, or at least, avoid looking 'deeply uncool' (fear). See E-Marketing Insights box (below). In fact, being over sociable or sharing too much 'stuff' can irritate other people as your 'stuff' clogs up their newsfeed, which may end up with several friends 'unfriending you'.

There are also many FUDS (Fears, Uncertainties and Doubts) about using Facebook Connect, such as:

- What exactly happens when I connect?
- What data is shared between my Facebook account and a web site that invites me to connect via Facebook?
- Can I disconnect? Is it easy to disconnect?
- What is the benefit of connecting?
- Will this new web site have access to my friends?

So, many sites explain carefully (as does Facebook) what exactly happens.

On a more positive note, excellent marketers understand their customers' fears and phobias and take actions to minimize them. The leading e-tailers not only have a great proposition, but they are perceived by the customer as low-risk because they eliminate customer fears.

E-MARKETING INSIGHT

Overshare and friends might hide you or 'defriend' you

There are now new social fears arising from social media; e.g. if you accept a friend request too quickly, does it mean you are over-eager, 'deeply uncool' and desperate for friends and therefore a loser? In an MTV study, *Millennials, Decoded*, half of smartphone-toting millennials said they were 'very concerned' that if they responded too quickly, they'd 'look like they had nothing better to do'. This generation are using each device or platform in ever-more specialized ways – for example, phone only for emergencies, IM for working together on homework. Millennials also relate digital communication to its real-life intimacy counterpart, and see it as an equal way of connecting. Mallory, 22, said that 'sending an email is like going out to dinner and Facebook is like getting coffee or just seeing someone at the store'. By contrast, many Gen-Xers were already into their 20s before email became part of everyday life – and maybe into their 30s before the BlackBerry did (Shore, 2011).

Marketers alone cannot change some of the negative feelings about the Internet. The Internet makes great copy for the newspapers; it seems that the Internet is a scapegoat for many events that occur in modern society, whether this is babies being adopted over the Internet, discontented employees running amok, racism or indeed any immoral or illegal activity.

What marketers can, and must do, is to reassure customers that the problems they perceive are unlikely and act responsibly to minimize the risk of problems happening.

Follow these guidelines to achieve reassurance, gain trust and build loyalty:

1 *Provide clear and effective privacy statements.* Visit the sites like easyJet (www.easyjet.com) for plain privacy statements which directly address customers' fear and phobias.

2 *Follow privacy and consumer protection guidelines in all local markets.* In 2003, the European Electronic Communications Regulations came into force to supplement existing European data protection laws. The essence of this law, implemented in the UK as the Privacy and Electronic Communications Regulations Act, is to make permission-based email marketing a legal requirement. *Opt-in and opt-out* are both legal requirements for email marketing to consumers (individual subscribers) in the UK. For B2B email communications in the UK, this isn't yet (2012) a requirement, but it is in many European countries with fines of hundreds of thousands of euros in some countries. It is also necessary to have clear privacy statements which inform users about *cookies* and *web analytics* tracking.

3 *Make security of customer data a priority.* This is a requirement of data protection law. For example, you should offer the strongest encryption standards possible and use firewalls and ethical hackers to maximize the safety of customer data.

4 *Present independent site certification.* Companies can use independent third parties which set guidelines for online privacy and performance. The best known international bodies are TRUSTe (www.truste.org) and VeriSign for payment authentification (www.verisign.com). Other UK certification bodies include SafeBuy (www.safebuy.org.uk), and the IMRG hallmark (www.imrg.org).

5 *Emphasize the excellence of service quality in all communications.* This is explained in Section 4.3 on meeting customers' expectations.

6 *Use content on the site to reassure the customer.* Explain the actions they have taken. Ask them to confirm. Allow them to revoke or cancel an action. Amazon takes customer fears about security seriously, judging by the prominence and amount of content it devotes to this issue.

7 *Leading-edge design.* Marketers should challenge their site designers to make the customer experience as easy as possible with customer-centred site design. Intuitive, easy-to-use sites, where customers experience flow help to counter fears and phobias. Customers become comfortable more quickly and word of mouth spreads positive messages.

New approaches are needed to build trust in the networked world since conventional ways of gaining trust such as personal contact are no longer practical. Credibility and trust must be built at Internet speed. Time is of the essence. For some FMCG brands, trust was built over two generations; Gap did it in ten years and Yahoo! in five years. In contrast, note that some studies show that trust is also a long-term proposition that builds slowly as people use a site, get good results and don't feel let down or cheated.

SECTION SUMMARY 4.4

Fears and phobias

The typical online customer has many anxieties and FUDS. Companies that succeed in reassuring customers by clearly addressing these, by communicating their security, privacy and ease of use backed up by real quality of service, will reap the rewards through customer loyalty.

4.5 Online information processing

By the end of this section, you will understand how customers process information – what gets through and what doesn't.

E-MARKETING INSIGHT

Information processing is changing

Although 'markets are changing' is a bit of a cliché, it is true because customers are changing – even changing the way they process information. Some customers are suffering information fatigue syndrome (too much information makes them ill), social network fatigue, deals fatigue and 'follow fatigue' (Twitter), which presents new challenges to marketers.

> *Once liberal with their likes, retweets, and follows, consumers are becoming much more guarded and realistic. Therefore brands will now have to more effectively listen to markets to make more informed decisions about how social media impacts the enterprise and in turn customer experiences. When asked what consumers want from brands, knowledge and entertainment soared to the top of the list . . . Listening leads to a more informed business. Engagement unlocks empathy and innovation. But it is action and adaptation that leads to relevance. And, it never ends.*
>
> *(GlobalWeb Index, 2011)*

This section is structured around Charles Hofacker's five stages of on-site information processing (Hofacker, 2001; and see Chapter 3, Section 3.6 for more on information processing models). The five stages are: (1) exposure; (2) attention; (3) comprehension and perception; (4) yielding and acceptance; (5) retention. Each stage acts as a hurdle, since if the site design or content is too difficult to process, the customer cannot progress to the next stage. The e-marketer fails.

Figure 4.1 'Session map' showing an individual's eye movements

Source: Etre Limited (www.etre.com)

The best web site designs take into account how customers process information. Some companies use eye tracking and heat maps to try to understand how customers actually process information presented on a web page (Figure 4.1).

Figure 4.2 provides a 'session map' showing an individual's eye movements across a web site (using sophisticated technology that monitors eye movements across the screen). The blue dots show the user's eye fixations, while the connecting blue lines illustrate eye movements. This information reveals where the customer looks, what he or she pays the most attention to, and most importantly, what he or she misses (e.g. the big red Sale Banner).

Figure 4.2 Erratic eye movements suggest that a user was confused

Source: Etre Limited (www.etre.com)

Figure 4.3 Eye movements suggest the user understands the page

Source: Etre Limited (www.etre.com)

Watching a user in real time is interesting, but the speed of movement makes it hard to keep track of what users see and what they miss (Figure 4.3). That's why specialists like Etre Limited (www.etre.com) produce an individual session map at the end of each session to show the sum total of all their visual activity. Each numbered circle represents a point that the user's eyes fixated on. The larger the circle, the longer the fixation. In Figure 4.2, the series of erratic eye movements suggests that a user was confused by a disorganized layout.

While a series of controlled eye movements show that a user was reading, the density of these movements helps us to establish their level of concentration and comprehension (Figure 4.3).

Figure 4.4 A 'heat map' reveals the hottest parts of a web page (and the parts that are ignored)

Source: Etre Limited (www.etre.com)

Once all users have been through the process, the aggregated results are converted into heat maps which reveal the behaviour of an entire group of people. The graded colour scheme shows visual activity. Warmer colours reveal areas that most users looked at, while colder colours show areas that few users noticed. Black reveals areas that no one looked at. In Figure 4.4, you can see that no one noticed the £4.99 SALE, despite its size and vibrant colours. This type of information is invaluable whether you are creating a new site or just evaluating the existing one.

Good e-marketers are aware of how the messages are processed by the customer and of the corresponding steps we can take to ensure the correct message is received. So now let's explore each of Hofacker's five stages of on-site information processing.

The first stage is *exposure*. This is not as straightforward as it used to be. If the content is not present for a long enough time, customers will not be able to process it. Think of splash pages, banner adverts or shockwave animations. If these change too rapidly, the message will not be received. However, ads can now follow customers as they move around the web; the same ad appears in different places. Marketers can now 'remarket' and place their ads in front of people who have already expressed an interest in a particular brand (maybe visited its web site, signed up for a newsletter, abandoned a shopping cart, or even bought the brand once).

The second stage is *attention*. The human mind has limited capacity to pick out the main messages from a screen full of single-column text format without headings or graphics. Movement, text size and colour help to gain attention for key messages. Note, though, that studies show that the eye is immediately drawn to content, not the headings in the navigation systems. Of course, we need to be careful about using garish colours and animations as these can look amateurish. Or they can look like loud advertisements which many customers simply screen out as indicated in the heat map in Figure 4.4 above.

Comprehension and perception are the third of Hofacker's stages. These refer to how the customer interprets the combination of graphics, text and multimedia on a web site. The design will be most effective if it uses familiar standards or metaphors since the customer will interpret them according to previous experience and memory. Once relevant information is found, visitors sometimes want to dig deeper for more information. However, selective perception means we screen out a lot of information around us (as demonstrated by the example of the violinist in the subway in Section 3.6 on information processing models in Chapter 3).

Fourth, *yielding and acceptance* refer to whether the information you present is accepted by the customer. Different tactics need to be used to convince different types of people. Classically, a US audience is more convinced by features rather than benefits, while the reverse is true for a European audience. Some customers will respond to emotive appeals, perhaps reinforced by images, while others will make a more clinical evaluation based on the text. This gives us the difficult task of combining text, graphics and copy to convince each customer segment.

Finally, *retention* – how well the customer can recall their experience. A clear, distinctive site design will be retained in the customer's mind, perhaps prompting a repeat visit when the customer thinks, 'Where did I see that information?' and then recalls the layout of the site. A clear site design will also be implanted in the customer's memory as a mental map which they will be able to draw on when returning to the site, increasing their flow experience.

Figure 4.5   Lastminute.com attracts attention

Sites with excellent design use a range of techniques. Examine Figure 4.5 and then read more in Chapter 6 to see how the concepts in this section have been applied.

E-MARKETING INSIGHT

Jakob Nielsen on graphics

Jakob Nielsen (2007) says: 'when they arrive on a page, users ignore navigation bars and other global design elements: instead they look only at the content area of the page' (www.useit.com/alertbox/20000109.html).

Studies show that e-customers are very goal-driven and tend to ignore banner ads while focusing completely on their task. Eye-tracking studies confirm the existence of 'banner blindness' where the user's gaze never rests in the region of the screen occupied by advertising (www.useit.com/alertbox/990221.html).

Nielsen says:

> *[T]he most common behaviour is to hunt for information and be ruthless in ignoring details. But once the prey has been caught, users will sometimes dive in more deeply. Thus, web content needs to support both aspects of information access: foraging and consumption. Text needs to be scannable, but it also needs to provide the answers users seek.*
> *(Nielsen, 2007: www.useit.com/ alertbox/20000514.html)*

A good compromise is to have small rectangular animated banner ads to the right of the screen which highlight the special offers. But remember about 'banner blindness'.

SECTION SUMMARY 4.5

Online information processing

Understanding how customers process information through the stages of exposure, attention, comprehension and perception, yielding and acceptance, and retention can help us design sites – sites that really help us get our message across and deliver memorable messages and superior customer service.

4.6 The online buying process

By the end of this section, you will understand the stages buyers go through and how to ensure you address all of these stages online. You simply have to understand how customers use the information in their purchase decision making.

The buying process should be catered for both online and offline (*mixed-mode buying*; see Chapter 2 and also Section 3.7 for more on low-involvement customer buying models). Each stage of the purchasing process should be supported both online and offline. Let us consider a 'high-involvement' purchase such as a car or a house. Assuming this follows a simple linear buying model, what occurs at each stage?

1 *Problem recognition*. This can occur through changed circumstances such as a new job, new money or the existing car breaks down, etc. Peer pressure or clever advertising or editorial (online or offline) which highlights the problem (or the need or the want) can also help the customer to recognize it themselves.

2 *Information search*. Having established a need – i.e. the problem is recognized – the customer gathers information. We need to understand how customers gather information – online and offline. Online, the web is increasingly used for searching. Remember there is a difference between searching and surfing. Think about the timing and frequency of when online

customers seek information. Get the timing and the targeting right and you create 'relevance' which allows the information through the customer's perceptual filters. Get it wrong and your information gets screened out by an uninterested audience.

3 *Evaluation*. We need to use the content on our site to communicate the features and benefits of the brand in what may be a fleeting visit to the site or an in-depth analysis. Independent reports prominently positioned on-site may save the buyer from having to search elsewhere. We also need to think about how to cater for different customer buying behaviour according to Internet experience. Remember that search behaviour will differ according to familiarity with the Internet, the organization and its web site.

4 *Decision*. Some car buyers may have already physically test-driven several cars and now want to decide and buy online. Some sites help the decision by offering payment facilities that match the customer's personal financial situation. Once the decision has been made to purchase, we don't want to lose the customer at this stage, so make purchasing slick and simple. And if the customer has anxieties, give them the choice of buying through other channels by prompting with a phone number or a call-back facility.

5 *Action (sale)*. Often an appropriate incentive to 'buy now' either online or offline helps to push the buyer over the edge and into the sale. The purchase can be made online, particularly if suitable reassurances are made.

6 *Post sale*. Then the real marketing begins. The sale is only the beginning of the relationship (i.e. relationship marketing and lifetime customers). Lifetime customers generate repeat sales which, in turn, generate much higher profits (some estimates suggest five times higher profits on repeat sales than on new customers). Use email and the web site to provide customer service and support.

But think about how the online environment has changed buyer behaviour, generally speaking:

- Search marketing has compressed the cycle – the buying process often starts with a generic search
- Supplier search is now also compressed by a few visits to comparison sites which often feature well in search engines
- Recommendations from other customers through user-generated content has a significant impact on conversion rates as we saw in the previous chapter (Section 3.7).
- Brand has become more important at later decision stages since it provides trust.

Figure 4.6 summarizes how content on-site can support the buying process. Produce a map for how your site supports the buying process.

Obviously the process above applies best to high-involvement purchases like a car, rather than to low-involvement purchases like a can of cola. Here the model is about awareness, trial and reinforcement (ATR), followed by availability, availability, availability. Rock band Oasis followed an interesting ATR approach to promote and sell their CD *Heathen Chemistry*. To satisfy the hunger for previews (before release) and reduce the number of illegal downloads from the Internet . . . seven days prior to the release of the CD, four tracks were offered to readers of *The Sunday Times* as a cover-mounted CD which was encrypted so it could only be played four times.

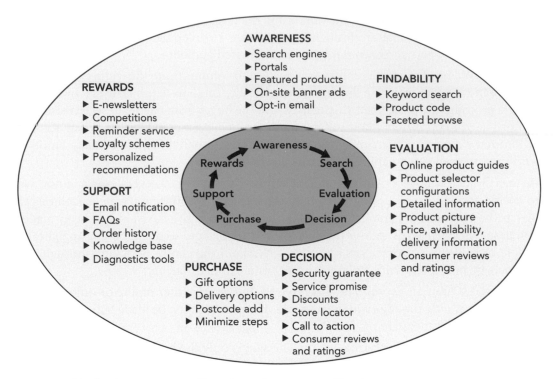

Figure 4.6   The buying process and how it can be supported by site content

After that, the CD was automatically wiped and the user directed to HMV (www.hmv.com) to buy the album. HMV donated 50p to the Prince's Trust charity – Big Time Cultural Bank.

Business-to-business buying models have a specification and tender stage built in before sellers can tender or present their bids (and product information). Often, only pre-selected or preferred suppliers' information is considered. Note that information search tends to be 'directed' or 'focused' rather than browsing or surfing. In fact, five different types of search behaviour have been recognized and we should cater for each in site design and communications, but with the emphasis on the predominant groups.

E-MARKETING INSIGHT

Using the psychology of persuasion

American psychologist Robert Cialdini (2006) identifies six 'weapons of influence' that you can use to influence site visitors and viewers of ads through the use of appropriate messages. The six weapons were originally developed with reference to personal interactions rather than web marketing, but we have summarized them as a checklist in Table 4.2 together with our recommendations on how you can apply them to your web communications.

Table 4.2 Summary of the online implications for Cialdini's six weapons of influence

Influencer	Online marketing implication
☑ 1 Reciprocity	Offer valuable, exclusive content or offers and your audience will remember you and will recommend you through bookmarks, links or by telling their friends. Encourage this behaviour through prompts on the site.
☑ 2 Commitment and consistency	Get initial commitment by encouraging visitors to drill deeper, search, subscribe or engage with product selectors. 'Set their alarm clock' by providing regular reasons to return, such as new promotions, content highlighted on-site and within e-zines.
☑ 3 Consensus	Your audience will believe others more than they believe you! So use reviews, case studies, testimonials and rewards as we described in Chapter 2.
☑ 4 Affinity (liking and credibility)	People are persuaded by other people they like or who are like them, so again use recommendations or endorsements by people who are known by your audience or to whom they can relate.
☑ 5 Authority	Unless you are a well-known brand, you need to prove your authority. So if you are a blogger, for example, you need to show off your authority, expertise and status. Companies need to show off satisfied customers or, in the B2B services example, their employees, qualifications and reputations!
☑ 6 Scarcity	The fear of loss is more powerful than that of gain, so show site visitors what they could miss. For example, in links to its site in offline communications, in its PPC ads, its email communications and, of course, on its site, Dell makes use of time-limited offers.

E-MARKETING INSIGHT

Identifying hunters, trackers and explorers

The E-consultancy (2004) classification of online retail shopping behaviour still has currency to test how well the web site design matched the different behaviours.

Three types of potential behaviour were identified: the tracker, hunter and explorer. Note that these do not equate to different people, since according to the type of product or occasion, the behaviour of an individual may differ. Indeed, as they research a product, they are likely to become more directed.

1 *Tracker.* Defined as follows:

> *knows exactly which product they wish to buy and uses an online shopping site to track it down and check its price, availability, delivery time, delivery charges or after-sales support.*

i.e. the tracker is looking for specific information about a particular product. The report says: 'If they get the answers they are seeking they need little further persuasion or purchase justification before completing the purchase.' While this may not be true since they may compare on other sites, this type of shopper will be relatively easy to convert.

2 *Hunter*. Defined as follows:

> *doesn't have a specific product in mind but knows what type of product they are looking for (e.g. digital camera, cooker) and probably has one or more product features they are looking for. The hunter uses an online shopping site to find a range of suitable products, compare them and decide which one to buy.*

The hunter needs more help, support and guidance to reach a purchasing decision. The report says:

> *once a potential purchase is found, they then need to justify that purchase in their own minds, and possibly to justify their purchase to others. Only then will confirmation of the purchase become a possibility.*

3 *Explorer*. Defined as follows:

> *doesn't even have a particular type of product in mind. They may have a well-defined shopping objective (buying a present for someone or treating themselves), a less-resolved shopping objective (buying something to 'brighten up' the lounge) or no shopping objective at all (they like the high street store and thought they would have a look at the online site).*

The report suggests that the explorer has a range of possible needs and many uncertainties to be resolved before committing to a purchase, but the following may be helpful in persuading these shoppers to convert: 'Certain types of information, however, are particularly relevant. Suggested gift ideas, guides to product categories, lists of top selling products and information-rich promotions (What's New? What's Hot?) – these could all propel them towards a purchasing decision.'

Leading companies use web analytics data to see how activity and repeat visits vary through each day, week, month and year. A financial services provider found a traffic peak on Monday lunchtime when people looked to find out more after reviewing alternatives in the Sunday newspapers. A B2B company found a peak at the start of each month that corresponded with new sales promotions. A monthly competition was launched, timed to coincide with the traffic peak.

Amazingly, research by BT showed that customers seem to use the Internet and telephone more before a full moon, but how marketers can tap into this behaviour is unclear!

The online buying process

We have to support customers through each stage of the buying process: problem iden-tification, information search, evaluation, decision, action and post sales.

We need to think about how we can combine online and offline communications to support the customer through each stage of the buying process and also support mixed-mode buying at each stage. We also need to be self-critical about how we profile customers. What are the underlying variables that might influence the customer's product purchase and usage patterns and can we track these patterns? Techniques to achieve this are described in Section 4.10 on researching the online customer. Finally, some customers want to search, compare and buy online. Others just want to browse. Does your web site accommodate all stages of the buying process?

4.7 Online relationships and loyalty

By the end of this section, you will understand the importance of lifetime customers, relation-ship marketing and loyalty. You will also know how to begin to explore setting up loyalty marketing schemes.

Look at the statistics. Retaining existing customers is five times more profitable than acquiring new customers. Interestingly, Laurent and Eltvedt (2005) suggest that online repeat customers are actually ten times more profitable. According to Reicheld (1996), US corporations realized they were losing half their customers every five years. Arguably all markets have accelerated into hyper-competition with more aggressive attrition rates. Even your own opt-in email lists rapidly deteriorate with estimates suggesting that if your list is left unused for 12 months, it can deteriorate by up to 66 per cent. Even when active, you lose 5 per cent of your list every three months. The list is most responsive when it's freshly recruited; i.e. within the first few months.

All marketers know that building long-term relationships with the 'ideal customer' is essential for any sustainable business. Failure to build relationships largely caused the dotcom failures. Research shows that by retaining just 5 per cent more customers, e-companies can boost their profits by 25 per cent to 95 per cent. This section describes techniques to build and maintain relationships with customers using a combination of online and offline techniques.

We want to move customers up what Considine and Murray (1981) originally referred to as the 'Ladder of Loyalty'. From suspects to prospects to customers to clients to advocates who are totally loyal and are happy to spread the word about our products and services.

Remember, some customers are more likely to be loyal than others. Companies need to focus on those ideal customers who are likely to become loyal rather than the promiscuous, loss-making customers who grab incentives and run.

Many companies now only proactively market to 'ideal' customers since it has been thought that, on average, only 20 per cent of existing customers are 'ideal' and generate most of your profits (however, see Section 4.1 for an alternative 'long tail' view). Some customers break even, while other, disloyal, promiscuous customers are loss-makers. They cost you money. Low loyalty has a high cost.

In Seth Godin's now classic book, *Permission Marketing* (1999), he suggested that marketers should 'Focus on share of customer, not market share – fire 70% of your customers and watch your profits go up!' Some companies go further – they actually stop 'bad customers' from becoming customers. They also invest in acquiring and keeping ideal customers. For many businesses, it can take at least two years before a company recoups its initial acquisition costs.

So how can we form relationships and keep customers loyal? Godin suggests that online relationships can be likened to the relationships built through dating, with incentives important at every stage. Lindstrom and Andersen, authors of *Brand Building on the Internet* (2000), encourage e-marketers to think of loyalty as virtual love.

Research summarized by Reicheld and Schefter (2000) showed that acquiring online customers is so expensive (20–30 per cent higher than for traditional businesses), that start-up companies may remain unprofitable for at least two to three years. The research also shows that by retaining just 5 per cent more customers, online companies can boost their profits by 25 per cent to 95 per cent. They say: *'but if you can keep customers loyal, their profitability accelerates much faster than in traditional businesses. It costs you less and less to service them.'*

Note that the relationship between customer loyalty and profitability has been questioned, notably by Reinartz and Kumar (2002), who discovered through analysis of four company databases that: 'there was little or no evidence to suggest that customers who purchase steadily from a company over time are necessarily cheaper to serve, less price sensitive, or particularly effective at bringing in new business'.

However, existing customers do not have an acquisition cost and that's why they are more profitable than new customers. After acquiring a new customer, it is best to plan a contact strategy to nurture them into repeat loyal customers.

As in any relationship, the early stages are crucial. In relationship marketing, the first 90 days are crucial. Maintaining online customer relationships is difficult. Laurie Windham (2001) says: 'That's what's so scary about customer retention in the online space. We've created this empowered, impatient customer who has a short attention span, a lot of choices, and a low barrier to switching.'

E-MARKETING INSIGHT

The *Cluetrain Manifesto* on developing relationships

The authors of the ground-breaking *Cluetrain Manifesto* (Levine *et al.*, 2000) suggest that we should not conceive of the Internet as an impassive network of hardware and software, but as a means of creating global conversations within markets – a new dynamic dialogue.

The book refers to a large organization being unable to listen or respond to the 'clues' from customers demanding better service and response. Clues include high churn, rising complaints and the success of more responsive competitors.

To illustrate the danger of continuing with push marketing, the authors say:

> *Conversations among human beings sound human. They are conducted in a human voice.*
>
> *Most corporations, on the other hand, only know how to talk in the soothing, humorless monotone of the mission statement, marketing brochure, and your-call-is-important-to-us busy signal. Same old tone, same old lies. No wonder networked markets have no respect for companies unable or unwilling to speak as they do.*
>
> *(Levine et al., 2000)*

Corporate firewalls have kept smart employees in and smart markets out. It's going to cause real pain to tear those walls down. But the result will be a new kind of conversation. And it will be the most exciting conversation business has ever engaged in.

DEVELOPING LOYALTY

So how do you develop loyalty and strong relations with customers?

First, target and acquire the right type of customer – the ideal customer. Second, delight them. Don't just satisfy them. Ground-breaking research by Xerox some years ago revealed that between 65 per cent and 85 per cent of customers who defected from Xerox were actually 'satisfied customers'.

E-MARKETING INSIGHT

Customers are more savvy and less susceptible

Customers used to be a more malleable bunch. Before the recession of 2008, the nod of a discount or the wink of a mass-appeal reward for purchase used to be enough to provoke a sale. Post-recession, the customer is more savvy and less susceptible (Sever, 2012).

'As a customer perceives their strategic power, the value of the relationship diminishes. For a win-win relationship, you need to offer an ongoing service that your customers want' (Robert Nuttall, Rolls-Royce vice-president, strategic marketing, cited in Sever, 2012).

So, we need to excel beyond the five 'primary determinants of loyalty' identified by Reicheld and Schefter (2000):

1 Quality customer support
2 On-time delivery
3 Compelling product presentations

4 Convenient and reasonably priced shipping and handling

5 Clear trustworthy privacy policies.

And then delight the customer with:

1 *Extra service and added value.* There are a host of other opportunities constantly to delight and surprise the customer. Start by asking: 'What interests, passions and needs do my customers have? How can I help them?' Then see how you can add value. The difficult bit is finding the time to think about these and then time to implement them. There is no limit to relevant, timely added-value ideas – many of which do not cost that much, but have a high value.

2 *Personalization.* Personalization and mass customization can have a high value. They can be used to tailor information in both the web site and opt-in email. Extranets can be used to provide value-added services for key accounts.

3 *Community creation.* Community creation can engage the customer and provide a hook that keeps them returning. It can be used to create a new form of added value built around the brand. Section 4.8 deals with communities.

4 *Integration.* Integration into the customer's own systems – e.g. enterprise resource planning (ERP) – reducing duplication of work and increasing 'lock-in' which creates a switching cost should a customer ever want to leave.

5 *Incentivization.* Traditional retention methods such as loyalty schemes and sales promotions work well. But remember – be consistent with your page layout so that your customers know where to find the special offers section. Opt-in email can also alert customers to special offers and events. For both B2B and B2C organizations, think about the potential for online events. There are an infinite number of opportunities.

There are many different approaches, but basically they embrace the same principles – focus on good customers, treat them individually and serve them excellently and outstandingly.

E-MARKETING EXCELLENCE

Dell identifies loyalty drivers

Reicheld and Schefter (2000) reported that Dell Computer has created a customer experience council which has researched key loyalty drivers, identified measures to track this and put in place an action plan to improve loyalty (Table 4.3).

Table 4.3 Relationship between loyalty drivers and measures to assess their success at Dell Computer

Loyalty drivers	Summary metric
1 Order fulfilment	Ship to target. Percentage that ships on time exactly as the customer specified.
2 Product performance	Initial field incident rate – the frequency of problems experienced by customers.
3 Post-sale service and support	On-time, first-time fix – the percentage of problems fixed on the first visit by a service rep who arrives at the time promised.

Source: Based on examples referred to in Reicheld and Schefter (2000)

SECTION SUMMARY 4.7

Online relationships and loyalty

To summarize, we need to keep 'ideal' customers for life by building strong emotional and rational bonds. Constantly listen to them and find out more about their needs, serve them and then plant seeds and relevant incentives to keep them coming back again and again.

4.8 Communities and social networks

By the end of this section, you will understand the benefits of building communities, be able to assess the suitability of techniques used to foster online communities and know how to build active and lively online communities that improve brand equity and foster customer retention. We introduced the concept of social networks in Chapter 3, where we looked at the main types of social network and why they have proved so popular.

Man is a sociable animal. Communities or social networks are important. Whether stock-brokers or punks – people tend to group together into communities. Can your brand immerse itself within a community and thereby strengthen its relationship with customers? Communities of buyers, users, lovers, even haters, can pop up all over the Internet. Better to work with communities than against them. Wouldn't it be great if you could listen to your customers and prospects talking about your brand and related issues? Imagine occasionally dropping in and asking the community a question.

Imagine them telling you their current and future needs – what they like and don't like about your company. Imagine your brand at the hub of a community? Imagine your customers using your brand as a virtual meeting place? Imagine your customers getting great value from talking to each other?

Community potential has been a key feature that distinguishes online e-marketing from traditional offline marketing. But why is community important? John Hagel said:

The rise of virtual communities *in online networks has set in motion an unprece-dented shift from vendors of goods and services to the customers who buy them. Vendors who understand this transfer of power and choose to capitalize on it by organizing virtual communities will be richly rewarded with both peerless customer loyalty and impressive economic returns.*

(Hagel and Armstrong, 1997)

What is the reality behind this vision? How can we deliver the promise of community? The key to successful community is customer-centred communications. It is customer-to-customer (C2C) interaction. Customers, not suppliers, generate the content of the site, email list or bulletin board.

Taken to the extreme, communities can create new business models, a kind of marketing utopia where decisions are made by customers who subsequently buy the products and services they (the customer community) generate. See the Ladder of Engagement and social business models in Chapter 3, Section 3.10.

COMMUNITY AND SOCIAL NETWORK BUILDING STRATEGIES

A key question to ask before embarking on a community-building programme is: 'Can customer interests be best served through a company-independent community?' If the answer to this question is 'Yes', then it may be best to form a community that is a brand variant, differentiated from its parent. For example, Boots the Chemist has created handbag.com as an independent community for its female customers. Another tip, and a less costly alternative, is to promote your products through sponsorship or co-branding on an independent community site or portal. Or, at a minimum, get involved in the community discussions.

Roger Parker, author of *Relationship Marketing on the Web* (2000), lists eight useful questions to ask when considering how to create a community for your customers:

1 What interests, needs or passions do many of your customers have in common?

2 What topics or concerns might your customers like to share with each other?

3 What information is likely to appeal to your customers' friends or colleagues?

4 What other types of business in your area appeal to buyers of your products and services?

5 How can you create packages or offers based on combining offers from two or more affinity partners?

6 What price, delivery, financing, or incentives can you afford to offer to friends (or colleagues) [whom] your current customers recommend?

7 What types of incentives or rewards can you afford to provide [for] customers who recommend friends (or colleagues) who make a purchase?

8 How can you best track purchases resulting from word-of-mouth recommendations from friends?

We add:

9 What similar communities or groups already exist on social media platforms? What information or discussion topics generate most interest (responses)?

What about specific approaches for the B2B community? The B2B community offers great potential for high-involvement business services.

E-MARKETING EXCELLENCE

Overcoming community problems

These are examples of how companies have overcome problems with their communities.

1 *Empty communities.* A community without any people isn't a community. You need to apply your traffic-building skills. What is the online value proposition of your community and how are you communicating it? Perhaps it is best if existing brands tap into a third-party, independent community rather than starting your own that may not gain critical mass. For example, a baby toy manufacturer is likely to be better served by getting involved on community sites such as Babyworld (www.babyworld.com) and Babycentre (www.babycentre.co.uk) rather than starting its own community which may never gain critical mass since it is not perceived as neutral.

2 *Silent communities.* A community may have many registered members, but a community is not a community if the conversation flags. This is a tricky problem. You can encourage people to join the community, but how do you get them to participate? Here are some ideas.

- Seed the community – use a moderator to ask questions, or have a weekly or monthly question written by the moderator or sourced from customers. Have a resident independent expert to answer questions. Visit the communities on Monster (www.monster.co.uk) to see these approaches in action and think about what distinguishes the quiet communities from the noisy ones

- Make it select – limit it to key account customers or set it up as an extranet service that is only offered to valued customers as a value-add. Members may be more likely to get involved

- Use email – with email groups such as Yahoo! Groups (http://uk.groups.yahoo.com), participants don't need to revisit the web site, it is always in their email inbox.

3 *Critical communities.* Many communities on manufacturer or retailer sites can be critical of the brand. For example, the Egg Free Zone (www.eggfreezone.com) from bank Egg had to be closed because of critical comments about its services and retailers. Think about whether this is a bad thing. It could highlight weaknesses in your service offer to customers and competitors, but enlightened companies use communities as a means to understand their customers' needs better and the failings with their services. Community is a key market research tool. Also, it may be better to control

and contain these critical comments on your site, rather than have them voiced elsewhere in newsgroups where you may not notice them and can less easily counter them. The computer-oriented newsgroup on Monster shows how the moderator lets criticisms go so far, and then counters them or closes them off. Particular criticisms can be removed. So, a moderator is clearly needed for any company-run communities.

SECTION SUMMARY 4.8

Communities

Well-run communities strengthen relationships, trust and loyalty as well as maintaining brand awareness in the minds of the community members. Communities also allow a unique opportunity to stay close to customers, their concerns, their worries and their desires. Despite these benefits, building an active community can be time-consuming, expensive and difficult. Careful moderation and seeding of topics from a subject expert may be required. An alternative approach is to hook up to an established community that has greater independence. Either way, communities are part of the dynamic dialogue and the dynamic opportunities that today's marketer enjoys.

4.9 Customer profiles

Marketers need to know their customer profiles. What is the ideal customer's profile? We need to know who's online. What are their profiles? We need to know each customer segment and the proportion of customers who use various digital channels.

We need to know the proportion of customers who:

1 Have access to which channel or channels?
2 Are influenced by using which channel or channels?
3 Purchase using which channel or channels?

Let's consider each of these now.

PROFILING B2C CUSTOMERS

1 *Access to channel* (includes the usual geographic, demographic, psychographic variables). E-commerce provides a global marketplace, and this means we must review access and usage of the Internet channel at many different geographic levels: worldwide, between continents and countries. Also we must evaluate demographic differences in access – the stereotype of the typical Internet user as male, around 30 years of age and with high disposable income no longer holds true. Many females and more senior 'silver surfers' are also active.

To understand online customer behaviour and how customers are likely to respond to messages, we also need to consider the user's access location, access device and *'webographics'*, all of which are constraints on site design.

Finally, we mustn't forget the non-users, who comprise more than half of the adult population in many countries.

2 *Influenced online*. Next we must look at how our audience is influenced by online media. Finding information about goods and services is a very popular online activity, but we need to capture data about online influence in the buying process for our own market.

3 *Purchased online*. Customers will only purchase products online that meet the criteria of de Kare-Silver's electronic shopping test. We know that an increasing proportion of people are prepared to buy online. For e-planning, you need to know this data for your segment. Although we can use this information when building e-plans and when calculating the channel contribution to revenue, we still need some psychographic information to understand online customers better.

E-MARKETING INSIGHT

Today marketers can target behavioural profiles and geo-targeted profiles

As described further in Chapter 7, behaviourally targeting and geo-targeting ads to visitors who have purchase intent is a powerful technique to increase conversion as visitors to a destination site see targeted ads (based on their previous interest) on third-party publisher sites which may remind them to buy. This retargeting (or remarketing, as it is known in Google Adwords) is a powerful technique to increase conversion.

Services like Merchenta (www.merchenta.com) can also create targeted dynamically personalized ads for, say, plumbers in Leicester to 'high quality'[1] potential customers who are actually looking[2] for plumbers in Leicester[3]. The ads also can contain positive reviews[4] of the plumber.

(1) 'High quality' prospects are identified by calculating a consumer quality score using a range of behavioural indicators plus things like time of day/season/day of week, etc. – score is 0–100 where 100 indicates maximum purchase intent.

(2) Actually looking for plumbers' services – previously showed purchase intent for plumbers' services (as they previously visited the plumbers' section on www.ratedpeople.com, etc.).

(3) Living in Leicester – geo-targeting only those people within the relevant delivery area.

(4) Positive reviews – reviews are sentiment analysed in real time to ensure a positive emphasis in reviews, which means the reviews are authentic, but have a positive emphasis and negative 5* reviews (5* reviews with very rude or negative comments) are excluded to avoid polluting a brand with contradictory 5* reviews.

PROFILING B2B CUSTOMERS

How should we profile online business users?

Think about the information you would want to collect when designing an online form to profile registered-site B2B users. Users may be asked to enter the following organization characteristics:

- Size of company (employees or turnover)
- Industry sector and products
- Organization type (private, public, government, not for profit)
- Division
- Country and region.

We also need to know the following customer variables:

- Name
- Role and responsibility from job title, function or number of staff managed
- Role in buying decision (purchasing influence)
- Department
- Product interest
- Demographics: age, sex and possibly social group.

We can also add what stage in the buying cycle the customer is in. We can also add how interested they are; i.e. whether they are hot or cold prospects. A lot of this can be done through digital body language (in the old days, sales reps and marketers could see if a buyer was particularly interested or disinterested by the actual body language used). As more and more B2B business is done online, the sales rep cannot see the body language, but e-marketers can see the digital body language, which allows marketers to identify hot prospects and even large hot prospects and give them very tailored (highly relevant) responses and information. This is rules-based; e.g. if visitor X visited the product details and pricing page plus reviewed customer reviews, he or she would get a higher score than visitor Y who only visited the landing page. In addition, digital body language can aggregate visitors to see if a particular company has a heightened interest; e.g. if several staff from the same company spend time studying product specifications, it is likely they are at a more advanced stage in the buying process and require more advanced information. So digital behaviour builds profiles which allow marketers to deliver even more relevant information at just the right time.

Combine this with remarketing and these visitors can be served highly relevant ads whilst on other sites.

Once the ideal customer profile has been defined, customers can be tracked down and offered highly relevant information. For example, LinkedIn PPC ads can target prospects with any or all of the following profile variables:

- Job title
- Job function
- Industry
- Geography (country or city)
- Company size (staff)
- Company name

- Seniority (VP or owners)
- Age (18–24; 25–34; 35–54)
- Gender
- LinkedIn Group.

Similarly, Facebook PPC ads can target B2C prospects with all or any of the following profile variables:

- Age, even by birthday
- Interests
- City, country
- School or university, graduation year
- Connections (your fans/group members, anyone who RSVPs your events or has used your app in the last 30 days)
- Friends of connections.

So you can see the importance of identifying the ideal customer's profile. When searching for the ideal customer, what variables, or characteristics do you use? What is your profile of your ideal customer?

E-MARKETING EXCELLENCE

There are always new and interesting ways of defining customer profiles

'The market is divided into those willing to spend time to save money, almost all of whom buy hardware, and those willing to spend money to save time, almost all of whom buy service and support' (Jonathan Schwartz, chief executive, Sun Microsystems, cited in Anderson, 2008).

SECTION SUMMARY 4.9

Customer profiles

User profiles change as online penetration changes. Marketers can now target very precisely exactly which profile variables represent the ideal customer – as long as the marketer knows the profile of his/her ideal customer segments.

4.10 Researching the online customer

In our quest to understand online customers, we need to know how to research them. Before that we need to identify what we need to know. In this section, we look at the key questions and where to find the answers.

So what do you need to know about online customers? 'Who, Why and How' are good headings to remember. Who exactly are my ideal customers? Why do they buy or not buy? How do they buy? These can be elaborated into:

- Who are they – demographics, psychographics, behavioural?
- What do they want – their needs – why do they buy or not buy?
- How do they buy (online or offline or mixed mode)?
- When do they buy?
- How did they find us or our competitors?

In the context of the site, we need to know, in particular, what do visitors need before, during and after they go online and when they arrive at your site? We also need to know what kind of content customers want. One way of finding out is *personas and scenario-based design*.

Modelling personas of site visitors is a powerful technique for helping to increase the usability and customer centricity of a web site. Personas are essentially a 'thumbnail' description of a type of person. They have been used for a long time in research for segmentation and advertising, but since the mid-1990s, have also proved effective for improving web site design. Here are two simple examples for a music publisher wishing to sell music clips and sheet music to a business audience.

Persona 1– George: George is a 45-year-old violin teacher who has used the Internet for less than a year. He accesses the Internet from home over a dial-up connection. He has never purchased online before, preferring to place orders by phone.

Persona 2 – Georgina: Georgina is a 29-year-old ad exec who has been using the Internet for five years.

You can see that these are quite different types of people who will have quite different needs.

Customer scenarios are developed for different personas. In her book *The Customer Revolution* (2001), Patricia Seybold explains them as follows: 'A customer scenario is a set of tasks that a particular customer wants or needs to do in order to accomplish his or her desired outcome.'

You can see that scenarios can be developed for each persona. For an online bank, scenarios might include:

1 New customer – opening online account
2 Existing customer – transferring an account online
3 Existing customer – finding an additional product.

Each scenario is split up into a series of steps or tasks before the scenario is completed. These steps can be best thought of as a series of questions a visitor asks. These questions identify the different information needs of different customer types at different stages in the buying process.

The use of scenarios is a simple but very powerful web design technique that is still relatively rare in web site design. There is evidence of the use of scenarios and personas in sites when the needs of a range of audiences are accommodated with navigation, links and search to answer specific questions. Clear steps in a booking process are also an indication of the use of this approach.

The approach has the benefits of:

- Fostering customer centricity
- Identifying detailed information needs and steps required by customers
- Can be used to both test existing web site designs or prototypes and to devise new designs
- Can be used to compare and test the strength and clarity of communication of proposition on different web sites
- Can be linked to specific marketing outcomes required by site owners.

Effective customer research also uses pre-launch research techniques such as concept testing, competitor benchmarking and usability testing (Chapter 6) as well as post-launch research such as customer profiling and tracking.

E-MARKETING EXCELLENCE

Dulux uses personas to appeal to paint purchasers

We will illustrate the development of personas through a case study from Agency.com available through the IAB (www.iabuk.net). The objectives of this project were to position Dulux.co.uk as 'the online destination for colour scheming and visualisation to help you achieve your individual style from the comfort of your home'. Specific SMART objectives were to increase the number of unique visitors from 1 million p.a. to 3.5 million p.a. in three years and to drive 12 per cent of visitors to a desired outcome (e.g. ordering swatches).

Target audience based on research for user-centred design

- Would-be adventurous 25–44-year-old women, online
- Lack of confidence
- Gap between inspiration (TV, magazines, advertising) and lived experience (shopping in large DIY warehouses and potential nervous discomfort of shopping)
- No guidance or reassurance is available currently on their journey
- Colours and colour combining are key
- Online is a well-used channel for help and guidance on other topics
- 12-month decorating cycle
- Propensity to socialize
- Quality, technical innovation and scientific proficiency of Dulux is a given.

Examples of personas developed:

FIRST-TIME BUYER Penny Edwards, Age: 27, Partner: Ben, Location: North London, Occupation: Sales Assistant

PART-TIME MUM Jane Lawrence, Age: 37, Husband: Joe, Location: Manchester, Occupation: Part-time PR consultant

SINGLE MUM Rachel Wilson, Age: 40, Location: Reading, Occupation: Business Analyst

Each has a different approach to interacting with the brand. For Penny, it is summarized by the statement: 'I've got loads of ideas and enthusiasm, I just don't know where to start.'

A storyboard was developed which illustrates the typical 'customer journey' for each persona and these informed the final design (Figure 4.7).

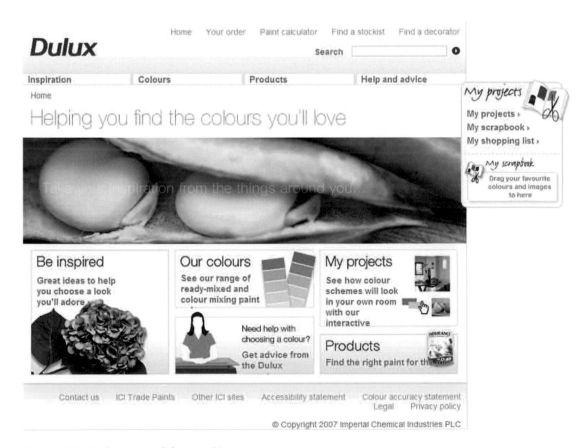

Figure 4.7   Dulux (www.dulux.co.uk)

E-MARKETING INSIGHT

Using personas and scenarios to inform web site design

These are some guidelines and ideas on what can be included when developing a persona. Start or end with giving your persona a name. The detailed stages are:

1 Build personal attributes into personas:

- Demographic: age, gender, education, occupation and for B2B, company size, position in buying unit
- Psychographic: goals, tasks, motivation
- Webographics: web experience (months), usage location (home or work), usage platform (dial-up, broadband), usage frequency, favourite sites.

2 Remember that personas are only models of characteristics and environment:

- Design targets
- Stereotypes
- Three or four usually suffice to improve general usability, but more are needed for specific behaviours
- Choose one primary persona whom, if satisfied, means others are likely to be satisfied.

3 Different scenarios can be developed for each persona as explained further below:

Write three or four, for example:

- Information-seeking scenario (leads to site registration)
- Purchase scenario – new customer (leads to sale)
- Purchase scenario – existing customer (leads to sale).

Once different personas have been developed who are representative of key site visitor types or customer types, a primary persona is sometimes identified. Wodtke (2002) says:

> *Your primary persona needs to be a common user type who is both important to the business success of the product and needy from a design point of view – in other words, a beginner user or a technologically challenged one.*
>
> *(Wodtke, 2002)*

She also says that secondary personas can also be developed such as super-users or complete novices. Complementary personas are those which don't fit into the main categories and that display unusual behaviour. Such complementary personas help 'out-of-box thinking' and offer choices or content that may appeal to all users.

RESEARCH TECHNIQUES

We can divide research techniques into primary data collection, where we collect our own data, and secondary data, where we use published research. For each we need to decide the best combination of online and offline.

The two main types of primary research are traditional marketing research methods and *web analytics* using server-based or browser-based techniques as shown in Table 4.4. Web analytics give undreamed-of visibility of customer behaviour: through click streams and page impressions, we can find out what a customer is or is not interested in and can measure the response to our online campaigns. Digital body language can build useful profiles and reveal how ready each visitor is for the next level of information (possibly delivered by email). We can also use data-mining software to profile different online behaviours.

We should note the weaknesses of log file analysis indicated in Table 4.4 and consider supplementing them with browser-based analysis methods. For large B2C sites, we can also use panel data to give customer numbers and profiles.

To understand the e-customer, we can use online versions of traditional marketing research techniques, but more rapidly and more cheaply than before. But remember there are many new issues involved with the design and execution of online questionnaires, focus groups and mystery shoppers and we need to assess the strengths and weaknesses of each technique.

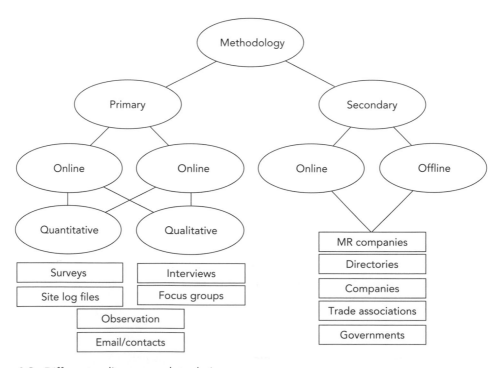

Figure 4.8   Different online research techniques

Table 4.4 A comparison of different online metrics collection methods

Technique	Strengths	Weaknesses
1 Server-based logfile analysis of site activity (web analytics) Examples: www.clicktracks.com www.webtrends.com	• Directly records customer behaviour on site plus where they were referred from • Low cost	• Doesn't directly record channel satisfaction • Undercounting and overcounting • Misleading unless interpreted carefully
2 Browser-based site activity data (web analytics) Examples: www.indextools.com www.google.com/analytics	• Greater accuracy than server-based analysis • Counts all users, unlike the panel approach	• Similar weaknesses to server-based technique apart from accuracy • Limited demographic information
3 Panels activity and demographic data Examples: www.netratings.com www.comscore.com www.hitwise.co.uk	• Provides competitor comparisons • Gives demographic profiling • Avoids undercounting and overcounting	• Depends on extrapolation from limited sample that may not be representative
4 Outcome data, e.g. enquiries, sales, customer service emails	• Records marketing outcomes	• Difficulty of integrating data with other methods of data collection when collected manually or in other information systems
5 Online questionnaires Customers are prompted randomly – every nth customer or after-customer activity or by email	• Can record customer satisfaction and profiles • Relatively cheap to create and analyse	• Difficulty of recruiting respondents who complete accurately • Sample bias – tends to be advocates or disgruntled customers who complete
6 Online focus groups; synchronous recording	• Relatively cheap to create	• Difficult to moderate and coordinate • No visual cues as from offline focus groups
7 Mystery shoppers. Sample customers are recruited to evaluate the site, e.g. www.emysteryshopper.com	• Structured tests give detailed feedback • Also tests integration with other channels such as email and phone	• Relatively expensive • Sample must be representative

For all research, we must devise a methodology to minimize sample bias. We need to make sure the sample is not made up solely of evangelists who love your service or critics who hate it. How do you counter this?

Remember also that the web also offers a fast, lower-cost method of researching the online customer using secondary data. Consider how well your organization uses the web to enhance its market intelligence using the sources given in the web links at the end of the chapter.

SECTION SUMMARY 4.10

Researching the online customer

Today's marketers have the most fantastic opportunity to research customers. We can track customers online, we can ask them questions online and we can have group discussions online. We can observe behaviour in reaction to new stimuli (new offers and/or new landing pages). We can gain a closer understanding of online customers. Metrics combine new research techniques such as digital body language and traditional techniques such as focus groups and questionnaires. Disciplined marketers will take the opportunity and improve their customer research by mixing online and offline research techniques.

4.11 The post-literate customer

Web access via PCs is declining as more people use mobiles, handheld devices, cars, clothes and Virtual Worlds to engage online. Here's a view of the future, its environment and what the post-literate customer might be like. By the end of this section, you will have a glimpse of the future and the customers within it. Let's step into the future now.

The post-literate customer may occasionally accept payment to view some ads. The rest are screened out by both filtering software and PVRs (Personal Video Recorders) – wall-to-wall-screen TVs. Neither governments nor society permit old-style intrusive advertising any more. No more intrusive evening telephone calls from script-reading intelligent agents. It is also illegal to litter anyone's doorstep or house with mail shots and inserts. Heavy fines stopped all that a long time ago. The only ads that do get inside are carried by the many millions of private media owners who rent out their cars, bikes and bodies as billboards.

The tedious task of shopping for distress purchases like petrol, electricity or memory storage is delegated completely to embedded intelligent shopping bots. Non-embedded bots (intelligent 3D hovering holograms appearing beside you) spun out of control some years ago when they first appeared – always at your side, always on, always double checking the best price for hire cars, hotels, even drinks at the bar. Some are programmed to be polite, others aggressive or even abusive. All are programmed to be intrusive whenever anything is being bought. Delays on buses and traffic jams regularly occurred when argumentative bots engaged in lengthy negotiations with bus drivers. Frustration broke out. Bots attacked bots, people attacked bots and bot owners. Eventually bots were banned from buses, planes, trains, 'bot-free' super-markets and 'bot-free' zones where virtual supermarkets appear in e.g. a subway train station (see Chapter 1, Figure 1.2 for Tesco's virtual store in South Korea).

Next came the great worm wars – programming bots so they only buy your brand – for life. But, unlike humans, bots can be reprogrammed by a competitor. The advertising agent worm was born. Agent eaters soon followed.

Despite being information-fatigued and time-compressed, the post-literate customer lives a lot longer than many bots. And certainly longer than most of the new brands that seem to come and go. The 150-year-old person has already been born.

Meanwhile, back at the ranch, microwaves insist on offering suggestions of ideal wines to go with your meal, offering instant delivery from the neighbourhood's wired-up 24-hour roving delivery van. Your fridge offers special incentives to buy Pepsi when you run out of Coke (or whichever brand owns or hires the 'infomediary' or the fridge-linked database). Children happily play chess and interact with their opponents on giant vertical screens (which are the side of the fridge). Voice-operated computers are considered noisy and old-fashioned as discrete, upmarket, thought-operated computers operate silently, but extremely effectively.

Think of a world without TV ads, billboards and direct mail – a world where customers choose the information they want to receive. How will businesses reach their target markets in this new environment?

And all the time, the technology, if truly mastered, can free up time to do the important things that give the post-literate customer a genuinely higher quality of life – like reading a book? Unlikely – as this might be a dying entertainment form – as described below.

In the last two editions of this book, we talked about the post-PC world; now we talk about the post-literate world. Here are some excerpts from an interview by Mary Kuntz with the author of a futuristic novel, *Super Sad True Love Story*. Gary Shteyngart portrays a very post-literate world. (In the following extracts, all emphasis is added.)

A POST-LITERATE WORLD

Credit poles are found on sidewalks in major metropolitan areas, and as you walk by they tell you what your credit rating is.

The apparat is worn around the neck as a pendant, and it has what's called RateMe Plus technology. Let's say you walk into a bar; it says, 'OK, you're the third-ugliest man in here, but you have the fifth-best credit rating', things like that. *Everyone is constantly ranked and constantly assessing everyone else's ranking, which is similar to the society we already live in.*

We all have credit scores. Those of us who have books out have Amazon scores. Those of us who teach have RateMyProfessors.com scores. So there's an endless amount of hierarchy. *In an insecure society, it becomes an obsession to constantly know where everyone stands*, and that's what this technology enables.

The rankings take over people's lives. Everyone wants to move their rating up, and everyone is obsessed with their number. *It's a very quantitative society.* Everything is about *enhancing one's numerical value.* Nothing is about the qualitative value. (He's) *constantly being told by his boss and everyone else to get his rankings up.*

They (books) haven't been banned. Oh no, they've just been abandoned. The *20th-century nightmare scenario where books were burned has been replaced by the 21st-century scenario, where nobody really cares enough to burn them. Literature is no longer considered a threat.* Literature's no longer considered to be something that can change the world, that can change the opinions of anyone, except for a very small group of intellectuals.

So everyone's attention span has been shot. We're no longer used to processing long strings of information. When a book is no longer a book but yet another text file, it's very hard to say, 'OK, I'm gonna devote myself to the 300 pages of text on my screen' when I have all this other stuff that I need to do.

They (web TV channels) *don't require textual immersion.* You just passively sit there and let these things happen on the screen.

And just the *inability to ever be alone.* You know, that's the difficulty. You want to read a book? That requires introspection. It requires time away from people and time away from *the constant need to communicate and to connect.*

(Shteyngart, 2010)

VIRTUAL CUSTOMERS IN VIRTUAL WORLDS

Now step into today's virtual worlds, where you can leave your body behind and become an entirely new virtual self – man, woman or hybrid. People can explore this 3D interactive opportunity to escape the confines of their bodies and explore the distant reaches of their minds, and meet other people in a new environment where you can play, talk, walk, run, fly,

Figure 4.9　PR Smith addressing a live audience in Belfast's Science Park (www.prsmith.org)

have sex, watch movies and do business all in a virtual, yet real, way. A world free from the dangers of disease – a 'post war, pre-aids innocence' (source unknown). Major businesses are exploring the possibilities with their own virtual islands, offices, shops and community areas as they learn more about the significance of virtual worlds and its 3D environment which gives glimpses of the next stage of online development, Web 3.0.

There are several virtual worlds including Second Life and Entropia Universe, with many more to come. In fact, some sites like O_2 already use 3D avatars to help customers. Combine this with augmented reality and Google's new glasses – the difference between virtual, augmented and real may decline as shoppers operate in all three simultaneously. The BBC has screened the *Money Programme* in Second Life; Sky News has opened a replica of its studio in Second Life; Reuters has a presence there; MTV premieres its TV shows inside Virtual Laguna Beach; Audi offers virtual test drives; IBM have sponsored a ballet; the Blarney Stone Pub (in Virtual Dublin) offers virtual Irish coffees. Northern Ireland has a vibrant digital community. The launch of its creative digital hub had a parallel virtual world launch as the 'real' event took place in the Science Park in Belfast (where the *Titanic* was built), with a screen showing a virtual world where the author (PR Smith) walked off the real stage and his avatar walked on-screen in Second Life to address the audience and introduce the Minister for Enterprise (avatar), who simultaneously addressed a virtual audience in Second Life and a real audience in the Science Park (see Figure 4.9 and 4.10).

The virtual world, Second Life, has had its first real-world millionaire who made her money from selling property in the virtual world. For more, see Smith and Zook (2011). Virtual worlds will continue in some manner, shape or form.

Figure 4.10 PR Smith's avatar addressing a virtual audience in Second Life beamed into the live audience in the Science Park (www.prsmith.org)

'Behaviour is a mirror in which everyone displays his own image' (Goethe, 1809, cited in Schifman and Kaunk, 1991).

SECTION SUMMARY 4.11

The post-literate customer

As Moore's Law (the observation made in 1965 by Gordon Moore, co-founder of Intel, that the number of transistors per square inch on integrated circuits had doubled every year since the integrated circuit was invented) continues to hold true, the time-compressed, information-fatigued, disloyal, post-literate customer seeks relationships not from brands themselves, but from databases that know, understand and seemingly care about them (witness the virtual girlfriend relationships in Japan), relationships with shops and vending machines. Oh, and relationships with people – real, quaint, touchy feely, physical people.

CHAPTER SUMMARY

1 Consumers are motivated to venture online for a range of reasons – social, shopping, entertainment. B2B customers are driven by cost savings, speed and selling.

2 We need to understand expectations for service delivery, making promises and then delivering.

3 Online customers have many fears and phobias such as security and privacy. Companies need to reassure them that with their services, the risks are minimized.

4 We have to support customers through each stage of the buying process: problem identification, information search, evaluation, decision, action and post-sales. We need to account for mixed-mode buying.

5 Understanding how customers process information through the stages of exposure, attention, comprehension and perception, yielding and acceptance, and retention can help us design effective sites.

6 Marketers must support the buying process online (and offline). Mixed-mode buying is not uncommon. The high-involvement buying model is explored online as are the six weapons of influence in online buying.

7 Achieving online relationships and loyalty involves defining the ideal customers, understanding their needs and meeting them through the five 'primary determinants of loyalty': quality customer support; on-time delivery; compelling product presentations; convenience and reasonable prices; and clear trustworthy privacy policies. We must delight the customer and add value through personalization, community, integration and incentivization.

8 Online communities and social networks can be effective in delivering *stickiness* and understanding customer motivations and fears. A key decision is whether communities are independent of, or integral to, the brand.

9 Profiling customers involves asking who they are (demographics and psychographics); what they need; why, how and when they buy; and identifying segments.

10 Research involves answering the profiling questions using a combination of online and offline primary and secondary techniques.

11 The post-literate customer. Companies will need to respond to new technologies to offer new forms of customer relationship that meet customer needs.

References

Adestra (2006) E-data unreliable. *Precision Marketing*, 9 June.

Ahonen, T. and Moore, A. (2007) *Communities Dominate Brands*. Future Text, London.

Anderson, C. (2006) *The Long Tail: Why the Future of Business is Selling Less of More*. Hyperion, New York.

Anderson, T. (2008) Giving away software makes good sense for Sun Technology. *The Guardian*, 21 February, p. 5.

Chaffey, D. (2004) Article on online value proposition. In the CIM's 'What's New in Marketing?', September 2004. Available from: www.davechaffey.com/E_marketing-Insights

Cialdini, R. (2006) *Influence, the Psychology of Persuasion*, 1st business edition. Collins, New York.

Considine, R. and Murray, R. (1981) *The Great Brain Robbery*. Pasadena, CA.

de Kare-Silver, M. (2000) *eShock 2000*. Macmillan, Basingstoke.

Dixon, M., Freeman, K. and Toman, N. (2010) Stop trying to delight your customers. *Harvard Business Review* Guest Edition, July–August at: http://hbr.org/2010/07/stop-trying-to-delight-your-customers/ar/1

EIAA (European Interactive Advertising Association) (2007) Europe online 2006–June 2007.

E-consultancy (2004) Online retail 2004, benchmarking the user experience of UK retail sites. Available from: www.e-consultancy.com

Fogg, B.J. (2009) How tags persuade Facebook users. Stanford University YouTube video at: www.youtube.com/watch?v=RWTZYq1QaDg

Gartner (2009) *Trip Report: Gartner Customer Relationship Management Summit 2009*. Gartner, Stamford, CT.

GlobalWeb Index (2011) *Wave 5 Trends*. Available at: http://globalwebindex.net/report-page/extended-wave-5-trends-report/

Godin, S. (1999) *Permission Marketing*. Simon and Schuster, New York.

Guest, T. (2007) *Second Lives: A Journey through Virtual Worlds*. Hutchinson, London.

Hagel, J. and Armstrong, A. (1997) *Net Gain: Expanding Markets through Virtual Communities*. Harvard Business Press, Boston, MA.

Hofacker, C. (2001) *Internet Marketing*, 3rd edition. Wiley, New York.

Kearon, J. (2008) Crowd pullers. *Marketing Age*, January/February.

Laurent, L. and Eltvedt, H. (2005) Beyond online advertising – lesson about the power of brand web sites to build and expand brands. Paper presented at ESOMAR Conference, Montreal.

Levine, R., Locke, C., Searls, D. and Weinberger, D. (2000) *The Cluetrain Manifesto*. Perseus Books, Cambridge, MA.

Lindstrom, M. and Andersen, T. (2000) *Brand Building on the Internet*. Kogan Page, London.

McGovern, G. (2010) Time is (still) money: increasing employee productivity (Part 1). 9 May, at: www.gerrymcgovern.com

Nielsen, J. (2007) Banner blindness: old and new findings. At: www.useit.com/alertbox/banner-blindness.html

Parker, R. (2000) *Relationship Marketing on the Web*. Adams Streetwise, Holbrook, MA.

Penn, D. (2005) Brain science, that's interesting, but what do I do about it? Paper presented at Market Research Society Conference.

Reicheld, F. (1996) *The Loyalty Effect: The Hidden Force behind Growth, Profits, and Lasting Value*. Harvard Business School Press, Boston, MA.

Reicheld, F. and Schefter, P. (2000) E-loyalty: your secret weapon on the Web. *Harvard Business Review*, July/August, pp. 105–13.

Reinartz, W. and Kumar, V. (2002) The mismanagement of customer loyalty. *Harvard Business Review*, July, pp. 4–12.

Schifman, L.G. and Kaunk, L.L. (1991) *Consumer Behaviour*, 4th edition. Prentice Hall International, London.

Sever, J. (2012) How to win your customers' loyalty. *The Marketer*, January/February.

Seybold, P. with Marshak, R. (2001). *The Customer Revolution*. Crown Business, New York.

Shore, N. (2011) Five tips for marketers from MTV's study of Millennials' digital habits – it's not just a medium, it's an ingrained part of the younger generation's culture. *Ad Age*, 20 July.

Shteyngart, G. (2010) *Super Sad True Love Story*. Granta Publications, London.

Shteyngart, G. (2011) Social media run amok: an interview with Gary Shteyngart (interviewed by Mary Kuntz). McKinsey & Company, What Matters blog, 26 October.

Smith, P.R.and Zook, Z. (2011) *Marketing Communications – Integrating Offline and Online with Social Media*. Kogan Page, London.

Soames, C. (2012) Is your website fast enough? Smart Insights, 13 March at: www.smartinsights.com/search-engine-optimisation-seo/index-inclusion/is-your-website-fast-enough-2/

Tagman blog (2012) Just one second delay in page-load can cause 7% loss in customer conversions. Blog post, 14 March at: http://blog.tagman.com/2012/03/just-one-second-delay-in-page-load-can-cause-7-loss-in-customer-conversions/

Windham, L. (2001) *The Soul of the New Consumer. The Attitudes, Behaviours and Preferences of E-Customers*. Allworth Press, New York.

Wodtke, C. (2002) *Information Architecture: Blueprints for the Web*. New Riders, Indianapolis, IN.

Wright, R. (2006) *Consumer Behaviour*. Thomson Learning, London.

Further reading

Godin, S. (1999) *Permission Marketing*. Simon and Schuster, New York. An interesting, influential book which raises direct marketers' hackles.

Google (2010) New GfK ROPO study with Vodafone. Google Barometer blog, 20 October at: http://googlebarometer.blogspot.com/2010/10/new-gfk-ropo-study-with-vodafone.html

Jayawardhena, C., Wright, L.T. and Dennis, C. (2007) Consumers online: intentions, orientations and segmentation. *International Journal of Retail & Distribution Management*, 35(6), pp. 512–26.

Kukar-Kinney, M., Ridgway, N.M. and Monroe, K.B. (2009) The relationship between consumers' tendencies to buy compulsively and their motivations to shop and buy on the internet. *Journal of Retailing*, 85(3), p. 298.

Mayfield, A. (2010) *Me and My Web Shadow*. A&C Black, London.

Web links

Market research

Sources to find more about consumer adoption and usage of digital media:

Eurostat (http://epp.eurostat.ec.europa.eu). European commission.
http://stakeholders.ofcom.org.uk. Consumer adoption of technology in the UK.
Market Research Society (www.mrs.org.uk).
www.emarketer.com. Digital market research studies and reports.
www.forrester.com. Digital and technology market research studies and reports (free content on blog).
www.research-live.com. Research news.
www.statistics.gov.uk. UK market information.

Self-test

1 What are the main reasons why customers venture online and how should marketers use this customer knowledge?

2 How should organizations meet the expectations of online customers?

3 Given that the main fears about using the Internet are security and privacy, how should companies reassure customers?

4 Draw a diagram that summarizes the online buying process and actions that can be taken at each stage to help move the customer through the process.

5 Explain what is meant by each of these five stages of on-site information processing: (1) exposure; (2) attention; (3) comprehension and perception; (4) yielding and acceptance; (5) retention.

6 Can you map out an online buying model for a high-involvement purchase?

7 How can customer loyalty be improved using online tools and techniques for your organization?

8 Explain how to overcome the problem of empty communities, silent communities and critical communities.

9 Identify the key variables by which you need to profile visitors to your organization's web site.

10 What are the research options for determining customers' opinions and feelings about a web presence?

11 How do you think the post-literate customer will live and what will this mean for marketers?

Chapter **5**

Social media marketing

Brands are either part of the conversation or they're not and as a result, they're either part of the decision-making cycle or they're absent from the heart, mind, and actions of the connected customer.

Solis (2011a)

OVERVIEW

We're excited about the potential of social media marketing! It's one of the biggest opportunities in marketing we've seen for years. But, if it's ad hoc or unmanaged, it won't be fully effective and can even be damaging. It definitely cannot be ignored and warrants its own strategy. That's why we've devoted a separate chapter showing you how to create a structured plan for social media marketing.

OVERALL LEARNING OUTCOME

By the end of this chapter, you will be able to:

- Review the impact and potential of social media adoption on marketing
- Understand customer and business requirements for social media
- Create a strategy and plan to manage social media marketing.

CHAPTER TOPIC	LEARNING OBJECTIVE
5.1 What is social media marketing and why is it important?	Understand the relevance of social media to business
5.2 Benchmarking and setting goals for social media marketing	Define methods to set goals for social media and measure its effectiveness
5.3 Create strategy and plan to manage social media	Identify the components of a social media strategy
5.4 Social listening and online reputation management	Review options for listening to customer conversations
5.5 Develop the content marketing and engagement strategy for your brand	Define methods to use different forms of content to engage online audiences
5.6 Define social media communications strategy	Demonstrate how social media can be integrated into communications strategy
5.7 Define approaches for the core social media platforms	Develop an understanding of practical approaches to improve marketing on the main social networks
5.8 Social media optimization (SMO)	Understand approaches to increase the returns from social media marketing

5.1 What is social media marketing and why is it important?

Social media means different things to different people, so let's start at the beginning . . . social media, that's Facebook, Google+, LinkedIn and Twitter? Well yes, but success in social media is not so much about the different social networks, your tools, but your strategy for how to use them as part of inbound marketing (Shah and Halligan, 2009). To apply them effectively for communications, we have to recognize that socializing online is all about participation in discussions and sharing of ideas and content.

We think the CIPR Social Media Panel described social media well:

> *Social media is the term commonly given to Internet and mobile-based channels and tools that allow users to interact with each other and share opinions and content. As the name implies, social media involves the building of communities or networks and encouraging participation and engagement.*
>
> *(CIPR, 2011)*

This definition shows that the most important feature of these social media channels is that we encourage our prospects and customers to interact and create user-generated content (UGC). Social media can be used as another broadcast-only channel, but that's a mistake!

To simplify it to its essence of why social is social, we can say: social media are digital media which encourage *audience participation*, *interaction* and *sharing*.

Social media marketing has to be focused on using these media to help achieve your marketing objectives – both protecting and expanding your brand: 'Monitoring and facilitating customer–customer interaction, participation and sharing through digital media to encourage positive engagement with a company and its brands leading to commercial value. Interactions may occur on a company site, social networks and other third-party sites' (CIPR, 2011).

Note that some commentators also discuss *social CRM* as part of a broader transformation needed to support social media marketing. We discuss this concept more at the start of Chapter 9.

WHAT ARE THE MAIN SOCIAL PLATFORMS?

In practice, social media sites are amongst the most popular sites on the Internet, along with search engines. To help you develop a strategy for social media, we've identified these key types of social media platforms, each of which needs managing in our social media marketing radar.

Smart Insights (2012) created a 'social media marketing radar' that summarizes the options to help you discuss with colleagues or agencies which sites warrant or deserve most attention in the different categories (Figure 5.1). A similar categorization of social media sites has been created by Weinberg (2010). Sites or services that are agreed to be more important, which warrant more resource, should be positioned towards the centre.

These are the main types of social platforms available to you:

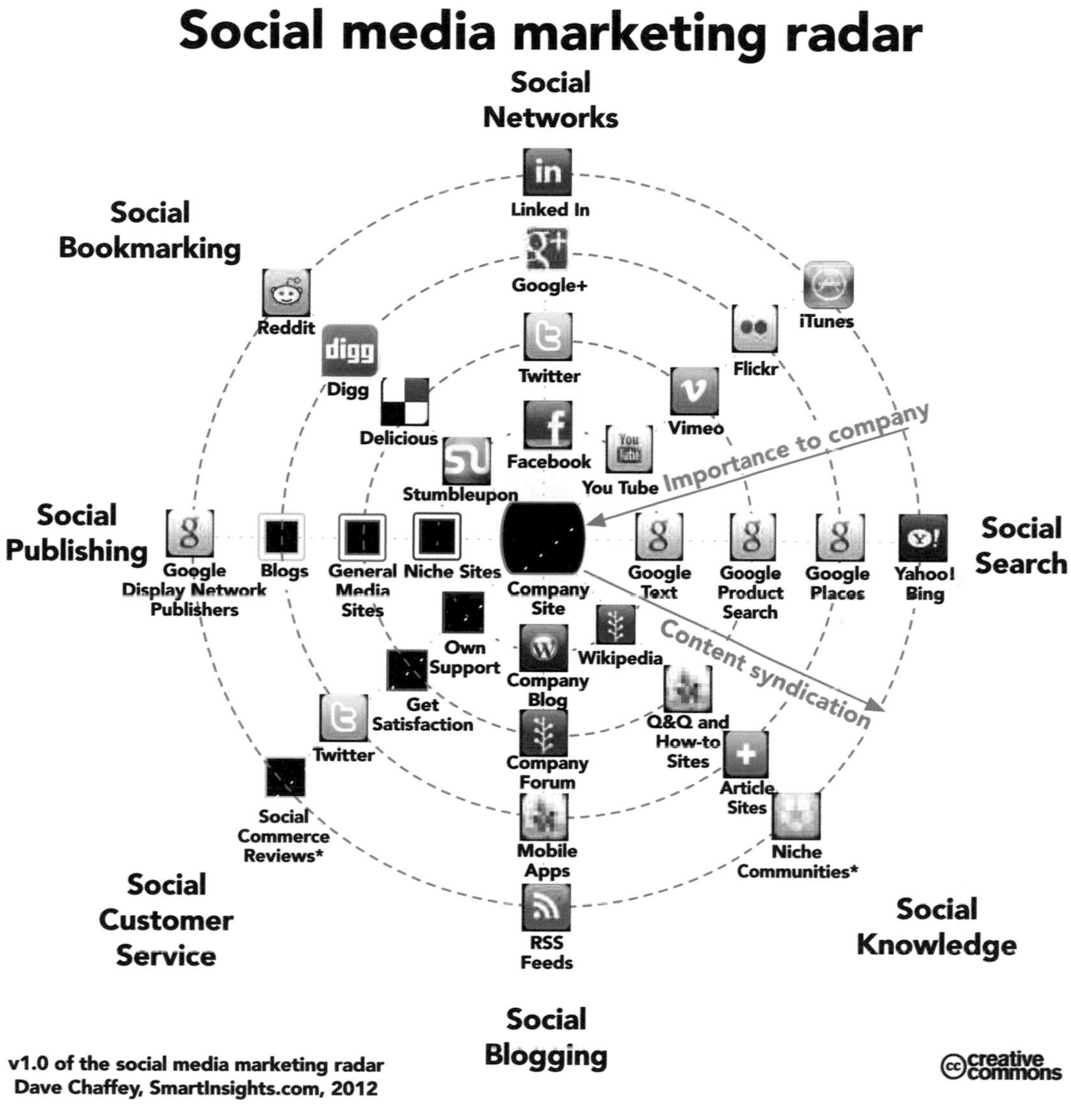

Social media marketing radar

v1.0 of the social media marketing radar
Dave Chaffey, SmartInsights.com, 2012

Figure 5.1   Social media marketing radar

Smart Insights (2012)

1 *Social networks* – in most countries, the core social platforms where people interact through social networks are Facebook for consumer audiences, LinkedIn for business audiences, and Google+ and Twitter for both.

2 *Social publishing and news* – nearly all newspapers and magazines, whether broad or niche, now have an online presence with the option to participate through comments on articles, blogs or communities.

3 *Social commenting in blogs* – a company blog can form the hub of your social media strategy

and you can look at tapping into others' blogs, whether company or personal or through blog outreach.

4 *Social niche communities* – these are communities and forums independent of the main networks, although these do support sub-groups. You can create your own community this way.

5 *Social customer service* – sites like Get Satisfaction (www.getsatisfaction.com) as well as companies' own customer-support forums are increasingly important for responding to customer complaints.

6 *Social knowledge* – these are reference social networks like Yahoo! Answers, Quora and similar, plus Wikipedia. They show how any business can engage its audience by solving their problems and subtly showing how products have helped others.

7 *Social bookmarking* – the bookmarking sites like Delicious (www.delicious.com) are relatively unimportant in the UK except if you are engaging technical audiences.

8 *Social streaming* – rich and streaming media sites including photos (e.g. Pinterest), video and podcasting.

9 *Social search* – search engines are becoming more social with the ability to tag, comment on results and, most recently, vote for them through Google+1.

10 *Social commerce* – mainly relevant for the retail sector, social commerce involves reviews and ratings on products and sharing of coupons on deals, and can be facilitated by social log-in as used, for example, by Sears Social.

We haven't identified mobile platforms or apps separately since all of these options will be available through smartphones. However, proximity services like Foursquare and Gowalla are specialist networks that should be considered and we've shown them in the social network section.

WHY IS SOCIAL MEDIA MARKETING IMPORTANT?

The importance of social media marketing is that it represents both a challenge and an opportunity. The challenge of social media is simple; when we socialize, we're hanging out, spending time with our friends, family or colleagues, so we probably don't want to be interrupted by ads from brands.

E-MARKETING EXCELLENCE

Burberry and transformation to the Social Business

Many of the leading brands which use social media successfully have clear statements of their vision for social and digital media to transform their brand, using BHAG (big hairy audacious goals) to support these.

This example of *vision* from Burberry CEO Angela Ahrendts (Figure 5.2) shows this perfectly, we think. She says:

1 *We have a vision – to be the first (fashion) company that is fully digital end-to-end*

2 *The experience is that the customer will have total access to Burberry across any device, anywhere . . . they will get exactly the same feeling of the brand, feeling of the culture, regardless of where, when and how they were accessing*

3 *To any CEO who is sceptical today about social enterprise, you have to be totally connected with everyone who touches your brand . . . if you don't do that, I don't know what your business model is in five years.*

(Ahrendts, 2011)

Figure 5.2   Burberry vision for social and digital media

Source: YouTube video, uploaded 30 August 2011

Christopher Bailey, chief creative officer of Burberry has also spoken about the importance of digital media. Speaking to Mashable when explaining how they used local Twitter takeovers for their 2011 'Tweetwalk', he said:

4 *Burberry is now as much a media-content company as we are a design company.*

5 *A brand is not just about product, it's about experience as well, and experiences need to come from the center of a community . . . I get excited about using all of those platforms to communicate to all of our different communities around the world about what we're doing.*

(Bailey, cited by Mashable, 2011)

Given the transformation that social media can offer, brands are increasingly looking at a broader scope of how it integrates with the business process, using labels such as the social enterprise, social business or social CRM.

But individuals do also socialize with brands and hang out with others who like these brands. In fact it gets better; the main reasons we go online aren't for commercial activities like shopping and doing business; rather we go online to spend time learning, having fun or socializing.

E-MARKETING EXCELLENCE

Princess Cruises' integrated social campaign

Let's take an example now of how you can engage your audience through their interests as part of an integrated campaign. Princess Cruises used a classic 'blog to win' or 'share to win' campaign, asking readers about their favourite travel destination (Figure 5.3).

The campaign engaged the audience through their interest in travel destinations and used Facebook as the heart of this, but encouraged participation through seeding, using other digital marketing channels like blogs and email.

E-MARKETING INSIGHT

The Forrester POST methodology

POST is a framework that businesses can apply to help them develop a social media strategy, first summarized by Forrester in 2007:

● *People.* Understanding the adoption of social media by an audience is an essential starting point. The Forrester Social Technographics Ladder that we'll come to in

Section 5.2 is helpful. Of course, reviewing how competitors and intermediaries like publishers and comparison sites are using social media marketing is important too as part of situation analysis.

- *Objectives.* Setting goals for different options to engage customers across the customer lifecycle from customer acquisition to conversion to retention. Josh Bernoff of Forrester recommends that you *'decide on your objective before you decide on a technology. Then figure out how you will measure it'*.

- *Strategy.* How to achieve your goals. Bernoff suggests that because social media is a disruptive approach, you should imagine how social media will support change. He says: 'Imagine you succeed. How will things be different afterwards? Imagine the endpoint and you'll know where to begin.'

- *Technology.* Finally, decide on the best social media platforms to achieve your goals; we'll review these in a moment.

Figure 5.3
Princess Cruises
campaign example
(www.princess.com)

Social media marketing is based on how we can use consumer-to-consumer (C2C) interactions to increase awareness of our brand while minimizing negative mentions. Social media marketing has the potential to transform businesses to make them more customer-centric, but major transformation requires senior managers to lead, through defining the vision and supporting it through sufficient resources and the organizational changes needed.

5.2 Benchmarking and setting goals for social media marketing

Social media platforms like Facebook, Twitter and LinkedIn are no longer new. Most companies already have some form of presence and customers will be discussing your brand and related interests.

So start strategy development by checking the current situation of what social media is delivering to your organization against commercial goals.

Even if you're not established in your use of the social platforms, you should still start here by reviewing how your customers and others in your sector and beyond are using social media; it's all too easy to go straight to getting your business up and running on Facebook, LinkedIn or Twitter. The mantra is 'Listen first!' We'll go into more detail on the tools to use this later.

REVIEW BUSINESS GOALS FOR SOCIAL MEDIA USING THE 5 SS

With social media, it's especially important to think about how it will support your business, since it's all too easy to go straight to getting your business up and running on Facebook, LinkedIn or Twitter without thinking of what you want to achieve.

Start with the business goals; make these as specific as possible by understanding how customers are using social media now.

Set sell goals

Write down how your social media channels will influence sales and purchase intent by generating leads and sales that are activated both online and offline.

Sell goals are best defined through the Smart Insights PRACE framework (Chapter 1) so that they cover all customer contact points through the customer lifecycle:

- *Reach* – use social media to reach new prospects through amplification such as shared mentions in social media streams and advertising within social media
- *Act* – use social content or web site(s) and social outposts to encourage interaction leading to increased leads
- *Convert* – increasing conversion to sale through moving customers from interaction with your brand to purchase using social recommendations

- *Engage* – encourage your existing customers to act as advocates for your business through sharing and recommendations.

Set speak goals

Write down your broad aims in these five areas:

1 Encouraging ongoing engagement (this should come before company messages so that the 'sell–inform–entertain' balance is right)
2 Communicating brand perception and key brand messages
3 Communicating updates about new products and offers
4 Encouraging dialogue to find out more about products
5 Reputation monitoring and management.

Set serve goals

Define how social media will be used to deliver customer-service goals:

- To provide information to resolve customer-service issues
- To identify discussed customer issues and resolve them
- To encourage web self-service including collaborative self-service.

Set save goals

Cost savings are a less relevant part of the 5Ss since managing social media has incremental costs for which budget will need to be found from elsewhere. But it's as well that this issue of budget reallocation is considered here.

Set sizzle goals

These are closely related to the speak goals; they explain how to add value to customers through social media.

Now you have thought through the potential benefits of social media for your business, you should review what it's delivering now *and* how well the organization can support it.

For setting objectives, we think the Altimeter social media ROI pyramid (Altimeter, 2010) is valuable in helping to define the important types of objective. It employs the classic approach of using business or strategic measures owned by a senior manager at the top of the pyramid with operational measures at the base (Figure 5.4).

You can see that there are three levels of key performance indicators (KPIs); check that you include each of these:

The measures at the top of the pyramid are the most important, but the most difficult to measure. These KPIs include ROI and contribution to revenue through sales attributed to social

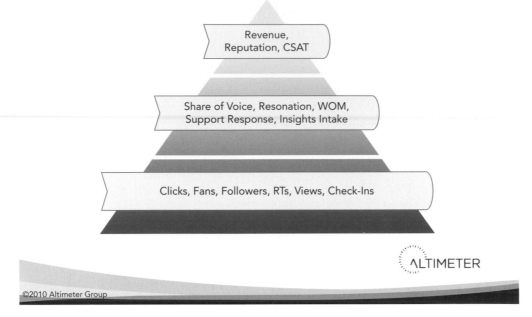

Figure 5.4   Social media KPI pyramid

Source: Altimeter (2010).

media. Softer measures include brand reputation and customer satisfaction (CSAT) – ask customers about the quality of social media for these interactions.

It's one thing to create a framework, it's quite another to be able to attribute investment in social media to return. To put in place a framework, you need to define:

- Cost of social media marketing activity – relatively easy to define
- Outcomes achieved through social media which can occur on your site or offline
- Value of outcomes online or offline; i.e. leads or sales influenced by social media.

> **E-MARKETING INSIGHT**
>
> **Using Google's Social Analytics feature to review goals**
>
> To set SMART objectives and report on social media marketing, we need to use the right systems and tools to collect insights. Here are some of the barriers:
>
> 1 *The 'last click wins' model.* By default, Google Analytics and other analytics tools measure outcomes based on the last visit to the site, but typically there will be repeated visits before sale. So we need to attribute these earlier visits where possible, using approaches like the Assisted Conversion Report.

2 *Direct visits and branded searches are still common ways to navigate to a site.* If you want to buy and you're already aware of a brand, you will often just type their name or URL direct into the search bar. Again, attribution using the Assisted Conversion Report can help here.

3 *Attribution is based on cookies. Customers delete and block cookies.* Attribution is based on use of cookies typically; if customers delete cookies, then multiple touch-points can't be measured.

4 *People use mobile devices and apps to visit sites prompted by social media.* If some of your users are using apps like Facebook, Twitter, TweetDeck or HootSuite on their mobile or tablet device, then these visits are not linked from another site, so they may not be registered as a visit inspired by social media.

5 *Multiple device usage.* It's common now for people to use multiple devices, so if a customer becomes aware of a brand through social media on one device, but later visits a site using another device, it's difficult to relate the two together.

While these don't really help you, it does give you a way to argue why the levels of leads and sales from social media marketing are lower than you might expect.

REVIEW CONSUMER DEMAND AND ENGAGEMENT FOR SOCIAL MEDIA MARKETING

It's important to understand what proportion of active social media participators you have in your type of audience for your type of market.

As an alternative approach to the Ladder of Engagement 3.10, Forrester provides two of the key tools to help understand how active your audiences are in using social media.

- *Social Technographics Ladder.* Use this to understand the range of audiences (Figure 5.5)
- *Social Media Profile Tool.* This enables you to see the different levels of audience involvement according to customer age, gender and location. There is also a B2B tool.

Their Social Technographics Ladder shows that the two key influencer audiences to understand are the creators and the critics, since they will help amplify your message.

Although we suggest focusing on the creators and critics, it's worth thinking about your goals for each of these audiences too. For example, think how you can activate each type of person:

- *Creators* – encourage them to feature you in their blogs, contribute to your site and then share their content
- *Critics* – encourage discussion in your blog or social outposts
- *Collectors* – share your content through social sharing
- *Joiners* – again, start to share your content through social sharing
- *Spectators* – encourage the move to Joiner or Collector
- *Inactives* – encourage the move to Spectator when you're communicating with them offline.

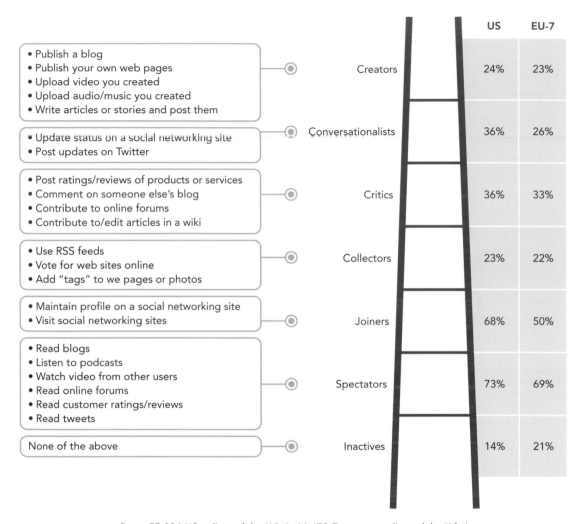

Base: 57,924 US online adults (18+); 16,473 European online adults (18+)

Figure 5.5   Social technographics for US and EU, 2011

Source: Forrester (2012)

Analysis of your own markets can give the best results. You can start with surveying your audience. Ask existing customers about their preferences for different platforms and how they'd like to see you using them – this is a great place to start.

You can also see how competitors have fared in encouraging interactions, which brings us to:

Benchmark competitor use of social media

To help review competitor use of social media, you need to find a standard method of reviewing competitors. We suggest creating a simple scorecard of how well your competitors are using social media. Here are some KPIs you can track for yourself and for competitors:

Reach and influence KPIs

- *Share of voice (number, per cent)* – number of people discussing brand and category keywords in social media
- *Sentiment (discussion polarity, per cent)* – how many are speaking positively about a brand.

Engagement KPIs

- *Network size and growth* – the obvious one – the numbers of fans or followers of the main social networks
- *Social sharing* – degree to which content is shared through the network – Retweets on Twitter, Likes on the other social networks.
- *Engagement (per cent)* – through user-generated content on-site.

SECTION SUMMARY 5.2

Don't just 'dive in' to social media through setting up a presence on Facebook and Twitter. Instead, listen to customer conversations. Watch how customers use social media and how competitors are using social media. Then review your business aims for social media across the 5Ss. In particular, think carefully about how social media will support the 5Ss.

5.3 Create strategy and plan to manage social media

In this section, we will cover six core social media marketing activities which together will form your strategy for social media marketing:

1 Listen and manage reputation
2 Transform the brand through social media
3 Acquire new customers
4 Increase sales to existing customers
5 Deliver customer service
6 Harness insights to develop the brand using social media optimization (SMO).

All activities should run on a continuous *and* campaign basis. To support them, they require both a content *and* a communications strategy which we cover in later sections of this chapter.

Activity 1. Define listening and reputation strategy

You need to understand social media usage for each of:

- *Your audience* – who they are, how they participate, what they're saying and sharing
- *Your activity* – through official social media channels and interactions through your site, but also through employee mentions

- *Your competitors* – for direct and indirect competitors, you need to review how their activities compare to yours

- *Online publishers and other key intermediaries* – these are a form of indirect competitor and are also important as influencers.

But listening is just listening, so at the same time you need to develop an approach on how to follow up for positive or negative mentions. Since this is a key topic in digital marketing, we cover listening and reputation management in more detail in the next section of this chapter.

Activity 2. Transform the brand through social media

To really exploit social media is not business as usual. For most companies, it will require big changes to their brand, company structure and how everyone in the company communicates.

Some key areas for delivering this transformation are:

1 *Set scope for social media activities.* Understand the intersection of social media and your business activities. It's not just about your Facebook, Google+, Twitter or LinkedIn presence, it cuts across all customer marketing activities.

2 *Review social media capabilities and priorities.* Social media marketing isn't new for most companies, they will already be using social media. But they won't be using it to the max. Benchmarking where you are now against where you want to be in the future is the key to future success.

3 *Governance: define who is responsible for social media.* We've seen that exploiting social media requires the involvement of many people in larger companies. So we need to decide who does what and how different groups work together. We'll see that in larger organizations, a social governance policy has to be created.

4 *Reviewing the personality of your brand and setting a vision.* Social media and content marketing give many opportunities to make your brand more engaging which have to be thought through. The whole personality of your brand may have to be revisited too.

Activity 3. Acquire new customers using social media

For most marketers, the ultimate appeal of social media marketing is to use it to increase sales through reaching new prospects and converting them to customers. In reality, for most businesses, social media marketing may be most important in serving existing customers or providing service, but you will set priorities according to what you think is important.

Acquiring new customers through social media marketing works best if you apply all aspects of our PRACE framework. You need to ask these questions:

- *Plan* – what is our strategy for making the best use of social media?

- *Reach* – how can we use social media to reach new prospects? Identification and outreach to key influencers will be part of this

- *Act* – which approaches on our web site(s) and social outposts will encourage interaction?

- *Convert* – how can we create sales through moving customers from interaction with our brand to purchase?
- *Engage* – which marketing activities will encourage our existing customers to act as advocates for our business? This will involve defining a content strategy to seed content that existing customers can share. Likewise, campaigns to encourage social sharing such as those run by McKay Flooring can help here.

The conversion funnel in Chapter 1, Figure 1.13 gives a visual representation of this cycle.

E-MARKETING EXCELLENCE

How a small business uses Instagram and Pinterest to grow awareness

McKay Flooring is a family business established for 40 years. It is a great example of how smaller businesses can be creative in using social media marketing to expand their reach.

What caught our interest was the way they use some of the newer social media marketing platforms like Pinterest and Instagram for competitions. These are all promoted through their blog, which is also a great example of how a blog can act as a social hub for campaigns, while also building the credibility of a company by using testimonials and linking to product categories on the main site (Figure 5.6).

The competition mechanic is straightforward:

- *Offer*: a prize draw to win a £100 Amazon voucher
- *Entry*: take a picture of the floor on Instagram (the iPhone and iPad app for easily sharing to Facebook or Twitter)
- *Campaign name*: a hash tag of #mckayflooring and #mywoodfloor has to be added to the post, which helps with branding.

McKay Flooring has also been active in using Pinterest. Their profile Pins (http://pinterest.com/mckayflooring) shows how you can use a range of techniques to build a brand:

- *Case studies* – demonstrate your expertise by showing previous work and how you solved a specific problem, perhaps using a customer testimonial video
- *Sell products* – you do this through showcasing products and potentially adding pricing to the Pin description
- *Develop brand personality* – use Pinterest to show company culture, the type of people who work for you, what your brand stands for and simply put a friendly face to your brand
- *Events/trade shows* – if you take part in lots of events and trade shows, why not entice your audience with sneak previews of your stand, let them know where you will be and when

- *Competitions* – run a contest to encourage visitors to create Pins of your projects/products/designs that they like and then choose the finalists and get others to vote for what they like.

Figure 5.6   Social media marketing campaign from McKay Flooring (http://blog.mckayflooring.com)

Activity 4. Increase sales to existing customers

Applying social media to increase sales to existing customers focuses on developing your customer communications strategy to encourage more social interactions on your site and on your social outposts. As with all communications strategies, this will cover:

- Your objectives
- Your target audiences
- Value to be offered through content and offers
- Integration of communications.

Tools and platforms that are important to support this communications strategy are:

- *Social outposts* – using the main public social networks to communicate offers, interesting content and to deliver service to improve experience of the brand
- *Your own community* – you may have your own community, either an explicit customer panel or forum or other techniques for getting customer feedback like reviews and ratings
- *Email marketing* – using e-newsletters and email campaigns to encourage more social interactions through customers
- *Mobile platforms* – using mobile apps and mobile web browsing to support all types of interactions.

Activity 5. Enhance customer service through social media marketing

Improving customer service through social media is not a major focus of this chapter since we focus on communications that directly increase sales through reaching or converting more of an audience.

However, to find out more about how customer service can be delivered through social media, we recommend reading the advice of consultant Guy Stephens of Foviance (Smart Insights, 2010). He talks about how specific customer-service activities should be managed, including:

- Social listening to identify customers requiring service
- Outreach to answer customer questions or resolve problems
- Using service to improve product and service offerings
- Management of a company's own service forums or other service platforms like GetSatisfaction.

Guy has a vision for 'anytime, anywhere' customer service in the context of customer need, as shown by this quote by John Bernier of Best Buy about their 'Twelpforce' Twitter service:

> *for us to enable customers to answer questions that come from anywhere so that the customer doesn't have to find us, we find them. We don't want someone to have to leave Facebook to ask a question, we want them to ask it there.*
>
> *(John Bernier, cited in Smart Insights, 2010)*

Activity 6. Harness insights to develop the brand using social media optimization (SMO)

Once you have your social media marketing up and running as you'd like, it's worth thinking more carefully about measurement and SMO which we'll cover in the final section of this chapter.

You may have the core of a social media strategy and have social media marketing up and running, but we can always find new methods to make our content work harder for us. This is optimization! Thinking from the customer perspective, SMO is about making brand interactions easier.

That's easier to:

- Discover
- Interact
- Share
- Return to through time
- Lead to purchase.

This is not just to make the process physically easier through navigation or buttons. Instead, it's understanding the psychology of motivation to interact and share.

SUMMARIZE HOW YOU WILL ALIGN STRATEGIES AND TACTICS TO BUSINESS GOALS

After you have reviewed your options for social media marketing, it's time to select the most important and summarize them. This is at the heart of your social media marketing.

TRANSFORMING YOUR BUSINESS

After you have identified the main social media marketing strategies, the final, crucial area to think through is how you will make the necessary change happen. This is where many companies fail to commit fully to social media since this change, as with all major business change, can only come if sponsored by the most senior managers as they buy into it. So in the final section for this step, we'll go into this in a bit more detail.

To help manage change, these are some key areas of delivering this transformation that we have seen in companies we have worked with and advised:

1 Set scope for social media activities to communicate to staff
2 Review social media capabilities and priorities
3 Governance: define who is responsible for social media
4 Review brand personality and vision.

Transformation factor 1. Set scope for social media activities to communicate to staff

Your people may understandably just believe that social media is about how the company uses Facebook and Twitter. To show its importance, it's best to define the breadth of social media to help explain why changes are needed.

- *Question: Is the scope of social media strategy defined?*

At first, social media may seem to be limited to a digital media channel like any other, such as affiliate, display ads or search. But this is a really narrow view and, if you take it, it is likely you will fail to exploit social media. Social media marketing can and should involve the whole business, wherever communications are involved.

Transformation factor 2. Review social media capabilities and priorities

Once you have a better understanding of the scope and business goals of social media, thinking through your current capabilities against where you want to be is useful. We like this assessment (Figure 5.7) developed by Paul Fennemore of Viapoint with Professor Moira Clark (Henley Business School College) and Dr Ana Canhoto (Oxford Brookes University).

We like this assessment since it can be applied to different types of company and acts a checklist of practical steps to improve digital marketing.

Transformation factor 3. Governance – who is responsible for our social media?

We've seen that exploiting social media requires the involvement of many people in larger companies. So we need to decide who does what and how different groups work together. This is more of an issue for large businesses, so do skip this part if you work for a smaller company and there are only a small number of people who need to 'get it', be approached and agree.

Social Media Adoption Framework

Eight Business Competencies		Experimental	Tactical	Strategic
	Leadership/ Direction	• Compelled involvement • Delegated	• Cautious • Centralised • No sponsor	• Vistionary • Distributed • Y Gen mentality • Involved/ownership
	Strategy	• Ad-hoc • Departmental	• Planned but tactical • Short term	• Social Commerce • Organisational • Aligned to business • Business value/KPIs
	Integration	• Separate function • Uncoordinated	• Marketing campaigns • Limited integration	• Systemic/multi-functional • Integrated & interactive • Aligned to all programs • Intranet/extranet/internet
	Culture & Governance	• Assumed/Tacit • Fear re loss of control • Stopped & blocked	• Censored • Highly moderated • Prescribed policy/Official	• Federated/everybody • Self regulating/enabling • Open/transparent/trust • Consistent Tone of Voice
	Resources	• Now ownership/No budget • Informal/part time	• Middle management • Marketing agencies • Minimal funding	• Community & conversation team • Digital/e-Commerce skills • Multi-functional • Financed against RoI/KPIs
	Community building	• Random postings • Limited engagement • Reactive	• Listening • Pro-active • Engagement/Supporting • Segment push approach	• Network weaving/viral/WoM • Merging audiences • Adding value & responsive • Segment pull strategy/SIM
	Content generation	• Not user generated • Overt promotions/display ads • Uncoordinated	• Over corporate/official • Broadcasted/limited media • Limited value to community	• Multimedia/mobile/rich/creative • Community/staff generated • Mix of owned, bought and earned • High frequency/contributing
	Data: CRM monitoring & managing	• Manual. Not integrated • Using new tools • Not applying analytics./No KPIs	• Some CRM correlation • Using mixed tools (free) • Applying analytics • Monitoring outcomes	• Using sophisticated tools • Improving outcomes/KPIs • SEM/Social CRM/CRM integration • Used for segmentation

Figure 5.7   Social media marketing capability assessment framework

Source: Viapoint (2012)

Define clear social media marketing responsibilities for each business function and each role within these.

Define how each business area contributes to improving social media marketing and the responsibilities they have. Define overall management of strategy, monitoring and improvement.

There are many governance issues to be considered across all types of company: these are some to consider. You may recognize these as the McKinsey 7Ss:

- *Strategy* – you'll have this covered through following the advice in this chapter.
- *Structure* – is a separate team (or resource) needed in a smaller company?
- *Systems* – are new ways of working, new processes required? These types of changes are arguably the biggest; they require a look at the process of new product development, customer service, marketing campaigns and brand development. Less important, systems can refer to new tools.
- *Shared values* – how are cultural shifts shared?
- *Skills* – are new team skills required?
- *Style* – change to organization culture?
- *Staff* – change in roles?

Having the right evaluation and monitoring tools and using them is also a key transformation success factor which relates to systems, skills and staff. We'll talk more about this in the next step.

US-based social media consultant Olivier Blanchard ('The BrandBuilder') recommends that social media management must be designed to plug into all business functions from market research to customer service so that they each have a role.

There does need to be a single point of control of the strategy and resources for managing activities, as suggested by the graphic (Figure 5.7), but there should be clear goals and responsibilities for social media marketing for each team:

- *Sales* – use to support lead generation, increase purchase frequency and category penetration
- *Customer support* – deliver immediate feedback and response, positive impact in public forums, cost reduction
- *Human resources* – manage employee social interactions, more efficient recruiting, online monitoring of employee behaviour
- *Public relations* – manage online reputation management, partner outreach to encourage advocacy, improved brand image via customer advocacy
- *Marketing* – understand customer needs, manage social communications, encourage social sharing, harness insight.

Even in smaller companies, where there isn't a separate function for each, someone needs to make sure these happen.

Transformation factor 4. Define or refine social media governance policy

Whether you're unleashing your workforce on social media as part of the brand or just letting them participate in social media on a personal level, having a governance policy in place allows everyone in the company to take part but within parameters set by you.

The debate has long raged about social media in the workplace and how it enables businesses to grow versus distracting employees and reducing productivity. Whatever your view, the facts are that we are in an ever-connected world; whether at a computer or through mobiles, employees can and will have access to the online social world.

A social media governance policy is a suite of polices, processes and educational resources to empower and manage your employees.

We recommend this database of social media governance policies where you can learn from approaches defined by others: http://socialmediagovernance.com.

Key areas you should ensure are covered as part of your social media governance policy are:

1 *Training and education* – this is the most fundamental area for any social media governance. Empowering employees with knowledge will prevent issues and also create new opportunities. Staff are likely to see this new knowledge and skills as an opportunity to further increase their performance. Set up training sessions with your team and show examples of how staff in other business have both helped and hindered the business. Ensure that you show staff how you monitor social media as a whole and how likely the tools/software are to pick up on their business/work-oriented posts as well. Give clarity on how this affects work/brand/business-related activity only; their personal posts are still private and confidential.

2 *Do's and Don'ts* – creating a top-level list of Do's and Don'ts will help staff understand the boundaries of their social media activity in the workplace. Make these playful; always bear in mind that if people want to access these networks they can, easily, on their personal phones. Restricting and blocking access to such items doesn't necessarily mean less time on them or increased productivity. Be clear that it's acceptable and no one will ever be questioned, as long as performance is where it needs to be and people are on schedule.

3 *Brand guidelines* – most large brands have a set of guidelines or books on how to communicate to represent the brand. Ensure that your social media policy is in this book/guidelines and that training and management personnel make sure it is understood and followed. The etiquette and running of the business will directly affect staff and therefore what they are likely to say about the brand in their own personal networks.

4 *Reviewing brand personality and vision* – this is what we have always called the brand essence; it's a positioning, but applied to what people engage with and want to experience. We think brand personality is a great way to think about it. For Jay Baer, author of the Convince and Convert blog, it's 'Your One Thing' . . . you seek to communicate.

We like the way Rohit Bhargava describes it as personality.

> *Personality is the unique, authentic, and talkable soul of your brand that people can get passionate about.*
>
> *Personality is not just about what you stand for, but how you choose to communicate it. It is also the way to reconnect your customers, partners, employees, and influencers to the soul of your brand in the new social media era.*
>
> *(Bhargava, 2008)*

A vision for the future

Here we're not talking about an overall vision or mission statement; instead, to get others on board, you need to show how social media can transform your organization as it's integrated with other channels.

E-MARKETING EXCELLENCE

EMC communicates social media vision to its employees through video

In this example from B2B technology hardware and services company EMC, a large company tackles the tough job of convincing sceptical employees who ask in a light-hearted way 'What's the point in social media?' As you can see, it shows that social media is nothing new, simply that technology now helps us to communicate in a way we always have since the time of the caveman.

Figure 5.8 shows the employee YouTube clip (http://youtube/ah8aHIsAJfc) from the blog of Keith Paul (@Kempipa, http://twitter.com/kemipa), the 'Chief Listener' at EMC.

Figure 5.8   EMC employee social media marketing benefits communication video

Source: EMC social media caveman, uploaded on 27 June 2011 (http://youtube/ah8aHIsAJfc)

SECTION SUMMARY 5.3

We reviewed these social media marketing activities which together will form your strategy for social media marketing:

1 Listen and manage reputation
2 Transform the brand through social media
3 Approaches to acquire new customers
4 Approaches to increase sales to existing customers
5 Approaches to deliver customer service
6 How to harness insights to develop the brand using social media optimization (SMO)

5.4 Social listening and online reputation management

In this section, we explain how to put in place the people, process and tools needed for effective listening.

'*Listen first!*' is the advice most social media consultants and agencies give when discussing the creation of a social media strategy. We agree! Improving the way you listen to conversations will help you through improving your insights on:

- *Market understanding*. Understand issues that your prospects and customers discuss for your market so you know which types of conversations are interesting to your audience, so that you can stimulate and participate in them. Market and customer needs should feed into new product development plans.

- *Brand mentions*. How popular is your brand compared to those of competitors (share of voice)? Which issues are discussed around your brand? What is the 'sentiment polarity'? This jargon term means the proportion of positive to negative mentions compared to competitors.

- *Influencer identification*. Influencers are core to your social marketing strategy; they help spread your brand to outposts beyond your current network. They give you instant reach, credibility and often are cheaper/more cost-effective than media spend in reaching your audience. An influencer could be an industry blogger with great content and good site traffic or a regular Twitter member with a large following. Identify the key influencers in your industry and using the steps below, look at how to utilize them appropriately

- *Partner development*. Related to influencers, this means identifying publishers or major sites you can use for strategic partnerships or to get involved in their discussions.

- *Content and campaign ideas*. Use social listening to find out which content assets or 'social objects' are shared – is it infographics, videos or images? How do companies run their campaigns? This relates, for example, to the frequency of campaigns, how they keep them sustained through repeating offers.

- *Negative comments*. Managing and responding to negative comments about your brand.

- *Sales opportunities*. Identifying leads and sales opportunities – particularly important for social media marketing.
- *Product and service development*. All of the above can help you understand customer needs.

There are two types of online listening, defined best by Stephen Rappaport, author of *Listen First!* (2011):

- *Social monitoring*. Tracking online brand mentions on a daily basis for PR, brand protection, operations and customer service outreach and engagement.
- *Social research*. Analysing naturally occurring online categories of conversation to better understand why people do what they do, the role of brands in their lives and the product, branding and communications implications for brand owners.

Each form of listening has a unique purpose. Social monitoring is continuous to enable reporting on conversation volume and to respond to events. For example, dealing with negative feedback or upset customers is one example of an outcome from social monitoring. Social research is more strategic and ad hoc and is used for campaign planning, new product development or improving the online experience.

There is also a third type of social listening, which is where you proactively ask existing customers or site visitors for their feedback in a structured way. We've identified five different types of online customer feedback tools to help you select the right tool:

1 *Voice of customer web site feedback tools and software*. These provide a permanent facility for customers to give feedback by prompts on every page. See http://bit.ly/smartfeedback
2 *Crowdsourcing feedback tools and software*. Put simply, this is crowdsourced structured social research. The example below from UserVoice shows how a brand asked selected customers to make recommendations for improvement to the brand
3 *Simple page or concept feedback tools*. Get feedback on a web site or visual design concept
4 *Customer intent–action tools*. Assess the success of and satisfaction with web site visits
5 *General online survey tools*. These are surveys that you encourage completion of through email marketing.

You may know the Dell IdeaStorm site (www.dellideastorm.com) where Dell gets ideas for improvements to products from users and then feeds back to them. Using tools such as UserVoice to complement social monitoring and social research offers amazing insights into your business from a customer's perspective. The beauty of tools such as UserVoice is that it not only allows you to put customers in the driving seat of your business, but you can also keep them informed on the progress of their ideas/feedback by updating the status.

WHAT SHOULD WE LISTEN TO?

A simple question, but it needs to be asked. You can't listen to everything and the tools aren't clever enough to do this automatically, so you have to set the scope of conversations you want to listen to. This means, that to start, you need to think about social media keyword analysis.

SOCIAL MEDIA KEYWORD ANALYSIS

The best approach to listening is to define a limited set of trigger words contained within phrases to listen out for.

We suggest three main types of keyphrase with these corresponding types of mentions:

- *Brand conversations about you.* Your brand name and sub-brands
- *Competitor conversations.* Your competitor brands
- *Market conversations.* Products and services you offer.

In addition to specifying keywords in these areas, check to see where keywords aren't relevant for use. These are similar to the 'negative matches' in Google Adwords. For example, if you're looking for phrases related to sportswear, but you don't offer ski clothing, you should exclude this.

THE MAIN TYPES OF SOCIAL LISTENING TOOLS

To refine your social media listening, you can use these tools:

1 Search engines

- free: Google Realtime, Blog, Discussion, Alerts, Reader
- free: Twitter Advanced Search.

These are simple, free tools for top-level review, but they don't include sentiment analysis. Still, a process needs to be in place to extract the insights and set up the appropriate action.

2 Specialist social media monitoring and analysis (see also Emarketing Insight box below on selecting tools for social media listening and online reputation management).

These include bother-free and paid options:

- free: WhosTalkin.com, Social Mention
- paid (low-cost): Viralheat, UverVu, Trackur (these services may be better value when they are included as part of search marketing analysis tools; for example, Raven Tools or SEOmoz)
- paid (enterprise tools): Radian6, Alterian SM2, Sysomos.

This type of listening tool varies a lot in terms of features and therefore potential uses. These tools generally offer some social research features as well as monitoring features, meaning you can usually extract more value from them by tweaking the configuration.

3 Customer communities: currently, there are relatively few tools in this category. The two primary tools in this area are UserVoice (www.uservoice.com) and UserEcho (www.userecho.com) because they are based on crowdsourced ideas and feedback, which is different to Kampyle and the like which are much more 'score our business'-oriented.

These tools operate solely in the structured research area, but complement other listening tools.

EMARKETING INSIGHT

Checklist – selecting tools for social media listening and online reputation management

Consider these ten points before deciding which tool(s) are most relevant for you.

☑ 1 *What's included in the data sets*? Does it cover blogs (via RSS feeds or crawlers), Tweets, Facebook Likes, reviews, comments, forums, etc.?

☑ 2 *What are the data sources and how does harvesting occur*? Is the data taken from third-party providers or is the data collected in-house through a crawler (similar to the way that Google crawls the web). An important point to consider is if the provider offers the ability to go back in time over 30 days or six months as data is regularly dropped out by third-party providers, thus providing a diluted view of days gone by.

☑ 3 *How is the data cleaned and prepared*? What process does the provider go through to manage duplicates, SPAM, forum threads, etc. You want to avoid double-counting or duplicating responses to customers.

☑ 4 *How is the data organized or segmented*? Is the remaining content relevant to the business questions being asked? What are the base, volume and discussion sources being included for classification? How is the data being segmented so it contains the most pertinent consumer discussions around your specific area of interest?

Key ways of grouping or filtering information are:

- By brand
- By product category or type
- By country.

Basic tools will only report against individual keywords or long lists of keywords. Grouping is essential to compare products. For example, Radian6 enables grouping of product-related keywords in its set-up and separate profiles for competitors.

☑ 5 *How is the data being analysed and are actionable insights delivered*? Is sentiment purely done by automated technology or by human analysis, or both? Can the system help you determine what the important topics are that lead volume or drive a particular sentiment? Does the system use an influence index of some sort to identify key persons around sectors/conversations?

☑ 6 *Can key influencers be readily identified?* To decide how to manage a negative mention, you need to see how important the site with it is. Tools vary in the way they assess influence and they don't all link to other systems like Klout. Mentions on Facebook or Twitter typically show the number of fans or followers. But for blogs, it can be harder to assess their influence – this may be based on Google PageRank, number of comments or number of links.

☑ 7 *How actionable are the insights and how should they be implemented?* Is there a consulting service so that information and data can be transformed into insight? Consumer-generated media is a vast and ever-changing form of media and many organizations need to rely on the expertise and experience of a well-seasoned research team. While data can be informational, consumer-generated media insights are powerful building blocks that can be used to transform and prepare an organization for the changing digital landscape.

☑ 8 *What workflow support is there?* Related to making the tool actionable, the better-quality tools enable you to manage follow-up through forwarding conversations to others in sales or support for action, and then their action taken and the outcome is included in the system.

☑ 9 *How much will it cost? What is the payment model for the service?* Most listening tools have a Pay Per Use service model based on the number of queries or searches done. This can make it difficult to evaluate the cost until you have done the keyword research. It will depend on the number of keywords you have defined in your category and how popular the competitors are. If Apple or Nike are your competitors, expect to pay.

☑ 10 *What are the hidden costs?* Configuring the keywords to monitor and customizing reports are often not quick to complete. There may be additional costs for training or report configuration which you should compare for different suppliers.

Smart Insights has a comprehensive analysis of more than 25 tools at http://bit.ly/smartlistening.

DEFINE APPROACH FOR RESPONDING TO BRAND MENTIONS

An obvious follow-on from social listening is responding; if you are listening and alert to customers' feedback, responding is a fundamental output in ensuring you are active and respected by your audience.

This could be responding to negative feedback or participating in active conversations.

How Dell responds to social media marketing mentions

Dell has created a process which, aligned to their brand guidelines, allows them to manage their social media presence as shown in Figure 5.9.

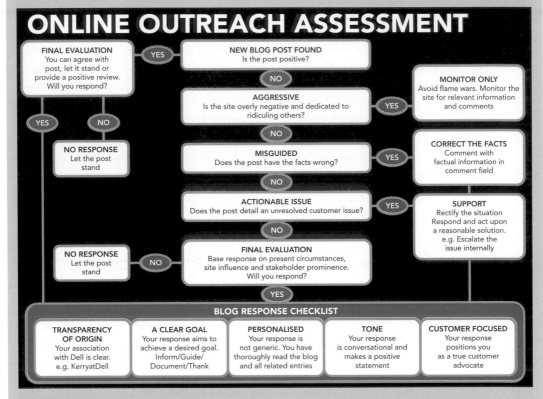

Figure 5.9   Social media governance process from Dell (2009)

Source: Presented by Kerry Bridge of Dell at an E-consultancy Masterclass

Building on these flow diagrams and aligning them to your brand guidelines is a key element both in becoming an active brand in social media, but also in empowering members of the business to be active on behalf of the brand.

Social listening is valuable not only to find negative mentions which may need to be responded to, but for finding potential influencers or media partners with whom you can work to 'spread your word'. There are many different types of tools for social media monitoring. The more expensive tools have features to enable filtering and follow-up on mentions.

5.5 Develop the content marketing and engagement strategy for your brand

You often hear the saying '*we need a social media strategy*', but to make the most of social media requires broader questions to be asked. For example, a customer engagement or communications strategy or content strategy is really part of a social media strategy. We believe you need to answer how you plan to engage customers with content as a core part of your social strategy. In addition to the Ladder of Engagement (3.10), using this approach gives a broader perspective, looking at how you engage customers across channels.

If we start with a definition of content marketing, you'll immediately see how important it is to social media.

We introduced content marketing in Chapter 1; in this chapter, we'll get Joe Pulizzi of the Content Marketing Institute to recommend how it is tackled.

E-MARKETING INSIGHT

Joe Pulizzi on content marketing

Joe describes content as: 'How a brand creates, delivers and governs original or curated content to attract and retain customers, positioning the brand as a credible expert and, ultimately, motivating a change in behaviour.'

Some of the key marketing principles that Joe Pulizzi espouses (Pulizzi and Barrett, 2010) are:

1 *Content must have intrinsic value.* Content is a key part of your online value proposition. You must define its relevance to customers – help them live their lives, do their work better.
2 *Understand what content customers value.* You need to do the research to understand the value.
3 *Content marketing strategy may completely or partially replace traditional advertising and marketing.* You need to prove the relative importance of content marketing within your budget, for your market.
4 *Get your customers to participate.* Yes, interaction is the name of the game online – don't just push, engage and share: comments, polls and surveys all help.
5 *Make it easy to buy.* Content must fit with your ultimate goal in investing in content.

Here are the key questions to ask, based on Joe Pulizzi's book *Get Content, Get Customers* (Pulizzi and Barrett, 2010), to help you develop a purpose for your content:

- *What do our buyers really need to know about our products, about information and anything relevant to what we have to offer?* There's what you want to say (or sell) and what the audience are looking for to make a decision.

- *What's the intersection between our expertise around the products or services and the information or entertainment needs of our consumer?* Map them to reveal the sweet spots.
- *How does what they need to know align with our unique expertise to create the best content?* What are the priority areas where there's a really great fit?
- *How do we position content for maximum impact and what media types will be most relevant?* Think back to personality and being authentic in how you communicate; it has to be natural too.
- *What will provide our consumers with most benefit personally or professionally?* Your aim is to add maximum value.

We think it's interesting that to answer these questions satisfactorily requires varied types of quality content which support product purchase decisions, customer service and customer engagement. So let's now take a look at the content.

Today, content is an integral part of many brands, so identifying the sweet spot for content to engage your audience and add value for them is crucial. Dan Bosomworth of Smart Insights recommends that you start by answering these questions (Smart Insights, 2012):

- *Do we have an overriding purpose for our content to deliver commercial goals through delivering relevance for the audience?*
- *How do we differentiate from the bland pack by having a perspective, a position, or if appropriate, a real attitude?*
- *Can we develop a personality that can shine through our online content, but really irrespective of the media?* This one is a key opportunity to engage your audience to comment and share your content. A great reference is Rohit Bhargava's site and book (2008) *Personality Not Included* (www.personalitynotincluded.com).

CREATING PERSONAS FOR CONTENT MARKETING

Experts increasingly emphasize the importance of knowing who your consumers are in order to increase the relevance of products. The concept also applies well to understanding customer content needs, and can be used to assess the relevance of content to different audiences.

We have covered the value and process of creating personas in Chapter 4.

To develop a content plan, you have to go back to basics, asking what content is used now by you and your competitors and for what purpose. You can then go on to look at particular formats and topics.

Auditing your current content and its effectiveness is the starting point on the journey to making content more effective, and it can also be crucial to prove to senior managers the value of investment so far in content marketing.

If your audience has a particular set of problems or issues and it is clear from the content gap research that your product or service can address it, then you'll want to focus there. Maybe there are immediately clear opportunities to help your product or service become more buyable, assuming your current content does not meet those needs already. It's a not so simple case of listing those priorities for the audience against the content you already have that is either missing from the site, or is available but is not being used well enough. Perhaps you have content, but in the wrong media format; maybe it's not findable on the site or just isn't resonating with your audience at all in communications terms.

CONTENT TYPES (FORMATS) TO FUEL CONTENT CAMPFIRES

Content formats vary and it's dependent on your story and the position that you want to take, and of course how your target market would find it easiest to consume, as to what can work for your brand. Logically, it's best to have content in a range of formats which work for different audiences. The key really is to be efficient with the media chosen and start with tangible and useful topics that your audience can understand.

Rather than simply re-posting content across several platforms, recreate fresh, supplemental content that answers questions and/or spurs discussion on a topic or idea in new ways. In her book *Content Rules*, Anne Handley (Handley and Chapman, 2010) talks about *'content campfires'*. Social media commentator Chris Brogan also uses this analogy and it's useful in visualizing the challenge. You layer on the *twigs, sticks and logs only when the fire is burning on tinder*. It's a useful metaphor to keep in mind when planning.

To get you thinking, here are some of the major content formats that we'd recommend that you can feature and seed within your social media marketing. Check them for relevance. Each can be used for consumer or business audiences, but some work better for B2B:

- Video – recorded and edited video including animated or explainer videos
- E-books or shorter guides including article content (web page, or short documents) and white papers
- Podcast and audio shared for iPod or MP3 player consumption. Think about the audio from videos for MP3 consumption as well as turning the audio to transcripts
- Webinars which can be recorded and streamed media
- Infographics – a flexible, shareable way to tell a brand story or explain a concept
- Q&As and FAQs.

Suitable formats to consider, with examples you can learn from within the digital marketing content area, are:

- Short-form news updates or opinion pieces (www.clickz.com or www.sethgodin.com)
- Long-form blog posts giving 'expert' guidance (www.viperchill.com or www.kaushik.net)
- Video blog posts (www.bannerblog.com.au, www.garyvaynerchuk.com)
- Image posts with statistics (www.wearesocial.net)
- Infographics (www.kissmetrics.com)

- Compilations aggregating other sites' content as a useful summary of statistics or tools (www.wearesocial.net, www.smartinsights.com)
- E-books, white papers and guides (www.hubspot.com and www.eloqua.com)
- Podcasts (www.boagworld.com)
- Surveys and polls (www.econsultancy.com and www.smartinsights.com)
- Questions and answers (www.linkedin.com).

CONTENT SEEDING AND OUTREACH

Creating the content assets is only one crucial part of social media marketing. The process of outreach and seeding to share these assets is an equally important aspect, but is perhaps less easy to control, so it is often useful to outsource this activity. In Chapter 7, we look at the example of Renault, which uses blogger relations to increase the reach of their social media campaigns. Later in this chapter, we see how Nokia uses its Nokia Connects blog to update its advocates. Seeding social media content like video and infographics to journalists of traditional publications is still important, particularly since the online sites of many publications now publish these types of assets.

SECTION SUMMARY 5.5

A content strategy defines the types of content assets you need to develop to engage your target audiences through the customer lifecycle. Examples of content types include infographics, white papers or guides, videos or image galleries.

5.6 Define social media communications strategy

You *can* use an ad hoc, reactive approach to communicating through social media. You will certainly get the benefits of interaction and sharing, but with more control on your approach, opportunities for interaction and sharing your brand assets more widely will be greater.

Smart Insights (2012) recommends that to gain this extra control, you structure your social media communications strategy around the areas of the PRACE framework of the customer lifecycle. Tackling it this way will help you keep your focus on the activities that matter:

1 *Plan*. Management of social media marketing, including reputation management and defining a content strategy.
2 *Reach*. How to increase the reach of your content as it is shared.
3 *Act*. Encouraging interaction and participation within your own blogs and sites and within social outposts.
4 *Convert*. The key question – how to make the transition from customer brand engagement with social media to generating more leads and sales.
5 *Engage*. Ongoing communications with consumers.

We will now review each of these activities in more detail.

1 PLAN – CREATING A SOCIAL MEDIA COMMUNICATIONS STRATEGY

We think that some form of communications strategy is needed to use this content within social networks. Many larger companies will already have customer communications guidelines, so you can expand upon these to include more within social media communications. We recommend you ask, and answer, these questions to check you have a sound plan:

Question 1. Is our social media communications plan integrated into a broader communications plan?

A communications strategy will be very familiar to marketers. One key difference with social media marketing is that you will be communicating much more frequently than with traditional press releases or e-newsletters, so you will have to source more content and develop an efficient publishing process that maintains quality, but isn't too much of a time sink.

Facebook have developed sample 'conversation calendars' for marketers that show the need for more frequent communication.

Question 2. What is a realistic content update frequency?

Let's start with frequency, since once you have decided on this, you can then think of the types of content to support this, but you may prefer to start with content types.

Deciding the frequency of content updates on your social media hub is a difficult challenge. You will decide the right frequency based on a balance of what your audience needs and expects; what you need to meet your objectives; and what's practical with the writing resources you have.

You shouldn't fall into the trap of feeling you should try to publish new content in lots of different formats every single day, but it is important to publish on a regular and ongoing basis in relevant formats and with consistent types of content.

E-MARKETING INSIGHT

How much content is sufficient?

Here are a sample of different strategies for content frequency update for your hub.

Which of these will work best for you? It will depend a lot on your market:

- *Multiple content updates per day* – typical for a news organization with many channels and many writers. It's also likely to be needed for a clothing retailer making constant changes to its collection and promotions. You will likely need a separate editorial team to create this.

- *One or two content updates per day* – this is the sweet spot for many organizations with a blog in a market which is dynamic – a retailer offering technology products, for example. It's also the right frequency for communicating through social media – it will keep your followers/fans interested. Of course, your updates can provide additional comments, dialogue and links to others' content. Creating content at this frequency can help provide sufficient content for a weekly e-newsletter. A single dedicated blogger putting part of their time into blogging can maintain this frequency.

- *One or two content updates per week* – this frequency may be right for you if you are posting occasionally to social media, but it's not a primary channel for you. It's also likely to be the right frequency if you have a monthly e-newsletter since it will help you develop sufficient content for this.

- *One or two content updates per month* – this frequency may be better for smaller companies with limited resources or in a niche that doesn't warrant so many updates, perhaps because repeat customer purchases are less common – financial services or will writing, for example!

A good example of the tactic of fewer quality updates is the Viperchill blog (www.viperchill.com), where the author, Glen Allsopp, just published one or two very detailed posts every month. Avinash Kaushik (www.kaushik.net) uses a similar approach on his blog about web analytics and has built up a passionate following.

If you adopt one of the shorter frequencies, remember that there is less potential for your content to be amplified. Higher frequencies tend to be best for growth of reach. However, there is a maximum frequency. Research by Dan Zarrella (www.danzarrella.com) shows that the optimum content frequency for Facebook seems to be about once per day.

Question 3. Content value: types, formats and proposition defined?

There is a tendency to get stuck in the rut of one format, but this works well for some, who become known for the format such as long-form or video blogs. But it can limit the appeal of the publisher. For example ClickZ tends to focus on short, limited-length posts. The Digital Buzz Blog just publishes case studies. These will engage, and it's useful to have a format you're known for, but it may not appeal to a range of audiences, so could limit your reach.

Great content solves problems for your audience, largely so they can make a decision about something (*you probably want the decision to be related to future purchase of something from you, at some point*). This should be self-evident from a visit to your hub or reading your content, but to drive people to the hub from elsewhere on the web or offline, it helps if you have well-thought-through messaging, explaining how the content will help solve problems.

Question 4. Do we have an editorial calendar and process to manage content formally, including integration between media?

An editorial calendar helps both to develop the right types of content and schedules for content production. Without an effective editorial calendar and a person to control it, content quality will definitely suffer.

Often, editors and writers are more interested in writing than in social media marketing and search keywords, so make sure that at least some of the content is targeting the keyphrases and types of searches that customers make.

Question 5. Do we have a content hub platform in place to manage publication and syndication of the content selected?

What do we mean by a hub? Essentially it's a place around which you can grow a network of interested individuals, *a place where interaction or engagement with your content and your brand can take place*. This interaction will happen because of the quality of your content marketing.

Think of the hub as the home for your content, a place for feedback and dialogue and the connector to a number of outposts where your brand is present (Facebook, SlideShare, etc.) and being shared and discussed. You can increasingly use a social network like Facebook as the place to build your hub, but Facebook is not an asset you can truly own in terms of features and functions, so that is risky (you never know!). Facebook also remains external to your main brand presence, so we'd suggest that a hub is the bridge between your commercial or main web site and external outposts like Facebook.

At the physical level of a site, the content hub can be:

- A blog – effectively the home page
- A customer magazine
- Your online news section
- A resource centre.

Does the label matter? Yes, it will vary by audience; so often in B2B, 'blog' or 'news' is the best approach, whereas consumers may not be so familiar with 'blog', so a 'magazine' may be the best label. A good example is www.asdamagazine.com; this uses the WordPress blog platform, but is positioned as a magazine.

Question 6. Have we defined internal resource to create and manage content and discussions in place?

We have separately identified internal and external resourcing, since we don't believe content creation for your social hub is a task you can completely outsource. You will have to decide which of the tasks are managed externally. In a small company, all tasks would typically be internal. Tasks to consider include:

- Define communications strategy – define content frequency, types and formats
- Define editorial calendar
- Create content – write copy, record videos, create infographics
- Review content
- Publish content on content hub

- Publish and syndicate content to other outposts
- Manage hardware platform
- Review results to improve performance
- Mark the ones that you think should be internal or external for you.

Question 7. Have we reviewed our options for external sourcing of content?

You will see that some of the content types above involve the creation of original content, and some are adding value or curating existing content by summarizing and/or aggregating it. Finding the internal resource for creating content is often a challenge. You may have experts who can contribute, but encouraging them to write in can be difficult.

Question 8. How is content syndication to other platforms managed?

This will be a combination of automation and manual interactions.

Smart Insights (2012) recommends that when new content is created, it can be automatically syndicated to the different social channels using the tools shown in Figure 5.10.

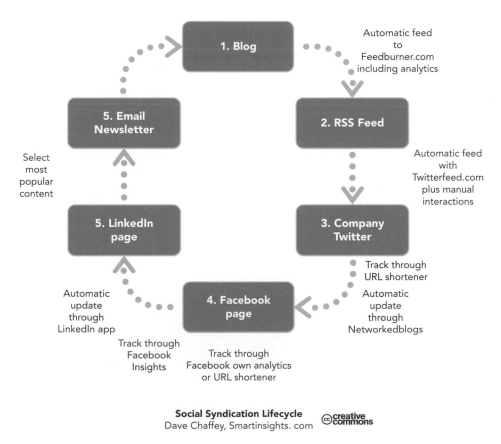

Social Syndication Lifecycle
Dave Chaffey, Smartinsights. com ©creative commons

Figure 5.10   Content syndication hub

Although we're advocating saving time here by syndicating, we need to be careful not just to push or SHOUT – the beauty of social media is that it's a two-way street enabling conversations and dialogue. So manual interactions with each of the social networks to ask and answer questions is also recommended, as we've said before.

Question 9. How is outreach to other sites and influencers managed?

There's a tendency to put the bulk of your personal time and the bulk of your budget and resource into your site, but reaching outwards is more important and more challenging.

We stressed the importance of seeding your content in Section 5.5; here, we'll go into more detail on this key part of your social media strategy. Great content will spread naturally, but it will reach more people through putting in the time to identify key influencers.

Seeding works best if you put resources into managing and communicating with your key influencers. But influencers will vary in importance and value, so as with working with other partners like affiliates, it's important to segment your influencers and lavish more attention on the most significant ones.

As an example of this need to prioritize, Nokia Connects is run by the Digital & Social Media division within Nokia with support from a specialist agency to create content and seed updates about new content and devices.

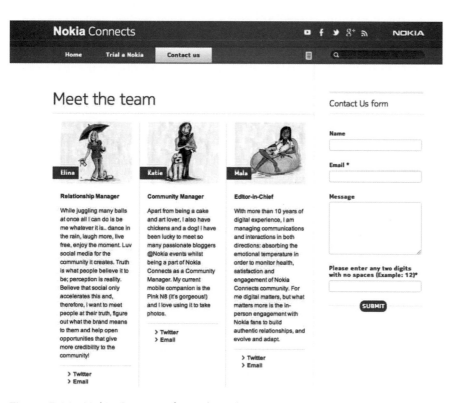

Figure 5.11   Nokia Connects for Nokia advocates (www.nokiaconnects.com)

E-MARKETING INSIGHT

Five steps to an influencer strategy according to Dan Bosomworth

In Smart Insights (2012), Dan Bosomworth makes these five recommendations to build an influencer strategy:

1 *Identify your influencers.* The most important influencers depend on a combination of popularity and expertise (perceived or real).

2 *What's in it 'for me'.* Consider your current relationship with your influencer; are they inactive or already an ambassador? Armed with this information, consider a means to engage and increase the influencer's involvement with you and value to you.

3 *Set goals and listen.* Work out what you are trying to achieve (traffic, word of mouth, product launch, better conversion). Before defining the right influencers to work with and how best to engage them, you need to be clear on the ambitions of your influencer programme.

4 *Develop relationships.* The most important part. Find out where your advocates congregate and open a dialogue. This takes time and persistence to get on the radar – be sure to consistently participate and offer information and insights that add value to the conversation. Read their discussion threads, blog posts and any other information you can lay your hands on. What are they saying, how they are saying it and why? What are their interests and motivations? You want to appear human and accessible to any customer you encounter online, step it up for the influencers that matter. Send them products, pitch ideas and ask for their opinions. Leave comments on blog posts. Send @ replies on Twitter. 'Like' a status update on Facebook. Again, focus on the primary influencers – the ones that get you traction – and remember that for each influencer, you need to choose the right way to start building a relationship. It might be best to engage them in their spaces – e.g. responding to their blog posts. Alternatively, you may want to contact them offline to arrange face-to-face meetings.

5 *Avoid self-promotion or direct marketing.* Some influencers are ready and willing to further your cause and are happy to agree a commercial arrangement to achieve this. Others eschew all commercial influence. If you are uncertain of which category someone fits into, take care in your first interactions. If they have a relationship with you that is already built on trust and respect, and you don't try to sell to them, but rather offer products, information and insight for their consumption, they're more likely to value what you give to them and share it with their own audiences, particularly if they believe your product or business can benefit their audiences.

Question 10. Communication through advertising, PR and email marketing of social media/community proposition/content proposition to existing customers and prospects?

This final planning issue is arguably the easiest to manage. It's about clarity and consistency of messaging to present your brand in a favourable, shareable way through social media. You should:

- *Demonstrate uniqueness.* It must be your story, something that no one else could tell. Work your story to create a distinct 'voice' and point of view – your personality is your differentiator. Don't aim to be the same, since you are then a part of the noise. Think about what your ideal product story sounds like – the components that make it a good story for your business; then figure out how you build on that. Stand for something, polarize the market and above all, be honest and genuine. People buy that.

- *Keep it relevant.* Relate back to your audience, their perspective, what they talk about, and what they're anxious about. Address those concerns by demonstrating that you 'get it'. Tell stories of ways your products relieved customer anxieties and demonstrate social proof where you can.

- *Demonstrate value.* Incorporate specifics to make your story credible and believable. Discuss results and benefits that are directly relevant to your target audience's needs.

- *Make it memorable.* Connect with the target audience on an emotional level. Be remarkable, inspiring even. Create something that is easy and fun to gossip about and, importantly, shareable. Remarkable can be as simple as changing to a video blog for valuable expert interviews once each month; it can be that you're co-creating content with a non-conflicting super-brand or celebrity, who knows.

- *Incorporate your brand.* Be sure to build on top of your brand tone of voice; brand is a bit vague, so specifically: your core promise, expectation, personality and how you aim to make people feel – the bit they have the relationship with.

- *Be human. The Cluetrain Manifesto* (Levine *et al.*, 2000) stated this over ten years ago. We're all human, so be that way. Be a little controversial, polarize the market, avoid jargon, break a few rules. You are also serving and solving problems in order to sell, so become a reliable and valuable resource. Of course, you have to be appropriate for your own audience, just push the boundaries – write differently, since words matter.

Well, these are the key questions to ask to help plan your social media strategy and its implementation. Next we look at specific approaches to engage customers through the PRACE customer engagement lifecycle.

2 REACH

With *planning* covered, look next at specific techniques you can use to reach new audiences through social media in a planned, structured way.

Technique 1. Target the most relevant audience segments

Your audience demographic, all the people that you could market to, vary in their importance in two key ways:

- *Commercial relevance* – is it likely buyers whom the content will drive closer to purchase?
- *Amplification relevance* – is it likely your content is going to motivate them to either share and amplify your brand, or drive them further towards purchase?

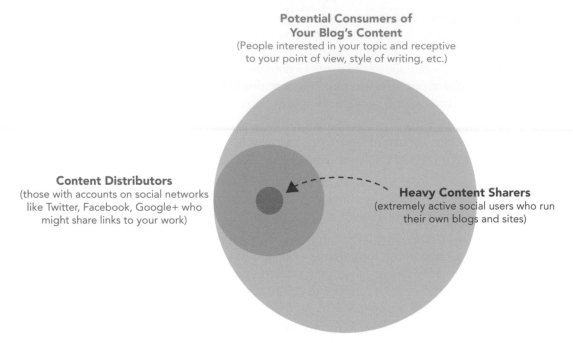

**Potential Consumers of
Your Blog's Content**
(People interested in your topic and receptive
to your point of view, style of writing, etc.)

Content Distributors
(those with accounts on social networks
like Twitter, Facebook, Google+ who
might share links to your work)

Heavy Content Sharers
(extremely active social users who run
their own blogs and sites)

Figure 5.12   A summary of the influence and activity of different blog audiences

Source: SEOmoz (2012)

Figure 5.12 by Rand Fishkin of SEOmoz shows this simple concept well.

Though you can try to appeal to lots of people, the reality of time and resources is that focusing on the audience most likely to amplify your message for you will probably give the best return on time and effort. How you do this is your influencer strategy, as outlined in the Emarketing Insights box above.

Technique 2. Fish where the fish are

This is one of our favourite social media expressions, although it's been used in areas as diverse as advertising, PR and direct marketing in the past.

Your core audience segments will differ from the masses, as will those influencers with the largest propensity to share – this means they're easier to connect with than you might think. You probably already know a few blogs, forums, web sites and/or social communities where discussions and content are being posted on your topic (and if you don't, a Google search will take much guesswork away). Take a targeted approach to finding your next customer, fish where the fish are.

An obvious free tool to help is the DoubleClick Ad Planner (see the web links at the end of the chapter).

When you do get involved in these marketing outposts, remember, of course, to add real value and be a good web marketer. That way you'll be rewarded with trust and, ultimately, traffic.

Spamming, trolling and aimless *'link-dropping''* will get you the boot, or worse, a bad reputation in a space where you want to build respect.

Technique 3. Listen up and leverage data

Think about the intelligence or insight that you can gather by collecting information that shows customer concerns in a market from multiple angles such as those key influencers, the topics that garner most traction – and why.

Social listening software is too powerful to mildly observe, make sure you follow up on new opportunities to grow your influence. This means doing social media keyword analysis as we described in the section on listening, so you find the conversations in blogs and forums that relate to your market.

Technique 4. Get involved in conversations the right way

When participating on blogs and forums, understand the language and terms that your audience uses. You need to keep your natural brand tone of voice, but moderate it, within reason, to be consistent with your audience.

Technique 5. Create relevant, rich content

This is creating and seeding quality content. Generally, people like short, snappy and consumable content that teaches, entertains, inspires – otherwise why are campaigns that entertain (Lynx, Old Spice, Tippex, etc.) so popular? – or that are informative infographics on particular topics.

Relevant entertainment and information are your opportunity, not just creating any content. Get under the skin of what will inspire your audience demographics to re-share your content. Don't create great content for everyone, create it for the right someone.

Technique 6. Participate to share ideas and content with your audience and peers

This sounds obvious – so where and how might you participate? Perhaps take a look back at the social media marketing radar (Figure 5.1) and then find the most relevant platforms for you.

Here are some more ideas:

- *Guest blog or re-share content.* Find related and influential sites (or site owners) and connect with them. Focus your efforts though, only go right for the most relevant blogs. Make sure you approach with ideas and a great example that's ready to publish – make it easier to get a yes.
- *Comment in others' blogs.* As above, choose carefully where you invest that time. Have a consistent name, picture and profile – we recommend setting this up in Disqus (*www.disqus.com*) which is the default standard across many blogs, in order to build your brand

reputation more effectively. You can find top bloggers in Google's blog search, for example, as well as Follower Wonk (www.followerwonk.com).

- *Social sharing through Reddit and StumbleUpon.* The golden rule is to add value, share what you like as well, your own content should not be the majority of what is shared. So don't spam with links – work hard to be relevant and leverage your great content to best effect.

- *Use Q&A sites.* These are gold so far as rich interactions go around things people want to learn. How can you position your content to make it genuinely useful and in turn ensure strategic opportunities, and so links, back to your web site? Examples include LinkedIn Q&A, Answers.com, Quora, Yahoo! Answers and Beepl.com.

Remember that the web is alive and driven by linking. So don't be afraid to always link back to great sources of information that you're referencing as well as your own content. The benefits are, of course, twofold – you drive traffic via the link as well as tell Google how important that content is if it's a followed link.

Technique 7. Promote through thinking guerrilla

Don't be averse to learning how competitors are getting their reach, campaigns, creative and links. Understand what works and deconstruct the success of others as best you can, using tools like Radian6 and Majestic SEO. If an influencer is participating in helping a competitor in some way, then in the spirit of offering choice to their reader or follower base, they're very likely going to be interested in helping you.

Promote yourself (and your content) at every opportunity, without being annoying. Success in social, content and search engine marketing is especially born from sustained effort in the right areas. Rome was certainly not built in a day; you have to earn your way into the market. Use content that best fits what you want to promote and what the user in those networks wants to learn about. Find this sweet spot.

Technique 8. Combining email and social media marketing

It's often the case that the audience you have built as email subscribers is larger than your social media audience. So if you get the basic *critical* factors of email marketing right, then you can encourage your audience to share more through social media and so boost your overall audience. Giving a great incentive or reason to share is key. Examples of email activity that can support your social media marketing include:

- Promotional emails supporting campaigns using a social network as the hub
- Customer review and testimonial emails, or more broadly, encouraging feedback about your brand and how it is experienced using these types of tools
- Recommendations to share with your network within the email.

3 ACT (ENCOURAGE INTERACTIONS)

In this section, we look at specific communications techniques to encourage interaction on your web sites or social outposts. You can think of Act in the context of the Forrester Social Technographics Ladder (Figure 5.5), where you are encouraging those that are watching or 'lurking' to interact by contributing, getting involved.

Think of these interactions as a means of:

- *Starting a dialogue on your site* – eventually giving rise to a user registration, sales lead or transaction
- *Generating user-generated content* – this can boost conversion through social proof and help with SEO
- *Encouraging the sharing of your brand* – in the form of content, in the social networks
- *Sparking interactions between people* – facilitating the discussion
- *Supporting buyer decision making* – the site visitor learns or realizes something of value, something inspiring, ideally.

Apply these practical tips to help increase participation and sharing amongst those visitors who haven't already interacted:

- *Engagement devices* – there is a tendency for calls-to-action to focus on generating leads and sales. But softer calls-to-action, encouraging interaction, have their place too. In the social world, these devices should encourage participants to share their results with others. For example, LinkedIn uses its Maps application to encourage interaction and sharing. Devices will include a lot of the ideas you developed through your content strategy.
- *Blog interactions* – a simple way to gain interaction. Assuming your blog has relevant and interesting content, this is all about frequency and being topical – manage this process well, have a publication schedule to help you keep on-brand, on-topic and on-time. Insert actions; for example, polls to be taken. Encourage comments within the post, ask for feedback and link to other pages on your site and forum pages, etc. Ensure every post is designed to do something.
- *Gamification* – to engage consumers, social gaming can be a great way to encourage interaction and therefore reach. The Wildfire Promotion Builder shows the types of engaging promotions that can be created in the social networks such as Sweepstakes, UGC content, coupons, Pick Your Favourites, Trivia and Quizzes, Instant Wins and Voting around topics.
- *Growing your communities* – today, you will have several communities on your preferred social networks or a community integrated into your site. Think about how you use messaging on the site and within email to encourage these.
- *Social network sharing page* – make it easy for web site visitors to find your social networks through promotional panels that give a feel for the benefits of joining your community. All social networks provide widgets you can embed on your web site to do this. Additionally, you may have a page devoted to social networks that you feature in your main navigation. It's surprisingly rare, although Dell has used this approach for a long time.

- *Social sharing buttons* – these are a straightforward feature to encourage sharing, most effective on a blog and home pages, but also for product pages where they are closely related to . . .

- *Social network integration* – integrating commenting on other networks into your site is becoming more popular through *social sign-on* through the Facebook API and tools such as Gigya and Janrain. These are independent tech web services that act as an intermediary between your domain and multiple social networks. Sears has created an impressive social commerce integration that you can read about in our post 'why social sign-on matters'' (Smart Insights, 2011b).

- *Product reviews and ratings* – another forum for social commerce. The popularity of TripAdvisor, Amazon reviews and retail site Reevoo show how we love to give our opinion. This form of user-generated content is fantastic in terms of assisting conversion and contributing to SEO, so it's a must-have for retail sites. Think about how you encourage and share comments. We think the Firebox product review page is a great example – they offer spot prizes for 'amazing' contributions and all comments are in Facebook to encourage amplification.

- *Encouraging commenting* – more general UGC comments can be encouraged on blogs, social network pages or other places throughout a site. But you need to work to encourage it. It's also important to respond to comments to encourage more comments. Make sure you have someone with time available to moderate and keep the discussion going.

- *E-newsletters and other email offers* – we know many consumers and businesspeople alike will subscribe to email if it offers unique value or convenience to them. Email is a great way of encouraging participation in many of the types of site or social network engagement we've described above. Make sure you make the most of email contact to encourage social interactions.

4 CONVERT

How can social media actually drive sales? This is a key question since we know social media can encourage interactions, but how do we encourage sales? Here are our recommendations:

1. Define the leads you're looking for

- *Create buyer personas* – these were around long before social media; direct marketers have long since found that having a good picture in mind of the target customer is beneficial in terms of how we write our content to connect with our audience. Apply that to blog marketing, for example, and you can have multiple categories of content topics and so you may find that certain categories speak more to certain personas than others. And certain Facebook and Twitter updates may appeal to certain types of user. Regardless of how you segment these groups, it's incredibly beneficial to share target persona information with whoever is developing content for your social media channels.

- *Be useful* – Kristina Halvorson (*Content Strategy for the Web*, 2010) and Joe Pulizzi (*Get Content, Get Customers*), both say that if our content isn't supporting the successful fulfilment of our business objectives and your users' goals, then it's a waste of time. 'Focus on the intersection between the two', recommends Joe (Pulizzi and Barrett, 2010). Kristina suggests adding two columns to a content inventory: value to user and value to business.

2. Your blog or 'social hub' is key to generating leads

- *Prioritize subscription* – an email subscription is step one in lead generation, yet is often overlooked in lieu of offering a blog RSS feed. RSS is fine, but it'll do next to nothing for helping you gain permission marketing. Email subscription must be front and centre, with the benefits clearly explained – what would the user receive via email? A weekly or monthly round-up of your best content with the latest offers?

- *Clear calls-to-action* – every blog post should include a relevant call-to-action that is related to what the post is about. It could be that you want to deepen engagement with subscribers and step them towards engaging with your products or services in a softer way – a webinar, for example – and/or ensure that there's clear information about how to buy, the next steps for those that are interested. If you don't ask, you don't get. Ensure that you've optimized landing pages from the email so that you can appreciate the user's journey with appropriate messaging.

- *Use ad space* – a common tactic with big publishers is to have formal ad containers in blogs and emails and then define the value of engaging with them. This supports the call-to-action and you're not sending mixed messages by virtue of using a well-established protocol of driving sales leads from content interest.

- *Test JavaScript pop-ups/lightbox subscriptions* – although many don't like the intrusion, there's so much evidence to say it works and so is worth testing. Emotionally, many of us will feel that it's the interruptive hard sell that damages user experience and it's not worth it (I'd agree). But! The fact is that if conversion increases can be believed, it may be worth trying – if you do, let us know! Please do, though, include rules in the session cookies so that users aren't repeatedly bombarded once they've said 'No', and keep the communications clear and fun.

3. Have great, shareable landing pages

- *Respect the process* – it's important to have landing pages showcasing your shareable content, marketing 'objects' that are dedicated to converting visitor to lead, not sale; and in turn, lead to sale. Here, the communications are totally different. You're focusing on a part of the process at any one time, not all of it.

- *Keep focus* – when thinking about lead conversion, keep the communications on a landing page short and focused; don't capture data because you can – data capture can be based on what will improve the relevance and quality of any future communications. You're data capturing for permission at this stage, not sale.

- *Test it* – a landing page is a key part of the conversion process and it's shocking how the art of button sizes, colours, images and messaging impact on a click conversion – don't underestimate it. Apply tools like Google Website Optimizer to test different versions of the page and its elements.

4. Clear brand messages and tone of voice

- *Purpose* – retaining that clarity on your brand's compelling purpose is a fundamental. I say this since it's easy to get all 'ad-men' about the promotional side of what you offer. The truth is that, via social media especially, you also need to be clear why your brand exists, what value it adds and then demonstrate that in your content, assets, web services and social interactions. Inspire commitment from a user to become a lead in the truest sense even when just creating a blog post, just as you would in your product or service.

- *Just be human* – the whole point of social media marketing is building relationships, it's not the sum total of the tools and tactics. Failure to just be 'regular people' is a killer. Companies like Zappos are famed for this very human way of interacting; real people at Zappos will interact with customers via the customer Twitter service. There's an old adage 'people buy people'; I'd suggest social media leverages that as a huge opportunity.

- *Familiarity breeds likeability* – so many social media initiatives struggle because marketers are leveraging tactics rather than thinking about the customer experience. Brands create expectation by having a Facebook page – the consumer assumes you're actually awake and interested in conversing, naturally. So, respond at least, answer questions whilst your competitors are still asleep! Then, proactively start the discussion as resources and confidence grow.

- *Listen to conversations* – monitor conversations about both your brand and competitors'. There are many social media listening tools that will help you keep a pulse on what's being talked about, and many will flag up potential sales leads for you. The more you know, the more responsive you can be and the more relevant your communications and content.

- *Develop a consistent brand attitude* – Guy Kawasaki's book (*Enchantment*, 2012) talks a lot about having a positive, can-do attitude within social media. It sounds obvious, but if you've got one person loving their job and one not, then you're going to get 50 per cent success at best. Social media is people-based. Zappos talk about how they made it easy for poor staff to leave by paying them! This has to typify their extraordinary commitment to the power of people and their recognition that enthusiasm is contagious.

5. Ensure content breadth and depth

- *Offer variety* – people, stories, images, video, audio and words all help us think about ways to engage more fully beyond 'a blog post'. Those types of content can be expressed through a range of media including e-newsletters, blogs, white papers, articles on marketing, case studies, online tutorials and webinars. Use a good mix of content; not all users will read a case study or watch an online video. You'll increase your odds of being seen by more people by using a mix that makes sense to your market and audience.

- *Thought leadership* – share your knowledge freely in blog posts and white papers. Some businesses are afraid they'll give away all of their secrets. Yet your knowledge remains a valuable asset; shared freely in a relevant format, it's also your key to permission and lead conversion. Giving information and knowledge freely now earns the permission to sell later. Worst case – those inspired fans or prospects become amplifiers for your communications.

- *Learn what content works* – where the first step to engaging a community of potential customers is sharing content, a simple social media update won't cut it. Include links with your updates that expand on key ideas, most easily achieved on your blog. Keep in mind that your goal is to create value for your fans and followers. Learn what your audience responds to and then adjust your updates and content mix.

6. Findability and reach

- *Remember Google* – your content and social media updates via your blog, Facebook page, tweets and YouTube channel appear in search results, too. The person searching is an active user looking for your knowledge and information to solve their problem. Market your content well to create the inbound effect that HubSpot is now famous for promoting. HubSpot provides some interesting recommendations: *'Businesses must produce enough content for their blog to kick off growth in leads, which starts with about 24 to 51 posts.'* HubSpot found that more indexed pages on Google also translate to more leads. They suggest that every 50 to 100 incremental indexed pages can mean double-digit lead growth. Also improve findability within your site by using signposts to highlight the main content.

- *Engage with influencers* – this is now the staple way to grow reach. Influencers will be a mix of journalists and bloggers specific to your market or niche. You don't have to be a big company to get picked up for a story – you do need to be findable (see above) and interesting. Build relations with those influencers over time so that when you have a story to share on a topic, offer the information to one or two contacts – not everybody! HARO (Help a Reporter Out; www.haro.com) is one good way to spread information; there's also the developing of a simple social media newsroom specific for the influencer audience.

- *Social sharing tools* – help users share your content and offer ways for people to like your content by using free tools such as AddThis and ShareThis. 'Likes' are valuable votes of confidence and go a long way with users who may have come to your site for the first time. Make your content easy to share.

- *Inspire an army or, if you prefer, a 'tribe'.* This is the most important tip – your customers are best placed to help you acquire more fans and followers, and so ultimately leads and sales. Focus on this. Why? If you can keep customers engaged and inspired, then not only do they feel good about future purchases, they are powerful amplifiers to share your story with. I think this is the most important point and yet, ironically, it's not about lead acquisition, it's all about thrilled customers.

5 ENGAGE

Consider these outreach approaches to engagement, which can be used both within your content hub and beyond, and on other sites:

- *Become part of the community.* Find ways to interact with the audience you want to reach. Monitor their online conversations and (crucially) identify the influential active members that are on your hub. Go to other sites that are active, participate in their conversations, and even comment on their blogs. Develop a blogging persona with whom they can connect and relate. Address their experiences and the issues they're facing. Assist them through your content. Talk about your brand, product and service only in the context of that larger topic; demonstrate how your offering is a practical part of the solution.

- *Shift control to your fans.* Help them expose others to your content, social objects and ultimately your brand. Provide them with the understanding, tools and inspiration to create content with you. Let them comment and write in their own voices, and let that independent perspective shine through. Give them ownership, and trust them to create good content that will resonate with the community. Promote their content, and help them to be successful through integrating free tools such as the Facebook Comments plug-in or paid versions such as Gigya (www.gigya.com).

- *Feed your fans.* Give them an incentive to be a fan and to evangelize. Make them feel good about being a fan. Listen to them, interact with them, and relate to their experiences. Use social media tools to converse in real time. Create community, identity and connection. Hear and implement their ideas and requests, and make good use of their contributions. Give them a sense of ownership in your successes. Show appreciation, and make big gestures. Demonstrate that you are thinking about them and their needs. Fashion company ASOS are very good at organizing events to help this.

- *It's a team job.* Disperse the responsibility for content creation among several individuals internally; even motivate individuals within your organization to contribute to the company blog by casually discussing potential ideas/topics with them, running contests, and getting key stakeholders (like the CEO) involved. Hire freelance talent to produce a volume of content more quickly on a regular basis – this may be important for a new launch or campaign.

- *Optimize your content.* It's important to remember why you're doing this – the commercial reasons. So ensure that you're tracking what works; pay attention to open and click rates to maintain a pulse on whether the content is resonating with your audience and influencing tangible outcomes like reach, fan, follower, lead and customer volumes that you can attribute back to all the content efforts. Link to your content from your various social media profiles to draw people back to your hub and build SEO – at the end of the day, we're still marketing.

Many of the techniques we covered in the section on encouraging interactions also apply within this section. For example, ASOS offers one-on-one style advice which is featured through Twitter and Facebook.

Delivering customer service through social media

Another key aspect of engaging customers is delivering customer service, yet the quality of response of many companies within social media often seems lacking.

Customer service in social media marketing

The importance of not neglecting customer service can be seen from a Social Media Leadership Forum report (Currah, 2012) which suggested how many people do complain or try to resolve a problem online. Over 44 per cent of adults now use the web to share grievances about products, with customers expecting to interact with companies online and get a speedy response.

The report emphasizes the need to put in place a sound way to manage new customer-service queries. This is the overall social CRM process it recommends – ten actions to put in place the right method to respond:

1 Appointment of an executive *team to oversee the transition* to social CRM, comprising representatives from a cross-section of the enterprise

2 A *detailed audit* of the social customer to understand where conversations take place that currently encompass and influence the company's brand

3 *Identify platforms* on which the company needs *to establish a presence*, adjusted for legal and regulatory obligations

4 *Create a multi-channel strategy for customer service*, taking into account capabilities of the existing operation

5 *Update staff training and communications guidelines* to incorporate desired best practices relating to customer engagement via social media

6 Review opportunities to *strengthen and streamline connections* between the customer-service operation and key business units

7 *Define the operational specifications of social CRM*, incorporating results of steps 3–6, as a basis to identify a shortlist of suitable vendors

8 *Evaluate the cost and features of chosen vendors*, including their ability to integrate media monitoring and/or community management platforms

9 *Consultation period with chosen social CRM vendor* to plan for the process of implementation and staff training

10 *Define metrics to assess the performance* of social CRM in terms of customer satisfaction and operating costs.

We applaud all of these, but opportunities to use social CRM to learn about new product/service requirements or develop advocacy aren't emphasized.

SECTION SUMMARY 5.6

The social media strategy details how content and process can be combined to facilitate C2B and C2C interactions that assist in progressing customers through a customer relationship we have discussed through the PRACE framework of Plan–Reach–Act–Convert–Engage.

5.7 Define approaches for the core social media platforms

Most companies already make use of brand pages on the main social networks like Facebook, Google+, LinkedIn or Twitter. Your company will likely have a presence and be posting status updates to share news and engage your followers. But how do you improve your use of these key social platforms?

In this section, we will show how you can review your existing presence; there are also issues to consider when creating a new presence on each of the networks. As part of this, we will cover lots of practical tips you can apply. We will do this first by reviewing general techniques you can apply across brand pages and second by recommending communications approaches across the social networks. In this section, we look at general principles of communicating using social platforms. We will get into the specifics of each of the platforms in a series of guides focusing on each network. So this section won't give you an in-depth guide to each network, but it will enable you to perform a quick health check of your performance on each.

Each social media platform can serve a different purpose for the individual, business or organization. You will find that for each brand, the platforms tend to attract different users and offer different features to engage them. The tone of voice used and interactions are quite different too, so a 'one-size-fits-all' communication strategy for each platform is definitely not the way forward. However, there are common issues to managing use of these platforms that need an agreed approach. There are also common tools to help communicate with your audience through each of these platforms.

DEVELOPING INDEPENDENT COMMUNITIES

It's also worth remembering that for some organizations that can offer a deeper interaction with their audience, it may be most effective to develop their own community. For example, the membership bodies CIM (www.cim.co.uk) and the Chartered Institute of Personnel and Development (CIPD; www.cipd.co.uk) both have active members' forums on their own site.

This may also be an option to consider for some major brands and publishers. However, many publishers prefer to make commenting possible via social sign-on to encourage amplification. For example, TechCrunch (www.techcrunch.com) uses Facebook commenting within its own site.

A good example of a business that has developed its own community to support its goals of increasing interaction with small business owners is American Express. It describes its proposition (Figure 5.13) as: 'A wealth of resources for business owners – videos, articles, blogs, podcasts, and expert advice to boost your business, sponsored by American Express OPEN'.

Review your strategy for brand-related communications across social platforms

The secret to success in making effective use of each social media platform is to work out which common approaches you can use across platforms and which approaches need to be unique for the platform. Some of the common issues will be defined in your communications strategy, covered in Section 5.6, i.e.:

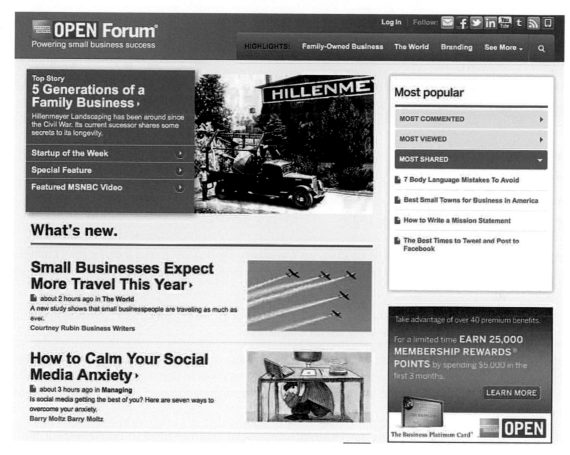

Figure 5.13   American Express OPEN (www.open-forum.com)

- Value provided through content of status updates
- Timing and frequency of updates
- Communicating the proposition to encourage people to follow or interact with the brand.

When you consider these in detail, there will be nuances for each platform in tone and style; for example, Twitter tends to require more frequent updates than Facebook and the interaction and content can differ – for example, it will be more support-related.

Select the social media platforms to prioritize on/find customer interaction preferences

You will find that each social platform will naturally differ in its importance to your business, so the first questions to answer are where are the priorities now and where to focus in the future.

Social networks are so important, it's worth doing extra research beyond the numbers from analytics to find out user intent – what do users want from the network? These can be simple 'tell us what you want' network updates or links to surveys posted as status updates or delivered through email marketing.

Profiling the audience for different social platforms

The analytics also generally won't tell you much about *who* your audience are. To determine this, use surveys as described above or take a sample of members to assess their demographics.

If you take a sample of 50–100+ users from each network, you should be able to determine their potential value to you by comparing them to your typical demographics or personas; i.e. group by:

- Gender
- Age
- Location
- Seniority and company types (B2B).

After completing this analysis, your ideas on the most relevant networks for you may change, since networks that are important by volume of fans or followers may not be so relevant in terms of potential value.

Define the proposition for your social outposts

It's simple: when someone arrives on your brand pages, they will decide whether to engage based on the experience you can offer them through the visuals, the messaging used plus the quality of the conversation evident on the wall or list of status updates. So these require urgent attention if they're not right.

Visuals and messaging showing the value of your social channel need to be consistent with the audience needs you established from your research, since audience will vary by channel. Some general things to think about: are they?

- Differentiated – from what others offer or your other channels
- On-brand – consistent with the brand
- Visually appealing – to get cut-through, this is as important as in TV ads.

We believe that the propositions for your social outposts are similar to those you offer through e-newsletters – they are both a stream of updates. The only (big) difference is that interactions and suggestions by your audience are much more important within social networks.

Explain your proposition for social updates – how you deliver value to subscribers, for example, through:

- *Saving time* – by providing a single, up-to-date source
- *Learning* – increasing knowledge and solving day-to-day problems
- *Saving money* – for instance, through regular, exclusive offers or deals
- *Entertaining* – regardless of the brand, social updates can and should be fun for their audiences – this is not only the preserve of consumer newsletters

- *Sizzle* – adding value to your brand through new ways of engagement and experiences. Burberry is brilliant at this through replicating offline experiences through the social networks.

Getting the sell–inform–entertain balance right

Getting the correct balance between using your social media outposts as a sales tool and adding other types of value is key to their success. In fact, if you over-sell you will fail – that's why we say consider the sell–inform–entertain balance in your communications. Think how this differs for your audience. Thinking generally about the difference between B2B and B2C, there are some common features. How you add value and engage will vary by audience, but there are some common features that many are looking for (Table 5.1). Work out which are key for your audiences.

Table 5.1 Different types of value to offer through social networks

B2B Proposition	B2C Proposition
Make my work easier	Make my life easier
Help me develop	Help me learn/have fun
Make me look good	Make me look good
Keep me up to date	Keep me up to date
Give me a great deal	Give me a great deal

Having clear goals around the types of value you want to offer through your updates will help staff managing your social media focus, and can also be used on the social network to encourage sign-up. Remember, it doesn't have to be original content – you can still add value by Alerting, Aggregating and Distilling about content from other brands. Indeed, this makes a brand feel like part of a wider community of sites. This is content curation.

E-MARKETING INSIGHT

Use of company brand pages on the main social platforms

Let's take one example from a business-to-business software company, Eloqua, who are well known for their use of content marketing – how they take advantage of the distinct nature of each channel for branding and to encourage interaction.

Twitter

Initially, brands using Twitter were limited to imagery in the left sidebar and what is added to the bio. Here, Eloqua (Figure 5.14) uses branded creative on the background to encourage interaction with key employees and showcase the Eloqua 'All About

Revenue' blog which is referenced in Twitter. (It is expected that Twitter will enhance their brand pages to be more like Facebook in future.)

Figure 5.14   Example of Twitter page for Eloqua (www.twitter.com/eloqua)

Facebook

Facebook pages offer more opportunities to explain your proposition through Views and Applications plus the timeline. The use of a 'Gated Like Page' encourages data capture through Applications within the Facebook company timeline. These Applications are shown below the company 'cover' (top right, Figure 5.15).

Figure 5.15   Example of Facebook page for Eloqua (www.facebook.com/eloqua)

Google+

Google+ and its company pages were launched in 2012. Figure 5.16 shows that initially they were limited in their use of creative options with communications limited to Facebook-style updates.

Figure 5.16   Example of Google+ company page for Eloqua (http://plus.google.com/114940452839274883041)

LinkedIn

LinkedIn is a more established network than Google, but it only offered company pages from 2011. These give the option for giving information on products and promotions as

Figure 5.17   Example of LinkedIn company page for Eloqua (www.linkedin.com/company/eloqua)

well as employee information (Figure 5.17). There is also a limited option for status updates where people can follow companies in a similar way to Facebook and Twitter; we can expect this to evolve further.

YouTube

YouTube offers companies the option for a branded YouTube channel which can be free or more sophisticated for advertisers. The Eloqua channel shows how featured playlists can be used to group certain types of content. The Eloqua example shows common examples for business-to-business marketing: best practices, demonstrations, tutorials, customer testimonials and recruitment (Figure 5.18).

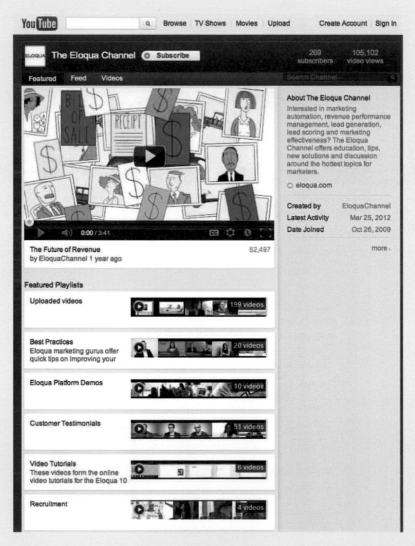

Figure 5.18   Example of YouTube channel for Eloqua (www.youtube.com/user/EloquaChannel)

Other popular social networks

Apart from the 'Big 5' social networks we have highlighted, which are popular in the 'Western world', there are many more specialist networks that may also give opportunities to reach and engage with audiences. There is a tendency for new networks to launch and, as they reach a tipping point, become rapidly popular, but they may then fade as Bebo and MySpace have done. Other networks which are popular at present are:

- *Flickr* (www.flickr.com) – an established image-sharing site owned by Yahoo! that is often used for social networks
- *Instagram* (www.instagram.com) – a method for iPhone and iPad users to rapidly share photos (see Figure 5.6 for an example)
- *Pinterest* (www.pinterest.com) – this network became popular in 2012 as a method of sharing photos and infographics
- *GetGlue* (www.getglue.com) – sharing about entertainment
- *Tumblr* (www.tumblr.com) – a network of over 50 million simple blogs enabling you to post quotes, videos or images similar to a Facebook wall, but with the option for your own design. Many companies also use Tumblr for rapid sharing of photos or videos.

Countries may also develop local social networks that are popular; for example, China has Renren, Pengyou and Weibo.

CREATING AN EDITORIAL PLAN FOR SOCIAL CHANNEL COMMUNICATIONS

An editorial calendar will help you deliver on the promise of proposition you have defined through your messaging and visuals.

There are some common, commonsense approaches to social media communications that apply regardless of channel.

E-MARKETING INSIGHT

E-marketing checklist – social media profile requirements

This checklist shows some key features to consider for company social media profiles and status updates:

☑ 1 *Do our social messages add value to the audience?* This is the very first question, since your content has to make a difference to those who are following you if they are to continue to engage and share your content. Your posts have to inform, entertain or contain great offers, otherwise you won't get cut-through. . .

☑ 2 *Is each channel offering its own unique value?* Online users, like customers everywhere, like exclusives, so think about social-channel-specific offers or deals

– such as a Twitter competition or a Facebook gated page campaign. ASOS (www.asos.com) has produced some fantastic versions of these. Of course, many messages communicated by channels will be similar, but it's worth having some differences.

☑ 3 *Are our profile pages communicating this value?* Of course, to gain subscribers, it's important that your profile summary shows why you're worth listening to *and* interacting with.

☑ 4 *Is our profile findable?* Naturally, the benefits of your social profiles should be communicated on your site, other profiles and in offline communications. Offer choice and subscribers will choose the channel that suits them best, or maybe more than one. There are some options for getting listed on directories which will give your channel some search benefit, if you're near the top of the list; it may gain you some new subscribers too.

☑ 5 *How valuable are our messages compared to competitors?* You can only answer the first two questions by checking out what the other guys are doing, so you audit these – we recommend setting up competitor auditing on another channel. It also suggests the need for good old-fashioned customer research. Ask them what they want through surveys or get them to give feedback on how you stack up against the competitors.

☑ 6 *Are we interacting?* It's all too easy to go into broadcast mode on social channels, particularly if you use tools to facilitate this. So check that you are interacting, which means as a minimum replying to questions, but it's better also to reach out and interact with others – some following, some not.

☑ 7 *Is the frequency right?* The right frequency is about getting the balance right between too many and too few messages and considering the resources needed to create content and send messages to alert subscribers to the content. You'll need to test this, it varies by channel. For example, some recommend one message a day via Facebook, others say this is too few. Certainly on Twitter, you would expect a business profile to be more active, if you have something worthwhile to say.

☑ 8 *Is the timing right?* This also needs testing. You will find times when your audience is more active and when your message is more likely to be read and shared. We have found that with our audience, first thing in the morning and just before lunch are effective.

☑ 9 *Do we send reminders about the good/important stuff?* As with many other media, reminders about key messages are worthwhile. This is particularly the case with social media since there is such a short half-life (Smart Insights, 2011c).

☑ 10 *Are we using the facilities of the network for a viral effect?* In Facebook, the Likes should happen without prompting if the content is good. Likewise the Shares or + in Google+. In Twitter, some recommend adding a 'Please RT', but we're not personally fans of this – it looks desperate unless it's for an ethical cause. In Twitter there are also hash tags; you need to include these to extend your reach, but not always – they work best for breaking news, campaign names and niche topics, we think.

☑ 11 *Are we integrating channels?* If you like the logic of offering something different via each channel, then it makes sense to communicate when these offers are available, since people may want to follow you on more than one network. But don't overdo it, as people will have their preferred channels.

☑ 12 *Are we using the unique benefits of each network?* Each network has its own style, its own vibe, its own etiquette. If we always send the same message across each network, we're certainly missing out on interactions.

☑ 13 *Are we using the right tools to make us efficient?* Using a common social communications tool that enables messages to be sent across all the networks is smart, essential really. There are many other advantages too, such as common tracking, scheduling and the ability to share the workload between team members. For example, we use HootSuite (www.hootsuite.com).

☑ 14 *Are we using the wrong tools/approach?* With a management tool, it's all too easy to just broadcast – too many identical messages across all the channels.

☑ 15 *Are we responding to customer comments?* Research suggests that many companies don't have the resources or process to respond to customer comments in social media channels. So make sure you can respond as appropriate.

SECTION SUMMARY 5.7

Success in engaging an audience on each social network is similar; it involves finding the best range of content and frequency for each network. The audience for each network is different, so different content should be used to reflect this. Don't forget to respond to comments in your stream when relevant and don't over-automate – you need human comments to keep it human.

5.8 Social media optimization (SMO)

The term social media optimization was first coined in 2006 when the search engine marketer Danny Sullivan first used it. We think it remains relevant today, and it's a good approach to show others in your business that social media is an 'always-on' activity which needs continuous efforts to improve it.

Since social media marketing is relatively new and an ongoing activity, there is a risk that it won't be managed in an integrated way to improve effectiveness; that's why SMO will become a key activity which needs management as part of content strategy.

Once you have social media marketing in place, SMO is a logical next step to improve its effectiveness.

So what is SMO? People have different views on what SMO involves, depending on whether their background is more in SEO or social media marketing. We prefer a broad definition, involving a structured approach to improving social media through a 'test–learn–refine' approach. We need to use social media to help people find our content, participate in conversations about it and then share it.

Since SMO centres on the distribution of social objects and their ability to rise to the top of any related search query, it's closely related to content marketing and SEO.

Brian Solis (2011a) believes that: 'SEO + SMO = Amplified findability in the traditional and social web'.

We think that's a great way to summarize it (but only if you're a fan of jargon).

At the centre of an SMO programme are social objects. Social objects represent the content we market via social media – images, videos, blog posts, comments, status updates, wall posts, and all related activity that creates the potential for online conversations. It follows, then, that the goal of SMO is to measure, monitor and improve the visibility of social objects as a means of connecting with individuals who are proactively seeking additional information and direction.

Social objects are contextualized through keywords, titles, descriptions, and/or tags.

REVIEW THE KEY SOCIAL MEDIA OPTIMIZATION ACTIVITIES

So what does SMO involve, what activities need to happen? We think it's useful here to look at the five new rules of SMO developed by Rohit Bhargava of Ogilvy New York (Bhargava, 2010).

As we run through each area, we'll add our recommendations on which SMO issues we think are important to consider. You will notice that several of these recommend looking at analysis by Dan Zarrella, the self-styled 'Social Media Scientist'; it's worth subscribing to his blog (www.danzarrella.com) if you're a specialist.

1 *Create shareable content.* As we have said before in this guide, this is fundamentally content marketing, so in SMO, it's about determining the content that your audience prefers to share across different social media platforms.

   You can learn from what Dan Zarrella has found through his analysis of the most shareable topics on Facebook:

   - *Web users like to learn about the most popular topics* – 'most', 'big' and 'best' are popular – these are often used in blog list posts which we know are popular
   - *Help readers learn and develop* – 'how' and 'why' are some of the most popular terms
   - *Making it personal can help engagement* – include 'you' in the headline – email copywriters will know this also works well in the body copy
   - *Some content types are a turn-off* – the analysis also shows that 'poll', 'review' and 'vs' are not shared so widely.

This is straightforward. The main services are:

- AddThis
- ShareThis
- Native service plug-ins.

We recommend the third approach since the top two tools, while easy to use, do not update to show shares from other sources such as social media management systems like HootSuite or TweetDeck. The native services of Facebook, Twitter and so on will check in real time to see what the latest number of counts are. Plug-ins are available for content management systems (CMS) such as WordPress.

2 *Reward engagement.* It's commonplace now to reward 'Liking' or 'Tweeting' through a promotional or content offer, so this can look at the best offers to do this. Rohit Bhargava also says that this should look at a longer term of encouraging deeper engagement and conversations.

3 *Proactively share content.* This covers the process and format for sharing beyond your central hub. This can include syndicating articles to other partners or platforms like SlideShare or Scribd. Some also create their own widgets or use ad widgets for embedding or sharing on other sites (atomization).

4 *Encourage the 'mashup'.* Rohit says that this is encouraging folks to take and remix your content, so it becomes user-generated content. This activity can effectively be built into campaigns.

We think these rules are really useful for reviewing your approach to integrating social media marketing into a web site, but think there's more to it. Other options to test and refine content through analytics and AB/multivariate testing include:

1 *Test effectiveness of sharing and content types on business outcomes.* Ask which sharing activities and types of promotions lead to business results, leads, sales or changes in brand preference.

2 *Review how well your content marketing supports SEO.* This is determining how content marketing and social media can support SEO activities, since the amount of social sharing of content is a ranking signal and encourages backlinks.

3 *Review preferences of different audiences using different social media platforms to convert and share different types of content and offers.* Some content and offers will naturally work best for different audiences, so it's good to have an understanding of what works and what doesn't. You can also demonstrate the relative effectiveness of how different social and digital marketing channels combine with content marketing through looking at relative propensities to convert.

4 *Optimum frequency for initiating sharing.* Determine how often you should share content. This will vary on different platforms – you should engage more frequently on Twitter than on Facebook, for example. Consider the half-life of your social communications, which is the time taken for an online communication to get half the clicks. Research from Bitly (2011) shows that typical values are:

- Twitter = 2.8 hours
- Facebook = 3.2 hours
- Direct sources (email or IM) = 3.4 hours.

This suggests that ideally, you should post several times per day to maintain sharing.

5 *Best methods for identifying influencers and seeding content.* Reaching out to other sites and influencers is a key success factor for content marketing, so it's good to examine how effective you are in this.

6 *Approaches to integrate sharing of content through different social platforms, web, mobile and email channels.* This is working out how you can engage your audience across different channels by linking between them.

Ensuring that you are visible

Content is the base for getting a good position in the search engine results pages (SERPs), and content is what is shared in social media and ultimately also appears in search results. The more relevant content you have, in the more relevant places, the more likely you are to be found by prospective buyers at the right time. The important part about being findable is to think multiple touchpoints, multiple web sites and at multiple times.

Content is the core for natural search results, and content is what is shared in social media and ultimately what also appears in search results in Google; it also converts better than any other traffic – so we want more of it. Search engine optimization is an integrated process, not a stand-alone set of tasks – it's certainly too important to be left to SEO experts. Fundamentally, content connects with search and social.

There are a lot of ways that people can view your content: the marketing model has shifted from a pure, 'How do we push messages to drive more traffic?' to 'How do we publish and become findable in more places including SERPs?'

You're seeking not only to optimize site content, but also off-site content on third- party web sites and social networks that have better potential to rank highly in the SERPs than you do – as well as increasing your reach to a much wider audience in the process: this includes image and video search, not just text. Links back from other sites and social networks are hugely important.

Manage your content with blog software, use posts that link back to relevant pages (especially product pages) – this is good for users and for Google; add content to categories, to product pages, optimize it (think keywords).

The question is, 'How do I make my content awe-inspiring and then shareable so that it has the best chance to go viral?' Hugh MacLeod of Gaping Void described this well when he said:

> *The most important word on the internet is not 'Search'. The most important word on the internet is 'Share'. Sharing is the driver. Sharing is the DNA. We use Social*

Objects to share ourselves with other people. We're primates. We like to groom each other. It's in our nature.

(MacLeod, 2007)

Making your content shareable

Shareable content is important for two reasons – first, for natural search and link building, and second, because the way people are finding and consuming content (product, entertainment, news, learning information) is fast-changing. Optimizing for both search and social media is now equally important. Think of your web site as the hub or heart of your marketing, pumping content outwards but with a backflow of comments and interactions.

We still want traffic coming to our web sites, of course, and if we do it right, then visitors will come. But if we value the creation of more entry points to connect with our brand across the Internet, then we must increase the reach of our content in and beyond the SERPs and into social referral traffic.

How can you increase sharing and social referral traffic?

There are three key factors at play here:

- How fascinating, valuable, informative or entertaining your content is
- How easily shareable you have made it (hint: not just for Facebook!)
- How much time you are spending interacting on third-party sites and social networks, sharing your story and interacting with your current and potential current audience

If you can inspire someone, then their friends are more likely to be interested in the same thing ('birds of a feather flock together'), so you're likely to be reaching and then leveraging a well-targeted audience.

Think about these five approaches to make your content more shareable:

1 *Make tagging, bookmarking and sharing easy.* Before Facebook's tools became so ubiquitous, widgets were the primary tool that allowed others to grab your content and share it on their blogs, Facebook profiles and social bookmarking sites. Examples of these widgets include the ShareThis or AddThis plug-ins.

   Each social media site has its own range of share buttons and badges or plug-ins; they are very similar to widgets, though they focus on one application, of course – for example, Facebook's 'Share' or StumbleUpon's 'Stumble', and Twitter's 'Retweet'!

2 *Enable others to help your content travel further.* Great content gets shared naturally. Back in the day, it was pretty much forwarding by email – now it's wider: RSS subscribers, content syndication, email newsletters, status updates, social bookmarks, Facebook promotions and tweets – they all improve reach and need to be employed with the big idea in mind, and as you create the content.

You will have heard, no doubt, the idea of encouraging people to 'mash-up', or augment and curate, your content – this further increases the reach and appeal of what you've done and drives traffic back. The classic example here is YouTube's cut-and-paste web code to embed video (your video) into any web page. So, encourage re-use and sharing – it will all flow back to you, the originator.

3 *Form a connection.* You want to attract visitors and you really want the visitor to register in some way – why? Connected visitors tend to engage more than anonymous visitors, and they've already engaged once by registering. You will most likely see more time on site, more page views, lower bounce rate and, if you're operating an e-commerce site, increased sales.

A traditional long and cluttered registration form can, however, limit interactions. Use social sign-in as an option to help reduce this.

4 *Encourage interaction.* A user leaving a comment on your site is great, sharing that comment with their social network is going to drive traffic. Today, through web services like LiveCycle, Facebook Connect, Gigya, Janrain and Disqus, you can easily encourage people to share their comments more broadly.

5 *Remember the real purpose.* What are you setting out to do at the business level? Build sales, influence or credibility, maybe? Align those business goals with the customer needs and ensure that that manifests as relevant content, specifically for your audience (not everybody). Get involved, online conversation is at the heart of social media, not just 'listening'. Be the go-to resource, even link to competitors and cement your position as a trusted and valued reference.

Think of it like some kind of 'content = social karma'; you've got to give to get, so just concentrate on doing an honest-to-good job of providing what your market really, really values. Is this not what you wish some brands would do for you? Of course, be real and even a bit humble in the process – most of us value that authenticity

Think small for accessibility and mobile content

With the smartphone market growing at a prolific rate, and tablets like the iPad the gadget to have, the concept of accessible content for devices beyond a desktop PC is important for broadening reach and maintaining brand relevance through social media, as described in Chapter 6.

SECTION SUMMARY 5.8

Social media optimization (SMO) is a structured approach to increasing engagement and sharing within social media marketing. It involves testing different content, messages and frequency with a view to increasing leads and sales generated through social media marketing.

CHAPTER SUMMARY

1 Social media are digital media which encourage audience participation, interaction and sharing.

2 Social media marketing can be defined as '*Monitoring and facilitating customer–customer interaction, participation and sharing through digital media to encourage positive engagement with a company and its brands leading to commercial value. Interactions may occur on a company site, social networks and other third-party sites*' (CIPR, 2011).

3 Social media marketing should start by listening to online conversations and should be driven by customer needs and business goals rather than the social platforms. The Forrester People–Objectives–Strategies–Technology (POST) mnemonic emphasizes this.

4 The Forrester Social Technographics Ladder suggests you should develop strategies to engage users according to their level of interaction with social media: Creators; Critics; Collectors; Joiners; Spectators or Inactives.

5 Social media marketing, social business and social CRM require a transformation in many staff, involving: setting a scope for social media activities to communicate to staff; reviewing social media capabilities and priorities; governance: defining who is responsible for social media; and reviewing brand personality and vision.

6 Ensure appropriate tools are in place to listen to and follow up on different 'social mentions', including brand conversations about you; competitor conversations; your competitor brands and market conversations; and products and services you offer.

7 Social media engagement should be based on a sound content strategy. Remember: content must have intrinsic value; content is a key part of your online value proposition; you must define its relevance to customers – help them live their lives and do their work better.

8 Use the PRACE framework to help develop a social media strategy. PRACE is Plan, Reach, Act, Convert and Engage.

9 Success in engaging an audience on each social network is similar; it involves finding the best range of content and frequency for each network. The audience for each network is different, so different content should be used to reflect this. Don't forget to respond to comments in your stream when relevant and don't over-automate – you need human comments to keep it human.

10 Social media optimization (SMO) is a structured approach to increasing engagement and sharing within social media marketing. It involves testing different content, messages and frequency with a view to increasing leads and sales generated through social media marketing.

References

Ahrendts, A. (2011) Burberry vision for social and digital media. YouTube video, 30 August.

Altimeter (2010) Framework: the social media ROI pyramid. Blog post by Jeremiah Owyang, 13 December at: www.web-strategist.com/blog/2010/12/13/framework-the-social-media-roi-pyramid/

Bhargava, R. (2008) *Personality Not Included: Why Brands Lose Their Authenticity – and How Great Companies Get It Back*. Available from: www.personalitynotincluded.com

Bharvaga, R. (2010) The 5 new rules of SMO. Blog post, 10 August 2010 at: www.rohitbhargava.com/2010/08/the-5-new-rules-of-social-media-optimization-smo.html

Bitly (2011) You just shared a link. How long will people pay attention? Blog post, 6 September 2011 at: http://blog.bitly.com/post/9887686919/you-just-shared-a-link-how-long-will-people-pay

CIPR (2011) Social media marketing best practice guide, May 2011 edition. Created by the CIPR Social Media Panel. At: www.cipr.co.uk/sites/default/files/CIPR_social_media%20_best%20_practice%20_guidance%20_2011_1_0.pdf

Currah, A. (2012) Future of customer service: the rise of the social customer report. Social Media Leadership Forum. At: http://socialmedialeadershipforum.org/index.php/blog/news/future-of-customer-service-the-rise-of-the-social-customer-report/

Forrester (2007) The POST method, a systematic approach to social strategy. Blog post by Josh Bernoff, December 2011 at: http://forrester.typepad.com/groundswell/2007/12/the-post-method.html

Forrester (2012) Global social technographics update 2011: US and EU mature, emerging markets show lots of activity. Blog post by Gina Sverdlov, 4 January at: http:// blogs.forrester.com/gina_sverdlov/12-01-04-global_social_technographics_update_2011_us_and_eu_mature_emerging_markets_show_lots_of_activity

Halvorson, K. (2010) *Content Strategy for the Web*. New Riders, Berkeley, CA.

Handley, A. and Chapman, C. (2010) *Content Rules: How to Create Killer Blogs, Podcasts, Videos, eBooks, Webinars (and More) That Engage Customers and Ignite Your Business*. John Wiley & Sons, New York.

Kawasaki, G. (2012) *Enchantment: The Art of Changing Hearts, Minds and Actions*. Portfolio/Penguin, New York.

MacLeod, H. (2007) More thoughts on social objects. Blog post, 24 October at: http:// gapingvoid.com/2007/10/24/more-thoughts-on-social-objects/

Mashable (2011) Burberry's evolving role as a media company. Blog post by Lauren Indivik, September 2011 at: http://mashable.com/2011/09/21/burberry-media-fashion-company

Pulizzi, J. and Barrett, T. (2010) *Get Content, Get Customers*. McGraw-Hill, Columbus, OH.

Rappaport, S. (2011) *Listen First! Turning Social Media Conversations into Business Advantage*. John Wiley & Sons, New York.

SEOmoz (2012) 21 ways to increase blog traffic. Blog post, 17 January at: www.seomoz.org/blog/21-tactics-to-increase-blog-traffic-2012

Shah, D. and Halligan, B. (2009) *Inbound Marketing: Get Found Using Google, Social Media and Blogs*. John Wiley & Sons, Inc., Hoboken, NJ.

Smart Insights (2010) Using social media and online channels to deliver customer service. Interview with Guy Stephens, 5 October at: www.smartinsights.com/customer-relationship-management/customer-service-and-support/online-customer-service/

Smart Insights (2011a) The social media marketing radar. Blog post by Danyl Bosomworth, 6 March at: www.smartinsights.com/social-media-marketing/social-media-strategy/social-media-marketing-radar/

Smart Insights (2011b) Why social sign-on matters. Blog post by Dave Chaffey, 26 September at: www.smartinsights.com/social-media-marketing/social-media-strategy/why-social-sign-on-matters/

Smart Insights (2011c) Do you know how scary the half-life of your online comms is? Blog post, 8 September at: www.smartinsights.com/email-marketing/email-marketing-analytics/did-you-know-how-scary-the-half-life-of-your-online-comms-is/

Smart Insights (2012) *Seven Steps to Social Media Marketing*. E-book by Dave Chaffey and Dan Bosomworth, available at: www.smartinsights.com

Solis, B. (2011a) *End of Business as Usual: Rewire the Way You Work to Succeed in the Consumer Revolution*. Wiley, New York.

Solis, B. (2011b) *Engage: The Complete Guide for Brands and Businesses to Build, Cultivate, and Measure Success in the New Web*. Wiley, New York.

Viapoint (2012) The social media capability maturity framework. Created by Paul Fennemore, published at: www.viapoint.co.uk

Weinberg, T. (2010) *The New Community Rules: Marketing on the Social Web*. Wiley, Hoboken, NJ.

Further reading

Halvorson, K. (2010) *Content Strategy for the Web*. New Riders, Berkeley, CA. Content marketing described from the perspective of the web manager.

Levine, R., Locke, C., Searls, D. and Weinberger, D. (2000) *The Cluetrain Manifesto*. Perseus Books, Cambridge, MA. The book (available online at www.cluetrain.com), which laid the foundation for social media marketing.

Pulizzi, J. and Barrett, T. (2010) *Get Content. Get Customers*. McGraw-Hill, Columbus, OH. A practical guide to content marketing.

Viapoint (2012) The social media capability maturity framework. Created by Paul Fennemore, published at: www.viapoint.co.uk

Web links

Brian Solis (www.briansolis.com). A foremost commentator on the development of social media marketing and its application in business.

Chris Brogan (www.chrisbrogan.com). A foremost commentator on the development of social media marketing and its application in business.

Convince and Convert (www.convinceandconvert.com). Analysis of social media marketing concepts by US commentator Jay Baer.

Dan Zarrella (www.danzarrella.com). Dan summarizes experiments on what engages audiences through the main social networks.

Digital Buzz Blog (www.digitalbuzzblog.com). Daily inspiration with examples of social media campaigns on this video blog.

DoubleClick Ad Planner (www.google.com/adplanner). Use this to find sites related to your sites, competitor sites and relevant media sites. Review the most popular sites within different interest categories.

Mashable (www.mashable.com). Site focusing on developments and statistics related to social networks.

Personality Not Included (www.personalitynotincluded.com). Site supporting the book by Rohit Bhargava, showing examples of how brands are transforming their personality to support social media engagement.

Smart Insights (www.smartinsights.com/social-media-marketing). Covers all developments in social media marketing to support this chapter.

Social Media Governance (http://socialmediagovernance.com). We recommend this database of social media governance policies where you can learn from approaches defined by others.

Viral and Buzz Marketing Network (www.vbma.net). A European-oriented community of academics and professionals for discussion of the applications of connected marketing.

Word-of-Mouth Marketing Association (www.womma.org). A US-oriented community of word-of-mouth marketing specialists.

Self-test

1 Explain and give examples of the main types of social media platform that can be used to engage with customers and influencers.

2 What types of goal is it important to define for social media marketing?

3 Which criteria would you use to assess a company's capability for adoption of social media?

4 Outline approaches to social listening.

5 Explain the principles and purpose of content marketing.

6 Give examples of different types of content that can be used for content marketing and explain how they may be used through the purchase decision.

7 Show how social media communications can support the areas of the PRACE framework as part of a social media communications plan.

8 What are common communications approaches that need to be applied by marketers across the major social media marketing platforms?

9 Explain approaches for assessing the return on investment of social media marketing.

10 Explain the principle and activities of social media optimization (SMO)

Get updates on
this chapter

Chapter **6**

Site design

A website attempts to deliver just three types of Outcomes: Increase revenue. Reduce cost. Improve customer satisfaction/loyalty. That's it. Three simple things.

Kaushik (2009)

OVERVIEW

This chapter will make you think about different forms of company online presence a little differently. We go beyond best practice in usability and accessibility, to show how to design commercially led sites which deliver results. Commercially led site designs are based on creating compelling persuasive experiences which really engage visitors through relevant messages and content, encouraging them to stay on the site and return.

OVERALL LEARNING OUTCOME

By the end of this chapter, you will:

- Know what makes an excellent online experience on different platforms
- Be able to review site effectiveness when designing an enhancement
- Understand the rules to follow and the mistakes to avoid
- Be able to converse with any web master, marketer or chief executive about improving your web site
- Be able to explore options for added value through dynamic facilities.

CHAPTER TOPIC	LEARNING OBJECTIVE
6.1 Introduction	Identify the main objectives of effective site design
6.2 Integrated design	Ensure web sites are integrated with the rest of the business
6.3 Online value proposition	Develop an online value proposition (OVP)
6.4 Customer orientation	Be able to translate customer needs into site design
6.5 Dynamic design and personalization	Explore options for added value through dynamic facilities
6.6 Aesthetics	Identify different aspects of aesthetic design
6.7 Page design	Understand and apply best practice for page layout
6.8 Content strategy and copywriting	Managing content quality and applying the fundamental principles of copywriting for web sites
6.9 Navigation and structure	Assess best practice for navigation and structure
6.10 Interaction	Assess best practice for interaction (including conversion optimization)
6.11 Mobile site design	Review considerations for design of mobile sites

6.1 Introduction to site design

In the early days of the web, the only sites we had to manage were web sites. Today, companies have to deliver effective experiences across a range of platforms. From web sites to mobile-optimized sites, to mobile apps, to a presence on social networks as branded company pages. The design challenge is certainly bigger, through offering customers choice and increasing your digital footprint, but the same principles of developing a user experience apply. When we make recommendations about improving 'sites' in this chapter, we refer to the full range of online customer experiences.

The imperative to produce a customer-centric online presence is suggested by Alison Lancaster, at the time the head of marketing and catalogues at John Lewis Direct and subsequently marketing director at Charles Tyrwhitt (www.ctshirts.co.uk) who said:

> *A good site should always begin with the user. Understand who the customer is, how they use the channel to shop, and understand how the marketplace works in that category. This includes understanding who your competitors are and how they operate online. You need continuous research, feedback and usability testing to continue to monitor and evolve the customer experience online. Customers want convenience and ease of ordering. They want a site that is quick to download, well-structured and easy to navigate.*
>
> *(Lancaster, no date; unpublished)*

ESSENTIAL ELEMENTS OF CREATING EFFECTIVE ONLINE EXPERIENCES

Site design = Function + Content + Form + Organization + Interaction

Combining these elements into a site design presents a challenge few have mastered, since success requires a range of skills and the right decisions to balance all of these elements. Companies need to harness internal skills and/or use specialist agencies on all of the success factors for web site design which we will review in this chapter:

- *Accessibility* – this should be built into all web sites since it is a legal requirement under disability and discrimination law. An accessible design supports visually impaired site users and other disabled users with limited limb movements. It also helps users accessing the site with a range of different web browsers, using different devices such as mobiles or tablets, and it also indirectly assists search engine optimization.

- *User-centred design and usability* – with a user-friendly site, visitors can find the information they are seeking, have a satisfactory experience and complete actions efficiently. User-centred web site design is an essential approach to ensure that the web site meets visitors' needs. Research to identify appropriate personas, customer journeys and relevant content is a key activity.

- *Information architecture and findability* – analysis and design to create a sound system of structure and labelling of content in headings and navigation are essential to help findability through standard navigation and on-site search.

- *Search engine optimization (SEO)* – if SEO isn't considered in site design and within content management systems, search robots may be unable to crawl content and the relevance of different pages will be unclear.
- *Web standards* – complying with standards to produce consistency in the way sites are coded and displayed in different browsers as promoted through the World Wide Web consortium (www.w3.org) and the Web Standards Project (www.webstandards.org).
- *Persuasion to deliver commercial results* – your design should emphasize specific content and *customer journeys* through the site in order for your site to meet its objectives such as *conversion rate optimization (CRO)*. Users should not be offered unlimited choice to visit any content; instead you should prioritize your most valuable content in a similar way to a supermarket using merchandizing to promote specific products. Remember too, that mixed-mode journeys are still commonplace; not everyone will buy online, many are just researching, so facilitate these journeys through prominent features like a store locator or in-store promotions.

We also need to study the psychology of customer engagement (Chapters 1 and 4) to understand the content, messages and visual design that influence customer perceptions (remember Robert Cialdini's six 'weapons of influence' from Section 4.6).

- *Visual design* – the experience of a brand and a site will not be memorable and positive if the visual design isn't energizing and doesn't fit with what the visitor would expect from a brand.
- *Web analytics* – analysis of site visitor journeys can help improve navigation and conversion to different site goals.
- *Legal requirements* – site owners need to check that they comply with the many laws to control a web presence.
- *Digital marketing planning and improvement process* – the web site must fit within the wider world where it supports different organization goals, integrates with other sales channels and is continuously reviewed and improved.

WEB SITE GOALS

Clarifying the key objectives and purpose of the site helps to determine the functions and content of the site. In turn, content drives form (the way it looks) and finally, form drives the organization of the web site. We will also look at how interaction should be built into the site to improve the visitor experience.

So what is the purpose, or objective, of your site? First, in order to help customers or other stake holders, ask '*How can my site help my customers?*' For example:

- Help them buy something they need
- Help them find information
- Help them to save money and time
- Help them to talk to the organization
- Help them to enjoy a better web experience.

These are the 5Ss – Sell, Serve, Speak, Save and Sizzle – introduced in Chapter 1, as seen from the customer perspective. Site design can help achieve the 5Ss, as follows:

- *Sell* – growing sales can be achieved through effectively communicating a crystal-clear online value proposition (OVP, Chapter 4) and through making e-commerce and lead generation easier.
- *Serve* – we can add value through designing easy-to-use interactive services that help customers to find relevant, up-to-date information quickly.
- *Speak* – we can use the site to converse with and get closer to customers by providing tailored content and designing interactive facilities to create a dialogue through email marketing or chat (or even a trialogue, when customers talk to each other), as well as learning about their needs.
- *Save* – costs are saved through delivering online content and services that may have previously been achieved through print and post or face-to-face service and sales transactions.
- *Sizzle* – an excellent site design helps build the brand and reinforces the brand values through the type of content, interactivities and overall style, tone or feel.

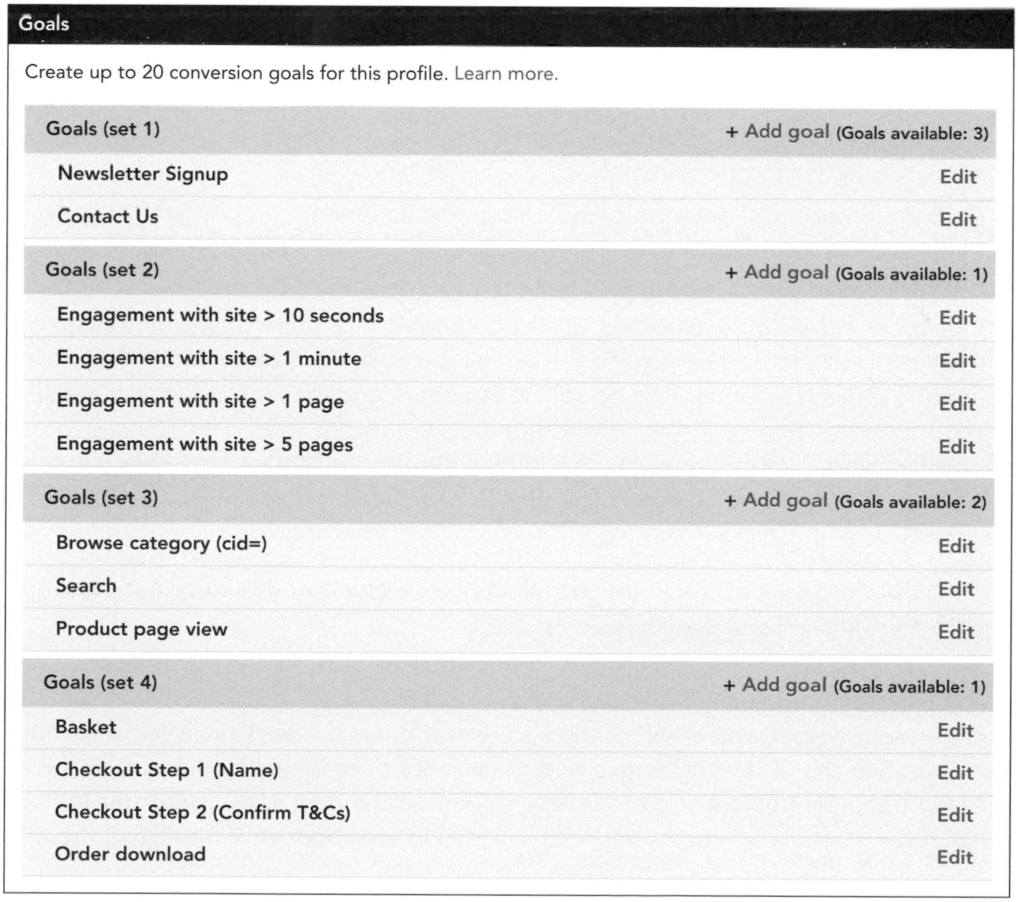

Goals	
Create up to 20 conversion goals for this profile. Learn more.	
Goals (set 1)	**+ Add goal** (Goals available: 3)
Newsletter Signup	Edit
Contact Us	Edit
Goals (set 2)	**+ Add goal** (Goals available: 1)
Engagement with site > 10 seconds	Edit
Engagement with site > 1 minute	Edit
Engagement with site > 1 page	Edit
Engagement with site > 5 pages	Edit
Goals (set 3)	**+ Add goal** (Goals available: 2)
Browse category (cid=)	Edit
Search	Edit
Product page view	Edit
Goals (set 4)	**+ Add goal** (Goals available: 1)
Basket	Edit
Checkout Step 1 (Name)	Edit
Checkout Step 2 (Confirm T&Cs)	Edit
Order download	Edit

Figure 6.1   Using Google Analytics to set up marketing goals

PRACTICAL E-MARKETING TIP

Conversion goals and value events

You should define conversion goals for your site to check that you are achieving your objectives. Visits to certain pages such as an e-newsletter registration, where-to-buy or sales confirmation page are more valuable than others.

These are also known as value events and you should create a tracking and scoring system to evaluate them by using web analytics. Google Analytics makes it easy to set up conversion goals (Figure 6.1, above, shows how different types of goals should be grouped) and track them and even better, show pages or referrers that influence them. Non-transactional sites should have value assigned to their goals. For example, travel company i-to-i (www.i-to-i.com) knows the value of everyone who downloads a brochure from research about conversion rates from download to sale in their conversion funnel. With a value assigned to the goal, the company can then work out which referrers to the site and which pages on the customer journey assist with conversion.

Design priorities do vary, but many companies use the objectives of customer relationship management to serve as objectives for their site; for example, through the PRACE framework introduced in Chapter 1 or the three key aspects of the customer lifecycle:

- *Customer acquisition* – acquisition means winning customers – converting prospects (visitors) into customers on-site.
- *Customer retention* – retention means keeping customers – ensuring they repeat buy. Timely, personalized and relevant emails and offers can bring them back to you via the site.
- *Customer extension* – extension means extending the share of wallet. Selling other relevant products and services to the same customer. For example, the database can identify similar customers who bought A but not B, and then make recommendations.

For each of these, design can help *convert* the visitor to the required marketing outcome. Achieving site *stickiness* increases the chance of achieving these objectives.

PRACTICAL E-MARKETING TIP

Bounce rates

You should use your web analytics tools to review bounce rates to analyse and improve the effectiveness of landing pages and the quality of referrers to a page. This is particularly important where you are investing in digital media such as Google Adwords since, if the majority of visitors bounce, you may as well burn your money.

Bounce rates are the percentage of visitors to a page or site that exit after visiting only a single page. We're often asked, 'What is a good bounce rate?'; of course, the answer is 'It depends'. To answer this in a meaningful way, you have to segment in the analytics through different visitor types like brand or direct visits, new versus returning visitors, generic or long-tail search visits. But generally, what we have found are bounce rates in this range; if you are way outside this range, you could have a problem:

- Home page (depends on strength of brand): 15 per cent to 25 per cent
- Category or product page (of course, this depends on the product, service and deal): 35 per cent to 55 per cent
- Landing page (created for bought media): 25 per cent to 40 per cent
- Blog post (many read, then leave): 60 per cent to 80 per cent.

E-MARKETING EXCELLENCE

Harley-Davidson uses the web to achieve diverse objectives

Some sites, like Harley-Davidson (Figure 6.2), are designed with a range of objectives including acquiring new customers through detailed product information about the core product and extended product such as guarantees and rentals; developing additional revenue streams such as rentals, tours and courses; and saving through making efficiency gains by helping dealers with warranty claims – thereby generating cost savings and better customer service. Communicating the experience and image possible through owning the brand is important, although this may not always be possible with accessibility goals.

Figure 6.2   Harley-Davidson (www.harley-davidson.co.uk)

Figure 6.2 shows a Quick start option offering content for different audiences, a good example of customer orientation. The main carousel has campaigns encouraging more interaction with the brand online. The three panels at the base encourage marketing outcomes.

KEY VARIABLES FOR WEB DESIGN OBJECTIVES

Christodoulides *et al.* (2006) have tested the importance of a range of variables that are indicators of online brand equity for online retail and service companies. This analysis was performed across these five dimensions of brand equity, assessed by asking the questions below – they provide an excellent framework which can be applied to assess and benchmark the quality of brand experience for different types of web site:

1 *Emotional connection*

   Q1: I feel related to the type of people who are [X]'s customers
   Q2: I feel as though [X] actually cares about me
   Q3: I feel as though [X] really understands me

2 *Online experience*

   Q4: [X]'s web site provides easy-to-follow search paths
   Q5: I never feel lost when navigating through [X]'s web site
   Q6: I was able to obtain the information I wanted without any delay

3 *Responsive service nature*

   Q7: [X] is willing and ready to respond to customer needs
   Q8: [X]'s web site gives visitors the opportunity to 'talk back' to [X]

4 *Trust*

   Q9: I trust [X] to keep my personal information safe
   Q10: I feel safe in my transactions with [X]

5 *Fulfilment*

   Q11: I got what I ordered from [X]'s web site
   Q12: The product was delivered by the time promised by [X].

How would you add to this framework for requirements for a customer-centric site? We would add the importance of relevant quality content (implied by Q6) and the presence of a community where user-generated content is shared (suggested by Q1).

PRACTICAL E-MARKETING TIP

Increasing landing page conversion rate

Remember that many visitors do not enter via your home page; we find that often more than half of visitors arrive from search engines and other sources not on the home page, but on campaign landing pages (Figure 6.3). Use your analytics to find which are the most important, both for entry and during the journey through the site, and then focus your optimization efforts here.

The implication is obvious: designers need to treat every page as the entry point to clearly explain their proposition and aim to convert to action. Here is a checklist of questions to ask to check your landing page effectiveness against specific goals.

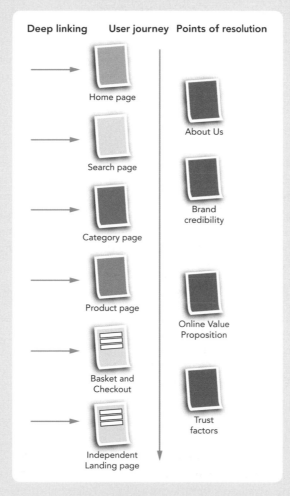

Figure 6.3   Entry pages for site visits on different customer journeys

☑ *Aim 1 Generate response (online lead or sale and offline callback)*

Does the page have a prominent call-to-action such as a prominent button above the fold, repeated in text and image form?

☑ *Aim 2 Engage different audience types (reduce bounce rate, increase value events, increase return rate)*

Does the page have a prominent headline and sub-heads showing the visitor is in the right place? Does the page have scent-trail trigger messages, offers or images to appeal to different audiences? For example, Dell has links on its site to appeal to consumers and different types of businesses. A landing page containing form fields to fill in is often more effective than an additional click since it starts committed visitors on their journey.

☑ *Aim 3 Communicate key brand messages (increase brand familiarity and favourability)*

Does the page clearly explain who you are, what you do, where you operate and what makes you different? Are your core proposition and online value proposition compelling? Figure 6.4 shows a company with clear, carefully considered brand messaging. Laser eye-treatment site Ultralase (www.ultralase.com) used to feature the top ten FAQs on its home page, but it has now reduced this to three key concerns (quality, cost, trust), for which it uses a simple carousel at the top of the home page to communicate the key message. The three main customer journeys and OVP are communicated through the green bar. Also ask whether you can use customer testimonials or ratings to show independent credibility as Ultralase does. To help with this, use run-of-site messages (on all pages) across the top of the screen or in the left or right sidebars. Figure 6.9 (below) is also an excellent example of this, since it has the 'Why choose us?' message to differentiate it. Many sites keep this hidden on the 'About us' or home page, but here it's obvious when a visitor arrives from a search engine or affiliate.

☑ *Aim 4 Answer the visitors' questions (reduce bounce rates, increase conversion rates)*

Different audiences will want to know different things. Have you identified personas (Chapter 4) and do you seek to answer their questions; e.g. do you use FAQs or messages which ask 'Are you a new customer?' (so you can explain the proposition)?

☑ *Aim 5 Showcase range of offers (cross-sell)*

Do you have recommendations on related or best-selling products and do you show the full range of your offering through navigation?

☑ *Aim 6 Attract visitors through search engine optimization (SEO) and paid search*

How well do you rank for relevant search terms compared to competitors? Do your navigation, copy and page templates indicate relevance to search engines through on-page optimization? Review the example of Figure 6.9, which has effective landing pages for SEO and which also has a high *Quality Score* in Google Adwords because the page title, headlines and copy all focus on the main search term, as explained further in Chapter 7.

Figure 6.4   Ultralase (www.ultralase.com)

USABILITY AND ACCESSIBILITY

Effective web site designs are informed by two key approaches used by professional designers. These are usability and accessibility.

Usability is an established concept that is applied to the design of a range of products and services which describes how easy they are to use. ISO 9241 defines standards for the ergonomics of human–computer interaction, including usability which it defines as:

> The *effectiveness*, *efficiency* and *satisfaction* with   which   specified *users* achieve specified *goals* in particular *environments*.

- *effectiveness:* the accuracy and completeness with which specified users can achieve specified goals in particular environments
- *efficiency:* the resources expended in relation to the accuracy and completeness of goals achieved
- *satisfaction:* the comfort and acceptability of the work system to its users and other people affected by its use.

You can see how the concept can be readily applied to web site design – web visitors often have defined goals such as finding particular information or completing an action such as booking a flight or viewing an account balance.

The same principles hold true today. In practice, usability involves two approaches. First, *expert reviews* are often performed at the beginning of a redesign project as a way of identifying problems with a previous design. Second, *usability testing* which involves:

1 Identifying representative users of the site
2 Asking them to perform specific tasks such as finding a product or completing an order
3 Observing what they do and how they succeed.

The use of *personas* and *scenario-based design* which we looked at in Chapter 4 (Section 4.10) is a key approach to inform usability. There are many other customer feedback tools which will assist with the process (see the compilation at http://bit.ly/smartfeedback).

Jakob Nielsen (2003) explains the imperative for usability best in his article 'Usability 101'. He says:

> On the web, usability is a necessary condition for survival. If a web site is difficult to use, people leave. If the homepage fails to clearly state what a company offers and what users can do on the site, people leave. If users get lost on a web site, they leave. If a web site's information is hard to read or doesn't answer users' key questions, they leave. Note a pattern here?
>
> *(Nielsen, 2003)*

For these reasons, Nielsen suggests that around 10 per cent of a design project budget should be spent on usability, but often, actual spend is significantly less.

PRACTICAL E-MARKETING TIP

Site customer feedback tools tell you why, while web analytics only show you what and where

Web analytics systems will only tell you so much about customer journeys. They will tell you the customer journeys followed, but not the opinions of visitors. Feedback tools are essential partners to web analytics since they help to get you closer to customers. These are the tools we use on projects and recommend. You can see a full listing of the categories of tools here: http://bit.ly/smartfeedback.

1 4Q
2 Kampyle (Figure 6.5)
3 Get Satisfaction
4 UserVoice.

Figure 6.5   Kampyle feedback system for Smart Insights (www.kampyle.com)

Web accessibility

Web accessibility is about allowing all users of a web site to interact with it regardless of disabilities they may have or the web browser or platform they are using to access the site. The visually impaired or blind are the main audience that designing an accessible web site can help, although often the site will also become easier to use for sighted users due to clearer navigation and labelling.

This quote shows the importance of accessibility to a visually impaired user of a web site who uses a screen-reader which reads out the navigation options and content on a web site. Lynn Holdsworth, a web developer and programmer, says: 'For me being online is everything. It's my hi fi, it's my source of income, it's my supermarket, it's my telephone. It's my way in' (Holdsworth, cited in RNIB, no date).

Remember that many countries now have specific *accessibility legislation* to which you are subject. This is often contained within disability and discrimination acts. In the UK, the relevant act is the Disability and Discrimination Act (DDA) – now part of the Equality Act 2010.

Recent amendments to the DDA make it unlawful to discriminate against people with disabilities in the way in which a company recruits and employs people, provides services or provides education. Providing services is the part of the law that applies to web site design.

Providing accessible web sites is a requirement of Part II of the Disability and Discrimination Act published in 1999 and was required by law from 2002.

Links on accessibility guidelines and standards are given at the end of the chapter.

E-MARKETING INSIGHT

From AIDA to persuasion marketing

In addition to usability and accessibility, web site designers need to add persuasion into the design mix; to create a design that delivers results for the business.

ClickZ columnist Bryan Eisenberg (www.clickz.com) has been called a 'conversion guru'. He advocates persuasion marketing alongside other design principles such as usability and accessibility. He says:

> It's during the wireframe and storyboard phase we ask three critical questions of every page a visitor will see:
>
> 1 What action needs to be taken?
> 2 Who needs to take that action?
> 3 How do we persuade that person to take the action we desire?

SECTION SUMMARY 6.1

Introduction to site design

Well-designed sites have clear objectives. The 5Ss can help you to choose objectives. Asking 'How can my web site help my customers?' also helps. But remember, the highest priority marketing objectives or purpose should determine the web site design. Well-designed sites have regularly updated, quality, content. Both content and context are 'king'. Good sites are also designed for usability and accessibility, but remember the principle of persuasion.

6.2 Integrated design

In this section, we look at the importance of integrating the web site into all communications, customer buying modes and with the databases that help to support relationships with customers.

THE WEB AND INTEGRATED MARKETING COMMUNICATIONS

Although web sites do more than just communicate (remember the 5Ss), they must integrate with all other communications tools, both online and offline. The web site's brand messages must be consistent with those in offline advertisements and mail-shots. Equally, new offers and major announcements such as awards won should be communicated consistently both online and offline. As the organization and the web site grows, this job gets more difficult, but space should be reserved within the page template for these key messages, which help show credibility and reinforce perceptions received through other channels.

At a basic level of integrated communications, all offline communications should carry the web site address or *URL* and describe the *online value proposition*. Equally, for customers who prefer other forms of contact, the web site should cater for *inbound communications* by carrying prominent and efficient telephone numbers, 'Contact us' forms, and where relevant to support sales questions, callback and Livechat systems.

It is worth remembering that different customers prefer different communication tools, channels or modes, particularly when buying.

THE WEB AND BUYING MODES

The web site should integrate with different buying modes. We must take account of customers' preferences of browsing, comparing, selecting or buying products either online or offline, as shown in Figure 6.6. Completing some activities of the buying process offline and some online is referred to as *mixed-mode buying* or *multi-channel behaviour*. The site design and offline marketing communications should be integrated to support mixed-mode buying.

Common buying modes include:

- *Online purchase* – some customers want to search, compare and buy online. Does your web site accommodate all stages of the buying process? Few products can be delivered online, so fulfilment is usually offline.
- *Online browse and offline purchase* – *mixed-mode buying* is when customers like to browse, look or research online and eventually purchase *offline* in a real store or in a real meeting. Some of these customers might like to browse online, but purchase via fax or telephone because of security and privacy issues. Does your site have fax forms and telephone numbers for

Offline
Online
Choose
Choose
Buy
Buy
Fulfil
Fulfilment (digital)

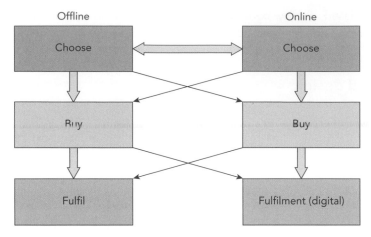

Figure 6.6 Alternative buying modes in mixed-mode buying

placing orders or taking further enquiries? Does your site integrate with other communications channels? Some sites also have *callback facilities* which allow visitors to request a telephone call from a sales staff member to complete the purchase.

Within these buying modes, there are different forms of customer decision making that need to be considered.

Brian Eisenberg, a US-based conversion optimization specialist, has developed a useful framework to help us think through the different decision-making styles of different web users (Figure 6.7). How well does your landing page support this range of styles?

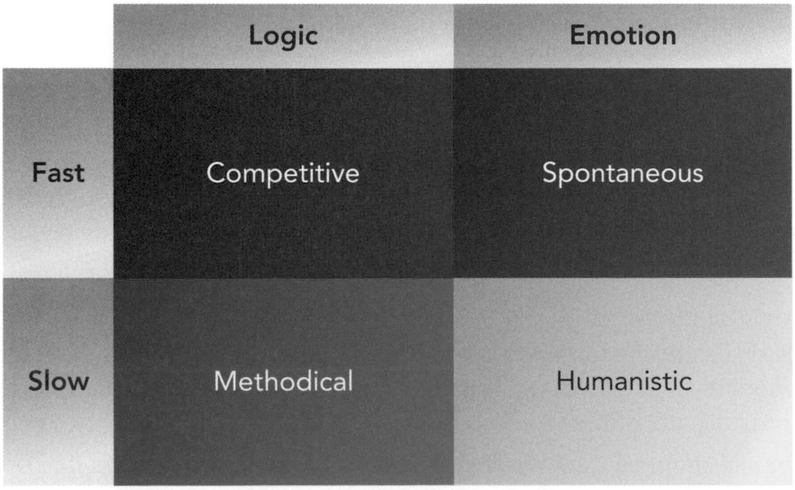

Logic
Emotion
Fast
Competitive
Spontaneous
Slow
Methodical
Humanistic

Figure 6.7 The four types of web purchase-making decisions according to Eisenberg

Source: Eisenberg (2006)

The *Methodical* focuses on HOW-type questions:

- What are the details?
- What's the fine print?
- How does this work?

The *Humanistic* focuses on WHO-type questions:

- How will your product or service make me feel?
- Who uses your products/service?
- Who are you? Tell me who is on your staff, and let me see bios.

The *Spontaneous* focuses on WHY- and sometimes WHEN-type questions:

- How can you get me to what I need quickly?
- Do you offer superior service?
- Can I customize your product or service?

The *Competitive* focuses on WHAT-type questions:

- What are your competitive advantages?
- What makes you the superior choice?
- What makes you a credible company?

E-MARKETING INSIGHT

How Dell supports mixed-mode buying

Dell supports a common buying mode: *offline awareness, then online selection, then offline purchase.*

This is done through communications tools that facilitate customer transition from offline to online and vice versa:

- *Offline choose to online choose* – if a customer reads about a particular model of a Dell computer in a magazine, it provides e-codes. These are typed in on the site's 'As Advertised' page, so avoiding the need for the customer to navigate to the particular product page.
- *Online choose to offline purchase* – if the customer decides to proceed with the purchase, but is uncomfortable about providing their credit-card details online, Dell facilitates this transition by providing a prominent telephone number on each page. This phone number is web-specific, so Dell knows that all inbound calls to this number

are in response to web research. Dell also uses different web-specific phone numbers on different parts of the site which have different audiences, to help connect callers to the right person and track site effectiveness.

HOW SHOULD THE WEB INTEGRATE WITH THE DATABASE?

Mixed-mode buying requires good systems. A web site database should, ideally, be integrated with the old, legacy, database and an email database. An integrated database can help sales reps know which web visitors have requested a real visit or a telephone call.

Furthermore, the database and the actual design of the web site can also help to nurture marketing relationships. The database remembers customer names, preferences and behaviours. The days of being able to build an effective web site using simple HTML code are long gone. An integrated database can personalize the experience and make relevant offers that match the needs of customer types.

E-MARKETING EXCELLENCE

A planned user-centred design approach

Effective web design requires a sound planning approach; success is not simply down to the creative skills of the designers. As with many marketing activities, research should be at the core of the web design process, so when briefing and evaluating web suppliers, make sure you gauge the user-centred design process. Don't reinvent the wheel, since there is an established standard for planning a web site improvement project: *ISO 9241–210: Human-centred design processes for interactive systems* (Figure 6.8).

The standard is based on four principles of human-centred design:

1 Active involvement of users and a clear understanding of user and task requirements
2 Appropriate allocation of function between users and technology, i.e. providing tools which automate user tasks
3 Iteration of design solutions through prototyping and user review, i.e. test, learn, refine
4 Multi-disciplinary design meaning the design team should have skills across all design aspects that affect the customer experience and the business results.

The different stages which relate to the techniques we will cover in this chapter are shown in Figure 6.8

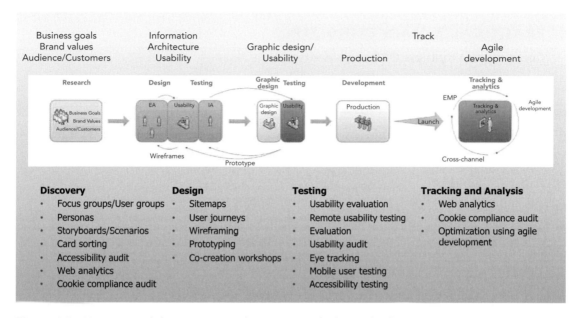

Figure 6.8   User-centred design process showing typical relationship between ISO 9241–210 and web site design phases

Source: Foviance (www.foviance.com)

SECTION SUMMARY 6.2

Integrated design

Web activities on their own won't work. Isolated web sites are ineffectual. They need to be integrated at several different levels:

1 Communications – consistent communications whether online or offline
2 Buying modes – marketers must facilitate customer transitions between online and offline information sources during the buying process
3 Databases – databases must be integrated to achieve a consistent view of the customer in order to build long-term relationships.

6.3 Online value proposition

The web gives the ultimate in customer choice. There are millions of sites to choose from and thousands of new domain names are still added every day. How will you stand out?

We saw in the first section of this chapter that good sites have good content, are regularly updated, easy to use and fast to download. In addition to all of these, your site has to have a clear and strong proposition. A proposition to your visitor. A unique proposition. An *online value proposition (OVP)*.

PRACTICAL E-MARKETING TIP

Communicate multiple OVPs run-of-site

You need to communicate your OVP, not only on your home page and the 'About us' page, but across your whole site through careful design of messages within the masthead or sidebars, as we saw in Figure 6.4. You also need to develop different OVPs for different audiences – the Dulux site (www.dulux.co.uk) does this well through use of four key personas. E-retailers need to think of their OVPs for different types of buyers from hunters and trackers through to explorers (see Section 4.6 in Chapter 4).

So reviewing your page template design for OVPs in different site sections during the web design and build process is crucial – you need mockups of all your site sections, not just the home page. This way you can communicate different OVPs to different audiences at different points in the buying process. For example, within the checkout process of a site, visitors need to be reassured about security, additional costs, delivery and returns.

Why should a customer visit, stay and even revisit your site? What does your site propose to visitors? Can you summarize the proposition for your site? Try to identify the proposition as you visit other web sites. Can you summarize their OVPs? Refer to Chapter 2, Remix, since the OVP will refer to different aspects of the marketing mix. The OVP should be clearly evident to the visitor. If you don't clearly know why a customer should visit and revisit your site, how likely is it that customers will understand?

The OVP is similar to the traditional unique selling proposition used in advertising, although advertising executives can have great debates about how the cyber world is different. Ideally, you need to try to find a proposition that explains what your organization or site is offering that:

● Is different from your competitors

● Is not available in the real world

● Makes a difference to your customers' lives.

At the very least, the proposition should clearly show the services you are offering and your credibility to deliver.

You then need to devise a tag line that accompanies your brand identity and URL to drive home your web proposition in all communications, both web-based and real-world.

So, we have our proposition. What next?

1 First, we need to leverage the proposition in traffic building. The proposition can be combined with the *URL* or web address and be in all advertising, as an email signature and included in all marketing collateral. As we see in Chapter 7, you can craft the message in the search results – this is important since it's often the first place a searcher finds out about you.

2 We need to state the proposition clearly on-site. Many sites are designed so that their proposition is prominent on the home page and may be referred to on every page at the top or top left as part of the organization's identity. Others make the visitor work too hard to understand the proposition.

3 We need to deliver on the proposition through all interactions a customer has with us including online and offline fulfilment and service.

E-MARKETING EXCELLENCE

Swiftcover communicates its online value proposition throughout the customer journey

Insurance company Swiftcover has thought carefully about the message it wants to deliver and then communicates it effectively through the customer journey; not just on its home page.

1 Communication starts in Google in the page description and site links (see Chapter 7 for discussion of these).

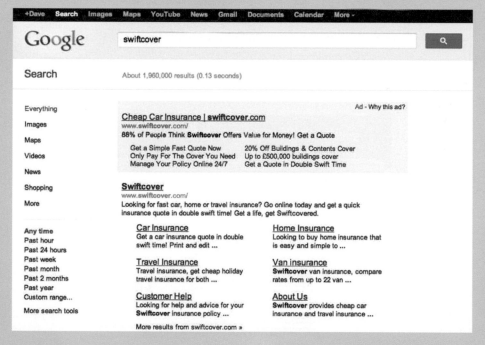

Figure 6.9   Swiftcover in the Google search results (www.swiftcover.com)

2 Communication of the OVP on the home page occurs both in the central panel above the fold and in the right sidebar through a 'Why choose us?' panel. It is a mistake to

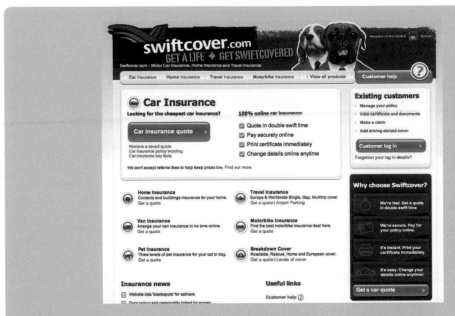

Figure 6.10   Swiftcover value proposition on the home page (www.swiftcover.com)

think people will go to 'About us' to answer this message, it needs to be on the home page and throughout the site where visitors may land.

3 Deeper in the site like this product page, Swiftcover communicates value through its testimonials – a different way of communicating value.

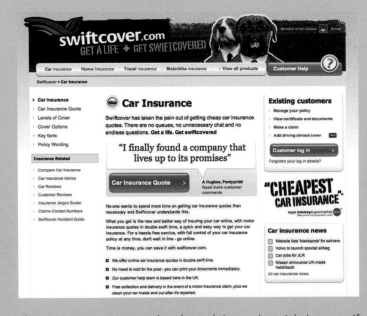

Figure 6.11   Swiftcover communicates value through its testimonials (www.swiftcover.com)

The following section on customer orientation examines what customers want, what's important and what's affordable.

E-MARKETING INSIGHT

Different views on the value proposition

These comments epitomize traditional meanings of the 'value prop' which can all be translated into an online environment.

A conventional view of the value proposition is provided by Knox *et al.* (2003) in their review of approaches to customer relationship management. They say a value proposition is: 'an offer defined in terms of the target customers, the benefits offered to these customers, and the price charged relative to the competition'.

Similarly, Rayport and Jaworski (2004) suggest that construction of a value proposition requires consideration of (1) target segments, (2) focal customer benefits, (3) resources to deliver the benefits package in a superior manner to competitors. However, branding advocates believe that the value proposition is more than the sum of product features, prices and benefits. They argue that it also encompasses the totality of the experience that the customer has when selecting, purchasing and using the product. We will see that these customer experiences and also service quality are very important online. For example, Molineux (2002) states that: 'the value proposition describes the total customer experience with the firm and in its alliance partners over time, rather than [being limited to] that communicated at the point of sale'.

To summarize, we can say that:

1 The offer forming the OVP should be developed specifically for specific target customer segments (see the Firebox example in Figure 6.12).

Figure 6.12   Firebox (www.firebox.com)

2 The OVP is not limited to the customer experience on-site, but involves how it links to other channels as part of a multi-channel buying process.

3 The product or service offer and experience that form the OVP must be based on in-depth research of which factors govern purchase and loyalty behaviour, and refined according to actual experience of the OVP by customers.

What should be the specific elements of an OVP? Remember from Chapter 4, Section 4.2 on motivations the six Cs that e-customers demand: Content, Customization, Community, Convenience, Choice and Cost reduction. These can all be built into the OVP.

SECTION SUMMARY 6.3

Online value proposition

In addition to good content, regular updates, ease of use and downloads, good sites need to have clear and strong online value propositions. OVPs require a lot of thought and refining. The hard work is rewarded, as a good OVP distinguishes your site and also, simultaneously, helps to focus the marketing effort and the customer's mind.

6.4 Customer orientation

Defining, first, the purpose of your web site and second, your audience, are fundamental stages of web site development. The answers drive the kind of content required; content drives the form required; and form drives the structure of the site. Usability and accessibility as defined at the start of this chapter are also key elements of customer orientation.

There are many different types of audience, including your competitors, shareholders, employees, the press and customers, to name a few (Table 6.1). *Customer orientation* is about trying to achieve the impossible – trying to provide content to appeal to a wide range of audiences. It's also about prioritizing your content for your key audiences and their key needs. Look at www.cisco.com, www.ibm.com and www.ni.com as examples of B2B sites that efficiently connect their audience with the information they need. In this section, we focus on the core audience – different types of customer.

As far as customers are concerned, you must remember that your web site exists for one reason and one reason only – to help customers. The big question is 'How can my web site help my customers?'

A customer-orientated web site starts with customers and their needs. The site will not only fulfil basic customer needs, it may even delight customers by fully understanding and satisfying the different needs that different customers have. So ask customers! Use live feedback tools like those we mentioned in Section 6.1. Try thinking about the types of services you can offer

Table 6.1 Different types of web site audience

Customers vary by	Staff	Third parties
New or existing prospects Personas (Chapter 4)	New or existing	New or existing
Size of prospect companies (e.g. small, medium or large)	Different departments	Suppliers
Market type, e.g. different vertical markets	Sales staff for different markets	Distributors
Location (by country)	Location (by country)	Investors
Members of buying process (decision makers, influencers, buyers)		Media students

customers. Identify their key tasks and goals and make these options prominent. These may be services you offer already such as giving the status of an order, new added-value services that don't cost much, or there may be new services that customers can operate themselves. Also ask customers what they think of your existing site. Ask them how you can improve your web site – what would they like to see there?

Rosenfeld and Morville (2002) suggest four stages of research that help achieve customer orientation:

1 Identify different audiences
2 Rank importance of each to the business
3 List the three most important information needs of each audience
4 Ask representatives of each audience type to develop their own wish lists.

Customer orientation can create competitive advantage. Customer-oriented web sites are relatively rare compared to product-orientated web sites. Product-oriented web sites tend to show lots of products (or services) and their features. Benefits are buried, as are any attempts to identify customer needs. Product benefits are never matched tospecific customer needs. These sites never ask 'How can I help my customer?'

Although we have said we want to provide content to appeal to a wide range of audiences, providing detailed content to all audiences may well be undesirable (since our messages to priority target segments may be diluted) or impractical (resources are limited). So we need to ask on which key audiences should we concentrate resources? A good starting point is to ask the question, 'Who is my ideal customer?'

Distinguish potential buyers from other types of site visitor

Bryan Eisenberg, author of *Call to Action* and *Waiting for your Cat to Bark*, recommends distinguishing potential buyers from other types of site visitors. He says (2011): 'Stop thinking of your traffic in terms of number of visits or visitors. That metric sucks! All that matters is potential buyers and actual buyers. Everything else just inflates egos.'

There are *three types of visitors* who can come to your web site:

1 *Buyers* – you know who they are because they converted to a sale or lead.
2 *Potential buyers* – these are visitors who are in the market for what you offer, but for any number of possible reasons, don't buy. They may be at earlier stages in the buying process, doing research to sell it internally, not adequately persuaded, driven away by bad usability, etc. The upshot is, there are countless numbers of changes/improvements you can test and make to bump these visitors from potential into actual buyers.
3 *Disqualified traffic* – these are visitors who wouldn't buy no matter what (maybe they arrived at your web site by accident – they typed shingles and were looking for the medical condition, not what you put on roofs, or maybe they don't have the type of budget your product or service needs, etc.).

On a typical web site, 3 per cent of visitors are buyers and the other 97 per cent are distributed among the potential buyers and disqualified traffic.

You should be asking yourself these two key questions:

1 Of your non-buyers, what percentage are potential buyers? And how can you increase those?
2 What marketing efforts are bringing ample *amounts* of traffic, but with poor *quality* traffic; i.e. what's driving a disproportionate amount of disqualified traffic?

SECTION SUMMARY 6.4

Customer orientation

A customer-oriented site provides easy access to content and services tailored for a range of audiences. But resources for content development should be targeted at ideal customers.

Site design should allow for different levels of experience or familiarity amongst its audience, including familiarity with the Internet, the organization, its products and its web site.

6.5 Dynamic design and personalization

The most important sound in the world is your own name. Remembering customer names and their needs is a personal thing. Web sites can get personal. Internet-based personalization delivers customized content and services for the individual, either through web pages, email or push-technology. In this section, we are going to look at what *personalization* is and what its components are. This topic is also reviewed from a different perspective in Section 8.6 where the concepts of *customization, mass customization* and *individualization* are explained.

Marketers have a dream opportunity – to personalize their services, and web sites in particular. Web technology, combined with database technology, increase the marketer's memory so that any number of customers can be recognized, their preferences remembered and served immediately. Cookies are the key to web personalization. When a new visitor arrives on a site, a *cookie* or small text file is placed on their computer which contains an identifier unique to them (it does not contain personal data as is commonly thought – this is securely stored in a database). When they return, they are recognized by the cookie and a personal message is automatically displayed within the page template according to their profile. Although some users do delete their cookies, if they are openly used with the option to 'remember me', they can provide a seamless, personalized experience, of which Amazon is arguably still the best example. Remember, sites are legally obliged to ask the visitor's permission to add cookies.

Personalization also helps to Sell, Serve, Speak and Sizzle:

1 *Sell* – personalization can make it easier for customers to select their products. A customer of an online supermarket does not want to select a new shopping basket of goods each time they shop. Example: Tesco (www.tesco.com).

2 *Serve* – a customer who uses an online travel booking service does not want to have to key in the same journey details if it is a common itinerary. Instead, personalization enables them to save their itinerary. Example: Expedia (www.expedia.com).

3 *Speak* – through personalization, a customer can select the type of communications they want to receive from a company as part of permission marketing. For example, a customer may just want to hear about major product launches via email, but not receive a weekly email. Example: Amazon (www.amazon.com).

4 *Sizzle* – all of the above can help add value, strengthen the brand and develop the relationship. Example: Dulux (www.dulux.co.uk). The Dulux brand enables visitors to save colour swatches and products to a scrapbook or project area for later access.

Note, though, that we missed out Save, since web-based personalization tends to be expensive to create and maintain. A less costly, email-based approach may be best for many companies. Personalized emails can be pushed out to customers reminding them and helping them in many different ways.

E-MARKETING EXCELLENCE

Customizo uses effective personalization to reduce bounce rates and lift conversion rates

Customizo's Online Design Studio offers anyone from sports teams to large businesses the opportunity to use their logos and proprietary designs to create their own apparel and accessories (Figure 6.13). Customizo (www.customizo.com) even allows its customers to share their creations online among their group in order to collaboratively edit, review, vote on and finalize a design.

Since recently revamping its Online Design Studio and adding new functionality with Adobe Scene7 customization features, Customizo has seen online user engagement metrics soar.

Within a month of its new web site going live, the company had increased page views by 340 per cent and conversion rates by 400 per cent. In addition, the company was able to decrease bounce rates by a dramatic 95 per cent. 'Using Scene7 to improve the way customers design, preview, and complete their orders, we saw more online conversions in just two weeks than in the 18 months on our old website with our previous, more manual, solution and processes', explained Ryan Saunders, the CEO of Customizo.

Figure 6.13   Customizo (www.customizo.com)

OPTIONS FOR PERSONALIZATION

Personalization can occur through displaying different information, depending on customer-specific or dynamic environment variables. Examples, many of which are illustrated by Figure 6.13, include:

- *Customer or company name.* A site can be personal on a simple level by referring to returning customers by name (using cookies to remember, for which permission is required in many EU countries).

- *Country.* Sites can identify the origin of a visitor based on their *IP address* and deliver content accordingly. IBM (www.ibm.com) automatically *redirects* customers to their own country site. Amazon recommends a local site if a visitor is on www.amazon.com.

- *Customer preferences.* Personalization of content on a web site can be set up by a customer clicking or selecting different types of content. This can be used to build data collected via registration forms, questionnaires, cookies and, of course, purchases.

- *Recommendation algorithms.* This approach, often known as *collaborative filtering*, uses automatic prediction (filtering) about the interests of a visitor by collecting preference information from different users. This is arguably the most effective personalization since it is unobtrusive; Amazon is the best-known example since it gives recommendations of books based on past purchases by customers with similar interests without requiring the user to register their preferences, using techniques described in *IEEE Internet Computing* (Linden *et al.*, 2003). The basic approach outlined in the paper is:

```
For each item in product catalog, I₁

    For each customer C who purchased I₁_

        For each item I₂ purchased by customer C

            Record that a customer purchased I₁ and I₂

    For each item I₂

        Compute the similarity between I₁ and I₂
```

- *News and events.* Results, surveys or press releases can be automatically posted to the site.

- *Viral personalization.* Here a user interacts with a site and personalized video clips are delivered based on a lookup of keywords typed by visitors. Early examples of this are the Burger King Subservient Chicken viral and the Mini Aveaword campaign, where it was combined with email to send a personalized video clip urging a friend to try the Mini, based on their geography, gender, job, hobbies, name and sexual preferences (straight or gay, etc.).

- *Referrer string.* Content can potentially be personalized according to which site the visitor previously visited and, in particular, the keyphrase typed into a search engine; e.g. an insurer has used the type of insurance searched for to tailor messages for new visitors.

- *Location.* Internet phones enabled with WAP make it possible to send promotions to a customer as they pass a shop. Whether this is desirable is another matter!

- *Multivariate real-time, conversion-optimized personalization*. Some systems use a combination of the variables above and then use a series of promotional containers to present the most relevant promotion, which is predicted to have the highest clickthrough rate, conversion rate or average order value for an individual customer. An established example of these approaches is Omniture's Touch and Target. Note, however, that personalization can be expensive to implement. It requires complex software and up-to-date databases. As such, it is most commonly used by retailers and major media owners that hope to have frequent interactions with customers and can demonstrate the returns. However, we predict that lower-cost personalization approaches will become widespread.

ONLINE RETAIL MERCHANDISING

For online retail site owners, merchandising is a crucial activity, in the same way that it is for physical retail store owners. In both cases, the aims are similar – to maximize sales potential for each store visitor. Online, this means presenting relevant products and promotions to site visitors which should help boost key measures of site performance such as conversion rate and average order value. You will see that many of these approaches are related to the concept of *findability*. Some of the most common approaches used are:

- *Expanding navigation through synonyms*. Through using a range of terms which may apply to the same product, the product may become easier to find if a site visitor is searching using a particular expression.

- *Applying faceted navigation or search approaches*. Search results pages are important in online merchandising since conversion rates will be higher if relevant products and offers are at the top of the list. *Faceted navigation* enables web site users to 'drill down' to easily select a relevant product by selecting different product attributes.

- *Featuring the bestselling products prominently*. Featuring strongest product lines prominently is a common approach, with retailers such as Firebox (Figure 6.12) showing 'Top 10' or 'Top 20' products.

- *Use of bundling*. The classic retail approach of buy-one-get-one-free (BOGOFF) is commonly applied online through showcasing complementary products. For example, Amazon discounts two related books that it offers. Related products are also shown on the product page or in checkout, although care has to be taken here since this can reduce conversion rates.

- *Use of customer ratings and reviews*. Reviews can be important in influencing sales. See 3.7 for Reevoo.com. Meanwhile, research in 2006 from online ratings service Bazaarvoice showed that for one of its clients, CompUSA, the use of reviews achieved:

  - 60 per cent higher conversion
  - 50 per cent higher order value
  - 82 per cent more page views per visitor.

- *Use of product visualization systems*. These systems enable web users to zoom in and rotate on products.

Dynamic design and personalization

Personalization delivers customized services through web pages and email and rich media containers. Personalization can be triggered through several dynamic variables, including: customer preferences, dates, events and locations. The jury is still out on the value of personalized web sites. It may work for some situations such as media sites, portals or complex e-tail catalogue sites. Remembering names shows respect. Recognizing customers and their preferences sows the seeds of good relationships and better business. The database is vital to this.

6.6 Aesthetics

$$\text{Aesthetics} = \text{Graphics} + \text{Colour} + \text{Style} + \text{Layout and Typography}$$

As we noted at the start of this chapter, effective web site design includes both form and function. Form means the aesthetics created by the visual design and function means interaction, navigation and structure. In this section, we're going to look at aesthetics – its components and the constraints. A site with powerful aesthetic appeal can help communicate a brand's essential values. The use of graphics, colour, style, layout and typography creates aesthetics. Together, these create a personality for the site.

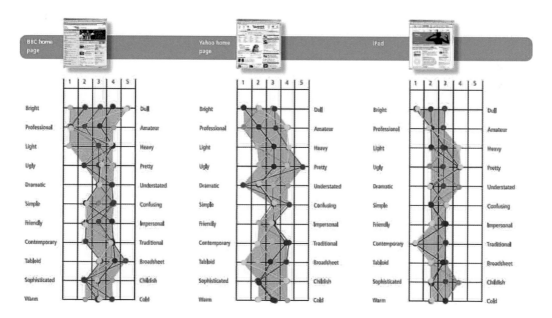

Figure 6.14   Emotional response testing example

Source: cScape (www.cscape.com)

SITE PERSONALITY

Words we could use to describe site personality are just as for people: formal, fun or engaging, entertaining, or professional and serious. This should be consistent with the brand. Emotional response testing can be completed by comparing well-known sites in a category against existing or proposed site sections as part of user-centred design. Figure 6.14 shows how this can be analysed through research of customer perception.

We like the way Rohit Bhargava of Ogilvy New York describes brand personality.

> *Personality is the unique, authentic, and talkable soul of your brand that people can get passionate about.*
>
> *Personality is not just about what you stand for, but how you choose to communicate it. It is also the way to reconnect your customers, partners, employees, and influencers to the soul of your brand in the new social media era.*
>
> *(Bhargava, www.personalitynotincluded.com)*

We think the examples of Ultralase (Figure 6.4) and Swiftcover (Figure 6.10) are good examples of a visual design with personality. But personality as Bhargava describes it is more than this; it also makes the brand shareable. Harley-Davidson (Figure 6.2) is a better example of this, perhaps.

SITE STYLE

Some sites are information-intensive and other sites are graphics-intensive. *Information-intensive sites* may appear cluttered because of the amount of text blocks, but the intention is to make best use of screen real estate and project an image of information depth and value to the visitor. Retail sites often fall into this category. Tests by Amazon showed that they generate best average order value with a design with many containers in left and right sidebars and with the option to scroll several times – there is simply more opportunity to connect a diverse audience with relevant products and promotions as they scan and scroll. However, where product range is more limited, as with Ultralase and Swiftcover, it is often found that simplicity is more effective, particularly at the level of the home page. With *graphics-intensive* sites, there is relatively little text; graphics and animations are used to create an impression. Fast-moving consumer goods (FMCG) brand sites often use this approach also. It's a matter of balance, that is best established through testing.

WHAT ARE THE DESIGN CONSTRAINTS?

There are many design constraints or challenges under which web designers operate. Unfortunately, the list of constraints is long and sometimes neglected, to disastrous effect:

1 *Modems and download time*. Although broadband access is growing rapidly, good designers optimize graphics for fast downloading and then test, using a slow modem across phone lines. Remember, the top sites download in less than a second. Also remember the 4-second

rule of thumb which shows that the majority of initial visitors to a site will not hang around to wait for it to download if it takes longer than this.

PRACTICAL E-MARKETING TIP

Decreasing download times – does your site pass the 4-second rule

Research from Akamai (2006) shows that content needs to load rapidly – within 4 seconds, otherwise site experience suffers and visitors will leave the site. The research also showed, however, that high product price/shipping costs and problems with shipping were both considered more important than speed. However, for sites perceived to have poor performance, many shoppers said they were less likely to visit the site again (64 per cent) or buy from the e-retailer (62 per cent). Surprisingly, slow download speeds are still a problem which impacts on conversion. Smart Insights (2012) gives the example of Walmart which showed that the conversion rate fell dramatically from 1 to 4 seconds, but due to technology constraints, one in two visits had at least one page download in more than 4 seconds.

These practical tips for designers developed by accessibility specialist Trenton Moss (2004) show how approaches to coding pages can make a difference. So make sure your site designers optimize for speed, not simply focusing on visual design.

1 Lay out your pages with CSS (Cascading Style Sheets), not tables
2 Don't use images to display text
3 Call up decorative images through CSS
4 Use contextual selectors (use classes to format)
5 Use shorthand CSS properties
6 Minimize white space [within code], line returns and comment tags
7 Use relative call-ups
8 Remove unnecessary META tags and META content
9 Put CSS and JavaScript into external documents
10 Use / at the end of directory links.

2 *Screen resolution.* Today a tiny proportion of desktop users have lower screen resolutions of 640 x 480 or 800 x 600 pixels; the majority have 1024 x 768 pixels or greater. But if designers use resolutions much greater than the average user, the screens may be difficult to read for the majority and, as we will see in the final section of this chapter, mobile design is becoming more important. *Fluid designs* (also known as adaptive design) may be best for retail sites where the design maximizes the space on the screen – fitting more above the fold on higher screen resolutions. However, designers of brand sites often prefer *fixed designs* where they have more control over the visuals. Some site designs, such as Kelkoo, give users the choice.

3 *Number of colours.* Some users have monitors capable of displaying 16 million colours, giving photo-realism, while others may only have the PC set up to display 256 colours.

4 *Browsers.* Different types of *web browser* such as Microsoft Internet Explorer, Mozilla Firefox and Apple Safari and different versions of browsers such as version 6.0 or 7.0 may display graphics or text slightly differently. An e-commerce site tested under one browser may fail completely under another. Make sure your designers test their designs against different versions of web browsers using a tool like BrowserCam (www.browsercam.com). Many don't, but should!

5 *Plug-ins and download time.* If the site requires *plug-ins* that the user doesn't have, you will be cutting down the size of your audience by the number of people who are unable or unprepared to download these plug-ins. Only use standard plug-ins such as Macromedia Flash or Windows Media Player which are pre-installed on PCs.

6 *Font sizes.* Choosing large fonts on some sites causes unsightly overlap between the different design elements. The facility for the user to change font size is required for accessibility, so test tolerance of a design for text resizing.

7 *Platform.* Sites are increasingly viewed via mobile phones or handheld devices like the PlayStation Plus. Different stylesheets can be provided for different platforms or view modes, such as printing or without images. But effectively, web pages have to be repurposed for mobile use.

As a result of these constraints, design of web sites is a constant compromise between what looks visually appealing and modern and what works for the older browsers, with slower modems; i.e. the *lowest common denominator*.

What are the implications of all these constraints? Although many professional site designers will work within these constraints, it is best to be upfront about the platforms you are targeting. The briefing or requirements specification should specify the target environments such as screen resolutions, browsers and platforms.

VISUAL DESIGN

As the Emarketing Insight box below shows, first impressions are important, whether it's meeting in the real world or via a web site. The visual design of a site is important to establishing trust and sets the tone for the future experience.

The biggest error with visual design is getting the balance wrong. Designers need to create a balanced visual design which is visually appealing, but also works for accessibility, usability, persuasion and branding! One way to help achieve this is to use different parts of the screen to achieve these elements. It used to be said by Jakob Nielsen himself (2000a) that 'Flash is 99% bad, but it is increasingly common to use Flash elements to engage an audience and to show the brand experience', but of course, at the time of writing (2012), Flash doesn't work on Apple iOS, so it can limit interactions with the substantial number of iPhone and iPad owners. Take a look at sites from chocolate brand www.divinechocolate.com, business software companies like www.salesforce.com or www.microstrategy.com which use a Flash banner, or PR company Ketchum (www.ketchum.com) which has an overlay of a team member literally engaging the audience. However, using a site which is 100 per cent Flash is still rarely a good idea, except for niche entertainment sites such as games, since there is little content for search engines to crawl.

COLOUR

The combination of colours used is important since they create a feeling about the site and brand. Colour schemes need to be right; i.e.

- Right for a personality which fits the target audience
- Right for a colour scheme that fits the brand
- Right for usability and accessibility.

Different colour temperatures evoke different feelings – between warm reds and oranges and cold blues and greens which can be helpful to give a more professional look. Of course, each colour has a different meaning or symbolism. For example, in Western cultures, red is vibrant and passionate, indicating love and danger, while blue contrasts and indicates reliability. But you need to be careful about local interpretation. See www.princetonol.com/groups/iad/lessons/middle/color2.htm for examples of colour symbolism in different cultures.

Complementary colours which are opposite each other on the colour wheel need to be used carefully and may cause problems with accessibility. The primary complementary colours are: red and green; blue and orange; and yellow and purple. Contrasting colours which are not necessarily opposite each other on the colour wheel tend to produce a vivid (if not garish) effect. When considering text on a background colour, for accessibility, high contrast is positive; tinted background boxes are also useful for highlighting content you want visitors to read such as a call-to-action. The Unilever corporate site (www.unilever.com) shows how a dominant colour can be used in each site section and this site also makes use of contrast.

Another issue to consider is white space (or background tints). White space can increase the visual appeal of a page and increase usability. However, it is again a balance, since the site visitor will need to scroll down more for content.

But whatever colour scheme you use, you need to make sure it's tested for accessibility; for example, through colour-blindness simulators such as www.etre.com/tools/colourblindsimulator/ which tests for the three types of colour blindness (protanopia, deuteranopia, tritanopia).

E-MARKETING INSIGHT

How long do you have to make an impact?

Research suggests that visitors can decide ultra-fast on whether they like a site, not in 2 seconds, but 50 milliseconds (that's 0.05 of a second). A summary of the research by Gitte Lindgaard (Lindgaard *et al.*, 2006) of Carleton University in Ottawa, published in the *Journal of Behaviour & Information Technology*, says:

> *The lasting effect of first impressions is known to psychologists as the 'halo effect': if you can snare people with an attractive design, they are more likely to overlook other minor faults with the site, and may rate its actual content more favourably.*
>
> *This is because of 'cognitive bias'. People enjoy being right, so continuing to use a website that gave a good first impression helps to 'prove' to themselves that they made a good initial decision.*
>
> *(Lindgaard et al., 2006)*

The research by Lindgaard *et al.* (2006) presented volunteers with a glimpse of web pages previously rated as being either easy on the eye or particularly jarring, and asked them to rate the web sites on a sliding scale of visual appeal.

Even though the images flashed up for just 50 milliseconds, roughly the duration of a single frame of standard television footage, their verdicts tallied well with judgements made after a longer review.

Further research by Haynes and Zambonini (2007) has shown a curve of visitors to museum sites that shows a peak (of visitors clicking) at about 2–3 seconds after page load. So this is a good indication of how long you have to get your message across. Based on this, a boxing analogy seems apt – you need to achieve a one-two punch. First you need a high-impact home page, which is relatively simple, but then follow up with a knockout punch on a second-level page or further down the main page, which is the detailed proposition which prompts conversion through the range of benefits, features, and testimonials that your offer is so good it will convince visitors to buy.

TYPOGRAPHY

The power of typography in adding to the visual appeal and persuasive power of a web site is often underestimated. Here are some practical tips to consider.

PRACTICAL E-MARKETING TIP

Typography Do's and Don'ts

Econsultancy (2007) recommends these approaches to typography best practice.

1 Use a consistent typography throughout a site. This will typically be enforced through cascading stylesheets.
2 Limit the use of different font types and sizes.
3 Sans-serif font styles such as Arial or Verdana tend to work best on the web, as they look sharper on the screen and are therefore easier to scan and read (unlike print

where the reverse is true). Sans-serif is by far the most popular approach online. But a visit to the *New York Times* (www.nytimes.com) shows that the use of serif fonts can make the site appear more distinguished – it affects the site personality.

4 Left-justified text works best in web browsers and is best for legibility.

5 The widespread use of images for rendering text in headlines and navigation is generally discouraged for accessibility and search engine optimization reasons (search engines read text, not images), but exceptions include text used in branding, promotions and certain sites where an immersive experience is required.

6 Where images are used for text captions, alternative text commonly known as 'alt tags' should be provided for accessibility reasons.

7 Create separate design requirements and a test schedule for the rendering of fonts in different browsers.

CHECKLIST FOR EXCELLENCE IN WEB TYPOGRAPHY

☑ 1 Never use underline in body text as a reader will think it's a hyperlink.

☑ 2 Avoid extensive use of italics as it is difficult to read on screen, but they can add variety.

☑ 3 Agree a standard for capitalization of headlines and link text. Generally, sentence case: 'Amazing new product released' is best since it is most scannable. Title case 'Amazing New Product Released' and all caps are ugly (and more difficult for readers to scan). However, all caps can be attention-grabbing if selectively used.

☑ 4 Headlines longer than three or four words may work best for SEO purposes, so ensure that font type size is not too large to support this, or allow the design to support wrapping or sub-headlines.

☑ 5 Remember that many web browser users will increase their type sizes, so check that the design renders gracefully as type is enlarged (at least by a small amount).

☑ 6 The difference between heading point sizes has a distinctive effect on design. Use a small difference between them for a smooth effect and a large difference for a more distinct design.

☑ 7 Where possible, avoid pages where the text content stretches across the full width of the browser, especially in fluid layout designs. Splitting the content into columns will vastly increase readability and is more in line with how people read articles and content in newspapers and magazines.

☑ 8 Standard fonts should be specified in the stylesheet(s), which allows a designer/developer to specify the font order in which the web browser should try and render the size. Using CSS also allows for simple and quick site-wide changes to the fonts displayed.

☑ 9 sIFR (or Scalable Inman Flash Replacement) is available for implementing non-standard fonts in site headings. sIFR (www.mikeindustries.com/sifr/) is an SEO-friendly approach for using more imaginative typography on sites. For headings, which are important for SEO and the main application of sIFR, the text is still specified as <h1>, <h2>, etc.

E-MARKETING EXCELLENCE

Using CSS to separate site style from design and create more engaging experiences

Visit css Zen Garden (www.csszengarden.com) (Figure 6.15), which shows how CSS can be used to separate presentation from content. Select the different designs from the right sidebar on the site to see how the design changes radically while the content remains the same.

Cascading style sheets (CSS) enable different style elements to be controlled across an entire site or section of site. Style elements that are commonly controlled include:

● Typography
● Background colour and images
● Borders and margins.

Figure 6.15   css Zen Garden (www.csszengarden.com)

For example, CSS will use this syntax to enforce the standard appearance of body copy on a site:

```
body {
margin:0;
padding:0;
color:#666666;
background-color:#f3f3f3;
font-family:Arial, 'Trebuchet MS', Verdana;
font-size:70%;
background-repeat:repeat-x;
background-position:top;}
```

The benefits of CSS are:

- *Bandwidth* – pages download faster after initial page load since style definitions only need to be downloaded once as a separate file, not for each page.
- *More efficient development* – through agreeing site style and implementing in CSS as part of page templates, it is more efficient to design a site.
- *Reduces updating and maintenance time* – presentational markup is stored in one place separate from the content, making it quicker to update the site globally with less scope for errors.
- *Increased interoperability* – by adhering to World Wide Web Consortium (W3C) recommendations; this helps with support of multiple browsers.
- *Increases accessibility* – users can more readily configure the way a site looks or sounds using browsers and other accessibility support tools. The site is more likely to render on a range of access platforms like PDAs and smartphones.

Most experienced designers will use CSS today, but it's worth exploring how CSS can be used to develop different styling for different sections of a site. This opportunity is used surprisingly rarely. Visit the different sections of the BBC site (www.bbc.co.uk) and the Natural History Museum (www.nhm.ac.uk) to see how different styling can be used in different sections to create a more engaging experience.

SECTION SUMMARY 6.6

Aesthetics

Aesthetics comprises graphics, colour, style and personality. Many web sites indulge in over-elaborate graphics and ignore their audiences' capability, and patience, to view them. Web designers must consider the constraints of variable modems, screen resolutions, colour displays, browsers and, of course, audiences. Many designers don't like designing for the lowest common denominator, but it does give you the widest audience.

6.7 Page design

In this section, we will explore the components of good page layout. Page layouts are implemented within *Content Management Systems* as *page templates*. Typically, the design will be more effective if there is a different page-template design for different site sections which have different objectives. For example, it is common to have different page templates for these key page types:

- Home page
- Product or service pages
- Product category and sub-category pages for sites with multiple products
- On-site search results page
- Landing pages for bought media such as Google Adwords or marketing campaigns
- Content marketing pages, often missed, but useful for sharing resources, advice or entertainment
- Social hub page (integrating feeds and updates from different networks)
- Blog page
- Utility pages (a standard template for 'About us', 'Contact us', etc.).

Of course it is necessary for different layouts to be consistent, so common across the site are:

- Company name and logo for identity (this should link to home page)
- Menu (and sub-menus) for navigation
- Footer for reference to copyright and privacy information (usually in small text)
- Page title for content; e.g. product information.

Each of these elements should be carefully considered, not only for usability, but also for SEO, since what the text headings and links contains is important to successful SEO as we will see in Chapter 7.

Using a capable CMS is essential to the consistency and management of any large site since it will enable *content owners* in different parts of the organization to update the content they are responsible for. Some good open-source content management systems are now available, such as WordPress, Drupal and Magento (for retail sites), which offer substantial savings without compromising quality.

A good page template design will achieve:

- An aesthetic, visually pleasing layout
- Clear emphasis of different content types

- Visual hierarchy showing the relative importance of different content through size
- Prioritization of marketing messages and calls-to-action for different audiences and products for persuasion purposes
- Clear navigation options to a range of content, services and visitor engagement devices.

A mistake often made is to use a symmetrical design in which page elements don't stand out; instead, *persuasive design* advocates that users should be guided on relevant paths by larger page elements. A good rule of thumb is to achieve a 'Focus on Five' key areas of screen (or six or seven), as shown by the designs in Figure 6.4 (Ultralase) and Figure 6.10 (Swiftcover), for example.

Wireframes are used by web designers to indicate the eventual layout for web page templates by showing where navigation elements and different types of content will appear on the page. The example of a wireframe in Figure 6.16 shows that the wireframe is so called because it just consists of an outline of the page with the 'wires' of content separating different areas of content or navigation, shown by white space. Wireframes are essential for agencies and clients to discuss the way a web site will be laid out without getting distracted by colour, style or messaging issues which should be covered separately as a creative planning activity.

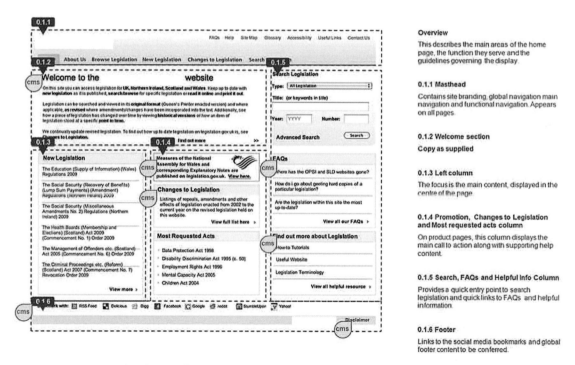

Figure 6.16   Example of a wireframe

© Bunnyfoot (2012) (www.bunnyfoot.com)

E-MARKETING INSIGHT

Craig Sullivan of Belron (www.autoglass.co.uk)

Craig Sullivan (2011), writing on the Simple Contraption blog, shows how wireframing can limit design through not showing interaction potential.

We do basic wireframes but quickly move direct to HTML for most of our work, as our developers are brilliant. Using agile iterations and lots of rapid changes, we take the design through several cycles of test and rebuild.

We often try stuff out or fake interfaces, pretend things – to gain insight or push the design forward. All of course with the wonderfully rich interaction and feedback.

This saves us lots of time, as we can make rapid pivots or changes without so much overhead. Pivotal tracker really works as the glue for this process, keeping everyone totally in the loop as we bring it together.

So – we'll often be racing to fit in maximum fidelity or indeed things we're interested in exploring in the next test. Sometimes we've worked until the mornings to get stuff into 'test shape' – and by this I mean the maximum level of leap in fidelity or fixes from the previous version.

Once we're good enough, we go live in a split test and measure metrics (conversion, customer Net Promoter Scores, times, downstream conversion). We then go into a further cycle of optimisation. This will involve rapid rounds of using analytics, ClickTale (to view customer sessions), browser testing and generally a lot of sleuthing to find uplifts. We jockey the metrics by improving persuasion, removing browser compatibility issues that may still lurk (customers' machines are different to test PCs) and generally tightening up copy, emotion handling and any interesting stuff ClickTale finds (a lot!).

Wodtke (2002) describes a wireframe (sometimes known as a schematic) as:

> *a basic outline of an individual page, drawn to indicate the elements of a page, their relationships, and their relative importance.*

As well as the position of navigation, wireframes should also consider announcements or special offers, which can be more effective if they occupy a consistent position on-screen. Examples include: links to product and service information; special offers or promotions; incentives to register; contact phone numbers; company news and PR.

The limited space on a page requires: concise writing (more so than brochures); chunking or breaking text into units of five to six lines at most; use of lists with headline text in a larger font; generally never including too much on a single page.

E-MARKETING INSIGHT

Users spend most of their time on other sites

Jakob Nielsen says:

> *Users spend most of their time on other sites. This means that users prefer your site to work the same way as all the other sites they already know . . . Think Yahoo and Amazon. Think 'shopping cart' and the silly little icon. Think blue text links.*
>
> *(Nielsen, 2000b)*

Web site designers face a difficult challenge in that they want their site to be memorable and differentiated from competitors. On the other hand, for ease of use, standardization of web features that users are familiar with is desirable. Think about the merit of these features of standardization:

- Widely used standards for labels such as Home, Main page, Search, Find, Browse, FAQ, Help, 'About us' and 'Contact us'
- Logo top left, hyperlink to home pages
- Main menu left margin or at top
- Signposts of content at top or top left of page
- Don't use non-standard text hyperlinks; e.g. non-underlined links.

E-MARKETING INSIGHT

Using eyetracking to improve page layout design

According to Lucy Carruthers, usability consultant at Foviance (www.foviance.com), the benefits of eyetracking are as follows:

> *Usability evaluations typically involve think-aloud protocols – whereby users describe their thoughts and actions as they carry out a set of tasks. This gives the facilitator a good view of the reasoning and driving factors behind the participant's actions.*
>
> *However, some types of behaviours are difficult to measure efficiently with think-aloud alone because participants may not be able to verbalize part of their thought processes and/or because some behaviours never reach consciousness.*
>
> *With eye tracking, however, we can provide insights into web design based on rigorous quantitative measures that are not possible using more traditional usability techniques.*

The heatmap example in Figure 6.17 shows that the location of headings and content pods will influence where people look. You can also see that the first part of headings and paragraphs are particularly important as visitors scan the page.

Bear in mind when evaluating a page template, that eyetracking studies of gaze trails typically show that visitors' eyes follow this path:

● Start in the centre
● Move to top left
● Move to top centre
● Move down the right column or navigation, if present
● Move to the bottom of the page.

However, these general patterns are influenced by the layout.

Figure 6.17   Example of a eyetracking heatmap

© Bunnyfoot (2012) (www.bunnyfoot.com)

Page design

Consistent layout is important. Key messages, menus, links, page size and frames versus tables all need to be considered carefully for effective web use.

6.8 Content strategy and copywriting

To create effective sites for marketing such resources requires a content strategy, since there is the challenge of delivering so many different types of content, in different forms, to different places and on different access platforms.

We define content strategy as:

> *The management of text, rich media, audio and video content aimed at engaging customers and prospects to meet business goals published through print and digital media including web and mobile platforms which is repurposed and syndicated to different forms of web presence such as publisher sites, blogs, social media and comparison sites.*

The definition suggests these elements of content management that need to be planned and managed:

1 *Content engagement value*. Which types of content will engage the audience – is it simple product or services information, a guide to buying product, or a game to engage your audience?
2 *Content media*. These include plain text, rich media such as Flash or Rich Internet Applications or mobile apps, audio (podcasts) and hosted and streamed video. Even plain text offers different format options from HTML text to e-book formats and PDFs.
3 *Content syndication*. Content can be syndicated to different types of sites through feeds, APIs, microformats or direct submission by email. Content can be embedded in sites through widgets displaying information delivered by a feed.
4 *Content participation*. Effective content today is not simply delivered for static consumption; it should enable commenting, ratings and reviews. These also need to be monitored and managed, both in the original location and where they are discussed elsewhere.
5 *Content access platform*. There are various digital access platforms such as desktops and laptops of different screen resolution and mobile devices. Paper is also a content access platform for print media.

Halvorson (2010) describes the importance of these activities. It can be seen that managing the creation of quality content is part of a broader customer engagement strategy which looks at delivering effective content across the whole customer lifecycle. As such, it is an integral part of the e-CRM strategy development which we cover in more detail in Chapter 8. It is also an important marketing activity affecting conversion optimization, social media engagement and SEO, so increasing attention is now directed at content strategy.

To help implement a content strategy requires a change of mindset for many companies (Pulizzi and Barrett 2010). They need to think more like a publisher and so invest in quality content that's superior to that of their competitors. This requires:

☑ Quality, compelling content – content is still king!
☑ Quality writers to create quality content who may be internal staff or external freelance writers
☑ An editorial calendar and appropriate process to schedule and deliver the content
☑ Investment in software tools to facilitate the process
☑ Investment in customer research to determine the content their different audiences will engage with
☑ Careful tracking of which content engages and is effective for SEO and which doesn't.

Pulizzi and Barrett (2010) recommend creating a content marketing roadmap which is underpinned by the BEST principles. BEST stands for:

☑ *Behavioural.* Does everything you communicate with customers have a purpose? What do you want them to do as a result of interacting with content?
☑ *Essential.* Deliver information that your best prospects need if they are to succeed at work or in life.
☑ *Strategic.* Your content marketing efforts must be an integral part of your overall business strategy.
☑ *Targeted.* You must target your content precisely so that it's truly relevant to your buyers. Different forms of content will need to be delivered through different social platforms.

COPYWRITING

Copywriting for the web is an evolving art form, but many of the rules for good copywriting are as for any media. This section explores the basic rules.

Possibly the most important rule is: don't assume your visitors have full knowledge of your company, its products and services. So, don't use internal jargon about products, services or departments and avoid indecipherable acronyms!

So what should you do? How should you write copy for your web site? A simple mnemonic for web copywriting is CRABS: aim for Chunking, Relevance, Accuracy, Brevity and Scannability.

Chunking, Brevity and Scannability go together. Many visitors briefly scan pages looking for headlines; follow these by short, brief, digestible, chunky paragraphs of five or six lines maximum which can be hyperlinked to further detail for those who want to 'drill down' for more information. Other visitors scan, move on and quickly find what they need elsewhere on the site. Section 6.9 on structure and navigation explores this in more detail.

In addition to chunky, brief and scannable, the copy must be relevant and useful to the target audience. This is where 'content is king' becomes 'context is king' – relevant information available at the right time in the right place. The copy must satisfy their needs and not yours; i.e. start with benefits instead of features. You can create benefits out of features by adding the three magic words: 'which means that . . .' after a feature.

Remember that you are copywriting not only for your human audience, but also the search engine spiders or robots which read (index) the words you use in your copy. So words used should include keyphrases that users are likely to search on within search engines (see Chapter 7 on search engine optimization).

And as with any genuinely good writing, it must be accurate to win credibility and loyalty in the long term. Don't promise what you cannot deliver. Do not cheat customers. It kills repeat business as well as new, referred business.

So, use CRABS (chunky, relevant, accurate, brief and scannable) to write good web copy. And remember, don't leave the best until last because, first, readers who scan will miss it; and, second, some readers won't scroll.

You should also check how persuasive your copy is against Cialdini's six 'weapons of influence' which we referenced in Section 4.6.

And last, but not least – don't forget nomenclature, or names, used for headings and signposting. Different nametags and signposts can give a very different feeling. Eyetracking research (www.poynter.org/extra/Eyetrack) suggests that on the web, customers' eyes are drawn first to the headings rather than the graphics. Test different headings to see which give the best *clickthrough*.

E-MARKETING INSIGHT

Gerry McGovern's top ten rules of copywriting

These are ten copywriting rules from Gerry McGovern (www.gerrymcgovern.com). As you read through these, think about whether these rules apply for other media and also whether your organization achieves them on your web site.

1 *Be honest.* Paper never refused ink. Web sites never refused hype. If you can't deliver within twenty-four hours, then don't promise to.

2 *Be simple, clear and precise.* Time is the scarcest resource, so never use five sentences when one will do. Avoid jargon. People are confused enough today.

3 *State your offer clearly.* What exactly is it that you sell?

4 *Tell them about your products' limitations.*

5 *Have a clear call to action.* If they like what you have to offer how do they go about buying it?

6 *Tell them quickly if they're not a customer you can supply.* There's nothing I find more frustrating than finding out at the last moment that they can't deliver.

7 *Edit! Edit! Edit!* There has never been an article that cannot be made shorter.

8 *Give them detail.* If they feel like finding out more about a particular product feature, then give them that opportunity. (That's what hypertext is for!)

9 *Write for the web.* Avoid the customer having to download Word documents, PowerPoints or PDFs unless offered as an alternative for convenience. (Note that Google and other search engines do now index these documents.)

10 *Leave it at nine!* If you want to create a 'Ten Rules' but can only find nine, leave it at nine.

SECTION SUMMARY 6.8

Copywriting

Copywriting for web sites is different to brochures and mailshots – think CRABS: chunky, relevant, accurate, brief and scannable. Watch the detail – even words used in signposts create a different feel or give a different personality to the site.

6.9 Navigation and structure

$$Ease\ of\ use = Structure + Navigation + Page\ layout + Interaction$$

Ease of use is number two of the key factors that make customers return to web sites. To achieve ease of use, we need to structure our site so that users can easily navigate. *Navigation* describes how users move from one page to the next using navigational tools such as menus and hyperlinks. We also need a suitable page layout that makes it easy for visitors to find information on the page and the right types and amounts of interactivity.

This section examines structure and navigation to ensure that first, all sections of your web site are easily accessible; and second, visitors enjoy the satisfying experience of finding what they want.

SITE STRUCTURE

Web site *structure* is the big picture of how content is grouped and how different pages relate to others. Without a planned structure, a site can soon end up as a 'spaghetti site'. This may leave visitors dazed, disoriented, confused and frustrated. If they cannot achieve *flow control*, they may not return.

A planned site structure with clear hierarchies will allow the user to build up a 'mental map' of the site. As we will see later, this can be reinforced by clear sign-posting and labelling.

There is a formal process that professional site designers use to create an effective structure known as an *information architecture*. Rosenfeld and Morville (2002) point out the importance of designing an information architecture when they say:

It is important to recognize that every information system, be it a book or an intranet, has an information architecture. 'Well developed' is the key here, as most sites don't have a planned information architecture at all. They are analogous to buildings that weren't architected in advance.

They describe an information architecture as:

1 *The combination of organization, labelling and navigation schemes within an information system.*

2 *The structural design of an information space to facilitate task completion and intuitive access to content.*

3 *The art and science of structuring and classifying web sites and intranets to help people find and manage information.*

4 *An emerging discipline and community of practice focused on bring principles of design and architecture to the digital landscape.*

Rosenfeld and Morville (2002)

Creating an information architecture requires specialist techniques. For example, *card sorting* or *web classification* categorizes web objects (i.e. documents and applications) in order to facilitate user task completion or information goals. *Blueprints* are then produced which show the relationships between pages and other content components, and can be used to portray organization, navigation and labelling systems. They are often thought of, and referred to, as site maps or site structure diagrams and have much in common with these, except that they are used as a design device clearly showing grouping of information and linkages between pages, rather than a page on the web site used to assist navigation.

The depth of the site is one aspect of creating an information architecture. This is important since it will determine the number of clicks a user has to make to find the information they need. The balance is between shallow and deep.

A good rule of thumb is that, even for a large site, *three clicks* should be sufficient to enable the user to find their area of interest. Placing an order should never be more than three clicks away. That said, the analytics show us that many who buy in a considered way will take many more clicks to buy. How deep is your site?

However, site design is an art, not a science. If you selected the deep structure, you will have had your reasons – the user has more simple choices at each stage in comparison with the shallow structure. In fact, the correct answer is probably a compromise between the two!

ACHIEVING FLOW

Good web designers try to enable '*flow*'. Flow is a concept that describes the degree of control or power a consumer has over the site. If customers can easily find the information they want through clicking on menu options and graphics, they will feel in control and this will be an enjoyable experience. We can use buttons and hyperlinks within copy to help achieve flow, but this is often neglected.

Site designers need to provide a choice for site visitors in browse mode or search mode. Many retail sites now use *faceted navigation* where the number of options in eachcategory or sub-category are shown. Retail sites also invest in *search analytics* to assess and improve the conversion rates from searches to sale. They will assess, for example, how many searches result in zero results following different types of product searches.

NAVIGATION RULES

Here are three navigation rules for a navigational template that is used throughout the site:

1 *Keep it simple.* Not too many buttons. Psychologists who have analysed the behaviour of computer users in labs say the magic number is seven (or fewer). Any more than seven and the user will find it difficult to choose. Seven or fewer keeps it simple. You can use nesting or pop-up menus to avoid the need for too many menus or too many menu items. Simplicity is necessary to avoid confusing the user.

2 *Be consistent.* Consistency is helpful since we want to avoid a user seeing different menus and page layouts as they move around the site. For example, the menu structures for customer support should be similar to those you encounter when browsing product information.

3 *Signposts.* Signposts help visitors by telling them where they are within the web site.

Cater for customers at different stages of the buying process – some want to see more, some want to try a sample and some want to buy right now. So 'See, Try, Buy' options can help. These can be presented in different formats – particularly when catering for customers who prefer to receive information in different formats; e.g. video (demonstration), text (often a PDF article) or actually speaking to a human (callback technology).We also need to clearly label the different folders or directories on the site so they act as a reference point for describing particular types of content on the site. A *URL strategy* specifies how different types of content will be placed in different folders.

A further example is where site owners have to make a decision how to refer to content in different countries – either in the form of sub-domain:

http://<country-name>.<company-name>.com or the more common http://www.<companyname>com./<country-name>.

E-MARKETING INSIGHT

Jakob Nielsen on navigation

Nielsen (2000c) suggests that the designer of navigation systems should consider the following information that a site user wants to know:

- *Where am I?* The user needs to know where they are on the site and this can be indicated by highlighting the current location and clear titling of pages. This is *context*. *Consistency* of menu locations on different pages is also required to aid cognition.

Users also need to know where they are on the web. This can be indicated by a logo, which by convention is at the top or top left of a site.

- *Where have I been?* This is difficult to indicate on a site, but for task-oriented activities such as purchasing a product, it can show the user that they are at the nth stage of an operation such as making a purchase.
- *Where do I want to go?* This is the main navigation system which gives options for future functions.

NAVIGATION TYPES

Most web sites have several types of navigation. These include:

- *Global navigation* – these are site-wide navigation schemes. Examples for a B2B site are: Products, Solutions, Clients, Support. They often occur at the top or bottom of a site, but may occur down the side.
- *Local navigation* – more detailed navigation to find elements in an immediate area – for example, 'Products' may be accessed through a faceted navigation, or a carousel on a home page is a common approach (Figure 6.19).
- *Contextual navigation* – navigation specific to a page or group of pages which may be in the body copy or in slots such as 'Related products'.
- *Breadcrumbs* – used to indicate where the visitor is on the site. For an example, see: www. smartinsights.com/social-media-marketing/facebook-marketing/. As you navigate around this site you will see, just below the top menu, a list of pages showing where you are and allowing you to easily visit a higher point in the structure. These are so named from the trail of breadcrumbs Hansel and Gretel left in the forest to go back to their house.

On a customer-facing web site, there are a number of alternative approaches to navigation. The most important are:

- Product-based
- Organization-structure-based
- Visit-based: first-time/repeat visitor
- Task-based or need-related
- Relationship-based: customer/non-customer
- Customer-type-based
- Company need

  - Calls-to-action
  - Campaign-related
  - Branding.

Figure 6.18   An effective carousel with labelled tabs at Coblands (www.coblands.co.uk)

How many of these are appropriate to your web site? How many are you missing? Note that many companies only adopt some of these, with the product-centric or organization structure common. Often, key navigation approaches may be missed, such as task-, relationship- or customer-type-based. It is always a balance between accommodating a range of audience needs and avoiding confusing visitors through too many navigation options.

SECTION SUMMARY 6.9

Navigation and structure

So navigation and structure can in themselves satisfy or dissatisfy customers. You need a strong information architecture. Well-thought-through navigation options are needed to promote flow experiences. Keep the page layout simple, consistent and clearly signposted, and you're on your way to success.

6.10 Interaction

Interaction helps to engage web site visitors by giving them some two-way communications plus greater involvement and control over their web experience. This section explores the types and benefits of interactions.

DIFFERENT TYPES OF INTERACTION

We can identify several basic interactive mechanisms:

- A simple mouse click on an image or an arrow to find more information or to look at the next item in a sequence (mouse event)
- Placing the mouse over a text menu option may give feedback by changing the colour of the text (mouse rollover)
- Selection from drop-down boxes
- Drag and drop
- Typing requirements into a box and then searching through a catalogue
- Slider, same choice: small, medium or large.

Remember also that there are many other types of interactions that add value to the user experience such as simulations, calculators, crosswords, quizzes, helpful information and turbine optimizers (see Chapter 1, Section 1.8).

Good interactions reinforce brand values – like FedEx's delivery update service. In addition to all of these automated interactions, web sites can also have real staff interaction; e.g. where *callback* technology invites a customer to request phone contact, *live chat sessions* or *co-browsing* involving a real-time web dialogue.

USING INTERACTIVITY TO MOVE CUSTOMERS THROUGH THE BUYING PROCESS

Now consider how interactions and two-way communications can help move a customer through several stages of the buying process, which was introduced in Chapter 4.

1 *Learning*. Help customers learn about you – your company, your products, features and their benefits. Interaction helps a customer to learn because involvement deepens the learning process. Interactive techniques include:

- Simulations or interactive demonstrations of products; e.g. the National Instruments Product Advisor (www.ni.com/advisor)
- Animations that explain different features or benefits of a product (e.g. www.nike.com)
- Tailoring – by product category or segment; e.g. Dell asks users to state whether they are a small, medium or large company. The site tailors itself accordingly (www.dell.com)
- Selection choice – online toy e-tailers allow selection by age of child, by type of toy and by brand (e.g. www.fisherprice.com)
- Downloads of detailed technical sheets, often presented as *PDF* files; e.g. business-to-business resources libraries with white papers to support different people involved in the buying decision for a complex product, such as an expensive software service
- Testimonials or case studies; e.g. www.accenture.com has client successes for each of its offerings
- 'Email a friend' facility; this can be used to alert a colleague or make them aware of a product or service.

2 *Deciding*. There are many kinds of interactions that can help customers to choose your product. Here's a small selection:

- An *interactive product selector* or sales adviser (Figure 6.20). This will help customers choose between different options if it is well-designed and not too interruptive.
- *Callback facility*. Human advice may be helpful in guiding the user through selection.

   To achieve this, some sites include callback facilities where a customer types in their name and phone number and specifies a time when the company should ring back.
- *Chat facility*. Some companies also include chat facilities where a human customer-service representative types an immediate response to the customer's queries. This approach is more efficient than bouncing emails between suppliers and customers over a long period. LivePerson (www.liveperson.com) illustrates this type of interaction. Co-browsing or screen-sharing can also help.
- *On-site search engines*. These help customers find what they're looking for quickly.

   They are popular features and some companies have improved conversion to sale greatly by improving the clarity of the results they return. Site maps are a related feature.
- *'Email a friend' facility*. This can be used to alert a colleague or friend or to help accelerate a shared decision on a purchase within an organization.

   Some e-tailers such as Lands' End (www.landsend.com) use a range of communications techniques to interact with the customer, including email, callback and chat (Lands' End live) – all helping the customer to decide.
- *Customer rating systems*. Incorporating star ratings and comments can add authenticity to a site and help increase conversion rates. Additional, fresh content can also help with SEO. See Superbreak (www.superbreak.com) for an example.

3 *Buying*. Leading the customer through the purchase (as shown by Figure 6.3) can help break down reluctance to buy online or *shopping cart abandonment*. Established e-tailers use techniques such as:

Figure 6.19   MyWebPresenters

- Leading the customer through the purchase in clearly numbered stages
- Minimizing the number of stages
- Offering an incentive to 'buy now'
- Understanding purchasing objections and information needs at each stage of the checkout process and providing appropriate information within the checkout area
- Location selection tool – find your nearest dealer by typing in a postal or ZIP code
- Voucher systems that are printed out on a customer's printer, then redeemed in store
- Including a phone number on-site to encourage purchase by phone where the customer prefers this
- Detailed content to reassure about security and privacy.

This remains an important, but hugely challenging, area despite the use of techniques such as usability analysis and web analytics.

4 *After-sales support.* After-sales support techniques for interactive support include:

- *Searchable FAQs* – easyJet (www.easyJet.com) has worked at improving its FAQs by analysing online and offline customer-service queries and then presenting FAQs when the customer selects the 'Contact us' option

- *Interactive support tools* – Epson allows customers to diagnose their problems with printers by prompting them to select their problem from pre-configured choices and then suggesting solutions (www.epson.co.uk/support)
- *Customer feedback* – after customers have used the interactive support tool, they have the option of interacting via a questionnaire on how useful the support was

The methods used for product selection, namely callback, chat or community discussion forums, can also be used. Some companies such as Cisco have found that customers can help solve other customers' problems.

Increasingly, interaction such as product selectors (Figure 2.3) is delivered using a *Rich Internet Application (RIA)* using techniques such as *Ajax* (Asynchronous JavaScript and XML) and/or Flash. While these applications can provide a compelling customer experience, care has to be taken with respect to search engine optimization (SEO) since the search engines may not index and link to specific product pages as readily.

Finally, all the interaction techniques we have reviewed in this section can also be viewed as a means of collecting marketing research. Web stats or web logs from your site reveal customer preferences, responses and problems.

E-MARKETING EXCELLENCE

Using interactions for research

Consider these examples of how interactions can be used to gather customer intelligence:

- *Customer preferences* – for example, Dell can see the proportion of users clicking on 'small, medium and large' customers to gain an appreciation of the role of the Internet in reaching these segments.
- *Responses to promotions* – when the Carphone Warehouse analyses response to online vouchers they can see regional differences in use of the Internet and response to promotions.
- *Customer problems* – Epson can use information from its interactive support tool to find out the type of problems customers experience with products and feed this information through into both customer service and new product development.

SECTION SUMMARY 6.10

Interaction

Appropriate interactions add satisfaction, value and flow to the web site. They help customers to learn about features and benefits, choose products and enjoy better after-sales service. It's worth considering!

6.11 Mobile site design

MOBILE AND SOCIAL SITE DESIGN CONSIDERATIONS

Making sure the mobile experience is right for users and site owners is a major consideration in site design. In the future, the majority of web access will be by mobile – principally smartphone and tablet users. This is already the case in many developing countries.

In this section, we'll show how a mobile-optimized site is becoming essential for mobile users.

How do consumers use mobile?

Research on UK smartphone use (Google, 2011) showed that smartphones are already regularly used for web activities, with 51 per cent browsing the Internet, 42 per cent using a mobile search engine, 38 per cent using an app and 18 per cent watching videos in a seven-day period. The triggers for usage include 65 per cent who pass the time when waiting, 52 per cent as a quick source of information, while only 7 per cent have no other Internet access.

Co-consumption of mobile content with other media is common, with 53 per cent watching TV ('dual screening'), 49 per cent listening to music and 18 per cent reading a newspaper or magazine.

Research also shows that mobile access is the most common form of web access during the early morning and evening.

Mobile marketing options

When reviewing the requirements for mobile design, it's worth remembering the full range of mobile marketing options since this shows the context of use. We identify eight main mobile marketing options.

1 *SMS*. Due to data protection laws, you can only send a marketing SMS (text message) to someone who has 'opted in' and agreed for you to send them a message. This makes it most effective for marketing to existing customers or prospects. For example, insurance brand Confused.com uses SMS to remind prospects to act on quotes they have been given. It's important that the follow-up from these is on a landing page and forms designed for mobile.

2 *Quick Response codes (QR codes)*. QR codes allow smartphone users to access a site rapidly from a smartphone, so if you use QR codes, again, offering users a mobile experience is essential.

Here are some examples of how they've recently been used for marketing – there are some fantastically creative ways to use them:

- Lacoste recently used QR codes in their shop windows. When users scanned the code, they were shown further information on the collection and other pieces in the range.

- Many magazines and billboards now use QR codes to extend the offer on the page or to encourage an impulse buy offline. This is extremely valuable for offline marketing campaigns.

- QR codes on in-store products to add value to the product; i.e. adding a QR code to a frying pan that gives the user recipes. A QR code scanner is needed (you can get one in mobile app stores).

3 *Bluetooth*. Bluetooth isn't a major marketing application. Bluetooth has limitations; you need to be in close proximity to a Bluetooth transmitter to receive information from it. It's also a barrier that a user has to switch on their Bluetooth before they can receive any messaging . . . Then there are the privacy/permission options of *bluespamming* and *bluejacking*.

Bluetooth ads can come in a variety of formats: text, images, audio, video and, in some cases, even stuff like games. Early adopters like Wembley Stadium and Arsenal Football Club tested the platform, but they never really saw a return. We see QR codes as a more effective method of achieving interaction and response today.

4 *Mobile applications*. The launch of the Apple app store in 2007 and the exponential growth of the app and smartphone market have turned mobile applications into an extremely credible marketing opportunity, which we will look at in more detail in the next sub-section.

5 *Mobile site*. With a mobile-optimized site, the images are large, the navigation is large and easy to use. The whole experience is completely different to a standard web site. Many companies have still not invested in a mobile-specific site. But take note that the leaders like Amazon, eBay and many leading UK retailers have done so.

6 *Mobile site and app advertising*. Mobile banners work in a similar way to web banners in terms of metrics, and ads are mainly bought through specialist ad networks. Of course, Google supports mobile advertisers through its Adwords product. You can see how many are advertising on mobile through its Keyword Tool.

7 *Location-based advertising*. Geo-location or proximity-based marketing allows you to target a customer or potential customer at the exact time that they are in the vicinity of your premises with the aim of enticing them in to your shop, cafe, bar, etc.

8 *Social network-based advertising*. We mention this option separately since, a lot of mobile web access is within social networks, so it's another opportunity to reach your mobile audience.

E-MARKETING INSIGHT

Mobile design requirements

Mobile marketing specialist Rob Thurner (2012) recommends these tips for brands launching mobile sites.

Best practice requirements include: content must be quick and easy to find, as mobile browsers have limited time, and often, an immediate 'intent'. Navigation is critical.

Content should always be accessible within three clicks, and mobile sites should be built 'on-tracks'; i.e. scrolling should be vertical only, not horizontal. Consistency with convention will help usability. However, Thurner notes that many retailers use a standard approach where they simply list product categories with a banner promotion; the approach is not personalized.

Checklist

☑ 1 *User experience is fundamental.* Make sure content is quick to find and easy to navigate

☑ 2 *Use handset detection software.* Once detected, redirect to a mobile-optimized site matching that handset's capabilities

☑ 3 *Ensure that all other media channels drive traffic to your site.* Add SMS calls to action or QR codes on above-the-line media, mailers, point of sale materials

☑ 4 *Use personalization.* Personalized content, derived from full integration with your CMS, encourages return visits

☑ 5 *Evaluate payment options and optimize checkout.* Minimize steps in the checkout process to reduce drop off

☑ 6 *Test!* Test the site prior to launch to remedy errors; test text and layout variables to optimise user experience

☑ 7 *Monitor!* Monitor traffic and page views constantly, and refine content in real time.

Taking the mobile site versus app decision

Despite advances in web development frameworks such as CSS, the challenge of developing for different platforms has increased with the advent of new platforms such as smartphones and tablets. Consequently, key technology options include:

● Mobile-optimized version of full site using a fixed-width, e.g. for smartphone screen resolution or a responsive design that adapts automatically for different screen resolutions and sizes including desktop, tablet and smartphone?
● Mobile version of site (most popular pages linking through to traditional pages)?
● Separate mobile app?
● Which device formats and so screen sizes do we support?
● Which mobile operating systems and mobile browser versions do we support? For example, Android, Apple iOS, Symbian, Windows Mobile platforms, etc.?

Since apps can provide a more tailored experience than mobile sites, eBay and Amazon both promote the app experience preferentially. Figure 6.20 shows how eBay uses the mobile targeting capabilities of Google Adwords to encourage download.

When users first arrive on the site, they are also encouraged to get the eBay iPhone app (Figure 6.21).

It will only be cost-effective for the very largest organizations to design for all of these target platforms and devices, so companies need to balance the costs against the benefits and select carefully. The decision is complicated by the improving quality of screen resolution through smartphones and tablets. Many of these now have a size that enables viewing of sites designed for desktops, although zooming and panning can be frustrating.

The challenge has been nicely summarized by former eBay designer, Luke Wroblewski, now lead designer at start-up Bagcheck, who says:

> *As use of mobile devices continues to skyrocket across the globe, we're seeing more ways to tackle the challenge of creating great web experiences across multiple devices. But which approach is right for any given project?*
>
> *For us site performance and speed of development were crucial. So many of the decisions we made were designed to make both of these as fast as possible. As part of our focus on performance, we also had a philosophy of 'just what's necessary'. This meant [that] sending things to devices (and people) that didn't actually need them made us squeamish. We liked to optimize. With a dual template system we felt we had more optimization of: source order, media, URL structure, and application design.*
>
> *(Wroblewski, 2011)*

SECTION SUMMARY 6.11

Interaction

Appropriate interactions add satisfaction, value and flow to the web site. They help customers to learn about features and benefits, choose products and enjoy better after-sales service. It's worth considering!

CHAPTER SUMMARY

1 Site design should be determined by clear marketing objectives. Key concepts for an effective design are usability, accessibility and persuasion.

2 Web site design needs to be integrated with other marketing activities – in particular, outbound and inbound communications, buying modes and databases.

3 Each site should have a clear online value proposition (OVP) that differentiates the site from those of competitors and defines services not available in the real world which positively impact on the customers' lives. The OVP should be communicated offline, online and on the site itself and should be delivered.

4 Customer orientation involves grouping access to content and services that meet the needs of an audience made up of different stakeholders and customer segments, with different degrees of familiarity with the Internet, the organization, its services and its site.

5 Customized services can be delivered through personalization of web pages and email. These help to build relationships as data can be gathered about customers' needs and services provided that these match needs more closely.

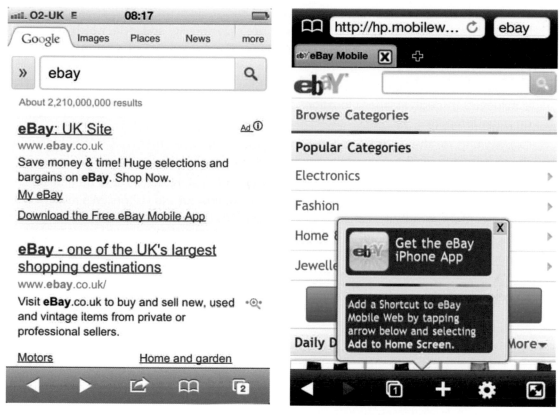

Figure 6.20   eBay within the mobile search results

Figure 6.21   eBay UK mobile site

Figure 6.22   Bagcheck.com – an example of a site where different desktop and mobile experiences have been implemented

6 Site aesthetics are an important consideration in design since the combination of graphics, colour, style, layout and typography define a site's personality and style, which are important in branding. Designers have to work under the constraints of, and test for, many technology variations including download speed, screen resolution, browsers and plug-ins.

7 Page layout is important to providing a clear consistent message throughout the site. This is achieved through standard locations for menus, logos, names, signposts and content on page templates.

8 Copywriting for the web shares much in common with other media. 'CRABS' highlights the importance of Chunking, Relevance, Accuracy, Brevity and Scannability.

9 Ease of use is achieved by creating a sound information architecture, and then designing navigation tools and structures that enable a smooth flow for site visitors. Minimizing clicks to find content, simplicity, consistency and signposts can all help achieve this.

10 Providing interactive content in addition to static content can help support the customer throughout the buying process through product selection tools, callback facilities and direct or indirect customer-service tools.

11 Develop a usable mobile experience, considering the relevance of apps.

References

Akamai (2006) Akamai and Jupiter Research identify '4 seconds' as the new threshold of acceptability for retail web page response times. Press release, 6 November at: www.akamai.com/html/about/press/releases/2006/press_110606.html.

Bhargava, R. (2008) *Personality Not Included: Why Brands Lose Their Authenticity – and How Great Companies Get It Back*. McGraw-Hill, New York. Available from: www.personalitynotincluded.com

Christodoulides, G., de Chernatony, L., Furrer, O., Shiu, E. and Temi, A. (2006) Conceptualising and measuring the equity of online brands. *Journal of Marketing Management*, 22(7/8), pp. 799–825.

Econsultancy (2007) *Best Practice Guide to Effective Web Design. Improving your Online Customer Experience through Results-led Web Design and Development*. Lead author: Dave Chaffey. Econsultancy, London. Available at: http://econsultancy.com/uk/reports/web-design-best-practice-guide.

Eisenberg, B. (2006) Dishing out what the customer really wants. Blog post, 1 April 2006 at: www.grokdotcom.com/topics/copywritinghype2.htm

Eisenberg, B. (2011) How many 'potential buyers' are you driving to your website? Blog post, February 2011 at: www.bryaneisenberg.com/how-many-potential-buyers-are-you-driving-to-your-website/

Google (2011) Mobile consumer evolution. Understand UK smartphone users. White paper with Ipsos MediaCT. Available at: www.google.co.uk/ads/mobile/m/insights.html#research-reports

Halvorson, K. (2010) *Content Strategy for the Web*. New Riders, Berkeley, CA.

Haynes, J. and Zambonini, D. (2007) Why are they doing that!? How users interact with museum web sites. In *Museums and the Web 2007: Proceedings*, eds J. Trant and D. Bearman,

Archives & Museum Informatics, Toronto. Available at: www.archimuse.com/mw2007/papers/haynes/haynes.html

International Organization for Standardization (2008) *ISO 9241. Part 151: Guidance on World Wide Web user interfaces.* International Organization for Standardization, Geneva.

International Organization for Standardization (2010) *ISO 9241. Part 210: Human-centred design for interactive systems.* International Organization for Standardization, Geneva.

Kaushik, A. (2009) *Web Analytics 2.0. The Art of Online Accountability and Science of Customer Centricity.* John Wiley & Sons.

Knox, S., Maklan, S., Payne, A., Peppard, J. and Ryals, L. (2003) *Customer Relationship Management: Perspectives from the Marketplace.* Butterworth-Heinemann, Oxford.

Linden, G., Smith, B. and York, J. (2003) Amazon.com recommendations: item-to-item collaborative filtering. *IEEE Internet Computing,* January/February, pp. 76–80.

Lindgaard, G., Fernandes, G., Dudek, C. and Brown, J. (2006) Attention web designers: You have 50 milliseconds to make a good first impression! *Behaviour & Information Technology,* 25, pp. 115–26.

Molineux, P. (2002) *Exploiting CRM. Connecting with Customers.* Hodder & Stoughton, London.

Moss, T. (2004) Ten ways to speed up the download time of your web pages. Article at: http://websitetips.com/articles/optimization/speed/

Nielsen, J. (2000a) Flash: 99% bad. *Jakob Nielsen's Alertbox,* 29 October at: www.useit.com/alertbox/20001029.html

Nielsen, J. (2000b) End of web design. *Jakob Nielsen's Alertbox,* 23 June at: www.useit.com/alertbox/000623.html.

Nielsen, J. (2000c) Details in study methodology can give misleading results. *Jakob Nielsen's Alertbox,* 21 February at: www.useit.com/alertbox/990221.html.

Nielsen, J. (2003) Usability 101. *Jakob Nielsen's Alertbox,* 25 August at: www.useit.com/alertbox/20030825.html

Pulizzi, J. and Barrett, T. (2010) *Get Content. Get Customers.* McGraw-Hill, Columbus, OH.

Rayport, J. and Jaworski, B. (2004) *Introduction to E-commerce,* 2nd edition. McGraw-Hill, New York.

RNIB (no date) Royal National Institute for the Blind web accessibility guidelines. At: www.rnib.org.uk/accessibility

Rosenfeld, L. and Morville, P. (2002) *Information Architecture for the World Wide Web,* 2nd edition. O'Reilly, Sebastopol, CA.

Smart Insights (2012) Is your website fast enough? Blog post by Chris Soames, 13 March at: http://www.smartinsights.com/search-engine-optimisation-seo/index-inclusion/is-your-website-fast-enough-2/

Sullivan, C. (2011) Wireframes must die. Post on Matt Conway's Simple Contraption blog, 13 March at: www.simplecontraption.com/wireframes-are-old-we-need-new

Thurner, R. (2012) Is your mobile user experience fit for purpose? Blog post, 13 February at: www.smartinsights.com/mobile-marketing/mobile-design/is-your-mobile-user-experience-fit-for-purpose/

Wodtke, C. (2002) *Information Architecture: Blueprints for the Web.* New Riders, Indianapolis, IN.

Wroblewski, L. (2011) Why separate mobile and desktop web design? Blog post, 1 September at: www.lukew.com/ff/entry.asp?1390

Further reading

Eisenberg, B. and Eisenberg, J. (2006) *Call to Action: Secret Formulas to Improve Online Results*. Thomas Nelson. Many practical tips on improving conversion for e-commerce sites.

Krug, S. (2005) *Don't Make Me Think*, 2nd edition. New Riders, Berkeley, CA. The classic common-sense introduction to this topic.

Lynch, P. and Horton, S. (2009) *Web Style Guide. Basic Design Principles for Creating Web Sites*, 3rd edition. Yale University Press, New Haven, CT. A great online resource available at: www.webstyleguide.com

Rosenfeld, L. and Morville, P. (2006) *Information Architecture for the World Wide Web*, 3rd edition. O'Reilly, Sebastopol, CA. A structured, fairly academic description of how to approach information architecture.

Van Duyne, D., Landay, J. and Hong, J. (2007) *The Design of Sites. Patterns, Principles, and Processes for Crafting a Customer-centered Web Experience*, 2nd edition. Addison-Wesley, Reading, MA. An in-depth analysis of web site design with many examples. All web site designers will learn some new tips from this book.

Web links

A List Apart (www.alistapart.com). Explores the design, development, and meaning of web content, with a special focus on web standards and best practices.

Boxes and Arrows (www.boxesandarrows.com). A collection of best practice articles and discussions about information architecture.

Equality Act (formerly Disability and Discrimination Act) information (http://www.equality humanrights.com/). Code of practice including reference to web sites.

Jakob Nielsen's Use It (www.useit.com). Despite the antiquated design, the detailed guidelines (Alertboxes) and summaries of research into the usability of web media are still referenced widely.

Royal National Institute for the Blind (www.rnib.org.uk/professionals/webaccessibility/Pages/web_accessibility.aspx). Web accessibility guidelines.

SitePoint (www.sitepoint.com). Online publisher with a range of blog articles in all web design categories.

Step Two (www.steptwo.com.au). This design company has introductory outlines and more detailed articles on information architecture and other aspects of usability.

UsabilityNet (www.usabilitynet.org). A portal about usability with good links to other sites and an introduction to usability terms and concepts.

Usability News (www.usabilitynews.com). A compilation of articles from different sources, plus jobs and events.

User Interface Engineering (www.uie.com). Articles on usability that often provide a counterpoint to those of Nielsen.

Webby Awards (www.webbyawards.com). The Oscars for the web – international.

Web Standards Project (WASP) (www.webstandards.org). A consortium that promotes web standards.

World Wide Web Consortium (www.w3.org/WAI). Web accessibility guidelines.

Zeldman.com (www.zeldman.com). The blog of web standards advocate, Jeffrey Zeldman.

Self-test

1 Explain the linkage between site design and marketing objectives.

2 Describe a scenario where on-site and offline marketing communications can be integrated to support mixed-mode buying.

3 Explain how OVP differs from USP and define the OVP for your organization.

4 How would you assess whether a web site had good customer orientation?

5 Describe the benefits of different types of personalization.

6 What are the constraints on using graphical elements to produce a site with strong visual appeal?

7 Draw a diagram summarizing the main page elements of your organization's web site.

8 Write down six rules for effective web copywriting.

9 Describe the link between web site design and supporting customers through stages of the buying process.

10 Explain the options for developing customer experiences on mobile devices. Outline the considerations which should affect the choice of option.

Chapter **7**

Traffic building

The web is different. Instead of one-way interruption, web marketing is about delivering useful content at just the precise moment a buyer needs it. What visitors really want is content that first describes the issues and problems they face and then provides details on how to solve those problems.

Meerman-Scott (2007)

Sadly it's not always the best products that succeed, but rather, reasonably good ones that (a) everyone knows about; and (b) everyone can easily find when they need them. The same is true of web sites. This chapter shows you how to build traffic – how to acquire the right visitors to your site or other forms of online presence in order to achieve the right marketing outcomes for you. You will get a briefing on the different digital communications channels including search engine marketing, online PR, online partnerships, interactive advertising, opt-in email and viral marketing. We will also show you that to succeed with your online communications also means gaining different forms of visibility on partner sites which are themselves successful in traffic building.

OVERALL LEARNING OUTCOME

By the end of this chapter, you will be able to:

- Evaluate the range of options for traffic building
- Develop a plan to balance the options for traffic building
- Identify success factors for different online communications tools
- Review options for achieving positive representation on third-party sites.

CHAPTER TOPIC	LEARNING OBJECTIVE
7.1 Introduction	Assess different options for traffic building
7.2 Search engine marketing	Use different approaches to improve a site's listing in search engines including search engine optimization (SEO) and Pay Per Click (PPC)
7.3 Online PR	Manage your reputation online through supporting journalists and maximizing your representation on portals and social networks
7.4 Online partnerships	Use link building, affiliate marketing and online sponsorships to exploit the network effect of the Internet
7.5 Interactive advertising	Identify the elements of a successful online display ad campaign
7.6 Opt-in email	Build traffic and relationships through opt-in email
7.7 Viral marketing	Assess the relevance of viral marketing
7.8 Offline traffic building	Create a balance between offline and online promotion techniques

7.1 Introduction to traffic building

Generating traffic is vital to achieving e-marketing objectives, no matter whether the aim is Sell, Serve, Speak, Save or Sizzle (see Chapter 1). What are the key characteristics of effective traffic building? In this section, we will introduce three key aspects of traffic building:

1 *Targets* – specific objectives for traffic building need to be developed before embarking on a traffic building campaign.

2 *Techniques* – traffic building involves combining new online *digital media channels* and traditional offline communication techniques to promote the web site proposition and so encourage visits. Achieving the correct mix of traffic building techniques is vital, but difficult. Use your *web analytics* systems as your ally to understand which elements of your communications mix are effective.

3 *Timing* – when should traffic building occur? Smart e-marketers include specific campaigns, perhaps to launch a site, new product or promotion, but they also make investment in a continuous *'always-on communications'* process of attracting visitors by search or affiliates. After all, online customers are looking for products, services and experiences throughout the year, not only when your campaign is live.

E-MARKETING INSIGHT

Reviewing different types of traffic sources with web analytics

Web analytics tools like Google Analytics show the range of traffic sources and you can drill down to find individual *referring sites* or search terms by which visitors find your site.

Figure 7.1 shows a compilation across all sites globally that use Google Analytics.

- *Search traffic* – this includes both natural and paid search (Google AdWords)
- *Referral traffic* – this is traffic from other sites which have direct links to your site
- *Direct traffic* – direct traffic results from URL type-ins, bookmarks or when email marketing or social media links from apps aren't tracked

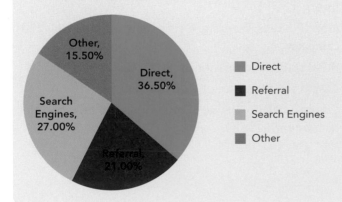

Figure 7.1 Average traffic sources for sites using Google Analytics

Source: Smart Insights (2011a)

- *Other/campaigns* – other digital marketing channels like affiliates, display ads and email campaigns. Best practice is to define marketing campaign tags associated with the link to the landing page – search Google for 'Analytics URL Builder' to see how this works.

If you use Google Analytics, you need to make sure traffic sources are tracked using the relevant five standard dimensions for campaign tracking; these need to be incorporated into the query string of the URL, which is after the question mark for each ad placement, as this example shows:

http://www.domain.com/landing_page.php?utm_campaign=spring-sale&utm_medium=banner&utm_source=publisher_site_name

The campaigns report in Google Analytics will then enable you to compare media. The table below explains each of these five dimensions which refers to this example:

A summary of the campaign tracking parameters in Google Analytics

Variable	Explanation
utm_campaign Recommended	The name of the marketing campaign; e.g. Spring Campaign
utm_medium Required	Media channel (i.e. email, banner, CPC, etc.)
utm_source Required	The publisher or partner site name
utm_content Optional	The version of the ad (used for A/B testing) or in AdWords. You can identify two versions of the same ad using this variable. This is not always used and is NOT included in the above example
utm_term Optional	The search term purchased (if the link refers to keywords). This is not always used and is NOT included in the above example

Note that each analytics vendor has its own format for marketing source codes; we give the example of the most widely used system.

TARGETS

Typical traffic targets include the quantity, quality and cost of traffic. Although a successful site is often referred to in terms of quantity, such as the number of visitors, it is the traffic quality that really indicates the success of each media channel.

Remember that generating traffic is not limited to driving visitors to your own web site. Traffic building can also be effective on the third-party sites that your audience use, including social networks. For example, a manufacturer of nappies may decide to create or sponsor a microsite on a third-party site.

Traffic quality can be assessed by asking two questions about site visitors. First, are they within the target audience for the web site? Second, do they respond in line with the communications objectives; i.e. do they engage with your content, do they receive the key messages about your brand and convert to the site outcomes you require? Remember from Section 6.1 (Practical E-Marketing Tip box) that *bounce rate* is an excellent way to compare the quality of different referrers to different *landing pages*.

Cost can be considered in terms of the cost of getting the visitor to the site, and the cost of achieving the outcomes during their visit. Experienced online marketers control their traffic building through managing the Cost Per Acquisition (CPA) (sometimes called Cost Per Action). Depending on context and market, CPA may refer to different outcomes.

Typical cost targets include:

- Cost Per Acquisition – of a visitor *(Cost Per Click, CPC)*
- Cost Per Acquisition – of a lead
- Cost Per Acquisition – of a sale *(allowable customer acquisition cost)*.

CPA is typically equivalent to Cost Per Sale (CPS), but may also apply to cost per visitor, lead or enquiry, or other type of outcome since direct product sales are not practical or appropriate for all web sites. For a car manufacturer, for example, CPA might refer to the cost of generating a brochure or test-drive request.

The value of sales should also be considered. Online retailers calculate sales value in terms of the value from the first sale *(average order value, AOV)* and campaign *return on investment (ROI)*. Companies should also model *customer lifetime value (LTV)*. Leading e-marketers select online referrers (i.e. choice of portal) not only by minimizing CPA, but also through maximizing new visitors with the highest potential LTV.

TECHNIQUES

The traffic-building techniques we will cover are summarized in Figure 7.2 (above) and will give you a good framework for planning your traffic-building or digital marketing campaign activities. These are now commonly referred to by agencies as digital media channels (or digital channels for short). The skill in traffic building is using the correct mix of online techniques such as viral marketing, affiliates and search engine optimization which best fits the media consumption of your audience and minimizes Cost Per Acquisition (CPA). The promotional mix for traffic building typically includes a range of online and offline techniques, each with their own strengths and weaknesses, which will be explored in later sections of this chapter. Van Doren *et al.* (2000) provide an overview of the range of techniques.

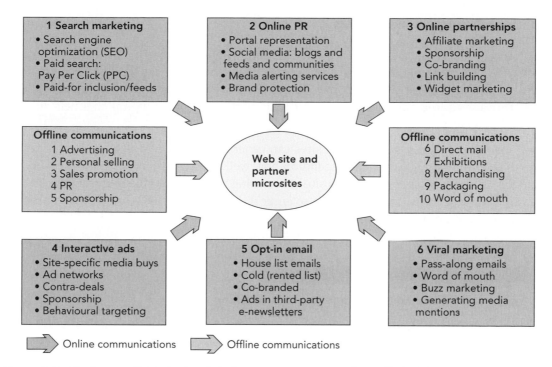

Figure 7.2 Options available in the digital communications mix for traffic building

Traditional advertising is based around campaigns that run for a fixed duration. Specific campaigns are also used for traffic building. These are often tied into a particular event such as the launch or relaunch of a web site. For example, a banner advert campaign may last for a period of two months following a relaunch. In addition to campaigns, there are also 'always-on' or *continuous traffic-building activities*. Companies should ensure that there is sufficient investment in continuous online marketing activities.

SECTION SUMMARY 7.1

Introduction to traffic building

Targeting, techniques and timing are three key aspects of traffic building and their relevance should be assessed for all techniques described in this chapter. It is traffic quality, not quantity, that really indicates the success of a traffic-building campaign. Traffic quality is high if site visitors are within the target audience for the web site and if they respond in line with the communications objectives.

7.2 Search engine marketing

Search engine marketing is arguably the most important digital marketing channel for customer acquisition. We all now naturally turn to a search engine when we are seeking a new product, service or entertainment. We also turn to search when we become familiar with a new brand, either through offline advertising or direct mail or through other digital channels such as graphical display ads.

In our experience, some transactional sites can generate over half of all their new business through search, although this will depend on how well known a brand is. For a well-known brand, users may navigate directly to a site via entering the URL into the browser address bar, but they will often use the search engine to enter the brand name URL or brand and product (known as a navigational search).

PRACTICAL E-MARKETING TIP

Assess your brand health in search, avoid hijacking

Assess how many of your visitors arrive at your site on brand-related searches and how this varies when you run cross-channel campaigns. You will need to protect your brand from brand-hijacking, where affiliates or competitors may advertise on your brand name if you don't take steps to protect it.

The importance of effective search marketing is suggested by Figure 7.3. The graph on the left shows that you really have to be on the first of the search engine results pages (SERPS). The chart on the right shows that the first few positions are important in driving visitor volume for the search phrases you are targeting.

We will now review the two main search engine marketing techniques for making a company and its products visible through search engines:

1 Search engine optimization (SEO)
2 Paid search marketing or Pay Per Click (PPC).

SEARCH ENGINE OPTIMIZATION (SEO)

Search engine optimization (SEO) involves achieving the highest position or ranking practical in the *natural or organic listings* on the search engine results pages after a specific combination of keywords (or keyphrase) has been typed in. In search engines such as Google and Bing the natural listings are on the left as shown in Figure 7.3 with Pay Per Click or sponsored links to the right above these. The position or ranking is dependent on an algorithm used by each search engine to match relevant site page content with the keyphrase entered. There is no charge for these listings to be displayed or when a link relevant to your site is clicked upon. However, you may need to pay a search engine optimization firm to advise or undertake optimization work to make your web pages appear higher in the rankings.

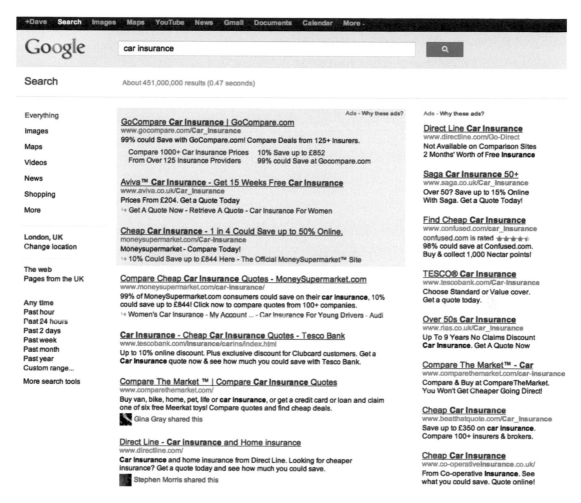

Figure 7.3   Google search engine results page (SERP) for car insurance

How are the search engine results pages produced?

To optimize your position in different search engines, it is essential to understand the basis on which SERPS are generated and ordered. Marketers who understand the ranking processes can boost their position higher than their competitors and so achieve higher levels of traffic. We believe that SEO is too important to just be left to an agency, and success in search involves training content owners and editors within a company to create content which fits the criteria used by search engines to assess relevance. Figure 7.4 shows that search technology involves these main processes:

1 *Crawling*. The purpose of the crawl is to identify relevant pages for indexing and assess whether they have changed. Crawling is performed by *robots* (bots) which are also known as *spiders*. These access web pages and retrieve a reference URL of the page for later analysis and indexing.

2 *Indexing.* An index is created to enable the search engine to rapidly find the most relevant pages containing the query typed by the searcher. Rather than searching each page for a query phrase, a search engine 'inverts' the index to produce a lookup table of the documents containing particular words.

3 *Ranking or scoring.* The indexing process has produced a lookup of all the pages that contain particular words in a query, but they are not sorted in terms of relevance. Ranking of the document to assess the most relevant set of documents to return in the SERPs occurs in real time for the search query entered. First, relevant documents will be retrieved from a runtime version of the index at a particular data centre, then a rank in the SERPs for each

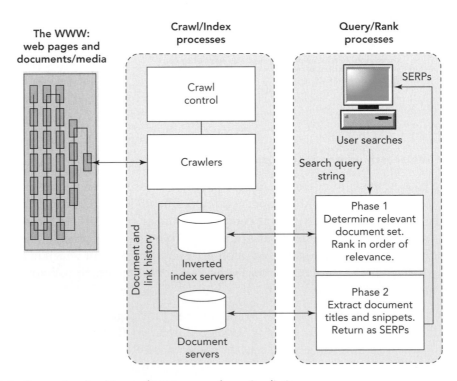

Figure 7.4   Stages involved in producing a search engine listing

PRACTICAL E-MARKETING TIP

Index inclusion

You can check which of your pages are indexed with a search engine by:

1 Reviewing web analytics data from log files which will show the frequency with which the main search robots crawl your site.

2 Using web analytics referrer information to find out which search engines your site visitors originate from, and the pages they land on.

3 Checking the number of pages that have been successfully indexed on your site.

   For example, in Google, the search 'site:www.smartinsights.com' lists all the pages of the site indexed by Google and gives the total number in the top right of the SERPS. This syntax is also useful for reviewing that you have the right brand messages in the SERPs, which as Figure 7.3 shows, is dependent on the title and description entered into the content management system. It's important that CMS users are trained so they know how the words they enter will appear in the SERPs; otherwise they will be missed.

4 Using the Webmaster Tools from Google and Bing referenced at the end of the chapter. You can upload a sitemap and see which pages are in the index and which are not.

If a page is identified as being similar to others, it may be classed as *duplicate content* in which case it will not be included in the index or it will be downweighted. You should check with your agency as to how they assess the level of duplicate content on your site and how they work to minimize it.

Sites wishing to reach an international audience should check index inclusion and ranking for different countries, particularly across different English-language versions of sites for countries such as Australia, Canada, the United Kingdom and the United States. Typically, using a separate local company domain, such as www.company.fr or www.company.de, which is also hosted locally in a country is often the most reliable approach for Google.

New sites without any external links indicating their reputation tend to be less trusted than existing sites (a phenomenon sometimes known as the 'Google Sandbox effect') which means that great care should be taken by start-up companies or new marketing campaign sites since these cannot compete effectively with similar sites in a sector which have more backlinks. For a campaign microsite, it is often best to host the campaign on the main company site even if a separate campaign URL is used which redirects visitors to the site content.

document will be computed, based on many ranking factors – we highlight the main ones below.

4 *Query request and results serving*. The familiar search engine interface accepts the searcher's query. The user's location is assessed through their IP address and the query is then passed

to a relevant data centre for processing. Ranking then occurs in real time for a particular query to return a sorted list of relevant documents, and these are then displayed on the Search Results Page.

Google uses around 200 factors or signals within its search ranking algorithm. These include positive ranking factors, which help boost position, and negative factors or filters which are used to remove search engine SPAM from the index where SEOs have used unethical approaches to 'game' the Google index. We will explore the most important ranking factors in a moment.

Site submission

How do you submit a new site? This is still a common question. It is recommended that automated submission tools are not used since these can be considered a *search engine spamming technique*. In fact, when launching a new site such as a campaign site, if you have links from other sites that are already indexed by a search engine, many search engines will automatically index your site without the need to submit a URL.

Keyphrase analysis

The key to successful search engine optimization and Pay Per Click is achieving *keyphrase* relevance, since this is what the search engines strive for – to match the combination of keywords typed into the search box to the most relevant destination content page. Notice that we say 'keyphrase' (short for keyword phrase), rather than 'key word' since search engines such as Google attribute more relevance when there is a phrase match on a page. Despite this, many search companies and commentators talk about optimizing your 'keywords' and, in our opinion, pay insufficient attention to *keyphrase analysis* to summarize the main consumer search behaviours.

We recommend these stages for analysis and goal-setting:

A. *Demand analysis*. Identifying the popularity of each search term, its relevance to the products or services, qualified by the 'intent of the searcher' indicated by the keyphrase, and the competition on it. We recommend using two free Google tools: the Google Keyword Tool and Google Insights for Search which are great for giving estimates on the popularity of searches for different products and brands online. A list of keyphrase analysis tools in different categories is kept updated at http://bit.ly/smartgap. You can see an example of the output from the Google Keyword Tool for terms related to car insurance in Figure 7.5.

When using this tool for analysis, it's important to realize that there are three different forms of estimate. First, broad match which shows all variants of searches related to a search term. Phrase match then shows all phrases *containing the term in sequence, for example 'cheap car insurance'*. Exact match, shown by square brackets [car insurance], gives the best idea of searchers for this phrase; this is important since a broad match gives an exaggerated idea of the number of searches. You can also see the importance of mobile search volume and it's possible to target these searches differently.

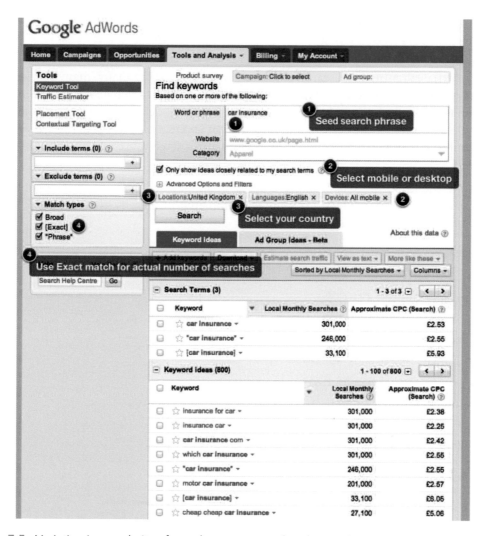

Figure 7.5 Variation in popularity of searches on terms related to car insurance

Source: Google AdWords Keyword Tool

Other sources for identifying keyphrases include your market knowledge, competitors' sites, key phrases from visitors who arrive at your site (from web analytics), the internal site search tool. When performing the keyphrase analysis, we need to understand different qualifiers that users type in so that we can target them in our SEM.

1 *Comparison/quality* – compare car insurance
2 *Adjective (price/product qualifiers)* – cheap car insurance, woman car insurance
3 *Intended use* – high mileage car insurance
4 *Product type* – holiday car insurance
5 *Vendor or brand* – Churchill car insurance
6 *Location* – car insurance uk

7 *Action request* – buy car insurance

8 *Provider type* – car insurance company, car insurance supermarket.

It's also worth evaluating local search potential (point 6) – for the many, many services where searchers need a local supplier, like a plumber, solicitor or pizza delivery. This type of search behaviour is particularly important for local businesses. Google offers services called Places and Google+ where businesses can add information about their local presence. If a business rates favourably and has images uploaded, it will benefit from more prominence as shown in Figure 7.6.

To illustrate the importance of different types of qualifiers, according to the Google Keyword Tool for a single month in 2011, for searches completed in the UK, the most popular exact phrases related to car insurance were:

- car insurance, 550,000
- cheap car insurance, 201,000
- car insurance quotes, 110,000
- compare car insurance, 49,500
- cheapest car insurance, 40,500
- car insurance comparison, 40,500
- temporary car insurance, 33,100
- car insurance groups, 27,100

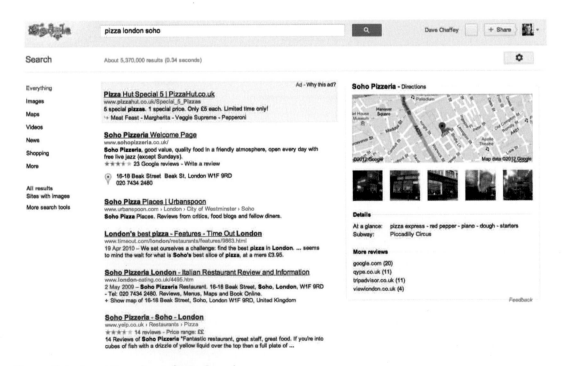

Figure 7.6   Local Search results in Google

- short term car insurance, 27,000
- car insurance for young drivers, 22,200
- classic car insurance, 22,200.

These data suggest the importance of ranking well for high-volume keyphrases such as 'cheap car insurance' and of considering products and services that target a need such as 'temporary' or 'short term insurance'.

B. *Performance analysis*. This assesses how the company is currently performing for these phrases. With the right tracking tools and tagging, it should be possible to report average position in natural and paid listings (see http://bit.ly/smartranking for our suggestions on rank-checking tools); click volume referred from search; click quality (conversion rates and, ideally, bounce rates to compare landing page effectiveness); outcomes (sales, registrations or leads); costs (CPC and CPA); profitability (based on cost of sale or lifetime value models).

C. *Gap analysis*. Identifies for each phrase and product where the biggest potential for improvement is, so you can target your resources accordingly (see http://bit.ly/smartgap for further information).

D. *Set goals and select keyphrases*. You should identify the different types of keyphrase you want to be visible for. Particularly important are the strategic keyphrases which are critical to success.

Improving search engine ranking through SEO

The challenge for SEOs is that there are many ranking factors and they are constantly changing! Google references over 200 main ranking factors which means hundreds of detailed changes to the way pages are evaluated and represented in the search results places happening each year. The importance of SEO is clear from Figure 7.7, since if you are not in the first few positions, you will not generate many clicks, with the first position being particularly important.

See, for example, SEOmoz (2011) for the latest updates (www.seomoz.org/google-algorithm-change).

Fortunately there are four common factors that influence search engine rankings, that can be managed as part of an SEO strategy:

1 On-page optimization
2 External linking or off-site optimization
3 Internal link structures
4 User behaviour signals.

Let's look at these in a little more detail:

1 *On-page optimization*. The most basic test of relevance by the search engines is the number of times the phrase appears on the page.

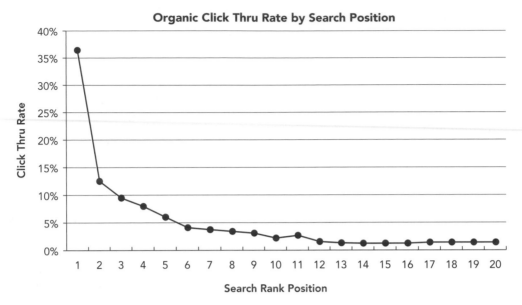

Figure 7.7   Organic clickthrough rate by search position

Source: Optify (2011)

However, there are many other factors that can also be applied. In its guidance for webmasters, Google (2012) states: 'Google goes far beyond the number of times a term appears on a page and examines all aspects of the page's content (and the content of the pages linking to it) to determine if it's a good match for your query'.

These other factors include:

- Frequency
- Occurrence in headings <h1>, <h2>
- Occurrence in anchor text of hyperlinks
- Markup, such as bold
- Density (the number of times)
- Proximity of phrase to start of document and the gap between individual keywords
- Alternative image text (explained below)
- Document meta data (explained below).

Alternative image text

Graphical images can have hidden text associated with them that is not seen by the user (unless graphical images are turned off or the mouse is rolled over the image), but will be seen and indexed by the search engine.

For example, text about a company name and products can be assigned to a company logo using the 'ALT' tag or attribute of the image tag as follows:

<IMG NAME = 'Logo' SRC = 'logo.gif ' ALT = 'Car insurance'>

Due to search engine spamming, this factor is assigned limited relevance, although it is still worthwhile for images that link to another page within the site. However, it is best practice to use this approach for significant images, since it is also required by accessibility law and screen-readers used by the blind and visually impaired read out the ALT tags (see Section 6.1 on web accessibility).

Document meta data

The three most important types of meta data are the document <title> tag, the document 'descriptions' meta tag and the document 'keywords' meta tag. You should try to make these unique for each page on your site(s), as otherwise Google may assess the content as duplicate and some pages may be downweighted in importance.

i *The document title.* The <title> tag is arguably the most important type of meta data since each search engine places significant weighting on the keyphrases contained within it *and* it is the call-to-action hyperlink on the search engine results page. If it contains powerful, relevant copy, you will get more clicks and the search engine will increase your position in the listing accordingly relative to other pages which are getting fewer clicks.

ii *The 'description' meta tag.* A meta tag is an attribute of the page within the HTML <head> section which can be set by the content owner.

The 'description' meta tag denotes the information which will typically be displayed in the search engine results page (see Figure 7.3). If it is absent or too short, relevant 'snippets' will be used from within the body copy, but it is best to control your messages. If it or the title are missing or identical, then this can result in duplicate content as described above: this can be checked for within Google's Webmaster Tools.

So the page creator can modify this to make a stronger call-to-action in the search engine listings as in this case:

<meta name = 'description' content = 'Direct Line offers you great value car insurance by cutting out the middleman and passing the savings directly on to you. To find out if you could save, why not get a car insurance quote? Breakdown Cover Insurance also available'.>

iii *The 'keywords' meta tag.* The keywords meta tag is used to summarize the content of a docu-ment based on keywords. Some unscrupulous SEOs can still be heard to say to potential clients ('we will optimize your meta tags'). But this is a waste of time since the keywords meta tag is relatively unimportant as a ranking factor (Google has never used them), although these keywords may be important to internal search engines.

Example:

<meta name = 'keywords' content = 'Car insurance, Home insurance, Travel insurance, Direct line, Breakdown cover, Mortgages personal loans, Pet insurance, Annual holiday insurance, Car loans, uk mortgages, Life insurance, Critical illness cover'>

E-MARKETING INSIGHT

Understanding PageRank

When Google founders Larry Page and Sergey Brin first developed Google at Stanford University, a key feature in their approach was to use backlinks or links into a page from other pages as an assessment of the quality of sites. They called this approach PageRank™, after Larry Page. If we ignore the science behind PageRank, essentially the more links you have from sites which themselves have high PageRank, the more this will increase the 'link popularity' of your site. The PageRank of an individual page is presented in the Google toolbar from 0 to 10 if you download it. It is not a regular scale; it is widely believed to be a logarithmic scale, similar to the Richter Scale for earthquakes. The average business is in the range 4 to 6, with larger businesses and organizations in the range 5 to 8. Media owners and publishers like the portals and the BBC are in the higher echelons of 8 to 10. Of course, what is important is how your PageRank compares to your traditional competitors and those media owners that rank well for search terms used by your potential customers.

Some SEO commentators dismiss PageRank, saying its importance is overstated since the quality and trust of sites is more important; and they point out that it is out of date when presented in the Google toolbar. This is true, but PageRank is a simple way of benchmarking against competitors, and it is important to assess its distribution within a site and is a crude way of assessing the value of backlinks.

Universal or blended search

When Google launched, the only presence you had to worry about within the search engines was the text listing. But today, text results are only one type of search, albeit the most important one for most products and services. Videos, images and social media mentions are all important too, so think about how you look in the universal or blended search listings. Google Places, which we showed in Figure 7.6 is one example of the blended listings.

Since search is becoming more visual, it's no longer only about the text results, so make sure you gain visibility within images, maps and videos according to which will work best for your market. Blended search is market- and phrase-specific, depending on how Google assesses the relevance of universal content for the query. For example, a search on 'jewellery' may not present any universal results, while 'designer jewellery' may include images.

2 *External linking.* Boosting external links is vital to your SEO efforts, although it is less easy to control and often neglected. The founders of Google realized that the number of links into a page and their quality was a great way of determining the relevance of a page to searchers, especially when combined with the keyphrases on that page. Although the Google algorithm has been upgraded and refined continuously since then, the number and quality of external links is still the most important ranking factor.

While natural links will be generated if content is useful, a proactive approach to link building is required in competitive markets. We recommend these steps to help boost your external links. There are more link-building tips in Section 7.4.

i *Identify and create popular content and services.* The starting point for both natural and proactive link building has to be to think of the value of your site and different types of content or services on different pages. The acid test is whether your visitors will bookmark a page of your content or tell a friend about it. Think not only about the home page, but also about other pages within the site.

By creating more valuable content and then showcasing it within your navigation, or grouping it within pages such as a 'Resource Centre' or blog, you can encourage more people to link to your content naturally; or approach them and suggest they link not only to the home page, but directly to the useful tools that have been created.

ii *Identify potential partner sites.* There are several options to find partner sites. It is helpful to try to identify the types of site that you may be able to link with; for example:

- Directories of links (often less valuable)
- Traditional media sites
- Niche online-only media sites
- Trade associations
- Manufacturers, suppliers and other business partners
- Press release distribution sites
- Bloggers including customers and partners
- Social networks.

Smart Insights (2012) recommends reviewing 12 options for creating more quality links, as shown in Table 7.1:

Table 7.1 Twelve options for creating more quality links

Area	Action needed
1 Linkbait creation	Production of *linkbait* assessed on full review of linkbait options
2 PR and marketing campaign integration	Potential of marketing campaigns for SEO planned at outset?
3 Blogging, guest blogging and blogger outreach	Effective blogger outreach? • Target partners reviewed and contacted? • Resource defined for managing partners?
4 Backlinking between company-owned and partner sites	Review options to improve links between company sites • Backlinks improved from strategic partners?
5 Press release distribution	Effective press release SEO?

Table 7.1 *(Continued)*

Area	Action needed
	• Guidelines for press release creation defined? • Syndicating through relevant press release services?
6 Video marketing	Potential of video marketing defined? • Use of hybrid host (included in own site) or post on a third-party site; e.g. YouTube defined? • Use of niche video sites reviewed?
7 Article syndication	Partners and process for article syndication reviewed?
8 Social network participation	Use of social networks to encourage backlinks from other sites Note: the use of 'nofollow tags associated with hyperlinks' means that direct links from social network sites are of limited value
9 Forum SEO	Options for benefits of SEO participation in forums reviewed? • Example – we're members of one forum which gives backlinks when members have posted a certain number of links and/or they pay for membership
10 Social bookmarking	Use of social bookmarking and StumbleUpon
11 Directory submissions	Directory options in market reviewed for relevance? Especially niche directories? • Free directories • Paid directories
12 'Buying links'	Options for buying links which cannot be identified as bought links by search engines reviewed? Not recommended, high risk.

Source: Smart Insights (2012)

PRACTICAL E-MARKETING TIP

Link anchor text and 'nofollow' in title

When setting up links, it is important to use specific suitable anchor text for the link. Links deep into the site, specific to a particular product, are often more valuable. It is also worth remembering that Google won't follow links which have the rel='nofollow' link on them, so check for these.

PRACTICAL E-MARKETING TIP

Finding out who links to you and your competitors

The best free way to find link associations for you and your competitors is the Open Site Explorer (www.opensitexplorer.org). For your own site, we would strongly recommend using the Google Webmaster Tools (www.google.com/webmasters/) which provide a useful set of tools just for sites owned and verified by their owners including internal and external links. To benchmark link growth, we recommend Majestic SEO (Figure 7.8) and its backlink history, since the unique linking domains are a key ranking factor. You can also drill down to see who links to you and your competitors and the anchor text used.

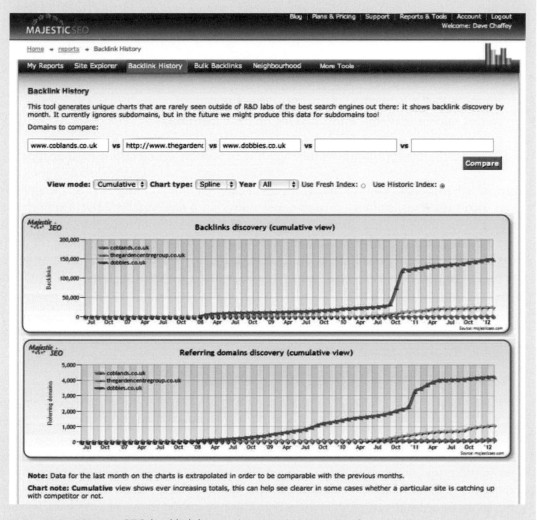

Figure 7.8   Majestic SEO backlink history (www.majesticseo.com)

THINK LINK QUALITY NOT LINK POPULARITY

Today, Google assesses not just the number of links into a page, but also uses the concepts of hubs and authorities to assess the relevance of a page about a particular topic. This approach was originally described by Google engineers Bharat and Mihaila (1999). Essentially, a hub page (actually referred to as an 'Expert page' in the paper) is a page which contains many quality outbound links about a particular topic. An authority page, referred to as a 'target' in the paper, contains many inbound links about a topic. Expert pages (hubs) are given more weighting to identify authority pages.

The context or theme of the linking page is also very important, with the search engines needing to determine hubs and authorities based on an assessment of the context of the link for the page, based on the phrases it contains.

In the paper by Bharat and Mihaila, there is a direct indication of the factors used to assess the theme of a page. They suggest the importance to good ranking of a searcher's keyphrases occurring in:

- The page title phrase (part of on-page optimization)
- Headings within documents (again, on-page optimization)
- Hyperlink anchor text (the words making up the hyperlink).

We describe different approaches to link building in Section 7.4 on online partnerships.

3 *Internal link structures*. Many of the principles of external link building can also be applied on your own sites. This is often a missed opportunity, since here you have the benefit that you have control of the linking, although the impact is less than from links from external sites. The most important principle is to include keyphrases used by searchers within the anchor text of a hyperlink to point to relevant content. It's also important to consider how you can increase the number of internal links to pages which you want to rank well. A meshed structure with lots of interlinks can work better than a simple hierarchy.

PRACTICAL E-MARKETING TIP

Analysing PageRank and internal backlink distribution

PageRank varies across a site. The home page is typically highest, with each page deeper within the site having a lower PageRank. This has several implications. First, it is helpful to include the most important keyphrases you want to target on the home page, or at the second level in the site hierarchy. Second, pages that feature in the main or secondary navigation (text link menus referencing the keyphrase in the anchor text are best) are more likely to rank highly than pages deeper in the site that don't have many internal backlinks because they are not in the menu. Third, you need to review whether there are pages deeper within the site which feature products or services that are important and which you need to rank for. If so, you need to find a method of increasing the number of backlinks (internal or external), perhaps by including a link to them in the footer or sidebars of the site which are separate from the main navigation. The Google Webmaster Tools have reports on internal and external links which are excellent diagnostic tools.

PRACTICAL E-MARKETING TIP

Improve your link anchor text

The importance of hyperlink anchor text isn't always realized by content authors, with many sites having hyperlinks which read 'click here' or 'read more' rather than referring to the target document's content. This is often a constraint/feature of content management systems, but body-copy links can be used to refer to the target document, using a meaningful link such as: 'Read more about search engine optimization best practice which is also better from a user experience point of view'.

E-MARKETING CHECKLIST – INTERNAL LINK BUILDING

☑ 1 *Links from standard navigation.* These are most effective if text-based rather than image menus. As well as the main navigation categories, conventionally placed across the masthead, providing more navigation links within the left or right sidebars can help with indicating to search engines the themes of pages.

☑ 2 *Links from ancillary navigation (e.g. page footers).* These can be varied in different site sections.

☑ 3 *Links from document listings.* (Including publishing search results or lists of news items.)

☑ 4 *Sitemaps.* These are useful for both human visitors and search robots – Google recommends creating these. They are most effective if broken down into different categories which are themed on specific topics.

☑ 5 *Body copy.* These 'editorial links' are particularly important to SEO today since Google now evaluates them as more important than 'run-of-site' links.

☑ 6 *Image links.* These were discussed in the section on document meta data.

4 *User behaviour signals.* Through time, search engines have introduced methods to assess the relevance of content based on how users interact with it. This is important to the search engines to maintain quality within their search results, since other ranking signals such as page optimization and backlinks can be manipulated. The main user behaviour signals that are used are:

i *Engagement with content.* If a user clicks through on a search result to a site and then immediately returns to the search engine and repeats a search, then the search engine can detect if this happens frequently for a site and so downweights its assessment of value.

ii *Bookmarking*. Search engines can detect bookmarking to favourites, and it has been speculated that this has been used as a ranking signal.

iii *Social sharing*. Both Google and Bing have acknowledged that they can use the number of 'Shares' on social networks and whether sharing occurs by more influential social networkers.

PAID OR PAY PER CLICK (PPC) SEARCH MARKETING

Paid search marketing or Pay Per Click (PPC) is similar to conventional advertising; here a relevant text ad with a link to a company page is displayed when the user of a search engine types in a specific phrase. A series of text ads usually labelled as 'sponsored links' are displayed to the right of the natural listings, as in Figure 7.3 (above).

Note that it is common for search agencies to describe paid search marketing as 'search engine marketing or SEM' to distinguish it from SEO. This can be confusing since others, including ourselves, prefer search engine marketing to include both SEO and PPC.

Although many searchers prefer to click on the natural listings, a sufficient number do click on the paid listings (typically around a quarter to a third of all clicks) so that they are highly profitable for companies such as Google, and a well-designed paid search campaign can drive a significant amount of business for the search companies.

Google has been working hard to increase the relevance of the paid search ads, particularly for retail where product and price information can now be displayed (Figure 7.9).

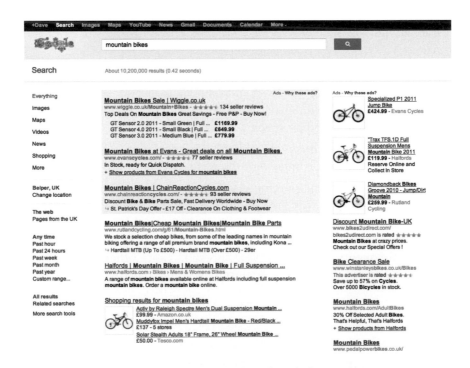

Figure 7.9   New ad extension formats within Google Adwords for retailers

Google AdWords (http://adwords.google.com) is the name of the Google advertising programme, with Microsoft Search Marketing the equivalent from Bing and Yahoo! If you advertise in markets where other search engines are dominant, such as Baidu in China, you will have to consider advertising within these.

Each of these programmes has to be managed individually through an online service; or alternatively, large campaigns can be managed and evaluated through a *bid management service*.

There are two significant differences between PPC and conventional advertising, which are the former's main advantages:

1 *The advertiser is not paying for the ad to be displayed*. Cost is only incurred when the ad is clicked on and a visitor is directed to the advertiser's web site. Hence, it's a *Cost Per Click (CPC) model*! However, there are increasingly options for paid search marketing using other techniques; Google also offers CPM options on its *content network* (e.g. the Google Display Network), where contextual ads are displayed on third-party sites relevant to the content on a page. This form of advertising accounts for around a quarter of Google's ad revenue. It is important to use a different form of creative and targeting within the display network to get the best results.

2 *PPC advertising is highly targeted*. The relevant ad with a link to a destination web page is only displayed when the user of a search engine types in a specific phrase (or the ad appears on the content network, triggered by relevant content on a publisher's page), so there is limited wastage compared to other media. Users responding to a particular keyphrase or reading related content have high intent or interest and so tend to be good-quality leads.

The relative ranking of these 'paid performance placements' is not simply based on the highest CPC bid for each keyword phrase, as is often thought by those unfamiliar with CPC. Additionally, Google, and now the other search engines, also take into account the quality of the listings. Within Google, this is known as the *Quality Score*.

E-MARKETING INSIGHT

Mastering Quality Score

Understanding the Quality Score is the key to successful PPC marketing. You should consider its implications when you structure the account and write copy. Google developed the Quality Score because the company understood that delivering relevance through the sponsored links was essential to their users' experience, and their own profits. In their AdWords help system, Google explains:

> *The AdWords system works best for everybody; advertisers, users, publishers and Google too when the ads we display match our users' needs as closely as possible. We call this idea 'relevance'.*

> *We measure relevance in a simple way: Typically, the higher an ad's Quality Score, the more relevant it is for the keywords to which it is tied. When your*

> *ads are highly relevant, they tend to earn more clicks, move higher in Ad Rank and bring you the most success.*
>
> *(Google, 2007)*
>
> The current formula for the Google Quality Score is:
>
> Quality Score = (keyword's clickthrough rate, Ad Text Relevance, Keyword Relevance, Landing Page Relevance and other methods of assessing relevance)
>
> So, higher clickthrough rates achieved through better targeted creative copy are rewarded, as is the relevance of the landing page (Google now sends out AdBots-Google to check them out). More relevant ads are also rewarded through Ad Text Relevance which is an assessment of the match of headline and description to the search term. Finally, the Keyword Relevance is the match of the triggering keyword to the search term entered.
>
> If you have ever wondered why the number of paid ads above the natural listings varies from none to three, then it's down to the Quality Score – you can only get the coveted positions for keywords which have a sufficiently high Quality Score – you can't 'buy your way to the top', as many think.

In addition to performance-based payment and well-targeted prospects, PPC has other advantages:

1 *Good accountability.* With the right tracking system, the ROI for individual keywords can be calculated.
2 *Predictable.* Traffic, rankings and results are generally stable and predictable. This contrasts with SEO.
3 *Technically simpler than SEO.* Position is based on a combination of bid amount and Quality Score, whereas SEO requires long-term, technically complex work on page optimization, site restructuring and link building.
4 *Speed.* PPC listings get posted quickly, usually in a few days (following editorial review).

   SEO results can take weeks or months to be achieved. Moreover, when a web site is revised for SEO, rankings will initially drop while the site is re-indexed by the search engines.
5 *Branding.* Tests have shown that there is a branding effect with PPC, even if users do not click on the ad. This can be useful for creating awareness and demand for the launch of products or major campaigns. Paid search ads on the display network can include display ad formats and YouTube 'promoted videos' or 'pre-roll' ads.
6 *Remarketing.* Google offers retargeting through cookies placed on the searcher's computer to display reminder ads on the display network after someone has clicked on a paid search ad, as a reminder to act. These reminders can be effective in boosting the conversion rate to lead or sale.

YouTube – the second largest search engine in many countries

Since YouTube features a lot of searches, it's worth checking to see the number of searches related to your brand – YouTube also features a keyword tool. Opportunities for paid advertising can then be reviewed. For example, Figure 7.10 shows how an ad giving a customer testimonial can be displayed when a searcher is investigating options for laser eye treatment.

Figure 7.10 Google Promoted Video ads within YouTube

However, PPC has these disadvantages, which do need to be managed:

1 *Competitive and expensive.* Since Pay Per Click has become popular, some companies may get involved in bidding wars that drive bids up to an unacceptable level. Some phrases such as 'life insurance' can exceed £10 per click.

2 *Inappropriate.* For companies with a lower budget or a narrower range of products on which to generate lifetime value, it might not be cost-effective to compete.

3 *Needs specialist knowledge.* PPC requires a knowledge of configuration, bidding options and of the reporting facilities of different ad networks. Internal staff can be trained, but they will need to keep up to date with changes to the paid search services.

4 *Time-consuming*. To manage a PPC account can require daily, or even hourly, checks on the bidding in order to stay competitive. This can amount to a lot of time. The tools and best practice vary frequently, so to keep up to date is difficult.

5 *Irrelevant*. Sponsored listings are only part of the search engine marketing mix. Many search users do not click on these.

Managing Pay Per Click

Different advertisers bid on particular key words through a web-based management interface provided by the network to achieve the listing that they want. The structure of Google AdWords account management is shown in Figure 7.11. Setting up a sound account structure is important since it determines how closely you can target your paid search activities.

Campaigns provide a way to manage ads for related products. You should set a daily budget, which will often correspond to budgets for different product groups (categories) and geographies. Generic search terms and brand terms often also have their own campaigns, as compared to more specific product campaigns. Within each campaign, Ad Groups will be set up which contain keywords that will trigger the ad to be displayed when it is searched upon. Advertisers decide on the maximum Cost Per Click (CPC) they are prepared to pay for each keyword or Ad Group. Figure 7.12 shows an example of an Ad Group created for a model of mobile phone. In this case, there is a single keyword which, when typed, will trigger a targeted message for which different versions can be served for testing.

The Cost Per Acquisition (CPA) can be calculated as follows:

$$\text{Cost Per Acquisition} = (100/\text{Conversion rate }\%) \times \text{Cost Per Click}$$

Given the range in costs, two types of strategy can be pursued in PPC search engine advertising. If budget permits, a premium strategy can be followed to compete with the major competitors who are bidding the highest amounts on popular keywords. Such a strategy is based on being able to achieve an acceptable conversion rate once the customers are driven through to the web site. A lower-cost strategy involves bidding on lower-cost, less popular phrases. These

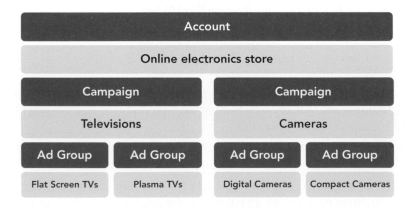

Figure 7.11   AdWords account structure

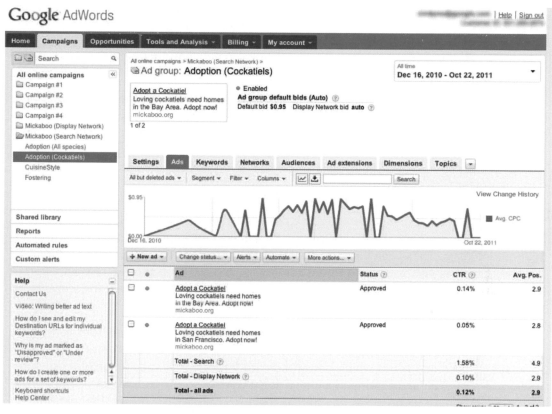

Figure 7.12   An example of an Ad Group within the Google AdWords campaign management tool

PRACTICAL E-MARKETING TIP

Google AdWords account structure

Your ads will tend to be more relevant to searchers if you create many focused Ad Groups in each campaign, which each target a particular type of searching. Each Ad Group shouldn't have too many diverse, unrelated keywords since you will be less able to deliver relevance, and so your clickthrough rate will be low and your price bid will have to be high compared to competitors to get the listing position you need. A good rule of thumb is 10 to 20 keywords maximum per Ad Group.

It is easy to test alternative creative/copy – check that your agency has developed the best messages through testing. To save time, you can use dynamic content insertion to tailor the ad. For example, in Google, the syntax {Keyword: <Default phrase>} is used to activate this 'dynamic keyword insertion' feature when defining the ad headline or description. This typically results in greater relevance and higher clickthrough rates since the phrase entered matches that typed.

It is also useful to create separate campaigns for the content network; then you can treat this differently by using different messages. As a first-time advertiser, it is usually best to switch off the content network initially, so you can concentrate on getting advertising right within the main search results.

With PPC, as for any other media, media buyers carefully evaluate the advertising costs in relation to the initial purchase value or lifetime value they feel they will achieve from the average customer. As well as considering the Cost Per Click (CPC), you need to think about the conversion rate when the visitor arrives at your site. Clearly, an ad could be effective in generating clickthroughs or traffic, but not achieve the outcome required on the web site such as generating a lead or online sale. This could be because there is a poor incentive or call-to-action or the profile of the visitors is simply wrong. One implication of this is that it will often be more cost-effective if targeted microsites or landing pages are created specifically for certain keyphrases – to convert users to making an enquiry or sale. These can be part of the site structure, so clicking on a 'car insurance' ad will take the visitor through to the car insurance page on a site rather than a home page. This is not a form of advertising to use unless the effectiveness of the web site in converting visitors to buyers is known.

Table 7.2 shows how Cost Per Click differs between different keywords from generic to specific. It also shows the impact of different conversion rates on the overall CPA. It can be seen that niche terms which better indicate interest in a specific product such as 'women's car insurance' demand a higher fee (this may not be true for less competitive categories where niche terms can be cheaper). The table also shows the cost of PPC search in competitive categories. Advertising just on these four keywords to achieve a high ranking would cost €33,000 in a single day! Some advertisers target lower positions in the SERPs, since visitors are thus better value and lower cost.

Table 7.2 Variation in Cost Per Click for different keyphrases in Google UK

Keywords	Clicks/Day	Average CPC	Cost/Day	Average position	CPA @ 25% conversion	CPA @ 10% conversion
Overall	5,714	€5.9	€33,317	1.3	€23.4	€58.4
'insurance'	3,800	€5.4	€20,396	1.3	€21.5	€53.7
'car insurance'	1,700	€6.6	€11,119	1.2	€26.2	€65.5
'cheap car insurance'	210	€8.4	€1,757	1.1	€33.5	€83.7
'women's car insurance'	4.1	€10.5	€43	1.0	€42.2	€105.4

will generate less traffic, so it will be necessary to devise a lot of these phrases to match the traffic from premium keywords.

Optimizing Pay Per Click

Each PPC keyphrase ideally needs to be managed individually in order to make sure that the bid (amount per click) remains competitive in order to show up in the top of the results. Experienced PPC marketers broaden the range of keyphrases to include lower volume phrases. Since each advertiser will typically manage thousands of keywords to generate clickthroughs, manual bidding soon becomes impractical.

Some search engines include their own bid management tools, but if you or your agency is using several different Pay Per Click services such as Overture, Espotting and Google, it makes sense to use a single tool to manage them all. It also makes comparison of performance easier. *Bid management software* can be used across a range of PPC services to manage keyphrases across multiple PPC ad networks and optimize the costs of search engine advertising. The current CPC is regularly reviewed and your bid is reduced or increased to achieve a goal of profitability or sales volume.

Some bid-management tools such as Efficient Frontier use historical click, cost, impression and position data to model the whole campaign in a portfolio-style approach similar to those used by stock market traders. For each keyword and each position, these tools predict the required bid, the actual CPC (Cost Per Click), the click volume and the conversion rate.

As more marketers have become aware of the benefits of PPC, competition has increased and this has driven up the Cost Per Click (CPC) and so reduced its profitability. We will soon reach the point where those bidding at the top will be the companies with the most efficient web sites for conversion to outcome and the highest potential lifetime value for cross-selling.

As we mentioned at the start of this section, it's important to optimize the Google Display Network through different forms of targeting and creative that work to engage when the visitor is not directly seeking information in the search engine. The Google Placement targeting tool and Google AdPlanner can be used for targeting as shown in Figure 7.13.

Making your ad creative effective

We have seen how important creative ad copy is to Quality Score and minimizing costs. Compare our tips checklist against the ads in Figure 7.5. Your copywriting techniques need to work within the many editorial guidelines.

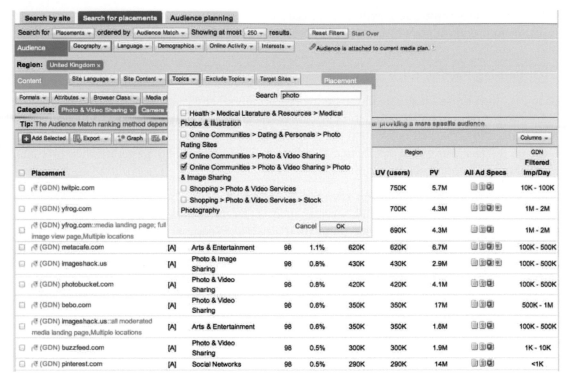

Figure 7.13   Targeting the Google Display Network with the Placement targeting tool

Emarketing best practice checklist – effective paid search ad creative

☑   1   Deliver relevance by including search term keywords in headline and body

☑   2   Be specific on the offer

☑   3   Include specific benefits; e.g. free delivery costs

☑   4   Differentiate – explain what is unique about your offering

☑   5   Include numbers as appropriate since they stand out when visitors scan the page

☑   6   Use CAPS (capitalize first letters and use acronyms where appropriate)

☑   7   Space can be good – sometimes relatively short text can have a higher impact

☑   8   Use characters (sensibly): !, ?, :, &

☑   9   Be quirky!

☑   10   Use distinctive words

☑   11   Try to squeeze in a call-to-action

☑   12   Capitalize display URLs (the web address shown) and consider including a sub-folder that highlights the product or a benefit.

Beware of the fake clicks

Whenever the principle of PPC marketing is described to marketers, very soon you can see 'a light bulb come on' and they ask, 'So we can click on competitors and bankrupt them?' Well, actually, no. The PPC ad networks detect multiple clicks from the same computer (IP address) and say they filter them out. However, there are techniques to mimic multiple clicks from different locations such as software tools to fake clicks, and even services where you can pay a team of people across the world to click on these links. It is estimated that in competitive markets, one in five of the clicks may be fake. While this can be factored into the conversion rates you will achieve, ultimately this could destroy PPC advertising. We believe that in the longer term, PPC will move to something similar to an affiliate model where marketers only pay when a sale or some other outcome on a site occurs.

SECTION SUMMARY 7.2

Search engine marketing

Ensure you employ someone who is knowledgeable to optimize your position with search engines. Remember, the main techniques are:

1 Ensure your sites are included in the indexes of the main search

2 Complete keyphrase analysis to identify phrases relevant to your market

3 Start a search engine optimization initiative. This may involve restructuring your site to make it more accessible to search engines and including relevant keyphrases in the body copy, title tag and other page elements.

4 Maximize quality links from and to different sites – run a link-building campaign

5 Review the relevance of Pay Per Click advertising and be sure to devote sufficient resources to deliver ROI from these.

7.3 Online PR

Online PR or e-PR leverages the network effect of the Internet. Remember, the term 'Internet' is a contraction of 'interconnected networks'! Mentions of your brand or site on other sites are powerful in shaping opinions and driving visitors to your site. Furthermore, as we saw in the section on search engine optimization, the more quality backlinks there are from other sites to your site, the higher your site will be ranked in the natural or organic listings of the search engines.

The UK's Chartered Institute of Public Relations (CIPR, 2011) defines PR as follows:

> *Public relations is about reputation – the result of what you do, what you say and what others say about you. Public relations is the discipline which looks after repu-tation, with the aim of earning understanding and support and influencing opinion and behaviour. It is the planned and sustained effort to establish and maintain*

goodwill and mutual understanding between an organisation and its publics [its target audience including potential customers and stakeholders].

(CIPR, 2011)

Online influencer outreach is now an important activity to identify companies or individuals with a strong online following and then using these partners to influence an audience. Minimizing unfavourable mentions – for example, monitoring and influencing conversations in blogs and social networks through *online reputation management* – is also a key activity of online PR. These activities are closely related to social media marketing which we reviewed in Chapter 5.

Ranchhod *et al.* (2002) identify four key differences between online PR and traditional PR:

1 *The audience is connected to organizations.* Previously, there was detachment – PR people issued press releases which were distributed over the newswires, picked up by the media and then published in their outlets. These authors say:

> *[T]he communication channel was uni-directional. The institutions communicated and the audiences consumed the information. Even when the communication was considered a two-way process, the institutions had the resources to send information to audiences through a very wide pipeline, while the audiences had only a minuscule pipeline for communicating back to the institutions.*
>
> (Ranchhod et al., 2002)

2 *The members of the audience are connected to each other.* Through publishing their own web sites or through email, information can be rapidly distributed from person to person and group to group. The authors (2002) say: 'Today, a company's activity can be discussed and debated over the Internet, with or without the knowledge of that organization. In the new environment everybody is a communicator, and the institution is just part of the network.'

3 *The audience has access to other information.* Often in the past, the communicator was able to make a statement it would be difficult for the average audience member to challenge – the Internet facilitates rapid comparison of statements. The authors say:

> *It takes a matter of minutes to access multiple sources of information over the Internet. Any statement made can be dissected, analyzed, discussed and challenged within hours by interested individuals. In the connected world, information does not exist in a vacuum.*
>
> (Ranchhod et al., 2002)

4 *Audiences pull information.* This point is similar to the last one. Previously there were limited channels in terms of television and press. Today there are many sources and channels of information – this makes it more difficult for the message to be seen. The authors (2002) say: 'Until recently, television offered only a few channels. People communicated with one another by post and by phone. In these conditions, it was easy for a public relations practitioner to make a message stand out.'

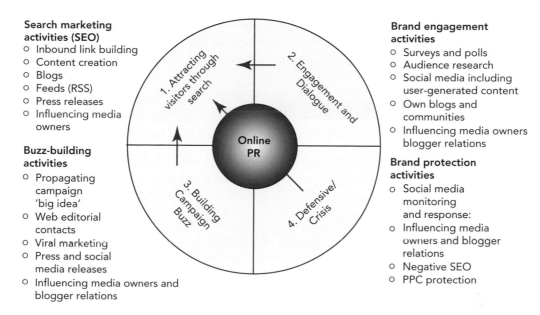

Search marketing activities (SEO)
○ Inbound link building
○ Content creation
○ Blogs
○ Feeds (RSS)
○ Press releases
○ Influencing media owners

Buzz-building activities
○ Propagating campaign 'big idea'
○ Web editorial contacts
○ Viral marketing
○ Press and social media releases
○ Influencing media owners and blogger relations

Brand engagement activities
○ Surveys and polls
○ Audience research
○ Social media including user-generated content
○ Own blogs and communities
○ Influencing media owners blogger relations

Brand protection activities
○ Social media monitoring and response:
○ Influencing media owners and blogger relations
○ Negative SEO
○ PPC protection

1. Attracting visitors through search
2. Engagement and Dialogue
3. Building Campaign Buzz
4. Defensive/Crisis

Online PR

Figure 7.14   Online PR options

There are many activities that need to be proactively managed as part of online PR which we have summarized in Figure 7.14. We recommend you create a plan for e-PR in four key areas:

1 *Search marketing activities (SEO)*. We have covered these in the previous section. As Figure 7.14 suggests, many of the other techniques involve creating *backlinks* which will also assist with this.

2 *Brand engagement activities*. Engagement is all about creating interaction or dialogue with online audiences to help understand audience needs and potentially influence them. This may be on your own site or on third-party sites through *business blogs* and communities which we will discuss more below.

3 *Buzz-building activities*. Here we use online and social media to create a noise about a campaign or message and then help the message to spread through viral marketing as described in Section 7.7. Naturally, web addresses should also be quoted for all offline PR activity to complete the campaign's objective in driving traffic to the site. This activity will include communicating with media (journalists) online who increasingly use the Internet as a new conduit to access press releases through e-mail alerts and RSS feeds. Options include setting up a press-release area on the web site; creating e-mail alerts about news which journalists and other third parties can sign up to; and submitting your news stories or releases to online news feeds. Examples include: PR Newswire (www.prnewswire.com); PRWeb UK (http://ukservice.prweb.com) and Free Press Releases (www.freepressreleases.co.uk)

Forming relationships with publishers of media online gives a way to expand the reach of a brand. These influencers may include traditional journalists, but as the case study about Renault shows (see Emarketing Excellence box), also bloggers or celebrities.

Journalists can be influenced online through alerts setting up a press-release area or social media newsroom on the web site. *Widgets* can also be used to extend your reach and build buzz as described in the Emarketing Excellence box below.

E-MARKETING EXCELLENCE

Renault uses influencer outreach to support new product launch

In 2010, Renault launched a new range of zero emission vehicles. Renault's objective was to get people talking about the range, and especially the star model, the Twizy. Renault wanted to create links with opinion leaders sensitive to the automotive sector, but also to ecology and new technologies.

To reach influencers and help spread the word about the new model, agency BuzzParadise (2010) organized a special meeting at an international event, LeWeb. The idea was for Renault to use this platform to set up viral advertising aimed at a target audience sensitive to technological advances.

Invitations were sent to 13 bloggers from France, Germany, Great Britain, Italy and Spain writing about high-tech, trends, innovation and scientific themes. These partners met for a conference session and for tests of vehicles in the ZE range.

As a result, 22 articles were created across the blogs and, through these, 900,000 exposures to the message were generated. This increased visibility for Renault and its Twizy in the European blogosphere, social networks (Facebook, Twitter) and SEO (Google). The amplification effect of a relatively small number of bloggers is illustrated well by this reach figure. But it's worth remembering that visibility on blogs and social networks like this is usually ephemeral, meaning that the message is only visible for a short time within the blogosphere. So other techniques are also needed to give a more sustained delivery of messages and reminders to the audience. This is where traditional advertising and remarketing through display advertising to those who have already visited a company microsite play an important role.

4 *Defensive and crisis PR*. Defensive PR overlaps with many of the activities mentioned above.

It is necessary to track the health of a brand online through reputation management tools and then respond accordingly. Crisis PR involves a proactive approach to manage a potentially negative incident such as hardware which has a major flaw or an oil company that has a major incident.

CREATING BUSINESS BLOGS AND FEEDS

Web logs, known as *'blogs'*, were first known as a method of publishing personal web pages which are online journals or diaries. But the power of business blogs, which are created by people within an organization, is often underestimated. Let's take a look at some examples and the benefits:

- Showcases a company's expertise on a topic – commonly used by analysts; for example, the Forrester Marketing blog (http://blogs.forrester.com/interactive_marketing). Blogs can also showcase the quality of a supplier's data, the approach taken by Hitwise (www.hitwise.com).
- Gives the company views on issues, so is useful for reaching journalists who today scour the web for stories.
- Can help attract visitors from searchers on the different categories that are blogged on; for example, B2B marketing agency B2B International has a great blog (www.b2binternational.com/b2b-blog).
- Use as a branding and sales promotion tool: Asos achieves both through its blogs. If you take a look at these feeds, you will see they are updated very frequently – more frequently than many traditional publishers.

Business blogs can be created by individuals, but they often work best with features from different columnists on different types of topic, who can specialize on different features or viewpoints just as for a magazine. If you think this way, they are a means of making an e-newsletter more interactive and more topical.

Blogging software is incredibly good value, with many free tools. It is relatively cheap if set up on a separate domain as for the ASOS blog, which is effectively a low-cost in-house magazine. It can become more expensive the more closely integrated it is with the main site, since this will require additional development costs for coding. A good template style that reflects the brand is important, but these themes can often be applied using similar cascading style sheets (CSS) to those for the main brand, and therefore should not be expensive to create because of the limited number of page types.

The main blogging tools for marketing blogs, in rough order of popularity, are:

1 Movable Type (www.movabletype.org) from Six Apart is a download for management on your servers. Paid service.
2 TypePad (www.typepad.com), also from Six Apart, who offer it as an online service similar to most of those below, which is easier for smaller businesses. Paid service.
3 Blogger (www.blogger.com), purchased by Google some time ago.
4 WordPress (www.wordpress.org), an open source alternative which can be used as a web service or downloaded. Highly configurable.

5 Other open source content management systems are more often used for corporate sites; e.g. Plone, Drupal and Mambo or corporate content management systems such as Microsoft Office SharePoint Server.

The blogging format enables the content on a web site to be delivered in different ways. We'll use the Econsultancy blog (www.econsultancy.com/blog/) as an example, since this has a lot of rich content which can be delivered in different ways:

- By topic (in categories or topics to browse) – example: online PR category
- By tag (more detailed topics – each article will be tagged with several tags to help them appear in searches)– example: 'blogs and blogging' tag
- By author (features from different columnists who can be internal or external) – example: guest column from Andrew Girdwood on SEO
- By time (all posts broken down by the different methods above are in reverse date order). This shows the importance of having a search feature on the blog for readers to find specifics – this is usually a standard feature.

These features are great from a usability viewpoint since they help visitors locate what is most relevant to them. They are also great for SEO, since they provide pages focused on a particular topic – e.g. online PR – which are regularly updated with fresh content. That said, there are many basic blogs which don't have any other option than breaking down by archives.

There are also risks to blogs which may have put many companies off blogging, but these can be countered:

1 *Damage to reputation*. Non-company staff or even company staff can write negative posts or comments or defame others – moderators are needed or a sign-up process which limits contributors. Alternatively, comments can even be switched off, although you then lose the benefits of interactivity.
2 *SEO SPAM*. Blogs will have SEO SPAM comments with links in the post name to other sites unless these are edited using a service like Akismet or Disqus for WordPress.
3 *Poor levels of traffic*. If you prominently label your blog on your site, then you should get a proportion of traffic to visit and maybe they will bookmark the blog. Blogs should attract natural search activity, but as with any SEO activity, they require the keywords of posts to reflect searcher behaviour and they need work to attract links in.

PRACTICAL E-MARKETING TIP

Options for setting up and creating marketing blogs

To summarize, here is a checklist of ten options to consider when creating a blog for marketing.

☑ 1 *Moderation*: either open or closed to comments, with or without a moderator. Star rating of posts is a good option.

☑ 2 *Frequency*: 5 to 20 posts per month would be typical for a company site unless posted in multiple categories for a new site.

☑ 3 *Authorship:* do you have a single author (e.g. head of company), different contributors or guest contributors?

☑ 4 *Topics:* for usability and SEO, remember to place blog postings of a main blog in categories to enable tagging by different keywords. Alternatively, you may separate out blogs on different topics.

☑ 5 *Integration with web site including SEO:* links to the blog should be clearly labelled as 'blog' across run-of-site. Article categories should reflect keyphrases you are optimizing for on the main site. Keyphrases within categories and individual posts should show up clearly in <h1> and <title>.

☑ 6 *Email digest/e-newsletter integration.* Can you include some blog postings in your e-newsletter or can the two overlap?

☑ 7 *Linking to third-party sites.* You have the choice of using the rel= 'nofollow' on comments – I would advise this to discourage comment link SPAM. Also consider the availability of plug-ins to make blog management easier.

☑ 8 *Images and rich media.* Blogs should easily allow images or videos to be integrated. The CIPD blog (www.cipd.co.uk/blogs/) focuses on topical podcast interviews.

☑ 9 *RSS feeds and syndication.* Really Simple Syndication (RSS) is an extension of blogging where a blog, news or any type of content is received by specialist reader software integrated with a browser (e.g. Firefox Live Bookmarks) or email package (we recommend Attensa for Outlook). These offer a method of receiving news that uses a different broadcast method to email, so is not subject to the same conflicts with SPAM or SPAM filters. Feeds should be made available for the blog overall or in different categories for interested readers to subscribe to. RSS feeds also enable you to distribute your content for use on other sites – so my feeds, for example, are included on the Amazon site.

☑ 10 *Next steps/monetization.* Since blogs like that from ASOS are often set up on a separate sub-domain (http://subdomain.company.com) with a different style, links through to the main site may not be clear. It will help if links to the main site (or ads) are in the left or right sidebars or at the top/bottom of each post where they will be most visible. Also remember to put links back to the main site from within the blog stories – the ASOS blog links to search results for particular fashion items, for example.

E-MARKETING INSIGHT

Use PR to increase PR

Mike Grehan, a UK search engine marketing specialist, stresses the importance of the web to PR. He puts it this way:

> *Both online and off, the process is much the same when using PR to increase awareness, differentiate yourself from the crowd and improve perception.*
>
> *Many offline PR companies now employ staff with specialist online skills. The web itself offers a plethora of news sites and services. And, of course, there are thousands and thousands of newsletters and zines covering just about every topic under the sun.*
>
> *Never before has there been a better opportunity to get your message to the broadest geographic and multi-demographic audience. But you need to understand the pitfalls on both sides.*
>
> *(Grehan, 2004)*

In the article he also emphasizes the importance of link-building activities to build Google PageRank – the 'PR' referred to in the title.

PORTALS

Understanding *your online marketplace and different portals* on which to gain visibility is important to successful online PR and link building. We described an approach to this in Section 3.3.

SECTION SUMMARY 7.3

Online PR

1   Online PR is maximizing favourable mentions of your company, brands, products or web sites on third-party web sites that are likely to be visited by your target audience.

2   An important part of this is online reputation management, which is controlling the reputation of an organization through monitoring and controlling messages placed about that organization.

3   There are four main differences between online PR and traditional PR: the audience is connected to the organizations; the members of the audience are connected to each other; the audience has access to other information; audiences pool information.

4   Activities that can be considered as online PR include: communicating with media (journalists) online; link building; blogs and RSS feeds; managing how your brand is presented on third-party sites; creating a buzz – viral marketing.

7.4 Online partnerships

We showed in Chapter 2 that partnerships are an important part of today's marketing mix. The same is true online. Resources must be devoted to managing your online partners. Many large organizations have specific staff to manage these relationships. In smaller organizations it is often neglected – a big missed opportunity. There are three key types of online partnership that need to be managed: link building, affiliate marketing and online sponsorship. All should involve a structured approach to managing links through to your site.

LINK BUILDING

Link building is a key activity for search engine optimization. It's simple logic! More quality links from relevant sites mean more quality visitors and more marketing outcomes.

Here is our checklist of six best practice approaches to link building:

☑ 1 *Achieve natural link building through quality content* – through creating 'must-have' resources and guides and using social bookmark tools, such as AddThis (www.addthis.com), to encourage visitors to bookmark these documents; this creates inbound links from sources such as Delicious.

☑ 2 *Request inbound-only or one-way links from partners* or through running a link-building campaign.

☑ 3 *Reciprocal linking – reciprocal links* are agreed between yourself and another organization. These are less valuable than one-way links, but from trusted sources are usually better than no links at all. Use Majestic SEO or Opensite Explorer to identify potential link partners by assessing your own or rival sites.

☑ 4 *Buying links* – through directories and link purchase exchanges (these are not recommended since such sites are widely believed to be penalized by Google when identified). However, Google is unlikely to be able to identify agreements between site owners . . .

☑ 5 *Creating your own external links* – on blogs and in community forums – not typically successful since many forums have introduced an attribute tag on outbound links known as rel='nofollow' which means that the search engine can potentially ignore these links.

☑ 6 *Generating buzz through PR* – optimize and distribute your press releases or create articles which contain links back to your site which can be syndicated to third-party sites.

E-MARKETING INSIGHT

Ken McGaffin on why linking matters

McGaffin (2004) provides a great introduction to link building. The main principle of link building is, as he says: 'Create great content, link to great content and great content will link to you.'

However, a structured link-building campaign is also needed to maximize the number of quality inbound or backlinks which are from sites that have a high PageRank and from pages with the right content and anchor text. Ken McGaffin recommends these stages in his report at www.linkingmatters.com:

1 *Who links to you now?* Set up Google Webmaster Tools for the best indication of links.

2 *Who links to your competitors?* Use these backlink checking tools to find out: http://bit.ly/smartlinkcheck

3 *Which sites could link to you?* It helps to categorize the types of site when building links – you will have relationships with many already. For example, directories, media sites, customers, partners and suppliers.

4 *Understand why external sites would link to you.* It also helps to list all the types of content that could encourage links – in particular, content which naturally attracts links, which is known as *linkbait*. Examples include helpful tips, insightful articles and even lists of useful links (don't be afraid to link out from a site). Viral content that people will discuss in blogs is particularly valuable.

5 *Set objectives.* Ask how much you hope to improve your PageRank, the number of links you will seek to gain and how this translates to visitors and competitive positions. This is particularly difficult since one quality link may be more worthwhile than ten poor-quality ones which could be discounted by the search engines, or even damage your reputation.

6 *Make sure your site is link-friendly.* You should have a URL strategy which means clear URLs that others can use on their site. Facilitating social media is part of this, with many sites now having options to bookmark a site with Delicious or Google Bookmarks.

7 *Which links are on your site?* Having sections or articles with links out can encourage others to link to you. It is sometimes suggested that reciprocal links are 100 per cent bad, but this is not the case so long as they are not part of link-exchanges. It is also sometimes suggested that links out are 100 per cent bad, but this is not the case if they are useful for visitors and they can lead to you being seen as a hub by search engines.

8 *Ask for inbound links.* Although Ken and link-building experts such as Eric Ward (www.ericward.com) will rightly say that the best links are natural and generated by valuable content, obtaining links proactively is still a key aspect of link building.

9 *Track and improve.* Use Google Analytics and the backlink checking tools (see point 2 of this list) to review link quality and traffic delivered from different sources.

But remember that it is link quality, not link quantity – you need to gain links from sources which the search engines trust.

AFFILIATE MARKETING

Affiliate marketing is the ultimate form of marketing communications since it's Pay Per Performance – it's a commission-based arrangement where the merchant only pays when they make the sale or get a lead. Compare this to the wastage with traditional advertising or direct mail! It can also drive a volume of business in a range of sectors – many banks, travel companies or online retailers get more than 10 per cent of their sales from a well-run affiliate marketing programme. It's not so suitable, though, for business products or lower-priced consumer products since it won't be sufficiently profitable for the affiliates.

Figure 7.15 summarizes the affiliate marketing process. To manage the process of finding affiliates, updating product information, tracking clicks and making payments, many companies use an *affiliate network* or *affiliate manager* such as Commission Junction (www.cj.com) or Tradedoubler (www.tradedoubler.com). Since the affiliate network takes a cut on each sale, many merchants also try to set up separate relationships with preferred affiliates often known as 'super affiliates'.

Many of the benefits of affiliate marketing are closely related to search engine marketing since affiliates are often expert at deploying SEO or PPC to gain visibility in the natural search results. The main benefits of affiliate marketing are:

- Gaining more visibility in the paid and natural listings of the SERPs (increase 'share of search').
- You can use different affiliates to target different audiences, product categories and related phrases.
- Affiliates may be more responsive than your in-house or agency teams in terms of algorithm changes for SEO or changes in bidding approaches for PPC. They are also great at identifying gaps in your search strategy. For example, they may be quicker at advertising on new products, or may use keyphrase variants that you haven't considered.
- Enables you to reach customers on generic phrases (e.g. 'clothing') at a relatively low cost if the affiliates secure better positions in natural listings.
- Increasing the reach of your brand or campaign since affiliate ads and links featuring you will be displayed on third-party sites.
- Can be used to generate awareness of brand or new products for which a company isn't well known.

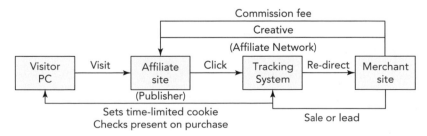

Figure 7.15 The affiliate marketing model (note that the tracking software and fee payment may be managed through an independent affiliate network manager)

- Use of affiliates reduces the risk caused by temporary or more fundamental problems with your SEM management.
- Pay Per Performance – the costs of acquisition can be controlled well.

But there are substantial downsides to an affiliate marketing programme which arise from the fact that your affiliates are mainly motivated by money. It follows that some of them may use unethical techniques to increase their revenue. Potential disadvantages are:

- *Incremental profit or sales may be limited*. You may be cannibalizing business you would have achieved anyway, as shown in the Emarketing Excellence box below.
- *Affiliates may exploit your brand name*. This is particularly the case where affiliates exploit brand names by bidding on variations of it (for example, 'Dell', 'Dell Computers' or 'Dell laptop') or by gaining a presence in the natural listings. It is important to prevent this, and many affiliate programmes exclude brand bidding, although affiliates can have a role in displacing competitors from the listings for brand terms.
- *May damage brand reputation*. Your ads may be displayed on sites inconsistent with your brand image such as gambling or pornography sites. Alternatively, creative may be out of date which could be illegal.
- *Programme management fees*. If you use an affiliate network to manage your campaigns, they may take up to 30 per cent of each agreed affiliate commission as additional 'network override'.
- *Programme management time*. Affiliate marketing is founded on forming and maintaining good relationships. This cannot be done through the agency alone – marketers within a company need to speak to their top affiliates.

E-MARKETING EXCELLENCE

Is affiliate marketing right for us?

The disadvantages of affiliate marketing mean that some marketers may avoid or stop using affiliate marketing.

Dabs marketing director Jonathan Wall (cited by Brooks, 2005) explains how Dabs.com reappraised their use of affiliate marketing. He said:

> *We stopped all our affiliate and price-comparison marketing in February because we wanted to see what effect it had on our business and if we were getting value for money.*

> *It was proving a very expensive channel for us and we've found [stopping] it has had virtually no effect, because we're seeing that people will still go to Kelkoo to check prices and then come to our site anyway. It's like they're having a look around first and then coming to a brand they know they can trust. We're continuing with paid-for search on Google, but that's all we're doing with online marketing at the moment.*

More recently, in 2007, affiliates were famously described by Nick Robertson, the CEO of online designer clothing store ASOS as *grubby little people in grubby studios* (Econsultancy, 2007).

BEST PRACTICE E-MARKETING TIP

Watch your EPC!

Success in affiliate marketing is based on selecting the right commission levels for different products, which have different levels of awareness, and will have different lifetime values for the retailer. The affiliates or publishers are obsessive about their average Earnings Per Click (EPC) – usually measured across 100 clicks since an average is needed over this number of clicks.

This is a crucial measure in affiliate marketing, since an affiliate will compare merchants on this basis and then usually decide to promote those with the highest EPC, which will be based on the commission levels and the conversion rates to sale for different merchants. It also depends on the cookie expiry period agreed on – the time between visitor clicking the affiliate link and the sale being accredited to the affiliate. Common times are 7, 30 or 90 days. A longer cookie period will result in a higher EPC. Of course, you don't typically want to pay multiple affiliates for a single sale – although that will boost your EPC. Instead, it is usually the last referring affiliate who is credited or a mix between first and last.

You can compare your EPC for different products against competitors using the affiliate networks, which is a valuable insight which you may miss if all affiliate marketing is outsourced. You may also be able to use this to benchmark your conversion rates.

For example, at the time of writing (2012), this is how Tesco.com used affiliates for different products (for more information, see www.tradedoubler.com):

- E-diets commission from £12 on 1–9 sales to £20 on 61+sales
- Wine at 2 per cent on lowest tier to 3 per cent on the Gold tier of sales of >£2,500
- Grocery and utilities – flat fee of £5.

Fees are relatively low on groceries for which Tesco.com is well known, but less so for diets and wine where awareness of the product offering may be lower or competition higher.

Different categories of affiliate site

Online marketers also need to be selective in choosing the right forms of affiliate marketing – not all may be desirable. These are the options for affiliate marketing models for you to consider.

1 *Aggregators* – these are the big comparison sites like Kelkoo, Shopzilla and MoneySupermarket. com. These aren't strictly affiliates since most charge per click, but Google Product Search (formerly Froogle) is a free option and you should definitely consider creating a product feed for some of these comparison sites.

2 *Review sites* – you'll know the CNET UK reviews or maybe start-ups like Reevoo or Review Centre. These all link to merchants based on Cost Per Click or Cost Per Acquisition deals.

3 *Rewards sites* – with names like Greasypalm or QuidCo, you get the idea. These split the commission between the reward site and their visitors.

4 *Voucher code sites* – MyVoucherCodes or HotUKDeals are typical. If you have some great deals to entice first-time shoppers, you should generate business, although many search by well-known brand.

5 *Uber-bloggers* – Martin Lewis's MoneySavingExpert.com is an incredibly popular site due to his PR efforts and great content. Although he has no ads, he is an affiliate for many sites he recommends.

6 *Everyone else* – they don't tend to be high-volume super-affiliates like all the above, but they're collectively important and you can work them via affiliate networks like Commission Junction or Tradedoubler. They often specialize in SEO or PPC. Don't expect this option to be easy since affiliates often only promote a few well-known merchants who maximize their Earnings Per 100 Clicks (EPC).

WHAT ARE WIDGETS?

Widgets are different forms of tools made available on a web site or on a user's desktop. They either provide some functionality, like a calculator, or they provide real-time information; for example, on news or weather.

They are often placed in the left or right sidebar, or in the body of an article. They are relatively easy for site owners to implement, usually requiring a couple of lines of JavaScript, but this does depend on the content management system.

E-MARKETING INSIGHT

Different types of widgets?

A widget is a badge or button incorporated into a site or social network space by its owner, but with content typically served from another site. They deliver content such as up-to-date information or even mini applications. There are now many types which offer to help a site owner spread their message beyond their own site. In a word, they're about reach. You can encourage partners to place them on their sites and this will help educate people about your brand, possibly generate backlinks and also allow people to engage with your brand when they're not on your site (which is the majority of the time). They offer your partner sites the opportunity to add value to their visitors through the gadget functionality or content, or to add to their brand through association with you (co-branding) and through affiliate arrangements.

1 *Web widgets*. Web widgets have been around for years for affiliate marketing, but they are getting more sophisticated, enabling searches on a site, real-time price updates or even streaming video.

2 *Google gadgets*. Different content can be incorporated onto a personalized Google home page.

3 *Desktop and operating system gadgets*. Vista, the new Microsoft OS, makes it easier to create and enable subscription to these widgets and place them into sidebars.

4 *Social media widgets*. You see these everywhere; for example, to encourage site visitors to subscribe to RSS or to bookmark the page on their favourite social media site like Delicious, Digg or Technorati.

5 *Facebook applications*. Facebook have opened up their API (application programming interface) to enable developers to create small interactive programs that users can add to their space to personalize it. Charitable giving site JustGiving has a branded API with several hundred users.

ONLINE SPONSORSHIP

Online sponsorship is not straightforward. It's not just a case of mirroring existing 'real-world' sponsorship arrangements in the 'virtual world'. There are many additional opportunities for sponsorship online which can be sought out, even if you don't have a big budget at your disposal.

Ryan and Whiteman (2000) define online sponsorship as: 'the linking of a brand with related content or context for the purpose of creating brand awareness and strengthening brand appeal in a form that is clearly distinguishable from a banner, button or other standardized ad unit'.

For the advertiser, online sponsorship has the benefit that their name is associated with an online brand that the site visitor is already familiar with. So, for users of the ISP Wanadoo, with whom they are familiar, sponsorship builds on this existing relationship and trust. Closely related is online 'co-branding' where there is an association between two brands.

Paid-for sponsorship of another site, or part of it, especially a portal for an extended period, is another way to develop permanent links. Co-branding is a lower-cost method of sponsorship and can exploit synergies between different companies.

A great business-to-business example of online sponsorship is offered by WebTrends which sponsors the customer information channel on ClickZ.com (www.clickz.com/experts). They combine this sponsorship with different ads each month, offering e-marketers information about different topics such as search marketing, retention and conversion marketing through detailed white papers and 'Take 10' online video presentations by industry experts which can be downloaded by registered users. The objective of these ads is to encourage prospects to subscribe to the WebTrends *WebResults* e-newsletter and to assess purchase intent at sign-up, enabling follow-up telemarketing by regional distributors. WebTrends reported the following results over a single year of sponsorship:

- List built to 100,000 WebResults total subscribers
- 18,000 'Take 10' presentations
- 13,500 seminar attendees.

SECTION SUMMARY 7.4

Online partnerships

We reviewed three key types of online partnership:

1 *Link building*: obtaining links from third-party sites to a company site. This should be performed in a structured manner to maximize visitors from third-party sites and to help increase PageRank within Google.
2 *Affiliate marketing*: a commission-based arrangement where referring sites are paid a fee for sales, leads or visitors. It is potentially a large source of quality traffic for e-retailers.
3 *Online sponsorship*: a long-term arrangement to associate a brand with a site, or part of a site.
4 Widgets can be applied to extend your reach via each of these three arrangements.

7.5 Interactive advertising

A visitor who clicks on an *interactive (banner) ad* at an ad site is then *referred* through to the site of the company which paid for the banner ad which links through to a *destination site* as indicated by Figure 7.16. Many organizations link interactive ads to a specific campaign *microsite* or, on Facebook, to their business page. This provides content tailored to the campaign that appears immediately on clickthrough without the distractions of a link to the standard site. The microsite can be independent of the media owner's site, or it can be part of it, which can potentially improve response.

But ad clickthrough rates (CTR) for non-video formats average less than 0.1 per cent. The microsite approach is somewhat ineffective. Instead, today, the name of the game is interaction and engagement. Many ads will encourage the media site visitor to interact through a prompt to 'rollover', and another Flash creative will then be loaded which may offer a clear brand message rendered in large font, a response form such as an insurance quote, or a request to obtain a SIM or a game or poll. The effectiveness of the ad campaign can then be assessed through the *IR* or *interaction rate* which will typically be ten times higher than the clickthrough rate if the targeting, offer and creative are right.

Although display advertising is often thought of simply as a traffic-building technique, there are several alternative objectives which were first summarized by Cartellerieri *et al*. (1997):

- *Deliver content*. Information on-site to help communicate a company's offering.
- *Enable transaction*. An e-tailer intending to use banner ads to increase sales.
- *Shape attitudes*. An advert that is consistent with a company brand or that features a new product can help build brand or product awareness. Research services such as Dynamic Logic

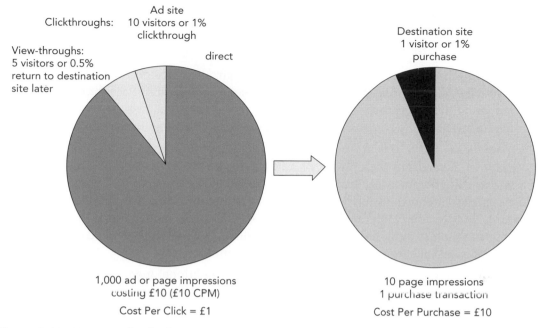

Clickthroughs:
Ad site
10 visitors or 1%
clickthrough

View-throughs:
5 visitors or 0.5%
return to destination
site later

direct

Destination site
1 visitor or 1%
purchase

1,000 ad or page impressions
costing £10 (£10 CPM)

Cost Per Click = £1

10 page impressions
1 purchase transaction

Cost Per Purchase = £10

Figure 7.16   Measures for display ads

(www.dynamiclogic.com) are used by savvy online advertisers to assess the effectiveness of creative in terms of traditional branding metrics such as message association, brand awareness and purchase intent.

- *Solicit response*. An advert may be intended to identify new leads or as a start for two-way communication.

- *Encourage retention*. The advert may be placed to remind site visitors about the company and its service.

Some marketers have had a bad experience of online advertising, and certainly there are weaknesses to be aware of, including:

1 *Poor and diminishing clickthrough rates*. Partly as a result of 'banner blindness', there has been a dramatic decline in average clickthrough rates (CTR) from 25 per cent on the first banner in 1994, which simply said 'Click here', to an average of 0.1 per cent, although higher for rich media as video streamed ads.

2 *Relatively high costs*. Relative to some other online marketing tools, such as search engine marketing and affiliate marketing which also have the advantages of being performance-based, interactive advertising costs can be relatively high, with media costs of around £10 per thousand ads served (£10 CPM), plus creative costs.

3 *Branding effect is difficult to quantify*. Although it is possible to pre-test and post-test online advertising effectiveness, there are relatively few providers in this area. It is a relatively costly discipline.

But before you move on to the next section, online advertising has developed a lot from the early banners and CPM-only deals. Consider these advantages of today's display advertising; for example, for a car manufacturer:

1 *Ads are highly targeted*. Media buyers can select the right site or channel within a site to reach the audience (e.g. a specialist online car magazine or review site or the motoring channel within an online newspaper or TV channel site). Audiences can also be targeted via their profile through serving personalized ads, or ads in email if visitors have registered on a site.

2 *Ad networks can reduce costs*. Ad networks from suppliers such as BlueLithium or 24/7 Real Media give advertisers the options of advertising across a network of sites to reach a particular demographic – e.g. female 18–25 – but at a lower cost, since the actual site used for the ad placement isn't known (hence these are sometimes known as blind network buys). Lower CPMs are achievable and in some cases, CPC or CPA payment options are available. Site owners such as publishers use ad networks since it gives them a method of gaining fees from unused ad inventory which has not sold at premium rates.

3 *Behavioural retargeting options*. It is well known from traditional media campaigns that the impact of an ad in terms of its ability to shape brand awareness, ad recall and purchase intent is dependent on the ad frequency or the number of times it is seen on average. This effect can be magnified if an ad is served preferentially, to someone who seems to have an interest in a topic from the content they consume. Effectively the ad follows the viewer around the site. For example, if someone visits the car section of a site, then the ad is served to them when they view other sections of the site. Retargeting can work across an ad network too and can even be sequential, where the messages are varied for an individual the more times they are exposed to the ad. Search retargeting offers the option to display an ad after a visitor has searched on a particular term such a car marque. Tracking of individuals is achieved through use of *cookies*.

4 *New ad formats can increase response*. In the early days of online advertising, most ads were simply banners of 468 × 60 dimension. Today, if you view ads served by rich media companies such as Tangozebra (www.tangozebra.com) in their labs, you will see that there is a wealth of Flash-based ad formats, including expandable banners and skyscrapers, where if the user rolls over the ad, a new ad can be triggered which might include a streamed video clip, audio, a personalized message or a form prompting someone to order a brochure, book a dealer appointment or perform a search on a site. Effectively the ads are serving a microsite or delivering their web site through an advert!

NEWER FORMS OF DISPLAY ADVERTISING

Real-time bidding (RTB) accounts for an increasing proportion of display advertising, enabling more precise targeting. It is often applied in combination with *remarketing* to remind web users who have previously interacted with a brand about relevant offers. It is dependent on cookies to identify individual user's preferences as they access different sites in an *ad network*.

To help understand RTB, you can think of it as a way of buying media similar to Google Adwords, except a bid is made for each ad impression on a publisher site rather than a search within Google. Indeed, Google's own Display Network (GDN) can be thought of as an RTB system where targeting is based on keywords and previous sites visited (AdWords Remarketing) and the advertisers bid for the placement on the site.

E-MARKETING INSIGHT

Consumer concern over remarketing

Some media and privacy campaigners have been critical of this form of targeting since it involves tracking the users across multiple sites. For example, the *New York Times* (2010), in what can only be described as a 'scaremongering ad' described how mother of two from Montreal, Julie Matlin, saw shoes on Zappos.com that were 'kind of cute', but she wasn't ready to buy, so left the site. The article went on to describe how

> *the shoes started to follow her everywhere she went online . . . an ad for those very shoes showed up on the blog TechCrunch. It popped up again on several other blogs and on Twitpic. It was as if Zappos had unleashed a persistent salesman who wouldn't take no for an answer.*
>
> **(New York Times, 2010)**

The article goes on to explain how other ads have caused problems too. Bad as it was to be stalked by shoes, Ms Matlin said that she felt even worse when she was hounded recently by ads for a dieting service she had used online. 'They are still following me around, and it makes me feel fat', she said.

The Electronic Frontier Foundation (www.eff.org) and Don't Track Us (http://donttrack.us) have been active in campaigning against the use of this behavioural information.

The advent of RTB has been greeted enthusiastically since its introduction as it offers the potential for granular one-to-one targeting, in theory reducing wastage compared to the time when ads were bought on the Cost Per Thousand (CPM) basis with the ad not relevant to many of the bidders. Let's take the example of targeting for a car manufacturer who is marketing an 'eco-friendly' car.

Options for targeting through RTB include:

- *Demographics* – while our car manufacturer could target based on demographics alone, this would result in a high level of wastage
- *Content viewed on a publisher site* – if an article reviews the advantages and options of 'eco-friendly cars', this will be stored against the user for subsequent advertising
- *Content previously viewed across an ad network* – if a user has viewed content related to cars on other publisher sites, this can also be used for targeting
- *Searches* – either performed on-site or before visiting a site
- *Previous interactions with a brand* – for example, visits to their site including product pages (*remarketing*)

- *Browser settings* – in some cases, it may be useful to target users with more or less advanced technology set-ups.

Demand-side platforms (DSPs) are a technology used as part of RTB to enable advertisers to place and manage ads from different ad exchanges and different *ad networks* through a single interface or trading desk.

E-MARKETING EXCELLENCE

Online video advertising best practice

Online video can generate higher response rates of 1–4 per cent, according to the compilations of ad serving companies such as ADTECH (www.adtech.de), but they need to use the right approach to achieve more influence. Research by Dynamic Logic summarized in *Admap* (Moorey-Denham and Green, 2007) understandably advises 'Keep it short and simple'. The authors say:

> *While a repurposed 30-second TV commercial may be of some benefit, shorter units may have an even greater impact. Short ads may reach a broader audience by communicating a simple message before viewers have the opportunity to become irritated or impatient and stop the player.*
> *(Moorey-Denham and Green, 2007)*

Online ads are one of the main revenue models for online media owners so there is a lot of research into how to make them effective. Here we will summarize the issues involved in interactive advertising by setting out five questions to ask when working with agencies when first exploring interactive advertising.

Q1. Mix of offline and online media (are we spending enough?)

The first question to ask is how much are you spending on online elements of campaigns; or, put another way – what is your optimal media mix to increase awareness and purchase intent within your target markets?

Table 7.3 Optimum media mix suggested by ground-breaking XMOS studies

Brand	TV %	Magazine %	Online %
Colgate	75	14	11
Kleenex	70	20	10
Dove	72	13	15
McDonald's	71	16 (radio)	13

Source: IAB (2004)

For any given campaign, media selection and the proportion of spend on online media will often be left to the media planner. But, depending on the agency used, they may play it safe by putting the ad spend into what they are familiar with and what may be most rewarding – offline media. Many *cross-media optimization studies (XMOS)* (e.g. IAB, 2004) have shown that the optimal mix for low-involvement products is surprisingly high, with online advertising at 10–15 per cent of total spend.

E-MARKETING INSIGHT

XMOS studies show the importance of online spend

XMOS research is designed to help marketers and their agencies answer the question 'What is the optimal mix of advertising vehicles across different media, in terms of frequency, reach and budget allocation, for a given campaign to achieve its marketing goals?' The mix between online and offline spend is varied to maximize campaign metrics such as reach, brand awareness and purchase intent. Table 7.3 (IAB, 2004) summarizes the optimal mix identified for four famous brands. For example, Dove found that increasing the level of interactive advertising to 15 per cent would have resulted in an increase in overall brand awareness of 8 per cent. The proportion of online is small, but remember that many companies are spending less than 1 per cent of their ad budgets online, meaning that offline frequency is too high and they may not be reaching many consumers.

Q2. Are we exploiting the full range of ad formats?

The classic 468 × 60 rotating GIF banner ad is virtually dead: many online users suffer from 'banner blindness' – we simply filter out this content. Media owners now provide a choice of larger, richer formats which web users are more likely to notice. Research has shown that message association and awareness building is much higher for Flash-based ads, *rich media* ads and larger format rectangles and skyscrapers. Visit the rich media ads at www.eyeblaster.com or www.tangozebra.com and you will agree that they definitely can't be ignored.

Other online ad terms you will hear include '*interstitial*' (intermediate adverts before another page appears); and '*superstitials*' (pop-up adverts which require interaction by the user to close them down). Online advertisers face a constant battle with users who deploy pop-up blockers or, less commonly, ad-blocking software. This is one reason why, in the UK in 2004, 40 per cent of online ad spend was in PPC – it is more visible, it can't be blocked (yet). Some media sites such as *The Guardian* now charge a premium for those users who don't want to see ads.

Q3. Are your ad buys smart?

Banner advertising is purchased for a specific period. It may be purchased for the ad to be shown or served on:

- The run-of-site (the entire site) and roadblocks
- A relevant section of site
- According to keywords entered on a search engine (the PPC model described earlier in Section 7.2 on paid or Pay Per Click search marketing).

Payment is typically based on the number of customers who view the page as a cost per thousand (CPM or CPT) ad or page impressions. Typical CPM is in the range of £10–£50. Other options that benefit the advertiser if they can be agreed are: per clickthrough – e.g. ValueClick Media (www.valueclick.co.uk); or per action such as a purchase on the destination site.

Placements on individual pages are also important – an ad is less likely to be viewed below the fold or in a masthead which is above the main menu of a site. Placements which are integrated with the content tend to be most effective and, increasingly, editorial is bought as part of the deal.

BEST PRACTICE E-MARKETING TIP

Frequency

As for other media, repeated exposure of a web user to an ad will make it more effective until the point of diminishing returns where each view of the ad has no additional impact. Research suggests that campaigns should be capped at four. Ask your ad agency to report not only on the average frequency, but also on the frequency distribution.

Q4. Are you using all the targeting options?

Online ads can be targeted through:

1 Purchasing on a site (or part of a site) with a particular visitor profile
2 Purchasing at a particular time of day or week
3 Online behaviour – the ultimate in *dynamic ad targeting* according to types of content used. For example, the *Financial Times* online (www.ft.com), using software from AudienceScience, can identify users in eight segments: business education, institutional investor, IT, luxury and consumer, management, personal finance, travel and private equity.

Banner ad networks provide the facility to advertise on a range of properties and target in a range of ways, as shown in the E-marketing Excellence box below.

Effective online advertisers build in flexibility to change targeting through time. Best practice is to start wide and then narrow your focus – allow 20 per cent of your budget for high-performing ad placements (high CTR and conversion).

E-MARKETING EXCELLENCE

Options for targeting advertising

Leading online media owners such as MSN (www.msn.com) and the *Financial Times* online (www.ft.com) offer a range of options for targeting:

1 *Content targeting.* Placement of advertising messages on a particular interest site or within an entire interest category such as: automotive, business and finance or health.

2 *Behavioural targeting.* An audience can be targeted according to how they use the web or an individual site. For example, advertisers can select business users by delivering advertisements on Monday to Friday between 9 am and 5 pm, or leisure users by targeting messages in the evening hours. Ads can be targeted according to the types of content viewed, even when in a different part of the site.

3 *User targeting.* This enables advertisements to be placed according to specific traits of the audience including their geographic location (based on country or post code), domain type (e.g. educational users with addresses ending in .edu or .ac.uk can be targeted), business size or type according to SIC code or even by the company they work for, based on the company domain name. This is possible where users create a profile on a site such as Yahoo! (www.yahoo.com) or the *Financial Times* online (www.ft.com) or through automated analysis of the type of content they consume.

4 *Tech targeting.* This is based on user hardware, software and Internet access provider.

Q5. Are you using creative effectively?

Avantmarketer (www.avantmarketer.com) summarizes these tips for effective online creative:

- Brand the first frame with a brand identity (or the top of skyscrapers)
- Tell a story, but each frame should stand alone
- Ditch 'Click here!', instead use an action verb such as 'Sign up now' or 'Download our white paper' (many would advise using 'Click here' for some ad types)
- Use high contrast
- Keep it simple – only use a few elements in ad creative
- Include a human face where possible
- Flash makes producing higher-impact ads more practical.

Choosing creative for different ad placements is difficult to predict and requires hard work. In an iMediaConnection interview, ING Direct vice president of marketing, Jurie Pieterse, highlighted the following:

> *Another lesson we learned is the importance of creative. It's critical to invest in developing various creative executions to test them for best performance and constantly*

introduce new challengers to the top performers. We've also learned there's no single top creative unit – different creative executions and sizes perform differently from publisher to publisher.

(Pieterse, cited in iMediaConnection, 2003)

Finally, consider your options for online sponsorship which is closely related to interactive advertising (online sponsorship is covered in Section 7.4 on online partnerships).

SECTION SUMMARY 7.5

Interactive advertising

Interactive advertisements can help build site traffic, but also have a role in building brand recognition. Rich media and large format ads are effective in targeting visitors through placements on specialized portals and dynamic or behavioural ad targeting. Acquiring customers by banners paid for by CPM is relatively expensive and alternative forms of promotion or payment according to results are preferable.

7.6 Opt-in email

Savvy e-marketers understand that *opt-in email* is a powerful online communications tool. As with direct mail, it is most widely used for direct response, but e-newsletters in particular can also achieve branding objectives. It enables a targeted message to be pushed out to a customer to inform and remind, and they are certain to view at least the subject line within their email inbox, even if it is only to delete it. Contrast this with the web – a pull medium where customers will only visit your site if there is a reason or a prompt to do this. But there is a problem: in the minds of many Internet users, email is evil. It is *SPAM*, unsolicited email sent by unscrupulous traders. Some say SPAM stands for 'Sending Persistent Annoying Email', but it actually originates from the Monty Python comedy sketch. Remember that SPAM is now outlawed in many countries.

To achieve the potential benefits of opt-in email, marketers should take careful measures to avoid SPAM. This section explains how to achieve this.

Opt-in is the key to successful email marketing. Customer choice is the watchword. Before starting an email dialogue with customers, companies must ask them to provide their email address and then give them the option of 'opting into' further communications and selecting their communications preferences; for example, the frequency of email and type of content. Privacy law in many countries requires that they should proactively opt in by checking a box (showing consent in some way). Email lists can also be rented where customers have opted in to receive email.

Opt-in email options for customer acquisition

For acquiring new visitors and customers to a site, there are three main options for email marketing. From the point of view of the recipient, these are:

1 *Cold email campaign*. In this case, the recipient receives an opt-in email from an organization which has rented an email list from a consumer email list provider such as Experian (www.experian.com), Claritas (www.claritas.com), IPT Limited (www.myoffers.co.uk); or a business email list provider such as Mardev (www.mardev.com), Corpdata (www.corpdata.co.uk) or trade publishers/event providers such as VNU. Although they have agreed to receive offers by email, the email is effectively cold. For example, a credit-card provider could send a cold email to a list member who is not currently their member. It is important to use some form of *'statement of origination'*, otherwise the message may be considered SPAM. Cold emails tend to have higher CPAs than other forms of online marketing, but different lists should still be evaluated.

2 *Co-branded email*. Here, the recipient receives an email with an offer from a company that they have a reasonably strong affinity with. For example, the same credit-card company could partner with a mobile service provider such as Vodafone and send out the offer to their customer (who has opted in to receive emails from third parties). Although this can be considered a form of cold email, it is warmer since there is a stronger relationship with one of the brands, and the subject line and creative will refer to both brands. Co-branded emails tend to get a better response than cold e-mails to rented lists since the relationship exists and fewer offers tend to be given.

3 *Third-party e-newsletter*. In this visitor acquisition option, a company publicizes itself in a third-party e-newsletter. This could be in the form of an ad, sponsorship or PR (editorial) which links through to a destination site. These placements may be set up as part of an interactive advertising ad buy since many e-newsletters also have permanent versions on the web site. Since e-newsletter recipients tend to engage with them by scanning the headlines or reading them if they have time, e-newsletter placements can be relatively cost-effective.

Opt-in e-mail options for customer retention

For most organizations, email marketing is most powerful for developing relationships with customers as part of e-CRM. We explore options for using email marketing to build relationships with customers through Chapter 8 and specifically in Section 8.5.

E-MARKETING EXCELLENCE

WH Smith uses sequential remarketing to increase conversion

This remarketing was a classic abandoned shopping cart follow-up email, but with three alternative follow-ups which were tested with these results:

1 *Generic branded follow-up email*: +10 per cent conversion rate
2 *Personalized remarketing email with a promotional code for a 5 per cent discount time limited to 72 hours*: +100 per cent conversion rate

3 *Personalized remarketing email with a promotional code for a 5 per cent discount time limited to 48 hours*: +200 per cent conversion rate.

(Smart Insights, 2011b)

WH Smith also conducted a survey of those customers identified as having clicked through from the remarketing emails and then made a purchase, but who hadn't actually used the promotional codes! Interestingly, they found:

- These customers had still reacted to the remarketing email as a prompt to return to the WH Smith web site.
- It was the expiry date of the call-to-action that had prompted them to return, even though they then did not take advantage of the 5 per cent discount promo code.

EMAIL MARKETING SUCCESS FACTORS

Effective email marketing shares much in common with effective direct email copy. We suggest you use the mnemonic 'CRITICAL' as a checklist for email marketing success factors. CRITICAL is a checklist of questions to ask about your email campaigns (Chaffey, 2006). It stands for:

- *Creative* – this assesses the design of the email including its layout, use of colour and image and the copy (see below).
- *Relevance* – does the offer and creative of the email meet the needs of the recipients?
- *Incentive* (or offer) – the WIFM factor or 'What's in it for me?' for the recipient. What benefit does the recipient gain from clicking on the hyperlink(s) in the email? For example, a prize draw is a common offer for B2C brands.
- *Targeting and timing* – targeting is related to the relevance. Is a single message sent to all prospects or customers on the list or are emails with tailored creative, incentive and copy sent to the different segments on the list? Timing refers to when the email is received; the time of day, day of the week, point in the month and even the year; does it relate to any particular events? There is also the relative timing – when it is received compared to other marketing communications – this depends on the integration.
- *Integration* – are the email campaigns part of your integrated marketing communications?
- Questions to ask include: are the creative and copy consistent with my brand? Does the message reinforce other communications? Does the timing of the email campaign fit with offline communications?
- *Copy* – this is part of the creative and refers to the structure, style and explanation of the offer together with the location of hyperlinks in the email.
- *Attributes* (of the email) – assess the message characteristics such as the subject line, from address, to address, date/time of receipt and format (HTML or text). Send out Multipart/ MIME messages which can display HTML or text according to the capability of the email reader. Offer choice of HTML or text to match the user's preferences.

- *Landing page* (or microsite) – these are terms given for the page(s) reached after the recipient clicks on a link in the email. Typically, on clickthrough, the recipient will be presented with an online form so the company can profile or learn more about them. Designing the page so the form is easy to complete can affect the overall success of the campaign.

Designing direct email copy is as involved as designing direct mail and many similar principles apply. Effective email should:

- Grab attention in subject line and body
- Be brief and be relevant to target
- Be personalized – not Dear Valued Customer, but Dear Ms Smith
- Provide opt-out or 'unsubscribe' option by law
- Hyperlink to web site for more detailed content
- Have a clear call-to-action at the start and end of the message
- Be tested for effectiveness
- Operate within legal and ethical constraints for a country.

SECTION SUMMARY 7.6

Opt-in email

Email is an effective push online communications method. It is essential that email is opt-in, otherwise it is illegal SPAM. Consider options for customer acquisition including cold email, co-branded emails and placements in third-party emails. For house list emails, experiment with achieving the correct frequency, or give customers the choice. Consider automated event-triggered emails. Work hard on email design and maintaining up-to-date lists. Stay within the law.

7.8 Viral marketing

We covered social media marketing in depth in Chapter 5, so in this section, we just take a brief look at viral marketing.

Ideally, viral marketing is a clever idea, a shocking idea, or a highly informative idea which makes compulsive viewing. It can be a video clip, a TV ad, a cartoon, a funny picture, a poem, song, political or social message, or a news item. It's so amazing that it makes people want to pass it on.

Viral marketing harnesses the network effect of the Internet and can be effective in reaching a large number of people rapidly in the same way as a computer virus can affect many machines around the world.

Like most buzz words, 'viral marketing' means different things to different people. A viral marketing initiative certainly needs to create a buzz to be successful. The two main forms of viral marketing are best known as 'word ofmouth' and 'word of mouse'. Both rely on networks of people to spread the word. Viral marketing also occurs in social networks.

To make a viral campaign happen, Justin Kirby of viral marketing specialists DMC (www.dmc.co.uk) suggests there are three things that are needed (Kirby, 2003):

1 *Creative material* – the 'viral agent'. This includes the creative message or offer and how it is spread (text, image, video).
2 *Seeding*. Identifying web sites, blogs or people to send email to – to start the virus spreading.
3 *Tracking*. To monitor the effect and to assess the return from the cost of developing the viral agent and seeding.

We distinguish between these types of viral email mechanisms.

1 *Pass along email viral*. This is where email alone is used to spread the message. It is an email with a link to a site such as a video or an attachment. Towards the end of a commercial email, it does no harm to prompt the first recipient to forward the email along to interested friends or colleagues. Even if only 1 in 100 responds to this prompt, it is still worth it. The dramatic growth of Hotmail, reaching 10 million subscribers in just over a year, was effectively down to pass-along as people received emails with a signature promoting the service. Word of mouth helped too.

Pass-along or forwarding has worked well for video clips, either where they are attached to the email or the email contains a link to download the clip. If the email has the 'WOW!' factor, of which more later, a lot more than 1 in 100 will forward the email. This mechanism is what most people consider to be viral, but there are the other mechanisms that follow too.

2 *Web-facilitated viral (email prompt)*. Here, the email contains a link/graphic to a web page with 'email a friend' or 'email a colleague'. A web form is used to collect data of the email address to which the email should be forwarded, sometimes with an optional message. The company then sends a separate message to the friend or colleague.

3 *Web-facilitated viral (web prompt)*. Here it is the web page such as a product catalogue or white paper which contains a link/graphic to 'email a friend' or colleague. A web form is again used to collect data and an email is subsequently sent.

4 *Incentivized viral*. This is distinct from the types above since the email address is not freely given. This is what we need to make viral really take off. By offering some reward for providing someone else's address, we can dramatically increase referrals. A common offer is to gain an additional entry into a prize draw. Referring more friends gains more entries to the prize draw. With the right offer, this can more than double response. The incentive is offered either by email (option 2 above) or on a web page (option 3). In this case, there is a risk of breaking privacy laws since the consent of the email recipient may not be freely given. Usually only a single follow-up email by the brand is permitted. So you should check with the lawyers if considering this.

5 *Web-link viral*. But online viral isn't just limited to email. If you click on any of the links in this chapter – that can also be considered to be online viral marketing, or you could call it

online PR. Links in discussion group postings or *blogs* that are from an individual are also in this category. Either way, it's important when seeding the campaign to try to get as many targeted online and offline mentions of the viral agent as you can.

SECTION SUMMARY 7.7

Viral marketing

With viral techniques, traffic is built either through using email (virtual word of mouth) or real-world word of mouth to spread the message from one person to the next.

7.8 Offline traffic building

In this section, we will see that offline communications are still a key component of the e-communications mix. In most sectors, companies still spend more in offline channels than online. For example, IAB (2012) estimates that around 30 per cent of communications budgets are spent online in the UK. Remember that even Google, which famously grew initially by word of mouth alone, now relies on TV, print and outdoor ads to grow awareness and adoption of its Google Chrome and Google+ services, and it even invests in direct mail to encourage adoption of its Adwords amongst advertisers.

Companies need to decide on whether advertising is *incidental* or *specific* – whether specialist messages need to be communicated and the mix of techniques used. All ten offline communications tools from Smith and Taylor (2004) can and should be used to build online traffic. These ten tools are referred to in Table 2.1. They are: advertising, selling, sales promotion, PR, sponsorship, direct mail, exhibitions, merchandising, packaging and word of mouth – all can be used to communicate or promote in the online or offline world.

How significant is offline promotion? After evaluating the range of online promotion techniques available, you may be asking yourself, 'If all these online techniques are effective, why do companies spend so much on offline advertising?' In fact, the spend on online advertising is dwarfed by the spend on advertising in traditional media such as print, TV and radio. In 2011, the UK Internet Advertising Bureau research showed that online ad spend had exceeded 27 per cent, but 73 per cent spend offline is still significant!

PRACTICAL E-MARKETING TIP

Assessing the effectiveness of offline communications as a traffic driver

Web analytics is again your ally in assessing the effectiveness of offline ad spend. You should consider how you will track campaign effectiveness before you start. Some options include:

● Landing page entries direct to the URL promoted in the campaign

- Number of visitors to site arriving after searching on your brand name or products, campaign names mentioned in the ad (some of these searches will be influenced by offline spend too)
- Increment in number of direct visitors to the site or section of site promoted in the campaign compared to level of business (i.e. same period) last month or last year
- Number of visitors arriving from new links to the site referencing the campaign.

To summarize, a key decision for e-marketers is deciding on the balance of spend between online and offline promotion.

WHAT ARE WE COMMUNICATING OFFLINE?

Important aspects of the online brand to communicate are:

- The brand name and URL (of course). Offline campaigns should result in an uplift to brand searches and direct visits which can be measured through analytics. In print, using a subfolder in the URL (www.domain.com/campaignname) can help direct users to the relevant section
- Online value proposition (see Section 6.3). The ad creative should give a specific benefit for immediately visiting the site
- Traditional brand values
- Sales promotions and offers.

Let us now briefly consider four of the main tools: advertising, word of mouth, PR and direct mail.

Advertising

Early attempts by many traditional clicks-and-mortar companies to advertise their online offering were limited to *incidental advertising* where the company's web site address was added as a footnote to the advert with no attempt to explain the online proposition or drive a web response. For dotcoms, it is vital to use offline advertising to communicate their *online value proposition* in specific adverts, and traditional companies are increasingly using this approach as more sales are achieved online. Online recruitment agency Monster.com saw its traffic quadruple in the 24 hours following adverts in the prime US Super Bowl spot. Many organizations now run *web response ad campaigns* where one of the main objectives is to achieve web site or social presence visits. The web may be used to request a sample, enter a competition, find further information or, if appropriate, buy online. Enlightened FMCG brands are now using offline advertising in conjunction with the web to get customers to interact with their brand, profile them and add value.

Word of mouth

Word of mouth is a powerful technique of offline promotion. An urban myth is that if someone successfully buys a book online, they will tell ten other people, but if fulfilment is poor, they will tell 20 people! Offline communications techniques such as PR and advertising should be aimed at stimulating word of mouth, and online viral techniques can also promote this.

PR

PR is a powerful and relatively low-cost form of offline communications. There is a good demand amongst the general and specialist media for stories about e-everything. PR can leverage events such as site launches and relaunches with new services, particularly when they are first in a sector. Press releases can be issued through normal channels, but using email linked to the full story on the web site to get information to the journalists faster. Options for getting mentions on the new online-only news sources should be explored. Some defensive, reactive PR may be necessary by scanning press releases on other company sites. The scope for PR stunts related to web sites is limitless. In the United States, a town has been renamed as Half.com, to be the first dotcom town.

Direct mail and physical reminders

Physical reminders about web site offers are important since most of our customers will spend more time in the real world than the virtual world. What is in our customers' hands and on their desk will act as a prompt to visit your site and overcome the weakness of the web as a pull medium. Examples include brochures, catalogues, business cards, point-of-sale material, trade shows, direct mail, sales promotions, postcards (in magazines), inserts (in magazines), password reminders (for extranets).

E-MARKETING INSIGHT

Understanding the opportunities of integrating digital media channels

Digital media, as with other media, are most effective when combined with a range of media. A useful way of characterizing the benefits of integrated communication are the 4Cs of Pickton and Broderick (2000):

- *Coherence* – different communications are logically connected
- *Consistency* – multiple messages support and reinforce, and are not contradictory
- *Continuity* – communications are connected and consistent through time
- *Complementary* – synergistic, or the sum of the parts is greater than the whole!

To help you think of the opportunities for integrating digital media into your communications, refer to Table 7.4.

Table 7.4 Marketing communications terminology

Marketing communications term	Definition	Examples
Medium (media)	'Anything that conveys a message.' The carrier of the message or method of transmission. Can be conceived as the touchpoint with the customer.	Broadcast (television, radio), press, direct mail, cinema, poster, digital (web, email, mobile).
Discipline	'A body of craft technique biased towards a facet of marketing communication.' These are traditionally known as 'promotion tools' or the different elements of the communications mix.	Advertising, direct marketing, public relations, market research, personal selling, sales promotion, sponsorship, packaging, exhibitions and trade shows.
Channel (tools)	The combination of a discipline with a medium.	Direct mail, direct response TV, television brand advertising. Digital channels: different forms of search marketing, affiliate marketing, display advertising, email marketing, social media, blogs and feeds.
Vehicle	A specific channel used to reach a target audience.	TV (ITV, Channel 4), newspaper (*Sun*, *Metro*, *Times*), magazine (*The Economist*, *Radio Times*), radio (Virgin Radio, BBC Radio 5) and their web equivalents. Different search engines such as Google fit, or aggregators such as MoneySupermarket. com fit here.

When discussing marketing communications, there are many ways to refer to the different facets of campaigns that marketers can control.

Within a team working on a campaign, it is helpful if there is clarity about the opportunities for integrating different media and different agencies involved at the outset. For terminology, the approach recommended by Jenkinson and Sain (2003) of the Centre for Integrated Marketing (CFIM) is sound. They say:

A variety of concepts and terms are used across both academics and practitioners. For example, within our research into media neutral planning, some people referred to media, some to contact points or channels as methods of distributing communication. Similarly, some referred to tools and others to channels, disciplines or methods as the techniques by which the media could be used.

(Jenkinson and Sain, 2003)

In practical terms, a sound process is essential for integrating and refining different media throughout the campaign. The checklist developed by ISBA/IPA (2007) is helpful.

☑ 1 Briefing and strategy: all agencies briefed together and strategy agreed upfront

☑ 2 Budgets: discuss, budget accurately and allow for contingencies

☑ 3 Roles and responsibilities: a single point of approval works best

☑ 4 Timings and project planning: plan early

☑ 5 Design and development: stretch yourselves

☑ 6 Tracking and measurement: measure only what matters

☑ 7 Trafficking and campaign launch: plan for quality assurance testing

☑ 8 Produce back-up inventory: saves white space embarrassment – and money

☑ 9 Optimization, reporting, updates: monitor and nurture your campaign in-flight

☑ 10 Learning from analysis of results: test and refine.

SECTION SUMMARY 7.8

Offline traffic building

Specific offline communications are vital to traffic building for both dotcoms and clicks-and-mortar companies. Traditional advertising, PR and direct mail are all essential to communicate the URL and OVP. Remember that although we have reviewed online and offline traffic building techniques separately, they need to be part of integrated e-marketing communications.

CHAPTER SUMMARY

1 Traffic building or visitor acquisition is dependent on defining the appropriate *targets* of traffic quantity and quality, using the correct combination of online and offline *techniques* and using both campaign-based and continuous *timing*.

2 An organization's presence on a range of search engines should be achieved and then optimized by using specialist techniques such as rewriting copy, redesign and link building. Pay Per Click marketing can be essential to achieve visibility in competitive markets.

3 Organizations should consider their online reputation and visibility by reviewing options for online PR and their representation on a range of portals: horizontal, vertical and geographic.

4 You should review your potential online partners to drive visitors by link building, affiliate marketing and online sponsorship.

5 A wide range of different types of interactive ads, including skyscraper, large rectangle and rich media formats – can be used to refer traffic to the site and can also be used for brand building.

6 Opt-in email is an effective method of communication since it is a push method delivering information to the mail inbox of the audience. Email options include newsletters, promotional campaigns and as a conversion tool.

7 Viral e-marketing techniques involve transmitting a marketing message using word of mouth or online word of mouth (email and chat).

8 Offline communications are essential to achieve reach amongst an audience to increase awareness and explain the online value proposition.

References

Bharat, K. and Mihaila, G. (1999) Hilltop: A search engine based on expert documents. At: www.cs.toronto.edu/~georgem/hilltop/

Brooks, G. (2005) Perfect match. *New Media Age,* 29 September.

BuzzParadise (2010) PR 2.0 for Renault. Case study at: www.buzzparadise.com/case-studies/pr-2-0-event-for-renault-le-web-2010/

Cartellerieri, C., Parsons, A., Rao, V. and Zeisser, M. (1997) The real impact of Internet advertising. *The McKinsey Quarterly,* 3, pp. 44–63.

Chaffey, D. (2006) *Total E-mail Marketing,* 2nd edition. Butterworth-Heinemann/Elsevier, Oxford.

CIPR (2011) What is PR? Definition from the Chartered Institute of Public Relations web site at: www.cipr.co.uk/content/careers-cpd/careers-pr/what-pr

Econsultancy (2007) Affiliates close ranks after ASOS CEO calls them grubby. Blog post, 13 March at: www.e-consultancy.com/news-blog/362851/affiliates-close-rank-after-asos-ceo-calls-them-grubby.html

Google (2007) Understanding the Quality Score. At: http://support.google.com/adwords/bin/answer.py?hl=en-GB&answer=2454010.

Google (2012) Webmaster Tools Help. General guidelines: Google Friendly sites. At: http://support.google.com/webmasters/bin/answer.py?hl=en&answer=40349&topic=2370419&ctx=topic

Grehan, M. (2004) Increase your PR by increasing your PR. *E-marketing News,* November. At: www.e-marketing-news.co.uk/november.html#pr

IAB (Interactive Advertising Bureau) (2004) *IAB Cross Media Optimisation Study.* At: www.iab.net/xmos

IAB (2011) 2010 Online ad spend full year factsheet. At: www.iabuk.net/research/library/2010-online-adspend-full-year-factsheet

IAB (2012) 2011 Online ad spend full year factsheet. At: www.iabuk.net/research/library/2011-online-adspend-full-year-factsheet

iMediaConnection (2003) Interview with ING Direct VP of Marketing, Jurie Pieterse. At: www.imediaconnection.com/content/1333.asp

ISBA/IPA (2007) Best practice guide for online campaign development. IPA Digital/ISBA Online Action Group.

Jenkinson, A. and Sain, B. (2003) Getting words clear – marketing needs a clear and consistent terminology. Available from Centre for Integrated Marketing (www.integratedmarketing.org.uk).

Kirby, J. (2003) Online viral marketing: next big thing or yesterday's fling? *New Media Knowledge*, March.

McGaffin, K. (2004) Linking matters. How to create an effective linking strategy to Promote your web site. Report published at www.linkingmatters.com

Meerman-Scott, D. (2007) *The New Rules of Marketing and PR: How to Use Social Media, Online Video, Mobile Applications, Blogs, News Releases, and Viral Marketing to Reach Buyers Directly.* John Wiley & Sons, Hoboken, NJ.

Moorey-Denham, S. and Green, A. (2007) The effectiveness of online video advertising. *Admap*, March, pp. 45–7.

New York Times (2010) Retargeting ads follow surfers to other sites. 29 August at: www.nytimes.com/2010/08/30/technology/30adstalk.html

Optify (2011) The changing face of SERPS: Organic clickthrough rate. White paper, spring 2011 at: www.optify.net/wp-content/uploads/2011/04/Changing-Face-oof-SERPS-Organic-CTR.pdf

Pickton, A. and Broderick, D. (2000) *Integrated Marketing Communications.* Financial Times/Prentice Hall, Harlow.

Ranchhod, A., Gurau, C. and Lace, J. (2002) On-line messages: developing an integrated communications model for biotechnology companies. *Qualitative Market Research: An International Journal*, 5(1), pp. 6–18.

Ryan, J. and Whiteman, N. (2000) Online advertising glossary: Sponsorships. ClickZ Media Selling Channel, 15 May.

SEOMoz (2011) Google algorithm change history. At: www.seomoz.org/google-algorithm-change

Smart Insights (2011a) How balanced is your traffic mix? Blog post by Dave Chaffey, 4 July at: www.smartinsights.com/digital-marketing-strategy/customer-acquisition-strategy/how-balanced-is-your-traffic-mix/

Smart Insights (2011b) Email remarketing – an example of how to test. Blog post by Dave Chaffey, 18 May at: www.smartinsights.com/email-marketing/email-targeting/email-remarketing-an-example-of-how-to-test/

Smart Insights (2012) *Seven Steps to SEO Success*. E-book published by Smart Insights for Expert Members. Available at: www.smartinsights.com/guides/search-engine-optimisation-seo/seo-7-steps-to-success-guide/

Smith, P.R. and Taylor, J. (2004) *Marketing Communications – An Integrated Approach*, 4th edition. Kogan Page, London.

Van Doren, D., Fechner, D. and Green-Adelsberger, K. (2000) Promotional strategies on the World Wide Web. *Journal of Marketing Communications*, 6, pp. 21–35.

Further reading

Hoffman, D.L. and Novak, T.P. (2000) How to acquire customers on the web. *Harvard Business Review*, May–June, pp. 179–88. Available at: http://ecommerce.vanderbilt.edu/research_papers.htm

Web links

A4UForum (www.a4uforum.co.uk). Used by affiliates to discuss approaches and compare programmes.

AM Navigator (www.amnavigator.com/blog). Advice on managing affiliate programmes from Geno Prussakov.

Bing Webmaster Tools (www.bing.com/toolbox/webmaster). A service to help site owners review their visibility in Bing.

ClickZ (www.clickz.com). An excellent portal for the online marketer to learn more, with channels for different e-tools such as email marketing, search and ad buying.

Dave Chaffey Digital Marketing Strategy Guides (www.davechaffey.com/guides). A summary of strategy and tools available for the full range of digital marketing channels.

Google Webmaster Tools Help (http://support.google.com/webmasters). Provides a useful set of tools for sites verified by their owners including index inclusion, linking and ranking for different phrases in different locations.

iMedia Connection (www.imediaconnection.com). 'State of the art' articles and guidance on interactive advertising techniques.

Internet Advertising Bureau (US: www.iab.net; UK: www.iabuk.net). The widest range of studies about Internet advertising effectiveness.

Mashable (www.mashable.com). Site focusing on developments and statistics related to social networks.

O'Reilly Radar (http://radar.oreilly.com). Commentary on the development of Web 2.0 approaches from publishers O'Reilly, whose founder Tim O'Reilly coined the term Web 2.0.

Search Engine Land (www.searchengineland.com). Blog by Danny Sullivan, the leading commentator on the search engine industry, containing updates on all major and many minor developments.

Searchenginewatch (www.searchenginewatch.com). This is the premier source for keeping up to date on the significance of different search engines and the techniques they use.

Smart Insights (www.smartinsights.com). Updates on digital marketing methods on-site, edited by Dave Chaffey.

Word of Mouth Marketing Association (www.womma.org). A US-oriented community of word-of-mouth marketing specialists.

Self-test

1 Define appropriate measures for traffic-building quantity and quality for a campaign for your organization's site.

2 Distinguish between the operation of a search engine and a directory. What are the implications for promotion of a company?

3 List the relevant portals your company *should be* and *is* represented on. Include horizontal portals, vertical portals and geographical portals.

4 What approaches should be used in a link-building campaign?

5 Assess the relevance of banner advertising to your organization through reviewing their advantages and disadvantages.

6 Summarize the elements of effective opt-in email.

7 List the different types of viral marketing campaigns for which you have been a recipient. Which could be effective for your own organization?

8 Explain why offline communications are significant. What should be their aims?

Chapter **8**

e-CRM

Processes companies have for handling customer feedback are often weak and fragmented and are not supported by systems. Today, social networks provide a more powerful source of feedback – for both customers and suppliers, but usually customers are better at handling them than suppliers!

Stone (2012)

OVERVIEW

Online customer relationship management is packed with fundamental common sense principles. Serving and nurturing customers into lifetime customers makes sense as existing customers are, on average, five to ten times more profitable. At the heart of this is a good database – the marketer's memory bank, which, if used correctly, creates, arguably, the most valuable asset in any company. In this chapter, we show you how to develop integrated contact strategies to deliver relevant messages throughout the customer lifecycle. *Social CRM* is today a key aspect of CRM, but we focus discussion on *content marketing* to build relationships with prospects and on delivering customer service and developing advocacy with customers in Chapter 5 on social media.

OVERALL LEARNING OUTCOME

By the end of this chapter, you will be able to:

- Apply basic customer relationship management (CRM) principles online
- Appreciate the careful planning required to create the perfect database
- Begin to develop and nurture a properly integrated, multi-channel database.

CHAPTER TOPIC	LEARNING OBJECTIVE
8.1 Introduction	Understand the significance of e-CRM
8.2 Introduction to relationship marketing	Explain the basic principles of relationship marketing and the importance of coherent contact or communications strategies
8.3 Database marketing	Grasp the basic principles of database marketing
8.4 e-CRM	Show how new media enhance CRM
8.5 Profiling	Know how to approach profiling
8.6 Personalization	Know the options for personalizing web sites, opt-in emails, prices and promotions.
8.7 Email marketing	Develop a strategy for managing inbound email, outbound email marketing campaigns and e-newsletters
8.8 Control issues	Develop control mechanisms
8.9 Cleaning the database	Assess approaches to database cleaning
8.10 Making it happen	Identify the steps to deliver excellent e-CRM

8.1 Introduction to e-CRM

This section introduces *e-CRM*, explains what it is, how it is inextricably linked with database marketing, why e-CRM is so important to delivering competitive advantage, yet often under-used, and how the other sections in this chapter fit together.

So first, what is e-CRM? Customer relations management with an 'e'. Ultimately, e-CRM cannot be separated from CRM, it needs to be integrated – and seamlessly. However, some organizations do have specific e-CRM initiatives or staff responsible for e-CRM. Both CRM and e-CRM are not just about technology and databases, it's not just a process or a way of doing things; it requires, in fact, the whole organization to develop a real customer culture.

In many ways there's nothing new here, since good marketers have been taking care of their customers for many decades now. What is new is the lack of CRM both offline (e.g. telephone) and online in this constantly changing marketplace where:

● Customer expectations are often higher than those of the offline world
● Customers' raised expectations are regularly crushed by previously successful offline companies
● Customer emails are left unanswered for days
● Fans' comments are ignored
● Immediate responses are expected, but more often than not, are not delivered
● Satisfying customers is simply not enough to keep them.
● Customers and prospects visit fewer sites but spend longer with them (a world of consolidating relationships for the successful brands).

We are still sitting on a customer service time bomb. Vast numbers of faulty web sites, millions of customer emails ignored, customer data lost and companies that don't even know who their customers are, let alone answer their emails. Have things got better since these damning reports? Half the FTSE 100 companies cannot profile their own customers (MORI, 2003). Two-thirds of European companies cannot track customer relationship history. Half of all CRM projects fail (Forrester, 2009). More than two-thirds of all IT projects fail (Tranfield and Braganza, 2007). The few CRM systems that do work focus on value restoration (dealing with complaints) rather than value creation (enhancing the customers' experience). And all the while customer expectations are rising. Yet 95 per cent of customer Facebook posts were ignored by brands (Rezab, 2011).

> #### Consumers are feeling baffled, berated and betrayed

'Processes companies have for handling customer feedback are often weak and fragmented and are not supported by systems . . . customers prefer to stand in queues in banks rather than deal with automated telephone systems' (Stone, 2004).

Has anything changed since 2004?

It gets worse. Overall, CRM is going backwards. Products have got better (e.g. rust-proof cars) but service has got worse.

Here are some CRM failure rates identified by Krigsman (2009):

2001, Gartner Group: 50 per cent

2002, Butler Group: 70 per cent

2002, Selling Power, CSO Forum: 69.3 per cent

2005, AMR Research: 18 per cent

2006, AMR Research: 31 per cent

2007, AMR Research: 29 per cent

2007, [The] Economist Intelligence Unit: 56 per cent

2009, Forrester Research: 47 per cent (in fact, 'more than 55 per cent of CRM projects deliver unacceptable results').

And in 2011, 95 per cent of questions on Facebook are unanswered (Rezab, 2011).

Lousy CRM: brands killing the Facebook conversation, damaging their brands

800m users, and 50% of those users being active every day, it's a very *active* network of users forming or maintaining relationships. Yet 95% questions unanswered! Some companies blocking user comments & just using social media as another 'traditional' media.

(Rezab, 2011)

Consequently, the US$100m CRM projects appear to have died off over the last decade. However, there are signs of a growing interest in investing in CRM as central to an organization's success. 'The $100m CRM project is quite rare now but they are starting to appear again,' says Ed Thompson (Gartner, 2010).

THE GOLDEN OPPORTUNITY

The good news is that this presents a golden opportunity to create competitive advantage by developing an integrated CRM system that adds value to customers' experiences, brings them closer to us, listens to them, collects data and serves their needs better than ever before. Some American organizations are forecasting the 'after-sale market' (after-sales service, consultancy, training) to be where many companies will find new growth. Other American companies are forecasting growth to come from 'share of wallet' (selling additional ranges of products and services to the same customer). Just look at Tesco – they can sell customers almost anything from pet insurance to DIY divorce kits (and groceries and petrol). Central to all of this is, of course, the relationship that customers have with the brand. This emphasizes the critical importance of CRM systems that work for customers first and the company second.

CRM is your best defence

'Customer relationships are the only thing that cannot be replicated by a competitor' (Hochman, 2008).

A key e-CRM concept is *sense and respond marketing* – the Sense, Respond, Adjust approach of delivering relevant, *contextual marketing* communications through monitoring customer behaviour. E-CRM enables digital marketers to create a multi-channel marketing process of:

- Monitoring customer actions or behaviours (clicks on specific emails or web site offers) and then . . .
- Reacting with appropriate messages, either online – for example, through an email follow-up; or offline – for example, a phone or direct mail follow-up to encourage response
- Monitoring response to these messages and continuing with additional reminder communications and monitoring.

The secret is to put the time into defining rules and testing automated follow-up communications which match the context. For example, an online shopper who has purchased a product can be sent a series of welcome emails in the context of their purchase to encourage future purchases.

The Gartner Group (Thompson *et al.*, 2011) identified five key trends in CRM applications:

1 *Operational CRM* is the automation of processes such as campaign management or case management. It represents more than 70 per cent of all CRM.

Figure 8.1   Sequence of automated emails forming a welcome strategy following initial purchase

2 *Analytical CRM*, which includes predictive analytics and segmentation applications, grew 9 per cent and according to Gartner, represents nearly 25 per cent of CRM spending.

3 *Social CRM* grew at over 50 per cent, but still represents less than 5 per cent of all CRM spending. Of this, 90 per cent is B2C and approximately 85 per cent of spending is initiated by companies based in North America. The 2012 forecast is US$1bn in revenue, up from US$600m in 2010.

4 *Software-as-a-Service* (SaaS) delivery represented approximately 26 per cent of all CRM application spending in 2010.

5 In *sales applications*, where it is now widely viewed as a mainstream model, almost 50 per cent was delivered via SaaS.

In terms of *enquiry traffic*, social CRM is the hottest area of interest in customer service and marketing departments, followed by related areas like digital marketing and e-commerce. Gartner points out that social CRM is used both within and outside an organization.

1 per cent increase in satisfaction = US$100m+ sales

'In fact, when we looked at the top 100 e-retailers, we saw that increasing satisfaction by just one point drove over $112 million in additional sales' (Atchinson, 2008).

Note that this is consistent with IBM's research, in previous years, which revealed that each percentage point improvement in customer satisfaction translates into US$500m more revenue over five years (Smith and Zook, 2011).

SOME E-CRM BENEFITS AND CHALLENGES

There is plenty of e-CRM software which enhances our ability to understand customers and enquirers, their needs, names, interests and a lot more. We can get closer to them. Speak with them. One of the 5Ss – the five fundamental benefits of e-marketing (see Chapter 1).

This is a dynamic dialogue that is instantaneous, relevant, value-adding and information-gleaning, that:

- Recognizes and remembers each customer by name and need
- Answers questions often automatically and, ideally, personally
- Asks questions, collects information and builds a better profile, particularly of those ideal lifetime customers.

The real advantage of online marketing lies in its potential to build relationships and create long-term value. Companies that have risen to the challenge of e-CRM have a '360 degree view of their customers'. This, in turn, generates real loyalty from lifetime customers who readily share valuable data with you.

Have you got the software to exploit the valuable data you can collect from customers? Many companies don't. Have you got the processes in place to ensure excellent service – that keeps customers coming back for more? On average, purchase intent sees a double-digit increase after someone has been to a site more than once (Flores and Eltvedt, 2005). Keeping existing customers coming back for more is more profitable than acquiring new customers. Flores and Eltvedt suggest it is ten times more profitable to serve an existing customer than recruit a new one. It therefore makes a lot of sense to nurture the captured customers into lifetime customers. CRM and e-CRM help to keep ideal customers. Customer retention can be improved by improving CRM. The returns on this investment are large.

The time-compressed, information-fatigued, impatient customer is unforgiving. Eighty per cent of consumers will never go back to an organization after a bad customer experience, up from 68 per cent in 2006 (Harris Interactive, 2007). Combine this with customers who talk back and who talk to each other courtesy of new social media or Web 2.0 and the goal posts have moved for many marketers. Social network sites facilitate customer discussions (Coca-Cola never asked for rockets, it just happened that customers discovered that mixing Coke and Mentos mints caused an explosive reaction and customers started posting videos of this phenomenon). User-generated content (UGC) is not totally controllable as Chevrolet and Nike discovered (when customers create negative Chevrolet ads and Nike shoes with negative tailored messages). Web 2.0 is here to stay. It will grow in line with the very human need for social contact. Customers have been mobilized by blogs, social network sites, invitations to create UGC, to name but a few Web 2.0 tools. The old CRM customer dialogue has evolved into the customer trialogue (see Section 3.5 in Chapter 3 on e-models).

'The hardest lesson to learn is that there are smarter people not working for your company than there are working for your company,' said Michael Boreel (2007), referring to customers and other stakeholders (including pressure groups) who generate content outside your control and all about your brand.

The online world presents new challenges when nurturing customer relationships. This e-CRM chapter has sections on the key elements, including two introductory-level sections on CRM itself plus relationship marketing and database marketing as well as personalization, profiling, managing incoming emails and implementing e-CRM.

Remember that CRM or e-CRM, in particular, is not about technology, it's not just a process or way of doing things; it requires, in fact, a complete customer culture. The challenge is yours.

Given these benefits of e-CRM, many companies have attempted to implement CRM technologies to help give a 'single view of the customer'. The challenge of CRM is that it is not just an immense technological challenge, but it is also a change management challenge, demanding changes in process and the roles of staff. In fact, Gartner Research (Radcliffe et al., 2001) suggests eight building blocks for CRM success:

1 CRM Vision
2 CRM Strategy
3 Valued Customer Experience
4 Organizational Collaboration
5 CRM Processes

6 CRM Information

7 CRM Metrics; and finally

8 CRM Technology (see Section 8.10).

E-MARKETING EXCELLENCE

Boots 'Change One Thing' campaign

This example shows how e-CRM can be built into a marketing campaign. In this campaign, the web site, database of customer preferences and email marketing were at the core of an integrated campaign based around the self-improvement proposition.

Offline communications delivered by TV and print ads plus editorial coverage were used to inspire an audience to take on a personal challenge such as losing weight or giving up smoking at the start of the year. These communications were used to drive visitors to the web where they could then select their challenge and interact with others with the same challenge.

Emails were sent to remind participants and help them sustain the challenge. Automated, personalized emails (and texts) were sent throughout the lifecycle of the relationship; for example, to:

1 Engage existing customers already signed up to e-newsletters

2 Encourage customers to select a personal challenge

3 Drive customers to the site to encourage them to commit to a challenge and update their progress

4 Encourage social interaction – share experience, encourage others

5 Subscribe to text reminder services to remind them when they hit a weak spot; e.g. time of day.

However, this campaign highlights a risk with short-term campaigns. A microsite was set up to maintain this dialogue, but if you went there mid-year, you found the microsite had been taken down and visitors were asked to wait until next Christmas! This shows the importance of obtaining resources to continue the dialogue and continue the momentum of a campaign. It is often best to integrate such campaigns into the main web site to deliver continuity and to help build awareness of the full online brand experience and other product offerings.

SECTION SUMMARY 8.1

Customer relationship management is well established as an approach to acquiring customers and then retaining them to develop a higher lifetime value for each customer. Managing CRM online and integrating it with offline CRM activities introduce new challenges. We need to think about how we can use online tools to have a more dynamic dialogue with the customer, answering their questions, understanding their needs, profiling them and then delivering appropriate services and communications.

8.2 Introduction to relationship marketing

By the end of this section, you should be able to see how relationship marketing and permission-based marketing are essential to CRM and e-CRM.

What is *relationship marketing*? Marketing is all about relationships – relationships with customers, lapsed customers and potential customers. There are also relationships with suppliers, partners and even internal audiences (staff). So although relationship marketing involves more than just customers, we're focusing on customers: CRM – customer relationship management. Real CRM involves treating each customer differently according to their characteristics as described in the E-marketing Insight box below.

Relationship marketing shifts marketing away from short-term *transactional marketing* (with one-off sales) towards developing longer-lasting relationships with people who, ideally, develop into lifetime customers. This obviously generates more profitable repeat business as well as increased 'share of wallet' (or customer share).

E-MARKETING INSIGHT

Peppers and Rogers on building one-to-one relationships

Peppers and Rogers, authors of the now classic one-to-one marketing book (1999) have applied their work on building *one-to-one* relationships with the customer to the web. They suggest (www.1to1.com) the IDIC approach as a framework for using the web effectively to form and build relationships. IDIC stands for:

1 *Customer Identification*. This stresses the need to identify each customer on their first web site visit and subsequent visits. Common methods for identification are the use of cookies or asking a customer to log on to a site.

2 *Customer Differentiation*. This refers to building a profile to help segment customers into groups which share characteristics and can be evaluated according to their value to the company. Peppers and Rogers suggest Most Valuable Customers, Most Growable Customers and Below Zero Customers.

3 *Customer Interaction*. These are interactions provided on-site such as customer service questions or creating a tailored product.

4 *Customized Communications*. This refers to personalization or mass customization of content or emails according to the segmentation achieved at the acquisition stage.

PERMISSION MARKETING

Building relationships is a delicate affair. Marketers have to gain permission first, then trust and, ultimately, loyalty. It's all common sense stuff. Stick to basic marketing tenets of identifying, anticipating and satisfying customer needs relentlessly: this helps to build relationships. But how do you do this? First, adopt a 'permission-based marketing' approach as developed in the now classic *Permission Marketing* by Seth Godin (1999). Seth originally talked about gaining permission via web sites to develop relationships. This is still really important, but new platforms such as social media platforms and mobile apps are increasingly important ways to gain permission. However, they can be limited compared to traditional permission marketing. For example, if someone follows your brand on Twitter, you have little context or profile information compared to web sign-up. So savvy companies realize that gaining permission via a web site is more effective in some senses.

There are several steps towards permission marketing:

1 *Gaining permission.* The first step is to get the customer's permission to give them information. Winning this permission, in the customer's time-compressed world, is a valuable asset, so a range of offers will be more powerful, as shown by the Ultralase example in Figure 8.2.

2 *Collaboration.* Marketing is a collaborative activity – where marketers help customers to buy and customers help marketers to sell. The customer forum and testimonials used by Ultralase are an example of this.

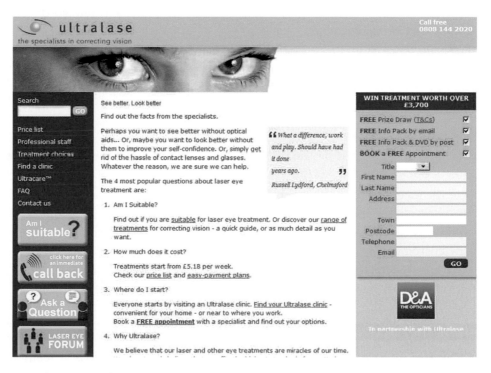

Figure 8.2   The design of the Ultralase eye treatment provider emphasizes gaining permission (www. ultralase.co.uk)

3 *Dialogue–trialogue*. A dialogue emerges whether via web site emails, discussion rooms or real conversations in focus groups, or even real meetings between customers and sales reps as well as among customers themselves (trialogue).

Permission marketers develop the relationship and get permission to talk on a regular basis. Some excellent permission-based marketers even get permission to place orders on the customer's behalf. Other permission-based marketers even deliver right into the customer's building without the customer opening the door! They become part of the customer's systems.

In developing the relationship there is a series of stages through which the customer moves. There are several approaches, one of which is the Ladder of Loyalty (Considine and Murray, 1981) from Suspects to Prospects to Customers to Clients to Advocates.

When a customer *'opts in'* for further email, they give permission to be emailed. This is a first step in using their permission to develop the relationship. Do not abuse this permission. Do not pass their details on to other marketers. Ensure that your future contact with the customer always adds value.

Remember you have to respect this relationship – this special permission you have. It is a moral and legal requirement to offer the customer the option to *'opt out'*. The number of existing customers that opt out from further contact is known as the *'churn rate'*. Obviously, good marketers watch the churn rate closely, and try to understand why it varies and how to reduce it.

The concept of permission marketing is best summarized by these three words from Seth Godin: 'anticipated, relevant and personal'.

We could add 'timely', since context is important in following up on initial permission.

Godin (1999) goes on to describe the essential concepts of permission marketing as 'Dating the Customer':

1 Offer the prospect an incentive to volunteer [Achieve opt-in]
2 Using the attention offered by the prospect, offer a curriculum over time, teaching the consumer about your product or service [Enable the customer to learn more]
3 Reinforce the incentive to guarantee that the prospect maintains the permission [Offer opt-out, but minimize the likelihood for this]
4 Offer additional incentives to get even more permission from the consumer [Learn more about the customer through time]
5 Over time, leverage the permission to change consumer behaviour towards profits [Deepen the relation through converting from prospect to customer and trialist to loyalist].

MANAGING THE DIALOGUE THROUGH CONTACT STRATEGIES

Too much contact can wear out the relationship. The key to building the best relationship is to have the right number of contacts of the right type at the right time for specific customers. This is a *contact strategy* – determining which kinds of customers and enquirers get which sequence of contacts. Most organizations require coherent contact strategies that span online and offline media. For example, some garages maintain contact with their customers via email, or SMS (text messages), sending them reminders when their car is due for a service. If no response is generated, then this triggers a prompt for staff to make a phone call to see whether the customer still wants to receive reminders. Other organizations ask their customers how they prefer to be updated about special offers, reminders and announcements. The database stores their preferred media (including, if email, whether text or HTML is preferred) and ensures that they are contacted in the preferred manner. So organizations vary their contact strategy depending on how customers (and prospects) react.

Your contact strategy should define an initial *welcome strategy* when the prospect is first added to the database, based on the best interval and sequence of messages as shown in the example (Table 8.1). The contact strategy should then be extended for later stages in the customer lifecycle with messages designed to convert them to purchase (from shopping basket abandons), encourage repeat purchases or trial of new products or to reactivate customers when their interest wanes.

A business-to-business supplier sends an automated email two weeks after a customer has registered initial interest in the company. Such emails can help companies educate customers about their offering and engage them through digital assets such as a calculator – which fits the permission marketing model of 'learning more through time'. Renault has a good B2C example of a welcome strategy. Over the initial six-month period of purchase consideration, they use a container or content pod within their e-newsletter to deliver personalized information about the brand and model of car the prospect is interested in. This is updated each month as the customer gets to know the brand better and the brand gets to know the customer better!

Table 8.1 Example of a template for email contact strategy

Message type	Interval/trigger condition	Outcomes required	Medium for message/ Sequence
1 Welcome message	Guest site membership sign-up Immediate	• Encourage trial of site services • Increase awareness of range of commercial and informational offerings	Email, post transaction page
2 Engagement message	1 month: inactive (i.e.<3 visits)	• Encourage use of forum (good enabler of membership) • Highlight top content	Email, home page, side panels deep in site
3 Initial cross-sell message	1 month: active	• Encourage membership • Ask for feedback	Email
4 Conversion	2 days after browsing content	Use for range of services for guest members or full members	Phone or email

For another example, see how Tesco's contact strategy varies according to new customers' responses to previous contacts (see E-marketing Excellence box in Section 8.4) and Section 8.5 for other contact strategies. Some organizations consider some web facilities as part of the dialogue; e.g. an on-site search engine preceded with a friendly face or question 'Tell us what you are looking for'. Virtual assistants, real-time live web chat and callback facilities also facilitate a dialogue. Ironically, some under-resourced companies, while holding customers in a telephone queue suggest that they might prefer to get a quicker answer online at the web site. Online contact varies as web sites carry FAQs, blogs (with clearly labelled topics), and sometimes customer forums actually facilitate self-servicing by the customer amongst other customers. Some of these are also mentioned in Chapter 2, Section 2.9 ('Delivering online service'). Markets are always changing, so your communications need to be flexible and capable of individualized, personalized, responses.

Don't forget that relationships have traditionally been two-way conversations (dialogues). Today they are trialogues, with customers talking to each other, generating PR, informing ads, designs and discussions about products. It involves as much listening as talking, emailing, mobile messaging, telesales, advertising, etc. Watch clickthroughs on different e-newsletter topics, news pages, special offers and forums as well the incoming flow of communications. Give the customer a chance to talk to you and to other customers, taking the time to listen and tell the other party how what they have told you has been acted upon, or at least heard! Today's marketers listen a lot more.

Tell customers what they have told you, maybe in the form of an order acknowledgement or consolidated feedback from surveys, etc. Showing them how this has changed what you do or how you do it is an important part of building a relationship – all part of the ongoing dialogue. Remember, 'Markets are conversations!' Database-driven marketing allows the dialogue to become a dynamic dialogue – responsive, relevant and fast-moving.

E-MARKETING INSIGHT

Practical e-permission marketing guidelines

How can Seth Godin's original principles of *Permission Marketing* be applied by today's online marketer?

1 *'Offer selective opt-in to communications'*. Offer choice in communications preferences to the customer to ensure more relevant communications. Some customers may not want a weekly e-newsletter; rather they may only want to hear about new product releases. Remember that opt-in is a legal requirement in many countries. Four key opt-in options, selected by tick-box, are:

- *Content* – news, products, offers, events
- *Frequency* – weekly, monthly, quarterly, or alerts
- *Channel* – email, direct mail, phone or SMS
- *Format* – text versus HTML.

2 *Create a 'common customer profile'.* A structured approach to customer data capture is needed; otherwise some data will be missed, as in the case of the utility company that collected 80,000 email addresses, but forgot to ask for the postcode for geo-targeting! This can be achieved through a common customer profile – a definition of all the database fields that are relevant to the marketer in order to understand and target the customer with a relevant offering. It sounds obvious, but. . .

3 *Offer a range of opt-in incentives.* Many web sites now have 'free/win/save' incentives to encourage opt-in, but often it is a 'one incentive fits all visitors'. Different incentives for different audiences will generate a higher volume of permission, particularly for business-to-business web sites. We can also gauge the characteristics of the respondent by the type of incentives or communications they have requested, without the need to ask them.

4 *'Don't make opt-out too easy'.* Our view is that we often make it too easy to unsubscribe. Although offering an easy opt-out or 'unsubscribe' is now a legal requirement in many countries due to privacy laws, a single click to unsubscribe is perhaps making it too easy – the relationship is over too abruptly. Instead, wise permission marketers like Amazon or First Direct have the option of more granular communications preferences, where it is possible to unsubscribe, but also to control the frequency and type of email content received. If customers definitely want to unsubscribe, then this is made easy, with the option of commenting on the reason for the 'unsubscribe' and many do, providing useful information on improving e-CRM for others.

The use of 'My Profile' can be tied to the principle of 'selective opt-in' – you could call it selective opt-out.

5 *'Watch, don't ask'.* The need to ask interruptive questions can be reduced through the use of monitoring of clicks to get a better understanding of customer needs and to trigger follow-up communications. Here are some examples:

● Monitoring clickthrough to different types of content or offer
● Monitoring the engagement of individual customers with email communications
● Follow-up reminder to those who don't open the email first time
● Monitoring the day and time of typical clickthrough to send emails when the customer is most receptive.

6 *Create an outbound contact strategy.* Online permission marketers need a plan for the number, frequency and type of online and offline communications and offers. This is a contact or touch strategy. The contact strategy should indicate:

1 Frequency (e.g. minimum once per quarter and maximum once per month)
2 Interval (e.g. there must be a gap of at least a week or a month between communications)
3 Content and offers (we may want to limit or achieve a certain number of prize draws or information-led offers)

4 Links between online communications and offline communications

5 A control strategy (a mechanism to make sure these guidelines are adhered to; for example, using a single 'focal point' for checking all communications before creation dispatch).

(Chaffey, 2007)

MANAGING COMPLAINTS – ENHANCING RELATIONSHIPS

Welcome complaints. Encourage complaints. It is much better for a customer to complain than not complain to the company, while complaining to other customers via social media. Managing complaints is an important part of contact management, or contact strategy.

Complaint management is one of the 5Ss (Speak) (see Chapter 1) as organizations need systems and processes to listen, rank and respond to complaints. 'They should be solicited rather than unsolicited, easy to make, quickly responded to, with both the problem of the consumer and the cause fixed', says Professor Merlin Stone (2011). He continues:

> *Improved complaint management produces a good return on investment. This is via improvements in consumer retention, market share and positive word of mouth – turning negative into positive experiences and improved branding, consumer loyalty, improved design of the service experience and improved product design.*
>
> *(Stone, 2011)*

Support is the new sales since how you manage a complaint determines the relationship and subsequent sales and word of mouth. But support needs resources and systems. As Gerry McGovern says:

> *Support communities need care and attention. You can't just leave customers on their own. Done properly these communities build your brand and help sell your products in a far more effective way than most of your marketing campaigns will. Some support communities are truly excellent. For example, Cisco (which I do work for) has a range of superb communities. Real experts from Cisco answer questions quickly.*
>
> *(McGovern, 2012)*

Customers can and do help each other to solve problems via communities and forums. However, Google has closed its Android developer complaint forums and asked for complaints to be submitted directly to Google as it feels the basic P2P (peer-to-peer) solutions phase has passed, since many developers previously needed basic help on how to use the service and peers could often provide that basic support. Now the basics are widely understood, so the remaining problems are more likely to require Google's direct intervention.

'Developers were reported to have "ranted and raved" re missing payments. Although the issue was subsequently resolved, it's possible Google prefers to deal with these issues directly' (Ray, 2011).

'Negative experiences are our biggest opportunity'

Samsung's small team of four prefer to find negativity and have a chance to fix it and change that consumer's perception. They focus on locating, identifying and solving real problems that real customers have.

> *Anyone in a marketing role who has suffered through never ending meetings about social media without a real vision or tangible outcome will easily be able to imagine how nice a feeling it is to actually solve real problems and the sense of accomplishment that would offer on a daily basis.*

> *(Bhargava, 2011)*

There is clearly a lesson here about the necessity of integrating marketing and customer service more closely.

NURTURING NEW RELATIONSHIPS VIA FACEBOOK CONNECT

Facebook Connect is an API (application programming interface) which can deliver better extended service to blog or web site visitors. It enables users to *enjoy* better service, as once the user's account on a web site becomes 'Facebook connected', you:

- Can share information much more easily from that web site to your friends via the Facebook 'liking', 'sharing', etc.
- Don't have to log into a web site (as you can log in via Facebook Connect) – this is 'social sign-on' which means you have one less log-in to remember. Many Facebook users are perpetually logged in anyway, or they regularly log in with their log-in information already committed to memory.
- Don't have to register and upload all your information to a new site.

f Connect with Facebook

Figure 8.3   Facebook Connect button

With Facebook Connect, users can take their friends with them to new web sites. They can also bring their profile information, profile photo, name, friends, photos, events and more with them to any partner web site using a trusted authentication method. Users can also control what they want to share with their Facebook network.

AMAZON.CO.UK

When you connect your Facebook account with, say, your Amazon account, you can see a list of your friends' birthdays, with gift suggestions, what's popular amongst your friends (see below) as well as the usual Amazon suggestions. You can also deliver an Amazon.com Gift Card via Facebook.

Figure 8.4   Connect Amazon to Facebook

Source: www.amazon.com

Amazon also states its terms of use front and centre when you connect your accounts:

- Amazon will not share your individual information from your account with Facebook.
- Amazon will not share your individual purchase history with Facebook.
- Amazon will not attempt to contact your Facebook friends.
- Amazon will never post anything to your Facebook Wall without your consent.

Levi's use Facebook Connect slightly differently by allowing visitors to 'view a personalized selection of Levi's products that their friends have "liked" (and also remembers their birthdays)' (see Figure 8.5).

Levi's does not suggest products for Friends (as Amazon does). Users are encouraged to update their newsfeed when they find interesting products 'hopefully to start a discussion with Friends' (Hubspot, 2011). Other retail web sites also use 'F- Commerce'.

Some brands really naturally lend themselves to Facebook like Groupon and Eventbrite. Groupon encourages users to share the deals they find with their friends via Facebook since 'daily deals' are newsworthy and local friends appreciate being alerted. Eventbrite encourages sharing of event announcements and ticket purchases among friends. Incidentally, Eventbrite estimates the value of a single Facebook 'share' to be US$2.52 in new ticket sales.

Figure 8.5   Levi's use Facebook

Source: http://store.levi.com/

Many more major brands are integrating their web sites with Facebook to create a 'social shopping experience'; for example, Macy's Magic Fitting Room is a Facebook-connected fitting room with virtual try-outs. Gap used Facebook Deals to give the first 10,000 Friends checking-in with Facebook to a Gap Store a free pair of jeans; all others received 40 per cent off all regular priced merchandise (see Figure 8.6).

Mazda used Facebook Deals for a UK launch – customers who checked-in with Facebook to a Mazda dealer on their mobile handset got 20 per cent off a Mazda roadster.

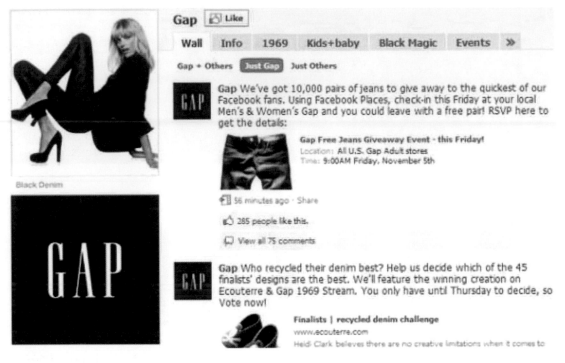

Figure 8.6   Gap Facebook page special offer for a 10,000 pairs of jeans give-away

Source: www.facebook.com/gap

Ending relationships boosts Burger King relationship?

Even the King must obey the rules. Probably the best-known and most controversial contest occurred in January 2009, back when Facebook still needed the publicity. Entrants could get a free Burger King Whopper for de-friending ten Friends. Close to 234,000 'friendships' promptly ended and user feeds made it clear as to just who was being sacrificed in exchange for 1/10th of a Whopper. While it was a great example of a business engaging their Facebook base, the thought of Friend connections being severed probably didn't sit well with Facebook. They eventually disabled the promotion. The grounds? Apps are not allowed to post 'de-friending' incidents (Hubspot, 2011).

So relationships are valuable (despite the Burger King case); organizations today acknowledge the importance of relationships and some brands are starting to nurture them in more structured processes.

SECTION SUMMARY 8.2

Relationship marketing

Relationship marketing is at the heart of e-CRM. It requires a longer-term perspective, a lifetime-value perspective built on upon permission and trust, listening, and responding to customers to build longer, lasting success.

8.3 Database marketing

The database and *database marketing* are at the heart of e-CRM. By the end of this section, you will understand what a database is, the complications that can arise, the types of data fields and the importance of linking it all to a clear marketing programme.

It has been said that the driving force underlying modern CRM systems is the customer database. This is the repository of information on customers and prospects from all sources and channels – whether web sites, interactive TV, sales reps or customer-service staff.

The database and profiling software is a vital part of e-CRM since it enhances our ability to understand customers and enquirers, their needs, names, interests and a lot more. We can get closer to them.

It helps achieve the dynamic dialogue of permission marketing, which:

- Recognizes and remembers each customer by name and need
- Answers questions often automatically and, ideally, personally
- Asks questions, collects information and builds a better profile, particularly of those ideal lifetime customers
- Delivers communications which are instantaneous, relevant and value adding.

WHAT IS STORED IN THE DATABASE?

A database is more than a list of names. A database is distinguished by the amount and quality of relevant marketing data held on each customer or prospect. It should identify best ('ideal') customers and worst customers. The worst customers have 'negative value'; these are customers who claim early on insurance, are bad debtors, or just intensive users of free services. There are two types of information kept on a database which a simple mailing list does not provide: historical data and predictive data. Smith and Zook (2011) describe *historical data* as 'transactional' or 'back' data which include names, addresses, recency and frequency of purchases, responses to offers and value of purchases. They say *predictive data* identify which groups or subgroups are more likely to respond to a specific offer. This is done through statistical scoring: customer attributes (e.g. house type, business type, past behaviour, etc.) are given scores that help to indicate their future behaviour.

This begs the question – what kind of data, or 'fields' should be captured? In addition to capturing a customer's name and address, there are obviously other kinds, or 'fields', of data worth capturing – for first, a B2C business; and then second, a B2B business. *FRAC* is a useful mnemonic. It stands for: Frequency, Recency, Amount and Category of purchase.

For example, RFM analysis can be applied to targeting using email, according to how a customer interacts with an e-commerce site. Values could be assigned to each customer as follows:

Recency:

1 – over 12 months
2 – within last 12 months

3 – within last 6 months

4 – within last 3 months

5 – within last 1 month.

Frequency:

1 – more than once every 6 months

2 – every 6 months

3 – every 3 months

4 – every 2 months

5 – monthly.

Monetary value:

1 – less than £10

2 – £10–£50

3 – £50–£100

4 – £100–£200

5 – More than £200.

Customers can be combined in different categories and then appropriate message treatments sent to encourage purchase. Simplified versions of this analysis can be created to make it more manageable; for example, a theatre group uses these nine categories for its direct marketing:

Oncers (attended theatre once)

- Recent oncers – attended <12 months
- Rusty oncers – attended >12<36 months
- Very rusty oncers – attended 36+ months.

Twicers

- Recent twicer – attended <12 months
- Rusty twicer – attended >12<36 months
- Very rusty twicer – attended in 36+ months.

2+ subscribers

- Current subscribers – booked 2+ events in current season
- Recent – booked 2+ last season
- Very rusty – booked 2+ more than a season ago.

There are a lot of other useful data worth collecting also such as promotions history (responses to specific promotions), share of wallet or customer share (potential spend), timing of spend and more. In B2B, we are interested in business type, size of business, holding companies and subsidiaries, competitive products bought, etc. You can segment customers by their activity or responsiveness levels and then develop strategies to engage them. For example, Novo (2003) recommends the use of *hurdle rates* which are the percentage of customers in a group (e.g. in a segment or on a list) who have completed an action. Hurdle rates can then be used to compare the engagement of different groups or to set targets to increase engagement with online channels, as the examples below show:

- 20 per cent of customers have visited in past 6 months
- 5 per cent of customers have made three or more purchases in year
- 60 per cent of registrants have logged on to system in year
- 30 per cent have clicked through on email in year.

Whether B2C or B2B, managing the activity levels of your subscribers is key – you need to manage email list decay.

E-MARKETING INSIGHT

Managing email engagement decay

It is inevitable that email list subscribers have their highest levels of engagement with a brand when they are first added to a database and that this will decay through time. Dom Yeadon (2009) of The Marketing Bureau (www.tmb.uk.com/) has analysed a sample of B2C and B2B lists that show the extent of email list decay. He summarizes the implications of the research as follows:

- You could lose 5% of the whole list every 3 months
- Your list loses 2/3rds of its value in 12 months
- Fresh emails (0 to 3 months old) are each worth three times as much as older emails (12 months old).

You can evaluate your email list using Dom's formula based on different aspects of email response:

Engagement Index = $(D \times V \times CTR \times 100)$ where D = Deliverability, V = Views (Opens) and CTR = Clickthrough rate

He gives these examples:

- Email engagement Index, 0–3 months = 11

  - Delivery rate = 90%

- Views = 35%
- Clickthroughs = 36%

$$[.9 \times .35 \times .36 = .11 \times 100 = 11]$$

- Email engagement Index, 9–12 months = 4

  - Delivery rate = 73%
  - Views = 31%
  - Clickthroughs = 18%

$$[.73 \times .31 \times .18 = .04 \times 100 = 4]$$

So what to do about email decay?

E-MARKETING BEST PRACTICE CHECKLIST – LIST DECAY

Here is our checklist for managing email list decay:

☑ Develop a welcome programme where over the first three to six months you deliver targeted auto-triggered emails to educate subscribers about your brand, products and deliver targeted offers.

☑ Think about how you can reactivate list members as they become less responsive.

☑ Segment list members by activity (responsiveness) and age on list. Assess your level of email list activity (ask what percentage of list members haven't clicked within the last three to six months – if they haven't, they are inactive and should be treated differently, either by reducing frequency or using more offline media).

☑ Follow up on bounces, using other media to reduce problems of dropping deliverability.

☑ Best practice when renting lists is to request only emails where the opt-in is within the most recent six to nine months when subscribers are most active.

WHICH SOFTWARE TOOLS ARE REQUIRED?

Every organization has lots of useful data on its customers. These can be very simple and well-organized, or incredibly complex – usually the latter. Unfortunately, many organizations have several databases, each set up at different times with no ability to cross-reference the data within them. Typically, there is the old *'legacy'* database or customer contact management system for traditional direct mail and a completely separate database for web site visitors containing registration information in a profile and purchase information for an e-commerce site. There is usually a separate system for managing email marketing which contains customer profile details and information on how they responded to each campaign.

CHOOSING AN EMAIL MARKETING SYSTEM

There are several options for sending marketing emails to customers:

1 *Standard office software*. Using Microsoft Outlook, for example. We don't recommend this option since it is only really practical for relatively small lists since each contact has to be added and removed manually. No tracking is available with this approach and all bounced emails have to be processed manually.

2 *Desktop mailer software*. With this approach, email lists are managed and emails broadcast using a software application running on the user's PC. These have the advantage of low cost and there is no fee for each message sent. They offer some personalization and now have additional tracking packages. But we still don't recommend this option, in favour of option 4 which is the route most companies follow.

3 *List-server software*. For businesses requiring higher volumes of email broadcast from an internal server, there are options such as Lyris HQ (www.lyris.com). Such tools have many options for personalization, tracking and automation of contact strategies; but if hosted internally, it will require support from IT and there may be problems with deliverability if the reputation of the broadcaster becomes compromised. Some of the email services also provide the capability for their application service provider (ASP) solutions to be installed in-house.

4 *Email service providers (ESPs)*. ESPs are web-based services that can be used by a client to manage their own email activities. Rather than buying software that you host and manage on your server, the software is effectively used on a subscription basis and runs on another company's server. In other words, it provides all the technical infrastructure that is needed to run the campaign, but is managed by an outside company. You can see a list we have compiled of the most popular services at http://bit.ly/smartesps. From a user experience point of view, the user logs in to a web-based 'booth' such as that shown in Figure 8.8 and from this one point, is able to create the email, select the targeting, broadcast and track the results in real time.

5 *SMTP mail relays and web services based on API interfaces*. Companies, app developers and ESPs are increasingly turning to services such as SendGrid as a method to outsource delivery and tracking of email while they manage segmentation and targeting internally. Web-based services such as GetSatisfaction, Foursquare and SlideShare all use this service.

There are four main requirements or tasks involved with managing email campaigns and e-newsletters. Here is our checklist of issues to consider when selecting an email service provider (ESP).

E-MARKETING BEST PRACTICE CHECKLIST – CHOOSING AN EMAIL SERVICE PROVIDER

The main email management activities are:

1 *Creating the content*

    ☑ Are predefined templates available?

    ☑ Is there an integrated WYSIWYG (what you see is what you get) editor in which content and images can be edited within a template, or does it require a separate web editing programme like Adobe Dreamweaver?

- ☑ Can different permissions be assigned to limit access according to skill level?
- ☑ How easy is it to add a personal salutation?
- ☑ How easily can dynamic content be included according to database criteria?
- ☑ Can e-newsletters easily be archived on site?
- ☑ Can e-newsletter features be provided as RSS feeds if required?

2 *Managing the list*

- ☑ Can subscriptions and 'unsubscribes' be managed through a web site?
- ☑ Are bounces managed such that the marketer only receives genuine replies, not undelivered messages and out-of-office autoreplies, etc.?
- ☑ Do the standard database fields apply for basic activity?
- ☑ Is it easy to add new fields to the standard fields?
- ☑ What are the options for integrating with other databases of customer/campaign/sales information? The options to achieve data integration are:

  a Ad hoc import/export process; i.e. customer profile information for personalization is exported from the customer database before a campaign as required, and changes to communications preferences are updated after each campaign.

  b Regular batch synchronization process: the system can be set up to exchange data at a regular time – daily, weekly or monthly.

  c Real-time synchronization process: direct communications are set up to occur between the email database and customer database using application programming interfaces (APIs).

3 *Broadcasting the message*

- ☑ Is smart broadcasting used to reduce the volume to avoid a high-volume SPAM signature?
- ☑ Is there a unique IP available for each client (not essential and expensive)?
- ☑ Can auto-response notifications be easily set up?
- ☑ Can predefined automated touch strategy emails be set up for behavioural or contextual marketing (Sense and Respond)?
- ☑ Can future email broadcasts be scheduled (e.g. for next day)?

4 *Tracking/reporting the results*

- ☑ Is deliverability and response tracked by the ISP/webmail provider to identify problems?
- ☑ Is closed-loop reporting of inbox delivery and complaints integrated with ISP/webmail providers?

☑ How easy is it to set up A/B or multivariate testing cells?

☑ What metrics are available (after the click); i.e. tagging on the web site to show number and type of pages accessed? Can the tagging integrate with a web analytics system?

☑ Can response be tracked at an individual level?

☑ Can response be tracked across time/multiple campaigns?

☑ Can response be tracked for different demographic profiles?

☑ Is there text and/or visual reporting on which links were clicked?

☑ Can viral pass-alongs be easily monitored?

☑ Can response be integrated with options (a) to (c) above?

Then comes the really interesting software – *data mining* software that drills down into the data warehouses to find correlations and profiles buried deep within the layers of data. Data mining can reveal surprising correlations, some of which help to profile your own customers and then look for similar types elsewhere.

There is an increasing growth in complex database generation because of the obvious links between data capture and web marketing – when you have a visitor to your web site, you have a great opportunity to capture data about that visitor, especially if you use *cookie* technology. But remember, data captured for data's sake does not make a good database. What will you do with the data? If, for example, key predictive data identify a customer who is likely to defect – what is the strategy? How will you separate offers between ideal and negative value customers? It is important to be clear about why you are creating a database in the first place. If there are no clear objectives, then the database is an expensive, unused toy.

Rohner (2001) says: 'Without a corresponding marketing programme, database marketing should not be introduced.' You must be clear what you want to do with the database. What kind of *contact strategy* will you have? A sequence of *opt-in* emails, snail mails, telephone calls, personal visits or what? What kind of responses and offers will be date-triggered (e.g. three months after purchase), event-triggered (e.g. Christmas time), purchase-triggered (bought Item A, but not Item B). What is the sequence of contacts for each of these? Be clear about what you want to achieve with your e-CRM system.

Active database marketers know that databases deteriorate over time – people die, change job, move house. So the database asset has to be maintained, cleaned or updated. The cleaning process costs resources, but is crucial if the database is going to be used to its optimum. See Section 8.9 on cleaning the database.

Finally, it is essential to have a seamless, integrated database that works across all different platforms. So a customer is recognized and remembered and serviced in a personalized way, whether they access the company by telephone, web site, interactive TV, mobile phone. Integrating the databases presents a big challenge.

SECTION SUMMARY 8.3

Database marketing

Although the database and database marketing are at the heart of e-CRM, it goes way beyond simply collecting data. You now know the importance of linking the database to a clear marketing programme; the types of data fields – the complications that can arise; how mining can help to profile different types of customer (including best and worst); and the importance of maintaining and cleaning the database. A carefully planned, integrated and managed database can reap huge rewards.

8.4 e-CRM

This section shows how e-CRM draws on the basic principles of CRM, relationship marketing and database marketing. By the end of it, you will also know how to (a) list the CRM stages; and (b) keep the relationship alive.

WHAT DOES THAT 'E' ADD TO CRM?

Relationship marketing is all about building relationships with all external parties involved in marketing. CRM focuses specifically on the relationship with customers, and e-CRM focuses even further on the electronic relationship with customers.

CRM software is used to manage these electronic relationships. There are many different types of CRM software, but the common denominators are systems that plan and analyse marketing campaigns, identify and categorize prospects/sales leads as well as manage customer contacts and call centres.

More specifically, here is an e-CRM checklist which shows the options for an e-CRM programme.

E-MARKETING BEST PRACTICE – MANAGING AN E-CRM CHECKLIST

- ☑ Using the *web site and social media for customer development* from generating leads through to conversion to an online or offline sale using email and web-based information to encourage purchase

- ☑ *Managing email list quality* (coverage of email addresses and integration of customer profile information from other databases to enable targeting)

- ☑ Applying automated triggered *email marketing* to support contact strategies aimed at customer development (welcome, purchase, upsell, cross-sell and after sales), as shown by the Tesco.com example below

- ☑ *Data mining* to identify new segments and improve targeting

- ☑ Providing online personalization or *mass-customization* facilities to automatically recommend the 'Next best product'

☑ Providing *online customer service facilities* (such as Frequently Asked Questions, callback and chat support)

☑ Managing *online service quality* to ensure that first-time buyers have a great customer experience that encourages them to buy again

☑ Managing the *multi-channel customer experience* as they use different media as part of the buying process and customer lifecycle; i.e. providing clear linkages and seamless transition between online and offline channels or touchpoints as part of the relationship.

These facets of e-CRM mean that marketers can potentially deliver cheaper, faster and more flexible CRM. *Cheaper* – since although software can be expensive initially, if it is carefully chosen and utilized fully, it can deliver significant savings, particularly when much of the dialogue is both personalized and automated. *Faster* – since much e-CRM is automated and so responses are almost instantaneous; e.g. when visitors register on a web site, acknowledgement is now almost instantaneous. Similarly when customers place orders via web sites, most sites now automatically respond by acknowledging the order immediately. Many e-customers expect this now. *More flexible* – CRM systems should be readily updated to accommodate new products and new promotion techniques for new media.

The CRM software also enables permission marketing so that the relationship is founded on customer permission, and communications, in particular, become *more relevant*, *more personalized* and often *more interactive*.

With its customer orientation, CRM helps marketers by growing longer-lasting customer relationships. So both lifetime value and customer 'share of wallet' grow. The best relationships are those where both partners feel they are equal and can build respect for each other through mutual understanding. From the customer's point of view, it means that the relationship – and communications, in particular – are more relevant, tailored and often interactive. Speedy responses and considered responses are always appreciated by customers. In fact, complaining customers can become friends for life if their problems are dealt with swiftly and professionally. So it follows that resources (people, money, time) have to be allocated towards monitoring customer feedback and dealing with the specific non-standard problems on a one-to-one basis. For example, many companies have found that online chat (LivePerson) and telephone callback systems activated when customers fill in an online form are effective for moving customers from a virtual-world relationship to a more involving real-world relationship with contact-centre staff. However, such systems are resource-intensive and customer expectations must be met so that they don't have to wait for that chat session or phone call.

E-CRM software is also important to *automate* the way the dialogue with the customer is initiated and then the relationship built through a series of targeted, tailored, timed email and direct mail communications. The E-marketing Excellence box ('Tesco.com automates relationship building', opposite) shows how this is achieved.

Tesco.com automates relationship building through web, email and direct mail

Tesco.com uses software to monitor events which occur in the customer lifecycle. The examples below show that a sequence of follow-up communications is triggered after an event. Communications after event 1 are intended to achieve the objective of converting a web site visitor to action; communications after event 2 are intended to move the customer from being a first-time purchaser to a regular purchaser; and communications after event 3 are intended to reactivate lapsed purchasers.

Trigger event 1: Customer first registers on site (but does not buy)

- Auto-response (AR) 1: 2 days after registration, email sent offering phone assistance and £5 discount off first purchase to encourage trial

Trigger event 2: Customer first purchases online

- AR1: Immediate order confirmation
- AR2: 5 days after purchase, email sent with link to online customer satisfaction survey asking about quality of service from driver and picker (e.g. item quality and substitutions)
- AR3: 2 weeks after first purchase, direct mail offering tips on how to use service and £5 discount on next purchases intended to encourage re-use of online services
- AR4: Generic monthly e-newsletter with online exclusive offers
- AR5: Bi-weekly alert with personalized offers for customer
- AR6: After 2 months, £5 discount for next shop
- AR7: Quarterly mailing of coupons.

Trigger event 3: Customer does not purchase for an extended period

- AR1: Dormancy detected – reactivation email with survey of how the customer is finding the service (to identify any problems) and a £5 incentive
- AR2: A further discount incentive is used in order to encouraged continued usage after the first shop after a break.

KEEPING THE RELATIONSHIP ALIVE

Think about your own relationships. What makes them work? All relationships can get stale unless you work hard at them. This means that your web site needs to be updated and kept fresh and tailored – your offerings need to be more attractive than the competition's. How can you keep the relationship alive – without changing so much that you are no longer the organization they wanted to have a relationship with in the first place? DRAMA – that's how!

- *Dialogue.* An organization should offer customers ways to talk to them – every message sent should allow for a response. Every unsolicited communication from them should receive a swift and relevant response. The organisation *must* show that it listens and can talk and tell too!

- *Relevancy.* The beauty of e-CRM is that mass communication can be personal and made relevant to the recipient; indeed, the customer's expectation of relevance will be so high that it is dangerous to send bulk messages that are not tailored to that one person's/company's needs.

- *Accuracy.* E-CRM opens the door for poor information management as does any other form of direct communication – but this time the problem might well have originated with the customer themselves; e.g. they misspell a name, enter digits incorrectly, etc. when data are captured. Data must be checked, must be updated and must be kept 'clean'. Equally, any information you give to customers must be double-checked (as in all good communication) to ensure total accuracy.

- *Magic.* This is what makes the difference – the extra dimension that makes people want to be your customer. There is much talk of Customer Delight – go one better and aim for Customer Amazement! The Internet allows for special effects, deliveries of technically advanced packages of personalized information presented in very appealing ways – animation, sound, interaction, prizes, incentives, collection schemes; these are sometimes expected by customers nowadays, so what will you do that is different? Will it be your creative execution? The links with famous personalities whom you sponsor or hire? The very personal touch of a one-to-one adviser, whether delivered by a virtual *avatar* adviser (Figure 8.7) or a human online chat?

Figure 8.7   Avatar delivered by IKEA (www.ikea.co.uk)

As with any relationship, an occasional gift is a pleasant surprise. Given the lifetime value and potential share of wallet, some marketers realize that it is worth treating their customers with surprises. Note that some countries restrict gift giving (e.g. German B2C markets and now also UK B2B markets, as the Bribery Act 2010 limits the value of gifts given to B2B buyers). *Magic* is what should be the goal – and never guess what it might be, carry out research to find out what your customers want it to be.

- *Access.* 'I feel like we're drifting apart!' Don't let your relationship wither due to lack of contact, but also be sure you are not smothering the relationship with over-attentiveness! If you have a scheme to get your customers to visit you regularly (let's say they have to visit you every week for a year to collect all the cards in a deck to get an opportunity to have a free trip to Las Vegas, you must keep them going with spot prizes, because a year is a very long time to wait!), then be sure there is something worth seeing when they do visit! Getting someone to visit your site is one challenge; the next challenge is to get them to come back (the second visit is usually the start of a beautiful relationship). So ask yourself: 'What are we doing to get visitors to come back to the site? Do we give them a reason to come back?'

So now let us get down to the nitty-gritty of e-CRM – what are the specific stages? There are many different approaches to the CRM or e-CRM stages or cycle such as the Ladder of Loyalty (Considine and Murray, 1981) or the customer development cycle of selection, acquisition, retention and extension (and now we have the new Ladder of Engagement – see Chapter 3, Section 3.10). Here is another approach to the CRM cycle.

1 *Attract!* Obviously, this is where traditional offline communication as well as online communication about your offering are being designed to bring customers to your site. From TV advertising to banner ads and hotspots, getting them to your site will only be possible if (a) they know what you are offering and are interested; (b) they know where you are and how to get to you.

2 *Capture data.* The Internet is a splendid mechanism for capturing data – the prospect has the keyboard and screen in front of them and you can incentivize the giving of data.

3 *Get closer.* Get to know them better. It is not surprising that there is reluctance on the part of many individuals to give away personal data while online. So it is often better to gather more information about a person slowly and over time, as the trust builds between you and them.

4 *Embrace them.* Make your customer feel loved! Approach them with offers, prizes, rewards, incentives and information as well as experiences that show them you are thinking about *them*.

5 *Golden handcuffs.* Once you get them to show some loyalty, build a system whereby things are too good for them to leave! Tailor information or services to suit them specifically. Or offer services that integrate with the customer's own systems or lifestyle. These switching costs make leaving less likely.

E-CRM

E-CRM draws on the basic principles of CRM, relationship marketing and database marketing. There is a clear set of stages in CRM development. You have to work hard at keeping the relationship alive (DRAMA). There are many benefits including lifetime customers and increased share of wallet which help to grow your business.

8.5 Profiling

Profiling helps you to know your customers better. By the end of this section, you will know what profiling is, how it works and how it can help marketers.

Profiling can combine explicit data (customer information collected from registrations and surveys) and implicit data (behavioural information gleaned from the back end; i.e. through the recorded actions of customers on your site). Good strategies combine both implicit and explicit data continually. It is important to have a clear understanding of the target markets, the characteristics that define each segment and how you want to serve each segment. For example, certain car buyers might have different demographic profiles, show interest in particular features of a car (on particular pages) and request a test drive. If this group of visitors (or segment) fits the ideal customer profile, then they may get a DVD and an immediate incentive to buy now. Whereas another group, or segment, of visitors with a less likely profile may only get an e-newsletter once a month.

We can observe visitors as they leave an audit trail of what they did, what they looked at and for how long. As the cookie enables us to trace which pages you access, we can establish your profile according to what you're interested in (pages visited x duration spent there) and everything you put into your shopping basket and ultimately what you did or did not buy.

BEST PRACTICE E-MARKETING TIP

Review response by segment

Don't only review the overall response to your email campaigns as measured by open, click and purchase rates. Drill down deeper and see how well different segments respond to different offers or features in a newsletter – then you will know how well the relationship is working with different groups of customers.

The database can help you to find out who your most profitable customers are and whether they have any similar characteristics (e.g. came from a certain type of site or search engine; searched using a particular keyphrase; or spent a certain amount of time on particular pages). It makes sense to build up profiles of both customers and enquirers and segment them according to their different interests/enquiries/requirements or purchases.

The better the profiling, the better the results because the more accurately you target your marketing efforts on particular profiles or segments, the less your efforts will be wasted. Different customers have different needs. It is actually easier to satisfy them if you divide them into groups sharing similar needs (segments) and then treat each segment differently.

The more you know about customers, the better. It's as simple as that. Therefore a well-used database as part of a CRM system can create a competitive advantage as you grow your own mini monopoly (customers on your database).

Today, we can build sophisticated consumer profiles based on previous purchasing decisions and even identify the consumer hierarchy of criteria – whether quality, speed of delivery, level of service, etc. This enables us to target tailored offers that match the specific needs of segments on our database. Get this right and this 'virtuous cycle' delivers superior service and simultaneously creates competitive advantage that protects us from losing our customers to the inevitable, new, competitive offers looming on the horizon.

WHICH INFORMATION IS NEEDED FOR PROFILING?

Who is your customer? This is a classic marketing question. Do you really know who they are? What are your customers' key characteristics? What characteristics separate your *ideal customers* from your average customers? What is the profile of your ideal customer? Is it different from your worst, *negative value customers*? Surprisingly, many companies cannot answer these questions. If you don't know your customer profiles, how can you (a) satisfy them better; and (b) find other customers like them?

A *customer profile* can take everything you know about the customer and everything you know about people who are like that customer. It can then be layered with all the psychological and sociological theory that suggests how that person will react to a specific offer or promotion. This helps you to tailor offers that work better for both your customers and your business.

E-MARKETING INSIGHT

London Fire Brigade data analytics predict fires through profiling

Database mining can even be used for non-marketing purposes, such as fire prevention. Take the London Fire Brigade. It carries out 65,000 home safety visits each year, but with over 3 million homes in London, it would take over 50 years to cover everyone. More than 60 different data elements are fed into the model, including census data and population demographics, broken down into 649 geographical areas (ward level), plus type of land use, data on deprivation, Mosaic lifestyle data, historical incidents and past prevention activity. The model predicts where fires are most likely to occur. The London Fire Brigade uses the information to predict where there is a high risk of fire – e.g. in a small estate of houses or industrial buildings – so they can then send in an assessor to investigate and perhaps circulate information, set up some advisory services and ultimately reduce the number of fires (Smith and Zook, 2011).

APPROACHES TO PROFILING

Profiling is a continuous activity – continually collecting customer information, mining it and using it to profile and target more successfully. It is crucial to know what fields or data should be collected.

A simple example of this is the classic, timeless, grandfather clock story. A marketer with a huge database decided to market a limited-edition upmarket grandfather clock. After some consideration, they targeted 45–65-year-olds, upper income, living in large detached houses. They ran a test mailing which generated 60 orders. They then used the 60 responses to build a better profile of the actual customer. Using a more accurate customer profile, they then targeted a different segment of their database and sold every single clock!

Profile data can be gathered from several sources: internally from the customer's own input on a web form, tracking mechanisms and questionnaires; or externally from research companies and data bureaux. Data can be complex and of massive volume – it might be that you have to hire a computer bureau to crunch the data to turn it into useful information. An example of building a profile through an online conversation with customers is given in the E-marketing Excellence box below ('Tektronix build customer intimacy with virtual conversations with their customers', opposite).

One of the toughest jobs is to know which data matter most – especially where there are conflicting data. Some customers will give you incorrect information – consciously or unconsciously. You have to come up with ways to:

1   Acquire the information in the first place
2   Make it useful to your organization.

The issue of the invasion of privacy is a difficult one. Laws, ethics and codes of practice come into play. Ethics have a role, but the main arbiters of 'how much contact is too much contact' are the customers themselves. They will show you how ready they are to be communicated with by their response. You have to gain their permission.

Asking for information is a delicate affair. You cannot be too greedy. Beyond the basic information, you may need to offer incentives for more information, or simply wait for the relationship to develop and permission to ask for more. But remember that customers value their privacy. Let your customers see your privacy policy posted clearly on your web site and any other access point customers may have with you.

E-MARKETING INSIGHT

Using behavioural analysis to predict lifetime values

Internet gaming company Victor Chandler used SAS (www.sas.com) to do a behavioural analysis to predict lifetime values of new customers. For example, if a new customer comes in and bets on casinos (instead of poker tables), the company can predict whether that customer is more likely to become a long-term customer or a short-term, expensive, loss-making customer. The predictive analysis suggests which customers are worth investing in (with regular contact and regular incentives) and which are not worth investing in – those loss-making 'bonus seeker' customers, whose profile is: young male, tight betting (as opposed to betting all of their stash), declining betting frequency, infrequent betting, and middle-aged female. If visitors display these characteristics, they'll stay 3 weeks and leave and therefore do not warrant any relationship-building efforts (i.e. no regular contact or incentives). The other customers are worth investing in, and it is worth developing 'retention activity' (a regular attractive incentivized contact strategy) for them. Predictive analytics use historical data to highlight and optimize marketing messages that work better for certain social networks (Smith and Zook, 2011).

Of course, it is one thing to collect profile information, it is quite another to use it and derive value from it. Many organizations of all sizes, shapes and sectors today acknowledge that their most valuable asset is their customer information. Ironically, it also seems to be one of the least understood and most poorly managed areas. Often, no one is in overall charge of the data and there is a failure to invest in developing processes and systems to help staff contribute to data collection, quality and usage; e.g. far too often, the same message and creative are sent to everyone on a list.

E-MARKETING EXCELLENCE

Tektronix builds customer intimacy with virtual conversations with their customers

B2B Test and measurement company Tektronix (www.tektronix.com) uses email as a strategic communications tool to build relationships with its customers. Tektronix uses regular e-newsletters and periodic personalized email 'e-blasts' about product launches and promotions based on a detailed personal 'myTek' profile. Tektronix also uses a novel form of email marketing to create greater intimacy with its customers. This uses technology from I-OP (www.i-op.com) to generate a dialogue with the email recipient rather than completion of a simple online form.

The goal in using email in this way is to:

- Increase registration-form completion rates to get more leads
- Pre-qualify leads so the sales team don't waste their efforts
- Build intimacy by educating leads with useful materials on products that are right for them.

When the customer receives an email, it links to a form titled 'A virtual conversation with Tektronix' (Figure 8.8). They are then led through a series of questions on different forms to help the company better understand their characteristics and needs and offering relevant white papers in return. The questions are carefully tuned so that different customers see different questions and are offered different white papers according to their interests. With these 'skip patterns', the average respondent sees around eight questions, although there may be 20 or so in total.

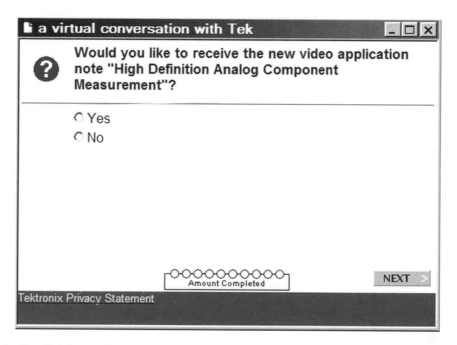

Figure 8.8   Email dialogue for Tektronix (www.tektronix.com)

SECTION SUMMARY 8.5

Profiling

Profiling helps you to:

- See your customers more clearly
- Identify customer segments
- Separate your best from your worst customers
- Tailor tempting offerings so that they are more relevant to specific customer profiles
- Build lifetime relationships
- Enjoy lifetime value and grow share of wallet.

8.6 Personalization

Specialized software combined with an up-to-date and well-cleaned database allow marketers to personalize communications such as emails, voice mails (voice- activated emails), snail mails (traditional direct mail), SMS text messages (for mobiles) and, most interestingly, web sites – personalized web sites. Chapter 6 on site design includes a section (6.5) dedicated to personalized web sites.

In 2010, the UK Prime Minister, Gordon Brown, said: 'Everyone in the country will be given their own personal web site page within four years in order to cut down the cost of dealing with officials' (Prince, 2010).

Some recent examples of personalized web sites include Asda (recommended shopping lists based on past buying behaviour); Google (search results modified by previous search behaviour); Groupon (offers vary according to your location); the UK's National Autistic Society (tailored content determined by user profile); and, of course, Nike (design and purchase of individualized products; but see E-Marketing Insight box ['HSBC uses personalization to deliver tailored propositions'] for a more in-depth example). The pioneers of all of this, Amazon, now claims that some 35 per cent of its sales come from suggested products (based on collaborative filtering; e.g. if customer X buys Johnny Wilkinson's rugby book and another 100,000 buyers of Wilkinson's book have also bought Martin Johnson's rugby book, then it is quite possible that customer X might buy Martin Johnson's book, if suggested).

E-MARKETING INSIGHT

Amazon gets more personal via Facebook Connect

By connecting to your Facebook Profile and Social Graph, Amazon can recommend products that match your interests and those of your friends beyond the clickstream, in addition to the purchase data it has from on-site Amazon behaviour.

Using the Facebook Open Graph, Amazon now offers recommended products based on the 'Likes' of Facebook Friends, along with upcoming birthdays. They can also base recommendations on the personal preferences expressed on Facebook (Hubspot, 2011).

WHY PERSONALIZATION?

The most important sound in the world is . . . your own name! We all appreciate it when people remember our names. It's personal. It's a compliment – an expression of respect. Web sites, blogs and Facebook pages today have to think about 'Giving Attention' and not just 'Getting Attention' from customers. By the end of this section, you'll know how personalization helps to build relationships and the issues that arise. Some call it affectionately, 'the personal touch', when a restaurant remembers your favourite wine or preferred table. The database enhances the marketer's memory of customer names, needs, interests and preferences.

Personalization enhances the relationship. Personalized web pages help to create a sense of ownership. Not 'of the customer by the marketer', but 'of the site by the customer'!

When you make a customer feel that their home page is truly theirs, that the offers you make available to them are theirs, that the information they access is put together just for them, then you allow the customer to own you.

This enhanced service helps to sell while also providing the platform for ongoing dialogue ('Speak') and enhancing the brand personality. So personalization delivers 4 of the '5Ss' benefits of e-marketing ('Sell', 'Serve', 'Speak' and 'Sizzle'). Which 'S' is missing? 'Save' – personalization software does cost money. And the larger the customer base gets, the more complex the personalization becomes. For this reason, many organizations stick with a less sophisticated mass web site.

APPROACHES TO PERSONALIZATION

There are three distinct approaches to personalization: customization, individualization and group characterization. *Customization* is the easiest to see in action: it allows the visitor to select and set up their specific preferences. *Individualization* goes beyond this fixed setting and uses patterns of your own behaviour (and not any other user's – they know it's you because of your log-in and password choices) to deliver specific content to you that follows your patterns of contact. In *group characterization*, you receive a recommendation based on the preferences of people 'like' you, using approaches based on collaborative filtering and case-based reasoning.

Mass customization is where different products, services or content are produced for different segments – sometimes hundreds of different segments.

Personalization is different. It is truly one-to-one. Particularly when not only the web site and communications are personalized, but the product is personalized.

As always, collecting the right data is critical in order for real segmentation and subsequent personalization to occur. In addition to analysing product purchases, data collection (and analysis) include: clickstream, site searches, and engagement including comments on blogs, links clicked within emails. Business-to-consumer (B2C) segments will include the usual demographics (age, gender, marital status) and socio-economic variables; while B2B will include industry sector, job/position, location, etc. (Linossi, 2011).

E-MARKETING INSIGHT

HSBC uses personalization to delivered tailored propositions

When HSBC Bank International Limited (HBIB) refined its web site, it wanted to use personalization, with the goals of delivering specific offers and servicing different customer segments, and encouraging customers to move into more valuable segments. This would enable it to capitalize on sales opportunities that would otherwise be missed. This was a challenge: since '60% of total weekly visitors to offshore.hsbc.com log on to the internet banking service, HSBC wanted to market to them effectively while they were engaged in this task, disrupting their banking experience without infuriating them'. Business rules were created to serve promotions dependent on the type of content accessed and the level of balance in the customer's account.

HSBC was successful in meeting its goals and the results show the benefit of personalized, targeted banners. On average, it was reported that the new banners had an 87.5 per cent higher clickthrough rate than non-personalized banners (6.88 per cent versus 3.67 per cent). The number of savings accounts opened via Internet banking increased by 30 per cent (based on 6 months pre- and post-launch). And the number of non-Premier customers upgrading to Premier accounts (requiring a balance of £60,000 or more) increased by 86 per cent (based on 4 weeks pre- and post-launch of the targeted banners).

Although the concept appears powerful, as with everything, there are always exceptions where things go wrong: Murphy's Law – what can wrong, will go wrong! Here are two examples where personalization goes wrong – passwords and personalized products. Take personalized sites – many of them require users to log in with a password which they inevitably lose. So the personalization is lost in the frustration of having to remember, find or recreate a password. Many visitors give up and leave the site. The use of cookies here can avoid the need for passwords and log-ins. Note that privacy laws now require marketers to explain the use of cookies within the privacy policy and seek permission before placing a cookie on the end-user's

Figure 8.9   Viva Las Vegas weddings

Source: www.vivalasvegasweddings.com/

device (PC, laptop, iPad, smartphone). Now consider personalized products and possible problems . . . Nike's web site invited customers to personalize or make their own shoes by stitching on their own personal logo. One customer filled out the online form, sent the US$50 and chose 'sweatshop' as a personal logo. Nike refused. The publicity soared. In addition, personalization incurs costs such as personalization software, human resources to measure the results, manage rules and optimize the system. It used to be said that 'Good navigation can replace personalisation in most cases' (Festa, 2003); today, marketers have to weigh up the pros and cons carefully.

One company that uses another form of personalization is Viva Las Vegas Wedding Chapels (see Figure 8.9), where couples can have their own web page with live, web-streamed video broadcasting of their wedding, in real time, so the family can watch and share the special moment from anywhere in the world. Couples can also keep track of developments before the wedding, invite friends, add photos or blog posts (CD-Traveller, 2012).

E-MARKETING INSIGHT

Gartner on personalization

There are many options for online personalization – these are some, from simple to complex, recommended by Gartner (www.gartner.com). How many of them do you use?

- Addressing customers personally:

  - Address customers/prospects by name in print communication
  - Address customers/prospects by name in electronic communication.

- Real-time personalization:

  - Keyword query to change content
  - Clickstream data to dynamically change web site content
  - Collaborative filtering to classify visitors and serve content.

- Customer-profile personalization:

  - Geographic personalization to tailor messages in traditional media
  - Demographic personalization to tailor messages in traditional media
  - Give web site visitors control over content from set preferences
  - Demographic personalization to tailor online messages
  - Geographic personalization to tailor online messages
  - Registration data to change web site content.

Over-personalization leads to overfamiliarity

Although personalization is important, it is possible to over-personalize. American Express call centres discovered that customers resented being greeted in person before the customer had declared his/her own name; the practice was swiftly discontinued.

Likewise, e-CRM systems make it possible to identify an individual responding to an email and downloading product information or a price list on a web site. While a follow-up phone call is obviously well timed, the call needs to be scripted carefully. It sounds like Big Brother if you say 'We see you downloaded a price list this morning.' It is much better to talk more generally about checking to see whether the customer needs any assistance in selecting a product.

SECTION SUMMARY 8.6

Personalization

There are pros and cons for the different levels of personalization. It requires resources. It requires a well-kept database. It does create a feeling of ownership. It does have some specific challenges (Murphy's Law), but can, if well executed, enhance customer relationships.

8.7 Email marketing

A coherent email marketing programme which helps build relationships needs to combine excellence in devising effective outbound email campaigns and managing incoming emails to satisfactorily resolve customers' questions.

OUTBOUND EMAIL MARKETING

Email is most widely used as a prospect conversion and customer retention tool, using an opt-in house list of prospects and customers who have given permission to a company to contact them. For example, lastminute.com has built a house list of over 10 million prospects and customers across Europe. Successful email marketers adopt a strategic approach to email and develop a contact or *touch strategy* that plans the frequency and content of email communications.

Think of the many benefits of email marketing which show why it has been called 'direct mail on steroids'. . .

1 *Relatively low cost of fulfilment.* The physical costs of email are substantially less than those of direct mail.

2 *Direct response medium encourages immediate action.* Email marketing encourages clickthrough

to a web site where the offer can be redeemed immediately; this increases the likelihood of an immediate, impulsive response.

3 *Faster campaign deployment.* Lead times for producing creative and the whole campaign lifecycle tend to be shorter than for traditional media.

4 *Ease of personalization.* It is easier and cheaper to personalize email than for physical media or a web site.

5 *Options for testing.* It is relatively easy and cost-effective to test different email creative and messaging.

6 *Integration.* Through combining email marketing with other direct media which can be personalized such as direct mail, mobile messaging or web personalization, campaign response can be increased as the message is reinforced by different media.

E-MARKETING BEST PRACTICE CHECKLIST – PRACTICAL TIPS FOR EMAIL MARKETING

But email marketing brings its own peculiar set of challenges that need to be managed. Your email programme will fail if you are not managing these issues adequately:

☑ *Deliverability.* Difficulty of getting messages delivered through different internet service providers (ISPs), corporate firewalls and webmail systems. Make sure you check your deliverability into the inbox using a tool like Lyris Email Advisor for the different webmail services your customers may be using, like Hotmail or Gmail. The two main reasons your carefully crafted email may be classified as SPAM are: use of SPAM words within the email subject or body (use the Lyris ContentChecker to see whether your copy is classified as SPAM at www.lyris.com/resources/contentchecker); the reputation of your email sender is poor due to complaints, or the broadcast characteristics are consistent with SPAM (high volumes, sent rapidly; check your reputation using Return Path's Sender Score at www.senderscore.org). The better your reputation, then the less likely you are to be blocked for using copy such as 'free' or 'limited offer' which have proven effectiveness.

☑ *Renderability.* A horrible word! It refers to the difficulty of displaying the creative as intended within the in-box of different email reading systems. The most common problem here is when email creative is all image-based and so is not displayed by default in the email reader as an anti-SPAM measure. In this case, the email will be meaningless unless it has a powerful subject line, so the response rate will fall. Instead, best practice is to use the approach shown in Figure 8.10, which uses body copy that is still clear when images are blocked, with hyperlinks highlighting value and encouraging clicks. It also uses alternative text for images (the same 'alt tags' we mentioned for accessible web pages in Chapter 6) to highlight offers and what the email is about. Finally, at the top of the email, there is a link *'Can't see this email? Click here for a web version',* which some recipients may prefer. An additional problem is that different email readers display emails slightly differently, so they need to be coded and tested to look their best across different email readers, which are even less standardized than different web browsers!

☑ *Email response decay.* Email recipients are most responsive when they first subscribe to an email. It is difficult to keep them engaged. We discussed this issue and approaches to counter it, such as a defined welcome strategy, in Section 8.2.

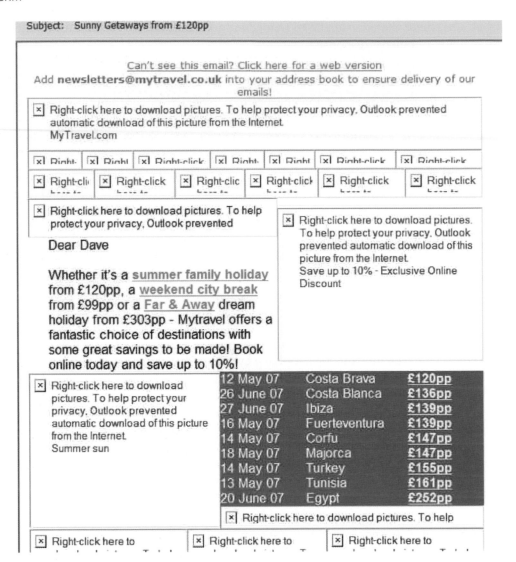

Figure 8.10   Best practice in countering blocked images from MyTravel

☑ *Communications preferences.* Recipients will have different preferences for email offers, content and frequency, all of which affect engagement and response. Some list members will naturally prefer more frequent emails. These can be managed through communications preferences.

☑ *Resource-intensive.* Although email offers great opportunities for targeting, personalization and more frequent communications, additional people and technology resources are required to overcome issues such as testing, deliverability and renderability.

OPTIONS FOR EMAIL MARKETING

When developing an email marketing programme, there are several options to be reviewed. Here is our checklist of options for using outbound email marketing as part of e-CRM:

☑ *Conversion email* – someone visits a web site and expresses interest in a product or service by registering and providing their email address although they do not buy. Automated follow-up emails can be sent out to persuade the recipient to trial the service. For example, betting company William Hill found that automated follow-up emails converted twice as many registrants to place their first bet compared to registrants who did not receive an email.

☑ *Regular e-newsletter type* – consider options of different frequency such as weekly, monthly or quarterly with different content for different audiences and segments.

☑ *House-list campaign* – these are periodic emails to support different objectives such as encouraging trial of a service or newly launched product, repeat purchases or reactivation of customers who no longer use a service. Although a newsletter is a good place to start with e-CRM, a problem with newsletters is that among the different features, your main message may be diluted, so you need a stand-alone email or 'e-blast' to have maximum impact.

☑ *Event-triggered email sequence* – these tend to be less regular and are sent out as part of an automated touch strategy to assist with customer development.

Think about which approaches you use now and which others you may consider. You can read more about how email is used strategically as part of customer relationship management in *Total E-mail Marketing* (Chaffey, 2006). We reviewed options for using email marketing for acquiring customers and creative best practice in Chapter 7, Section 7.6.

E-MARKETING INSIGHT

Rain triggered emails

In the US, bowling company AMF works with engagement marketing specialist, Silverpop, to take advantage of sudden changes of weather. Live weather feeds are used to trigger emails. So if rain is forecast for the weekend, emails are sent out to opted-in bowlers on AMF's database, offering discounts on and vouchers for the days in question. By making it clear that rain is likely and outdoor activities won't be as much fun, AMF has been able to boost participation and revenue.

Silverpop also works with Air New Zealand, putting live weather feeds into travel confirmation emails. Suggested activities for travellers to undertake once they reach their destination, provided by the airline's partners, are tailored depending on the predicted weather conditions (Gray, 2011).

MANAGING INCOMING EMAILS

Surprisingly, many major blue-chip companies insult their customers by ignoring or misman-aging their incoming emails – they lose sales, raise anger and damage the brands which they have spent fortunes building. By the end of this sub-section, you will know how to reduce the quantity of incoming emails and reduce the workload of outgoing responses, while growing strong customer relations.

Incoming emails can be sales enquiries, complaints, after-sales service requests and much more. They provide a direct conduit to the marketplace. Having made the effort to create a dialogue, you need to have the systems, procedures and resources in place to manage this communications channel. You must have systems in place that:

1 Receive, sort and route the incoming emails
2 Generate an 'auto-acknowledgement' response (automatic 'message received')
3 Provide a suitable response, regardless of the quantities of incoming emails.

This all sounds very simple, but it demands good planning and foresight. The quantity of incoming emails can be reduced, without jeopardizing the relationship, in the following ways:

1 FAQs allow for many issues to be dealt with without the customer contacting you directly.
2 Search facilities allow for customers to find out more about a topic without having to contact you directly.
3 Linked web sites and other locations can allow customers to research a topic across the web without having to contact you directly. It is worth looking at other web sites and their FAQs.

Even once you have removed many of the most repetitive reasons for email, there will still be some incoming communication that can be dealt with through fairly standard answers. This is where pre-prepared standard template responses (or 'canned messages') come in.

And template responses can be used without human input, thanks to intelligent software that matches words in incoming email to potential responses. So, for example, when the right count of critical words matches a certain topic, a specific relevant standard template response is sent. It can even be personalized. There are arguments for and against this type of response. It would be nice to think that nothing could match the way in which a human responds to another human, but this is not always the case.

When using real customer service or e-CRM staff, you need well-trained, knowledgeable staff who, if they don't know the answer to a question, at least know where to look to find it. There are always some emails that require a human response – so don't ignore human training as well as system design! And if your site has real-time text messaging facilities or live email answers or callback facilities (where the customer requests a telephone call from the company), remember that these require different skills – email skills and telephone skills.

Staff need to be managed. They need to be set goals for response, set performance standards, to be trained, motivated and monitored. Ignore people management at your peril.

Incoming emails

Systems help to categorize incoming emails. FAQs reduce the workload. Standard templates reduce workloads. Intelligent systems also use standard templates. Real staff also answer emails. They need to be trained and managed . . . if incoming emails are going to help customer relations to blossom.

8.8 Control issues

In this section, we examine six typical e-CRM control issues that confront marketers regularly:

1 Inexperience
2 Unintegrated systems
3 Information overload
4 High churn rate
5 Spiralling cleaning costs
6 Changing regulations.

By the end of this section, you will know how to begin to deal with them.

1 *Inexperience.* You have to start good management from within, but there is no reason why you can't try to learn some lessons from outside too! Some of these forms of advice come free, others have a fee attached. The best way to learn about the sort of information that is available for those setting up and managing database and e-CRM systems is to visit some of the organizations which offer such services.

2 *Unintegrated systems.* Having systems and sub-systems that don't talk to each other – either online or offline – this is one of the most common challenges, and one that has to be overcome without all the data, on all the systems, having to be recreated! The expensive way to tackle this is to get in new hardware and software and 'recapture' all the data. A better way is to work with a company that has the skills, scope and track record to do the job. There are many companies that offer to integrate your systems.

3 *Information overload.* Information overload means too much data. Even when your databases are integrated, the amount of data can grow too large to manage properly. Again, by using systems or data that have been designed to solve this issue, you can break down seemingly huge tasks into a series of smaller, more manageable tasks. This eases workflow and aids planning. For example, business-to-business company Actel provides its sales account managers with an email every Monday morning, listing prospects or customers to follow up who have engaged with an email the previous week. Even better, the list indicates which products they are interested in through summarizing links clicked or web pages visited. A simpler example is to include a field in the database which shows the date the customer last responded or interacted with an email, so it is possible to see how long ago they were last active.

4 *High churn rate*. Imagine this. Everything, it seems, is working well, but the 'churn rate', or customer defection rate, is high. The result of high churn rate is high recruitment costs (high customer acquisition costs) and high data capture costs, as well as increasing the required rate of cleaning. One solution is to investigate the reasons for the high churn rate; e.g. are your introductory offers too good to miss, but your subsequent offerings not meeting customer expectations?

5 *Spiralling cleaning costs*. Cleaning costs can escalate. Remember that a dirty database is a bad database. It is essential to maintain the integrity of the database. However, there can be pressure to reduce cleaning costs by either de-duplicating less often, or less thoroughly. While the relentless search for cost savings is constant, cutting costs here could well be your most expensive false economy.

6 *Changing regulations*. Industry rules and regulations keep changing or evolving (e.g. privacy laws) and therefore stop you being as creative as you would like. CRM, and especially the e-CRM industry, can only survive and thrive if it has the confidence of the customers. Every practitioner should strive to protect and enhance that trust in all their dealings. Don't forget to read up on the changing laws and regulations, particularly if you attract international customers.

E-MARKETING EXCELLENCE

Richard Beal of Direct Line on a single data view

For over a decade now, Richard Beal (Dempsey, 2000) has maintained that the key to effective control of CRM lies not in trying to enforce one single view of the customer (although Direct Line does have a large database of customer information). He uses a Japanese *kaizen* or continuous improvement approach, but this does not involve one huge team of call-centre agents employing a single approach to callers, but small groups of staff trying out different ways of handling calls.

For Richard Beal, the strategic goal of this CRM project is cross-selling. Direct Line has expanded into home insurance and now offers loans via the Internet. This approach gives it the ability to identify a loan application that comes from a customer who might also benefit from one of its credit-card schemes. The Chordiant software it uses allows a customer to bounce between web contact and a telephone conversation. Direct Line believes this flexibility is the key to converting queries into sales.

Richard Beal says, 'We have found that people want a hybrid, they will commence an inquiry over the Internet but do not feel comfortable carrying out the whole transaction online.'

Control issues

Be aware of some of the e-CRM issues that lie ahead of you, including:

1 Inexperience
2 Unintegrated systems
3 Information overload
4 High churn rate
5 Spiralling cleaning costs
6 Changing regulations.

Now is the time to learn more about dealing with them if you are to enjoy excellent customer relations.

8.9 Cleaning the database

The database is arguably a company's greatest asset; yet it can turn into a liability if not maintained properly, since databases start to decay as soon as they have been created (!) as people move house, change job, get sick, die, leave the country, change preferences, etc. By the end of this section, you'll know why and how databases can be maintained.

Your database is an asset. You must maintain its integrity. Like all assets, it needs to be maintained, otherwise it becomes a liability – harassing uninterested people, duplicating emails and snail mails, calling people by the wrong name, contacting people who have 'opted out' or asked not to be interrupted; in a word, making a nuisance of yourself and damaging your brand, not to mention wasting time and money. Horror stories abound.

The excuse that you have an old system – or worse, several old and unintegrated systems, which present too big a task – is a weak, although understandable, excuse. Some organizations manage to put off setting up effective cleaning systems for years by having some sort of committee or group looking into a new super-system, costing the project and then realizing that technological developments have moved ahead.

And all the time, the working group has been costing huge sums of money to operate and very little, if anything, has been invested in keeping the databases in question clean and up to date. This is a very poor, but frequently observed, business practice. You must try to keep cleaning, even while discussions about changes and upgrades continue.

There are many methods of keeping databases clean; some are proactive and some are responsive.

Let's start with the minimum requirement – responsiveness. Respond to changes in data. They need to be updated continually. And remember, as with any communication, online or offline, the recipient should be given the chance to inform you either (a) how their information should be corrected; or (b) if they want to be taken off your database. The web site is an obvious place to achieve this, through a communications preferences or customer profile form, but this facility is only usually offered by e-tailers.

Customers can self-help to clean a database if they are always invited to 'opt out' from future emails. 'Opt-outs' can be managed manually or automatically (by CRM and/or email software). Many countries' laws now insist that individuals should be able to 'opt out' of a list at any time. In the UK, the Email Preference Service (EPS) is available to companies for the sole purpose of removing opt-out email addresses from B2C lists. Organizations with large databases can ensure their database is clean in several ways.

One way to clean your database is by asking customers to keep opting in. Another way is to use suppression files. These are lists of people who have died, moved ('Gone away files') or simply asked to be taken off snail mail, email or telephone lists. Examples are Royal Mail's National Change of Address (NCOA®) Suppress file or the Direct Marketing Association's Mailing Preference Service, Telephone Preference Service and Email Preference Service.

Sometimes, members of your database don't want to opt out, but do want to tell you that they didn't like a specific mail-shot, or that they continue to receive three copies of something from you, or that they do not wish to receive emails about pet insurance, but they do want emails about car insurance, or even more unusual items that you simply cannot imagine. To maintain a good relationship, you must be flexible and allow for a wide-ranging dialogue. This requires good systems and procedures as well as trained customer-service staff.

A free-flowing and flexible dialogue can be encouraged by: freephone numbers, a dedicated web page, a dedicated email address and mail-back/fax-back special request sheets. The aim is to get any unusual request into the system quickly and accurately, allow someone to have responsibility for checking that it is routed within the organization to the right place/person and to be able to follow up should the database member request it.

PRACTICAL E-MARKETING TIP

Using a data bureau

You can use a data bureau to manage the process of matching or appending profile data from different databases or de-duplicating common customer records. They can also correct email addresses and add missing postcodes, for example, and other information through referencing other data sources. Another alternative is to use specialist list-cleaning software such as WinPure (www.winpure.com) in-house, or agencies such as CleverTouch (www.clever-touch.com) (Figure 8.11).

joined-up-marketing

About Us   What We Do   Our Clients   Resources   News

How can we help you?

→ Marketing Automation Optimisation & Campaign Delivery

→ Marketing Automation Consulting & Best Practice

→ **Data, Data Governance, Visualisation, Reporting & Analysis**

→ Inbound marketing - Social Media & PR

→ Integrated Engagement Marketing

tp://www.clever-touch.com/

Data, Data Governance, Visualisation, Reporting & Analysis

Big data and Data Visualisation is very much in vogue. This is good news as we have been at it for years.

No matter how captivating your creative is, if you are not targeting the right contacts in the right way, your campaigns will not work.

But it is so much more than that; with new data privacy laws in place the way you manage your customer and prospect data is as important to your reputation and brand management as the need for leads.

Enhanced data

At CleverTouch we employ a team of data modellers and data visualisation specialist to help our clients with data audits, data cleans-ups, data governance strategies, data modelling, preference centres set-up, and importantly campaign and marketing reporting.

Many of our clients ask us to manage their data and campaign reporting on a continuous basis because after a little while trends appear where we are able to predict

Figure 8.11   The importance of cleaning your data

Source: www.clever-touch.com

Sometimes it's not enough to listen – you have to go out and ask. Being proactive means you have much better databases because you take responsibility for your data being correct.

So:

1 Regularly contact (by mail or email) inactive database members
2 Regularly scan your records for possible duplication
3 Regularly cross-reference your new records against your old.

As with all business processes, you can do the cleaning yourself in-house, or subcontract, or outsource, the service; i.e. you can buy in the planning and design and then run it yourself. There are many companies that specialize in software that manages customer relationships via mail, email, telephone and sales force. It is worth having a look at some of them.

SECTION SUMMARY 8.9

Cleaning the database

The database is an asset. It needs to be maintained and cleaned. You can do it yourself in-house or subcontract outside. You can be responsive through customers helping to clean the database and you can be proactive by actively cleaning it yourself. Either way, cleaning is essential if your database is to remain an extremely valuable asset.

8.10 Making it happen

Given the list of failed CRM projects on record . . . how do you make it happen – how do you establish excellent e-CRM? Many organizations have to start from scratch. By the end of this section, you'll know what's involved when setting up an e-CRM system.

It is quite common for an inter-disciplinary team to be developed to create a database marketing and e-CRM system. They will have to develop project teams made up of the users of the system, analysts to understand their requirements, technical staff to create the system and a project manager with sufficient time to devote to the job.

When choosing a CRM system, you need to consider the current and future scale – how it can now, and in the future, integrate with other systems (like invoicing and debt collection). You also need to consider your budget which includes the 3Ms – 'men' (people) who will be involved in data capture, analysis and use; money – the budget required for software licences plus training and motivation schemes (to ensure staff buy into the new system); and minutes (time required to specify the brief, source it, test it, modify it, train the team and roll it out).

Systems development should follow a structured approach, going through several stages as shown in Figure 8.12. Note though, that just as for web site development, prototyping is the most effective approach since it enables the system to be tailored through users' experience of early versions of the system. Beware of 'scope creep' (adding extra requirements to the brief after the brief has been agreed). Ultimately, CRM is an attitude as much as a system. Success depends on a customer culture where all staff always ask, 'How can we help the customer?'

There are several approaches. The Gartner Group (2010) suggests a three-step process to create a CRM strategy:

1 *Set the destination*. Managers are urged to examine the various definitions of CRM, creating their own to gain buy-in and cohesiveness from those involved in the initiative. A vision for CRM that identifies why the organization wants the initiative and that defines its desired results should be established immediately. Teams that drive the initiative should be composed of three key roles: a sponsor, facilitator and project/programme manager.

2 *Audit the current situation*. Beginning with a full assessment of past CRM initiatives, participants should be asked what they thought needed to be changed in order to understand what did/did not work. The report also states that 'assumptions, business case, and goals of past projects remain valid, even if the execution was not as successful as hoped'. Readers are also warned to beware shortcuts in information gathering: 'Seek information from external sources first, and weight customer and consumer feedback highest.'

3 *Map the journey*. Identify the steps to achieve the vision. Core value propositions for customers and motivating factors for customer loyalty should be classified. The company should be revalued on the potential of its customer base rather than on current revenue or profits.

Figure 1
The Eight Building Blocks of CRM

1. CRM Vision: Leadership, Market Position, Value Proposition

2. CRM Strategy: Objectives, Sements, Effective Interaction

3. Valued Customer Experience

Understand Requirements
Monitor Expectations
Satisfaction vs. Competition
Collaboration and Feedback
Customer Communication

4. Organizational Collaboration

Culture and Structure
Customer Understanding
People: Skills, Competencies
Incentives and Compensation
Employee Communications
Partners and Suppliers

5. CRM Processes: Customer Lifecycle, Knowledge Management

6. CRM Information: Data, Analysis, One View Across Channels

7. CRM Technology: Applications, Architecture, Infrastructure

8. CRM Metrics: Value, Retention, Satisfaction, Loyalty, Cost to Serve

Source: Gartner Research

Figure 8.12 The eight building blocks of CRM

Source: Adapted from Radcliffe *et al.* (2001)

Processes and systems that can be altered rapidly and dynamically as individual customers move among segments should be built. Three to five top-line objectives for CRM initiatives should be established – more than five is considered unnecessary. The initiative should be communicated daily to sponsors and executives.

Some years previously Gartner unveiled the Eight Building Blocks of CRM (Radcliffe *et al.*, 2001; Figure 8.12). This still provides a useful template for teams to explore on their quest for CRM excellence. This framework was designed to help enterprises see the big picture, make their business cases and plan their implementations. The framework can be used for internal education, and to foster debate about the development of a CRM vision and strategy.

Marketers need to improve their skill sets. We need to get better at speaking the language of IT and develop a greater understanding of how technology can translate into improved customer knowledge and ultimately an 'improved customer experience'. As Hooly Wright (2007) says, 'IT people use scary language, and marketers step back from it'. But if marketers constantly brought conversations back to the benefits for the customer, that would help build a common language around the customer and put technology back in its place.

As they say: 'Front end is fun. Back end is business.' Marketers are reasonably good at developing web sites (front end), but we have to become experts with the database and the e-CRM systems (back end) required to build continual success.

MANAGING THE DATABASE

The database is the core of the CRM system. The database administrator/manager (DBA) has many responsibilities here:

1 *Database design* – ensuring the design is effective in allowing customer data to be accessed rapidly and queries performed.

2 *Data quality* – ensuring data is accurate, relevant and timely.

3 *Data security* – ensuring data cannot be compromised by attacks from inside or outside the organization.

4 *Data back-up and recovery* – ensuring that data can be restored if there are system failures or attacks.

5 *User coordination* – this involves specifying who has access to the information retrieval and who has access to information input. Too many uncontrolled inputs mean files get changed and deleted by too many different people. The database spins out of control.

6 *Performance monitoring* – checking the system is coping with the demand placed on it by users.

There's one more part of the DBA's job – to communicate with clarity to the rest of the organization the advantages of database marketing.

COSTS AND TIMESCALES

Projects range from several hundred thousand customer records to several million (or in some cases, 40 million records). A data integration, data-mining campaign optimization and a full direct marketing suite from companies like SAS range from £500,000 to £5m, with social media customer link analysis starting at around £250,000. (Note that Gartner (2010) reported that average US$100 m CRM projects are coming back again in the United States after having 'dried up'.)

When it comes to the crunch question of 'How much does it all cost?', there are many variables to consider:

1 The set-up costs of the system

2 The type of system

3 The scope of the system

4 The size of the system

5 The choice made about the database management system (DBMS)

6 The maintenance programme

7 The use you make of it!

8 Where your physical database management system is geographically located.

It's a complex job, but once all these variables are taken into consideration, a task breakdown can be performed and analysis, design, set-up, maintenance and running schedule of costs can be calculated.

What's missing? Staff – customer-service staff. They are a key component, particularly when handling wide-ranging, non-standard requests or complaints. Here's a crucial question. How many customer-service staff should you employ?

Some organizations employ thousands of CRM staff. Some are also shifting staff from telephone service to social media service – using Facebook, in particular, to reduce response times, increase customer satisfaction and cut costs.

The other key question is 'How long does it take to set up an e-CRM system?' The variables are similar to cost:

1 Time allowed for investigative stage
2 Time allowed for design
3 Time for writing programmes
4 Time for data capture/reassessment/input
5 Time for trials, piloting, testing and de-bugging.

Then decide how good your commitment to CRM is by using the Customer Sensitivity Quotient (Table 8.2):

Table 8.2 Customer Sensitivity Quotient

Are your customers getting the service they deserve? Answer the following questions 'yes' or 'no' to find out how your organization is doing.	Yes/No

1 Do you know what percentage of customers you keep each year?
2 Do you know what percentage of customers you lose each year?
3 Do you know the top three reasons your customers leave?
4 Do you know your customers' number one service expectation?
5 In the past three months, have you personally contacted ten former customers to find out why they left?
6 Do you (and everyone else in your company) understand the lifetime value of a customer?
7 Do you have written customer service quality standards (that your people helped you develop, so they own them)?
8 Do you articulate your quality standards in understandable and measurable terms?
9 In the past six months, have you checked to see if any of your customers' expectations have changed?
10 Do you know how many members of your staff serve internal versus external customers?
11 Are your customer service performance standards tied to any incentives?
12 Is everyone in your company required to take a minimum number of hours of customer care training programmes each year?

Table 8.2 *(Continued)*

If you scored . . .	You are . . .
12	A CSQ legend!
10–11	A CSQ star!
7–9	Jo(e) Average
4–6	A benchwarmer
Below 4	In the penalty box

SECTION SUMMARY 8.10

Making it happen

An effective CRM programme needs a strong project manager who can unite the business and technical team members. A defined database administrator is also required who will champion the system and own it to ensure appropriate data quality, security and performance. Planning using the systems development lifecycle provides a framework for costing, scheduling and monitoring the project. Remember also that CRM programmes should never end; they evolve.

CHAPTER SUMMARY

1 *E-CRM* operates in an environment where customers demand quality services from organizations. Since it is technology-based, it can be used to increase the speed, frequency and relevance of interactions, while remembering that human contact is the best for some situations.

2 *Relationship marketing* involves a long-term rather than transactional approach to customers. It is based on building up permission and trust, listening and then responding to customers.

3 *Database marketing* is key to e-CRM since the database can be used to understand customer needs through profiling and data mining, to segment customers and manage integrated marketing and direct marketing campaigns.

4 *E-CRM* provides DRAMA – Dialogue, Relevancy, Accuracy, Magic and Access – to marketing communications. A good approach to the CRM cycle is attract, capture data, get closer, embrace and attach golden handcuffs.

5 *Profiling* helps to identify groups of customers and rank them according to their importance to the company. Appropriate communications and offers can then be developed for these groups with the aim of building long-term relationships with them.

6 *Personalization* refers to tailoring of a range of communications from emails to web sites. These can be individual (one-to-one) or tailored to segments (mass customization). Personalization can occur due to user selection (customization), marketing rules (individualization) and group characterization such as collaborative filtering.

7 If *incoming emails* are mismanaged, this can destroy customer relationships. Procedures

must be put in place to sort and route the incoming emails, notify receipt and provide a suitable response. Contact strategies such as FAQs and using the phone where appropriate can minimize the volume of emails and maximize the clear-up rate.

8 *Control* is necessary to avoid e-CRM problems caused by inexperience, unintegrated systems, information overload, high churn rate, spiralling cleaning costs and changing regulations.

9 *Cleaning the database* is important to minimize marketing costs and improve relationships. Approaches are responsive where customer requests are implemented rapidly and proactive where regular planned cleaning occurs.

10 An *effective CRM programme* needs a strong project manager to achieve staff involvement across the business and ensure that the implementation is well planned, so it is delivered on time. A good-quality database administrator is important to champion the system and to deliver data quality, security and performance.

References

Atchinson, S. (2008) The ROI of customer satisfaction. Interview with Larry Freed, *ClickZ*, 24 July.

Boreel, M. (2007) Sogeti IT consultancy. *Marketing Age*, March.

Bhargava, R. (2011) 10 big brand lessons from the Corporate Social Media Summit, *Social Media Today*, June 22. At: http://socialmediatoday.com/clifffigallo/309088/10-big-brand-lessons-corporate-social-media-summit

CD-Traveller (2012) Viva Las Vegas Wedding Chapel launches free personalised sites. Submission by editor, 2 March at: www.cd-traveller.com/2012/03/02/viva-las-vegas-wedding-chapel-launches-free-personalised-websites/

Chaffey, D. (2006) *Total E-mail Marketing*.

Chaffey, D. (2007) Summary of an article by Dave Chaffey for *What's New in Marketing*. At: www.davechaffey.com/E-marketing-Insights

Considine, R. and Murray, R. (1981) *The Great Brain Robbery*. Pasadena, CA.

Dempsey, M. (2000) Direct Line: Strategic goal of this CRM project is cross-selling. Financial services case study. *Financial Times*, 7 June.

Feta, P. (2003) Personalised web sites are driving customers away. Silicon.com, 14 October.

Flores, L. and Eltvedt, H. (2005) Beyond online advertising – lessons about the power of brand web sites to build and expand brands. Published in *Proceedings of ESOMAR Online Conference, Montreal*.

Forrester Research (2009) *Answers to Five Frequently Asked Questions about CRM Projects*. Forrester Research, Cambridge, MA.

Gartner (2009) *Trip Report: Gartner Customer Relationship Management Summit 2009*. Gartner, Stamford, CT.

Gartner Group (2010) Three steps to create a CRM strategy. At: www.gartner.com/id=1298722

Gray, R. (2011) Here today. . . *The Marketer*, July/August.

Godin, S. (1999) *Permission Marketing*. Simon and Schuster, New York.

Harris Interactive (2007) *Second Annual Customer Experience Impact Report*. A Harris Interactive study sponsored by RightNow(R) Technologies.

Hubspot (2011) *The Facebook Marketing Update, Spring 2011*. E-book created by *Who's Blogging What?* and sponsored by Hubspot.

Hochman, L (2008) Guide to customer loyalty. *Marketing Age*.

Krigsman, M (2009) CRM failure rates: 2001–2009, *ZDNet*, 3 August.

Linossi, K. (2011) Website personalisation – why it pays off. *New Media Knowledge*, 30 June.

McGovern, G. (2012) Support is the new sales. *New Thinking*, 11 March.

MORI (2003) *Managing your Customer Insight Capability and the Drivers for Change – Client Managed, Cosourced, Insourced or Outsourced – A Survey of UK FTSE 1000 Organisations Commissioned by Detica*.

Novo, J. (2003) *Drilling Down: Turning Customer Data into Profits with a Spreadsheet*. Available from www.jimnovo.com

Peppers and Rogers (1999) *One-to-One Field Book*. Currency/Doubleday, New York.

Prince, R. (2010) Personalised website for everyone within four years. *Daily Telegraph*, 22 March.

Radcliffe, J., Kirkby, J. and Thompson, E. (2001) *The Eight Building Blocks of CRM*. Gartner Research, Stamford, CT.

Ray, B. (2011) Silent support costs more, but it's less embarrassing. *Developer*, 23 August.

Rezab, J (2011) Companies respond to just 5% of questions on Facebook. Econsultancy. Blog post, 17 October at: http://econsultancy.com/uk/blog/8149-companies-respond-to-just-5-of-questions-on-facebook

Rohner, K. (2001) *Marketing in the Cyber Age – the Why, the What and the How*. Wiley, New York.

Smith, P.R. and Zook, Z. (2011) *Marketing Communications: Integrating Offline and Online with Social Media*, 5th edition. Kogan Page, London.

Stone, M. (2004) Interview with PR Smith.

Stone, M. (2011) Literature review on complaints. *Journal of Database Marketing & Customer Strategy Management*, 18, pp. 108–22.

Stone, M. (2012) Interview with PR Smith.

Thompson, E., Maoz, M., Collins, K. and Dunne, M. (2011) What's 'hot' in CRM applications in 2011. Gartner Research. At: www.gartner.com/id=1595014

Tranfield, D. and Braganza, A. (2007) *Business Leadership of Technological Change – Five Key Challenges facing CEOs*. Chartered Management Institute, London.

Wright, H. (2007) Reclaiming the customer high ground. *The Marketer*, July/August.

Yeadon, D. (2009) Statistics published on an occasional basis on the web site of the Marketing Bureau (www.tmb.uk.com/)

Further reading

CCA Global Excellence Awards 2011. Best Use of Social Media: UCAS – winners. At: www.cca-global.com/gsx/content/awards/?contentid=58

Ebner, M., Hu, A., Levitt, D. and McCrory, J. (2002) How to rescue CRM. *The McKinsey Quarterly*, 4 (Special Edition: Technology).

Godin, S. (1999) *Permission Marketing*. Simon and Schuster, New York. An interesting and influential book.

Newell, F. (2000) *Loyalty.com*. McGraw Hill, New York. An accessible book, with US examples of the principle of loyalty.

Reicheld, F. and Schefter, P. (2000) E-loyalty: your secret weapon on the Web. *Harvard Business Review*, July–August, pp. 105–13. An essential, short summary of achieving customer loyalty using online techniques.

Seybold, P. (1999) *Customers.com*. Century Business Books, Random House, London. Describes a customer-centric approach to business strategy with many examples drawn from the United States.

Web links

ClickZ (www.clickz.com/experts). Email channels. ClickZ has expert articles within its channels on deliverability, email optimization and creative.

CustomerThink (www.customerthink.com). Forum, plus blog advice.

Database Marketing Institute (www.dbmarketing.com). Great practical guidelines and presentations on traditional database marketing and online marketing using email and web personalization.

DMA Email Marketing Council Blog (www.dmaemailblog.com). UK advice from the Direct Marketing Association,

E-Loyalty (www.mycustomer.com). An introduction to achieving online loyalty by Ellen Reid-Smith.

Email Experience Council (www.emailexperience.org). A US organization with compilations of practical tips on email marketing.

Email Marketing Best Practice (www.smartinsights.com/email-marketing). Advice on best practice.

Email Marketing Reports (www.email-marketing-reports.com). Articles and reviews on email solutions.

Email Marketing Tools (http://bit.ly/smartesps). A compilation of tools for managing email broadcast and deliverability.

JimNovo.com (www.jimnovo.com). Specializing in online CRM, Jim's site has many practical insights about analysing and following up according to online purchase behaviour, including the excellent *Drilling Down* guide.

MyCustomer.com (www.mycustomer.com). Portal focusing on traditional and online CRM.

Net Promoter Score Blog (http://netpromoter.typepad.com/fred_reichheld). Blog on achieving advocacy by Fred Reicheld and other specialists such as Paul Marsden.

Peppers and Rogers One to One Marketing (www.1to1.com). Contains interesting articles, case studies and supplier guides.

Self-test

1 How do database marketing, relationship building, direct marketing and CRM relate to each other?

2 Describe different staged approaches to relationship building.

3 Explain the concept of data mining.

4 How do we use DRAMA to keep customer relationships alive?

5 How, when and why should profiling occur for an organization you are familiar with.

6 Summarize the benefits and disadvantages of personalization.

7 Describe the management issues of incoming emails.

8 Explain these six typical issues of e-CRM control that confront marketers regularly: inexperience, unintegrated systems, information overload, high churn rate, spiralling cleaning costs and changing regulations.

9 Describe approaches to database cleaning.

10 Produce an outline list of the main activities that need to occur for e-CRM implementation and maintenance.

Chapter **9**

Managing digital marketing

Digital marketers need to make the business case to convince those who control the budgets that we require to implement our digital plans. Otherwise change won't be fast enough and the effectiveness of our marketing activity is likely to decline as consumers or business customers switch to new platforms; we risk 'missing the boat'.

Mike Berry (Berry and Chaffey, 2012)

OVERVIEW

Digital technologies and platforms are still relatively new compared to traditional communications. The options available evolve rapidly. This gives great opportunities to companies which are able to adapt to exploit these changes. For most companies, though, there are major challenges – how to manage digital marketing effectively through adapting existing organizational culture, structure and resourcing, both internal and external.

OVERALL LEARNING OUTCOME

By the end of this chapter, you will be able to:

- Understand key issues for managing digital marketing
- Be able to review the current digital marketing capabilities of an organization
- Prepare a business case and budget for investment in digital marketing
- Take actions to manage issues such as change management, resourcing, data quality and security.

CHAPTER TOPIC   LEARNING OBJECTIVE

CHAPTER TOPIC	LEARNING OBJECTIVE
9.1 Introduction	Understand the importance of processes to review the opportunities from digital technology and adapt to integrate them into the organization
9.2 Transformation to e-business	Assess the context of digital marketing activities within wider changes to use of digital technology within organizations
9.3 Creating the social business through implementing social CRM	Evaluate the impact of social media marketing on internal company activities
9.4 The endless journey – reviewing digital marketing capabilities	Review digital marketing capabilities using a range of different criteria
9.5 Budgeting for digital marketing	Understand approaches to setting appropriate budgets for digital marketing
9.6 Making the business case for e-marketing investment	Review methods of convincing others why investment in digital media is required
9.7 Selecting the right suppliers for digital marketing	Assess alternatives including traditional, general and specialist digital agencies
9.8 Change management for digital transformation	Review success factors for changes needed for effective digital marketing, including internal resourcing, structure and leadership
9.9 Measuring and optimizing digital marketing with digital analytics	Understand approaches such as A/B and multivariate testing and how to manage them

9.1 Introduction

When the applications of the Internet for marketing were first explored in the 1990s, some advocates urged adoption of Internet marketing since it was 'quick, cheap and easy'. Maybe this was true at the time, in a relative sense; it was possible to get an edge over slower-moving competitors.

Today, few would argue that e-marketing is 'quick, cheap or easy' since the popularity of digital technologies with consumers and businesses has made it such a popular medium which is highly competitive.

To be involved in e-marketing is certainly interesting since there are constant changes in features and functionality from all the major platforms such as Facebook, Google+ and Twitter. New platforms are rapidly adopted; for example, Foursquare, Instagram and Pinterest have all become popular since the emergence of the first social networks. The growth of mobile Internet usage through smartphones and tablets has further changed our options for marketing. We also have new options to optimize investments in familiar existing channels; for example, testing and improving the effectiveness of media like paid search or display, or conversion rate optimization of our web site.

These changes to platforms make e-marketing challenging to manage, since we have to constantly assess our e-marketing activity on new and existing platforms. When we decide, as marketers, we want to invest in technology, this is also challenging since we will probably have to persuade colleagues that the investment is worthwhile, source the right skills or agencies and suggest changes to ways of working. Organizational change is challenging, whatever the reason.

This chapter explores these challenges and changes involved in managing digital marketing. We will start by reviewing the moves to e-business and social business that are needed to transform organizations to enable them to make wider use of digital and social technologies. For many, these are uncharted waters, so we need to explore the best approaches and convince others to invest in our exploration.

SECTION SUMMARY 9.1

Introduction

Managing digital marketing requires a constant review of new digital marketing opportunities. A major transformation to e-business and social business in organizations is needed to fully implement these new capabilities.

9.2 Transformation to e-business

Commentators and companies offering services to help businesses navigate the new world of digital technology and media have always used labels to describe the new opportunities and approaches needed to manage them. These labels are useful since they can describe the scale of change needed and the ultimate goal, where digital technology is seamlessly integrated into all marketing and business activities.

E-business was one of the terms initially used to describe the use of digital technology to support processes throughout a business.

Here is IBM's definition from 1997 when they originated the term on their web site: e-business (e' biz' nis): 'The transformation of key business processes through the use of Internet technologies'.

We still hear this term today; indeed, many people work as e-business or e-commerce managers, endeavouring to build new ways of working through technology.

E-MARKETING INSIGHT

IBM coins the term e-business

[In 1997,] IBM Chairman Louis V. Gerstner, Jr. announces to IBM employees the debut of a major strategic campaign built around the IBM-coined term 'e-business'.

In his first major customer address on e-business – a speech considered by many as the first 'wake-up call' to Wall Street on the implications of the networked world – Gerstner describes to the Securities Industries Association the Internet's ability to challenge centuries-old business models and transform the nature of all important transactions between individuals and institutions.

(IBM, no date a)

E-business described how technology can transform key business processes out of the old *value chain* and into new, dynamic, *value networks*. This involves integration, automation and extension of processes both inside and outside a company. This usually means letting go – handing over information and empowerment to employees, strategic partners, customers, distributors and other stakeholders.

The old value chain started with the purchasing of raw materials and then moved to the production of goods and services, their distribution, marketing, sales and after-sales service. The new *value networks* reshuffle the sequence so that customers, distributors and partners are more involved as the business integrates into a flexible, faster-moving, customer-driven extended network of online partners.

Creating an e-business still offers a golden opportunity to analyse and improve your whole business – its operations, processes and procedures as well as strategic partners – a fresh opportunity to re-engineer a company.

Perhaps one of the greatest impacts of the Internet is that it has forced many business to rethink all of their 'cherished perceptions and ideas'. Building an e-business helps managers to adopt what the Zen Buddhists call 'the beginner's mind'.

Having said that, the term 'e-business' probably won't exist in a few years, as most businesses will be using 'e-business' as part of their normal procedures, although it's still used after 15 years! But reviewing business processes and re-engineering of companies will continue long after e-business has integrated itself into the business architecture.

So what is e-business? Let's keep it simple. Let's ignore legal departments, accounting, HR and IT departments and assume that they have to be integrated into any business system. So, let's just break up the business into those aspects that perform Buy-side, In-side and Sell-side processes (Figure 9.1). This identifies three key areas in which to achieve e-business performance. There are other approaches to this. But for now, let's just stick with this simple model.

So how does e-commerce relate to e-business? Are they similar? Certainly, but generally speaking, the e-commerce team in a business tends to focus more on the Sell-side, but it's really a matter of interpretation in each company.

Electronic commerce (e-commerce) is often thought simply to refer to buying and selling using the Internet; people immediately think of consumer retail purchases from companies such as Amazon. But e-commerce involves more than electronically mediated *financial* transactions between organizations and customers. E-commerce can be considered as *all* electronically mediated transactions between an organization and any third party it deals with. By this definition, non-financial transactions such as customer requests for further information would also be considered to be part of e-commerce.

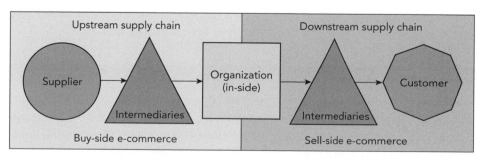

Figure 9.1   A simple framework for e-business

Kalakota and Whinston (1997) referred to a range of different perspectives for e-commerce which remains valid today:

1 *A communications perspective* – the delivery of information, products or services or payment by electronic means.
2 *A business process perspective* – the application of technology towards the automation of business transactions and workflows.
3 *A service perspective* – enabling cost cutting at the same time as increasing the speed and quality of service delivery.
4 *An online (transaction) perspective* – the buying and selling of products and information online.

BUY-SIDE E-BUSINESS

The buy-side is B2B – buying raw materials and/or services. It can include procurement, inbound logistics, and warehousing. Here, the business's *extranet* is used to open up certain aspects of the business (applications and data) to an exclusive audience of carefully selected suppliers to allow:

- Faster and easier trade with suppliers, manufacturers and/or distributors
- Collaboration with suppliers, manufacturers and/or distributors so that they move from 'independence to interdependence', sharing data to improve operational efficiency and ultimately customer satisfaction.

Reduced working capital is achieved as efficient systems allow 'just-in-time' deliveries, thereby avoiding having vast quantities of cash tied up in stock (working capital). This is an 'extended enterprise' where partner suppliers and distributors work much more closely together. Supply-chain management applications are commonly used.

IN-SIDE E-BUSINESS

The in-side is sometimes known as B2E – business to employee – involving internal processes and communications. This could be manufacturing, management or operations. Here the *intranet* empowers employees by opening up access to key information and applications. Any of these internal processes can be outsourced. Excellent B2E systems are vital if a small core internal team is going to run a tight ship. From a marketing point of view, intranets to share knowledge and respond to customer concerns have been a great innovation.

SELL-SIDE E-BUSINESS

The sell-side involves processes and applications that help you to sell to and service customers, whether directly or indirectly through intermediaries. E-CRM applications and selling-chain management applications are commonly used. Here the *extranet* provides exclusive use to strategic intermediary partners such as distributors and also to key account or registered customers. Extranets can be used to:

- Sell to customers directly and indirectly through intermediaries
- Move from online occasional sales to lifetime loyalty relationships
- Serve and manage customer relations better.
- Speak to them individually and tailor one-to-one offerings drawn from the database.

There are also many applications:

- CRM and social CRM
- ERP (enterprise resource planning)
- Supply-chain management
- Selling-chain management
- Operating resource management
- Enterprise application integration (EAI)
- Business analytics
- Knowledge management
- Decision support applications.

Remember that isolated, stand-alone applications will soon be history. For new e-businesses, options for *business models* and *revenue models* will also have to be reviewed. Some of the options for business models are shown in the E-marketing Insight box 'Paul Timmers on business models'. *Revenue models* specifically describe different techniques for generation of income. For existing companies, the standard revenue model is the income from sales of products or services. This may be either for selling direct from the manufacturer or supplier of the service or through an intermediary who will take a cut of the selling price. Other options for generating revenue include selling advertising space, and *affiliate* revenues.

E-MARKETING INSIGHT

Paul Timmers on business models

Almost 15 years ago, Timmers (1999) identified no less than 11 different types of business model that can be facilitated by the web. These still remain the core business models, although variants have been created.

1 *E-shop* – marketing of a company or shop via the web
2 *E-procurement* – electronic tendering and procurement of goods and services
3 *E-malls* – a collection of e-shops such as the now defunct Barclay Square. This model didn't prove sustainable. The nearest equivalent is price comparison sites which link through to retailers using an affiliate model (see Section 7.4 in Chapter 7).
4 *E-auctions* – these can be for B2C – e.g. eBbay (www.ebay.com); or B2B – e.g. Alibaba (www.alibaba.com)

5 *Virtual communities* – these can be B2C or B2B communities such as the social networks or independent company communities like the American Express OPEN Forum (see Chapter 5, Section 5.7).

6 *Collaboration platforms* – these enable collaboration between businesses or individuals; e.g. Yammer (www.yammer.com).

7 *Third-party marketplaces* – marketplaces such as EC21 (www.ec21.com).

8 *Value-chain integrators* – offer a range of services across the value chain.

9 *Value-chain service providers* – specialize in providing functions for a specific part of the value chain, such as the logistics company UPS (www.ups.com).

10 *Information brokerage* – providing information for consumers and businesses, often to assist in making the buying decision or for business operations or leisure (affiliates are also involved here).

11 *Trust and other services – an example is* TRUSTe (www.truste.org) which authenticates the quality of service provided by companies trading on the web.

SECTION SUMMARY 9.2

Transformation to e-business

E-business gives a broader perspective on e-marketing; it involves managing the application of digital technologies on the buy-side, in-side and sell-side. New business and revenue models are explored as part of this.

9.3 Creating the social business through implementing social CRM

In Chapter 5, we saw how there is a diverse range of goals of applying social media, with many companies looking to use social media to reach new prospects through the amplification effect of sharing. See 3.10 for social business models and the Ladder of Engagement.

Since success in social media requires involvement of departments and functions across the business, social media can't just be owned through marketing, PR or IT, it has to be a collaborative, shared ownership.

We think it's interesting that IBM, which coined the term 'e-business', today promotes the use of 'social business' which they describe in terms of the power of internal and external connections.

> *Social business is the next step in the overall evolution of business. As our global network of people becomes more instrumented, interconnected and intelligent, dramatic shifts are taking place. The ways in which people interact, relationships form, decisions are made, work is accomplished and goods are purchased are fundamentally changing.*
>
> *Consumers now wield unprecedented power over how brands are perceived and purchases are made. Crowdsourcing is changing industry landscapes by levelling the*

intelligence playing field at an extraordinary rate. In addition, employees are demanding social tools in the workplace, and are actively sidestepping established hierarchies and IT processes to use them. As a result, the world finds itself at a transformative point with regard to how business is done. We believe it is the dawn of a new era – the era of the social business.

(IBM, no date b)

Other key IT service vendors, such as Salesforce and Oracle use a similar term to describe their services today, although the term doesn't fit so well in some countries where 'social business' describes an ethical business contributing to the community.

E-MARKETING INSIGHT

Altimeter defines the scope of social CRM

Within the narrower application of marketing, *social CRM* (Figure 9.2) has been used to describe the integration of social applications across the customer lifecycle and value chain. This model is created by marketing analysts, Altimeter, but consultants such as Accenture and PricewaterhouseCoopers (PwC) use a similar term.

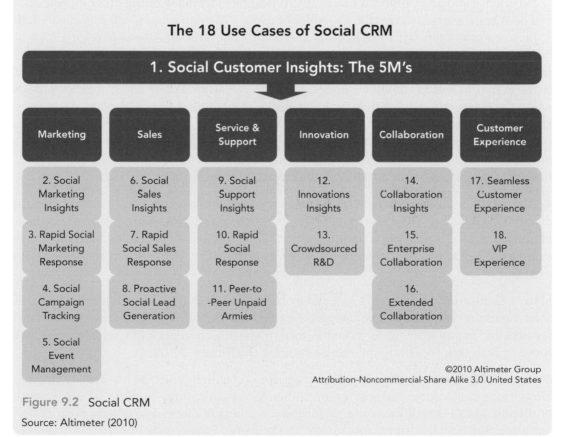

The 18 Use Cases of Social CRM

1. Social Customer Insights: The 5M's

Marketing	Sales	Service & Support	Innovation	Collaboration	Customer Experience
2. Social Marketing Insights	6. Social Sales Insights	9. Social Support Insights	12. Innovations Insights	14. Collaboration Insights	17. Seamless Customer Experience
3. Rapid Social Marketing Response	7. Rapid Social Sales Response	10. Rapid Social Response	13. Crowdsourced R&D	15. Enterprise Collaboration	18. VIP Experience
4. Social Campaign Tracking	8. Proactive Social Lead Generation	11. Peer-to -Peer Unpaid Armies		16. Extended Collaboration	
5. Social Event Management					

Figure 9.2 Social CRM

Source: Altimeter (2010)

A social CRM strategy can be developed by reviewing and prioritizing options in each of the six business applications below.

1 *Marketing* – monitoring, analysis of and response to customer conversations through social listening tools. We think the Altimeter report misses a discussion on integration of social marketing into other campaign tactics like email marketing.

2 *Sales* – understanding where prospects are discussing selection of products and services offered by you and competitors and determining the best way to get involved in the conversation to influence sales and generate leads. Within B2B, LinkedIn is an obvious location that should be monitored.

3 *Service and support* – customer self-help through forums provided by your own site and neutral sites.

4 *Innovation* – using conversations to foster new product development or enhance online offerings is one of the most exciting forms of social CRM.

5 *Collaboration* – this is e-business collaboration within an organization through an intranet and other software tools to encourage all forms of collaboration which support business processes.

6 *Customer experience* – this references the use of social CRM to enhance the customer experience and add value to a brand, which is implied by many of the other aspects above. The Altimeter report gives the examples of using VIP programmes, offering collaboration between customers with shared characteristics to add value and create advocacy.

In the social business, organizations create online communities (both internal and external), social networks and collaborative groups. Research reveals that more and more companies are using the extranet's collaborative facilities to engage customers in new product development and collaborative self-servicing (through shared servicing solutions like Get Satisfaction [www.getsatisfaction.com]). There is also proactive social listening to 'reach out' to customers airing their own grievances. Dell estimates that 80 per cent of its Twitter service consists of finding customers who are registering dissatisfaction through tweeting.

Today, many organizations use collaborative product development tools, such as initiating discussions in blogs to test ideas, or virtual development tools involving customers in the use of collaborative design tools (allowing external designers and engineers to collaborate, using a company's exclusive development software), or testing how well products sell within virtual worlds.

Many organizations (two-thirds in a survey by McKinsey, 2007) use online tools to involve their customers in product development. Each industry sector is different; e.g. both financial services and manufacturing, for example, focus on testing concepts and screening ideas, while those in high tech focus on generating new ideas (McKinsey, 2007).

Crowdsourcing, or more formally *'open innovation'*, facilitates access to a marketplace of ideas from customers, partners or inventors for organizations looking to solve specific problems. LEGO is well known for involving customers in discussion of new product developments. See 'Social business models and the Ladder of Engagement' (3.10).

Figure 9.3   InnoCentive (www.innocentive.com)

InnoCentive (Figure 9.3) is one of the largest commercial examples of crowdsourcing. It is an online marketplace which connects and manages the relationship between 'seekers' and 'solvers'. Seekers are the companies conducting research and development that are looking for new solutions to their business challenges and opportunities. Solvers are the hundreds of thousands of registered members of InnoCentive who can win cash prizes ranging from US$5,000 to US$1m for solving problems in a variety of domains including business and technology.

The social business is not just about having a new dialogue between the brand and the customer, but having a 'trialogue' where customers talk to each other and the brand can then be a small part of billions of conversations. Customers want to talk to each other, to participate and create, and to hear what other customers have to say. Witness book reviews, uploading photos in Pinterest (http://pinterest.com) or Flickr (www.flickr.com), writing comments on people's walls in Facebook, reading blogs, posting comments, and on it goes.

'This is the point where user generated content meets brands – an area fraught with difficulty for the unwary and rich with opportunity for the creative' (Walmsley, 2007).

The extranet helps to integrate suppliers, distributors and stakeholders efficiently into the value network. An organization's intranet has huge potential to increase operational efficiencies and boost teamwork. However, if it isn't sold properly to senior management, and consequently senior managers don't engage, then mismanagement is almost inevitable. Well-managed intranets deliver time – the most limited of all three key resources (the 3Ms – men (and women), money and minutes/time).

Intranets help staff to carry out basic tasks such as finding product information; finding experts; locating forms and processes. However, this requires constant care and attention. Your intranet is not a massive heaving 'rough-and-ready' library where stuff gets stored. Caution is urged when considering using wikis for internal document storage as, without very careful management, they can grow to become a heaving mass of unedited and only partially organized information.

Gerry McGovern says:

> *Your intranet can be a goldmine, so don't sell it like a coalmine. The gold-dust of the intranet is productivity. A great intranet will save time whenever a staff member carries out a common task. These time savings will lead to greater operational efficiency and a more competitive organization (saving five minutes here and two minutes there).*
>
> *(McGovern, 2007)*

Today, using tools like Yammer, companies like Suncorp (www.suncorp.com.au/) are creating internal social networks which help staff integrate across the functions shown in Figure 9.2 (above).

E-MARKETING INSIGHT

Suncorp uses Yammer for internal social collaboration

This case study is adapted from Yammer (2010).

The Suncorp financial services group manages 25 brands in Australia and New Zealand, spanning banking, insurance, investment and superannuation. Suncorp has over 219,000 shareholders, over 16,000 employees and around 7 million customers.

Suncorp uses enterprise social networking tool Yammer (Figure 9.4) to help geographically dispersed people and teams to connect, share, discuss and innovate. It has also helped Suncorp to create a culture where collaboration is more natural, by enabling people to interact online in an open, informal and transparent way. Within a matter of months, Yammer membership grew from a handful of early adopters to over 1,700 users and continues to grow.

Jeff Smith, CEO at Suncorp explains the benefits of Yammer, as follows: 'Yammer has enabled us to harness the wisdom of our people who are spread across multiple teams, geographies and brands to help achieve our purpose of delivering business solutions for competitive advantage.'

The benefits of applying a tool like Yammer to Suncorp can be summarized as:

Figure 9.4   Yammer (www.yammer.com)

- Increased informal knowledge flow across the organization through microblogging
- Overcoming barriers to collaboration, providing instant connection for people, teams, informal networks, communities of practice and other shared interest groups
- Improved alignment between executives and employees by use of broadcast message to communicate messages and quickly crowdsource to get ideas, suggestions and answers to questions
- Helped to stimulate greater sharing and discussion among common role groups; e.g. developers, architects and testers.

Facebook encourages businesses to be social by design

The three elements of social design

According to Facebook (2012), 'social design' defines how we understand ourselves and each other and can be broken down into three core elements: *community, conversation* and *identity*.

- **Community** *refers to the people we know and trust and who help us make decisions. Facebook profile data can be used to personalize the user experience in your app so that it feels familiar, relevant and trusted by default.*

- **Conversation** *refers to the various interactions we have with our communities. Build tools and experiences that give people the power to connect and share, allowing them to effectively listen and learn from each other.*

- **Identity** *refers to our own sense of self and how we are seen by our communities. Users share and interact with others because self[-]expression feels good and rewarding. Help them learn more about themselves and curate their identity.*

(Facebook, 2012a)

In Facebook's IPO filing (Facebook, 2012b), there is a lengthy, impassioned letter from CEO and founder Mark Zuckerberg. It explains how Facebook sees the future of social business on their platform:

> *We think a more open and connected world will help create a stronger economy with more authentic businesses that build better products and services.*

> *As people share more, they have access to more opinions from the people they trust about the products and services they use. This makes it easier to discover the best products and improve the quality and efficiency of their lives.*

> *One result of making it easier to find better products is that businesses will be rewarded for building better products – ones that are personalized and designed around people. We have found that products that are 'social by design' tend to be more engaging than their traditional counterparts, and we look forward to seeing more of the world's products move in this direction.*

> *Our developer platform has already enabled hundreds of thousands of businesses to build higher-quality and more social products. We have seen disruptive new approaches in industries like games, music and news, and we expect to see similar disruption in more industries by new approaches that are social by design.*

SECTION SUMMARY 9.3

Creating the social business through implementing social CRM

The social business involves enhanced communication both internally and externally to gather and respond to feedback and share ideas. It involves providing rapid feedback to customer service requests and using crowdsourcing, where customers can help to shape and promote new products and services.

9.4 The endless journey – reviewing digital marketing capabilities

Like a web site (which is a small part of the e-business or social business), the transformation to e-business is a journey, not a destination. The aim is to enhance the brand by helping customers, followed by suppliers, partners and distributors. Combine this with a drive for continual improvement and you can see why it's an ongoing journey.

EVOLUTIONARY STAGES IN THE DEVELOPMENT OF DIGITAL MARKETING

This journey takes most organizations through several evolutionary stages. Most organizations' web sites evolve from the early-stage, one-way communications sites sometimes called brochureware (listing products and prices), to two-way sites that can interact with customers via making sales transactions and having two-way communications whether sales, emails, discussions or automated interactions.

Today, we add in social or collaborative facilities and it becomes a lot more interesting. As shown in Chapter 5, we need to use APIs and plug-ins to integrate our web site with relevant social networks to encourage sharing and discussion related to a brand. As Mark Zuckerberg of Facebook has said (Facebook, 2012b), we need to be 'Social by Design'. There may then be further evolution into an e-business system with the web site often at the hub of all processes.

A five-year analysis of leading consumer web sites supported the notion that web sites are making the transition from a mere spoke in the marketing wheel to the hub itself (Flores and Eltvedt, 2005).

Web sites are moving beyond just helping customers to helping internal staff (intranet), and external customers, distributors, suppliers and strategic partners (extranet).

E-MARKETING INSIGHT

Digital capability maturity models

A *capability maturity model* shows the series of common stages that organizations pass through during their adoption – and increasing refinement – of digital marketing.

In a digital marketing context, 'capability' refers to the processes, structures and skills you adopt for planning and implementing digital marketing.

Capability maturity models can help you to:

● Review current approaches to digital marketing to identify areas for improvement
● Benchmark against competitors who are in the same/different sector/industry
● Identify best practice among more advanced adopters
● Set targets and develop strategies for improving capabilities.

Carnegie Mellon SEI

One well-known capability maturity model has been devised by Carnegie Mellon Software Engineering Institute (www.sei.cmu.edu) to help organizations improve their software development practices.

While your field of application is quite different, the concept is readily transferable. The Carnegie Mellon SEI describes its role as: 'To identify best practices useful in helping organizations increase the maturity of their processes.'

A detailed stage model which businesses can use to benchmark their e-commerce capabilities was developed by Dave Chaffey for Econsultancy (2005, 2008), based on research with marketing directors and e-commerce managers in a range of companies.

The capabilities evaluated are presented in Table 9.1. This was based on research designed to identify the challenges faced in managing e-commerce and the approaches used. Since the model was created, social media and social business have increased as concerns, so these should also be included at higher levels of capability. Such is their importance that it could be worthwhile reviewing social media marketing capability using a framework like that introduced in Chapter 5 (Figure 5.5).

SECTION SUMMARY 9.4

The endless journey – reviewing digital marketing capabilities

Capability maturity models are useful for showing the position of a company on its journey to e-business or social business. Through reviewing and benchmarking, a roadmap for future implementation can be developed.

9.5 Budgeting for digital marketing

Budgeting for digital marketing involves many different media channels like search marketing and social media marketing, and many platforms such as the desktop web site and the mobile web site. It also requires the development of the content assets that are so important to the user experience and content marketing.

Table 9.1 Stage model of e-commerce adoption based on Econsultancy research

E-commerce capability level	(A) Strategy process and performance improvement	(B) Structure: organizational location of e-commerce	(C) Senior management buy-in	(D) Marketing integration	(E) Online marketing focus
1 Unplanned	*Limited.* Online channels not part of business planning process. Web analytics data collected, but unlikely to be reviewed or actioned.	*Experimentation.* No clear centralized e-commerce resources in business. Main responsibility typically within IT.	*Limited.* No direct involvement in planning and little necessity seen for involvement.	*Poor integration.* Some interested marketers may experiment with e-communications tools.	*Content focus.* Creation of online brochures and catalogues. Adoption of first style guidelines.
2 Diffuse management	*Low-level.* Online referenced in planning, but with limited channel-specific objectives. Some campaign analysis by interested staff.	*Diffuse.* Small central e-commerce group or single manager, possibly with steering group controlled by marketing. Many separate web sites, separate online initiatives; e.g. tools adopted and agencies for search marketing, email marketing. E-communications funding from brands/businesses may be limited.	*Aware.* Management becomes aware of expenditure and potential of online channels.	*Separate.* Increased adoption of e-communications tools and growth of separate sites and microsites continues. Media spend still dominantly offline.	*Traffic focus.* Increased emphasis on driving visitors to site through Pay Per Click search marketing and affiliate marketing.
3 Centralized management	*Specific.* Specific channel objectives set. Web analytics capability not integrated to give unified reporting	*Centralized.* Common platform for content management, web analytics. Preferred-supplier list of digital agencies. Centralized, independent e-commerce function, often a	*Involved.* Directly involved in annual review and ensures review structure involving senior managers from marketing, IT,	*Arm's-length.* Marketing and e-commerce mainly work together during planning process. Limited review within	*Conversion and customer experience focus.* Initiatives for usability, accessibility and revision of content management

Table 9.1 (Continued)

E-commerce capability level	(A) Strategy process and performance improvement	(B) Structure: organizational location of e-commerce	(C) Senior management buy-in	(D) Marketing integration	(E) Online marketing focus
	of campaign effectiveness.	profit-centre, but with some digital-specific responsibilities by country/product/brand.	operations and finance.	campaigns. Senior e-commerce team-members responsible for encouraging adoption of digital marketing throughout organization.	system (including search engine optimization) are common at this stage.
4 Decentralized operations	*Refined.* Close cooperation between e-commerce and marketing. Targets and performance reviewed monthly. Towards unified reporting. Project debriefs.	*Decentralized.* Digital marketing skills more developed in business with integration of e-commerce into planning and execution at business or country level. E-retailers commonly adopt direct channel organization of which e-commerce is one channel. Online channel P + L sometimes controlled by businesses/brands, but with central budget for continuous e-communications spend (search, affiliates, e-communications).	*Driving performance.* Involved in review at least monthly.	*Partnership.* Marketing and e-commerce work closely together through year. Digital media spend starts to reflect importance of online channels to business and consumers.	*Retention focus.* Initiatives on analysis of customer purchase and response behaviour and implementation of well-defined touch strategies with emphasis on email marketing. Loyalty drivers well known and managed.

5 Integrated and optimized	Multi-channel process. The interactions and financial contribution of different channels are well understood and resourced and improved accordingly.	Integrated. Majority of digital skills within business and e-commerce team commonly positioned with-in marketing or direct sales operation. Supporting process of 'front-end' systems development skills typically retained in a central e-commerce team which is more likely to be a cost centre.	Integral. Less frequent/in-depth involvement required. Annual planning and 6-monthly or quarterly review.	Complete. Marketing has full complement of digital marketing skills, but calls on specialist resource from agencies or central e-commerce resource as required. Online potential not constrained by traditional budgeting processes.	Optimization focus. Initiatives to improve acquisition, conversion and retention according to developments in access platform and customer experience technologies. May use temporary multi-disciplinary team to drive performance.

Budgeting involves achieving the best balance of investment between these traffic-building and other e-marketing activities. Other aspects of resourcing that must be balanced are between online and offline promotion and between campaign and continuous ('always-on') traffic-building activities.

KEY MARKETING COSTS

As a starting point for a new digital marketing investment, you need to be clear on the right balance between expenditure on:

1 Creating the user experience – this is the initial web site design and build (including mobile apps and creation of company social pages including Facebook apps)
2 Ongoing content creation and optimization
3 Traffic building or reach, covering the paid, owned and earned media we introduced in Chapter 1 (see Figure 1.11).

In previous editions of this book, we suggested that many European sites have allocated resources between build, optimization and traffic in the ratio 5:2:1. However, for many US sites, these were in the order 1:2:5; i.e. with the emphasis firmly on traffic. You need to review carefully what is right for your business. We believe the biggest mistake made by companies, particularly small to medium-sized companies, is to create a site and not update it, because budget or resource isn't available for ongoing content creation and optimization. So try to plan for this.

SELECTING THE BEST COMMUNICATIONS MIX

Deciding on the best communications mix for an online campaign is perhaps more of an art than a science, because there are so many elements (which we introduced at the start of Chapter 7) which should influence your decision. As a reminder, when selecting each digital marketing channel, you should assess its:

- *Cost Per Acquisition* (CPA). You will naturally be looking to minimize this, it will depend on the combination of media costs, delivery of the right target audience and conversion rates.
- *Volume*. More campaign expenditure will typically go into the channels that drive volume – often paid search, which can also have a well- controlled CPA. However, having a low-CPA channel is not helpful if it doesn't drive volume because it is not possible to purchase sufficient media.
- *Conversion*. Not all digital channels convert equally; for example, paid search tends to convert slightly more highly than natural search since searchers have sought out the paid ad. Similarly, paid search tends to convert better than display ads since with the former, searchers have higher intent and are more directed, while with display ads, they may have clicked more out of impulse.
- *Branding impact*. Channels such as display advertising or editorial coverage may not result in

high clickthrough rates, but testing shows they do build awareness of products, services and promotions.

- *Flexibility*. This is important for larger campaigns; is it possible to build in tests and amend the creative to gain better results, as is the case with paid search and display ads?

- *Frequency*. Does the channel enable you to retarget to repeat messages as is the case with behavioural retargeting and paid search?

- *Risk*. Is it a tried-and-tested channel with which you can be confident of delivering results? Viral marketing, for instance, or renting an email list are both high-risk strategies; display advertising and paid search are lower-risk.

E-MARKETING INSIGHT

Zed Media on assessing the right online marketing mix

Selection of the right type of e-tools will vary according to whether your campaign is focused on creating direct response, which is more typical for transactional categories such as finance, travel and retail; or whether awareness is more important, which is more typical for many business-to-business categories or consumer goods.

Figure 9.5 shows how one agency estimates that the mix can vary according to type of campaign. You can see that for direct response, paid search and affiliate marketing are often most suitable with lower budgets, while display advertising is a relatively small part of the mix. This is reversed for brand awareness campaigns.

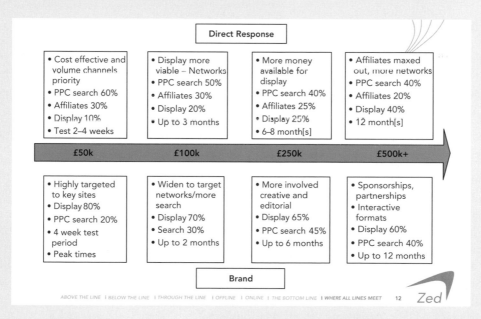

Figure 9.5   Options for varying the mix for direct response and brand awareness campaigns

Source: Zed Media

BALANCE BETWEEN ONLINE AND OFFLINE PROMOTION

Defining the correct balance between investment in online and offline promotion is another key aspect of resourcing. The appropriate balance is determined by many factors, but the most important is the percentage of sales that are informed or completed online. In the foreseeable future, investment in offline communications will still dominate overall, because of its power in creating awareness and demand for brands which will often then give rise to site visits.

BALANCE OF CAMPAIGN AND CONTINUOUS TRAFFIC BUILDING

It would be a mistake to spend an entire promotion budget on campaigns. A proportion should be left for expenditure required every month of the year for search engine re-registration and updating; updating copy to improve search engine positions; link building; managing long-term sponsorship arrangements and direct opt-in email.

SECTION SUMMARY 9.5

Budgeting for digital marketing

Budgeting is about achieving the right balance of: promotion, service and design; online and offline promotion and campaign activities; and continuous traffic building. For campaigns, resourcing decisions include: banner run length, ad-weighting, targeting and campaign size.

9.6 Making the business case for e-marketing investment

As an e-marketer, you will believe in the power of digital marketing to get results and you will want to try new techniques. But your colleagues may be more cynical and rightly so. They will have seen different marketing approaches come and go and will be reluctant to change from tried-and-tested approaches – 'We've always done it this way'.

For your own and your colleagues' benefit, you need to find ways to *prove* the value that e-marketing can generate for an organization.

Although digital marketing has been described as 'the most measurable medium ever' (Bughin *et al.*, 2008) it is often not so easy to prove the value of digital marketing investment. Yes, you can determine for a Google Adwords or email marketing campaign the clicks through to a retail site which generate a sale, but not all marketing is that simple. We know from Chapter 2 that many customers take several visits to convert, responding to different stimuli, so we need to apply attribution modeling to determine the value. What if the site doesn't sell direct, but only generates leads which are fulfilled offline by phone; or if it does sell direct, but many visitors are only browsing the catalogue. Other investments such as social media or content marketing similarly lack a clear 'cause and effect' relationship.

In this section, we recommend different approaches that can be used for justifying digital media investment at the appropriate level. Which options work best will naturally depend on who you are trying to convince and the culture of the organization; does it support emotional or rational decisions?

TYPES OF DIGITAL INVESTMENT DECISION

There are different types of digital investment and the justification will vary according to these. The main types of investment decision are:

- *Media investment* – you'll be looking for a bigger piece of an existing pie or increasing the size of the pie.
- *Agency resource* – outsourcing creation of digital assets or management of digital marketing campaigns.
- *Internal resource* – new staff to work within marketing or IT.
- *Capital expenditure (CapEx)* – this is when businesses need to buy new equipment or a communications platform such as a server or invest in developing a new system. This spend can be amortized over several years. Software can be treated in this way too, according to accounting practices in a company or tax regimes.
- *Operational expenditure (OpEx)* – this includes the planning, designing and testing of a system. The creation of new services using an agile method can mean that a higher proportion of cost is treated as CapEx, compared to a traditional system where it is based on OpEx.
- *Different digital marketing activities* – the investment types described above can be applied across the digital marketing framework of PRACE – Plan, Reach, interAct, Convert and Engage (long-term).

METHODS OF JUSTIFYING INVESTMENT

1. Prove value through tests

The single best way to convince colleagues of the value of digital marketing is to prove the impact of digital marketing through a test in your own company. Many of the other methods such as modelling and benchmarking still require a 'leap of faith' to believing, so it's best if you can run a test.

It can be difficult to isolate the impact of a digital campaign if it also involves other media, so consider these forms of testing that can help with making the case for digital channels:

- *Online-only launch*. A new product or category can be launched in the online channel only or can have upweighted digital spend compared to a normal launch or campaign. This can help prove the impact of digital media.
- *Adjusting budgets through time*. If you vary the mix through time, this can help you see the impact of adding or removing elements to a mix through the campaign or year. For example, if practical, switch off an 'always-on' component such as search marketing or display advertising for one month. Since most prospects don't convert immediately, it may require several weeks of testing to achieve this. When reviewing the impact of these tests, it's important not only to look at visits generated, but other measures of brand awareness/favourability

such as brand search volume and conversion rates (which tend to be correlated with awareness and favourability generated by advertising).

- *Hold-out testing*. This approach involves a test group that does not receive a particular communication such as an email or a catalogue, to help in understanding the combination of channels that work best.

However, you do already need investment to run a test, so some of the later recommendations will help with this.

2. Piggy backing

This is not a technical term! We're recommending that you make use of agreed investments and projects to run tests which may justify other future investments. If, for example, there is already a focus on improving email marketing or social media marketing within a company, then how can these be used to make other changes – for example, investing in a content strategy or improving the use of attribution modelling.

3. Improve the quality of your digital analytics

Throughout *Emarketing Excellence* we have stressed the importance of making use of web analytics.

To prove value, you have to 'get your analytics house in order'. This means tracking a lead or sale to its origin, as far as is possible, by:

- *Detailed tracking using marketing source codes* – for example, make sure your social media, display advertising, affiliate marketing and email marketing is tracked through the relevant source codes

- *Use of attribution* – if you're using Google Analytics, use features like Multi-Channel Funnel Assists

- *Track offline outcomes* – for example, if you generate telephone calls from the web site, use call-tracking software to track these carefully.

4. Return-on-investment models

The commercial argument will be the strongest in many organizations, so we start here. You should create conversion-based models to illustrate the return on investment (ROI). Figure 9.6 shows an example where the impact of increasing the level of visitors or conversion rate by a percentage can be used to show the value generated.

These models can be refined and used for budgeting campaign investments by breaking them down into media investment and then further down into digital media channels such as display advertising and paid search (see Chapter 10, Table 10.3).

If a site doesn't directly generate revenue, the value of a lead or engagement with the site will have to be determined, and then average lead or engagement value can be used in the model.

	Performance measure	Scenario 1	Scenario 2
Acquisition	Current unique visitors to site or section per year	1,000,000	1,000,000
	Potential incremental visitors	1.00%	2.00%
	Cost of increasing visitors (Year 1)	£4,000	£20,000
	Potential incremental visits	10,000	20,000
	Potential future visits total	1,010,000	1,020,000
Conversion	Current conversion rate	2.00%	2.00%
	Incremental conversion rate change	20.00%	5.00%
	Cost of improving conversion (Year 1)	£20,000	£20,000
	New conversion rate	2.40%	2.10%
	Current sales	20,000	20,000
	Potential incremental leads or sales (from conversion)	4,000	1,000
	Potential future sales total (from visits and conversion)	24,240	21,420
Sales value	Current average order value	£50	£50
	Potential incremental average order value	10.00%	0.00%
	Cost of improving AOV (Year 1)	£10,000	£10,000
	New AOV	£55.00	£50.00
	Current revenue	£1,000,000	£1,000,000
	Potential incremental revenue (from AOV)	£100,000	£0
	Potential future revenue total (from visits, conv and AOV)	£1,333,200	£1,071,000
Returns	Current returns rate	10.00%	10.00%
	Potential incremental returns change	5.00%	3.00%
	Cost of improving returns rate	£5,000	£5,000
	New returns rate	9.50%	9.70%
	Current revenue (with returns)	£900,000	£900,000
	Potential incremental revenue (with reduced returns)	£905,000	£903,000
	Potential future revenue total (with all improvements above)	£1,206,546	£967,113
Channel profitability	Margin	15%	15%
	Current site profit	£135,000	£135,000
	Future site profit	£180,982	£145,067
	Change in profit (%)	34%	7%
	Incremental profit	£45,982	£10,067
	Total initiative costs	£39,000	£55,000
	Return on investment	18%	–82%

Figure 9.6 Simple conversion-based model

Source: Smart Insights (2012)

Mixed-mode purchases should also be assessed; for example, whether phone tracking or match backs between online users and catalogue buyers can be used to determine how offline purchases arise from online research (ROPO; see Figure 1.9 in Chapter 1).

Lifetime value models are even more powerful to help in justifying investment since they can be used to look at the value that new investments will deliver over a period of years and so calculate the break-even period.

Lifetime value (LTV) is the total contribution (sales price minus direct costs) that a customer or group of customers will provide a company over their total relationship with it.

See Kumar *et al.* (2007) for an explanation of LTV calculations. LTV modelling is based on estimating the income and costs associated with each customer over a period of time, and then calculating the net present value in current monetary terms using a discount rate value applied over the period.

Lifetime value modelling is a great technique since it answers the question: 'How much can I afford to invest in acquiring a new customer?'

If online marketers try to answer this from a short-term perspective, as is often the case – i.e. by judging it based on the profit from a single sale on an e-commerce site – there are two problems:

- We become very focused on short-term return on investment (ROI) and so may not invest sufficiently to grow our business.
- We assume that each new customer is worth precisely the same to us and we ignore differentials in loyalty and profitability between differing types of customer.

Lifetime value analysis enables marketers to:

- Plan and measure investment in customer acquisition programmes
- Identify and compare critical target segments
- Measure the effectiveness of alternative customer retention strategies
- Establish the true value of a company's customer base
- Make decisions about products and offers
- Make decisions about the value of introducing new digital technologies which will affect lifetime value.

E-MARKETING INSIGHT

An example of a simple lifetime value model

Figure 9.7 gives an example of a lifetime value model.

1 *Customers* – this is the number of initial customers (100,000). It declines each year dependent on the retention rate (row 5).

2 *Margin* – this is the profit (gross margin) contributed by this group of customers based on the typical type of product they purchase.

3 *Years* – lifetime value shows the revenue and cost for each year although it can be used for other time periods; e.g. a monthly subscription.

4 *Customers* – this is the number of customers in each year dependent on the retention rate (row 5)

	A	B	C	D	E	F
1	New customers in Year 1	100,000				
2	Margin	20%				
3		Year 1	Year 2	Year 3	Year 4	Year 5
4	Customers	100,000	50,000	27,500	16,500	10,725
5	Retention rate	50%	55%	60%	65%	70%
6	Average revenue per annum	£100	£120	£140	£160	£180
7	Total revenue	£10,000,000	£6,000,000	£3,850,000	£2,640,000	£1,930,500
8	Net profit	£2,000,000	£1,200,000	£770,000	£528,000	£386,100
9	Discount rate	1.000	0.860	0.740	0.636	0.547
10	NPV Contribution	£2,000,000	£1,032,000	£569,492	£335,808	£211,197
11	Cumulative NPV contribution	£2,000,000	£3,032,000	£3,601,492	£3,937,300	£4,148,497
12	Lifetime value at net present value	£20	£30	£36	£39	£41

Figure 9.7 A simple lifetime value model

5 *Retention rate* – the proportion of customers who stay with the company through time. In lifetime value modelling, this is usually found to increase year-on-year, since customers who stay loyal are more likely to remain loyal.

6 *Average revenue per annum* – likewise, typical spend increases through time.

7 *Total revenue* – calculated through multiplying rows 3 and 5.

8 *Net profit (at 20 per cent margin)* – LTV modelling is based on profit contributed by this group of customers; i.e. revenue multiplied by margin.

9 *Discount rate* – since the value of money held at a point in time will decrease due to inflation, a discount rate factor is applied to calculate the value of future returns in terms of current-day value.

10 *NPV contribution* – this is the profitability after taking the discount factor into account to give the net present value in future years. This is calculated by multiplying row 8 by row 9.

11 *Cumulative NPV contribution* – this adds the previous year's NPV for each year.

12 *Lifetime value at net present value* – this is a value per customer calculated by dividing row 11 by the initial number of donors in Year 1. This is the figure that is used to set an acceptable Cost Per Acquisition.

5. Competitor and industry benchmarking

Benchmarking is simply comparing your own capabilities or performance to other companies. It can be a blend of a rational argument and an emotional argument as you show what other companies are doing.

Table 9.2 gives some example of benchmarking applications for digital marketing.

Table 9.2 Types of digital marketing benchmarking and relevant sources

Benchmarking approach	Comments	Sources
Capability maturity modelling	Requires estimation of competitors' capabilities	See Smart Insights (2012) Healthcheck and Section 9.4
Site feature benchmarking	Review functionality	The e-CRM Egg (Chapter 4) provides a framework for this
Reach/site usage	Hitwise gives a paid version; the DoubleClick Adplanner is the best version for a larger site	Google DoubleClick AdPlanner http://bit.ly/smartsize
SEO performance	Based on ranking compared to competitors	Advanced Web Ranking is one tool recommended here: http://bit.ly/smartranking
SEO backlinks	The Majestic SEO tool gives	http://bit.ly/smartlinkcheck

Table 9.2 *(Continued)*

Benchmarking approach	Comments	Sources
	backlink history useful for benchmarking against competitors	
Media investment	For example, the IAB in the UK has a compilation of ad spend on digital media	The UK IAB: www.iabuk.net
Act	Compare length of visits	Compilation of bounce and duration from Google Analytics http://bit.ly/smartbounce
Conversion	Compare 'add to basket' and 'basket to checkout' conversion.	See Smart Insights conversion compilation http://bit.ly/smartconversion
Multi-channel conversion	Consider the Research Online, Purchase Offline (ROPO) for competitors	Other research studies may be available
Engage	Email and social media marketing benchmarking	www.smartinsights.com/email-marketing/ and http://www.smartinsights.com/social-media-marketing/

One of the difficulties with benchmarking is finding data from similar companies.

E-MARKETING INSIGHT

David Bowen of Bowen Craggs & Co on benchmarking

Bowen Craggs & Co (www.bowencraggs.com) produce the FT corporate site benchmarking for FTSE 500 companies.

In an interview, David Bowen explains more about the approach:

> **Who is the main audience/roles for applying your index to improve their corporate sites?**
>
> *Anyone with responsibility for big websites – corporate, public, NGO. The direct audience is likely to consist of web or digital managers, though people throughout the comms and marketing teams want to know what best practice is and what their rivals are doing. In some companies the heads of corporate comms, marketing, or even investor relations or finance directors, take a direct interest. It depends how important they believe online communications is.*

2011 overall position	2011 overall score	Company	Construction	Message	Contact	Serving society	Serving investors	Serving the media	Serving jobseekers	Serving customers	Total	2010 score	2010 position	URL	Country
1	217	Siemens	13	41	10	27	22	28	24	22	217	210	2	www.siemens.com	Germany
2	216	BP	49	36	10	28	26	21	24	22	216	210	2	www.bp.com	UK
3	213	Royal Dutch Shell	47	37	9	26	28	21	24	21	213	213	1	www.shell.com	UK-Netherlands
4	209	Eni	44	36	10	27	27	24	21	20	209	200	6	www.eni.it	Italy
5	206	Unilever	47	38	8	25	25	20	23	20	206	198	8	www.unilever.com	UK-Netherlands
6	204	Roche	39	41	9	22	22	25	23	23	204	209	4	www.roche.com	Switzerland
7	200	General Electric	43	39	8	25	18	21	23	23	200	199	7	www.ge.com	US
	200	Intel Corporation	47	31	9	25	26	19	22	21	200	189	24	www.intel.com	US
9	199	British American Tobacco*	46	36	10	25	25	19	16	22	199	194	13	www.bat.com	UK
	199	Novartis	47	37	10	19	22	23	19	22	199	191	21	wwwnovartis.com	Switzerland
	199	Wal-Mart Stores*	47	36	9	20	22	24	19	22	199	190	22	www.walmartstores.com	US
12	198	IBM	39	36	7	23	22	24	24	23	198	192	18	www.ibm.com	US
13	197	Chevron	45	38	10	26	24	16	20	18	197	192	18	www.chevron.com	US
14	196	Nestlé	40	36	7	25	23	25	17	23	196	195	12	www.nestlé.com	Switzerland
15	195	AstraZeneca	42	37	9	21	24	20	24	18	195	196	9	www.astrazeneca.com	UK
	195	Cisco Systems	36	28	9	24	24	26	24	24	195	193	15	www.cisco.com	US
	195	Procter & Gamble	48	34	7	24	21	21	21	19	195	196	9	www.pg.com	US
18	194	Rio Tinto	43	35	7	23	26	19	20	21	194	201	5	www.riotinto.com	Australia
19	191	GlaxoSmithKline	46	35	8	24	25	18	20	15	191	192	18	www.gsk.com	UK
	191	Statoil	44	39	3	24	24	22	19	16	191	186	27	www.statoil.com	Norway

Figure 9.8   Corporate site benchmarking

Source: Bowen Craggs & Co (www.bowencraggs.com)

Some companies get more detailed benchmarks of their own sites (including social media channels), which include recommendations and pointers to best practice inside the Index and elsewhere.

They will use these as working documents and set up a programme to implement improvements. Companies also use the database to spot best practice in specific areas, and to see what their competitors are doing. One client talks to non-competing companies directly, and also sees what we have said about these companies' sites – it finds this twin track approach comforting and helpful, especially as the two sources nearly always support each other.

Which learnings from effective corporate sites do you think smaller businesses could incorporate?

The rules of good website design are the same, whatever the size of the site or the company. Big companies are more likely to get the 'message' side right – they realise their website is their main window to much of the world, and put a lot of effort into making sure their brand values (not just visual ones) are reflected in it. It is worth looking at some of the best home pages – they are the most important square foot of real estate a company owns, and the immediate impression they give is vital.

It is worth seeing how big companies are using web technologies such as video and interactivity. If, say, Shell, is happy to embed YouTube videos in its sites, then arguably anyone should be – big does not necessarily mean spendthrift.

Although small companies are often more adept at using social media channels than big ones, it is worth looking at some of their efforts. Using Flickr as a photo library is a good example – again where the low cost approach may well be the most sensible one.

(Bowen, forthcoming)

6. Optimization

A/B and multivariate testing are a great opportunity to show how a 'test–learn–refine' approach generates more leads and sales.

A/B testing of two different versions of a landing page is a low-cost activity if you're using the Google Website Optimizer. Creating a story of how changes to the site layout, messaging and offer have improved results can help justify further investment.

See Section 9.9 for more detail on these approaches.

7. Market research studies

Traditional research to gain insights on customer motivations, preferences and behaviours is still important. This can show how many people buy offline after researching online, for example.

8. Forward planning

We find that many companies still don't have a clear e-marketing plan as discussed in Chapter 1, Section 1.1.

Creating a structured e-marketing plan as a stand-alone document or integrating it into existing plans can definitely help to give a focus to digital media. Creating such a plan is a reason to canvass colleagues, taking them through the stages of SOSTAC®. For example, involve colleagues in these ways:

- *Situation analysis* – ask them to review the current use of digital technology and multi-channel marketing – how do they rate the capabilities? Involve them in creating a SWOT analysis with a key issues summary.
- *Objective setting* – find a method of showing how digital channel objectives align with current business goals and strategic initiatives.
- *Strategy* – involve colleagues in reviewing the strategic options by asking them to score the value of different business options, considering the value to the business and the costs.
- *Tactics* – these are less relevant, but you can give illustrations of the different approaches.
- *Actions* – a roadmap can be created to show priorities and aid discussion of what should happen when.
- *Control* – use the analytics reporting not just to show trends, but make them actionable through aligning them with business goals. Use a risk assessment where risks are rated by impact and probability to show the potential consequences if there is insufficient investment.

Creating and reviewing a plan which is independent from existing types of plan gives a good opportunity for collaborative discussion. Different ways of discussion will be appropriate in different types of company; for example, review workshops or regular steering groups involving 'stakeholders' from across the organization.

Making the business case for e-marketing investment

Making the business case for digital marketing investment depends on the culture of the company and the attitudes of those you are looking to convince. Emotional arguments may work in some cases. But for business owners and financial directors, quantitative approaches based on conversion and lifetime value models are most likely to give you success.

9.7 Selecting the right suppliers for digital marketing

Selecting a communications agency is seldom straightforward. You have to choose between full-service agencies and numerous specialists – brand, direct marketing, media buying and advertising agencies.

Digital marketing has spawned a whole new plethora of specialist agencies, and many traditional agencies have extended their portfolios to include digital media.

When choosing suppliers, you need to consider the level and type of marketing expertise you require:

1   Strategy
2   Market research and analysis
3   Campaign creative concepts
4   Asset and content development
5   Campaign execution, including reporting analysis and adjustment
6   Infrastructure (e.g. web design and build, ad serving, email broadcasting, evaluation).

Suppliers are usually asked to undertake a range of campaign communications: web site design and build, online advertising, search engine marketing, email marketing and wireless or interactive TV campaigns.

The main digital supplier options are:

1   *Full-service digital agency (or a specialist unit within a traditional agency)* with expertise in:

- *The core digital media channels* – online advertising, search marketing and email marketing; with or without affiliate marketing and online PR
- *Display advertising* – concept, creative development, media planning and buying
- *Web site design and build* – full sites, mobile sites, company social site or campaign microsites.

2   *Specialist digital agency.* Appearances can be deceptive and in reality, there are a limited number of specialist agencies. Typical specialists include:

- Strategy and planning consultants
- Web site design and build – analysis, web site design, HTML coding and JavaScript plus programming
- Online ad creative and online ad buying
- Search engine marketing including SEO and paid search specialists, although most search agencies today offer both
- Mobile marketing and interactive TV specialists
- Social media and e-PR agencies
- Evaluation and improvement specialists – increasingly merging into units that provide: usability specialists, accessibility specialists, web analytics/web metrics evaluation, online customer research groups (online surveys and focus groups)
- Other rare specialist agencies, typically combined with other larger agency disciplines – email marketing, online PR, affiliate marketing.

3 *Traditional agency*. These range from providing a full service through to specialists for advertising, direct marketing, market research, sales promotion or PR.

4 *In-house resource*. Larger organizations may have in-house specialists who plan and execute campaigns, typically concerning web site design and infrastructure.

RESOURCING SEARCH MARKETING

One of your more difficult and most important decisions will be whether to hire an SEO specialist and a separate Pay Per Click specialist, or try to combine the two skills in one role. Since successful SEO today is more dependent on content and social media marketing than the technical factor, there is also a big overlap in resources for managing these with SEO. Indeed, in many companies, there is a joint responsibility for SEO and social media marketing – ideal if you can find someone with the hybrid skills.

Anne Holland of Marketing Sherpa (www.marketingsherpa.com) advises:

> *Your search campaign is like building a house. You need specialists like a carpenter and a plumber, and they can't do each other's jobs remotely well. You also need a contractor to oversee both and make sure the work fits together under the same roof and in the same budget.*
>
> *So, don't trust an agency rep who glibly says they can do both. Instead, ask to meet the specific specialists for yourself – and make sure that they are two different people in two different departments.*
>
> *The bigger firms have enough resources to have two departments plus account reps to supervise everything. However, there's a bigger price tag for this convenience.*
>
> *You may choose to be your own general contractor and hire two specialist firms instead. Just be sure to budget enough time in your schedule to manage them.*
>
> *(Holland, 2004)*

Here are some other perspectives on outsourcing SEM, based on some interviews with search agency staff and marketing managers by Dave Chaffey in 2008.

This need for specialism in different SEO activities is indicated by the staff roles of Greenlight (www.greenlightdigital.com), one of the largest UK/European agencies which has also opened offices in the United States. Andreas Pouros, COO at Greenlight, describes their key roles as SEO consultant/analyst; copywriter; link builder; account manager; social media specialist and SEO developers.

Andrew Girdwood, head of search at multinational SEM agency bigmouthmedia (www.bigmouthmedia.com) believes that having this range of skills on the client side is impractical. He said: '[A]n in-house team would need to be unfeasibly large in order to match an agency who has an SEO research department who trial new approaches and monitor SEO blogs, news and forums'.

Clare Brandish, sales & marketing director of Ragdale Hall spa, which uses agency MediaCo, believes in a different approach: she argues: 'We recognize that, in the past, today and going forward, search optimization is a specialism in an ever-changing landscape.' She adds that 'By collaborating with a good agency, we are confident of receiving knowledgeable, professional and up-to-date service.'

Of course, a 'mix and match' approach can also be used. Elliot Zissman, then director of multi-channel retailer Totally Fitness, believed that some activities such as keyword research and copywriting are best kept in-house, using initial guidance from an agency. But other aspects, such as technical site audits to ensure that the search engine robots are crawling the pages, together with link generation and online PR, are best outsourced to specialist agencies.

He explains:

> [W]e have gained a lot of knowledge from using an agency, but going forwards I envisage the majority of the work will be done in-house. This is because . . . we feel we gained good value for money initially, but that agency fees are hard to justify for what is relatively low-level work going forwards (link building, writing content, etc).
>
> (Zissman, 2008)

E-MARKETING INSIGHT

The virtual marketplace

There is now a wide range of online services to help you find and manage your out-sourced marketing sites. The four sites listed below are some of the more popular services used by people online.

They include an organized directory of freelancers. You would publish your brief/requirements and providers can then apply for that job. At this point, you can organize/sort through the applications in each site's interface. It is easy to filter by hours worked, cost and feedback rating.

1 *oDesk* (www.odesk.com). oDesk is a very well-established crowdsourcing platform with marketing activities placed.

2 *Elance* (www.elance.com). Elance is similar to oDesk, it is well-established, and has a large database of workers. The key difference, however, is that Elance has a larger focus on programming.

3 *Freelancer.com* (www.freelancer.com). Freelancer is a much more online marketing-oriented platform; with over 3 million members, it makes Elance look small. Examples of projects range from simple link-building tasks through to web site build and translation.

4 *99 designs* (http://99designs.com). 99 designs is an example of a niche outsourcing site, focusing purely on creative freelancers and therefore design/creative briefs.

SECTION SUMMARY 9.7

Selecting the right suppliers for digital marketing

We reviewed the options for selecting a digital marketing agency:

1 Full-service digital agency
2 Specialist digital agency
3 Traditional agency
4 In-house resource.

The importance of owning strategy, customer insight and analysis was discussed.

9.8 Change management for digital transformation

Figure 9.9 shows key aspects or levers of change that need to be assessed in order to maximize the benefits of e-business. The main change levers required are:

1 Market and business model
2 Business process
3 Organizational structure, culture and staff responsibilities
4 Technology infrastructure changes.

These are all major changes that are required for an organization to be agile enough to respond to marketplace changes and deliver competitive customer service.

A useful framework for reviewing an organization's capabilities to manage e-business-related change is shown in Table 9.3. This 7S framework was developed by McKinsey consultants in the 1970s and summarized by Waterman *et al.* (1980).

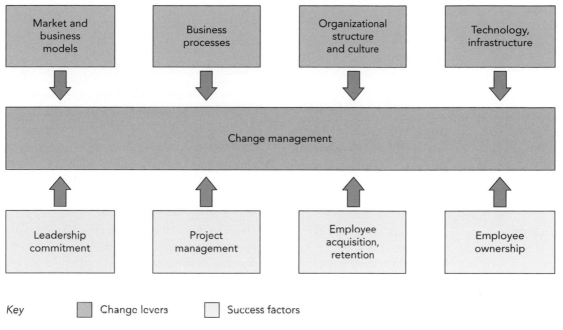

Figure 9.9   Factors governing the response to change

Table 9.3   The 7S strategic framework and its application to e-business management

Element of 7S mode	Relevance to e-business management	Key issues
Strategy	The contribution of e-business in influencing and supporting organizations' strategy	• Gaining appropriate budgets and demonstrating/delivering value and ROI from budgets. Annual planning approach • Techniques for using e-business to impact [on] organization strategy • Techniques for aligning e-business strategy with organizational and marketing strategy
Structure	The modification of organizational structure to support e-business	• Integration of e-commerce team with other management, marketing (corporate communications, brand marketing, direct marketing) and IT staff • Use of cross-functional teams and steering groups • Insourcing *vs* outsourcing
Systems	The development of specific processes, procedures or information systems to support Internet marketing	• Campaign-planning approach integration • Managing/sharing customer information • Managing content quality • Unified reporting of digital marketing effectiveness

Table 9.3 *(Continued)*

Element of 7S mode	Relevance to e-business management	Key issues
		• In-house *vs* external best-of-breed *vs* external integrated technology solutions
Staff	The breakdown of staff in terms of their background, age and sex and characteristics such as IT *vs* marketing, use of contractors/ consultants	• Insourcing *vs* outsourcing • Achieving senior management buy-in/involvement with digital marketing • Staff recruitment and retention. Virtual working • Staff development and training
Style	Includes both the way in which key managers behave in achieving the organization's goals and the cultural style of the organization as a whole	• Relates to role of the e-commerce team in influencing strategy – is it dynamic and influential or conservative and looking for a voice?
Skills	Distinctive capabilities of key staff, but can be interpreted as specific skill-sets of team members	• Staff skills in specific areas: supplier selection, project management, content management, specific e-marketing approaches (search engine marketing, affiliate marketing, email marketing, online advertising)
Superordinate	The guiding concepts of the e-commerce organization which are also part of shared values and culture. The internal and external perception of these goals may vary	• Improving the perception of the importance and effectiveness of the e-commerce team amongst senior managers and staff [that] it works with (marketing generalists and IT)

Source: Adapted from Waterman *et al.* (1980)

MANAGING CHANGE

Kotter and Schlesinger (1979) identified reasons for resistance to change:

• Parochial self-interest
• Lack of trust
• Different evaluation of the benefits and costs likely to result from change
• Low tolerance of change, perhaps as a result of culture or previous exposure to change.

They list six approaches for dealing with resistance to change which can usefully be applied to digital-marketing-related change:

1 *Education and persuasion.* These are needed to address parochial self-interest. The approach should use rational persuasion based on a reasoned argument, and an element of 'buzz' to get staff excited about the change.

Managers of digital change should spend sufficient time to educate colleagues through direct meetings with key stakeholders, talks to relevant people and workshops.

2 *Participation and involvement.* These can 'excite, motivate and help to create a shared perception of the need for change'. It is not necessary to interview all those affected, though opinion leaders and legitimizers should be involved. Staff can be surveyed to enable some input.

3 *Facilitation and support.* Fear and anxiety concerning change must be countered. Line managers must play an important role in listening to problems or frustrations (emotional support) and seeking to resolve problems where possible (practical support).

4 *Negotiation and agreement.* Rewards are helpful when resistance to change is high. A rewarding approach can also be used to encourage staff to share knowledge and enthusiasm for change.

5 *Manipulation and cooption.* Manipulation is covert, involving deliberate biasing of messages to persuade others. Manipulation can be on a one-to-one basis from line managers to staff, or from senior managers. Coopting involves getting the involvement of a key figure, even if they have relatively little to directly contribute to the change project. For example, someone who is perceived as a trouble-maker or project saboteur could be coopted to the project team to deflect their criticism.

6 *Direction and a reliance on explicit and implicit coercion.* Coercion involves the change managers forcing new behaviour through granting or withdrawing outcomes valued by employees. It can be achieved by including adoption of the new approach in the employee's performance-related contract.

E-MARKETING INSIGHT

E-commerce managers on the challenge of e-business transformation and digital marketing integration

Econsultancy (2005) surveyed UK e-commerce managers to assess their views on the main challenges of managing e-commerce within an organization. Their key challenges, which are still relevant in many companies today, include:

- *Gaining buy-in and budget* consistent with audience media consumption and value generated
- *Conflicts of ownership and tensions* between a digital marketing team, traditional marketing, IT, and finance and senior management
- *Coordination with different channels* in conjunction with teams managing marketing programmes elsewhere in the business
- *Managing and integrating customer information* about characteristics and behaviours collected online

- *Achieving a unified reporting and performance improvement process* throughout the business, including reporting, analysis and putting suggested changes into action
- *Structuring the specialist digital team* and integrating it into the organization by changing responsibilities elsewhere in the organization
- *Insourcing versus outsourcing online marketing tactics*; i.e. search, affiliate, email marketing, PR
- *Staff recruitment and retention* – there is a shortage of e-marketing skills, given the rapid growth in demand for these, which gives great opportunities for everyone reading this book!

The research showed that managing the interfaces between the e-commerce or digital marketing team and other parts of the organization was a major challenge for many organizations.

1 *Senior management.* Managing the senior management team interface was mainly an issue for less-evolved adopters of e-commerce. Leading adopters mentioned that it had been a problem, but they now felt they had achieved understanding of the strategic importance of online channels, and this was matched by financial resources and sufficient input into planning to achieve alignment between business objectives and e-commerce initiatives.

2 *Marketing: different brands, businesses or countries.* Similarly, this was more of an issue for the less-evolved organizations. Others had created processes for collaboration between e-commerce and marketing teams and defined responsibilities for e-commerce within these marketing teams.

3 *Information technology.* This interface was mentioned as a challenge by nearly every respondent – there was a belief that insufficient resource for applications development was limiting the potential of e-commerce to deliver value to customers and the organization.

In addition, the management of two more key groups should be considered:

4 *Agencies and external suppliers.* Concerns about managing external interfaces were voiced less frequently among respondents than concerns about senior management, marketing and IT interfaces.

   Indeed, several respondents referred to their use of digital agencies or external IT providers to circumvent internal resource problems.

5 *The internal team.* In this research, the main concern here was staff retention, since digital staff are in high demand.

STRATEGIC AGILITY

With digital strategy, it is particularly important to be responsive to marketplace change, since the competitive benefits of innovation may be short-lived. A more responsive strategy development approach is described as an emergent strategy approach or *strategic agility* – where strategic analysis, strategic development and strategy implementation are interrelated and occur on a more continuous basis.

Strategic agility is the capability to innovate and so gain competitive advantage by monitoring changes within an organization's marketplace; and then to efficiently evaluate alternative strategies and then select, review and implement appropriate candidate strategies.

To help create a more emergent approach to strategy, consider the approaches described in Table 9.4 for digital channel development.

This agile approach is best able to develop responses to sudden environmental changes which can open 'strategic windows'. Strategic windows may occur through changes such as introduction of new technology (different Web 2.0 applications such as feeds, mashups and widgets are an obvious example here!); changes in the regulation of an industry; changes to distribution channels in the industry; development of a new segment or redefinitions of markets (an example is the growth in leisure and health clubs during the 1990s).

Table 9.4 Summary of approaches used to support strategic agility

Aspect of emergent strategy	Approaches used to support emergent digital strategy
Strategic analysis	• Staff in different parts of organization encouraged to monitor introduction of new approaches by competitors in-sector or out of sector • Third-party benchmarking services report monthly or quarterly on new functionality introduced by competitors • Ad hoc customer panel used to suggest or review new ideas for site features. • Quarterly longitudinal testing of usability to complete key tasks (a time-intensive activity used by one large multinational direct retailer) • Subscription to audience panel data (comScore, NetRatings, Hitwise) – reviews changes in popularity of online services
Strategy formulation and selection	• Budget flexible to reassign priorities • Dedicated or 'ring-fenced' IT budget up to agreed limits to reduce protracted review cycles • Digital channel strategy group meets monthly, empowered to take decisions about which new web functionality to implement
Strategy implementation	• Use of agile development methodologies enable rapid development • Area of site used to showcase new tools currently under trial (e.g. First Direct Lab) • Customer feedback through standard services such as OpinionLab or regular satisfaction surveys. Should also promote listening to new ideas; e.g. Dell IdeaStorm, online customer feedback initiatives by McDonald's and Starbucks

SECTION SUMMARY 9.8

Change management for digital transformation

Managing the change needed for transformation to the e-business or social business needs careful thought.

'Transformation' is not a minor change; it will likely need changes to process, people and systems. These must be carefully managed since others in the organization may not believe in the reasons for the change; so education, education, education is the name of the game.

9.9 Measuring and optimizing digital marketing with digital analytics

We've referenced web analytics throughout *Emarketing Excellence* since this approach is crucial to improving results from e-marketing, whether it's traffic building or a web site.

The value of web analytics is suggested by the results of the *Web Analytics Industry Outlook Survey 2011* (Web Analytics Association, 2011). In this, 570 respondents were asked: 'What is the purpose of web analytics as a function in your organization?' Multiple responses were possible, but these are the main activities identified in order:

- Optimizing web site functionality and conversion (79.7 per cent)
- Analysis of past performance (73.7 per cent)
- Optimizing performance of, and conversions from, marketing campaigns (67.3 per cent)
- Determining the best creative executions through A/B and multivariate testing (49.8 per cent)
- Baseline information for site redesign (48.6 per cent)
- Predictive metrics for developing future marketing campaigns (41 per cent)
- Budgeting and planning for upcoming business objectives (32.7 per cent)
- Other (5.6 per cent).

As we go to print (summer 2012), the main industry body representing web analytics vendors and those who specialize in reporting analysis has changed its name. The Web Analytics Association is now the Digital Analytics Association (www.digitalanalyticsassociation.org). So we can expect everyone to gradually change to the new term. We think the name change is appropriate, since 'digital' better reflects the measurement and improvement of digital marketing beyond the web site to include media, mobile, social and multi-channel analysis.

In the remainder of this section, we will introduce digital analytics and then look at specific requirements to apply them – they're often not used to their full potential.

WHAT ARE DIGITAL ANALYTICS?

The early *web analytics tools* simply recorded 'site statistics' such as the volume of traffic, its source (referring sites) and which content was popular on site, including *clickstreams* of each visit.

Two alternative technical approaches are still commonly used to capture this information. Traditionally, server-based tools such as Webtrends were popular, particularly for large enterprise sites. These worked by summarizing, across different time periods, all the events recorded in a *transaction log file* every time a web page or graphic is downloaded for viewing by a site visitor. More recently, browser-based measurement tools, such as Google Analytics, Adobe Omniture and IBM Coremetrics, have become more popular since these are more accurate. Browser-based tools work by including a small piece of JavaScript in each page which records the page view on a separate (remote) server. Browser-based tools have the advantage that information can be accessed in real time, and visits to pages are recorded each time a page is viewed. This contrasts with the server-based approach where repeat visits may not be identified if the pages have already been loaded and are cached by the browser or a server. A combination of tools is often used since server-based tools are best for managing server load, page errors and identifying crawling by search robots.

The most valuable types of information available from web analytics systems to improve e-marketing include:

1 *Referring sites*. The proportion of visitors from different sites indicates the relative importance of referrers. This is useful for identifying potential link-partners. You can also segment site visitors by different types of visit, such as natural or paid search, brand versus non-brand terms, to see which drive the most valuable traffic. The use of such 'advanced segments' in Google Analytics is essential to driving results through Google Analytics.

2 *Referral time*. The most popular days and times of arrival of visitors can be used to plan the timing of future campaigns such as email campaigns.

3 *Search engine keywords*. Search engine keyphrases indicate the behaviour of customers trying to find your site and can be used to assess the success of your search marketing efforts.

4 *Conversion rates*. Conversion to key outcome pages such as registration pages or purchase pages can be calculated to understand the effectiveness of site design, messaging and incentives. In Google Analytics, these are called 'Goal Conversion pages'. Once you have identified them and set a monetary value against them, you can assess the value of different referrers and pages in driving this value. Google also tracks interactions such as video plays or clicks on buttons through 'Event Tracking' – this provides useful insight if the agency has set up event tracking.

5 *Stickiness*. The duration of visitors on different pages of your site can be used to assess whether visitors are finding what they require. Assessing the *bounce rates* of different landing pages and different referrers is also really helpful information that can be used to refine campaigns, site copy and creative.

6 *Repeat visits*. During a campaign we need to see whether what proportion of visitors on the site are new customers and what proportion are existing customers. Cookies or registration on a web site need to be used to estimate repeat visitors.

E-MARKETING INSIGHT

Eric Peterson demystifies web analytics

Eric, an analyst specializing in web analytics, defines it like this:

> *Web analytics is the assessment of a variety of data, including web traffic, web-based transactions, web server performance, usability studies, user submitted information (i.e. surveys), and related sources to help create a generalized understanding of the visitor experience online.*
>
> *(Peterson, 2004)*

Note that in addition to what are commonly referred to as 'site statistics', sales transactions, usability and researching customers' views through surveys are also included. The definition could also refer to comparison of site visitor volumes and demographics relative to competitors, using panels and ISP-collected data.

We believe, though, that the definition can be improved further – it suggests analysis for the sake of it – whereas the purpose of analytics should be emphasized. Our definition is: 'Web analytics is the customer-centred evaluation of the effectiveness of Internet-based marketing in order to improve the business contribution of online channels to an organization.'

In addition to measuring traffic directly from a site, it is also useful to use *panel data* to estimate your traffic, break it down by socio-demographic characteristics and compare it to competitors. A panel member is profiled in terms of socio-demographics and software is installed on their PC to monitor the sites they visit. Examples of online panel data providers are Nielsen NetRatings (www.nielsen-online.com) and comScore (www.comscore.com). Similar data are available from Hitwise (www.hitwise.com) which aggregates data from ISPs with which it has signed agreements to show the relative popularity of sites (online audience share) within a sector. Hitwise is particularly valuable since it gives information on competitors – e.g. which keyphrases they rank well for – shows which traffic sources drive visitors and clickstreams showing sites their audience visit before and after the evaluation of the site. The Google DoubleClick Ad Planner is also recommended for this information.

Customer feedback tools

Web analytics will show customer journeys through sites, but will miss key information about intent, preference and satisfaction. To gain this information. it's important to use these types of customer feedback tools:

Smart Insights (2010) identifies these five different classes of online feedback tools (http://bit.ly/smartfeedback):

1 *Website feedback tools.* These provide a permanent facility for customers to give feedback by prompts on every page. They are run continuously to enable continuous feedback including ratings on page content, but also products and services.

2 *Site user intent–satisfaction surveys*. These tools measure the gap between what the user had hoped to do on the site and what they actually achieved. For example, we recommend using the free 4Q survey (www.4QSurvey.com) that covers four questions to assess site effectiveness.

3 *Crowdsourcing product opinion software*. This is broader than web feedback, enabling customers to comment about potential new services. This is the approach used by Dell in the IdeaStorm (www.ideastorm.com).

4 *Simple page or concept feedback tools*. Again a form of crowdsourcing, these tools give feedback from an online panel about page layout, messaging or services.

5 *General online survey tools*. These tools like Zoomerang (www.zoomerang.com) and SurveyMonkey (www.surveymonkey.com) enable companies to survey their audience at a low cost.

A/B AND MULTIVARIATE TESTING

Site owners and marketers reviewing the effectiveness of a site, will often disagree, based on their personal experience, and the only method to be certain of the best-performing design or creative alternatives is through designing and running experiments to evaluate which is the best to use. Matt Round, then director of personalization at Amazon, speaking at the eMetrics Marketing Optimization Summit in 2004, said that the Amazon philosophy is: 'Data trumps intuition'.

A/B testing and multivariate testing are two measurement techniques that can be used to review design effectiveness to improve results.

A/B testing

In its simplest form, *A/B testing* (or AB testing) refers to testing two different versions of a page or a page element such as a heading, image or button. Some members of the site are served alternately, with the visitors to the page randomly split between the two pages. Hence it is sometimes called 'live split testing'. The goal is to increase page or site effectiveness against key performance indicators including clickthrough rate, conversion rates and revenue per visit.

Changes in visitor behaviour can then be compared, using different metrics such as clickthrough rates on page elements like buttons or images, or macro-conversion rates, such as conversion to sale or sign-up.

When completing A/B testing, it is important to identify a realistic baseline or *control page* (or audience sample) to compare against. This will typically be an existing landing page. Two new alternatives can be compared to a previous control which is known as an A/B/C test.

An example of the power of A/B testing is an experiment that Skype performed on its main Topbar navigation, where the company found that changing the main menu options from 'Call Phones' to 'Skype Credit' and from 'Shop' to 'Accessories' gave an increase of 18.75 per cent revenue per visit (a Skype representative was speaking at the 2007 eMetrics Marketing Optimization Summit). That's significant when you have hundreds of millions of visitors! It also shows the importance of being direct with navigation and simply describing the offer available rather than the activity.

Multivariate testing

Multivariate testing is a more sophisticated form of A/B testing which enables simultaneous testing of pages for different combinations of page elements that are being tested. This enables selection of the most effective combination or 'recipe' of design elements to achieve increased conversion (Figure 9.10). Common elements that can be tested on the page include:

- Page headline: message and typography
- Main (hero) image
- Button (size, colour, placement and call-to-action text plus arrow)
- Page copy
- Benefits messages.

Figure 9.10 Example of different test variants from Belron

Source: Craig Sullivan

MANAGING DIGITAL ANALYTICS

The use of web analytics to improve online marketing dates back to the 1990s when the first web analytics systems were developed. Yet recent research suggests that many companies are still failing to utilize core web analytics best practices and are therefore not getting the potential return from web analytics that they could.

The *Web Analytics Industry Outlook Survey 2011* (Web Analytics Association, 2011) gives insights on the specific challenges of performance management for digital marketing. The top five challenges for 2011 were:

- Actionability of the data (36 per cent mentioned it)
- Business decisions driven by analytics (35.3 per cent)
- Social media (34.9 per cent)
- Executive management awareness and support for web analytics (34.9 per cent)
- Failure to take action on the data (31 per cent).

In the 2009 survey, the largest hurdle that organizations predicted was funding; but by 2011, this wasn't in the top ten, suggesting more buy-in to use of web analytics. The report also shows that the majority are happy with the capabilities of their web analytics tools. Instead, the top two issues reported suggest the problems of performance management – taking action based on the data.

The frustrations are expressed in a more human way by these responses from those managing analytics in interviews with Dave Chaffey:

'There's just me as web analyst and 60 users of Google Analytics. They don't dedicate time to using it. They're too busy running campaigns . . .' (Web analyst, financial services)

'It's very frustrating. I've no time to go into any great depth. I don't know where to go to find information to show what's working and what's not.' (Brand manager, pharmaceuticals company)

'I use it primarily for monthly or weekly reporting. Due to the amount of data and lack of time I don't have time to do more.' (B2B e-commerce manager)

To succeed in a measured approach to improving results from digital marketing, we suggest that there are four main requirements (as shown in Figure 9.11) relating to the quality of the digital analytics processes. These include defining the right improvement measures, purchasing the right tools, and the management processes – such as putting in place a process where staff review results and then modify their marketing activities.

SECTION SUMMARY 9.9

Measuring and optimizing digital marketing with digital analytics

Control activities should target assessing the effectiveness of promotion campaigns against objectives of: traffic volume; traffic quality (marketing outcomes); cost of visitor and customer

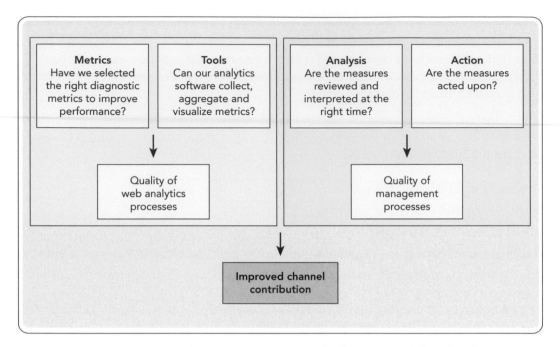

Figure 9.11   Key questions in evaluating the organizational effectiveness of digital analytics

acquisition for different promotional techniques. Digital analytics systems, panel data and customer feedback tools should be used together to make this evaluation.

Digital analytics offer the opportunity to get the most from e-marketing, but getting the value from them is not straightforward; it requires careful selection of measures, tools and, most important, training of people and improvement in process.

9.10 Automation

Automation is about improving digital marketing efficiency. It takes modelling and optimization to another level, where human intervention is minimized.

Automated control has, of course, been used for many years to control industrial processes. Digital technologies now enable the same principles to be applied to marketing communications and relationship management.

While human intervention is often still needed to assess and fine-tune the process, four areas where almost pure automation is possible are:

1 Pay Per Click
2 Creative optimization
3 Web service delivery
4 Automation of marketing messages.

1. Pay Per Click automation using bid-management software

Real-time automated control can be applied to bidding, such as Pay Per Click marketing.

Control is achieved using an *objective function* or target (e.g. minimize flooding, or achieve a set ranking in PPC) using three parameters:

- *State variables* or *inputs* (e.g. evaluation of water levels, or position of ad in listing)
- *Control or optimization variables* – varied to achieve the objective function (e.g. the amount of pumping that occurs, or the Cost Per Click bid)
- Defined *constraints* (e.g. minimum and maximum water levels, or minimum or maximum bid prices and budgets available in Pay Per Click).

Every PPC engine has similar control and state variables, but the way each calculates ad ranking (position) is different.

There are some interesting implications in how these tools will shape the millions being spent on PPC marketing:

1 Currently not everyone uses these tools, but what happens if and when they do? Will results depend on the quality of the tool as the different brands of software compete against each other?
2 For high-volume keyphrases, will manual tweaking always be worthwhile?
3 Bid-management tools are often expensive, costing thousands or even tens of thousands per month. However, Google now offers simpler capabilities as part of its service.

Behavioural ad targeting is another example of automation. This involves automating the ads served according to audience characteristics or behaviour.

2. Landing page optimization

In Section 9.9, we mentioned how A/B and multivariate testing can be used to test different 'recipes' of creative in different containers for content. This still requires manual management.

We can expect to see more automation used in this area. For example, tools from vendors such as Adobe Omniture Test & Target (www.adobe.com) and ATG/Oracle (www.oracle.com) optimize creative on a wide range of variables.

These tools can use different information about the visitor to tailor content in the containers according to a goal such as maximizing clickthrough or conversion rate. Information considered might include:

- First-time or returning visitor
- Content previously browsed on site
- Search phrase used or source of visitor
- Browser or hardware platform used to access site.

3. Automated service delivery

Another aspect of automation for digital marketing, with a lot of potential value attached, is service automation.

Service automation uses automated avatars or chat bots or 'Frequently Asked Questions' to reduce the need for human support staff. Automated tools answer routine queries, freeing up human operators for more complex issues.

Service delivery can be combined with promotion to provide automated 'Next best product' recommendations based on previous purchase behaviour.

4. Marketing automation for e-communications

Behavioural or event-triggered email marketing works by producing super-relevant emails, since they're sent in the context of previous customer behaviour, like signing up for an email, purchasing a product, doing a search or bailing out of a shopping basket.

As we described in Chapter 8 on e-CRM, all of these activities can be automated as part of a 'Sense and Respond' approach. Rules can be set up which determine which messages are sent based on which communications (Figure 9.12).

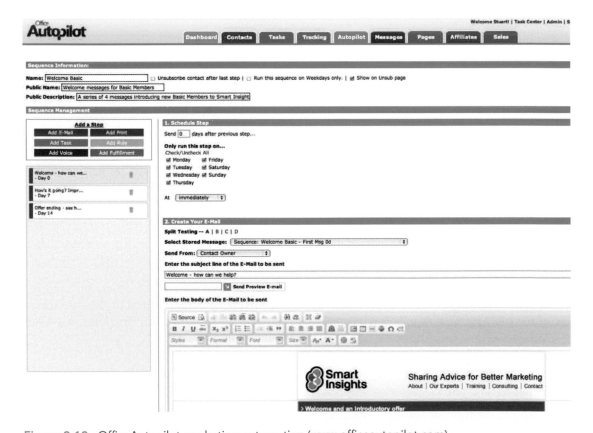

Figure 9.12   OfficeAutopilot marketing automation (www.officeautopilot.com)

Examples where these communications can be used include:

- Shopping basket abandoned
- Customer searches or browses a category and doesn't buy
- Welcome for a new customer (onboarding)
- Reactivation for a lapsed customer.

SECTION SUMMARY 9.10

Automation

Automation uses services to test or repeat different processes to find the most efficient process.

9.11 Implementing new systems

The complexity and evolving requirements for new sites, platforms, systems and apps give many businesses and agencies challenges in managing the deployment of new systems as this case study shows. In this section, we'll review some good practices for building systems.

E-MARKETING INSIGHT

The reasons behind a failed e-project

McLaughlin (2010) has reviewed a case study of a project where, after significant financial investment (approximately US$300m), and three years of development, the project was deemed a failure. The initiative was designed to link the sales, marketing, fulfilment, manufacturing and distribution systems together in order to reduce supply-chain stock levels, increase responsiveness to customer demands, and increase profit margins by providing a direct link to customers (circumventing business partners for some product lines).

The project was managed centrally from the North American headquarters, with input sought from the other geographies (Europe/Middle East/Africa, Asia Pacific and Latin America). The geographies had responsibility to respond to the central team on local aspects of the e-CRM project. The central team had responsibility for the overall scope of the project and the back office – or the e-CRM 'engine' – while the geographies had responsibility to ensure that the system, once deployed, considered local and cultural aspects of how the organization interacted with customers and business partners.

In this study, McLaughlin surveyed the level of employee awareness of the e-CRM system: employee buy-in; employee confidence in the e-CRM system; and employee awareness of barriers to successful implementation. Although most employees had heard of the e-CRM project, the depth of awareness was not consistent across the organization. From the surveyed population, 24 per cent had heard of e-CRM, but were unaware of what the project would deliver. Twenty-eight per cent understood the deliverables and received regular communications on the project's progress. But 48 per cent of the surveyed workforce, while understanding what e-CRM was about and what it was trying to achieve, did not receive any communications on a regular basis updating them on the project's progress. In effect, 72 per cent of the workforce was not aware of how e-CRM was progressing, and how the objectives and deliverables were changing.

PROTOTYPING

Prototyping is a common approach to the development of e-business systems to help avoid inaccurate requirements; its essence is that it is an iterative process in which web site users suggest modifications before further prototypes and the live version of the site are developed.

Prototypes are:

- *Rapid* – prototyping is part of a systems development approach known as '*RAD – rapid application development*', since the time from inception to completion is reduced to months rather than years. More rapid development is achieved through reducing the length of time of the analysis, design and build stages by combining them, in conjunction with the use of graphical software tools with which applications can be built quickly from pre-assembled components.
- *Simple* – skeleton applications are produced as *prototypes* that do not contain all the functions of a system, but are a framework which gives a good indication to users of the information available and the look and feel of an application. They can then comment on it and say, for example, 'this information is missing' or 'we like that feature, but it would be nice to do that also' or 'that feature isn't necessary, it's not what we meant'.
- *Iterative* – prototypes are produced often at a frequency of one every few days or weeks so that the comments from the last review can be fed into the evolving system.
- *Incremental* – each prototype incorporates the feedback from the previous review, so each version of the application has a limited number of new features.
- *User-centred* – users are involved at all stages of development, in describing the existing system, reviewing the prototypes and testing the system.

The prototyping approach is now ubiquitous since it reduces the risk of major design, functional or informational errors during the construction of the application that may be costly and time-consuming to fix at a later stage in development.

AGILE SOFTWARE DEVELOPMENT

Today, the concept of prototyping has been extended across the whole lifecycle for developing web site functionality or software applications, where it is known as *agile software development*. The goal of agile development is to be able to create stable releases more frequently than traditional development methodologies allow; i.e. new functionality will be introduced through several releases each month rather than a more significant release every few weeks, months or even years. The approach is sometimes known as 'permanent beta'. Another difference with agile development is the emphasis on face-to-face communication to define requirements rather than detailed requirements specifications.

Scrum is a methodology that supports agile software development. Scrum involves the *scrum master* who is effectively a project manager, the *product owner* who represents the stakeholders such as the business owners and customers, and the *scrum team* which includes the developers.

Scrum is based on focused sprints of a 15–30-day period where the team creates an increment of potentially releasable software. Potential functionality for each sprint is agreed at a *sprint planning meeting* from the *product backlog*, a prioritized set of high-level requirements. The sprint planning meeting is itself iterative, with the product owner stating his or her requirements from the product backlog and the technical team then determining how much of this they can commit to complete during the forthcoming sprint. The term 'scrum' refers to a daily project status meeting during the sprint. See www.softhouse.se/Uploades/ Scrum_eng_webb.pdf for an overview of the process.

The principles of agile development are encapsulated in the *Agile Manifesto* (http://agilemanifesto.org/), which was agreed in 2001 by proponents of previous rapid development methodologies including the Dynamic Systems Development Method and Extreme Programming. The Agile Manifesto is useful in illustrating the principles of agile programming which it contrasts with traditional approaches. The text of the manifesto is:

> *We are uncovering better ways of developing software by doing it and helping others do it.*
>
> *Through this work we have come to value:*
>
> - *Individuals and interactions over processes and tools*
> - *Working software over comprehensive documentation*
> - *Customer collaboration over contract negotiation*
> - *Responding to change over following a plan.*
>
> *That is, while there is value in the items on the right, we value the items on the left more.*

CHANGE MANAGEMENT

Siebel's (2003) six change-management levers borrow heavily from generic change management and can readily be applied to a CRM implementation:

1 *Compensation and rewards*

- Performance evaluation and improved structures – these need to be created to promote customer-centric behaviour. Better understanding of the customer enables better service delivery. For example, customer satisfaction might be added as an evaluation criterion for employee performance, in addition to the more traditional measures such as number of sales achieved or number of service calls resolved.

- Staff incentives to improve data quality – for example, a bank ran a competition to identify the member of its call-centre staff who collected the most customer email addresses, since this field in the database had poor coverage. Similarly, sales representatives can be given incentives to record details of customer visits more accurately.

2 *Boss's behaviour*

- The actions, attitudes and decisions of a supervisor, manager or executive effect change within an organization.

- It is incumbent on managers to be aware of their role in supporting change. A top-down approach, where the most senior managers actively support change and encourage this attitude in the managers who report to them, seems to be the most practical approach. This can then be cascaded down the different levels of a large organization.

- Performance review and evaluation can be used to control behaviour.

3 *Policies and processes*

- Changes to policies and processes required by a new system must be identified early, defined clearly and communicated to staff. It must be acknowledged that e-CRM is not just 'a new software tool', but also 'a new way of working'.

- The changes to sales processes need to be documented and the implications explained to staff. Examples of staff activities that need to be redefined concerning a sale system are initiating and closing sales opportunities, addressing customer complaints and managing partnership relationships.

4 *Training*

- Many e-CRM projects don't provide employees with adequate training.
- Formal software training is not the only approach; mentoring in the workplace by more skilled staff can be very effective.
- Adequate help systems, built into the software and available on the web systems, and access to organization-specific help-desk staff are also important.

5 *Communication*

- Communication should have sufficient frequency and depth. It should be ongoing, keeping staff informed throughout the implementation, including the phase when the system becomes live and problems are often encountered.

- Frequent communication can be achieved using diverse media – a mix of non-verbal and verbal communications including 'employee portals, emails, broadcast voicemails, newsletters, memos, videos, luncheons or breakfasts, meetings and speeches!'.

- Non-verbal communications are sometimes neglected, but are useful to communicate the importance of the new system.

- The importance of two-way communication is emphasized. Meetings should solicit feedback from employees on their concerns and explain their role in supporting and facilitating change.

6 *Organizational structure*

- The existing structure must support open communication to promote change – it must facilitate collaboration, aiming towards the ultimate goal of serving the customer better. Making minor adjustments to reporting lines and the mechanics of team collaboration is a sign that communicates senior managers' expectations that the people in the organization work together to achieve change.

- Cross-departmental collaboration during implementation is a further issue for e-CRM projects – it is often unclear where project ownership lies. Is it the marketing department, the operations department (for customer service), the IT department, the customer information manager or a member of senior management? To resolve this problem, it is important that one clear owner of the project is established and that he or she is at director level.

- A change or project team involving the different stakeholders needs to meet regularly to manage change and control the project.

To quote Siebel:

> *The influence of top executives is required to overcome the cultural resistance, organizational inertia, political battles, disagreements and other similar challenges that crop-up when considerable cross-organizational change takes place. Since resistance attributed to internal factors plagues CRM projects and frequently contributes to their failure, strong executive sponsorship and commitment to enforce change in the face of criticisms and organizational discomfort is an imperative.*
>
> *(Siebel, 2003)*

9.12 Managing data quality

Data quality is likely not the most interesting area of managing digital marketing, but as we highlighted in Chapter 8, Section 8.10, it is a common problem which limits companies' abilities to personalize their communications. The Econsultancy email marketing census (www.econsultancy.com/reports/email-census) regularly rates it as the biggest challenge in email marketing. We think this highlights a lack of ownership and management of data quality.

All marketing managers should understand the principles of data quality and put in place approaches to improve quality.

The list below gives the main attributes of data quality. For example, for a geographic location for a customer defined by a postcode or zip code, the aspects of data quality are as follows.

1 *Accuracy*. This means that the data correctly define the event or object which they describe. For a postcode, accuracy means does the postcode actually describe where the person lives? Data could be inaccurate if the customer has moved address since the data were collected; i.e. the data are out of date.

2 *Completeness*. This refers to whether all the data are present. A company could profile its postcode or zip code field for completeness. It may find that these are only recorded for 80 per cent of customers. This means that is difficult to identify where a fifth of customers live. This is important for targeting relevant communications to them which are often based on the lifestyle of people living in a particular area.

   This can be achieved through a common customer profile – a definition of all the database fields that are relevant to the marketer in order to understand and target the customer with a relevant offering. The customer profile can have different levels to set targets for data quality (Level 1 is contact details and key profile fields only, Level 2 includes preferences and Level 3 includes full purchase and response behaviour).

3 *Validity*. This means that the data fall between acceptable ranges defined by the business. For a postcode, there will be a standard format in every country that is required for valid data. Validity does not necessarily mean the data are accurate. For example, customer birth dates must be within a defined range such as from 1900 to the present day, but are inaccurate if the birth dates are not correct for some reason. Validity is sometimes defined as congruence with business rules. Form validation rules on a site can improve this.

4 *Consistency*. This means that the data elements are consistently defined and understood. With a UK postcode, for example, some people entering the postcode 'DE22 1GB' may not realize that a full postcode is required and may have entered just 'DE22' – the postal area. Consistency is particularly important where different sources of information are used in an analysis. For example, are customer enquiries measured in a similar way in different countries?

A structured approach to customer data capture is needed, otherwise some data may be missed, meaning we can't target accurately. Witness the case of the utility company that collected 80,000 email addresses, but forgot to ask for the postcode for geo-targeting!

SECTION SUMMARY 9.12

Managing data quality

The quality of data is important to enable targeting and the delivery of relevant communications, but often it isn't managed proactively. Make sure you have methods of defining data quality and responsibilities for reviewing and improving it.

9.13 E-business security

There are thousands of hackers, vandals and viruses at large at any given time. It's disturbing, whether you are concerned about the privacy of your personal data, or the potential risk to your organization. Businesses and customers get damaged. Kids, con-men, criminals and competitors – not to mention pressure groups, political groups, government intelligence agencies and many more – want to break through security systems.

In the corporate world, popular targets for activists include: large corporations, news outlets, banking/finance, hate groups, political sites, e-commerce, personal/credit-card data, computer security sites. What's left?

The excitement of building a new dynamic e-business, combined with the race to market, exposes many companies to significant new risks. This is because since the extended enterprise opens up systems and data to external parties. Poorly designed systems thrown together by technical whizz-kids often ignore the wide variety of risks lurking out there.

Organizations can be accused of negligence for breaches of privacy/security. So apart from damaging customers' trust in your organization, security lapses can mean that company directors end up in court, if they are deemed to be negligent in their responsibilities towards good security. In fact, Web 2.0 can actually make it easier for security breaches.

Although usability and accessibility are popular issues, we don't see much about security. Good web site management needs to build in security policies, security reviews, security testing and auditing, as well as planning for business continuity in case of 'disaster recovery' and emergencies. Remember, the earlier security is discussed, the cheaper it becomes to manage risks. Also integrate security into any testing programmes.

E-BUSINESS SECURITY THREATS SECURITY THREATS

Check the list of different types of security breach. You will know of some of these risks, but who is responsible for managing the threats to your organization and are they covering all the bases? These are some of the threats:

- *Credit-card fraud.* Imagine having your card details sucked into cyberspace and used by someone else. Or imagine customers denying receipt of goods delivered. Almost half of Visa's card disputes are Internet-related. Elsewhere it's higher. For the e-tailer, the percentage of fraudulent purchases on sites can run to double figures. Phishing attacks where SPAM emails encourage users of secure services, such as banks, to divulge their security details are still widespread because some new consumers fall for them.

- *Distributed denial of service (DDOS).* This effectively denies access to your site when hackers flood network routers from lots of different sites with an overwhelming amount of traffic to targeted web sites. They effectively shut down the sites.

- *Cyber graffiti.* Hackers can alter your web site, insert nasty images, false information, false testimonials, and even direct customers to another site. Non-hackers can put up rogue sites sounding very similar to your own and attract lots of your customers. Spot the difference between: Investsmartindia.com and Investmartindia.com.

- *Botnets or alien computer control.* If you have a permanent Internet connection (cable or ADSL), you're constantly open and vulnerable to the outside world. Any hacker can easily gain access to your computer by using network scanning tools which track poorly protected systems. Then an alien or remote third-party software controls your PC and forms a botnet of 'Zombies' used for phishing scams or DDOS. If you have the right contacts, you can hire a botnet at a few cents per PC!

- Your web site is used to *host and distribute other unauthorized software,* some of which may damage other users' computers (even a simple response form for an enquiry could have some hidden code placed by a hacker so that it deletes database information or sends emails to everyone in your address book). Remember that social media Web 2.0 can increase your vulnerability to hackers.

- *Chat room undesirables.* Even without permanent connections, your chat rooms can be invaded by uninvited and unwanted third parties such as racists. They post obscene messages or more subtle racist arguments to often vulnerable audiences.

- *Intellectual property theft.* On top of this, theft of intellectual property happens all the time – software, music, information downloaded, copied and passed on. Sometimes it's duplicated and sold commercially by unauthorized pirates. Worse still, pirating is effectively legal in some countries where there is no IPR law.

- *Competitive information.* Another type of intellectual property also gets stolen – sensitive company information, particularly competitive information and databases of customers.

- *Anything that damages your data can have huge legal implications,* since without properly used back-up systems, directors can be liable for any damage to their own business caused by a virus.

Apart from damage done to the business, security violations can also end in downstream negligence litigation.

We see much more about usability and accessibility nowadays than several years ago, but who asks about security?

E-BUSINESS SECURITY SOLUTIONS

Good security starts with a security policy. Do you have one? System security is part of a wider security policy that should include physical (lost laptop, stolen PC) and procedural security (to avoid disaffected employees deliberately formatting a disc or sending information out).

It's good to build security into the design of an e-business early as it's hard to retrofit security to an operational system under attack.

Tough decisions are required; e.g. convenience and security don't always work together; passwords are a nuisance, but do offer at least a minimal level of security. Equally, risk can be reduced by asking customers to pre-register before purchasing anything or clearing payment before goods are despatched.

There are many other technological, physical and procedural controls required:

- *Contracts*. Clauses that define the security processes to be used may have to be incorporated into contracts with companies you do business with online.

- *Trend and exception monitoring*. Visa contacts cardholders if any 'out of character' purchases are made and American Express offers temporary numbers that are valid for a predetermined (1–2 hours) shopping period and amount.

- *Public key technology and cryptography*. Web servers and browsers can be set up easily to encrypt or seal all communications. Public key encryption basically confirms the identity of an individual or company as established by an intermediary trusted by your company; it proves that a transaction originated with that individual or company, so it cannot subsequently be denied (often called non-repudiation) and seals data, such as transactions or emails, to prevent the contents being altered.

- *Intrusion detection routines*. These scan for attacks such as denial of service or access to a site via a competitor. They are often part of a *firewall* solution which is a specialized server at the gateway to a company that is used to keep out unwanted intruders.

- *Virus scanners*. These should be set up to monitor continuously and be kept updated to the latest version.

- *Audit trails*. You need to record good audit trails of key events, with particular security-related events and transaction records. Do you audit the information that should be retained to help resolution of disputed electronic transactions?

- *Back-up*. Back-up is crucial if your business depends on being online. Do you have good back-up and recovery procedures? Is your web site content stored separately?

The best systems in the world aren't going to help if people don't use them properly. A security solution is only as strong as its weakest link and lapses such as assigning 'no brainer' passwords like 'password' or the day of the week create gaping holes for even the most novice hacker.

SECTION SUMMARY 9.13

E-business security

There are many security challenges out there including:

- Credit-card fraud
- Distributed denial of service
- Web site defacing
- Computer viruses
- Undesirables populating your chat rooms
- Intellectual property theft
- Sensitive data theft.

Fortunately there are many solutions, from firewalls to filters and encryption. But remember, constant vigilance is required in this fast-changing online world.

> **CHAPTER SUMMARY**

1. Digital marketers need to be adept at change management. Identifying relevant changes, making the case for change and then implementing change within an organization.

2. To manage digital marketing in a medium to large sized organization, the integration with e-business services such as extranets and extranets need to be managed also through collaboration with colleagues.

3. Many companies are now considering social business and social CRM as a way to improve collaboration internally and to harness the insights from customer and partner interactions.

4. To help develop a roadmap of enhancements to marketing, capability assessment of the overall digital strategy and individual channels is a useful approach. Use this tool to help assess your capabilities: http://bit.ly/smarthealthcheck

5. To help make the case for digital marketing, quantitative models such as conversion budget models and lifetime value models are recommended.

6. Depending on the type of business and the competence of competitors, different supplier arrangements may be appropriate ranging from a full-service marketing agency through a specialist digital agency or one skilled in managing individual communications channels such as SEO or social media marketing.

7. Great tools existing for optimizing online customer experiences using techniques such as web analytics, AB and multivariate testing. The right people, process and tools need to be in place to make the most of these tools.

8. Likewise, tools for automating different aspects of online communications such as web personalization, email personalization and media buying are available, but their use needs careful planning to define the right business rules.

9. The digital marketer is a champion for providing great multichannel customers. As such they should ensure that data quality, privacy and security are adequate to meet the needs of customers and the brand.

References

Altimeter (2010) Altimeter report: the new rules of relationship management. Blog post by Jeremiah Owyang, 5 March at: www.altimetergroup.com/2010/03/altimeter-report-the-18-use-cases-of-social-crm-the-new-rules-of-relationship-management.html

Berry, M. and Chaffey, D. (2012) *Making the Business Case for Digital Marketing Investment*. Smart Insights e-book at: www.smartinsights.com/guides/digital-marketing-strategy/making-the-business-case-for-investment-in-digital-marketing/

Bowen, D. (forthcoming) Interview with Dave Chaffey. To be published on Smart Insights.

Bughin, J., Guggenheim Shenkan, A. and Singer, M. (2008) How poor metrics undermine digital marketing. *McKinsey Quarterly*, October. At: www.mckinseyquarterly.com/How_poor_metrics_undermine_digital_marketing_2220

Econsultancy (2005) *Managing an E-commerce Team: Integrating Digital Marketing into your Organisation*. Research report by Dave Chaffey. Available at: http://econsultancy.com/uk/reports/managing-an-e-commerce-team-integrating-digital-marketing-into-your-organisation

Econsultancy (2008) Managing Digital Channels Best Practice Guide. Research report by Dave Chaffey. Available at: http://econsultancy.com/uk/reports/managing-digital-channels-best-practice-guide

Facebook (2012a) Social design. At: http://developers.facebook.com/socialdesign/

Facebook (2012b) Form S-1 Registration Statement: Facebook, Inc. Letter from Mark Zuckerberg. At: www.sec.gov/Archives/edgar/data/13268

Flores, L. and Eltvedt, H. (2005) Beyond online advertising – lessons about the power of brand web sites to build and expand brands. Published in *Proceedings of ESOMAR Online Conference, Montreal.*

Holland, A. (2004) How much should you budget for search marketing? Marketing Sherpa article, 11 October at: www.marketingsherpa.com/article.php?ident=23744

IBM (no date a) E-business. IBM history archives, 1997 at: www-03.ibm.com/ibm/history/history/year_1997.html

IBM (no date b) Social business. At: www.ibm.com/socialbusiness

Kalakota, R. and Whinston, A. (1997) *Electronic Commerce. A Manager's Guide.* Addison-Wesley, Reading, MA.

Kotter, J. and Schlesinger, L. (1979) Choosing strategies for change. *Harvard Business Review,* March–April.

Kumar, V., Petersen, J. and Leone, R. (2007) How valuable is word of mouth? *Harvard Business Review,* 85(10), pp. 139–46.

McGovern, G. (2007) Intranets: getting senior management's attention, *Gerry McGovern Newsletter,* 26 August at: www.gerrymcgovern.com

McKinsey (2007) How companies are marketing online: a McKinsey global survey. Available at: www.mckinseyquarterly.com/How_companies_are_marketing_online_A_McKinsey_Global_Survey_2048

McLaughlin, S. (2010) Dangerous solutions: case study of a failed e-project. *Journal of Business Strategy,* 31(2), pp. 24 –33.

Peterson, E. (2004) *Web Analytics Demystified.* Self-published. Available from: www.webanalyticsdemystified.com.

Siebel, J. (2003) Applied change management: a key ingredient for CRM success. Siebel white paper, Siebel Resource Center.

Smart Insights (2010) Website feedback tools review. At: www.smartinsights.com/digital-marketing-software/website-feedback-tools-review/

Smart Insights (2012) Website conversion and revenue model calculators. Template by Dave Chaffey, January at: www.smartinsights.com/guides/conversion-optimisation/conversion-optimisation-calculator/

Timmers, P. (1999) *Electronic Commerce Strategies and Models for Business to Business Trading.* Series on information systems. John Wiley, Chichester.

Walmsley, A. (2007) New media – the age of the trialogue. *The Marketer,* September.

Waterman, R.H., Peters, T.J. and Phillips, J.R (1980) Structure is not organisation. *McKinsey Quarterly* in-house journal. McKinsey & Company, New York.

Web Analytics Association (2011) *Web Analytics Industry Outlook Survey 2011.* Digital Analytics Association, Wakefield, MA.

Yammer (2010) Suncorp case study. Accessed May 2010 from: www.yammer.com

Zissman, E. (2008) Interview with Dave Chaffey.

Further reading

Chaffey, D. (2004) *E-business and E-commerce Management: Strategy, Implementation and Applications*, 2nd edition. Pearson Education, Harlow. Free updates at www.davechaffey. com/E-business. Part 1 describes e-business concepts, Part 2 describes approaches to e-business strategy for buy-side, sell-side and in-side e-commerce, and Part 3 describes practical issues of implementation such as change management and user-centred design.

Deise, M., Nowikow, C., King, P. and Wright, A. (2000) *Executive's Guide to E-business. From Tactics to Strategy*. John Wiley and Sons, New York. Suggests approaches to e-business according to four snapshots and their impact on organizations, people, processes and technology. The snapshots are: channel enhancement, value-chain integration, industry transformation and convergence.

Kalakota, R. and Robinson, M. (2000) *E-business. Roadmap for Success*. Addison-Wesley, Reading, MA. A good introductory book on approaches to e-business divided into buy-side and sell-side.

Web links

Econsultancy (www.econsultancy.com). Research, best practice reports and supplier directory for online marketing.

European Commission Information Society Statistics (http://ec.europa.eu/information_society/digital-agenda/index_en.htm). Reports evaluating e-business activity and consumer adoption across the European Union.

Marketing Experiments (www.marketingexperiments.com). Gives examples and explains best practice for optimizing digital marketing.

MIT Center for Digital Business (http://ebusiness.mit.edu). Created by MIT's Sloan School of Management, it contains summaries of over 50 university-sponsored research projects on e-business and e-commerce.

Ofcom (http://stakeholders.ofcom.org.uk/). The UK Office of Communication has an annual Communications Market report on the adoption of digital media, including telecommunications and the Internet (including broadband adoption), digital television and wireless services.

Optimize and Prophesize (www.optimizeandprophesize.com). A blog focusing on practical optimization approaches for paid search and landing pages.

Self-test

1 Devise an explanation of e-business for a colleague in the context of your organization.

2 How should a company review its capabilities for digital marketing?

3 Explain and contrast the relevance of the concepts of social CRM and social business for an organization.

4 Outline approaches to make the business case for investment in digital marketing.

5 Describe the situations where you think a single digital marketing agency is preferable to the use of different specialists.

6 Describe some of the alternative structures for digital marketing within an organization.

7 Explain why data quality is important in e-marketing and approaches to manage it.

8 Summarize the main security threats to your business and describe solutions to each threat.

9 Make notes on success factors for managing change, explaining which are missing or not relevant to your business.

10 Outline the factors that may contribute to e-business failure (including IT projects failure).

Chapter **10**

E-planning

There's no point rowing harder if you're rowing in the wrong direction.

Ohmae (1999)

534

E-marketing planning involves marketing planning within the context of the e-business e-environment. So, not surprisingly, the successful e-marketing plan is based on traditional marketing disciplines and planning techniques, adapted for the digital media environment and then mixed with new digital marketing communications techniques. This chapter shows you how to create a comprehensive e-marketing plan, based on the well-established principles of the SOSTAC® Planning System (Smith, 1993).

OVERALL LEARNING OUTCOME

By the end of this chapter, you will be able to:

- Draw up an outline e-marketing plan
- Analyse the situation
- Draw up realistic objectives
- Begin to develop sensible strategies
- Develop appropriate tactics
- Execute the tactics with detailed action plans
- Control, monitor, measure, report and adjust.

CHAPTER TOPIC	LEARNING OBJECTIVE
10.1 Introduction	Describe the context and main components of an e-plan
10.2 Situation analysis	Assess your performance within the online and multi-channel marketplace
10.3 Objectives	Model and define SMART commercial and communications objectives for the e-marketing plan
10.4 Strategy	Explain the difference between strategy and tactics, and understand the components of strategy
10.5 Tactics	Select the relevant digital communications channels that can be deployed as part of tactics
10.6 Actions	Execute the tactics effectively
10.7 Control	Build in a review process to your plans based on web analytics and management dashboards
10.8 The 3Ms resources	Identify the key internal and external resources required and allocate these to achieve your e-marketing objectives

10.1 Introduction to e-marketing planning

By the end of this chapter, you will know what an e-marketing plan is, its key components and how they fit together. Without a realistic plan, an organization drifts unknowingly and can end up anywhere – usually sinking, without cash and without direction, just like so many of the 'dotbombs'.

Planning is essential. It helps you to stop constant fire-fighting, desperately searching for funds, panicking and paying higher prices (like rush rates). Planning puts you in control and reduces stress. It also gives direction to the team so they can work in harmony.

There are many types of plans. Corporate plans and business plans incorporate the long-term corporate strategy which includes diversification and acquisition strategies, systems and funding.Then there are marketing plans that must help to fulfil the overall corporate objectives. Then there are e-marketing plans which have to integrate with the offline, traditional marketing plan.

E-marketing plans do not occur in isolation, but are most effective when integrated with offline marketing communications channels such as phone, direct-mail or face-to-face selling. Online channels should also be used to support the whole buying process from pre-sale to sale to post-sale and the continuing development of customer relationships.

Although the e-marketing plan can span right across an organization's functions (e.g. customer feedback, customer service, product enhancement, sales, finance/payment, delivery, administration and marketing), e-marketing plans tend to be linked strongly to marketing communications plans. The reality is that any e-marketing plan needs to be a part of a marketing communications plan, and it also should be part of a broader marketing plan. Needless to say, the e-plan should also fit in with the overall business plan.

For a traditional business, an overall corporate or business plan covers systems, procedures, resources and structure, while a marketing plan covers the sales, distribution, communications and delivery of the product or service.

Figure 10.1 shows the typical relationship between different plans. The corporate plan guides the marketing and e-business plan, both of which, in turn, guide the e-marketing plan. The plans are integrated so that developing the e-marketing plan may give insights that help to impact on strategy in other plans. The e-marketing plan can highlight and review opportunities for business growth by targeting new audiences, new geographic markets or through introducing new products and services. Companies which have successfully used the web to grow sales have used a cost-effective web presence coupled with the right investment in digital media to exploit new opportunities. For example, airline easyJet and business-to-business retailer RS Components have launched new services in many countries where sales are serviced online.

> **Long- versus short-term plans**

Many organizations have short- and long-term plans or roadmaps. Ultimately they must integrate the goals, the timeframes and resources required. We can distinguish between short-term (one year) plans, medium-term (two to three year) plans and longer-term (three to five

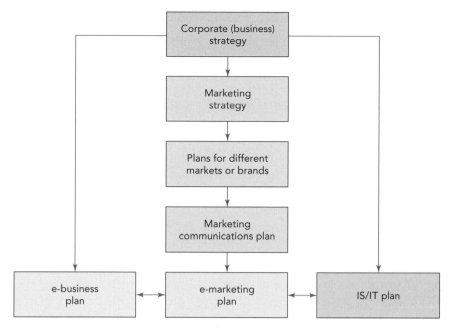

Figure 10.1   The relationship between different types of plans

year) plans. All these plans can use SOSTAC® (which is based upon PR Smith's 1996 original CD and its 2011 update as an e-book). For example, all these plans include strategy and tactics sections. Strategy gives clear guidance and direction for all subsequent tactical details. Strategy for a short-term plan summarizes how the one-year objectives will be achieved, while strategy for a long-term plan summarizes how the long-term objective will be achieved.

Some feel that strategy is, by definition, deemed to have a longer-term and a more enduring perspective, while tactics are shorter-term and more flexible.

Longer-term e-marketing plans should place emphasis on three key areas. First, early identification of significant changes/trends in the macro-environment and changes to competitive forces in the micro-environment. Second, developing and communicating value propositions for customers using online services as part of their buying process. Third, definition of the technology infrastructure and database architecture to deliver these value propositions.

New technologies such as a customer relationship management (CRM) system and integrated databases to deliver customized communications can take several years to specify, select and implement, and so need to go on a long-term roadmap. Database, CRM, integration of e-business architecture and business processes are all long-term when making plans and major decisions.

The shorter-term operational e-marketing plan can then address the mix of communications techniques such as search marketing and online advertising (Chapter 7), used to acquire new customers; and the tools used to engage and retain customers online such as incentive programmes and customer contact strategies delivered through opt-in email marketing integrated with traditional direct media such as phone and direct mail.

To help you, we'll structure this chapter by using a simple aide-mémoire, called SOSTAC®. *SOSTAC®* is used by thousands of professionals to produce all kinds of plans – corporate plans, marketing plans, e-marketing plans, advertising plans.

SOSTAC® stands for: Situation analysis, Objectives and Strategy, Tactics, Action and Control (see Chapter 1, Figure 1.1):

- *Situation analysis* means 'Where are we now?' For multi-channel marketers, how many of your customers are buying or influenced online? Full customer analysis answers the questions 'Who, Why and How' (see Chapter 4). What is the growth forecast? What are your competitors doing? What is the impact of the new intermediaries? What's working for them? What seems to work online and offline and what seems not to? How have you performed online? What's changing in the online world?

- *Objectives* mean 'Where are we going, or where do we want to be?' Why go online? What are the benefits, what is the purpose of going to all of this effort? Remember the 5 Ss (Sell, Serve, Speak, Save and Sizzle)? Good objectives are quantified and also contain strict timescales.

- *Strategy* means 'How do we get there?' Strategy summarizes how to fulfil the objectives. How will sales and other brand goals be delivered? Which trends are we responding to? What positioning will be chosen? Which segments will be targeted with which propositions? What communications strategies will be used to support customer acquisition, conversion and retention? Which media mix will be used to acquire new customers, and which contact strategy will be used for customer retention and 'share of wallet' growth?

- *Tactics* are the details of strategy (the marketing mix, communications mix and channel mix are the tactical tools) and here we add more detail. Highlighting on, say, a Gantt chart, exactly which tactics occur when; e.g. execution of Pay Per Click ads or a series of opt-in emails. What level of integration is there between tools, database and e-CRM? Tactics explain how to implement the strategy.

- *Action* is the detailed working out of tactics. Who does what, what processes are required to make things happen? Each tactical e-tool is a mini project that needs to be managed. What actions have to be taken to create and optimize a web site, to develop a Pay-Per-Click campaign, an opt-in email campaign? Everything degenerates into work! Arguably, this is the weakest part of the planning process for most companies (as identified by Bossiddy and Charan, 2004). Internal marketing is often the weakest link where managers forget to allocate time and resources to explain to their own staff and motivate them to execute the actions better.

- *Control* questions whether you know if you are succeeding or failing – before it is too late. This is where web analytics systems measure and monitor regularly the key online measurables – visitors, durations, enquiries, subscriptions, sales, conversion rates, churn rates, loyalty levels and more. Control needs to be built into a plan; i.e. who reports on specific control criteria (e.g. usability testing, web statistics analysis and external trend spotting) and how frequently.

Note: half the plan should be devoted to the situation analysis. Much of the detail can be put into appendices.

BEST PRACTICE E-MARKETING TIP

Integrated e-marketing planning

Your planning devices should integrate situation analysis, goal setting, strategy, tactics and control. Table 10.1, for example, shows how the e-SWOT of situation analysis can be used to generate ideas for corresponding strategies and tactics which can then be prioritized and selected as part of strategy definition. Another toolkit to facilitate integrated planning is to create a table made up of rows of different goals, with columns for corresponding objectives, drivers (based on situation analysis), strategies and key performance indicators (KPIs) used for control.

Table 10.1 An Internet SWOT analysis showing typical opportunities and threats sometimes presented online for an established multi-channel brand. It also acts as a strategic option generator and review toolkit

The organization	Strengths – S	Weaknesses – W
	1 Existing brand	1 Brand perception
	2 Existing customer base	2 Intermediary use
	3 Existing distribution	3 Technology/skills (poor web experience)
		4 Cross-channel support
		5 Churn rate
Opportunities – O 1 Cross-selling 2 New markets 3 New services 4 Alliances/ co-branding	**SO strategies** Leverage strengths to maximize opportunities – attacking strategy **Examples:** 1 Migrate customers to web strategy 2 Refine customer contact strategy across customer lifecycle or commitment segmentation (email, web) 3 Partnership strategy (co-branding, linking) 4 Launch new web-based products or value-adding experiences; e.g. video streaming	**WO strategies** Counter weaknesses through exploiting opportunities – build strengths for attacking strategy **Examples:** 1 Counter-mediation strategy (create or acquire) 2 Search marketing acquisition strategy 3 Affiliate-based acquisition strategy 4 Refine customer contact strategy (email, web)
Threats – T 1 Customer choice (price) 2 New entrants	**ST strategies** Leverage strengths to minimize threats – defensive strategy **Examples:**	**WT strategies** Counter weaknesses and threats: – build strengths for defensive strategy

Table 10.1 (Continued)

3 New competitive products 4 Channel conflicts 5 Social network	1 Introduce new Internet-only products 2 Add value to web services – refine OVP 3 Partner with complementary brand 4 Create own social network/customer reviews	**Examples:** 1 Differential online pricing strategy 2 Acquire/create pure-play company with lower cost base 3 Customer engagement strategy to increase conversion, average order value and lifetime value 4 Online reputation management strategy/e-PR

Your e-marketing plan should also be reviewed and revised frequently. Quick reactions are required. If something isn't working – find out why and change it. Constantly improve. In addition to regular detailed measurements, review your overall plan once a quarter and be prepared to revise and re-present it to senior management every six months.

Don't forget, a plan without resources will fail. So you need to budget for the 3Ms, the three key resources. These are:

● Men (and women) – human resources
● Money – budgets
● Minutes – timescales and time horizons for production, delivery, service, etc.

All aspects of SOSTAC® must be thought through. The next sections will take you through each of the SOSTAC® and 3Ms concepts. At the end, you will be able to plan your e-marketing with confidence.

SECTION SUMMARY 10.1

Introduction to e-marketing planning

E-marketing plans must support, and be integrated with, corporate/business plans and marketing plans. SOSTAC® stands for: Situation analysis, Objectives and Strategy, Tactics, Action and Control.

10.2 Situation analysis

Situation analysis is the first part of the e-marketing plan. It answers the question 'Where are we now?' After this you can define where you want to go (see Objectives in Section 10.3). We need to analyse both internally and externally (Figure 10.2): internally within the organization; and externally, the business environment affecting our online business situation.

The traditional tried and tested analytical areas are:

- *KPIs* – key performance indicators which identify the business's success criteria, results, data and measurements against benchmarks
- *SWOT analysis* – identifying internal strengths and weaknesses, as well as external opportunities and threats
- *PEST* – political, economic, social and technological variables that shape your marketplace
- *Customers* – how many are online, how many prefer iDTV – are there new channel segments emerging?
- *Competitors* – who are they? New online *pure play* adversaries or the same old *'bricks and clicks'* competitors as always?
- *Distributors* – are new online intermediaries (e.g. affiliate networks) emerging while old offline distributors migrate their services online?

'The real act of discovery consists not in finding new lands, but in seeing with new eyes' (Marcel Proust).

INTERNAL ANALYSIS

The internal analysis looks at key performance indicators (KPIs). Common KPIs used to assess online activities include:

- Enquiries or leads
- Sales
- Market share
- ROI (return on investment) (see Section 10.7)
- Online revenue or service contribution (see Section 10.3).

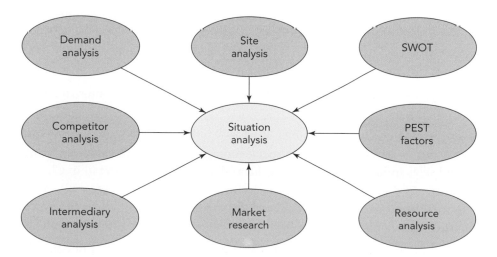

Figure 10.2   The different types of management information that should feed into your situation analysis

Other KPIs include:

- *Unique visitors* – the number of separate, individual visitors who visit the site (typically over a month).

- *Conversion rates* to different goals – the percentage of visitors converting to subscribers (or becoming customers). This is critical to e-marketing. Let's take an example. Say 2 per cent of 5,000 visitors to a site in a month convert to 100 customers who place an order. £10,000 cost divided by 100 conversions = £100 cost per order. Now imagine you can double your conversion rate, or better still quadruple it to 8 per cent; you then get £25 cost per order. The leverage impact caused by improved conversion rates is huge – revenues go up and percentage marketing costs go down. We saw in Chapter 2 how you should define and score different conversion goals for different types of outcome.

- Total numbers of *sessions* or *visits* to a web site (forget *'hits'* – these are a spurious measure, since when a web page is downloaded to the PC, a number of separate data transfers or hits take place, usually one for each HTML and graphics file. Techies need to measure hits because this helps them plan the resources needed to run the sites efficiently; as an e-marketer, you should measure *page impressions* because that's one measure of customer traffic to your site, and for an advertiser it equates with other familiar measures such as 'opportunities to view').

- *Repeat visits*. This is the average number of visits per individual. The total number of sessions is divided by the number of unique visitors. Update your site more often and people come back more often. *Cookies* can help track repeat visits. Remember to get permission before placing any cookies on someone else's PC.

- *Duration* – the average length of time visitors spend on your site (but remember that for some areas of the site, such as online sales or customer service, you may want to minimize duration). A similar measure is the number of pages viewed per visitor.

- *Most popular pages* or most popular product – can be identified by seeing which pages are attracting the most traffic and the longest duration. Some large e-commerce and media sites watch this every day or even hourly so that when they see something popular, they lift the offer onto the home page to boost traffic even more for a period.

- *Subscription rates* – number of visitors subscribing for services such as an opt-in email and newsletters.

- *Churn rates* – percentage of subscribers withdrawing or unsubscribing (after you have emailed them).

- *Clickthrough rates (CTR)* – from a banner ad or web link on another site to your own.

- *Social media engagement and ROI* – new social contacts, share of conversation, conversation polarity and sales influenced by social media as discussed in more detail in Chapter 5.

All of the preceding KPIs can be quantified and used as objectives, which can be constantly measured. Section 10.7 on control explains how frequently each KPI is measured and by whom.

Costs also need to be analysed. These metrics are also considered as part of control (Section 10.7). Internal analysis will also review the success of an organization's resources, processes and structure in delivering customer value, satisfaction and loyalty. Market research of customers and partners will be needed to determine their opinions.

Remember that numbers out of context are meaningless. Sales of £1m – is this good news or bad news? If last year's sales were £500,000, then this is good news; but if they were £2m, then this is bad news. Imagine the previous year's sales were £500,000, this year's sales are £1m and the market had quadrupled in size? Although your sales have doubled, your market share has halved! This is bad news in the long run. So remember all indicators are relative – backwards and across – backwards over time – to see the trend (compared over previous periods) and across your industry – to see how competitive you are.

Additional KPI ratios of engagement through time can be derived from ABC Auditing for any site which uses a web analytics system; for example, in any particular period, a report can confirm the number of: page impressions/volume (number of pages opened by all browsers) and unique browsers/reach (number of individual visitors on a particular device: note that one person accessing the site via mobile and then later via a laptop counts as two browsers) (see Table 10.2). Reports can also include average page views per visit and average number of visits per visitor. These can be related to site enhancements and marketing campaigns that occur at different times.

Table 10.2 Excerpt from the *Guardian* newspaper: ABC-audited traffic volume

Online Property: Certificate of Activity
For the period: 1 May 2012–31 May 2012

guardian.co.uk

Property Name: guardian.co.uk

Daily Activity: guardian.co.uk

Date	Unique Browsers	Page Impressions
01-May-12	3,495,183	13,744,485
02-May-12	3,617,010	13,489,528
03-May-12	3,519,229	13,300,644
04-May-12	3,932,135	14,467,646
05-May-12	3,017,140	10,931,014
06-May-12	3,163,706	12,439,151
07-May-12	3,525,095	13,209,013
08-May-12	3,563,617	13,880,280
09-May-12	3,949,013	14,165,682
10-May-12	3,430,261	13,497,055
11-May-12	3,212,854	12,505,642
12-May-12	2,609,720	9,920,796
13-May-12	2,945,786	12,672,639
14-May-12	3,748,934	15,188,670
14-May-12	4,047,248	15,319,161

E-MARKETING INSIGHT

Neil Mason of Applied Insights on measurement frameworks

As a consultant who helps customers improve their online business performance, Neil advocates the use of an online performance management framework to help focus an organization on its most important digital marketing KPIs or the 'measures that matter'. Table 10.3 (below) shows an example summarizing metrics for improving performance in different parts of the customer lifecycle from acquisition to retention. The rows indicate different forms of tracking metrics and performance drivers which will influence higher-level metrics such as the customer-centric key performance indicators (KPIs) and business-value KPIs. In the bottom two rows, we have also added in typical strategies and tactics used to achieve objectives, which shows the relationship between objectives and strategy. Note, though, that this framework mainly creates a focus on efficiency of conversion, although there are some effectiveness measures also such as reach, profit and advocacy. We have added strategies and tactics to show how these should be based on achieving goals set in measurement. Use this as a checklist to assess which goals are relevant for you at the objective-setting stage of SOSTAC and which KPIs should be used to assess performance at the control stage, using web analytics and management dashboards which include visual summaries of the KPIs.

STRENGTHS AND WEAKNESSES

A situation analysis usually includes an analysis of strengths and weaknesses. For a multi-channel business, the e-marketing plan should focus on comparing the strengths and weaknesses of the digital channel with other channels; i.e. it is an *Internet-specific SWOT or e-SWOT*. A sample e-SWOT is shown in Table 10.1. What do you think are your online strengths and weaknesses? Which tactical tools are you particularly good at using? You may review the following:

- Customer database – is it large, live, clean and integrated? Can you deliver personalized communications (one-to-one) through every communications tool both online and offline?
- Online customer care – is it sloppy or outstanding? Has your speed of response or speed of resolution increased or decreased? Do you measure it?
- Web site – is it a user-centred design that is effective in converting visitors to outcomes? Do you use customer scenarios and usability testing?
- Integrated database – does it link all online and offline tools together?
- Opt-in email campaigns – are these generating results?
- Web links – are *referrals* being generated from a range of sources?
- Display ads or sponsorship – are clickthrough rates and customer acquisition costs favourable?
- Mobile marketing – what are your experiences (if relevant) with mobile phone campaigns?
- Interactive TV – if it's relevant to your marketplace, have you any experience with it?

EXTERNAL ANALYSIS

The external analysis includes analysing customers (see Chapter 4), benchmarking competitors, and the uncontrollable opportunities and threats. E-marketing is overflowing with new opportunities and threats thrown up by the constant waves of change. We showed a number of tools you could use to assess your online marketplace in Table 10.1 You should create an e-marketplace map as we showed in Chapter 3 (Figure 3.1) to understand the dynamics and interactions of different customer types with search engines, different intermediaries and competitors. You can also use the social media sites to explore customer types, brands and competitors from a different perspective. These include Wikipedia (www.wikipedia.org) – the user-generated online encyclopaedia; Flickr (www.flickr.com) – user-generated pictures of products and their ads ; YouTube (www.youtube.com) – customer reviews and critiques, advertisements, spoof advertisements (including 'user-generated (dis)content' – or negative advertisements), press conference highlights; the Digg (www.digg.com) tech-news community – votes on stories they think are most interesting; Delicious (www.delicious.com) – an online favourite folder where members share their finds with other members. In addition, Google Alert and Google News track brands, companies and people or trends and deliver the headlines daily or weekly into your inbox. Lastly, the Wayback Machine (www.archive.org) allows you to see old web pages dating back to 1996 – if you were interested in tracking how an organization or a brand is changing over time.

Consider customers, how are they changing? How many are online? Do you have a similar proportion of your customers buying online? If not, why not? Figure 10.3 shows the type of picture you need to build up of customer activity showing demand for your online services. This compares the role of online channels, such as the web site, as a means of reaching, influencing and directly delivering sales. We need to ask – how many customers buy exclusively online? How many browse online and shop offline? How many use price comparison sites? How many are happy to give you permission to email them, text message them or even snail mail them? Are the numbers changing? You should repeat this activity for different segments requiring different products. It is also useful for multi-channel businesses to compare the

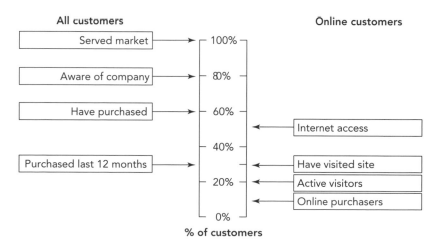

Figure 10.3 Assessing customer adoption of online services

demographic profile of their online B2C or B2B audiences with their traditional offline audiences, as this should inform strategies to encourage adopters or non-adopters of digital channels to purchase more.

What do your competitors offer on their web sites that you don't? Who are they? Are there new online players entering your market? What are their differentiators?

A further issue is distributors such as online intermediaries. Are there new intermediaries you could partner with, are your competitors already working with them?

So, effectively, the analysis is not a one-off annual analysis. It's an ongoing observation of your marketplace known as *environmental scanning* which includes regularly checking statistics, web sites, customer surveys, and reading reports.

OPPORTUNITIES AND THREATS

The OT in SWOT, the external 'opportunities and threats', are churned up by the relentless tide of change. They can arise from the PEST factors:

- Political – laws or regulations that affect your online marketing, such as the UK Privacy and Electronic Communications Regulations (PECR)
- Economic – variables impact on all markets
- Social – the trends that shape future online behaviour
- Technology – are you abreast with developments – have you got an overview of the emerging technology?

External opportunities and threats are also posed or presented by changes in aspects of the marketplace such as customer behaviour or new strategies pursued by intermediaries or competitors. We advocate summarizing the results of your situation analysis through an Internet-specific SWOT analysis. Remember, hyper-competition has arrived in many markets where border-less and category-less businesses (competitors from other industry sectors) have emerged. Even traditional competitors can compete in new ways such as targeting your customers via Facebook and LinkedIn.

> *Both Facebook and LinkedIn enable marketers to target their ads using the goldmine of demographic data they hold about users. Whether serving ads to users by age, interests or location, or targeting employees of a specific company or fans of a competitor brand.*
>
> *(Manning, 2012)*

BEST PRACTICE E-MARKETING TIP

Perform an e-SWOT to identify and select optional strategies

The form of SWOT shown in Table 10.1 is recommended since it not only summarizes the current situation, but can be used to help in developing strategy by placing optional strategies on it. It is not important in which cells the strategies are placed – some may overlap – but it is a method of formulating and then selecting strategies. Remember, the first strategy someone thinks of is rarely the best one. Hence strategic options need to be considered before choosing the best strategy.

SECTION SUMMARY 10.2

Situation analysis

Your situation analysis should include KPIs, customers, competitors and intermediaries as well as the uncontrollable PEST factors. Now you know where you are, the next section will help you to determine your online destiny – where you want to go (your objectives).

10.3 Objectives

While the situation analysis explains 'where you are now', objectives clarify where you are going – where you want to be. By the end of this section, you'll know what are the realistic objectives of an e-marketing plan, and what benefits each of these objectives can yield for your business.

There are five broad benefits, reasons or objectives of e-marketing. These can be summarized as the 5 Ss (see Chapter 1 for a description and Table 1.2). You must decide whether all, or only some, are going to drive your e-marketing plan.

- *Sell* – grow sales (through wider distribution to customers you can't service offline or perhaps a wider product range than in local stores, or better prices).
- *Serve* – add value (give customers excellent service and extra benefits online; e.g. product development in response to online dialogue).
- *Speak* – get closer to customers by tracking them, asking them questions, conducting online interviews, creating a dialogue, monitoring forums, groups, blogs and tweets and, most of all, listening and responding to this dialogue in a structured way (collecting usable customer insights).
- *Save* – save costs: of service, sales transactions and administration, print and post. Switching telemarketing customer support to Facebook customer support can be a lot more efficient and effective. Can you reduce transaction costs and therefore make online sales more profitable? Or use cost savings to enable you to cut prices, which in turn could enable you to generate greater market share?

- *Sizzle* – add some magical 'added value' that can only be delivered online; e.g. the Sistine Chapel online allows you to climb up the walls and study Michelangelo's paintings in detail. Extend the brand experience online in new ways. The web scores very highly as a medium for creating brand awareness and recognition.

Specific objectives are created for each. Consider sales – a typical objective might be: 'To grow the business with online sales; e.g. to generate at least 30 per cent of sales online within 6 months.' Or 'To generate an extra £100,000 worth of sales online by December.'

These objectives can be further broken down; e.g. to achieve £100,000 of online sales means you have to generate 1,000 online customers spending, on average, £100. If, say, your conversion rate of visitors to customers was a high 1 per cent, then this means you have to generate 100,000 visitors to your site. You can use the KPIs (key performance indicators) mentioned in Section 10.2 to help you quantify the main objectives and the subsequent detailed objectives.

Specific targets for the *online revenue contribution* for different e-channels should be set for the future, as shown in Figure 10.4. Objectives should be set for the percentage of customers who are reached or influenced by each channel (or brand awareness in the target market) and the percentage of sales to be achieved through the channel. The online revenue contribution should also consider *cannibalization* – are online sales achieved at the expense of traditional offline channels?

Another major objective might be to build brand awareness; e.g. to create brand awareness among 50 per cent of your target market through online activities. Equally, it might be to use the online opportunity to create some excitement around the brand ('sizzle'). Interactive TV and text messaging come to mind as do reactive viral marketing techniques.

Another major online objective might be to consolidate relationships and increase loyalty from 50 per cent to 70 per cent among a high-spending customer segment over a five-year period. Or would you prefer to do this in one year? If yes, this will affect your strategy.

There are many types of objective. They will, of course, be underpinned by either financial objectives (sales, number of new customers, retention rates, average revenue, profit margin, lifetime value – see Figure 10.5), or communications objectives (positioning, branding, awareness, e-CRM . . .).

Whatever the objective, it ultimately has to be measurable. Therefore your objectives need to be quantifiable and to have a deadline.

Finally, be realistic about what is achievable – interactive technology means that e-marketing offers enormous potential for data gathering and analysis, but many advertisers and marketers just expect too much!

So ask, are your objectives well-defined and properly thought through? Are they SMART – specific, measurable, achievable, realistic and time-related?

Online Media Mix model – based on percentage of budget – with example of 'average' clickthrough rates

Overall budget	£100 000

External online media

	Media costs					Media volume/response				Conversion to Opportunity			Conversion to Sale			
	Set-up/creative/Mgt costs	CPM	CPC	Media costs	Total cost	Budget %	Impressions or names	CTR	Clicks or visits	CRO	Opport-unities	CPO (cost per lead)	CRS	Sales	% of sales	CPS (CPA)
Online ad buys (CPM)	£0	£10.0	£5.00	£10 000	£10 000	10%	1 000 000	0.2%	2000	10.0%	200	£50.00	10.0%	20	1%	£500.0
Ad network (CPC)	£0	£20.0	£1.00	£20 000	£20 000	20%	1 000 000	2.0%	20 000	10.0%	2000	£10.00	10.0%	200	10%	£100.0
Paid search (CPC)	£0	£10.0	£0.50	£30 000	£30 000	30%	3 000 000	2.0%	60 000	10.0%	6000	£5.00	10.0%	600	30%	£50.0
Natural search (Fixed)	£0	£0.5	£0.05	£5000	£5000	5%	10 000 000	1.0%	100 000	10.0%	10 000	£0.50	10.0%	1000	50%	£5.0
Affiliates (CPS)	£0	£10.0	£1.00	£5000	£5000	5%	500 000	1.0%	5000	10.0%	500	£10.00	10.0%	50	3%	£100.0
Aggregators (CPS)	£0	£0.0	£0.00	£0	£0	0%	0	1.0%	0	10.0%	0	£0.00	10.0%	0	0%	£100.0
Sponsorships (Fixed)	£0	£100.0	£33.33	£10 000	£10 000	10%	100 000	0.3%	300	10.0%	30	£333.33	10.0%	3	0%	£3333.3
Online PR (Fixed)	£0	£100.0	£10.00	£10 000	£10 000	10%	100 000	1.0%	1000	10.0%	100	£100.00	10.0%	10	1%	£1000.0
Email lists (CPM)	£0	£10.0	£1.00	£10 000	£10 000	10%	1 000 000	1.0%	10 000	10.0%	1000	£10.00	10.0%	100	5%	£100.0
Total/Average	£0	£6.0	£0.50	£100 000	£100 000	100%	16 700 000	1.2%	198 300	10.0%	19 830	£5.04	10.0%	1983	100%	£50.4

Internal online media

	Set-up/creative/Mgt costs	CPM	CPC	Media costs	Total cost	Budget %	Impressions or names	CTR	Clicks or visits	CRO	Opport-unities	CPO (cost per lead)	CRS	Sales	% of sales	CPS (CPA)
In-house email list/DM	£1000	£0.0	£0.33	£0	£1000	n/a	100 000	3.0%	3000	15.0%	450	£2.22	30%	135	n/a	£7.4
Own-site ads (other footfall)	£1000	£0.0	£0.05	£0	£1000	n/a	1 000 000	2.0%	20 000	10.0%	2000	£0.50	25%	500	n/a	£2.0
Total/Average	£2000	£1.8	£0.09	£0	£2000	n/a	1 100 000	2.1%	23 000	10.8%	2450	£0.82	15.8%	635	n/a	£3.1

| **Overall total/Average** | £2000 | £5.7 | £0.46 | £100 000 | £102 000 | n/a | 17 800 000 | 1.2% | 221 300 | 11.2% | 22 280 | £4.58 | 18.2% | 2618 | n/a | £39.0 |

Figure 10.4 An e-communications mix for an annual plan – blue cells can be changed for a 'what-if' analysis

Source: Marketing Insights (www.marketing-insights.co.uk/spreadsheet.htm)

	A	B	C	D	E	F
1	New customers in Year 1	100 000				
2	Margin	15%				
3		Year 1	Year 2	Year 3	Year 4	Year 5
4	Customers (new)	100 000	50 000	27 500	16 500	10 725
5	Retention rate	50%	55%	60%	65%	70%
6	Average revenue per annum	£100	£110	£120	£130	£140
7	Total revenue	£10 000 000	£5 500 000	£3 300 000	£2 145 000	£1 501 500
8	Net profit	£1 500 000	£825 000	£495 000	£321 000	£225 000
9	Discount rate	1.000	0.860	0.740	0.636	0.547
10	NPV contribution	£1 500 000	£709 500	£366 102	£204 633	£123 198
11	Cumulative NPV contribution	£1 500 000	£2 209 500	£2 575 602	£2 780 235	£2 903 433
12	Lifetime value at net present value	£15	£22	£26	£28	£29

(a)

	A	B	C	D	E	F
1	New customers in Year 1	100 000				
2	Margin	0.15				
3		Year 1	Year 2	Year 3	Year 4	Year 5
4	Customers	=B1	=B4*B5	=C4*C5	=D4*D5	=E4*E5
5	Retention rate	0.5	0.55	0.6	0.65	0.7
6	Average revenue per annum	100	110	120	130	140
7	Total revenue	=B4*B6	=C4*C6	=D4*D6	=E4*E6	=F4*F6
8	Net profit	=B7*$B$2	=C7*$B$2	=D7*$B$2	=E7*$B$2	=F7*$B$2
9	Discount rate	1	0.86	0.7396	0.636	0.547
10	NPV contribution	=B8*B9	–C8*C9	–D8*D9	–E8*E9	–F8*F9
11	Cumulative NPV contribution	=B10	=B11+C10	=C11+D10	=D11+E10	=E11+F10
(b) 12	Lifetime value at net present value	=B11/$B$1	=C11/$B$1	=D11/$B$1	=E11/$B$1	=F11/$B$1

Figure 10.5   (a) Lifetime value model – blue cells show what can be changed for a 'what-if' analysis (b) Lifetime value model showing formulae corresponding to Figure 10.5 (a)

Source: Marketing Insights (www.marketing-insights.co.uk/spreadsheet.htm)

SECTION SUMMARY 10.3

Objectives

The 5 Ss (Sell, Serve, Speak, Save and Sizzle) are a useful starting point for objectives. Ultimately, objectives have to be SMART. Finally, objectives help you to focus on where you want to get to. Now you're ready to move on to how to get there; the next section shows you just how to do this – strategy.

10.4 Strategy

There is much confusion about the difference between strategy and tactics. Strategy summarizes 'How do we get there?' Objectives specify 'where we want to go'. Strategy summarizes how to achieve the objectives and guides all the subsequent detailed tactical decisions. Strategy is influenced by both the prioritization of objectives (Sell, Serve, Speak, Save and Sizzle) and, of course, the amount of resources available (see Section 10.8). It should embrace the aspects previously discussed – OVPs, contact strategies (databases and technology required) and overall trends affecting the marketplace. Strategy should also exploit distinctive competitive advantage. Play to your strengths (assuming the market/customers want your strengths).

BEST PRACTICE E-MARKETING TIP

The sales and profit delivered by each prong of the strategy (e.g. acquisition, retention or new product introduction) should be modelled using available information on customer and marketplace demand for products, along with competitors. Different scenarios should be reviewed to check that your strategies will deliver the objectives. This will be an iterative process with models revised during the goal setting and strategy selection and tactics.

So what goes into an e-marketing strategy? The answer – whatever it takes (within your resources) to achieve your objectives. The e-marketing strategy focuses on what you're going to do online. It can include propositions (which summarize the online mix). Will your online proposition be different to your offline proposition? Or integrated? Can you succinctly tell your boss what your strategy is? Strategy helps it all to fit together and avoids ad hoc tactical patchworks which usually, in the end, cause more complications. For some strategists, strategy is all about establishing an integrated database between your web site and all other communications points. For others, it is developing the web site from stage 1 to stage 2, stage 3 or stage 4 in the evolutionary stages of a web site (e.g. a fully integrated, automated, database-driven site linking opt-in email and direct mail). Others develop an Internet strategy, an intranet strategy and an extranet strategy. These are longer-term strategic perspectives. For a few, e-marketing strategies are just about traffic building – a shorter-term strategic perspective. Planning around customer lifetime value forces marketers to think long term and therefore more strategically. See lifetime value calculations in Figure 10.5.

Ideally, an experienced strategist would create strategy by thinking purely about how to achieve the objectives with the resources available (and in the context of competitor strategies – both existing and potential). Having generated several strategic options, the best strategy is carefully chosen and this then eventually cascades down into the tactical details. However, in reality, because there is little good solid experience of making strategies, many practitioners tend to move on to what they're good at – tactics; e.g. display ads, search marketing and opt-in email. Having developed a range of exciting tactics, they then sit back and try to make sense of it all or try to tie it all together, summarize it and then call it a traffic strategy (retrospective strategy making!). This can work if (a) it all integrates sensibly; and (b) you can test it against at least another two strategic alternatives.

Other strategists draw from marketing warfare; e.g. full frontal attack (comparative marketing on web sites); flanking attack using the web site to highlight areas of weakness among competitors (surround bigger players by creating an array of microsites and web rings around an area so that smaller players cannot complete).

PRACTICAL E-MARKETING TIP

Ensuring that strategies support objectives

To help ensure that strategies support objectives, you should create a linkage between the two as shown in Table 10.1, which also shows related tactics to deliver the strategies.

Strategy is crucial. Get it wrong and all your hard work is wasted. As Kenichi Ohmae (1999) said, 'There's no point rowing harder if you're rowing in the wrong direction.' Hard work is wasted if the strategy is wrong. Take some examples of absurd strategies. Imagine building an amazing WAP site, but none of your customers use WAP phones. Or imagine building a transactional web site to take orders, yet the majority of your market only browses online and always shops offline. Or missing the early adopters in your target market by avoiding interactive TV advertising. Or worse still, reaching them through interactive TV, but not having the back-office systems and fulfilment services required to, say, deliver pizzas within 30 minutes, or offer a test drive the next day. Domino's Pizza has successfully used interactive TV to reach its online audience and then created the infrastructure to serve them. Integrating procedures and redesigning business processes are strategic and tend to be longer term.

Strategy summarizes how the objectives will be achieved. So let us say the overall marketing objective is to achieve a 50 per cent increase in sales. The strategy that rolls out could be based on expanding the marketplace and securing new customers, attacking a particular competitor's customers, or simply reducing churn (lost customers) and getting more of your existing customers to reorder. Three different strategies: one for market expansion, one for competitor attack and one for customer retention.

COMPLEMENT OR REPLACE?

An e-marketing strategy should define the level of resources directed at different channels. Essentially, the question is: will the online channels complement the company's other channels or will they replace other channels? Gulati and Garino (2000) describe it as 'Getting the right mix of bricks and clicks'. If it is believed that sales through digital channels will primarily replace other channels, then it is important to invest in the technical, human and organizational resources to achieve this. A 'replace' strategy was chosen by airlines such as easyJet and Ryanair which now sell over 90 per cent of their tickets online. To assess the 'replace' versus 'complement' strategy alternatives, Kumar (1999) provides a framework. He suggests that replacement is most likely to happen when:

1 Customer access to the Internet is high

2 The Internet can offer a better value proposition than other media (i.e. propensity to purchase online is high)

3 The product can be delivered over the Internet (it can be argued that this is not essential)

4 The product can be standardized (the user does not usually need to view to purchase).

If at least two of Kumar's conditions are met, there may be a replacement effect. For example, purchase of travel services or insurance online fulfils criteria 1, 2 and 4.

STRATEGIC COMPONENTS – STOP AND SATIS

One way to remember some of the key components of any marketing strategy is the acronym STOP and SATIS –stop, think and develop a satisfactory strategy:

- Segments
- Target markets
- Objectives
- Positioning
  &
- Sequence
- Acquisition versus retention
- Tactical tools (the mix or selection)
- Integration
- Social media (includes content strategy).

First of all, all marketing strategies should embrace STP: *segmentation* (S), choosing *target markets* (T) and how the company or brand is going to be positioned (P).

Segments (S) and *Target markets (T)*. What segments are being targeted online? How do we break the market into segments and which ones are we going to target? Who is the target market?

Objectives (O) don't need to be explicitly repeated in strategy, but it is important to always bear them in mind. Keep asking 'Will this strategy achieve the basic objective that we're trying to achieve?' If not, drop the strategy.

Positioning (P) is a fundamental platform for the customer proposition or OVP (online value proposition). Possibly the most difficult part of strategy is developing a crystal-clear positioning in the market place; i.e. how exactly do you want to be perceived in the minds of your target audience? What exactly is the product, its price and perceived value in the marketplace? Can this be summarized into a strong proposition? Is it a source of differentiation – what is the *online value proposition*? Figure 10.6 shows how the details of an OVP are explained on a 'How it works' page for those who aren't convinced to immediately start a trial. Another question to ask for multi-channel organizations is 'Can new digital products or services be developed to compete with pure plays?'

Sequence (S) and stages embrace a couple of strategic e-issues. Sequence means there should be a sequence of tools; e.g. which comes first, building awareness (via online PR, sponsorship and ads) or trying to convert customers with Facebook and Foursquare sales promotions or affiliate marketing programmes? In addition, it is imperative to develop credibility before raising visibility; e.g. develop a credible web site that works before raising visibility and generating a lot of traffic. More importantly, should the business have a series of online stages of web evolution (see the evolutionary stages of Quelch and Klein, 1996)?

Acquisition (A) or retention? – that is the question. Is there an emphasis on acquiring new customers, or are there enough customers currently on board to really focus on keeping them happy, growing them into lifetime customers and also growing their share of wallet? Customer acquisition requires a different emphasis on tactical tools such as aggregators, natural search, paid search and display ads than the tools required for customer retention.

Tactical tools (T) – the choice and emphasis (mix) of some tactical tools are driven by strategy. Some brands have built themselves with large TV ad campaigns, while others grew through their viral aspect online. Some brands today are strategically reducing this emphasis away from TV and moving more into sponsorship and community building online. Remember, do not discount offline potential – it is still significant.

Integration (I) – can the customer be dealt with as a recognizable individual with unique preferences, regardless of how the customer comes into contact with the brand or organization? Are the web site processes and databases integrated and accessible, whether access is from social media sign-up forms, mobile-optimized web sites, apps or even telemarketing? Can the online activities be integrated with the offline processes and databases? What level of database integration is required to allow a dynamic dialogue using an array of tactical tools?

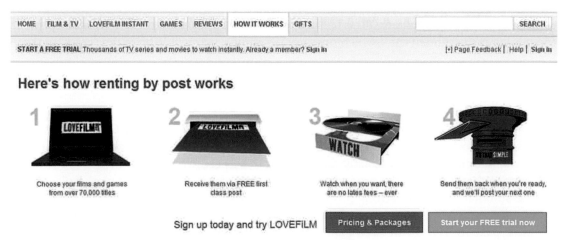

Figure 10.6   LOVEFiLM explains the details of its OVP on its 'How it works' page (www.lovefilm.com/how-it-works)

Social media (S) – is more than a tactical e-tool (although some use it just to shout and try to build awareness). It can become a platform for listening to and engaging with customers. It can also be used strategically to develop a completely new *modus operandi* as demonstrated by the Ladder of Engagement (see Section 3.10). For example, incorporating user-generated content (UGC) into the development of new products is a major strategic decision. Decisions about social media involve developing a 'content strategy', determining what topics will be published in which media on what platforms.

E-marketing strategy guides the choice of target markets, positioning and propositions which in turn guide the optimum mix – the sequence of e-tools (such as web sites, opt-in email, e-sponsorship, viral marketing), service levels and evolutionary stages (from brochureware sites to two-way interactive sites to fully integrated e-business systems). One ultimate (medium- to long-term) part of e-marketing strategy is the development of the dynamic dialogue (including a contact strategy) via the integrated database. Regardless of how the customer comes into contact, he or she must be dealt with as a recognizable individual with unique preferences. This affects customer retention which, in itself, is a strategic decision (e.g. to improve customer retention levels requires a complete integrated database and contact strategy, as explained in Chapter 8 on e-CRM). The strategy can also determine how social media will be used.

The overall balance of the marketing mix is strategic, while the details of the mix are tactical. For example, deciding whether to heavily discount prices and raise a high profile in a broad array of downmarket online web sites and communities is strategic. The tactical details would list the sites and communities and relevant prices..

POOR STRATEGY

'Bad strategy abounds. Senior executives who can spot it stand a much better chance of creating good strategies', says Richard Rumelt, Professor of Business and Society at the UCLA Anderson School of Management. Consider this strategy: 'Our fundamental strategy is one of customer-centric intermediation.' Rumelt rightly rips this to pieces:

> *Intermediation means that the company accepts deposits and then lends out the money. In other words, it is a bank. The buzzphrase 'customer centric' could mean that the bank competes by offering better terms and service, but an examination of its policies does not reveal any distinction in this regard. The phrase 'customer-centric inter-mediation' is pure fluff. Remove the fluff and you learn that the bank's fundamental strategy is being a bank.*

> *(Rumelt, 2011)*

E-marketing strategy is also found to be lacking in many businesses. This contributes to ad hoc tactical approaches that are short-term and often unfocused. Here's a selection of examples of some elements of e-marketing strategies that do not constitute a full strategy. You will see vastly different approaches to this crucial aspect of planning:

> 'by creating a seamless interface between online and offline, integrated by the underlying database . . .'

'by moving through the three evolutionary stages over an 18-month period means the race is on to get our e-strategy on track . . .'

'integrate website, database and CRM to efficiently automate a two-way dialogue between customers and our business . . .'

'by establishing a presence on several different portals . . .'

'to own a particular content sector online rather than try to sell a specific product'.

Bradley *et al.* (2011) list 'Ten timeless tests to help you kick the tires on your strategy, and kick up the level of strategic dialogue throughout your company'. However, we are only going to give you the top five since few strategies pass more than three of these tests.

- Test 1: Will your strategy beat the market?
- Test 2: Does your strategy tap a true source of advantage?
- Test 3: Is your strategy granular about where to compete? [Think 30 to 50 segments]
- Test 4: Does your strategy put you ahead of trends?
- Test 5: Does your strategy rest on privileged insights?

(Bradley *et al.*, 2011)

E-marketing strategy examples

Although there is a scarcity of examples of comprehensive e-marketing strategies, here is a selection where you can clearly see many of the STOP and SATIS components.

Intel (Bolger, 2011) decided to reposition the company from 'High quality technology products' to a 'Leader in technology breakthroughs', targeting Generation Y by associating Intel with innovation in music, art and lifestyle, using social media to leverage offline real events. . .

Unilever (source unknown) took a major strategic shift to change Persil from a product-centric corporate portal (product information) to customer-centric sites and social presences (two main sections: Time In and Time Out – lifestyle and time for yourself – relaxation, minding your skin, diet and kids, time with kids . . . tips for a happy family . . . 'get creative with kids' section). This is an online brand experience integrated into TV, press and Internet campaigns.

Unilever is also switching budgets from online advertising spend to social media content across all product ranges.

The digital marketing strategy of Bent Rail Boots (www.justinboots.com; American cowboy boots) had a social media emphasis (Falls, 2010): launch Bent Rail Boots by talking to the young target audience where they were: online – using branded pages on social media platforms and inviting fans to follow the music of its hip, young country music endorsees, developing exclusive, value-adding content especially for their youth audience and making the content compelling enough for people to share; driving people to specific calls-to-action to see, try or learn more about the new line of boots.

The Great Sportsmanship Programme (www.greatsportsmanship.org; Smith, 2012) was repositioned from a sportsmanship book (targeted at sports fans in the UK and Ireland) to a sportsmanship educational programme (including curriculum integration, teacher training, student and teacher resources [including the book], an ambassadorial programme and social media campaign focused around the Big 5 social media platforms: Facebook, Google+, Twitter, YouTube and LinkedIn, linking to blogs. The primary target is United Arab Emirates (UAE) secondary students learning English.

Implicit in all strategic choices is resource. The strategy will, in the end, be constrained by the resources available and their allocation (see Section 10.8). For example, when trying to allocate resources between web site design, web site service and web site traffic generation, whichever strategy you choose, try to generate a few strategic alternatives before deciding the final e-marketing strategy. Remember, the first strategy that comes to mind is not necessarily the best one.

You may generate different propositions (with different mixes) for different markets. This is perfectly acceptable. But ensure that each strategy includes the key components (STOP and SATIS) and works within the limited resources available (3Ms). Finally, determining how much you are prepared to invest in either acquiring a customer or retaining an existing one is a useful exercise; it is strategic insofar as it influences your contact strategy, integrated database, sequence of messages across a variety of tools as well as forcing you to think beyond the short-term, one-off transactional sale.

E-MARKETING EXCELLENCE

Beware: trading advocacy and loyalty for investigation and interest

> *Say we run a program that instead of engaging and growing relationships with our top fans, it's designed to get 10 million additional likes by the end of the month. Over the course of that month our metrics will show success. Additional likes per week will go up. Comments per post will go up. Impression numbers will be through the roof. Yet in the process we are also drowning out the voices of the advocates in a sea of folks who care only for the offer that got them there. We've essentially traded advocacy and loyalty for investigation and interest.*

> *(Knorp, 2011)*

In 2011, Pepsi's marketing strategy centred on its social media spend, an approach questioned by the Ad Contrarian (2011). 'We took the divergent path', explained Frank Cooper, chief consumer engagement officer for Pepsi. 'We wanted to explore how a brand could be integrated into the digital space.'

The idea behind the programme was that you, the consumer, got to engage with Pepsi by voting for the 'Refresh' projects you deemed most worthy.

According to Bob Hoffman (the Ad Contrarian, 2011), the Refresh Project accomplished everything a social media programme is expected to: over 80 million votes were registered; almost 3.5 million 'Likes' on the Pepsi Facebook page; almost 60,000 Twitter followers. The only thing it failed to do was sell Pepsi.

Massimo d'Amore, then chief executive of PepsiCo Americas Beverages had this to say: 'When my ancestors went from the Middle Ages to the Renaissance, they blew up the place, so that's what we are doing.' He also said: 'We need television to make the big, bold statement. . .'.

E-MARKETING INSIGHT

Timothy Cummings on competitive strategies

Cummings (2001) applies well-known military strategies to e-marketing. The strategies are not exclusive. They are:

1 *Full-frontal attack*: e.g. use of comparative marketing on web sites.
2 *Flanking attack*: e.g. use the web site to strike at areas in which competitors are weak such as price or service.
3 *Surround and cut-off*: e.g. larger companies use their resources to provide web site communications that are targeted at micromarkets. Smaller companies cannot compete with the resources needed.
4 *Blocking attack*: e.g. closing out competitors by offering additional services to customers.
5 *Guerrilla attack*: e.g. direct attack on competitors using guerrilla tactics such as online PR. The easyJet online competition to guess the losses of rival airline Go is an example of these tactics.
6 *Niche defence*: e.g. specializing through providing superior content or services to competitors.
7 *Territorial defence*: e.g. developing leading communities for particular segments or countries in advance of a competitor.
8 *Mobile defence*: e.g. developing new online functionality that is one step ahead of the competitors.
9 *Stealth defence*: e.g. minimizing web content about a new service, so existing players find it difficult to find out about the new service. The service is promoted through direct sales, networking and word of mouth.
10 *Diplomatic nous*: e.g. partnering with content providers to increase the value of your site compared to competitors.

One of the best books on e-marketing strategy was written over two thousand years ago by Sun Tzu, a Chinese military genius who was conscious of the environment and understood the importance of alliances and market intelligence (translated by Wing, 1989).

Strategy

Strategy is the big picture. It summarizes how you're going to get there. STOP and SATIS combined with resource allocation (constraints) present at least some of the components required as part of an e-strategy.

Now you're ready to move on to the details of strategy – tactics. The next section explores them in more detail.

10.5 Tactics

'The 21st century is not a place for tidy minds' (Sir Martin Sorrell, cited by Thomas, 2012).

Tactics are the details of strategy. You need to list all the e-tools you plan to use, in the sequence or stages guided by the strategy.

THE DIFFERENCE BETWEEN STRATEGY AND TACTICS

Tactics tend to be short term and flexible, whereas strategy is longer-term and more enduring. But tactics must also be developed only after the strategy is agreed and set. It is tempting to do the reverse: have a bright idea for a new marketing initiative or a new service offering and rush it into play without a strategic context. Tactics don't drive strategy. You don't plan the journey until you have decided where you want to go.

It is easy to muddle strategy and tactics. Here's an oversimplified example: let's say your strategy is to create an effective e-CRM programme (because one of you wants to increase repeat sales by increasing customer retention/reducing customer churn). To deliver this strategy, you decide to use four tactical tools – four moments of contact with each customer over the next three months: these will be an email acknowledging the order, a follow-up email to check delivery was OK, a real Christmas card (if it was a seasonal product), and a personalized email and newsletter. These are the detailed tactics that support the strategy.

You need to think through what happens when. The best tool for this is a Gantt chart that lists all the tactical tools throughout the weeks and months of the period. So you can see what's happening when. A simple Gantt chart (see Table 10.3) can be used to detail which tools are used when by inserting an 'x' in the appropriate column.

Table 10.3 Marketing tactics – displayed on a Gantt chart

	J	F	M	A	M	J	J	A	S	O	N	D	£000's
Web site	x	x											25,000
Forums			x										5,000
Social media			x	x	x	x	x	x	x	x	x	x	30,000

Table 10.3 *(Continued)*

	J	F	M	A	M	J	J	A	S	O	N	D	£000's
Advertising													50,000
Display ads/Banner ads													
Pay Per Click ads													
Other	x		x	x		x			x			x	
Sponsorship	x	x	x	x	x	x	x	x	x	x	x	x	10,000
Online sponsorship – communities, pages, sites, events													
Public Relations													
Online-optimized News Releases		x		x		x		x		x			10,000
Viral marketing													
Direct Mail													
Opt-in email (NB retention versus acquisition)			x			x			x				20,000
Event-triggered, time-triggered, behavioural triggers													
E-newsletters													
Sales Promotions													
Incentives and calls-to-action online in emails, web sites and social media			x			x		x			x		10,000
Sales Force – Field Sales and Telemarketing													
Affiliate and partner marketing		x	x	x	x	x	x	x	x	x	x		50,000
Exhibitions and Events													
Virtual exhibitions, virtual worlds like Second Life									x				5,000
Packaging													Nil
N/A other than packaging images on the web site													
Point of Sale													35,000
Web site, particularly calls-to-action; product photos and product users' photos													
Web site personalization (and landing pages optimization)													
Total													**£250,000**

We have taken the ten communications tools and their various online tactical tools and started to develop, for example, major work on the web site for the first two months followed by a continued social media campaign throughout the year. An 'always on' Pay Per Click campaign is used quarterly and so on. Total spend is £250,000.

Also, your strategy will have gone through approval and budget processes and will be set for a defined period. Whereas your ability to make swift and effective tactical responses to the changing environment will be a key factor in determining your success – especially in e-business and e-marketing, where change happens so quickly. For example, you may know at the start how you plan to implement the strategy; but what if a competitor steals a march, or an e-tool you were planning to use fails? You must think on your feet, be first to react.

E-MARKETING TACTICS

E-marketing tactics focus on deciding the optimum marketing mix. This was described in detail in Chapter 2 'Remix'. Here we simply look at decisions about the choice of tactical e-tools. And then there are traffic tools such as banner ads, text messages, opt-in email, viral marketing, search engine optimization – all discussed in Chapter 7 on building traffic.

PRACTICAL E-MARKETING TIP

Automated event-triggered emails

Don't forget the importance of devoting resources to planning your contact strategy to support the customer lifecycle (see Chapter 8 on e-CRM) for the different audiences you are targeting. For example, cosmetics brand Clinique (www.clinique.co.uk; Figure 10.7) has different emails for its male and female audiences and has a cleverly crafted welcome strategy that explains its OVP and encourages trial of its online services and products.

Customer relationship management tools

If you then provide benefits or added-value information through the opt-in email service, you can develop an integrated database of customers and prospects which can be exploited in further ways: send them gifts, invite them to enter contests, run a free draw for tickets to a sports or cultural event you sponsor – the trick is to use the connection with the customer to create ongoing relationships which give you regular access points where you can deliver a marketing message. See Chapter 8 on e-CRM.

MANAGING TACTICS

Who has control of tactics and implementation? This is a big question and the e-marketer must win the ownership argument. Take the web site: is it controlled by marketing or by the technical department or some other function? Many web sites actually damage brands with their broken links, dead ends, cumbersome downloads, out-of-date content, impossible navigation and

CLINIQUE
ALLERGY TESTED. 100% FRAGRANCE FREE.

| home | club clinique | what's new | bestsellers | gift centre | miss clinique |

| 3-step | skin care | makeup | fragrance | haircare | sun+body | men's |

Dear Zoe Chaffey,

Welcome!
We are delighted you have joined Club Clinique!

As a Club Clinique member, enjoy exclusive offers and special benefits customised just for you!

Plus, don't forget to take advantage of **FREE STANDARD DELIVERY** on your first online purchase. Simply enter offer code **CCNEW** at checkout.

The benefits of Club Clinique don't stop there...

FREE STANDARD DELIVERY on your first online purchase >>

You are now entitled to all of the following member privileges:

1 **Fast checkout**
Store your billing and delivery information for fast checkout every time.

2 **Shop from past purchases**
Clinique Online stores all your past orders, so reordering Clinique favourites is fast and easy.

3 **In-Store Bonus Time information**
Opt in to receive email alerts about Bonus Time and Special Events happening in a store near you!

4 **Samples at checkout**
Recieve a complimentary sample with every online purchase.

PLUS, if you haven't already, sign up for our newsletter to receive the following benefits:

New product news
Be the first to hear about new products before anyone else!

Exclusive shopping offers
Receive product sampling opportunities, complimentary delivery, gift wrap and other select offers only available to Club Clinique members.

Click here and enter 'my account' to update your personal information to ensure you receive the Clinique newsletter>>

Figure 10.7 Clinique welcome email. Subject line – Thanking you for registering at www.clinique.com From address: Clinique registration [infocl@clinique.co.uk]

unanswered emails (see Section 1.5 on sloppy e-marketing). No e-marketer would let this happen. You can usually tell from a site whether the webmaster is a 'techie' or a marketer. Many sites skip the cardinal rule of asking customers what they would like on a web site. Then, having put it up, they forget to check to see if they got it right. Regular reviews should not be devoted to reviewing the latest technology, but rather, focused on customer reviews. As an e-marketer, you'll want a site that is easy on the eye and clear to the reader and lightning fast to download. If that means dispensing with some of the techies' zanier ideas . . . well, the customer will thank you for it!

E-MARKETING EXCELLENCE

Apps versus mobile web site(s) – choice of tactical tools

Jon West, managing director at HRS UK & Ireland, has this to say:

The big mistake we made at HRS. We built these 240 different style sheets for every type of mobile application you can think of so that we could deliver WAP to any booker that wanted to come and book a hotel room. We tried to move that out to the partner portal as well and expand that business and after about 9 months we looked at what the revenue was for this and it was minuscule, it was a complete disaster.

We decided we needed to get into the app world. When we started to get into the App world we realised that we should have been there in the first place. We've now got a multi-million pound business using our apps that have been downloaded all over the globe and people are making their bookings through the leisure portal.

We also make those apps available to our corporate customers such as Google. If they are travelling around the world they might use their mobile app and they'll be trying to access HRS's hotel content but they need to have the Google negotiated prices that they've got on the hotels on their app. What they have to do is put in a customer number. You wouldn't believe it, but Google can't find the place they have to go to download the app that they need to use but that's how it works, so they arrive on our portal having gone past the page on their own intranet that tells them exactly where to download the app and start to search for the Google app so they can book their hotels.

Now, through using the clever MAGIQ technology, we can identify a 'Google' visitor by either their actions on the pages or the domain that they are coming from. We can now point them to a page we have set up especially for them that we call the Googlers so they can go onto that page, download the app and start making their booking. A second huge advantage to us.

(West, 2012)

E-MARKETING INSIGHT

Willcocks and Plant on tactics to achieve differentiation

Willcocks and Plant (2000) describe two dimensions to 'sustain the e-advantage through differentiation' that can be considered as e-marketing tactics:

● Merchandise dimension – for a car, this includes its characteristics such as performance, image and options. The web site can use content to differentiate by describing what the offer will do for the customer, the 'aura' – what the offer will say about the customer.

● Support dimension – differentiating features which help them in choosing, obtaining and using the offering. For a car, examples include availability of information, ease of test drive, ordering a brochure and the purchase mechanism via the web site. Personalization and expertise available via the web site can help enhance the support dimension.

SECTION SUMMARY 10.5

Tactics

Tactics are the details of strategy. Tactics list the events and e-tools that will be used over time. Now you have a tactical plan (Gantt chart) – now make it happen. The next section on actions shows you how.

10.6 Actions

'Everything must degenerate into work', said Peter Drucker – strategies and tactics eventually cascade into actions which become work that has to be carried out and eventually checked for any mistakes. According to John Stubbs (2006), former executive director of the Chartered Institute of Marketing, up to 40 per cent of marketing expenditure is wasted through poor execution.

As discussed in Chapter 1, Section 1.5, we are swimming in a sea of sloppy marketing and e-marketing. It is not surprising that Bossiddy and Charan (2004) suggested that 'execution is the missing key between aspirations and results'. So, the action stage, or execution, may be the weakest link in the planning process. For example, 'if Facebook is "always on" you need to plan accordingly and ensure you're staffed appropriately' (Scissons, 2011). Is there a process in place for managing this? Do you post messages saying you're finished now for the day, or do you schedule auto-releases for your blog and Twitter stream via, say, WordPress and HootSuite respectively, that automatically feed into your Facebook updates. How do you deal with queries or responses? Pre-emptive messages can intelligently guess what the issues are. Or do you just ignore it (95 per cent of Facebook questions remain unanswered) because there are no processes in pace, because no one decided to use Facebook to have a dialogue with or even just for market research purposes? Or do you hire people equipped with canned messages that can be tailored to respond to social platforms outside traditional office hours? What is the best way of setting up these processes or actions?

Cross-industry benchmarking can help since often the best source of new ideas can actually be standard operating procedures in a totally unrelated industry. 'Ideas that are routine in one industry can be revolutionary when they migrate to another industry, especially when they challenge the prevailing assumptions & conventional wisdom that have come to define so many industries' (Taylor, 2012). For example, physicians from Great Ormond Street Hospital for children redesigned many of their surgical procedures by studying how Ferrari's Formula 1 racing team handled pit stops (Taylor, 2012).

Tactics break down into actions – in fact, a series of actions that need to be managed. Each tactic becomes a mini project, requiring a series of actions or processes.

You need to produce a project action plan for each tactic project, with key steps allocated to specific people with specific timescales. Good project management skills are essential. Apply more Gantt charts, or critical path analysis, flow charts or whatever project management approach is best. Although most e-marketing plans would not necessarily contain a mini-project plan for every single tactic, these project action plans for each tactic will need to be drawn up at some stage, after the main e-marketing plan is completed.

Each tactical e-tool requires careful planning and implementation. Whether building a web site, search engine optimization (SEO), search engine management (SEM), a viral campaign or an opt-in campaign, good project management skills and diligent attention to detail are required.

Success in all these actions requires good implementation. The best strategy in the world will achieve nothing if it does not cascade down into detailed tactics which are carefully actioned if implemented. Good implementation only happens if you plan well and use your resources well. First of all, you have to communicate to get the plan approved and supported from above and below. The activities are going to include: project management schedules, meeting deadlines, meetings, memos, phone calls, chasing people, careful preparation, constant checking and attention to vast volumes of details.

RISK MANAGEMENT

Action, or implementation, also requires an appreciation of what can go wrong – from cyber libel to viruses, to mail bombs, hackers and hijackers to cyber squatting and much more . . . contingency planning is required. What happens when the server goes down or a virus comes to town? What happens if one of the e-tools is not working, or is not generating enough enquiries? Something has to be changed. *Risk management* involves:

- Brainstorming a list of all the things that could go wrong
- Assessing their impact and likelihood
- Creating contingency plans for the highest impact and most probable risks
- Continuous review, revising and refining during campaign execution
- Post-implementation reviews to learn from the successes and failures for the next project.

Note: in addition to the usual KPIs, Procter & Gamble ask their managers to report on their 'learning' from the marketplace.

Actions

Good project management skills are essential during the implementation or action stage. You are now ready to control your destiny by building control mechanisms into your e-plan.

10.7 Control

Are you feeling lucky? Without control mechanisms, e-marketing depends on luck. It's a bit like playing darts in the dark. How do you know if you are hitting the target or are just shooting blindly and wildly? How do you know if you're targeting the right customers? Who are they? What do they like? How many of them become repeat customers? Which e-tool works best? How much does each customer actually cost you? By the end of this section, you'll be able to answer these questions and begin to take control of your destiny instead of spinning out of control. Control also includes monitoring your competitors – what they're doing; what they're repeating; what works for them; what they're stopping doing.

Good marketers build in control systems to ensure they know what's working and what's not, early rather than late. Why wait until the end of the year? Why not have a system in place to keep track of key performance indicators?

You have done the work – specified the tactics, performed the actions . . . now, is the plan working? Have you achieved the objectives, is the strategy working, did you choose the right tactics . . . have you spent the money and time wisely? To find out, you must measure and review what you did – performance measurement. To do this, you need to determine what data you will look at each day, each week, each month, each quarter. This is the Control section of the e-marketing SOSTAC® cycle. Remember, we agreed in Section 10.3 that your objectives had to be SMART: specific, measurable, achievable, realistic and time-related. Now we test whether they were!

Essentially, all the objectives listed in the objectives section need to be measured and monitored – some of them quarterly, others monthly and others daily. This puts you in control. In addition, there are other controls that need to be in place: usability testing; concept testing; A/B testing.

Time has to be made for a regular review of what's working and what's not – performance diagnosis. Good marketers have control over their destinies. They do not leave it to chance and hope for the best. They monitor key metrics regularly – sometimes by the hour (see E-marketing Insight box on 'McDonald's Twitter hijacked'). They reduce risk by finding what works and what doesn't. Then, your e-tactics, or even strategy, can be changed through corrective action if necessary. Your plan should specify:

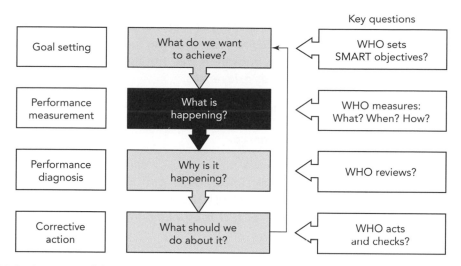

Figure 10.8 Summary of the control process for e-marketing planning

- The metrics
- The frequency of reporting
- Who measures and reports
- To whom
- Who takes appropriate actions arising.

And you don't want to wait for the year end to find out that something isn't working. If something is wrong, you need to have control systems (reviews) in place so that you find out and correct the problems early rather than late. Equally, if something is working unbelievably well, you need to know so you can learn and perhaps accelerate the success. Figure 10.8 shows the overall control process.

E-MARKETING INSIGHT

McDonald's Twitter hijacked – within 1 hour it's taken down

This story was reported on CNBC (Cheddar Berk, 2012).

Give consumers a microphone, and they'll have something to say – it just might not be what you want to hear. That's a lesson McDonald's learned once again, the hard way.

A McDonald's restaurant in San Jose, Calif. Earlier this month, the fast-food chain was forced to pull down a social media campaign it had launched on Twitter using the sponsored hashtag #McDStories. Hashtags are clickable links Twitter users can place on their posts to aggregate tweets on the same subject. McDonald's (MCD) had hoped to promote the quality of their ingredients. They first used the hashtag #MeetTheFarmers, and all was well, but then they switched to #McDStories, expecting fans would share positive experiences. Instead, the tag became a way for animal activists and less-than-satisfied diners to air their grievances.

McDonald's quickly pulled down the promoted hashtag, but it lives on. There's also a new one that's grown infamous – #McFail – which is being used by those discussing the fiasco.

Such is the way of social media marketing: It can backfire quickly and spectacularly. As the Financial Times points out, McDonald's is only the latest victim. There have been similar backlashes against social media campaigns from brands such as fast-food chain Wendy's and Australian airline Qantas.

McDonald's social media director, Rick Wion, told PaidContent.org: 'Within an hour, we saw that it wasn't going as planned. It was negative enough that we set about a change of course.' Wion said McDonald's carefully selects the words and phrases it uses in promoted tweets because it is inevitable both 'fans and detractors will chime in'.

In Wion's Twitter feed, @rdublife, he is still discussing the incident and he shared a statistic: On the day of the promotion, there were more than 72,000 mentions of McDonald's and only 2% were negative. A certain amount of negative feedback must be expected in every social media campaign.

THE METRICS

Performance is measured against detailed targets based on the objectives and strategy.

So you need to measure the KPIs that were detailed in Section 10.2 on situation analysis and Section 10.3 on objectives. Table 10.4 shows a list of typical KPIs. Whatever selection is used, it should match with the KPIs listed in Section 10.3 on Objectives.

Table 10.4 Control – the metrics

What do you need to watch?	How often (Daily, Weekly, Monthly, Quarterly)	Who will do it? Agency or staff?	What does it cost to measure this?

Sales
  – Units
  – Revenue
  – Market share

Table 10.4 *(Continued)*

What do you need to watch?	How often (Daily, Weekly, Monthly, Quarterly)	Who will do it? Agency or staff?	What does it cost to measure this?

Leads/Enquiries (number of)
- Unique visitors
- Repeat visitors
- Quality enquirers (Rank/Score) *
- Registrations
- Actual enquiries
- Value of enquiries

Conversion rates
- from enquiries
- from registrations
  (a) white papers
  (b) newsletters
- from trial purchases
- from channel sources
  (a) (a)
  (b) (b)
  (c)

Churn rates
- Attrition rate (cancelling contract)
- Unsubscribe (to email/newsletter)

Awareness levels
- (a) Brand
- (b) Brand benefits

Affection levels
- Sentiment analysis
- 'Shares'
- 'Likes'

Engagement levels
- Engagement ratio: Sum of 'Shares', Likes & Comments to Total 'Likes'

Social network analysis

- finding networks of influence

Customer satisfaction scores

Loyalty levels
- Net Promoter Score

ROI (Return on investment)

Source: Adapted from Smith (2011)

Sales, leads, awareness, attitude and ROI are the most common metrics used to manage or control the business. Regardless of which KPIs are used, remember that metrics are more useful when you compare first, across your industry (note: it is also interesting to compare with scores from excellent businesses outside your industry sector); and second, backwards to see any trend. So where do you get this information? Many of the metrics concerning visitor behaviour are available from *web analytics*. Collection by other information systems or processes is required for key measures such as sales, subscriptions, conversion and attrition rates. Standard practice should ensure that data from the different sources are compiled into a monthly or weekly report and are delivered *and* reviewed by the right people. Decide which metrics need to be reviewed daily, weekly or monthly, and by whom. The e-marketer must know which tools are working. That's why the 'channel source' of sales or enquiries is useful – if a particular banner ad doesn't pull customers, drop it and try another until you find one that does. This can be monitored in much more detail – measuring variations in each tactical tool.

Remember that all forms of measurement (or metrics) cost money – you'll have to factor in budgets and resources for any of these mechanisms:

● Monitoring customer awareness
● Monitoring customer satisfaction
● Monitoring customer attitudes.

Many of the above variables can be measured offline (street surveys) as well as online, as these variables are influenced by both online and offline tactics. Other forms of control like sales analysis only require your own time (and your team's time in compiling the reports). So how do you know if things are going well? Some objectives are easy to state and easy to measure: existing recording systems in the organization will produce the data to answer the question: so if the objective is to grow sales . . . well, what was the target for growth and the timetable for achieving it . . . and did you make it?

E-MARKETING INSIGHT

Sentiment analysis

Sentiment analysis identifies themes, sentiments and connections. It can:

> [R]eveal sentiments as positive, negative or neutral. NB Ask yourself: 'are there themes clusters or specific terms that are emerging? Should I be encouraging the conversation, responding or correcting?' An analytics tool should be able to show you: Trends in positive, negative & neutral activity & drill down & see the actual comments. . . Incorporate learning from online conversations into planning cycles.
>
> (Delahaye Paine et al., 2010)

> **What's your process for gleaning customer insights from conversations?**

Continually use customer insights from online conversations to improve performance. Do you have a systematic approach to doing this?

PERFORMANCE DIAGNOSIS

Some objectives require more careful study: in fact, when you set objectives and define strategy, you should consider what would be a successful outcome and how you are going to monitor this performance.

So if the objective is to create a dominant web-based brand (first stage) and then to make a profit within 18 months on advertising sales and sponsorship . . . well, what criteria can you set to define success, and how will you then measure against these criteria? You may need to implement data-recording systems and develop analysis tools.

Similarly, if the objectives revolve around getting closer to customers – customer relationship management or CRM – your measurement tools must be carefully defined and implemented.

Consider how the motor industry has adapted online. Many manufacturers are dealing directly with consumers, in terms of information provision and order taking: some dealerships should be worried, the process of disintermediation is going to squeeze them out. But how should the industry measure its success? By counting sales and sales leads directly generated online – that's the easy bit. And also by measuring conversion rates for people who visit the web site and choose your brand of car when they subsequently go to a dealer. This is difficult to measure, so you need to be capturing customer feedback scientifically and measuring levels of customer satisfaction – that's the hard part.

CORRECTIVE ACTION

Corrective action is used to revise the strategies and tactics to ensure that the objectives are achieved. Or perhaps the objectives need revising? To minimize the need for corrective action, good marketers can monitor e-tools before they are even rolled out by rigorous concept testing. E-marketers can reduce risk with relevant information so that their decisions are made upon fact instead of blind luck. This applies even to web site development – researching concepts and usability testing help to ensure the design is right and you don't have high termination rates.

So which of the e-tools are giving the best return on investment? See P&G's BeingGirl ROI calculation (below). It is possible to compare ROI across different channels. It is also possible to calculate Cost Per Enquiry and Cost Per Order (see Table 10.5) .

Remember that these simplified approaches ignore the previous effects of other marketing activities (see Chapter 3, Section 3.4 on attribution models).

Table 10.5 Cost Per Order and Cost Per Enquiry

	Volume of people/ size of audience	Total Cost £	CPT/ CPM (Cost per thousand people reached) £	% CTR Click through Rate/ Visit Web Site/ Enquiry	Unique Visitors	Cost Per Visitor / Lead £	Conversion Rate Visitors to Customers Say 1%	No. o͞ Orders	Cost Per Order £
SEO									
Blog									
Banner Ad									
PPC Ad									
Opt-In eMail									
Viral A									
Online Sponsorship									
E-zine/ E-newsletter									
Press Ad									
Direct Mail									
List A									
Telemarketing – outbound									
Exhibition B									

E-MARKETING INSIGHT

Feeding the Google money machine – cost per enquiry/lead?

When you consider that companies are paying US$5 to US$250 per lead, and the effective rate they're paying for clicks can be as high as US$2 to US$6, it just doesn't always seem worth the investment. While lead generation has improved via traditional marketing tactics, the truth is that much of this investment yields low results. Overall, only about 1–2 per cent of leads are qualified, and yet companies continue to feed the Google money machine, even though only a tiny fraction of that investment ever turns into sales (Fugetta, 2011).

E-MARKETING INSIGHT

Watch your engagement ratio

In 2012, Oscar Ugaz posted the following comments on iSportConnect (www.isportconnect.com):

> *Some months ago, a well-known sports brand reached 5 million fans on Facebook, so they posted on their wall to celebrate the happy event: 'Today is a magical date that we will never forget. Today we are going to reach 5 million fans in our football page. We only can say something to you: 5 MILLION OF THANKS.' They only received nine comments, eight of which were the usual mumblings, but one of them was happy to say what he thought: 'Today is also my birthday and that is more magical. The 5 million fans don't say anything to me. You guys are getting a little boring.'*

> *Last October [2011], Facebook Pages started displaying the new '[People] Talking About This' metric [Mashable, 2011], which measures the number of unique people who have created a story (comment, like, share) about a specific page during the last week. From this data derives another interesting one: the engagement ratio (ER) – a percentage that measures how many fans really interact with the page.*

> *Over the last three weeks, the average ER for the major European football clubs on Facebook (Real Madrid, FC, Barcelona and Manchester United) was 3.5% of an average fan base of more than 20 million each. I remember many meetings concerning the number of fans clubs have. Some people said: 'But, "Club A" have more fans than us. We must do something.' A second point of view was: 'What is important is not the size, but what we do with those fans.' The latter way of thinking is the one that produces great content and entertainment.*

> *(Ugaz, 2012)*

> **Are you in control? What is the value of all your social media efforts?**

Do you know the value of a 'Like' or a 'Share' or a Tweet or a review?

Eventbrite knows that a 'Like' generates US$1.34 in revenue (Hubspot, 2011); a Tweet generates US$0.80 in revenue (Hubspot, 2011); a link shared on Facebook generates US$2.52 in ticket sales (Halligan, 2011). Ticketmaster knows that a comment such as 'I bought a ticket from Ticketmaster' generates an additional US$5.30 on the site from a percentage of that person's friends (who presumably decide to go to the same event) (Halligan, 2011). PowerReviews found that when a person shares a customer review on Facebook in their newsfeed, it generates US$15.72 in sales (Halligan, 2011). In addition, Facebook users who utilize a 'Like' button visit 5.3 times more web URLs to engage with content, and on average have 2.4 times more 'Friends'. So providing a 'Like' button on a web site gives a brand access to these more socially engaged consumers and their networks. A 'Like' can start a conversation with both new and existing users and it can also drive more traffic to your page.

A Syncapse (2010) sample revealed that customers who are also Facebook fans spend, on average, US$71 more than customers who are not Facebook fans. And customers who are also Facebook fans are 28 per cent more likely to remain loyal to your brand. See Table 10.6. Do you believe this demonstrates the value that social media can generate? Many have argued that this doesn't isolate a causal effect and you would naturally expect fans to be higher value, since they are more likely to be customers anyway (and passionate customers).

So that is the additional revenue generated by investing in developing a Facebook following. How might this convert to ROI? Procter & Gamble (P&G) reportedly calculates a 200 per cent ROI from their BeingGirl web site. It is suggested that this is a four times better return than from traditional advertising. Here's how they calculate it.

Table 10.6 The value of a Facebook fan

	Average customer value of non-Facebook fans (US$)	Average customer value when Facebook fans (US$)
Nokia	63	171
BlackBerry	97	132
Motorola	69	160
Dove	57	141
Gillette	76	126
Adidas	73	125
Nike	83	205
Coca-Cola	120	190
Nutella	53	101
Red Bull	50	113
Pringles	60	133
Starbucks	110	235
McDonald's	150	310

Source: Syncapse (2010)

P&G's BeingGirl web site (www.beinggirl.com)

Each 'girl' customer has an estimated spend of US$5 p.m. on feminine care products for 40 years

Generates a lifetime value of: US$5 $\times$ 12 months x 40 years = [US$2,400] per girl

20 per cent margin (or contribution): 0.2 $\times$ US$2,400 = [US$480] margin per girl

Web site traffic (unique visitors): 1,875,000 girls

1 per cent yearly customer conversion rate = [18,750] new customers converted p.a.

18,750 new customers @US$480 lifetime contribution = [US$9,000,000]

Cost to run web site each year: US$3,000,000

Yearly profit: [US$6,000,000]

Return on Investment (Return/Investment)

Return (Profit/Margin/Contribution): US$6,000,000

Investment (cost of developing, maintaining and getting traffic to the site): US$3,000,000

ROI – 200 per cent.

Note: Next year they will recruit another 18,750 customers and the following year, etc. This is somewhat simplified as the future revenue stream (stream of contribution/margin) should be discounted to net present value. It is assumed (1) that their marketing is good enough to keep a customer for life; and that (2) every year they continue to recruit 1,875,000 new customers as new visitors grow into their market place. This calculation does cause some debate regarding its robustness, but at least it does provide an insight into how the lifetime value perspective changes how marketers see customers and the budgets they are willing to spend to acquire them and retain them. Of course, things do not always go according to plan, but good marketers build contingency plans for those 'what if' scenarios.

Contingency plans

Good marketers also have contingency plans. What happens if Plan A doesn't work? Or worse still, what happens if the competition cuts prices? Or worse still, what happens if the server goes down and your network crashes? Do you have a second server? Good marketers think things through.

On a more positive note, good marketers react quickly to emerging opportunities and threats. Some companies, when checking the daily web statistics, spot a lot of additional traffic on a particular page, or a particular item being purchased more frequently; they then highlight the page or the product on the main home page to boost even more traffic/conversions for a period until they spot some other, more popular, page emerging.

SECTION SUMMARY 10.7

Control

Control is about monitoring whether your objectives are being achieved and then modifying the tactics and actions to ensure that they are.

10.8 The 3Ms resources: 'men', money and minutes

Budgeting for the delicate balance of resources required to run an online operation is a science not yet fully understood by many. The late Professor Peter Doyle (1994) simplified this critical issue when he said: 'The resource allocation decision is the choice of which products and markets offer the best opportunities for investment.'

We are going to consider resource allocation among different products, markets and e-marketing tools by splitting the resource issue into three components – the 3Ms: men (and women; the human resource), money (budgets) and minutes (timescales and time horizons for production, delivery, service, etc.).

MEN (AND WOMEN)

How many bodies are required to deal with incoming email enquiries and outgoing telephone calls triggered by the 'callback' facility on the web site? Or can it be automated and personalized? How much time is needed to notify customers of deliveries? How much time and what skills are required to set up a project and integrate with the existing (legacy) database systems, etc.? There are some key questions in the area of people resources. Even at times when many tech companies are shedding staff, really able people who know what they are doing in terms of web site design, e-commerce delivery, e-business strategy, online media sales, etc. are not in huge supply. So you will have to call on a mixture of internal resources and external skills to deliver your plans.

It is often said that a company's greatest assets walk out of the door each night – i.e. the people.

Human resource allocation can be critical: if you can find existing resources to fulfil some of the e-marketing requirements, then you keep costs down and that reduces pressure on revenues.

Outsourcing or insourcing

To outsource or not to outsource – that is the question. Outsourcing continues to grow in popularity both in major strategic aspects of e-marketing and also in shorter-term tactical aspects of e-marketing. In Section 3.3, we explained how value networks and their dependence on excellent outsourcing management skills are becoming increasingly popular. Here are a few specific outsourcing questions to consider.

So you need to update your web site, build a new blog, grow a highly interactive Twitter following – do you do it in-house or contract out to an agency? And what balance should you strike between resources allocated to building the site and those required to maintain it on a regular basis, leaving a pot aside for a complete review and upgrade in three, six or nine months? Do not forget traffic – resources are also required to build traffic. Remember that out-of-date web sites can damage brands: who will trust you if the offers on the web site have expired?

Other resources to consider are customer service via social media like Facebook: are additional staff required or can the in-house team be retrained to do it? Who will do the e-marketing research? Who is going to analyse the data you get from the customer feedback, and who is going to produce the recommendations? Is it the existing team, or a new team – internal (staff) or external (agency)? If customers show that there is a need to change procedures, do you have the people to react and respond?

Don't underestimate the ability of customers to consume your people resources: if you offer an email response mechanism, who is going to answer the incoming emails? If you create a Facebook page, who will engage in conversations? But if you don't answer them, or don't even offer an email response, you are still locked into last century's marketing philosophy.

MONEY

Of course, to a large extent, the people resources at your disposal will be a function of the money resources. So once you have calculated the people requirements for your e-marketing plan . . . you need to work out how to get them: you need to find the skills, and you need the budget to pay for them.

Marketing costs money; e-marketing is no different. Your e-marketing plan must include a budget covering the costs you will incur and a clear benefit statement – what will the return on the investment be?

Be aware that the very nature of e-marketing means you may be expected to demonstrate a clear relationship between investment and return: if your budget is allocated in order to create an online service that generates sales, then you'll have to create a model showing the ratio of e-marketing cost to sales return, or return on investment (ROI) as in the P&G example earlier.

And be realistic in your expectation: if revenues fall short of the plan, you should assume this will bring pressure on the money resources left at your disposal! You may have to trim costs on the web site or reduce the online marketing spend.

Try therefore to get some sliding scale agreed, so that there is also an upside: develop plans for additional marketing activity if sales are going well, so you can quickly go up a gear and build on the success.

But with e-marketing, you also have some opportunities to generate some income: can you get sponsors for your web site or sell some banner ads? Can you partner with suppliers of other products and get a cut of their income? If you can do any of these, you can then approach the budget decision makers and negotiate to be able to spend some or all of the income you generate.

Also, don't forget the obvious: work out what you could usefully do for free. You may find a complementary business prepared to exchange banners and links; you must certainly ensure that you are well represented on search engines. Look around the web for opportunities to promote your sites and services or acquire names for your database which won't cost you a penny.

A specific warning too: don't underestimate the resources required to maintain a web site. Too often, companies go out and spend vast sums getting designer-rich agencies to build flashy and complex sites and then find that when it comes to updating the content and answering the customers, there is no resource left to cover this. Finally, don't forget that a wonderful site without traffic is a dead site. So budget is also required to generate traffic.

MINUTES

Time is often the most limiting of all of the resources. Does it ever seem that there are simply not enough hours in the day or days in the week?

Of course, the e-marketing world is used to shorter timescales: you might need three months to prepare a TV campaign or 12 months to create a new pack; but you could build a new web site in a lot less time. Or could you? How long would competitor analysis, focus group discussions, concept testing and usability testing take? Even simple banner ads take time to prepare. The creatives required for an online banner campaign are generally less complex than those for a print campaign; and, of course, booking times are shorter: you can, in theory, plan, design and deliver an online campaign in a matter of days.

So get the balance right: recognize that e-marketing has an expectation of being able to think, plan, react, change and respond quickly; that's the fun and excitement, and also the power of e-marketing. But don't be bullied into skimping on the planning, research, design and development just because timescales have been made arbitrarily or are artificially short.

E-MARKETING INSIGHT

5:2:1 versus 1:2:5

It has been suggested that UK companies tend to adopt a ratio of 5:2:1 (site design to site maintenance to traffic building), whereas the ratio tends to be 1:2:5 in the United States. The US approach makes sense, as there's no point having a wonderful (expensive) web site or social media platform if no customers or prospects bother to visit. In addition, as mentioned earlier, popular sites are frequently updated during maintenance (serviced) and quick to download even in a download world.

E-MARKETING INSIGHT

Gulati and Garino (2000) on restructuring to obtain resources

Gulati and Garino (2000) identified a continuum of strategic approaches from integration to separation. They describe the choices as:

1 *In-house division (integration).* Example: RS Components Internet Trading Channel (www.rswww.com).

2 *Joint venture (mixed).* The company creates an online presence in association with another player.

3 *Strategic partnership (mixed).* This may also be achieved through purchase of existing dotcoms; e.g. in the UK, Great Universal Stores acquired e-tailer Jungle.com for its strength in selling technology products and strong brand, while John Lewis purchased Buy.com's UK operations.

4 *Spin-off (separation).* Example: Egg bank is a spin-off from the Prudential financial services company.

The advantages of the integration approach, according to these authors, is being able to leverage existing brands, being able to share information and achieve economies of scale (e.g. purchasing and distribution efficiencies). They say the spin-off approach gives better focus, more flexibility for innovation and the possibility of funding through flotation. For example, Egg has been able to create a brand distinct from Prudential and has developed new revenue models such as retail sales commission. They say that separation is preferable in situations where:

- A different customer segment or product mix will be offered online
- Differential pricing is required between online and offline
- There is a major channel conflict
- The Internet threatens the current business model
- Additional funding or specialist staff need to be attracted.

SECTION SUMMARY 10.8

Resources: 'men', money and minutes

Your e-marketing plan must provide properly for the resources you will need to deliver:

- Men (and women) – you need to work out what people resources you will need and how to acquire these in a market where core skills are not abundant.
- Money – you need adequate budgets in order to achieve your plans; this will include a forecast for the return on investment (ROI) and a plan to be able to adjust costs if sales figures are higher or lower than expected.
- Minutes – your e-marketing plan must contain timescales, schedules and deadlines. And if you want it to work, your actions will stick to them!

1 E-marketing plans must support and be integrated with corporate or business plans and marketing plans. SOSTAC® stands for: Situation analysis, Objectives and Strategy, Tactics, Action and Control.

2 Situation analysis is the first part of the e-marketing plan. It explains 'where we are now'. It reviews internal resources and e-marketing performance, and external factors such as customer, competitor and intermediary activity. It also reviews the PEST factors – political, economic, social and technology.

3 SWOT analysis is part of the Situation analysis and is used to summarize strengths, weaknesses, opportunities and threats.

4 Objectives are set to define the direction of the plan. Objectives can be constructed by reviewing the 5 Ss: Sell, Serve, Speak, Save and Sizzle. Objectives must be checked to ensure they are SMART: specific, measurable, achievable, realistic and time-related.

5 Strategy summarizes how the objectives will be achieved. The key components are highlighted by STOP – segments (S), target markets (T), overall objectives (O), positioning (P); and SATIS – sequence or stages (S), acquisition versus retention (A), tactical tools (T), integration (I) and social media (S).

6 Tactics define how the strategy will be achieved. They describe the e-tools used and how they will be sequenced through time.

7 Action equals implementation plans. Actions should be defined to build traffic, gain customer response, gain sales and fulfil them, if appropriate, and foster e-CRM. Risk management should be used.

8 Control gives a feedback loop, starting with monitoring whether the objectives are achieved, assessing what the problems are and then revising the strategies, tactics and actions as appropriate.

9 Resources can be planned through the 3Ms of men (and women; i.e. the human resources), money (budgets) and minutes (timescales and time horizons for production, delivery, service, etc.).

References

Ad Contrarian, the (2011) Social media's massive failure. Blog post by Bob Hoffman, 21 March.
Bolger, M. (2011) Profile: Gail Hanlon, Expect the unexpected. *The Marketer*, September/October.
Bossiddy, L. and Charan, R. (2004) *Execution, the Discipline of Getting Things Done*. Crown Business, New York.
Bradley, C., Hirt, M. and Smit, S. (2011) Have you tested your strategy lately?
McKinsey Quarterly, Member edition, January at: www.mckinseyquarterly.com/Have_you_tested_your_strategy_lately_2711
Cheddar Berk, C. (2012) #McFail? McDonald's Twitter campaign gets hijacked. CNBC, 25 January. Available at: www.usatoday.com/money/industries/food/story/2012-01-28/cnbc-mcdonalds-twitter-backfire/52824472/1

Cummings, T. (2001) *Little e, Big Commerce: How to Make a Profit Online*. Virgin Publishing, London.

Delahaye Paine, K. and Chaves, M. (2010) Social media metrics: listening, understanding and predicting the impacts of social media. Paper presented at eMetrics Marketing Optimization Summit, 3–7 May, San Jose, CA.

Doyle, P. (1994) *Marketing Management and Strategy*. Prentice Hall, London.

Falls, J. (2010) From staid to social: a social media case study. *The Social Media Explorer*, 10 May. At: www.socialmediaexplorer.com/social-media-marketing/from-staid-to-social-a-social-media-case-study/

Fugetta, R. (2011) Five reasons you need to focus on earned media. *Ad Age Digital*, 18 May.

Gulati, R. and Garino, J. (2000) Getting the right mix of bricks and clicks for your company. *Harvard Business Review*, May–June, pp. 107–14.

Halligan, C. (2011) Facebook marketing: the four biggest blunders hurting your brand. *Ad Age*, 13 September.

Hubspot (2011) *The Facebook Marketing Update, Spring 2011*. E-book created by *Who's Blogging What?* and sponsored by Hubspot.

Knorp, B. (2011) What your social-media team should learn from direct-response folks. *Ad Age*, 18 July.

Kumar, N. (1999) Internet distribution strategies: dilemmas for the incumbent. *Financial Times Special Issue on Mastering Information Management*, No. 7: Electronic Commerce.

Manning, J. (2012) Digital: 5 social advertising endorsements. *The Marketer*, January/February.

Mashable (2011) Facebook's 'People Talking About It' metric. At: http://mashable.com/2011/10/02/facebook-people-talking-about/

Ohmae, K. (1999) *The Borderless World: Power and Strategy in the Interlinked Economy*. Harper Business, New York.

Quelch, J. and Klein, L. (1996) The Internet and international marketing. *Sloan Management Review*, spring, pp. 61–75.

Rumelt, R. (2011) The perils of bad strategy. *McKinsey Quarterly*, June.

Scissons, M. (2011) 5 things you need to understand for successful marketing on Facebook. *Ad Age Digital*, 18 November.

Smith, P.R. (1993). SOSTAC® is a registered trademark of PR Smith. See www.prssmith.org for more information.

Smith, P.R. (1996) Marketing Planning, the Marketing CDs. Available at www.prsmith.org

Smith, P.R. (2011) *The SOSTAC® Guide to Writing the Perfect Plan*. E-book, available at: www.prsmith.org and on Amazon.

Smith, P.R. (2012) The Great Sportsmanship Programme (www.greatsportsmanship.org).

Stubbs, J. (2006) In conversation with PR Smith.

Syncapse (2010) The value of a Facebook fan – an empirical review. White paper. Syncapse Corp, Toronto.

Taylor, B. (2012) Are you learning as fast as the world is changing? *Harvard Business Review* Blog Network, 26 January at: http://blogs.hbr.org/taylor/2012/01/are_you_learning_as_fast_as_th.html

Thomas, M. (2012) Why Aristotle's less authoritarian philosophy is the new spirit of business, *The Guardian*, 27 March.

Ugaz, O. (2012) Football & social media: why clubs need to change to stay relevant.

iSportConnect at: www.isportconnect.com/index.php?option=com_content&view=article&id=11223:football-a-social-media-why-clubs-need-to-change-to-stay-relevant-oscar-ugaz&catid=62:sports-marketing&Itemid=171

West, J. (2012) How HRS use MAGIQ's real-time personalisation and targeting technology. Presentation at Technology for Marketing and Advertising (TFM&A) conference, London, 29 February.

Willcocks, L. and Plant, R. (2000) Business Internet strategy: moving to the Net. In Willcocks, L. and Sauer, C. (eds) *Moving to E-business*. Random House, London.

Wing, R.L. (1989) *The Art of Strategy* (translation of *The Art of War* by Sun Tzu, c.480–221 BC). Aquarian Press, Wellingborough, Northants.

Further reading

Chaffey, D., Mayer, R., Johnston, K. and Ellis-Chadwick, F. (2005) *Internet Marketing: Strategy, Implementation and Practice*, 3rd edition. Financial Times/Prentice Hall, Harlow. This book covers a structured approach to e-planning in detail, with Chapters 2 and 3 looking at situation analysis and Chapter 4 at Internet marketing strategy.

Web links

Avinash Kaushik's blog (www.kaushik.net). As digital marketing evangelist at Google, Avinash is an expert in web analytics and his popular blog shows how web analytics should be used to control and improve return on e-marketing investments.

ClickZ (www.clickz.com). Articles on digital strategy and channel tactics.

Emarketer (www.emarketer.com). Digital market research studies and reports to inform planning decisions.

Forrester (www.forrester.com). Digital and technology market research studies and reports (free content on blog).

Harvard Business Review (www.hbr.org). Strategy advice.

IAB (Internet Advertising Bureau, UK) (www.iabuk.net). Statistics to support investment decisions on digital versus traditional media.

McKinsey Quarterly (www.mckinseyquarterly.com). Business strategy.

New Media Age (www.nma.co.uk). A UK digital marketing trade weekly which has interviews with practitioners discussing their strategic approach to digital marketing.

PR Smith.org (www.prsmith.org). The originator of SOSTAC®; more information on SOSTAC®.

Smart Insights (http://bit.ly/smartstrategy). Articles about the need for and methods of e-planning.

TheNextWeb (www.thenextweb.com). Digital technology developments.

Self-test

1 Summarize the relevance of the elements of a SOSTAC® e-plan for your organization.

2 What are the main factors of situation analysis that should be reviewed in the areas of internal and external review?

3 Summarize objectives for your organization for each one of the 5 Ss.

4 What are the elements of strategy summarized by STOP and SATIS?

5 Write down each of the e-tools used as part of tactics that are most relevant to your organization.

6 Which specific actions are required for you to build traffic, gain customer response, gain sales and fulfil them, if appropriate, and foster e-CRM?

7 What are the key measures of the effectiveness of your online presence?

8 Specify the main resource types required to develop an online presence.

Glossary

3G Third generation of mobile phone technology based on UMTS standard with high-speed data transfer enabling video calling and download.

4G Fourth-generation wireless, expected to deliver wireless broadband at 20–40 Mbps (about 10–20 times the current rates of ADSL broadband service).

A/B Testing A/B or AB testing refers to testing two different versions of a page or a page element such as a heading, image or button. The alternatives (A or B) are served alternately, with the visitors to the page randomly split between the two pages. Hence it is sometimes called 'live split testing'. Changes in visitor behaviour can then be compared using different metrics such as the clickthrough rate on page elements like buttons or images, or macro-conversion rates, such as conversion to sale or sign-up. A/B Testing is aimed at increasing page or site effectiveness against key performance indicators including clickthrough rate, conversion rates and revenue per visit. Since it doesn't consider combinations of variables tested, for best uplift, *multivariate testing* is increasingly used.

Acceptance (of customer) One of Hofacker's five stages of web site information processing. Does the customer accept (believe) the message?

Accessibility legislation Legislation intended to protect users of web sites with disabilities, including visual disability.

Acquisition cost Total promotional cost to gain a new customer.

Ad network A collection of independent web sites, each of which has an arrangement with a single advertising broker to place banner advertisements on a CPM, CPC or CPA basis.

Aesthetics of site design Graphics + Colour + Style + Layout + Typography.

Affiliate marketing A commission-based arrangement where referring sites (publishers) receive a commission on sales or leads from merchants (retailers).

Affiliate networks Brokers, known also as affiliate managers, who manage the form of links, tracking and payment between a merchant and a range of affiliates.

Aggregators A site featuring a range of product or service listings from suppliers; for example, a price comparison intermediary. Prices are usually updated by suppliers using *XML* feeds. Google Product Search is an example of an aggregator.

Agile development An iterative approach to developing software and web site functionality with emphasis on face-to-face communications to elicit, define and test requirements.

AIDA model Attention, Interest, Desire, Action. A model of hierarchy of responses to communications.

ALEA model Attention, Learning, Emotional response and Acceptance. A model of hierarchy of responses to communications.

Allowable customer acquisition cost (CPA)   The maximum acceptable cost for gaining a new customer, typically based on consideration of the initial profitability or *lifetime value* for gaining that customer type.

Always-on communications   A continuous investment in online communications to tap into continuous demand for products and services through a range of *inbound marketing* techniques – typically, search, display and affiliate marketing communications.

Animated ads   A *GIF* or Flash file is used to present a sequence of several different image frames to the viewer.

Application programming interfaces (APIs)   A method for automated data exchange through a feed in a defined format, enabling different systems or web services to integrate data.

Atomization   Describes a concept where the content on a site is broken down into smaller fundamental units which can then be distributed via the web through links to other sites. The use of *widgets* and the distribution of content via *RSS* feeds are examples of atomization. The small units of content contributed by participants within a *social network* can also be considered atomization.

Attention   One of Hofacker's five stages of web site information processing. Can the site attract the customer's attention?

ATR model   Awareness, trial and reinforcement.

Attribution modelling   The influence of different referring media in the 'path to purchase' is assessed to see which influenced conversion to sale. This compares to the simplistic approach of the *last-click model*.

Attrition rates   Percentage of site visitors that are lost at each stage in making an online purchase.

Auctions   A buying model where traders make offers and bids to sell or buy under certain conditions.

Auditing   An independent body verifies the number of *page impressions* and *visitors* for a *web site*.

Augmented reality   Blends real-world digital data capture, typically with a digital camera in a webcam or mobile phone, to create a browser-based digital representation or experience mimicking that of the real world.

Auto-responders   Software tools or 'agents' running on a *web server* which automatically send a standard reply to the sender of an email message.

Average order value (AOV)   The average amount spent for a single checkout purchase on a retail site for a particular customer group; e.g. first-time purchasers.

Backlinks   Hyperlinks which link to a particular web page (or web site). Also known as inbound links. Google *PageRank* and Yahoo! WebRank are methods of enumerating this.

Bandwidth   Bandwidth indicates the speed at which data are transferred using a particular network media. It is measured in bits-per-second (bps).

Banner adverts   A typically rectangular graphic displayed on a web page for purposes of brand building or driving traffic to a site. It is normally possible to perform a *clickthrough* to access further information from another web site.

Banner adverts, animated   Early banner adverts only featured a single advert, but today they will typically involve several different frames which are displayed in sequence to attract attention to the banner and build up a theme, often ending with a call-to-action to click on the banner.

Behavioural retargeting   Ads are displayed elsewhere on a site or other sites in an ad network after a customer has interacted with an initial ad or related content. A series of relevant ads developing the message can be displayed through behavioural retargeting.

Behavioural targeting   Personalized, relevant messages are delivered, for example, by email or web which relate to a customer's current interests. For example, if they review a specific product online, then they may receive an email or be served an ad which relates to their interest. Also known as *contextual marketing*.

Bid-management software   Software or web-based services which partially automate the management of paid search advertising across a range of paid search networks by applying rules to display ads for specific *keyphrases* at particular bids, positions and times to achieve specified business aims, such as ROAS, *ROI*, profitability, etc., while minimizing cost.

Blog   An online diary regularly updated by an individual or group with topical news and views.

Bluejacking   Sending a message from a mobile phone or transmitter to another mobile phone which is in close range via *Bluetooth* technology (without the user's permission).

Blueprints   Show the relationships between pages and other content components, and can be used to portray organization, navigation and labelling systems.

Bluetooth   A standard for wireless transmission of data between devices; e.g. a mobile phone and a *PDA*.

Breadcrumbs   An indication of position in site structure which also allow users to go up a level within the site.

Broadband   A term referring to methods of delivering information across the Internet at a higher rate by increasing *bandwidth*; e.g. fibre-optic cable access.

Bounce rate   Proportion of visitors to a page or site that exit after visiting a single page only, usually expressed as a percentage.

Brochureware   A web site where a company has migrated its existing paper-based promotional literature onto its web site without recognizing the differences required by this medium.

Business models   A summary of how a company will generate revenue, identifying its product offering, value-added services, revenue sources and target customers.

Business-to-business (B2B)   Commercial transactions between an organization and other organizations.

Business-to-business (B2B) exchanges   Virtual locations with facilities to enable trading between buyers and sellers.

Business-to-consumer (B2C)   Commercial transactions between an organization and consumers.

Buy-side e-commerce   E-commerce transactions between a purchasing organization, its suppliers and partners.

Callback   A direct response facility available on the web site for a company to contact a customer by phone at a later time as specified by the customer.

Cannibalization   Sales achieved via an e-commerce site replace sales traditionally made via other channels.

Card sorting or web classification   The process of arranging a way of organizing objects on the web sites in a consistent manner.

Channel conflict   A significant threat arising from the introduction of an Internet channel is that while *disintermediation* gives the opportunity for a company to sell direct and increase profitability on products, it can also threaten existing distribution arrangements with existing partners.

Churn rate   The percentage rate at which customers stop/lapse in the use of a service or product.

Clicks and mortar   A business combining an online and offline presence.

Clickstream   A record of the path a user takes through a web site. Clickstreams enable site designers to assess how their site is being used.

Clickthrough   A clickthrough (ad click) occurs each time a user clicks on *banner adverts* with the mouse to direct them to a *web page* with further information.

Clickthrough rates (CTR)   The clickthrough rate is expressed as a percentage of total ad impressions, and refers to the proportion of users viewing *banner adverts* who click on them. It is calculated as the number of *clickthroughs* divided by the number of ad impressions.

Cloaking   Serving different pages to a visitor than those indexed by a search engine. This is unethical, but surprisingly common. One example is using hidden text on the site that can't be seen by visitors; another is serving different pages to the searchers to those served to search engine robots by identifying the type of visitor.

Co-branding   An arrangement between two or more companies where they agree jointly to display content and perform joint promotion, using brand logos or a *banner advert*. The aim is that the brands are strengthened if they are seen as complementary. This is a reciprocal arrangement which can occur without payment.

Co-browsing   A customer's screen can be viewed by the call-centre operator in combination with *callback* or *real-time chat*.

Co-buying   Group buying enabling a reduction in price for a volume purchase.

Collaborative filtering   Profiling of customer interests coupled with delivery of specific information and offers, often based on automatic assessment of the interests of groups of similar customers.

Commoditization   Products are selected primarily on price due to minimal differences between competitive products.

Comprehension   One of Hofacker's five stages of web site information processing. Does the customer understand the message as intended?

Contact strategy   A defined sequence of integrated communications delivered by personalized email and web contacts plus traditional media such as direct mail and phone. Contact strategies will help provide contextual communications throughout the customer lifecycle or for different phases in a campaign.

Content   Content is the design, text and graphical information which forms a *web page*. Good content is the key to attracting customers to a web site and retaining their interest or achieving repeat visits.

Content management system (CMS)   A software tool/web application for creating, editing and updating documents accessed by intranet, extranet, or Internet.

Content marketing   The management of text, *rich media*, audio and video content aimed at engaging customers and prospects to meet business goals, published through print and digital media – including web and mobile platforms – which are repurposed and syndicated to different forms of web presence such as publisher sites, *blogs*, *social media* and comparison sites.

Content network   Sponsored links are displayed by the search engine on third-party sites. Ads are paid for on a PPC basis or on a CPM basis.

Content owners   Company staff, usually within the business, who are responsible for updating content.

Contextual ads   A paid search technique where ads embedded within a publisher's site are displayed on the content network according to the type of content. For example, an ad placed on a page about email marketing techniques will be related to email marketing services.

Contextual marketing   Personalized, relevant messages are delivered, for example, by email or web which relate to a customer's current interests. For example, if they review a specific product online, then they may receive an email or be served an ad which relates to their interest. Also known as *behavioural targeting*.

Continuous traffic building activities   Communications activities, such as *affiliate marketing*, search engine marketing and online sponsorship, intended to drive visitors to the site. These activities tend not to occur in short-burst campaigns, but across the year.

Convergence   A trend in which different hardware devices such as TVs, computers and phones merge and have similar functions.

Conversion goal   A page on the site such as e-newsletter registration or sales confirmation for which a visit shows that a business objective is being met. Site owners should track the number of conversion goals and the pages or referrers that influence them. Also known as a *value event*.

Conversion rate   Percentage of site visitors that perform a particular action, such as making a purchase.

Conversion rate optimization (CRO)   A structured approach to using marketing communications to maximize conversion of potential customers to actual customers, based on using qualitative research from customer surveys and quantitative data from tests and *web analytics*.

Cookie   Small text files placed on an end-user's computer to enable web sites to identify the user. They enable a company to identify a previous visitor to a *web site*, and build up a profile of their behaviour. They do not contain personal data which is securely held in a database and looked up via the unique identifier (customer code) in the cookie.

Cookie expiry period   The time stated in an affiliate marketing programme between that when a visitor clicks the affiliate link and that when the sale is credited to the affiliate. Common times are 7, 30 or 90 days. A longer cookie period will result in a higher *EPC*.

Cost Per Acquisition (CPA)   The cost of acquiring a new customer. Typically limited to the communications cost and refers to cost per sale for new customers. May also refer to other outcomes such as cost per quote or enquiry.

Cost Per Click   The cost of each click from a referring site to a destination site, typically from a search engine in Pay Per Click search marketing.

Cost Per Thousand (CPM)   Cost per 1,000 *page impressions* for a *banner* or display advert.

Countermediation   A response to *reintermediation* where an established organization creates or purchases a rival portal that is positioned as independent or part of an existing brand.

Customer engagement   Repeated interactions that strengthen the emotional, psychological or physical investment a customer has in a brand.

Customer journeys   Common or company-preferred paths through a site and/or across multiple sites, often considered as part of the 'path to purchase'.

Customer lifetime value (LTV)   A modelled future value of customers over a set number of years, based on future purchases and customer acquisition and management costs.

Customer orientation   Providing content, services and offers on a *web site* consistent with the different characteristicsof the audience of the site.

Customer-preferred channel   The customer prefers a particular channel for certain activities; e.g. phone to purchase, email for support.

Customer scenarios   Alternative tasks or outcomes required by a visitor to a web site. Typically accomplished in a series of stages of different tasks involving different information needs or experiences.

Customer-to-business (C2B)   The customer is proactive in making an offer to a business; e.g. the price they are prepared to pay for an airline ticket.

Customer-to-customer (C2C)   Interactions between customers on a web site; e.g. posting/ reading of topics on an electronic bulletin board.

Customer unions   The same as *co-buying*.

Database-driven marketing   The process of systematically collecting data about past, current and/or potential customers, maintaining the integrity of the data by continually monitoring customer purchases, by enquiring about changing status and using the data to formulate marketing tactics and foster personalized relationships with customers.

Data mining   Searching organizational databases in order to uncover hidden patterns or relationships in groups of data. Data-mining software attempts to represent information in new ways so that previously unseen patterns or trends can be identified.

Data warehouse   Data warehouses are large database systems containing detailed company data on sales transactions which are analysed to assist in improving the marketing performance of companies.

Demand-side platforms (DSPs) Technology used as part of *real-time bidding (RTB)* to enable agencies to manage data from different ad exchanges through a single interface or trading desk. They enable targeting of specific audiences based on behavioural targeting data.

Destination site   Frequently used to refer to the site that is visited following a *clickthrough* on a banner advert. Could also apply to any site visited following a click on a hyperlink.

Digital audio broadcasting (DAB) radio   Digital radio with clear sound quality with the facility to transmit text, images and video.

Digital media channel (digital channels)   Different forms of digital media used for online promotion such as affiliate marketing, paid search and display advertising.

Digital rights management (DRM)   The use of different technologies to protect the distribution of digital services or content such as software, music, movies, or other digital data.

Digital signage   The use of interactive digital technologies within billboard and point-of-sale ads. For example, videos and *Bluetooth* interaction.

Digital value   Offers or services that can only be accessed or delivered online.

Direct response   Usually achieved in an Internet marketing context by *banner ads, callback* services or *email* marketing.

Directories   A directory provides a structured listing of registered web sites in different categories. They are similar to an electronic version of the *Yellow Pages*.

Disintermediation   The removal of intermediaries such as distributors or brokers who formerly linked a company to its customers. It enables a company to sell direct to the customer by 'cutting out the middleman'.

Disruptive Internet technologies   New Internet-based communications approaches which change the way in which information about products is exchanged which impacts on the basis for competition in a marketplace.

Doorway pages   Pages deliberately created which are optimized for particular key phrases or search engines in order to increase listings in *SERPS* which often redirect to other pages in sites. Typically they are entry points that are not part of the main navigation. They are considered to be an unethical approach, known as search engine spamming. Ethical search marketers instead create search entry pages that are part of the main site navigation which are themed around particular phrases that customers are likely to use.

Duplicate content   This is where a search engine identifies different content pages as similar, so either doesn't include them in the index or downweights their importance.

Dynamic ad targeting   Specific ads are served in real time to visitor clusters according to their characteristics and behaviour as assessed by content types viewed.

Earnings Per Click (EPC)   An important measure that an affiliate uses to determine the value of each merchant or pages on their site. It stands for average Earnings Per Click and is usually measured across 100 clicks since an average is needed over this number of clicks.

E-business   All electronically mediated information exchanges supporting the range of business processes, both within an organization and with external stakeholders.

E-commerce   All electronically mediated information exchanges between an organization and its external stakeholders. Can refer to purchase transactions only.

Effective Cost Per Thousand (eCPM)   A measure of the total revenue the site owner can generate when 1,000 pages are served.

Email   Push sending of messages or documents, such as news about a new product or sales promotion.

Email, inbound   Emails received by a company from customers and other stakeholders.

E-marketing   Achieving marketing objectives through use of electronic communications technology.

Enterprise application integration (EAI)   The *middleware* technology that is used to connect together different software applications and their underlying databases is now known as 'enterprise application integration' (EAI).

Enterprise resource planning   Software providing integrated functions for major business functions such as production, distribution, sales, finance and human resources management.

Environment scanning   The process of continuously monitoring the environment and events and responding accordingly.

E-procurement   The electronic integration and management of all procurement activities including purchase request, authorization, ordering, delivery and payment between a purchaser and a supplier.

Expert reviews   Often performed at the beginning of a redesign project as a way of identifying problems with a previous design.

Exposure   One of Hofacker's five stages of web site information processing. Does the customer see the message?

Extended enterprise   Functions of an organization *outsourced* as part of a *value network*.

Extranet   Formed by extending the *intranet* beyond a company to customers, suppliers, collaborators or even competitors. This is password-protected to prevent access by general *Internet* users.

Faceted navigation   Used to enable users to rapidly filter results from a product search based on different ways of classifying the product by their attributes or features. For example, by brand, by sub-product category, by price bands.

Fast-moving consumer goods (FMCG)   The term says it all.

Findability   An assessment of how easy it is for a web user to locate a single content object or to use the browser's navigation and search system to find content. Like usability, it is assessed through efficiency – how long it takes to find the content; and effectiveness – how satisfied the user is with the experience and relevance of the content they find.

Firewall   A specialized software application mounted on a server at the point where the company is connected to the Internet. Its purpose is to prevent unauthorized access into the company from outsiders.

Fixed layout   The screen design has a fixed number of pixels width unlike a fluid layout or adaptive layout which dynamically resizes according to minimum screen resolutions.

Fluid designs   An adaptive web page or email design which makes use of all horizontal space as screen resolution increases. Fixed layouts have a fixed width in pixels.

Focus groups   Online, these take the form of a bulletin board or discussion group where different members of the focus group respond to prompts from the moderator and each other.

FRAC   A data analysis technique based on assessing the Frequency, Recency, Amount and Category of purchases by customers.

Frames   A technique used to divide a *web page* into different parts such as a menu and separate content.

General Packet Radio Services (GPRS)   A standard offering mobile data transfer and WAP access approximately five to ten times faster than traditional GSM access.

Geographical portal   A *portal* limited to a single country, area or city.

GIF (Graphic Interlaced File)   GIF is a graphic format used to display images within a *web page*. An interlaced GIF is displayed gradually on the screen, building up an image in several passes.

Globalization   The increase of international trading and shared social and cultural values.

Graphics-intensive sites   Sites in which white space or large images are mainly used to convey the message rather than text.

Group characterization   Web site communications are based on grouping people's preferences as part of *mass customization*.

Halo effect   The role of one media channel on influencing sale or uplift in brand metrics. Commonly applied to online display advertising, where exposure to display ads may increase *clickthrough* rates when the consumer is later exposed to a brand through other media; for example, sponsored links or affiliate ads. It may also affect conversion rates on a destination site through more exposure to the brand and message.

Hit   A hit is recorded for each graphic or block of text requested from a *web server*. It is not a reliable measure for the number of people viewing a page.

Horizontal portal   A *portal* with a wide audience or *reach*, offering general services; e.g. Yahoo!, MSN.

HTML   HTML (hypertext markup language) is a standard format used to define the text and layout of a *web page*. HTML files usually have the extension .HTML or .HTM.

Hubs   Alternative term for *B2B exchange*.

Ideal customer   Preferred customer who is targeted due to their potential for a profitable relationship.

I-MODE   A successful mobile standard originating in Japan that enables transfer of colour images between phones.

Inbound marketing   The consumer is proactive in seeking out information for their needs and interactions with brands, attracted through content, search and social media marketing.

Incidental advertising   Offline advertising where the web address is incidental to the main aim and creative.

Index inclusion   Ensuring that as many of the relevant pages from your domain(s) are included within the search engine indexes you are targeting to be listed in.

Indirect online contribution   Assesses the influence of the web site in generating offline purchases.

Individualization   Tailoring of content or offer to individual preferences.

Infobots   Software tools that collect information from the web for their users according to predefined preferences.

Infomediaries   An *intermediary* business whose main source of revenue derives from capturing consumer information and developing detailed profiles of individual customers for use by third parties.

Information architecture   The combination of organization, labelling and navigation schemes comprising an information system.

Information-intensive sites   Sites in which text is mainly used to convey the message rather than white space or large images.

Interaction rate (IR)   The proportion of ad viewers who interact with an online ad through rolling over it. Some will be involuntary depending on where the ad is placed on-screen, so it is highly dependent on placement.

Interactive banner ads   Banner ads where the user can type in information and receive a response; for example, loan interest for a particular loan.

Interactive kiosks   Fixed-site access to information about an organization and its services through a PC simplified through touch-screen access.

Interactive radio   Access to radio via a web site or digital radio.

Intermediary   Online sites that help bring different parties such as buyers and sellers together. They play a similar role to traditional brokers or channel partners.

Internet   The physical network that links computers across the globe. It consists of the infrastructure of network servers and communications links between them that are used to hold and transport information between the clients and servers.

Internet value proposition   See *online value proposition*.

Interstitial ads   Ads that appear between one page and the next.

Intranet   A network within a single company which enables access to company information using the familiar tools of the *Internet* such as *web browsers* and *email*. Only staff within a company can access the intranet, which will be password-protected.

IP address   The unique address of a computer accessing the Internet or a server used to host information (e.g. 207.68.156.58).

IPTV (Internet Protocol Television)   Digital television service delivered using Internet Protocol, typically by a broadband connection. IPTV can be streamed for real-time viewing or downloaded before playback.

JPEG (Joint Photographics Experts Group)   A graphics file format and compression algorithm, best used for photographs.

'Just-in-time'   An approach to operations management where inventory holding is minimized by manufacturing according to immediate demand.

Key influencers   Sites or individuals who have a large following for their writing, through their articles, *blog* posts or *social media* status updates.

Key performance indicators (KPIs)   Key measures collected to assess whether an organization's objectives are achieved.

Keyphrase   The combination of keywords typed into a search engine by a user.

Keyphrase analysis   A structured approach to identifying and selecting relevant combinations of keywords for *SEO* marketing and *PPC search marketing*.

Keyphrase density   The percentage importance of a keyphrase in comparison with the total number of words within a title, *meta tag* or web page.

Knowledge management   Techniques and tools for disseminating knowledge within an organization. Knowledge is used to apply staff experience to problem solving.

Last-click model of digital media channel attribution   The site which referred a visitor immediately before purchase is credited with the sale. Previous referrals influenced by other customer touchpoints on other sites are ignored.

Legacy systems   Old IT systems on which an organization is reliant, but they do not meet the current organizational requirements.

Lifetime value (LTV)   The estimated value of a customer or group of customers integrated across their past, current and future revenue.

Link anchor text   The text used to form the blue underlined hyperlink viewed in a web browser and defined in the *HTML* source. For example: Visit Dave Chaffey's web log is created by the HTML code: <A HREF = http://www.davechaffey.com>Visit Dave Chaffey's web log </A>

Linkbait   Content developed to encourage links to a site from other sites (and sharing of this content through social media, sometimes called 'sharebait').

Link building   A structured activity to include good-quality hyperlinks to your site from relevant sites with a good *PageRank*.

Link farms   Interlinked sites set up to increase PageRank. Considered to be *search engine spamming*.

Live chat sessions   A user asks questions of a company representative by typing into their browser. The representative replies in real time.

Localization   Designing the content of the *web site* such that it is appropriate to different audiences in different countries.

Location-based marketing   Location or proximity-based marketing is mobile marketing based on the GPS built into phones or based on interaction with other local digital devices.

Long tail, the   The long tail concept describes a frequency distribution showing the typical decline in popularity of items within a sector when a consumer has a choice in selecting these items. In search, the most common generic search terms (of the search head) for a site or market sector have much higher volumes than the less common phrases, which together are important in generating qualified visitors. The tail in retail refers to the capability of less popular products to generate sales and profitability.

Mass customization   Using technology to create tailored marketing messages or products for individual customers or a group of similar customers, yet retain the economies of scale of mass marketing or production.

Measurement   A process that collects metrics to indicate the effectiveness of Internet marketing activities in meeting e-marketing objectives.

Meta tags   Text within an *HTML* (hypertext markup language) file summarizing the content of the site (content meta tag) and relevant keywords (keyword meta tag) that are matched against the keywords typed into search engines.

Microsite   Specialized *content* that is part of a media owner's web site; e.g. ad-specific content for a company on an independent portal.

Middleware   Software used to facilitate communications between business applications including data transfer and control.

Mixed-mode buying   The process by which the customer switches between online and offline channels during the buying process.

Mobile apps   Software application designed for use on a mobile phone, typically downloaded from an app store. The best known are iPhone Apps, but all smartphones support the use of apps which can provide users with information, entertainment or location-based services such as mapping.

Mobile marketing   Marketing to encourage consumer engagement when using mobile phones (particularly smartphones) or tablet devices.

Modem   Device used to connect to the Internet via phone lines. Converts signals from digital to analogue.

Multi-channel behaviour   Customers use different traditional media or locations (phone, store, direct mail) in combination with different digital media (web, mobile, IPTV) to inform their purchase decision.

Multivariate testing   Multivariate testing enables simultaneous testing of web pages for all combinations and variations of page elements that are being tested. This enables selection of the most effective combination of design elements to achieve the desired goal.

Natural or organic listings   The pages listing results from a search engine query which are displayed in a sequence according to relevance of match between the *keyphrase* typed into a *search engine* and a *web page*, according to a ranking algorithm used by the search engine. Placements in the natural listings are targeted through *search engine optimization (SEO)* activity.

Navigation   Navigation describes the method of finding and moving between different information and pages on a web site. It is governed by menu arrangements, site structure and the layout of individual *web pages*.

Negative SEO   A company aims to decrease the ranking of other sites (usually indirectly) by gaining more favourable mentions above a negative listing in the natural search engine results.

Negative working capital   Working capital refers to money tied up in stocks and debtors. If *just-in-time* delivery occurs and customer payments are taken in advance of supplier payment, negative working capital can be created.

Net Promoter Score   A measure of the number of advocates a company (or web site) has who would recommend it compared to the number of detractors.

Offline promotion Offline promotion uses traditional media such as TV or newspaper advertising and word of mouth to promote a company's *web site*.

One-to-one marketing   Communication and tailoring of an offer at an individual level.

Online marketplace model   A description of the main audiences, intermediaries and destination sites within a specific market. It is used to assess consumer behaviour, competitor strength and the role of different intermediaries in influencing consumer purchases and media consumption.

Online PR   Maximizing favourable mentions of your company, brands, products or web sites on third-party web sites that are likely to be visited by your target audience.

Online promotion   Online promotion uses communication via the *Internet* itself to raise awareness about a *web site* and drive traffic to it; e.g. hyperlinks from other *web sites*, *banner adverts* or targeted electronic mail *(email)*.

Online reputation management   Controlling the reputation of an organization through monitoring and controlling messages placed online about the organization.

Online revenue contribution   An assessment of the extent to which the *Internet* contributes to sales is a key measure of the importance of the Internet to a company.

Online surveys   Surveys on-site through pop-up questionnaires.

Online value proposition   Defines an organization's online offering, distinct from offline or competitor offering.

On-page optimization   Writing copy and applying markup such as the <title> tag and heading tags <h1> to highlight to *search engines* relevant *keyphrases* within a document.

Onsite search engine   A search engine that is specific to a single site to help users find content.

Opt-in email   The customer is only contacted when they have explicitly asked for information to be sent to them (usually when filling in on-screen forms).

Opt-out   The customer is not contacted subsequently if they have explicitly stated they do not want to be contacted in future. Opt-out or 'unsubscribe' options are usually available within the email itself.

Outsourcing   Contracting an outside company to undertake e-marketing (or any) activities.

Page impressions   A page impression denotes one person viewing one *web page*.

Page template   A defined layout that is used throughout the site for different page categories (e.g. category page, product page, search page).

PageRank   An index used to assess the interconnections between web pages. A trademark of Google. Based on 'link popularity' or the number of *inbound links* and the PageRank of the linking sites.

Paid for inclusion (PFI)   The advertiser specifies pages with specific URLs for incorporation into the search engine *natural or organic listings*. There is a set-up fee and/or annual fee and *Pay Per Click* charge.

Panel   Members are recruited in order that their TV or web usage can be measured.

Panel data   Includes time and duration of access and content accessed for different geo-demographics.

Partner relationship management Management of marketing activities performed by downstream (or upstream) channel partners.

Pay Per Click (PPC) search marketing   This is when a company pays for text ads to be displayed on the search engine results pages when a specific key phrase is entered by the search users. It is called this because the marketer pays each time the hypertext link in the ad is clicked on.

Permission-based marketing   Customers agree (*opt-in*) to be involved in an organization's marketing activities, usually as a result of an incentive.

Personal digital assistants (PDAs)   Digital organizers with a touch screen that can be used to access the Internet and personal productivity applications.

Personalization   Delivering customized content for the individual either through *web pages*, *email* or push technology.

Personal video recorder (PVR) or digital video recorder (DVR)   Home consumer electronics device that records television shows to a hard disk in digital format.

Personas   A summary of the characteristics, needs, motivations and environment of typical web site users.

Person-to-person (P2P)   *Intermediaries* such as Napster which enable individuals to share information or files, similar to *C2C*.

Persuasion marketing (Persuasive design)   Using design elements such as layout, copy and typography, together with promotional messages, to encourage site users to follow particular paths and perform specific actions rather than giving them complete choice in their navigation.

Plug-in   A program that must be downloaded to view particular content such as an animation.

Portal   A web site that acts as a gateway to the information on the Internet by providing search engines, directories and other services such as personalized news or free email.

Price comparison intermediaries Sites like MoneySupermarket (www.moneysupermarket.com) and Expedia (www.expedia.co.uk) which allow a user to specify the features of the product they are looking for and then find the best deals from participating suppliers.

Price transparency   Prices can be readily compared by purchasers using the Internet, particularly through *shopping bots*.

Privacy   Concerns that affect an individual's or company 's personal details.

Profiling   Determining the customer key characteristics to enable *segmentation*.

Promotion   *Online promotion* uses communication via the Internet itself to raise awareness about a site and drive traffic to it. This promotion may take the form of links from other sites, banner adverts or targeted email messages. *Offline promotion* uses traditional media such as TV or newspaper advertising and word of mouth to promote a company's *web site*.

Proximity marketing   Marketing messages are delivered in real time according to customers' presence, based on the technology they are carrying, wearing or have embedded. *Bluecasting* is the best-known presence example where messages are automatically pushed to a consumer's *Bluetooth*-enabled phone or they request audio, video or text content to be downloaded from a live advert. In the future, ads will be able to respond to those who view them.

Prosumer   Typically, 'proactive consumer', but see the range of definitions in Section 2.5 (E-marketing Insight box, 'Alvin Toffler and the prosumer').

Prototype   A preliminary version of part or all of an information system reviewed by its users and business sponsors.

Prototyping   An iterative process in which web site users suggest modifications before further prototypes and the live version of the site are developed.

Pure play   An online only organization with no physical high-street presence or distribution, as opposed to a multi-channel or '*clicks and mortar*' organization which will have both an online and offline customer-facing presence. They may still use offline communications such as direct mail and advertising and have staff to manage inbound enquiries.

Quality Score   Influences a *Pay Per Click* ad's position on Google and the Google Network. It also partly determines your keywords' minimum bids. In general, the higher your Quality Score, the better your ad position (Ad Rank) and the lower your minimum bids (the bid needed to trigger an ad). *Clickthrough* rate is the main determinant of Quality Score, but a match between the triggering keyword and the ad copy, together with the relevance of the landing page, are also used to determine Quality Score.

Rapid application development (RAD)   An approach to information systems development that includes incremental development using *prototypes*.

Reach   The audience size of a web site as a percentage of total possible audience.

Really Simple Syndication (RSS)   An extension of blogging where a *blog*, news or any type of content is received as a 'feed' by specialist software such as RSSReader (www.rssreader.com). It offers a method of receiving news that uses a different broadcast method to email, so is not subject to the same conflicts with SPAM or SPAM filters.

Real-time bidding (RTB)   Online ads are served dynamically to the highest bidder according to a range of targeting criteria including, potentially, demographics, browser settings, searches performed, content previously viewed across an ad network, previous interactions with a brand (*remarketing*).

Real-time chat   A customer support operator in a call centre can type responses to a site visitor's questions.

Reciprocal links   Two organizations agree to link to each other's sites.

Redirects   A temporary web page or address is used, often for measurement purposes, before the required page is served to the user.

Referrals   The number of links from other sites.

Referring sites   A previously visited site from which the user followed links to reach the current site. Includes all the main digital media channels such as search engines, affiliates and display ads.

Reintermediation   The creation of new *intermediaries* between customers and suppliers providing services such as supplier search and product evaluation.

Relationship building   Consistent application of up-to-date knowledge of individual customers to product and service design which is communicated interactively in order to develop a continuous and long-term relationship which is mutually beneficial.

Remarketing A communications technique involving serving of ads to visitors who have already interacted with a brand through visiting their site, accessing specific content on the site, or interacting with an ad (see also *behavioural targeting*).

Repeat visits   A *tagged* visitor is recorded as visiting a site again.

Representation   Defines all the locations on the Internet where an organization is referred to or purchases can be made. Includes your own web site and intermediary sites.

Repurposing   Porting content from one digital platform to another; for example, web to interactive digital TV.

Return on investment (ROI)   A measure of the value derived from a marketing campaign (or any business activity) compared to its costs. There are many forms of ROI equation, but they can be simplified to: profit generated from activity divided by amount spent on activity (over a defined period of time).

Return path   An interaction where the customer sends information to the provider using a phone line or cable.

Revenue models   Different options for generating revenue from an online presence including sale, affiliate, subscription and advertising.

Reverse auctions   The buyer places a request for tender or quotation (RFQ) and many suppliers compete, decreasing the price with the supplier with the lowest price winning the contract.

Rich Internet Applications (RIA)   Interactive applications which provide options such as product selectors or games. They may incorporate video or sound also. Typically built using technologies such as Adobe Flash, Ajax, Flex, Java or Silverlight.

Rich media adverts   *Banner adverts* that are not static, but provide animation, sound or interactivity. An example of this would be a banner advert for a loan in which a customer can type in the amount of loan required, and the cost of the loan is calculated immediately.

Roadblocks   Where an advertiser buys all the available advertising space on a particular page.

Robots   A software tool employed by *search engines* to regularly index web pages of registered sites. Can also refer to any automated agent.

Satisficing behaviour   Consumers do not behave entirely rationally in product or supplier selection. They will compare alternatives, but then may make their choice based on imperfect information.

Scenario-based design   Site design and testing is based on a common path or flow of events or activities performed by visitors.

Scenarios   See *Customer scenarios*.

Scent trails   Cues such as text and image hyperlinks and page labels that *web browsers* follow to find content or services when navigating a site, typically associated with directed information seeking.

Screen resolution   Number of pixels (dots) displayed; e.g. 800 across by 600 vertical.

Scrum   A methodology that supports *agile software development* based on 15–30 day sprints to implement features from a product backlog.

Search analytics   The evaluation of the effectiveness of on-site search in order to increase its effectiveness.

Search bots   Software agents that search the web for information based on keywords.

Search engine   A specialized web site that uses automatic tools known as *spiders* or *robots* to index web pages of registered sites. Users can search the index by typing in keywords to specify their interest.

Search engine optimization (SEO)   A structured approach used to increase the relative ranking position of a company or its products in search engine *natural* or *organic* results listings on *search engine results pages* for selected *keyphrases*.

Search engine results pages (SERPS)   The pages generated and displayed by a search engine after a search engine user types in their *keyphrase*.

Search engine spamming   Unethical actions deliberately taken by marketers to mislead the search engines and give a higher ranking, such as repeated use of *keyphrases* and use of *link farms*, *doorway pages* and *cloaking*. Search engines may penalize marketers if they detect spamming.

Second-layer selling   Product is sold via an intermediary.

Secure Electronic Transaction (SET)   A standard for public key encryption intended to enable secure e-commerce transactions; lead-developed by MasterCard and Visa.

Secure Sockets Layer (SSL)   A commonly used encryption technique for scrambling data as it is passed across the Internet from a customer's web browser to a merchant's web server.

Security   Security attributes include:

1 *Authentication* – are parties to the transaction who they claim to be? This is achieved through the use of digital certificates.
2 *Privacy* and *confidentiality* – is transaction data protected? The consumer may want to make an anonymous purchase. Are all non-essential traces of a transaction removed from the public network and all intermediary records eliminated?
3 *Integrity* – checks that the message sent is complete; i.e. that it isn't corrupted.
4 *Non-repudiability* – ensures the sender cannot deny sending the message.
5 *Availability* – how can threats to the continuity and performance of the system be eliminated?

Segmentation   Identification of different groups within a target market in order to develop different offerings for the groups.

Sell-side e-commerce   E-commerce transactions between a supplier organization, intermediaries and its customers.

Sense and Respond marketing   Monitoring customer actions or behaviours and then reacting with appropriate messages and offers to encourage desired behaviours.

Share of wallet   Amount of customer income spent at a single organization as a proportion of all expenditure in a category; e.g. financial services.

Shopping bots   Software agents that find the lowest price for a specified product.

Short message service (SMS)   Also known as text messaging between mobiles.

Social media   Digital media which encourage audience participation, interaction and sharing.

Social media marketing   Monitoring and facilitating customer-to-customer interaction, participation and sharing through digital media to encourage positive engagement with a company and its brands, leading to commercial value. Interactions may occur on a company site, social networks and other third-party sites.

Social media optimization (SMO)   A systematic approach to improving content effectiveness in attracting visitors and leads and engaging existing audiences through testing techniques to increase the visibility, participation and shareability of content.

Social network   A site enabling community interactions between different consumers (C2C model). Typical interactions include posting comments and replies to comments, sending messages, rating content and tagging content in particular categories. Well-known examples include Bebo, Facebook, MySpace and (B2B) LinkedIn.

Social network company brand pages   Initially available on Facebook and now available on Google+, LinkedIn and Twitter, these enable services traditionally delivered via a company web site to be delivered on a social network.

SOSTAC®   SOSTAC® is a simple planning system covering Situation analysis, Objectives, Strategy, Tactics, Action and Control. Created by PR Smith in 1993, SOSTAC® is a registered trademark of PR Smith (see www.prsmith.org for more information).

SPAM   Unsolicited email (usually bulk mailed and untargeted).

Spamming   Bulk sending of SPAM.

Specific advertising   Offline ads that specifically highlight the *online value proposition*.

Spiders   Automatic tools known as spiders or robots index registered sites. Users search by typing *keyphrases* and are presented with a list of pages.

Spotlight tags   An outcome page on a site is marked as valuable for use in management information reports. Thetag is usually script which effectively updates a counter that this page has been viewed, often using a single pixel image referenced by the web analytics system. Spotlight was originally a proprietary term of DoubleClick DART, which has now been replaced by floodlight tags. These terms are now used more generally.

Statement of origination   A message in an opt-in email showing who has sent the message and why they have permission to send it.

Static ads   *Banner ads* that are not *animated*.

Stickiness   An indication of how long a visitor stays on a site.

Strategy, e-marketing   Definition of the future direction and actions of a company,defined as approaches to achieve specific objectives.

Superstitials   Pop-up ads that require interaction to remove them.

SWOT   Internal strengths and weaknesses, external opportunities and threats.

Tagging visitors   Tracking of origin of site visitors, their actions and spending.

Touch strategy   The sequence, frequency and content of outbound communications such as email and direct mail.

Traffic building   The use of *online promotion* and *offline promotion* techniques to increase the audience of a site (both new and existing customers).

Trialogue   The interaction between company, customer and other customers facilitated through online community, social networks, reviews and comments.

UMTS   Universal Mobile Telecommunications System. The standard for *3G* mobile access.

Unified message service   *Portal* offering combined access to mobile, landline and email messaging; e.g. emails can be heard by phone.

Uniform resource locator (URL)   A unique web address in the format, for example, http://www.company.com.

Unique visitors   The number of individuals who visit a web site in a fixed time period.

URL rewriting   A technique used to make complex web addresses for pages associated with dynamic content such as product catalogues or news articles visible to search engines.

URL Strategy   A defined approach to forming URLs including the use of capitalization, hyphenation, domain canonicalization and sub-domains for different brands and different locations. This has implications for promoting a web site offline through promotional or vanity URLs, search engine optimization and findability. A clean URL which fits many of these aims is http://www.domain.com/folder-name/document-name. Care must be taken with capitalization since Linux servers parse capitals differently from lower case.

Usability   An engineering approach to web site design to ensure the user interface of the site is learnable, memorable, error-free, efficient and gives user satisfaction. It incorporates testing and evaluation to ensure the best use of navigation and links to access information in the shortest possible time.

User-generated content (UGC)   Web users rather than the site owners create content. Examples include Wikipedia, personal blogs and reviews of products and companies.

User testing   Representative users are observed performing representative tasks using a system.

Value chain   A model for analysis of how supply-chain activities can add value to products and services delivered to the customer.

Value event   A visit to a web page such as e-newsletter registration or sales confirmation which indicates that a business objective is being met. Also known as a *conversion goal*. Site owners should track the number of conversion goals and the pages or referrers that influence them.

Value networks   The links between an organization and its strategic and non-strategic partners that form its external value chain.

Vertical integration   The extent to which supply-chain activities are undertaken and controlled *within* the organization.

Vertical portal   A *portal* with specialized content, often for a vertical market.

Viral marketing   Email is used to transmit a promotional message to another potential customer. 'Online word of mouth'.

Virtual assistants   Different types of software agents such as *shopping bots* and *infobots*.

Virtual business   An organization which uses information and communications technology to allow it to operate without clearly defined physical boundaries between different functions. It provides customized services by outsourcing production and other functions to third parties.

Virtual communities   A customer-to-customer interaction delivered via email groups, web-based discussion forums or chat.

Virtual integration   The majority of supply-chain activities are undertaken and controlled *outside* the organization by third parties.

Visitor session   One visit by a single customer. Visit ends after no activity for 30 minutes. The number of unique visitors is always less than the number of visitor sessions.

Visits, site   The number of visits to a web site in a fixed time period.

Voice portals   Portals that can be accessed by phone to hear information such as news or emails.

Web 2.0   Refers to a collection of web services which facilitate certain behaviours online such as community participation and *user-generated content*, rating and *tagging*.

Web 3.0   Next-generation web incorporating high-speed connectivity, complex cross-community interactions and an intelligent web where applications can access data from different services to assist searchers.

Web accessibility   Designing web sites so that they can be used by people with visual impairment, or regardless of the browser/access platform they use.

Web analytics   Techniques used to assess and improve the contribution of e-marketing to a business including reviewing traffic volume, referrals, *clickstreams*, online reach data, customer satisfaction surveys, leads and sales.

Web browsers   Browsers such as Netscape Navigator or Microsoft Internet Explorer provide an easy method of accessing and viewing information stored as *HTML* (hypertext markup language) web documents on different *web servers*.

Web log file   A log file analyser is a software tool used to summarize the information on visitor activity in a log file which contains a line defining the page, access time and *IP address* of the visitor.

Webographics   The web access characteristics of users such as place of access, connection speed and experience.

Web pages   A single page of a *web site*.

Web response ad campaign   An offline print or TV campaign where one of the main campaign objectives is to encourage ad viewers to visit the web site – for example, to request a sample, enter a competition, find further information or buy online.

Web servers   Used to store the *web pages* accessed by *web browsers*. It may also contain databases of customer or product information which can be queried and retrieved using a browser.

Welcome strategy   The sequence of personalized emails, web messages and offline communications intended to educate the customer about a brand and develop a relationship.

Widget   A badge or button incorporated into a site or *social network* space by its owner, but with content typically served from another site. Content can be updated in real time.

Wi-Fi ('wireless fidelity')   A high-speed wireless local-area network enabling wireless access to the Internet for mobile, office and home users.

Wireframe   Also known as schematics, a way of illustrating the layout of an individual web page.

Wireless application protocol (WAP)   Offers Internet browsing from mobile handsets. Mainly text-based sites developed in wireless markup language (WML).

World Wide Web   A medium for publishing information on the Internet. It is accessed through *web browsers* which display *web pages* and can now be used to run business applications. Company information is stored on *web servers* which are usually referred to as *web sites*.

XML or eXtensible Markup Language   A standard for transferring structured data, unlike HTML, which is purely presentational.

XML Product feeds   A standard format of product feature and pricing information that is uploaded by merchants to *price comparison intermediaries* to enable listing of all products in their catalogue.

XMOS (cross-media optimization studies)   XMOS research is designed to help marketers and their agencies answer the question 'What is the optimal mix of advertising vehicles across different media, in terms of frequency, reach and budget allocation, for a given campaign to achieve its marketing goals?' The mix between online and offline spend is varied to maximize campaign metrics such as reach, brand awareness and purchase intent.

Yielding   One of Hofacker's five stages of web site information processing. Does the customer accept (believe) the message?

Index